Translated from the German, *Einführung in das Neue Testament,* Chapters 1–6, by Helmut Köster, copyright © 1980 by Walter de Gruyter & Co., Berlin, Federal Republic of Germany, and New York, United States of America.

English translation copyright © 1982 by Fortress Press, Philadelphia.

Library of Congress Cataloging in Publication Data

Koester, Helmut, 1926–
    Introduction to the New Testament.

    (Hermeneia—foundations and facets)
    Translation of: Einführung in das Neue Testament.
    Includes bibliographies and indexes.
    Contents: v. 1. History, culture, and religion of the Hellenistic Age—v. 2. History and literature of early Christianity.
    1. Bible. N.T.—History of contemporary events.
I. Title. II. Series.
BS2410.K613   1982   225.9'5   82-71828
ISBN 0-8006-2100-X (v. 1)

TYPESET ON AN IBYCUS SYSTEM AT POLEBRIDGE PRESS

9597G82   Printed in the United States of America   1-2100

Volume One

INTRODUCTION TO
THE NEW TESTAMENT

HISTORY, CULTURE, AND RELIGION
OF THE HELLENISTIC AGE

HELMUT KOESTER

FORTRESS PRESS
PHILADELPHIA

WALTER DE GRUYTER
BERLIN AND NEW YORK

Hermeneia

FOUNDATIONS AND FACETS

HISTORY, CULTURE, AND RELIGION
OF THE HELLENISTIC AGE

Contents

§1. Historical Survey

Illustrations

Acknowledgments

Grateful acknowledgment is made for permissions to use a number of photographs in these volumes: to the Agora Excavations, Athens, Greece, for the photograph of the Library of Pantaenus Inscription (vol. I, p. 92); to the Fogg Art Museum, courtesy of the Sardis Excavation Office of Harvard University, for the photograph of the Synagogue of Sardis (vol. I, p. 221); to the Freer Gallery of the Smithsonian Institute, Washington, D. C., for the photograph of a page from Washingtonianus (vol. II, p. 28); to the Houghton Library and Semitic Museum of Harvard University for the photograph of Oxyrhynchus Papyrus 655 (vol. II, p. 151); and to the Institute for Antiquity and Christianity of the Claremont Graduate School for photographs of a page from Codex II of the Nag Hammadi Library and of the site of the discovery of that Library (vol. II, pp. 210 and 227).

Additionally, the author wishes to express his thanks for permission granted him to take photographs, also used in these volumes, at the following institutions: the Archaeological Museum, Thessaloniki, Greece (vol. I, pp. 163, 204, 305); the Byzantine Archaeological Administration, Thessaloniki, Greece (vol. II, p. 85); the National Museum, Athens, Greece (vol. I, p. 175); the Archaeological Museum, Verria, Greece (vol I, p. 330); the Louvre, Paris, France (vol. I, p. 125); the Staatliche Museen Charlottenburg, Berlin, German Federal Republic (vol. I, p. 37; II, pp. 243, 289); the Pergamon Museum, Berlin, German Democratic Republic (vol. I, p. 83; II, pp. 115, 339); the Museum für Kunst and Gewerbe, Hamburg, German Federal Republic (vol. I, p. 185); the National Archaeological Museum, Copenhagen, Denmark (vol. I, p. 7); the National Museum Numismatic Collection, Athens, Greece (vol. II, p. 75); Museum Ancient Ethesus, Turkey (vol. II, p. 249); Corinth Excavations of the American School of Classical Studies (vol. II, p. 123).

A final work of thanks is due the research team for Religion and Culture of the Lands of the New Testament (ASOR) who supplied the remaining photographs used in this volume.

FOUNDATIONS AND FACETS

FOREWORD TO THE SERIES

The publishers of *Hermeneia: A Historical and Critical Commentary on the Bible* are pleased to present the first volumes in a companion series to be known as *Hermeneia: Foundations and Facets*. The new series will include works foundational to the commentary proper and works treating facets of the biblical text.

At present *Foundations and Facets* is confined to the New Testament division of *Hermeneia*.

Foundations and Facets is designed to serve two related functions.

Much of the more creative biblical scholarship on the contemporary scene is devoted to facets of biblical texts: to units smaller than canonical books, or to aspects of the New Testament that cut across or exceed canonical limits. An intensive treatment of the sermon on the mount, for example, need not require a full commentary on Matthew, any more than a generic study of the great narrative parables of Jesus demands a complete study of Luke. *Facets* in this sense refers to any textual unit or group of such units that does not coincide with canonical books. Such units may be as short as an aphorism or as extensive as source Q, as limited as the birth and childhood stories or as diffuse as hymns in the New Testament. Again, tracking the various strands of the gospel tradition from the time of Jesus down into the second century can better be pursued independently of specific biblical books. In this second sense, *Facets* refers to strands or trajectories of early Christian tradition.

Further, *Facets* indicates features of biblical books themselves, such as the literary method of Luke, the use of irony in the Fourth Gospel, or the formal structure of the gospel as literary genre. While such features might well be included in the commentary proper, there may be reason to isolate one or more for special and extended consideration.

As it turns out, these creative and innovative impulses in current scholarship are linked to emerging new methods in biblical criticism or to the reconception of old ones. Accordingly, a second function of *Foundations and Facets* is to accommodate the creation or revision of correlative foundational instruments and tools. Such foundational works, properly conceived, will form the basis for the next phase of biblical scholarship.

The pioneering work of Martin Dibelius and Rudolf Bultmann in form criticism more than a half century ago rested on comparative evidence then newly acquired. Recent efforts to interpret the same oral forms—parables, pronouncement stories, miracle tales, and the like—have led to revised and expanded collections of comparative data. *Foundations and Facets* will be open to these primary materials, so that every student of the New Testament will be able to examine the comparative evidence firsthand.

Similarly, new methods allied with literary criticism, the study of folklore, and linguistics bring with them newly conceived grammars and lexica. Grammars include a poetics of biblical narrative, a handbook of hellenistic rhetoric, and a systematic hermeneutics. Other alliances with the social and psychological sciences are producing correlative new methodologies, which will themselves eventually require precise formulation. To be sure, older methodologies are being revised and refurbished as well. The cultural and religious milieu of the New Testament, together with its sociological and economic substratum, remain ingredient to an understanding of early Christianity and the literature it produced. And New Testament "introduction" is as pertinent today as it was when New Testament science assumed its modern form a century earlier, although it should by now be apparent that this traditional discipline must reorient itself if it is to lead into the text. It is fitting that the series should begin with a work of just this order: a classical form of scholarship with provocative new content.

The new series is thus aimed at both the *Foundations and Facets* of the biblical canon, seeking to harness mature as well as creative and innovative impulses impinging upon it.

The complete scope of *Foundations and Facets* has yet to be determined. It is the plan of the series to adapt itself as nearly as possible to the unfolding requirements of sound biblical scholarship. The series may thus eventually embrace works the exact dimensions of which are at present unknown, and it may well omit projected works for which suitable authors do not appear.

The expansion of biblical instruction into secular contexts, such as the public university, presents biblical scholarship with a fresh and serious challenge: in addition to exposition for the reader trained in the fundamental disciplines of biblical science, exegetes must now make the text in-

telligible for persons generally rather than technically literate. It is the
intention of the authors and editors of *Foundations and Facets* to meet this
challenge: they aspire to a mode of biblical scholarship that will illumine
the text for the general reader, while simultaneously serving the most
stringent requirements of the advanced student. If the series succeeds in
achieving this goal, it will have attained a new level of scholarly integrity.

Polebridge Press
Riverbend 1982

Robert W. Funk, editor

The concept of an "Introduction to the New Testament" in the form of a history of early Christianity in its contemporary setting, including a survey of the political, cultural, and religious history of the Hellenistic and Roman imperial period, stems from the predecessor of this book, the *Einführung in das Neue Testament* by Rudolf Knopf (revised edition by Hans Lietzmann and Heinrich Weinel) in the series "Sammlung Töpelmann" (now succeeded by "De Gruyter Lehrbücher"). Thus, the *Introduction* presented here in its English version does not aspire to be an "Introduction" in the technical sense nor a "History of Early Christian Literature" which treats the scholarship, date, integrity, and literary structure of each of the New Testament writings. To be sure, these questions are encompassed in the present work, but they are discussed within the context of a reconstruction of the historical development of early Christianity. My primary concern is to present the history of the early Christian churches, since it seems to me that the student of the New Testament must learn from the outset to understand the writings of the earliest period within their proper historical context.

It is obvious that this attempt to reconstruct the history of early Christianity requires one to relinquish some strictures of traditional introductions. I do not limit the discussion to the twenty-seven canonical books, but treat also sixty other early Christian writings from the first 150 years of Christian history, whether or not these writings are preserved fully or only in fragments. These non-canonical works are witnesses to early Christian history no less valuable than the New Testament. A historical presentation of these materials requires that clear decisions be made about authorship, date, and place of each writing; in other words, the results of historical-critical inquiry have to be consulted fully in each instance. I have also made an effort to discuss the problems in making such decisions. If these issues remain controversial with respect to some parts of the New Testament, they are even more difficult for non-canonical literature: traditionally scholarly debate has focused on the canonical literature, whereas the so-called "apocrypha" and other non-canonical writings have received only scant attention. Furthermore, quite a few of the latter have been discovered only recently, and their critical evaluation has just begun.

Nevertheless, it is much better to advance scholarship, and thus our understanding, through hypothetical reconstruction than to ignore new and apparently problematic materials.

In view of the present situation of New Testament scholarship, it would be misleading to suggest to the students of early Christian history that they can expect largely secure results. The New Testament itself furnishes evidence that the history of early Christian communities was a complex process, full of controversies and difficult decisions. Understanding this process requires critical judgment as well as the construction of trajectories through the history of early Christianity. The recent discovery of even more early writings not only demands a basic reorientation of our views, but will also enable the student to appreciate more fully the depths and riches of this formative period, especially as it is seen in the context of the general history of the culture in which Christianity began.

The scope of this book does not permit me to base my entire presentation upon the results of my own research. There are many topics in my survey of the Hellenistic and Roman world on which the specialist will have better insights and judgment. I am not only indebted to the published works of many scholars, but also owe much to my students at Harvard University, who have enriched this book in its various stages of writing and re-writing with their suggestions and criticisms, and equally to my colleagues, from whom I have learned a great deal during the last two decades in seminars and in discussions. I wish to express my special thanks to colleagues and friends: to Klaus Baltzer, of the University of Munich, and to Frank M. Cross, Dieter Georgi, George MacRae, Krister Stendahl, John Strugnell, and Zeph Stewart, all of Harvard University.

This book is the author's own translation of the German *Einführung in das Neue Testament,* published 1980 by Walter De Gruyter, Berlin and New York. Only in a few instances has the text been changed; one chapter was added (§6.3d). However, a number of minor errors and a few major mistakes were corrected. For this, I am particularly indebted to Eckhard Plümacher's review of this book (*Göttingische Gelehrte Anzeigen* 233 [1981] 1–22) and to the extensive notes which he kindly made available to me.

The bibliography has been redesigned so that editions and translations of texts are quoted first in order to encourage the student to read further in primary materials. English translations of texts are cited in the bibliographies wherever available. I am grateful to my colleague Albert Henrichs of Harvard University for suggestions regarding the revision of the bibliography. The bibliography is not meant to be exhaustive, but is designed to emphasize what is, in my opinion, the most valuable and more recent material, and what will best lead to further study. I have, however, included the most important "classics" which are still basic guides for scholarship today. For further reference, the reader should consult the standard reference works: *The Interpreter's Dictionary of the Bible* (especially its recently published supplement), *Reallexikon für Antike und Christentum, Der Kleine Pauly, Die Religion in Geschichte und Gegenwart,* and *The Oxford Classical Dictionary* (specific references to these works are normally not given in the bibliographies).

The English edition (as already the German work) would scarcely have been finished in such a brief time without the patience and interest of my wife and my children. Numerous persons have given their help in the various stages of translation and production of this work: Philip H. Sellew (editing, bibliography), Jonathan C. Guest (editing, copyediting, and proofreading), Gary A. Bisbee (maps), Pamela Chance (typing), Robert Stoops and Douglas Olson (bibliography). I am very grateful for their expert and untiring help. Rarely does an author enjoy such experienced and congenial production assistance as I had from my friends Charlene Matejovsky and Robert W. Funk of Polebridge Press at Missoula, Montana. Their dedication, care, competence, and advice accompanied every step of the book's production.

Inter Nationes, an agency of the government of the Federal Republic of Germany in Bonn, made a major grant to offset the cost of assistance for this translation. Thanks are due for this generous help.

This book is dedicated to the memory of my teacher Rudolf Bultmann. He encouraged me more than thirty years ago to deal more intensively with the extra-canonical writings from the early Christian period. His unwavering insistence upon the consistent application of the historical-critical method and his emphasis upon the investigation of early Christian literature in the context of the history of religions must remain basic commitments of New Testament scholarship.

Harvard University
Cambridge, Massachusetts
May 1982

Helmut Koester

Abbreviations

Serial and Journal Titles

AAWG.PH	Abhandlungen der Akademie der Wissenschaften zu Göttingen. Philologisch-historische Klasse
AB	Anchor Bible
ADAI.K	Abhandlungen des deutschen archäologischen Instituts, Kairo, Koptische Reihe
AHR	*American Historical Review*
AGSU	Arbeiten zur Geschichte des Spätjudentums und Urchristentums
AJP	*American Journal of Philology*
AKG	Arbeiten zur Kirchengeschichte
AnBib	Analecta biblica
ANRW	*Aufstieg und Niedergang der Römischen Welt*
ANTT	Arbeiten zur neutestamentlichen Textforschung
ASNU	Acta seminarii neotestamentici upsaliensis
AThANT	Abhandlungen zur Theologie des Alten und Neuen Testaments
AVTRW	Aufsätze und Vorträge zur Theologie und Religionswissenschaft
BAC	Biblioteca de autores cristianos
BEThL	Bibliotheca ephemeridum theologicarum Lovaniensium
BEvTh	Beiträge zur evangelischen Theologie
BFChTh	Beiträge zur Förderung christlicher Theologie
BHTh	Beiträge zur historischen Theologie
BibOr	Biblica et orientalia
BJRL	*Bulletin of the John Rylands Library*
BKP	Beiträge zur klassischen Philologie
BT.B	Bibliothèque de théologie, 3. Ser.: Théologie biblique
BWAT	Beiträge zur Wissenschaft vom Alten Testament
BZNW	Beihefte zur Zeitschrift für die neutestamentliche Wissenschaft
CBQ	*Catholic Biblical Quarterly*
CGTC	Cambridge Greek Testament Commentary
ConB	Coniectanea biblica
CRI	Compendia Rerum Judaicarum ad Novum Testamentum
EHS.T	Europäische Hochschulschriften. Reihe 23: Theologie
EKKNT	Evangelisch-katholischer Kommentar zum Neuen Testament
EPhM	Etudes de philosophie médiévale
EPRO	Etudes préliminaires aux religions orientales dans l'empire romain
ErJb	Eranos-Jahrbuch
EtBib	Etudes Bibliques

EtJ	Etudes Juives
EvTh	*Evangelische Theologie*
FKDG	Forschungen zur Kirchen- und Dogmengeschichte
FRLANT	Forschungen zur Religion und Literatur des Alten und Neuen Testaments
GBSNTS	Guides to Biblical Scholarship, New Testament Series
GCS	Die griechischen christlichen Schriftsteller der ersten drei Jahrhunderte
GLB	De Gruyter Lehrbuch
GRBS	*Greek, Roman, and Byzantine Studies*
GTB	Van Gorcum's theologische bibliotheek
GWU	*Geschichte in Wissenschaft und Unterricht*
HAW	Handbuch der Altertumswissenschaft
HDR	Harvard Dissertations in Religion
Hesp.S	Hesperia. Supplements
HeyJ	*Heythrop Journal*
Hist	*Historia. Zeitschrift für alte Geschichte*
HNT	Handbuch zum Neuen Testament
HNT.E	Handbuch zum Neuen Testament. Ergänzungsband
HSM	Harvard Semitic Monographs
HSS	Harvard Semitic Series
HThK	Herders Theologischer Kommentar zum Neuen Testament
HTR	*Harvard Theological Review*
HTS	Harvard Theological Studies
Hyp.	Hypomnemata. Untersuchungen zur Antike und zu ihrem Nachleben
ICC	International Critical Commentary
IDBSup	*Interpreter's Dictionary of the Bible. Supplement*
Int	*Interpretation*
JAC	*Jahrbuch für Antike und Christentum*
JAC.E	Jahrbuch für Antike und Christentum. Ergänzungsband
JAL	Jewish Apocryphal Literature
JBL	*Journal of Biblical Literature*
JEA	*Journal of Egyptian Archaeology*
JHS	*Journal of Hellenic Studies*
JQR.MS	Jewish Quarterly Review. Monograph Series
JR	*Journal of Religion*
JRomS	*Journal of Roman Studies*
JSHRZ	Jüdische Schriften aus hellenistisch-römischer Zeit
JTC	*Journal for Theology and the Church*
JTS	*Journal of Theological Studies*
KlT	Kleine Texte für (theologische und philologische) Vorlesungen und Übungen
LBS	Library of Biblical Studies
LCL	Loeb Classical Library
LHR	Lectures on the History of Religions, Sponsored by the American Council of Learned Societies
MAPS	Memoirs of the American Philosophical Society
MBPF	Münchener Beiträge zur Papyrusforschung und antiken Rechtsgeschichte
MH	*Museum Helveticum*
Mn.Suppl.	Mnemosyne. Bibliotheca classica/philologica Batava. Supplements
MThSt	Marburger theologische Studien

MThZ	*Münchener theologische Zeitschrift*
NAWG.PH	Nachrichten der Akademie der Wissenschaft in Göttingen. Philologisch-historische Klasse
NHS	Nag Hammadi Studies
NovT	*Novum Testamentum*
NovTSup	Novum Testamentum. Supplements
NTDSup	Das Neue Testament Deutsch. Supplementband
NTS	*New Testament Studies*
NTTS	New Testament Tools and Studies
NumenSup	Numen. International Review for the History of Religions. Supplements
OBO	Orbis Biblicus et Orientalis
OTS	*Oudtestamentische Studien*
PBA	*Proceedings of the British Academy*
Ph.S	Philologus. Supplement
PTS	Patristische Texte und Studien
PVTG	Pseudepigrapha Veteris Testamentis graece
RAC	*Reallexikon für Antike und Christentum*
RB	*Revue biblique*
RechSR	*Recherches de science religieuse*
RGG	*Die Religion in Geschichte und Gegenwart*
RechBib	Recherches bibliques
RPS	Religious Perspectives (series)
RVV	Religionsgeschichtliche Versuche und Vorarbeiten
SBLDS	Society of Biblical Literature Dissertation Series
SBLMS	Society of Biblical Literature Monograph Series
SBLSBS	Society of Biblical Literature Sources for Biblical Study
SBLSCS	Society of Biblical Literature Septuagint and Cognate Studies
SBLSS	Society of Biblical Literature. Semeia Supplements
SBLTT	Society of Biblical Literature. Texts and Translations
SBS	Stuttgarter Bibelstudien
SBT	Studies in Biblical Theology
SC	Sources chrétiennes
SCHNT	Studia ad Corpus Hellenisticum Novi Testamenti
SEÅ	*Svensk Exegetisk Årsbok*
SG	Sammlung Göschen
SHCT	Studies in the History of Christian Thought
SJ	Studia Judaica
SJLA	Studies in Judaism in Late Antiquity
SNTSMS	Society of New Testament Studies Monograph Series
SÖAW.PH	Sitzungsberichte der Österreichischen Akademie der Wissenschaften. Philosophisch-historische Klasse
SPB	Studia Post-Biblica
SQAW	Schriften und Quellen der Alten Welt
SQS	Sammlung ausgewählter kirchen- und dogmengeschichtlicher Quellenschriften
StANT	Studien zum Alten und Neuen Testament
STL	Studia Theologica Lundensia
StNT	Studien zum Neuen Testament
STRT	Studia Theologica Rheno-Trajectina

SUNT	Studien zur Umwelt des Neuen Testamentes
SVTP	Studia in veteris testamenti pseudepigrapha
TEH	Theologische Existenz heute
TF	Texte zur Forschung
ThBü	Theologische Bücherei
ThF	Theologische Forschung
ThHK	Theologischer Hand-Kommentar
ThLZ	*Theologische Literaturzeitung*
ThR	*Theologische Rundschau*
ThZ	*Theologische Zeitschrift*
TSJTSA	Texts and Studies of the Jewish Theological Seminary of America
TU	Texte und Untersuchungen zur Geschichte der altchristlichen Literatur
UB	Urban-Bücher
VC	*Vigiliae Christianae*
VTSup	Vetus Testamentum. Supplements
WdF	Wege der Forschung
WMANT	Wissenschaftliche Monographien zum Alten und Neuen Testament
WUNT	Wissenschaftliche Untersuchungen zum Neuen Testament
WZ (J)	*Wissenschaftliche Zeitschrift der Friedrich-Schiller-Universität Jena*
YCS	Yale Classical Studies
YPR	Yale Publications in Religion
Zet.	Zetemata
ZNW	*Zeitschrift für die neutestamentliche Wissenschaft*
ZThK	*Zeitschrift für Theologie und Kirche*

Works often Cited

Barrett, *Background*
C. K. Barrett (ed.), *The New Testament Background: Selected Documents* (London: SPCK, 1956; reprint: New York: Harper, 1961).

Bauer, *Orthodoxy and Heresy*
Walter Bauer, *Orthodoxy and Heresy in Earliest Christianity* (Philadelphia: Fortress, 1971).

Betz, *Galatians*
Hans Dieter Betz, *Galatians: A Commentary on Paul's Letter to the Churches in Galatia* (Hermeneia; Philadelphia: Fortress, 1979).

Bihlmeyer, *ApostVät*
F. X. Funk and Karl Bihlmeyer, *Die Apostolischen Väter* (SQS 2,1,1; 2d ed.; Tübingen: Mohr/Siebeck, 1956).

Black and Rowley, *Peake's Commentary*
Matthew Black and H. H. Rowley (eds.), *Peake's Commentary on the Bible* (London: Nelson, 1962).

Bornkamm, *Experience*
Günther Bornkamm, *Early Christian Experience* (London: SCM, New York: Harper, 1969).

Braun, *Studien*
Herbert Braun, *Studien zum Neuen Testament und seiner Umwelt* (3d ed.; Tübingen: Mohr/Siebeck, 1971).

Bultmann, *Exegetica*
Rudolf Bultmann, *Exegetica: Aufsätze zur Erforschung des Neuen Testaments* (ed. Erich Dinkler; Tübingen: Mohr/Siebeck, 1967).

Bultmann, *Existence and Faith*
Rudolf Bultmann, *Existence and Faith* (ed. Schubert M. Ogden; New York: Meridian, 1960).

Bultmann, *Theology*
Rudolf Bultmann, *Theology of the New Testament* (2 vols.; New York: Scribner's, 1951).

Calder and Keil, *Anatolian Studies*
W. M. Calder and Josef Keil, *Anatolian Studies Presented to William Hepburn Buckler* (Manchester: Manchester University, 1939).

CambAncHist 7–10
S. A. Cook, F. E. Adcock, and M. P. Charlesworth, *The Cambridge Ancient History,*

vol. 7: *The Hellenistic Monarchies and the Rise of Rome;* vol. 8: *Rome and the Mediterranean 218–133 B. C.;* vol. 9: *The Roman Republic 133–44 B. C.;* vol. 10: *The Augustan Empire 44 B. C.–A. D. 70* (New York: Macmillan, 1928–34).

Cambridge History of the Bible 1
P. R. Ackroyd and C. F. Evans (eds.), *The Cambridge History of the Bible,* vol. 1: *From the Beginnings to Jerome* (Cambridge: Cambridge University, 1970).

Cameron (ed.), *The Other Gospels*
Ronald D. Cameron (ed.), *The Other Gospels, Introductions and Translations* (Philadelphia: Westminster, 1982).

von Campenhausen, *Tradition*
Hans von Campenhausen, *Tradition and Life in the Church: Essays and Lectures in Church History* (Philadelphia: Fortress, 1968).

Cartlidge and Dungan, *Documents*
David R. Cartlidge and David L. Dungan (eds.), *Documents for the Study of the Gospels* (Cleveland: Collins, 1980).

Conzelmann, *Outline*
Hans Conzelmann, *An Outline of the Theology of the New Testament* (New York: Harper, 1969).

Cullmann, *Vorträge 1925–1962*
Oscar Cullmann, *Vorträge und Aufsätze 1925–1962* (Tübingen: Mohr/Siebeck, and Zürich: Zwingli, 1966).

Foakes Jackson and Lake, *Beginnings*
F. J. Foakes Jackson and Kirsopp Lake (eds.), *The Beginnings of Christianity* (5 vols.; London: Macmillan, 1920–33, and reprints).

Foerster, *Gnosis*
Werner Foerster, *Gnosis: A Selection of Gnostic Texts* (Eng. trans. ed. R. McL. Wilson; 2 vols.; Oxford: Clarendon, 1972–74).

Fraser, *Alexandria*
P. M. Fraser, *Ptolemaic Alexandria* (2 vols.; Oxford: Clarendon, 1972).

Grant, *ApostFath*
Robert M. Grant, *The Apostolic Fathers: A New Translation and Commentary* (6 vols.; New York: Nelson, 1964–68).

Grant, *Hellenistic Religions*
Frederick C. Grant (ed.), *Hellenistic Religions: The Age of Syncretism* (The Library of Religion 2; New York: Liberal Arts, 1953).

Haenchen, *Acts*
Ernst Haenchen, *The Acts of the Apostles: A Commentary* (Philadelphia: Westminster, 1971).

Haenchen, *Gott und Mensch*
Ernst Haenchen, *Gott und Mensch: Gesammelte Aufsätze* (Tübingen: Mohr/Siebeck, 1965).

Käsemann, *New Testament Questions*
Ernst Käsemann, *New Testament Questions of Today* (Philadelphia: Fortress, 1969)

Kee, *Origins*
Howard Clark Kee, *The Origins of Christianity: Sources and Documents* (Englewood Cliffs, NJ: Prentice Hall, 1973).

Kirche: Festschrift Bornkamm
Dieter Lührmann and Georg Strecker (eds.), *Kirche: Festschrift für Günther Bornkamm zum 75. Geburtstag* (Tübingen: Mohr/Siebeck, 1980).

Lake, *ApostFath*
  Kirsopp Lake, *The Apostolic Fathers* (LCL; 2 vols.; Cambridge, MA: Harvard
  University, 1912, and reprints).
Layton, *Rediscovery of Gnosticism*
  Bentley Layton (ed.), *The Rediscovery of Gnosticism* (Proceedings of the International
  Conference at Yale, New Haven, 1978; NumenSup 16; 2 vols.; Leiden: Brill, vol. 1,
  1980; vol. 2, forthcoming).
Lightfoot, *Apostolic Fathers*
  J. B. Lightfoot, *Apostolic Fathers: A Revised Text with Introductions, Notes,
  Dissertations, and Translations* (2 parts in 5 vols.; London: Macmillan, 1885–90).
Lipsius-Bonnet, *ActApostApoc*
  Richard Albert Lipsius and Maximilian Bonnet, *Acta Apostolorum Apocrypha* (2 vols;
  Leipzig: Mendelssohn, 1891–1903; reprint: Darmstadt: Wissenschaftliche
  Buchgesellschaft, 1959).
NagHamLibEngl
  James M. Robinson (ed.), *The Nag Hammadi Library in English* (Leiden: Brill, and
  New York: Harper, 1977).
Neusner, *Religions in Antiquity*
  Jacob Neusner (ed.), *Religions in Antiquity: Essays in Memory of Erwin Ramsdell
  Goodenough* (NumenSup 14; Leiden: Brill, 1968).
Nilsson, *Griechische Religion 2*
  Martin P. Nilsson, *Geschichte der griechischen Religion,* vol. 2: *Die hellenistische und
  römische Zeit* (HAW 5,2,2; 3d ed.; München: Beck, 1974).
Nock, *Essays*
  Arthur Darby Nock, *Essays on Religion and the Ancient World* (2 vols.; Cambridge,
  MA: Harvard University, 1972).
NTApo
  Edgar Hennecke, *New Testament Apocrypha* (ed. Wilhelm Schneemelcher; 2 vols.;
  Philadelphia: Westminster, 1963–65).
Robinson and Koester, *Trajectories*
  James M. Robinson and Helmut Koester, *Trajectories through Early Christianity*
  (Philadelphia: Fortress, 1971).
Schmithals, *Paul and the Gnostics*
  Walter Schmithals, *Paul and the Gnostics* (Nashville: Abingdon, 1972).
Morton Smith, *Clement*
  Morton Smith, *Clement of Alexandria and a Secret Gospel of Mark* (Cambridge, MA:
  Harvard University, 1973).
Vielhauer, *Geschichte*
  Philip Vielhauer, *Geschichte der urchristlichen Literatur* (GLB; Berlin: De Gruyter,
  1975).

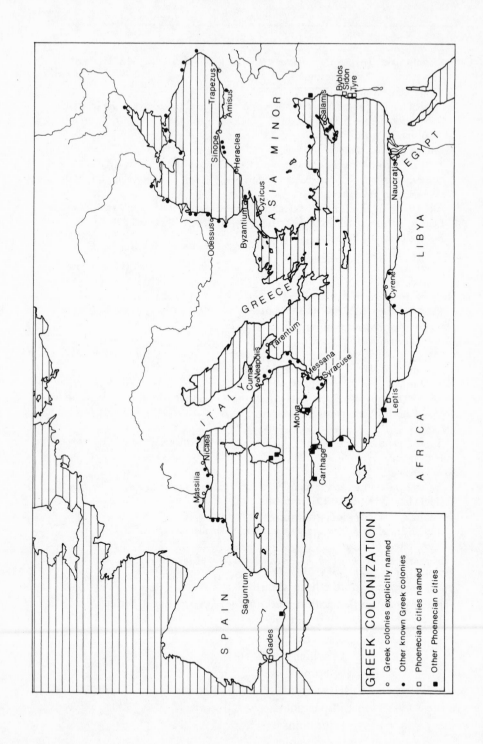

GREEK COLONIZATION

○ Greek colonies explicitly named
● Other known Greek colonies
□ Phoenecian cities named
■ Other Phoenecian cities

Trapezus
Amisus
Sinope
Heraclea
Byblos
Sidon
Tyre
Salamis

ASIA MINOR

EGYPT

Naucratis

Odessus
Byzantium
Cyzicus

GREECE

LIBYA

Cyrene

Tarentum
Neapolis
Cumae
Messana
Syracuse

ITALY

Motya
Leptis

Massilia
Nicaea

Carthage

AFRICA

SPAIN

Saguntum

Gades

HISTORY, CULTURE, AND RELIGION
OF THE HELLENISTIC AGE

The conquests of Alexander the Great led to the formation of a new
political and economic order of large dimensions, which was ruled first by
the Hellenistic kings and later, further expanded to the west and north, by
Rome. This new realm eventually encompassed all the countries of the
Mediterranean Sea and many far to the east. To a certain degree the
nations between Mesopotamia and India were also included, as well as
the regions far to the north, what is now France, Britain, West Germany,
and the countries of the Alps and along the Danube.

Christianity developed as part of the culture of this new world, one in
which important processes of cultural and religious interpenetration and
amalgamation had taken place during the Hellenistic period. Many
elements of different origin contributed to this process, but in philosophy,
art, literature, science, and religion the results appear to have been
determined primarily by the Greek element. Greek became the dominant
language, and even such world tongues as Latin and Aramaic had to take
second place. But this process, which is generally called Hellenization,
was not without conflict. Conflicts resulted from tensions between
traditional, particularistic interests and institutions on the one hand, and
universalizing forces which called for the creation of a world economy,
world culture, and world religion on the other. Particularistic interests,
however, did not arise only from the different older traditions of the
various nations and ethnic groups which, unable to escape from the
processes of Hellenization, still demanded that the emerging world
culture come to terms with their special contributions. Even more
important were those tensions which arose from the particularistic
interests of the cities which were at the same time the most important
supports of the development towards a new world culture. The cities
emancipated themselves from local and ethnic peculiarities and became
centers of the most important economic, cultural, and religious activities;
yet they had to solve questions of morality and religion that emerged from
worldwide political, economic, and social problems. It is exactly these
major Hellenistic cities in which early Christianity was formed and

developed its potential as a new world religion. A historically-oriented *Introduction to the New Testament* thus must begin with a consideration of the Hellenistic age in order to clarify the presuppositions for the formation and expansion of early Christianity.

HISTORICAL SURVEY

1. GREECE AND THE EASTERN MEDITERRANEAN BEFORE ALEXANDER

(a) Hellenization prior to the Fourth Century BCE

Ionian and Aeolian immigrants had begun to settle the western coast of Asia Minor in X BCE and founded a number of cities (Smyrna, Ephesus, Priene, Myus, Miletus, and many others). Under the rule of the Lydian kings during VII and VI BCE, these cities experienced their prime and became leading participants in the founding of new Greek cities in other areas of the Mediterranean. Miletus was culturally the most significant Greek city. The Greeks of this area were open to influences from the east, yet also contributed to the process of Hellenization in Asia Minor.

Greek colonies were also founded outside of the coastal areas of the Aegean and Propontis beginning in VII BCE. Only some of the more important cities can be listed here: on the coast of the Black Sea, Sinope, Trapezus, and Panticapaeum; in Sicily and southern Italy, Syracuse, Tarentum, and Naples; in southern Gaul, Massilia (Marseilles) and Nicaea (Nice); in North Africa, Cyrene and Naucratis, the only Greek city of Egypt in this early period. Most of these cities were founded as *apoikiai,* that is, founded through the emigration of part of the population from the mother city. Close political and economic ties were thus established between the newly founded colony and its mother city, connections which were often maintained for many centuries. The first result of the founding of these cities was economic: new markets were opened up for export, and the new cities served as centers for the importation of raw materials and grain into Greece. In the course of time, because of such ties, an intellectual, cultural, and religious exchange also took place that is clearly visible in the history and development of Greek culture and religion.

These colonies eventually became more or less independent of their founding cities, a tendency reinforced through political developments. In Asia Minor the rule of the Lydian kings was replaced by the more oppressive rule of the Persians. Many new cities began to produce their own manufactured goods with the raw materials they had formerly shipped to the mother city, where they had once bought the finished products they needed. This development began in v BCE in southern Italy and Sicily, continued in the following century in the colonies of the east, and was one of the main causes of the economic crisis of Greece in IV BCE.

(b) The Eastern Mediterranean before Alexander

Politically, culturally, and economically the opposition between Greeks and Persians dominated the eastern part of the Mediterranean. The Persians were able within a few years to conquer Syria, Egypt, and Asia Minor, including its Greek cities (an Ionian insurrection in 500–494 BCE failed), but their attempts to make the Greek homeland subject to their rule as well did not succeed. The victory of the Greeks over the Persians deeply impressed itself upon the Greek mind. This theme found manifold expression in Greek literature, in poetry and fiction as well as in political and scientific writings, and led to reflections about the fundamental differences between "East" and "West" that would remain significant for many centuries to come. The Greeks had successfully withstood the onslaught of an eastern superpower. The consciousness of the superiority of Greek education, Greek culture, and of the Greek gods formed not only the Greek mind, but also that of other nations, later including even the Romans, although they were to become the masters of the Greeks.

Greece and Persia were indeed fundamentally different. Greece was politically divided into a number of democratic, oligarchic, or aristocratic states; there were also several kingdoms, of which Macedonia would soon

Bibliography to §1: Comprehensive Studies of the Entire Period

W. W. Tarn, *Hellenistic Civilization* (3d ed.; rev. by author and G. T. Griffith; London: Arnold, 1952).

F. E. Peters, *The Harvest of Hellenism: A History of the Near East from Alexander the Great to the Triumph of Christianity* (New York: Simon and Schuster, 1970).

Hermann Bengtson, *Griechische Geschichte von den Anfängen bis in die römische Kaiserzeit* (HAW 3,4; München: Beck, 1969).

Arnold J. Toynbee, *Hellenism: The History of a Civilization* (New York and London: Oxford University, 1957).

Bibliography to §1.1a–b

Jean Bérard, *L'Expansion et la colonisation grecques jusqu'aux guerres médiques* (Paris: Aubier, 1960).

Edouard Will, *Le monde grec et l'orient*, vol. II: *Le IVe siècle et l'époche hellénistique* (Paris: Les presses universitaires de France, 1975).

Claude Mossé, *La colonisation dans l'antiquité* (Paris: Fernand Nathan, 1970).

Robert Cohen, *La Grèce et l'hellénistisation du monde antique* (Paris: Les presses universitaires de France, 1948).

A. J. Graham, *Colony and Mother City in Ancient Greece* (New York: Barnes and Noble, 1964).

become the leading power. All these existed side by side, their relations tense, rarely cordial, and often openly hostile. Persia, on the other hand, was an empire under a Great King whose central government maintained its rule over large areas through military power, even though the various provinces (satrapies) retained their cultural and religious independence. Greece, deeply divided, was incapable of organizing itself into a unified commonwealth. Nevertheless, various Greek city-states, not altogether dissimilar, developed an amazing economic power and extended their cultural influence far beyond their borders. Even though Persia had relinquished all plans to conquer Greece, it remained the only superpower in the eastern Mediterranean, but its empire lacked economic, cultural, and religious force. The power struggle in the West between Rome, Syracuse, and Carthage had barely begun.

(c) Greece

The golden age of classical Greece during the time of Pericles found a dreadful end in the confusions of the thirty years of the Peloponnesian war, and the condition of Greece grew continually worse during the following decades. Political disunion increased; the country was torn by never-ending internal wars. Attempts were made to replace the former hegemonies of Sparta and Athens by federal republics, but they had no lasting success. In the second half of IV BCE, the hegemony of Macedonia brought a short-lived solution; but new disorders arose, often caused by external powers, namely the Hellenistic empires and Rome.

The economic situation also worsened during IV BCE. To be sure, the process of industrialization begun in V BCE continued; through employment of slave labor, industrial manufacturing increased its output both of consumer goods and of the weapons and other equipment for war now in ever-rising demand due to continuous fighting. Shipbuilding was further developed and banking expanded, but there was no corresponding growth in the Greek foreign market. Archeological excavations have demonstrated that Syria, Egypt, and the Greek colonies on the coasts of the Black Sea and in the western Mediterranean replaced the goods which they had

Bibliography to §1.1c–d

J. B. Bury, *A History of Greece to the Death of Alexander the Great* (3d ed.; rev. Russel Meigs; London: Macmillan, 1975).

N. G. L. Hammond, *A History of Greece to 322 B.C.* (Oxford: Clarendon, 1959).

Hermann Bengtson (ed.), *The Greeks and the Persians* (New York: Delacorte, 1968).

Eduard Meyer, *Das Perserreich und die Griechen* (Geschichte des Altertums 4; Stuttgart: Cotta, 1944).

previously bought in Greece with their own products. Building activity in the Greek cities declined; major buildings projects often halted, only to be resumed in the time of Alexander or during the Roman period.

An impoverishment of the Greek population corresponded to these developments. The lack of natural resources, minerals, wood, and arable land was felt ever more strongly. These needs could not be satisfied through imports, because Greek exports, such as wine, olive oil, and pottery, brought returns insufficient to balance the foreign trade deficit. Imported luxury items, such as gold, spices, perfumes, and incense for the temple cults, became so expensive that only a small portion of the population could afford them. At the same time, the total population increased, deepening the contrast between rich and poor and aggravating the unemployment problem. A large portion of the middle class slid into poverty. Banishments and confiscations of property, a consequence of the political turmoil, weakened the upper classes in particular. Since those classes of citizens that in the past had been the main support of the state were diminished, the army became increasingly dependent upon mercenaries, who were primarily recruited from the lower classes. Greek mercenaries also served foreign powers, even in the time before Alexander.

(d) The Persian Empire

The eastern part of the Persian empire was primarily rural. This was the case in the Iranian heartland, the Persis, as well as in Media, where independent farmers lived side by side with landed proprietors raising cattle and horses. The recruits for the Persian army came from these regions; the families of the landed gentry supplied the officials for the Persian administration. The far eastern satrapies of Bactria and Sogdia also were rich agricultural areas. Further north, near the Caspian Sea and the Aral Sea, the inhabitants were nomadic tribes ethnically related to the Iranian people.

Immediately west of the Persian heartlands the situation was completely different. The ancient cultural center of Babylon was here, with its large cities, Babylon and Ur, which continued to exist under Persian rule, even though they declined visibly after the destruction of the great Babylonian sanctuaries by Xerxes (482 BCE). Though the temples and their priestly aristocracies retained a certain degree of economic power, they were dedicated primarily to the preservation of the inherited legal system and the perfection of astronomical mathematics. But they lost much of their influence upon the population, especially since large numbers of immigrants (mostly Persians, Medes, and Jews) settled in Babylonia. The highly developed agriculture of lower Mesopotamia continued to be a source of prosperity for this densely settled area with its numerous towns and villages, even though the Persian treasury and the large banks were the primary beneficiaries.

Assyria, to the northwest, had been only sparsely populated since the collapse of its empire at the end of VII BCE. Assur continued to exist, but Nineveh was in ruins. The area between the middle portions of the Euphrates and the Tigris was a barren steppe. But Syria, with its large population of various ethnic origins between the Euphrates and the Mediterranean Sea, was one of the most vital parts of the Persian empire. In its interior were centers of extensive international trade, the caravan cities of Damascus, Aleppo, and Palmyra; on the Syro-Palestinian coast were the powerful merchant cities of the seafaring Phoenicians, which also provided Persia with naval forces. The most important of these cities were Tyre, Sidon, and Byblos. With the exception of the insurrection of Sidon (350–344 BCE), Persian rule brought peace and prosperity to these countries, including the dependent Jewish temple state of Jerusalem as it was reconstituted by the Persian Kings (§5.1a).

Asia Minor was inhabited by many different peoples and nations with diverse economic and social structures. Primitive mountain tribes lived side by side with the descendants of nations that had once ruled large kingdoms and empires, such as the Hittites, Phrygians, and Lydians. There were also peoples who had immigrated from other parts of the Mediterranean (Carians and Lycians) and large Greek populations, especially in the coastal cities of the Aegean and the Black Sea. The western part of Asia Minor and its northern and southern coasts were tied to Greece through numerous bonds and had an important share in the culture, trade, and industrial production of the Mediterranean world. In the interior and eastern parts of Asia Minor, different forms of agricultural economy dominated, such as villages dependent upon temples or large estates owned by members of the Persian nobility; here economy and trade were linked to the caravan roads.

Egypt, heir to one of the oldest of cultures, was ruled by a centralized government with a centrally directed economy. The Persian rulers did not change these structures, and when Egypt again became independent in 405 BCE after more than a hundred years of Persian rule, it returned without difficulty to the established, ancient patterns of administration. In this last period of Egyptian independence, the country prospered until it was conquered once more by the Persians in 343 BCE, shortly before the arrival of Alexander the Great.

The Persian Empire was organized with a central government and regional administrations (satrapies) strengthened by standing army detachments that increasingly employed foreign mercenaries, especially Greeks and also Jews; the Jewish military colony in Elephantine in Upper Egypt is an example well known through the discovery of its papyri. But the Persians did not make any attempt to impose their culture upon the people they ruled, nor did they try to bind them to the ruling dynasty by religious institutions; there was neither a state religion nor a royal cult. Economy and trade were strengthened, though not through an active economic policy of the Persian court, but rather due to the maintenance of peace and security. The hoarding of immense amounts of gold and silver by the royal Persian treasury became an ever increasing encumbrance for the economy. There was no unified monetary policy, although barter trade was partially replaced by the money market.

At least in one respect the Persians created a bond of unity that continued to have its effects: they used the Aramaic language, spoken by many nations of Semitic origin, as the primary medium of their administration (so-called Imperial Aramaic). Western Aramaic was the dialect of this language spoken in Palestine at the time of Jesus, and Syriac and Mandean developed from its eastern branch.

2. ALEXANDER THE GREAT

(a) The Presuppositions for the Conquest of the East

The Macedonians were a nation closely related to the Greeks; indeed their language belonged to the family of Greek languages. But the Macedonians did not consider themselves to be Greeks and were distinctly different from them in many respects. Even geographically Macedonia was a country of different character: instead of the high mountains and narrow valleys which divide Greece into numerous separate units, Macedonia boasts of a large and fertile coastal plain with great rivers, the Axius and Haliacmon. Both rivers flow into the Aegean in Macedonia and with their tributaries make the more remote valleys accessible; thus the mountains of the hinterland do not block access to the inland regions, as is the case elsewhere in Greece. On the other hand, ancient Macedonia did not have good natural harbors, nor cities which were primarily oriented toward the sea.

To this geographical structure of Macedonia corresponded its political and sociological character, also quite different from that of the Greek city-

Bibliography to §1.2a

Paul Cloché, *Histoire de la Macédonie, jusqu'à l'avènement d'Alexandre le Grand (336 avant J.-C.)* (Paris: Payot, 1960).

Idem, *Un Fondateur d'empire: Philippe II roi de Macédonie (383/2–336/5 avant J.-C.)* (Saint-Étienne: Éditions Dumas, 1955).

Arnaldo Momigliano, *Filippo il Macedone* (Firenza: Monnier, 1934).

Marble Head of Alexander the Great
(Roman copy of a statue from Alexandria)
Alexander is presented with the characteristic ram's horns of the Egyptian god Ammon-Re, whom the Greeks called Zeus (cf. p. 10).

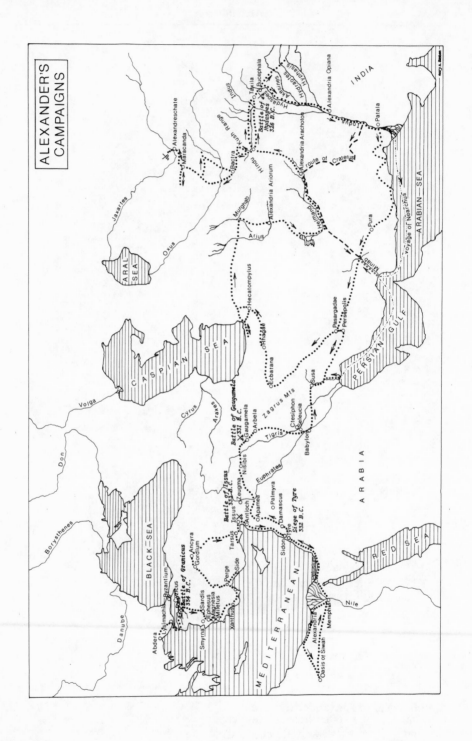

ALEXANDER'S CAMPAIGNS

states. Macedonia's mostly rural population did not share the petty-state consciousness of the Greek polis. Its king was the commander of an army recruited from all people in the country, and the continuous conflict of the Greek polis between tyrannic rule and democracy was as unknown as the employment of foreign mercenaries. Macedonia was self-sufficient economically, whereas the economy of the Greek city-states was dependent upon foreign trade.

To be sure, since v BCE Macedonia had increasingly begun to participate in the cultural developments of Greece, and Macedonian kings before Alexander had favored this development. It is no accident that Euripides spent the last years of his life at the royal Macedonian court in Pella, and that Aristotle was the teacher of the young prince Alexander. But when the Macedonians assumed political leadership in Greece during IV BCE, this did not simply represent the transfer of power from one Greek state to another, but rather a momentous transition to new political structures. Although the Macedonians were quite conscious that they had become heirs of the Greek tradition and that they had now taken responsibility for the Greek mission to the world, such inheritance and mission now appeared in a completely new perspective.

The victory of Philip II of Macedonia over Athens and its allies at Chaeronea in 338 BCE, through which Athens lost its hegemony over Greece once and for all, marks the beginning of a new epoch. Demosthenes, the famous Athenian orator, was no doubt correct when in his memorial speech for the fallen soldiers he lamented the freedom and glory of Athens, departed forever. Yet Isocrates, then ninety years old, also saw the signs of the times when he wrote to Philip: "Once you have made the Persian subject to your rule, there is nothing left for you but to become a god."

(b) Alexander's Conquest of the East

Alexander was born in 356 BCE. He was educated by Aristotle, the greatest philosopher of that time, beginning in 343. When his father, Philip II, was murdered in 336, the army proclaimed Alexander king of the Macedonians. His first action was to complete the conquest of Thrace begun by his father (336/5). In 335 he was forced to suppress a Greek insurrection; Thebes, the leading city of the revolt, was completely des-

Bibliography to §1.2b

Joh. Gust. Droysen, *Geschichte Alexanders des Grossen* (Düsseldorf: Dorste, 1966; first published 1833). The classic monograph and basis of modern scholarship.

W. W. Tarn, *Alexander the Great* (Cambridge: Cambridge University, 1948).

C. Bradford Welles, *Alexander and the Hellenistic World* (Toronto: Hakkert, 1970).

G. T. Griffith, *Alexander the Great: The Main Problems* (Cambridge: Hedder, 1966).

troyed. Still in the same year, Alexander crossed the Bosporus into Asia Minor, liberated in a triumphal procession the Greek cities of Ionia from Persian rule, and defeated the Persian army stationed in Asia Minor in the battle at the Granicus in 334.

The first great victory over the Persian king Darius III was won in 333 BCE at Issus, near the gateway leading from Asia Minor into Syria. The rest of Syria and Phoenicia, Samaria, and Jerusalem were taken without major resistance; only the conquest of Tyre involved a lengthy siege. Soon Egypt also submitted to Alexander's rule without battle, and in the Libyan temple of Ammon at Siwa, Alexander was greeted by the priest as the son of Zeus-Ammon. The founding of the new city of Alexandria in Egypt became the symbol for a whole new cultural epoch. Alexander's victory in 331 over Darius at Gaugamela, east of the upper Tigris, opened access to the central countries of the Persian realm. But the conquest of the northeastern sections of the Persian empire, including Bactria, entangled the Macedonian army in protracted battles. Finally, in the year 327, Alexander reached India (= modern Pakistan), but before he could advance to the Ganges river, his army forced him to turn back. Historians have variously evaluated the political significance of this expedition to India and the subsequent passage of Alexander's fleet through the Hydaspes, the Indus, and through the Arabian Sea to the Persian Gulf. Nonetheless, it is certain that these exploratory missions were a powerful stimulus, both to the development of Greek science and also for the literary imagination, the effects of which lasted for many centuries.

After his return west into the Persian heartlands, Alexander tried to reorganize the immense empire he had conquered. But Alexander failed in this effort, in part because he was unable to overcome the difficulties lying in his own personality, and also because of the complexity of the problems created through his conquests. Specific difficulties included Alexander's political meandering, often coupled with a want of moderation; his increasing unpredictability; the simultaneous alienation of the Persian nobility and of his Greek advisers and generals; and finally the ill-conceived and unrealistic policy of amalgamation of the Greco-Macedonian and Persian populations.

Victor Ehrenberg, *Alexander and the Greeks* (Oxford: Blackwell, 1938).

Ernst Badian, "Alexander the Great and the Greeks of Asia," in: idem (ed.), *Ancient Society and Institutions: Studies Presented to Victor Ehrenberg on his 75th Birthday* (Oxford: Blackwell, 1966) 37–69.

Idem, "Alexander the Great and the Unity of Mankind," *Hist* 7 (1958) 425–44.

Idem, *Alexander the Great: Collected Essays* (Chico, CA: Scholars Press, forthcoming).

Helmut Berve, *Das Alexanderreich auf prosopographischer Grundlage* (2 vols.; München: Beck, 1926).

These last years of Alexander also seem to have witnessed the beginnings of the divine veneration of the ruler, although not all traditional information about this process is reliable. But it is well attested that in the year 324 Alexander requested the Greeks to worship his deceased friend Hephaestion as a divine hero, and that Greek ambassadors appeared before Alexander wearing crowns fit for an audience before a god; divine veneration of the living ruler is thus presupposed. Contrary to former views, it is recognized today that such a ruler cult is not derived from "oriental" concepts imported into Greek culture, but is the genuine development of Greek ideas about the presence of the divine in extraordinary persons. Egyptian ideas may have played some additional role in the formation of the concept of the divine king (§1.5a–d).

In the year 323 BCE, Alexander, not yet thirty-three years old, fell ill with a fever and died in Babylon, which he had chosen to become the capital of his new empire.

(c) The Situation at the Time of Alexander's Death

At the time of his death, Alexander's empire was not threatened by any external enemies and indeed was protected by a strong army, but the problem of the inner consolidation of this vast realm was completely unsolved. A number of new Greek cities had been founded as colonies primarily serving the military and the civil administration; only later would these cities become significant culturally and economically. But the empire as a whole had not been given a new organization; the old Persian administration was simply taken over, with Greeks and Macedonians (also Persians later, in the east) appointed as satraps and financial administrators. Military concerns predominated in the administration, evident in the fact that it was mostly generals who were entrusted with the old Persian provinces, i.e., people who were unlikely to subordinate their personal ambitions to the common good of a new, united empire.

Immediate difficulties arose from the psychological effect of the news about the death of Alexander. As soon as that report arrived, Greece rose up in arms, involving the Macedonian administrator Antipater (an old general and minister of Alexander's father Philip II) in a difficult war. This event demonstrated that Greece was neither ready nor able to share responsibility for the new situation in the east which had been created by

Bibliography to §1.2c

Hermann Bengtson, "Die ptolemäische Staatsverwaltung im Rahmen der hellenistischen Administration," in: idem, *Kleine Schriften zur Alten Geschichte* (München: Beck, 1974) 304–22.

Fritz Schachermeyer, *Alexander in Babylon und die Reichsordnung nach seinem Tode* (SÖAW.PH 268; Wien: Kommissionsverlag der ÖAW, 1970).

Alexander. To be sure, in the following years numerous Greeks emigrated to the new cities founded in the lands of the former Persian empire and thus played a decisive role in shaping the newly formed empires into "Hellenistic" states. But the old Greek states never made the matter of the new empires their own concern.

That Alexander died without leaving an heir and successor proved to be disastrous; his son by the Bactrian princess Roxane was born after his death, and from the day of his birth was nothing but a pawn in various political intrigues. Alexander's younger brother Philip Arrhidaeus was completely incapable of filling the dead king's shoes. In any case, the Macedonian army, by no means committed to the house of the king for better or worse, would readily give allegiance to the most influential leader, whoever he was. Moreover, the Persian auxiliaries, who formed an important part of the army together with the Macedonian footguards, could not be expected to show any greater loyalty to the house of the foreign king.

3. THE DIADOCHI AND THE FORMATION
OF THEIR EMPIRES

(a) The Developments prior to the Death of Antipater

The battles which the successors of Alexander (= the Diadochi) fought among themselves have been described frequently and with more detail and thoroughness than is possible within the scope of this book. But the most important features must be repeated here, because they serve to demonstrate the different forces and tensions at work in the development as well as in the decline of the Hellenistic empires during the centuries to follow.

The decision about who was to succeed Alexander fell to the assembly of the Macedonian army in Babylon, which had assumed the role of the capital of his empire for the time being. It was already clear that the political center of gravity would never return to the Greco-Macedonian

Bibliography to §1.3

W. W. Tarn, "The New Hellenistic Kingdoms," in *CambAncHist* 7. 75–108.

Edouard Will, *Histoire politique du monde hellénistique (323–30 avant J.-C.)* (Nancy: Faculté des lettres et des sciences humaines de l'Université, 1966–67).

Horst Braunart, "Hegemoniale Bestrebungen der hellenistischen Grossmächte in Politik und Wirtschaft," *Hist* 13 (1964) 80–104.

Paul Cloché, *La Dislocation d'un Empire: Les premiers successeurs d'Alexandre le Grand (323–281/280 avant J.-C.)* (Paris: Payot, 1959).

Hatto H. Schmitt, *Die Staatsverträge des Altertums III: Die Verträge der griechisch-römischen Welt von 338 bis 200 v. Chr.* (München: Beck, 1969).

homeland. Perdiccas, who had held the position of the chiliarch (= commander of the royal guard) since the death of Alexander's friend Hephaestion, was confirmed in this office and remained in the east as regent
of the Asian part of the empire. Craterus, the most experienced of Alexander's generals, was leading the veterans of the army back to their Macedonian homes at the time of Alexander's death; he was appointed "guardian
of the royal interests," i.e., he was responsible for Arrhidaeus, Alexander's
incompetent brother, and for Alexander's yet unborn child, and became
commander-in-chief of the army in their name. Whereas Antipater was
confirmed as the *strategus* of Macedonia, an agreement was reached for a
new division of the former Persian satrapies: Antigonus Monophthalmus
("the one-eyed"), one of the Alexander's older generals, received Phrygia,
Pamphylia, and Lycia (i.e., the central and southern part of Asia Minor);
another senior officer, Lysimachus, took over Thrace; Eumenes of Cardia,
a Greek distinguished as an administrator, became satrap of Cappadocia.
Ptolemy the "Lagide" (son of Lagus), who belonged to Alexander's generation, had once been his bodyguard, and had proven to be an excellent
army officer, received Egypt. Ptolemy alone of the first generation of satraps was able to hold on to his original satrapy, a feat due not only to his
intelligence and cunning, but also to the isolated position of the country
which he received. Moreover, Ptolemy seems to have abandoned from the
very beginning any thought of reconstituting the unity of Alexander's empire and concentrated all his efforts upon the strengthening of his own position as the ruler of a separate kingdom. The primary interest of the other
Diadochi, in contrast, was the reunification of the whole empire under
their own leadership—an aim not always motivated by selfish ambition
alone. But this idea of a unified empire receded more and more into the
background during the wars of the following decades, until the building of
clearly defined, separate kingdoms finally became the only concern. But
there was still another reason for continuing battles among the Diadochi:
the maintenance of a direct connection with the Greek homeland proved to
be of vital importance for the Hellenistic kingdoms, as well as the control,
for economic but also for symbolic reasons, of at least some part of the old
Greek territories. Thus conflict was unavoidable with the old Greek city-
states, whose striving for freedom was repeatedly frustrated.

Perdiccas, supported by Eumenes, tried to establish the unity of the
empire under his own leadership, with Babylon as his capital, and had the
most powerful position during the first few years. But he was defeated and
killed when the other satraps formed an alliance against him. In a provi-
sional settlement, Antipater became regent in his stead (321 BCE), and
Seleucus, who had participated in the alliance against Perdiccas, received
Babylonia as his satrapy. Antigonus Monophthalmus sought to expand

his influence in Asia, but found that both Eumenes and Seleucus stood in his way. When Antipater died in 319, the settlement collapsed after lasting only two years.

(b) Events prior to the Battle of Ipsus

Before Antipater died, he appointed Polyperchon, an old, tested general, as his successor. However, Antipater's son Cassander, resentful at being passed over, revolted against this appointment. Cassander was supported by Eurydice, a granddaughter of Philip II, who meanwhile had married Alexander's brother Arrhidaeus. More important, the powerful Antigonus Monophthalmus also joined with Cassander; only Eumenes recognized Polyperchon as regent, who though legitimate, was quite incompetent. During the course of the ensuing wars, Polyperchon was expelled; Eumenes, who had most unselfishly supported the concept of the unity of the empire, was defeated and executed; and Arrhidaeus and Eurydice were poisoned by Alexander's mother Olympias, after returning from her exile. Seleucus fled to Ptolemy in Egypt, because he was threatened by Antigonus, now the sole ruler of Asia, while Cassander was left to establish himself as ruler over Macedonia and Greece. A preliminary peace was agreed upon in 311 BCE; Cassander sealed this treaty by executing the young son of Alexander, now officially the king, and his mother Roxane—both being held under his protection.

It appeared that there was no danger of a revival of dynastic claims and that a balance had been found among the rival Hellenistic kingdoms, each an economically viable unit. Asia Minor and Syria under Antigonus together formed the most powerful kingdom, which also possessed the greatest share of world trade. Egypt, which for a time also possessed southern Syria and the Cyrenaica, was able to strengthen its position. Seleucus had returned to Babylon in 312 and subjected the entire Iranian east to his rule, and even though he met resistance from the Indian king Sandrocottus (Tchandragupta), he was able to reach agreement with him.

In the west, Lysimachus ruled Thrace in relative peace. Cassander of Macedonia was the master of Greece proper. But the balance of power was soon disturbed by the ambitious design of Antigonus, who for the last time tried to reconstitute the unity of the whole empire of Alexander the Great. But the agreement would nonetheless have proven to be of short duration for another reason: two of the major kingdoms, namely Egypt and Babylonia/Persia, had no direct access to the Greek motherland.

War started again when Demetrius Poliorcetes ("the taker of cities"), son and coregent of Antigonus Monophthalmus, took Athens by a *coup de main*. This ended the last period of independent renewal of Athenian culture under the ten-year rule of the Peripatetic philosopher Demetrius of

Phaleron, now forced to flee to Ptolemy in Egypt (307 BCE). Shortly afterwards, Demetrius Poliorcetes defeated Ptolemy's fleet near Salamis on
Cyprus and thus achieved undisputed maritime superiority for a decade,
even after the final defeat of his father. Encouraged by his son's achievements, Antigonus claimed the title of king for them both, thus underlining
their claim to leadership in the attempt to reconstitute Alexander's empire. But the immediate result was only that Seleucus, Ptolemy, Lysimachus, and Cassander now also claimed the royal title for themselves, thereby instituting particularism.

In 305/4, Demetrius besieged Rhodes. But despite the deployment of
the most modern siege machinery he was unable to conquer the city which
was allied to Ptolemy of Egypt through a treaty of friendship. (The rise of
Rhodes to become a significant center of culture and trade continued without interruption from this time on.) Meanwhile the coalition of all the
other kingdoms of the Diadochi against Antigonus consolidated. In the
battle of Ipsus in Phrygia (301 BCE) Antigonus Monophthalmus, almost
eighty years old, lost his life and his kingdom. The last attempt to reconstitute the empire of Alexander the Great had failed.

(c) The Consolidation of the Hellenistic Empires

The second cause for the wars of the Diadochi assumed greater significance in this last phase of the military conflicts: neither the kingdom of
Seleucus, now enlarged by Syria, nor Ptolemaic Egypt had any share in
the rule over the Greek homeland. The Thracian king Lysimachus had
been able to add Asia Minor to his realm, and the Macedonian king Cassander controlled the affairs of Greece unchallenged. But access to Greece
was important for the other Hellenistic kingdoms; their administrations
and their armies needed new supplies of manpower from the homeland,
and their economies were closely intertwined with the Greek cities, especially for their exports. Moreover, domination over the Greek cities had
considerable symbolic value.

The first of the other kings who claimed sovereignty over Greece, however, was neither the Seleucid nor the Ptolemy. Rather, Demetrius Poliorcetes, the Antigonid who ruled over the eastern Mediterranean after
the death of his father as the "King of the Sea," endeavored to gain possession of Macedonia and thus also control Greece. Once more he conquered
Athens, where before he had received divine honors: the Athenians had
been the first people to worship him and his father as "Savior Gods."
Major portions of central Greece, Thessaly, and Macedonia fell to him;
Cassander, whose reign is still memorialized today through the city which
he founded and named after his wife Thessalonike, had died in 298 BCE.
However, Lysimachus, in alliance with the young king of Epirus, Pyrrhus

(who later was to become famous through his "Pyrrhic" victories over the Romans), challenged these conquests. Finally, Demetrius, the most enterprising among the Diadochi, after some initial success in Asia Minor, fell into the hands of Seleucus (286), in whose prison he died three years later. Egypt could now secure its access to Greece by seizing the inheritance of Demetrius as ruler of the sea, thus extending its dominion over the Aegean islands, and after the fall of Lysimachus over some coastal areas of Asia Minor as well.

Seleucus, however, could gain access to the Greek homeland only at the price of war with Lysimachus. This exemplary administrator and successful general, especially in his fight against the northern barbarians, had established a flourishing kingdom controlling access to the Black Sea. The incident which triggered the war was a family conflict: Lysimachus had his son Agathocles executed; his partisans fled to Seleucus. In the subsequent war Seleucus defeated Lysimachus in battle on the Corupedium, near Magnesia-on-the-Maeander (281), where Lysimachus was killed. Seleucus proclaimed himself king of the Macedonians and prepared for the conquest of Macedonia and Greece. Here for the very last time, perhaps, the idea of the reunification of the empire of Alexander was revived. But just as Seleucus made ready to set his foot on European soil, he was assassinated by Ptolemy Ceraunus, the oldest son of Ptolemy Lagide. Thus the last of the Diadochi died; the first Ptolemy had met his death two years earlier. But the Seleucid empire as well as Ptolemaic Egypt had thus reestablished their vital connection to the realm of the Greek homeland and its culture. The situation of Greece itself, however, was still quite unsettled and in lasting confusion.

4. The Empires and States of the Hellenistic World prior to the Roman Conquest

(a) Greece and Macedonia

In cultural and economic terms, the first half of III BCE was the prime period of the Hellenistic era. The Hellenistic kingdoms were governed by the sons of the Diadochi, all remarkable rulers: in Egypt, Ptolemy II; in Syria, Antiochus I; and a little later in Macedonia and Greece, Antigonus Gonatas. Greece proper, however, shared little in the generally fortunate condition of this period. Before the middle of III BCE, a Celtic invasion brought destruction and war to Greece and parts of Asia Minor. With the exception of Pyrrhus' short-lived adventures in southern Italy and Sicily, political developments in the Hellenistic East, including Greece, took little account of Rome and its steadily growing power. The interventions of

Rome at the end of this century therefore came as a real shock with far-reaching consequences. Macedonia and Greece, much weaker militarily and politically than the other Hellenistic countries, were the first to be surprised by Roman interventionist politics, and they were no match for the newcomers.

After the assassination of Seleucus, Ptolemy Ceraunus became the ruler of Macedonia; however, he was killed in 279 BCE in a battle against the Celts. The latter advanced as far as Delphi and caused widespread devastation, but withdrew due to the approaching winter and invaded Asia Minor instead. The anarchy now left in Macedonia and Greece in the wake of the Celtic invasion lasted several years and provided an opportunity for the Aetolian League to strengthen its position and influence. (The Aetolians, a league of tribes settled in the mountains of central Greece, had distinguished themselves in battle against the Celts.) In Macedonia, Antigonus Gonatas had clung to a small portion of the possessions of his father Demetrius Poliorcetes. He succeeded in subduing those Celts who had settled in Thrace, and during the following years brought all of Macedonia and parts of Greece under his control. He also defended his position against Pyrrhus of Epirus (§1.4c), who was killed in a street battle (272 BCE), and in the Chremonidean War Antigonus curtailed the Ptolemaic domination of the Aegean Sea, thus securing free access to Greece for

Bibliography to §1.4

M. Cary, *A History of the Greek World from 323 to 146 B.C.* (London: Methuen, 1951).

A. Aymard, *Les grandes monarchies hellénistiques en Asie après la mort de Seleucos Ier* (Paris: Centre de documentation universitaire, 1965).

Grace Harriet Macurdy, *Hellenistic Queens: A Study of Women-Power in Macedonia, Seleucid Syria, and Ptolemaic Egypt* (Johns Hopkins University Studies in Archaeology 14; Baltimore: Johns Hopkins, 1932).

Bibliography to §1.4a

W. W. Tarn, "Macedonia and Greece," in *CambAncHist* 7. 197–223.

Benedictus Niese, *Geschichte der griechischen und makedonischen Staaten seit der Schlacht bei Chaeronea* (Gotha: Perthes, 1893–1903).

J. A. O. Larsen, *Greek Federal States* (Oxford: Clarendon, 1968).

William Scott Ferguson, *Hellenistic Athens: A Historical Essay* (London: Macmillan, 1911).

W. G. Forrest, *A History of Sparta 950–192 B.C.* (New York: The Norton Library, 1969).

A. H. M. Jones, *Sparta* (Oxford: Blackwell, 1967).

Moses Hadas, "The Social Revolution in 3rd Cent. Sparta," *The Classical World* 26 (1932/33) 65–76

F. W. Walbank, *Aratos of Sicyon* (Cambridge: Cambridge University, 1933).

Idem, *Philip V of Macedon* (Cambridge: Cambridge University, 1940).

N. G. L. Hammond, *Epirus* (Oxford: Clarendon, 1967).

W. W. Tarn, "The Greek Leagues and Macedonia," in *CambAncHist* 7. 732–68.

much-needed grain imports. Antigonus Gonatas was not only an energetic
ruler, but also a student of philosophy, whose teacher had been Zeno, the
founder of the Stoa (§4.1d). Philosophers were welcome at his court, and
in his political actions he strove to follow the principles of Stoic philosophy. In his long reign he successfully strengthened the domination of
Macedonia over Greece, but experienced several setbacks in the last years
before his death (239 BCE): the major leagues of Greek states renewed
their efforts to achieve greater political independence, supported by
Egypt; Euboea and Corinth gained autonomy, and the organized piracy of
the Aetolians increased markedly.

MACEDONIA

(all dates are BCE)

Rulers		Events	
359–336	Philip II		
336–323	Alexander the Great		
317–297	Cassander	316	Founding of Thessalonike
	Antigonids:		
294–287	Demetrius I (Poliorcetes)		
283–239	Antigonus II Gonatas	279	Celtic invasion
239–229	Demetrius II		
229–221	Antigonus III Doson	222	Victory over Sparta
221–179	Philip V	220–217	"Social War"
		215–205	1st Macedonian War
		197	defeated by Rome at Cynoscephalae
179–168	Perseus	171–168	3rd Macedonian War
		168–149	Macedonia divided into four districts
		149	Insurrection of Andriscus
		after 148	Roman province

Gonatas' second successor, Antigonus Doson (229–221), was able to reestablish peace to some extent but this pacification was questionable for
two reasons. Antigonus Doson could achieve his goals only by subduing
Sparta, bringing to a premature end the social reforms begun by the Spartan king Agis IV and resumed by Cleomenes III, reforms which set an
example for other Greek cities. On the other hand, Antigonus was unable
to come to terms with the problem of Rome and the threat of its increasing
power. The aid of the other Hellenistic states would have been required,
since Macedonia was too weak to stand alone. But neither the Ptolemies
nor the Seleucids were willing or able to lend the needed support. The
question of Roman intervention in Greek affairs became a real issue dur-

ing the reign of Doson's successor, Philip V (221–179). The peace of Naupactus, which ended the war of Macedonia and Achaea against Sparta and the Aetolians (the Social War, 220–217), was the last peace treaty the Greeks achieved without Roman participation. In the first Macedonian War (215–205), when Pergamum and Aetolia stood as Roman allies against Macedonia, which was in league with Rome's arch-enemy Hannibal, Greece was still spared from a direct military intervention of the Roman forces. But when Philip sought to take control of the former Ptolemaic possessions in the Aegean in accordance with the Egyptian partition treaty he had made with Antiochus III, Rhodes and Pergamon appealed to Rome (201 BCE). Rome, strengthened in its self-assurance by its victory over Hannibal, decided to intervene for purely imperialistic reasons. A Roman army, supported by Macedonia's arch-enemies, the Aetolians, defeated Philip in the year 197 BCE at Cynoscephalae in Thessaly. Philip's domain was restricted to Macedonia, and the king was forced to surrender his fleet, to pay war indemnity, and to give up all his other possessions. The Romans proceeded to punish the Spartan king Nabis, who had attempted to resume the social reforms of Cleomenes. After they had sent a large number of Greek works of art home to Italy, the Romans proclaimed the freedom of the Greek states and withdrew.

Philip's son Perseus (179–168 BCE) sought to break the isolation of Macedonia imposed by Rome and established relationships with Bithynia, Rhodes, and Syria; he also tried to win the sympathies of Greece for the Macedonian cause. In spite of some success he was finally ruined through the insidious villainy of Rome: while offering its help, Rome was already planning a war to crush Macedonia once and for all. Though Perseus defended himself well against the Romans at the beginning of the war, he was ultimately defeated at Pydna by the Roman philhellene Aemilius Paullus (168 BCE). Macedonia and its Greek friends were severely punished. As an aftermath of the defeat of Perseus came the humiliation of Rhodes, which had sided with the Macedonians. Although Rhodes had not dared to begin open war with Rome, the Roman Senate gave in to the pressures of a strong business lobby to force the island to give up its possessions on the mainland of Asia Minor and to accept severe restrictions of its trade, to the benefit of Roman-dominated Delos.

Rome thus began its domination of Greece, but peace and quiet did not return immediately. A blacksmith named Andriscus, who claimed to be a son of Perseus, led an insurrection in Macedonia (149 BCE). After its suppression Macedonia became a Roman province. In 146 BCE the Achaean League went to war against Sparta, Rome's ally. Roman emissaries were insulted in Corinth, and after the defeat of the Achaean League the Romans completely destroyed that city. The site remained desolate until

Caesar refounded Corinth as a Roman colony and settled it with Italian colonists (44 BCE; see §6.3b). In this war, which led to the incorporation of a large part of the country into the new province of Macedonia, Greece suffered immensely. New miseries came through the wars of Mithridates with Rome (88–83 BCE; see §1.4b).

(b) Asia Minor

Only the western and southern parts of Asia Minor were conquered by Alexander the Great; the northern and eastern regions remained on the fringes of Hellenistic politics. The collapse of the kingdom of Lysimachus on both sides of the straits to the Black Sea allowed new possibilities for independent development in the western regions. The rise of more local-ized power centers was further encouraged by the decreasing strength of the Seleucid kingdom and the inability of Ptolemaic Egypt to maintain its control over the coastal areas of Caria, Lycia, and Cilicia (including such cities as Ephesus and Miletus).

Pergamum became culturally and economically the most important kingdom of Asia Minor during III and II BCE. Philetaerus, son of Attalus of Tios, had been installed by Lysimachus as commander of Pergamum (thus the designation "Attalids" for the later kings of Pergamum) but he deserted Lysimachus before the latter's final defeat (281 BCE) and sup-ported Seleucus. This led to the establishment of a small independent kingdom, whose capital was the fortress and city of Pergamum, strategi-cally situated in the Caicus valley of northwestern Asia Minor. Eumenes I, nephew and successor of Philetaerus, defeated the Seleucid king Antio-chus I near Sardis and expanded the rule of Pergamum over the entire Caicus valley and to the Aegean coast (263–241 BCE).

The reigns of the three successors of Eumenes I mark the century-long flowering of Pergamum. Attalus I Soter (241–197), a cousin of Eumenes I, was able to defeat the Celts, assumed the title king, and temporarily controlled all of southern Asia Minor as far as the Taurus mountains. He managed to reach an understanding with the Romans, whom he sup-ported against Macedonia. But Attalus' fame was established through his support of the arts and scholarship and through his splendid buildings. His son and successor Eumenes II Soter (197–159) made Pergamum a

Bibliography to §1.4b

David Magie, *Roman Rule in Asia Minor* (Princeton: Princeton University, 1950).

George M. A. Hanfmann, *From Croesus to Constantine: The Cities of Western Asia Minor and Their Arts in Greek and Roman Times* (Ann Arbor: University of Michigan, 1975).

Louis Robert, *Villes d'Asie Mineur* (Etudes Orientals 2; 2d ed.; Paris: Boccard, 1962).

major world power, not without the help and blessings of Rome, and reformed Pergamum's administration accordingly. The wealth and splendor of his rule were shown by buildings which achieved worldwide fame:
the Palace of Eumenes, the Library of Pergamum with over 200,000 volumes, the Altar of Zeus, as well as the Stoa of Eumenes in Athens. Thus
the Attalids became the most significant patrons of Greek art and scholarship in II BCE. Attalus II Philadelphus (159–138) continued the policies
and the building activities of his brother, best known through the Stoa of
Attalus in Athens. The last king of Pergamum, Attalus III Philometor
(138–133), died after a short reign and willed his country by testament to
the Roman Senate. With this territory the Romans established the province of Asia.

Bithynia, a Thracian country in northwestern Asia Minor on the Propontis and the Black Sea, was able to maintain its independence even after
the conquest of Asia Minor by Alexander the Great. The most important
ruler in III BCE was Nicomedes I, who founded the city of Nicomedia in
264 BCE. He defended himself successfully against the Seleucid king
Antiochus I and against Antigonus Gonatas of Macedonia; however, he
called to his aid the Celtic tribes which were to remain the terror of large
parts of Asia Minor, even after their forced settlement in the central
region of the subcontinent (Galatia). Nicomedes' successor Prusias I
(230–182) founded the city of Prusa. It was to the Bithynian king that
Hannibal fled after the failure of his designs against Rome in alliance
with Antiochus III of Syria. In Bithynia Hannibal committed suicide
(where later the Roman emperor Septimius Severus erected a large monument for him in Libyssa) in order to avoid extradition to the Romans (183
BCE). Yet this event also marks the growing Roman influence in this area.
In the following decades Rome intervened repeatedly in the affairs of
Bithynia, until the region came under Roman control in 74 BCE through
the testament of its last king in the same way in which Pergamum had
become Roman more than half a century earlier.

In northern Asia Minor, the Kingdom of Pontus, situated along the
Black Sea, was ruled by Hellenized Iranian princes. Several Greek cities
were established in its domain, such as Sinope and Trapezus. The first
known ruler of the Hellenistic period was Mithridates II Ctistes (302–
266 BCE). At first he was subject to Lysimachus, but after 281 BCE he
called himself king and successfully defended his independence against the
Seleucids. Pontus had a mixed population of Greeks, Iranians, and remnants of older Anatolian nations which were Hellenized only during the
later centuries. The Greek cities preserved their independence for a long
period, but Sinope was conquered by Pharnaces I (185–170 BCE) and became the capital of Pontus under his successor Mithridates IV. The desire

of the kings of Pontus to appear as the equals of other Hellenistic kings is evident in their Greek surnames; these were later supplemented by Roman honorary titles which demonstrated the growing influence of Rome even in this remote area: Mithridates IV Philopator Philadelphus (179–159 BCE) called himself "Friend and Ally of the Romans," a title which was also assumed by his son Mithridates V Euergetes (150–120), who supported Rome during the Third Punic War. Until this time the Romans let it be known that they had no objections to the further expansion of the realm of Pontus, but the conflict with Rome became unavoidable in view of the aspirations of the most talented and last king of Pontus, Mithridates VI Eupator Dionysus (120–63 BCE). This Hellenized Iranian attempted to make himself the advocate of the Greek inheritance and to establish a Hellenistic empire in the east which would halt Rome's imperialistic expansion; the result was decades of war during which the people of Greece and the Greek populations of Asia Minor were subjected to countless sufferings. Mithridates, the "Savior of the Greeks," began by conquering western Armenia (Armenia Minor) and thus became the master of northern and eastern Anatolia and almost all of the area bordering the Black Sea. In the first war with Rome, which now opposed the further expansion of the Pontian realm, Mithridates, enthusiastically hailed as the "New Dionysus" by many Greeks, conquered all of Asia Minor and Greece (86 BCE). This liberation of the Greeks was accompanied by the murder of 80,000 Italians in Asia Minor (the "Asian Vespers") and the sack of the Roman-dominated island of Delos. The new freedom of the Greeks did not last very long. Sulla (§6.1d) defeated Mithridates in several battles and forced him to give up all his new conquests. Athens, the first Greek city to make an alliance with Mithridates, was demolished and plundered by Sulla's army. But the wars with Mithridates continued, and it was Pompey (§6.1d) who finally defeated this last Hellenistic empire and initiated the establishment of a new order in Asia Minor according to Roman concepts of pacification (63 BCE).

Cappadocia, the eastern-most district of the Anatolian upland, at the upper course of the Halys river, became subject to Hellenistic rule under Alexander's successor Perdiccas. But it seceded during the latter part of III BCE under Ariaramnes, son of the last Persian satrap. Ariaramnes' son assumed the title of king in 225 BCE. During the following period Cappadocia remained on the fringes of Hellenistic influence, at times completely independent, at other times subject to Pontus, until it was conquered by the Romans under Pompey and became a Roman vassal kingdom. Later it became a Roman province and together with Pontus, Galatia, and Paphlagonia was administered by a Roman legate from 72 CE.

(c) Egypt

Geographically and economically Egypt was more homogeneous than other Hellenistic states. Wars with other countries usually concerned only its outlying territories in Syria, Asia Minor, and the Aegean islands, rarely Egypt itself. This secure situation of the central area of Ptolemaic rule was the foundation of its considerable economic wealth and prosperity and permitted its capital Alexandria to become the center of Greek art and science during the flowering of Hellenistic culture (§3.2b). Ptolemy I Soter ("Lagos" 323–283 BCE), first satrap and then king, laid the foundations for the reorganization of Egypt. He established a Greek administration which took over in part the lower ranks of the existing Egyptian administrative system. Economic productivity increased, due in large part to the transition to a monetary economy, replacing the barter trade which had been the rule in domestic transactions. At the same time, Egypt became a more active partner in Mediterranean trade. Ptolemy I also moved the capital from Memphis to the newly-founded Alexandria. The isolation of Egypt was prevented by the possession of southern Syria, Cyprus, the Cyrenaica, several areas and cities in Asia Minor (Miletus, Ephesus, Caria, Lycia), the domination of some islands (Samos, Lesbos, Thera, and parts of Crete) as well as by the protectorate over the league of the Aegean islands.

The Hellenistic empire of Egypt experienced its greatest flowering under Ptolemy II Philadelphus (283/2–246). To be sure, the long series of Syrian Wars was begun during his rule, in which Egypt fought with the Seleucids for possession of southern Syria, Palestine, and the Phoenician cities. But, for the time being, Egypt was able to defend its Syrian possessions; the influence of its culture and economy remained unbroken over the areas inhabited by the Jewish nation. To the south, expeditions into Arabia and Ethiopia expanded the area of Ptolemaic domination. Philadelphus also strengthened and improved the system of administration and economic control, the internal revenue service, geodetic surveys, irrigation, and the centralized regulation of agricultural production. In the year

Bibliography to §1.4c

Wilhelm Schubart, *Ägypten von Alexander dem Großen bis auf Mohammed* (Berlin: Weidmannsche Buchhandlung, 1922).

Edwyn Bevan, *A History of Egypt under the Ptolemaic Dynasty* (London: Methuen, 1927).

Alen Edouard Samuel, *Ptolemaic Chronology* (MBPF 43; München: Beck, 1962).

P. M. Fraser, *Ptolemaic Alexandria* (Oxford: Clarendon, 1972).

Theodore Cressy Skeat, *The Reigns of the Ptolemies* (München: Beck, 1954).

M. Rostovtzeff, "Ptolemaic Egypt," in *CambAncHist* 7. 109–54.

278 Philadelphus divorced his wife Arsinoë I to marry his sister Arsinoë II, who had been married to Lysimachus and afterwards to Ptolemaeus Ceraunus (§1.3c). Such a marriage was considered incestuous by the Greeks, but it was legal according to Egyptian and Achaemenid custom. Arsinoë II was the first great woman of the Hellenistic period who fully shared in the making of political decisions. Arsinoë and Philadelphus received divine honors during their lifetime as "Divine Brother and Sister" (§1.5c).

EGYPT

(all dates are BCE)

Rulers		Events	
		322	Alexander in Egypt: Founding of Alexandria
323–283/2	Ptolemy I Soter	ca. 300	Creation of cult of Sarapis
283/2–246	Ptolemy II Philadelphus	274–271	1st Syrian War
		260–253	2nd Syrian War
246–222/1	Ptolemy III Euergetes	246–241	3rd Syrian War
222/1–204	Ptolemy IV Philopator	219–217	4th Syrian War
204–180	Ptolemy V Epiphanes	195	Palestine comes under Syrian rule
180–145	Ptolemy VI Philometor	170–168	Antiochus IV in Egypt
145–116	Ptolemy VIII Euergetes II		Greek scholars expelled
116–107	Ptolemy IX Soter II		
107–88	Ptolemy X		
88–80	Ptolemy IX (see above)		
80–51	Ptolemy XI Auletes	55	Roman garrison in Egypt
51–30	Cleopatra VII	48	Pompey killed in Egypt
51–47	Ptolemy XIII		Caesar in Egypt
		30	Marc Antony commits suicide in Egypt

after 30 BCE Egypt Roman province

Under Philadelphus' successor, Ptolemy III Euergetes (246–222/1), Egyptian power reached its apex. Euergetes was a skilled diplomat, successful in war against the Seleucids, and also protected Egyptian trade with a strong navy. In war with Syria he advanced as far as the Euphrates, but was unable to hold his Syrian conquests, with the exception of the port city Seleucia, near Antioch. Egypt's situation began to deteriorate, however, under the next king, Ptolemy IV Philopator (221–204). Although the victory over Antiochus III of Syria at Raphia (217 BCE) once more confirmed Egyptian rule over Palestine, Nubian kings in the southern regions of the Nile were able to establish an independent realm (206–

185). The Mediterranean trade, vital for the Egyptian economy, suffered severely during the Second Punic War, and Egypt itself was tormented by repeated insurrections of the native Egyptian population—a problem which the government was never able to solve. After Philopator's death, when guardians governed for his son Ptolemy V Epiphanes, who was still a minor, Antiochus III of Syria and Philip V of Macedonia even made a partition treaty for the Egyptian possessions. Following the terms of this pact, Antiochus conquered southern Syria and Palestine, which thus became a part of the Seleucid empire (see also §5.1b).

During II BCE, Egypt was torn by repeated struggles over succession to the throne, conflicts in which the sister-wives Cleopatra II and Cleopatra III played important parts. Several times the Egyptian empire broke up into its constituent parts of Egypt, Cyprus, and Cyrenaica. Attempts to reconquer southern Syria failed, but rather enticed Antiochus IV Epiphanes to attempt the conquest of Egypt; only Roman intervention forced him to withdraw. Even the process of Hellenization suffered severe setbacks in the second half of II BCE. Ptolemy VIII Euergetes III (170-164, coregent with his brother; 145-116 king and second husband of his sister Cleopatra II) expelled the Greek artists and scholars from Alexandria. As a result, Rhodes and Pergamum achieved eminence as the new centers of Greek culture and learning. In the royal administration of Egypt, Hellenized Egyptians increasingly replaced members of the Macedonian upper class. At the same time, Egypt lost its political independence and became in fact a client state of Rome, although for the time being the Romans intervened only occasionally in the internal affairs of Egypt.

A Roman garrison was finally established in the year 55 BCE, when the Romans brought Ptolemy XII Neos Dionysus (called "Auletes" = "the flute-player"; 80-58 and 55-51) back to Egypt and restored him to the throne. From that time the Romans considered Egypt a possession at their free disposal. Pompey, after his defeat by Julius Caesar at Pharsalus (48 BCE), fled to Egypt where he was murdered at the instigation of Auletes' son, Ptolemy XIII. This last Ptolemaic king of Egypt drowned in the Nile when the Romans attacked his camp (47 BCE). His sister and wife, Cleopatra VII, the last of the house of Lagides, mistress of Caesar and later wife of Marc Antony, represented in her political astuteness the final inheritance of the Hellenistic rulers of Egypt. When all her plans had failed, she found death through the bite of a poisonous snake.

(d) The Seleucid Empire and Syria

The Seleucid empire comprised an immense area, extending from Bactria in the east to Asia Minor in the west. The constant dilemma of the Seleucid kings was to balance the security and defence of this vast realm with attention to the internal problems and economic development of their central provinces of Syria and Mesopotamia. Control of the important centers of trade and commerce on the Syrian coast, and thus of access to the sea routes in the eastern Mediterranean, was of crucial importance. However, southern Syria, Palestine, and Phoenicia were in Egyptian hands. Wars with Egypt over the possession of these districts were therefore to characterize the entire III BCE.

Antiochus I Soter (281–261; coregent with his father Seleucus from 293) was able to vanquish the Celts (275) and to settle them in Galatia. But he had no success in the first Syrian War against Egypt (274–271), and in his war with Pergamum he was defeated at Sardis by Eumenes I (262). Antiochus II (260–253; coregent from 266), in alliance with Antigonus Gonatas, regained some portions of Asia Minor during the second Syrian War (260–253). But under his successors Seleucus II Callinicus (246–225) and Seleucus III Soter (225–223), the Seleucid empire experienced a crisis which seriously threatened its existence. The Third Syrian War (246–241), caused by dynastic problems, led to the temporary loss of large areas in Asia Minor and Syria and strengthened the independent Anatolian kingdoms. The brother of Seleucus II, Antiochus Hierax, established himself as a rival king in southern Asia Minor with Sardis as his capital, although he was finally defeated by Attalus I of Pergamum and was killed while fighting the Celts in Thrace (266). The cousin of Seleucus III forced Pergamum to return some Seleucid possessions in Asia Minor, but then he also rebelled and made himself independent, with Sardis as his capital.

The difficulties which arose with the accession of Seleucus II to the Syrian throne had even more disastrous consequences in the eastern provinces. The satrap of Bactria, Diodotus, seceded from Syria, relying on aid from the flourishing Greek cities and the Iranian nobility of his realm. This independent Greek kingdom of Bactria survived for several centuries; around the year 200 BCE Bactria controlled a large realm, including

Bibliography to §1.4d

M. Rostovtzeff, "Syria and the East," in *CambAncHist* 7. 155–96.

Edwyn Robert Bevan, *The House of Seleucus* (London: Arnold, 1902).

Hatto H. Schmitt, *Untersuchungen zur Geschichte Antiochos des Grossen und seiner Zeit* (Historia, Einzelschriften 6; Wiesbaden: Steiner, 1964).

H. L. Jansen, *Die Politik Antiochus' des IV*. (Oslo: Kommisjon hos J. Dyswad, 1943).

Alfred R. Bellinger, *The End of the Seleucids* (Transactions of the Connecticut Academy of Arts and Sciences 38; New Haven: Connecticut Academy of Arts and Sciences, 1949) 51–102.

Glanville Downey, *A History of Antioch in Syria* (Princeton: Princeton University, 1961).

Sogdia, parts of northwest India, and perhaps some areas of Chinese Turkestan. Even after the collapse of the Bactrian kingdom the influence of Greek culture survived for a long time, as can be seen in the region's architecture and coinage.

SYRIA

(all dates are BCE)

Rulers	Events
312–281 Seleucus I Nicator	312 Founding of Seleucia on the Tigris
	300 Founding of Antioch on the Orontes
281–261 Antiochus I Soter	275 Defeat of the Celts
	262 Defeated by Pergamum
261–246 Antiochus II Theos	
246–225 Seleucus II Calinicus	240–226 Separate kingdom of Antiochus Hierax in Asia Minor
	ca. 240 Secession of Bactria Establishment of Parthian Kingdom
223–187 Antiochus III the Great	212–205 "Anabasis" of Antiochus
	195 Conquest of Palestine
	191/190 Defeated by Rome
187–175 Seleucus IV Eupator	
175–164 Antiochus IV Epiphanes	170–168 Conquest of Egypt
	168–164 Maccabean Revolt
164–139 Antiochus V, Demetrius I, Alexander Balas, Antiochus VI	140 Judea independent
139–129 Antiochus VII Sidites	
129–125 Demetrius II	
126–96 Antiochus VIII Grypus	
	83–69 Tigranes I of Armenia occupies Syria
	64 Pompey makes Syria a Roman province

While the developments in Bactria posed no direct threat to Seleucid power, the establishment of the Parthian kingdom meant the loss of the entire Iranian region east of the Seleucid empire. The Parni were an Iranian people comprised of horsemen from central Asia who conquered the satrapy of Parthia (east of the Caspian Sea) shortly after 250 BCE. Since this satrapy was their first center of established power, they called themselves "Parthians." In their further expansion, they not only claimed a relationship to the Persian (Achaemenid) heritage but also incorporated many elements of Greek origin. Both Greek and Aramaic were used as official languages in their administration. The privileges of the Greek cities were at least partially confirmed by the Parthian rulers. It was as a "Hellenistic" power that the Parthians became a constant threat to the

Seleucid empire. Arsaces I is known as the founder of the Parthian royal dynasty (the "Arsacids"), but more is known about his successor Tiridates I (ca. 247–210 BCE). Tiridates consolidated the Parthian rule in Parthia and Hyrcania (south of the Caspian Sea) and made further advances to the west, since the Bactrians prevented any expansion to the east.

Under Antiochus III ("the Great"; 223–187) the Seleucid empire finally recovered from its impotency. First, Antiochus turned against Egypt. But after some initial success he was forced to give up southern Syria and Phoenicia/Palestine after a brief occupation, because he was defeated by Ptolemy IV at Raphia (Fourth Syrian War, 221–217). Antiochus then turned to Asia Minor, where he defeated and executed the disloyal viceroy of Sardis, Achaeus (213). Antiochus was now ready for his great campaign into the east (the "Anabasis" of Antiochus). Armenia, Parthia, and Bactria were defeated and forced to recognize the supremacy of the Seleucid king (212–205). Thus he succeeded in reestablishing at least temporarily the Seleucid dominion over the east through a system of dependent vassal states.

As had been agreed in the treaty of the partition of Egypt with Philip V of Macedonia Antiochus occupied southern Syria and Phoenicia/Palestine as soon as the weakness of Egypt became evident after the death of Ptolemy IV (200 BCE). After Egypt had ceded to him all its possessions in Syria, Asia Minor, and Thrace, Antiochus moved west with his army and occupied the straits of the Black Sea. However, when a call for help by the Aetolians enticed him to invade Greece, the Romans decided that they must intervene. They defeated Antiochus at the Thermopylae, scattered his fleet twice in the Aegean, and followed him in his retreat to Asia Minor under the leadership of the brothers Scipio (Africanus and Asiaticus). At Magnesia-on-the-Maeander Antiochus suffered a crushing defeat. He was forced to withdraw entirely from Asia Minor; most of his former possessions now became Pergamene territory. The peace treaty of Apamea (188 BCE) imposed heavy war reparations upon Antiochus, a burden which caused immense financial problems for his country and severely impaired its stability. Antiochus was slain when he attempted to plunder the treasures of a temple (187 BCE).

After his son and successor, Seleucus IV Eupator (187–175), was assassinated by his chancellor, Seleucus' brother, who had spent fourteen years in Rome as a hostage, became his successor: Antiochus IV Epiphanes (175–164). When the conflict with Egypt for the possession of southern Syria flared up once more (Sixth Syrian War, 170–168), Antiochus Epiphanes conquered all of Egypt, with the exception of Alexandria. He was forced to return to Syria briefly (it was at this time that he "plundered" the temple treasures of Jerusalem), but then invaded Egypt once more. However, in a suburb of Alexandria, the Roman ambassador Popilius Laenas encountered him and relayed a message from the Roman Senate: he drew a circle around the king with his cane and requested, before the king stepped over the circle, an answer to Rome's demand that Antiochus return to Syria immediately and give up his Egyptian conquests. The king knew that prudence required him to yield. Shortly afterwards he died during a campaign in Armenia and Media.

The Maccabean Revolt (§5.1c), triggered by the Jews' embitterment over Antiochus Epiphanes' policies of Hellenization, must be understood in the context of the Seleucid empire's subsequent dissolution, for which the intervention of Rome was not the least cause. Never again was the Seleucid kingdom able to raise itself above the level of a petty Asian state; an unavoidable consequence was that former client states saw the opportunity to fight for independence. Dynastic quarrels severely impaired the power of the state after Antiochus' death, yet were only another symptom of the decline of the Seleucid rule.

Southern Syria had been under the authority of the Seleucids for only a few decades. The Maccabean insurrection resulted in the establishment of the Jewish state of the Hasmoneans, which survived until Pompey's conquest of Syria. East of the Jordan, the ancient Arab state of the Nabateans was reorganized with its capital in Petra. Not until 105 CE did parts of Nabatea become a Roman province.

The Parthians continued their westward advance after the year 160 BCE, conquering Media and Babylonia and the ancient Iranian countries to the south. Antiochus Sidites regained control over Media and Babylonia for a brief period, but his army was crushed by the Parthians in 129 BCE. Meanwhile Armenia, ruled by a branch of the royal Parthian family, also rose to become an independent country, further expanding its domain to the southwest. Part of Cappadocia was temporarily under Armenian rule, and in the year 86 BCE Tigranes I of Armenia conquered whatever was left of the Seleucid empire, now so weak militarily and economically that it succumbed without any formidable resistance. Armenia's rule over Syria lasted until the appearance of the Roman legions under Lucullus (69 BCE) and Pompey (64 BCE).

All successor states of the Seleucid empire, including some smaller domains which were able to gain independence during this period (e.g., Commagene and Adiabene), were Hellenized countries that understood themselves as heirs of the Greek tradition, which they combined with their own national heritage. In several instances they claimed the ancestry of both the Greeks and the Achaemenids. The Parthian rulers took over large parts of the existing Seleucid administration, and as they were Hellenized themselves, they had the right to appear as protectors and advocates of Greek culture (e.g., the Arsacid Mithridates I, 171–138 BCE, called himself Euergetes, Dikaios, and Philhellene). The political energies and aims of Hellenism still lived on to some degree in these successor states of the Seleucid realm until the Roman conquest marked the beginning of a new era.

(e) Sicily and Southern Italy

Greeks had inhabited Sicily and southern Italy (Magna Graecia) for centuries. But in the second half of IV BCE they experienced increasing pressure from the Italic tribes—ultimately from Rome—and from Carthage. The only attempt to unite the Greeks of this area that was at all successful was led by Agathocles. His home was Thermae, in western Sicily, where he was born ca. 360 BCE. He became a citizen of Syracuse, 319/18 *strategos,* and in 317/16 absolute sovereign of this the most important Greek city of Sicily. He first fought against Carthage on Sicily, but with little luck, and later without final success in Africa. In any case, he did succeed in uniting the Greeks of Sicily. After the peace with Carthage (306 BCE) he assumed the title "king" (following the example of the Diadochi) and lent his support to the cities of southern Italy in their fight against the Italic tribes. He died in the year 289 BCE, however, without having accomplished his goal of establishing a united Greek kingdom in Sicily and southern Italy.

The expedition of king Pyrrhus of Epirus to Italy against Rome did little if anything for the strengthening of the Greeks of Magna Graecia. After a variety of experiences (e.g., as hostage for Demetrius Poliorcetes at the court of Alexandria) Phyrrhus became king of the Molossians and leader of the Epirote League (297 BCE); after the death of Demetrius Poliorcetes he was even proclaimed king by the Macedonian army. In 280 BCE Pyrrhus invaded Italy in an attempt to support the Greek city Tarentum against the Romans, who had occupied Thurii. The whole campaign was organized at great expense and widely advertised as a pan-Hellenistic war, and in fact, Pyrrhus managed to defeat the Romans in two very costly battles ("Pyrrhic victories"). He advanced as far as the immediate environs of Rome, then went to Sicily and routed the Carthaginians almost completely from the island. But difficulties with the Sicilian Greeks, a last undecided battle with the Romans, and finally his aspirations to the Macedonian throne prompted Pyrrhus to withdraw from Italy (275 BCE)

Bibliography to §1.4e

M. I. Finley, *Ancient Sicily to the Arab Conquest,* in: idem and D. Mack Smith, *A History of Sicily,* vol. 1 (New York: Viking, 1968).
Erik Sjöqvist, *Sicily and the Greeks* (Ann Arbor: University of Michigan, 1973).
David Randall-MacIves, *Greek Cities in Italy and Sicily* (Oxford: Clarendon, 1931).

without achieving any lasting results. Yet he left behind an inheritance of a different kind: Rome never forgot the impression which Pyrrhus and his army had made upon them; it decisively formed their image of the Hellenistic empires and their rulers.

In the following years the Romans rapidly conquered all of southern Italy and parts of Sicily. Syracuse retained some degree of independence under king Hieron II (269/68–215) but was soon restricted to a narrow strip of land along Sicily's east coast and was compelled to pay tribute to Rome. In the First Punic War (264–241) the Romans occupied most of Sicily which became a Roman province in 227 BCE. During the last years of its independence, Syracuse once more enjoyed a flourishing culture. But the disorders following upon the death of Hieron prompted Rome to intervene; the Romans conquered Syracuse and incorporated it into their province of Sicily. The Greeks of southern Italy and Sicily henceforth played a significant role in the mediation of Greek culture to Rome and thus decisively influenced the development of Roman culture.

5. POLITICAL IDEOLOGY AND RULER CULT

(a) Basic Features of Hellenistic Political Ideology

The Hellenistic kings claimed to be the legitimate successors of the Achaemenids and the Pharaohs. Indeed the Seleucids took over from the Achaemenids the royal diadem, the signet ring, and the sacred fire. But for the Greeks, the legitimacy of the new dynasties was not founded in any such resumption of traditional Persian or Egyptian symbols. Rather, the idea of absolute monarchy, which became a reality in the establishment of the Hellenistic rulers, was rooted in very different presuppositions, name-

Bibliography to §1.5a

T. A. Sinclair, *A History of Greek Political Thought* (2d ed.; Cleveland: World, 1968).

V. Ehrenberg, *The Greek State* (2 vols.; New York: Norton, 1964) 2. 135–240.

Mason Hammond, *City-State and World-State in Greek and Roman Political Theory until Augustus* (Cambridge, MA: Harvard University, 1951).

Arnold Ehrhardt, *Politische Metaphysik von Solon bis Augustin,* vol. 1: *Die Gottesstadt der Griechen und Römer* (Tübingen: Mohr/Siebeck, 1959).

The Greek Political Experience: Studies in Honor of William Kelly Prentice (Princeton: Princeton University, and London: Oxford University, 1941).

Erwin R. Goodenough, *The Political Philosophy of Hellenistic Kingship* (YCS 1; New Haven: Yale University, 1928) 55–102.

Max Pohlenz, *Staatsgedanke und Staatslehre der Griechen* (Leipzig: Quelle u. Meyer, 1923).

Fritz Gschnitzer (ed.), *Zur griechischen Staatskunde* (Darmstadt: Wissenschaftliche Buchgesellschaft, 1969).

ly, the Greek beliefs regarding the lawful rights that an extraordinary and distinguished individual could claim. In Greece such people had always been honored as heroes after their death, and poets had praised them as divinely inspired human beings. The philosophers, to be sure, would speak of the "man of wisdom" whose charisma and education would qualify him to become king. But in the common perception it was simply the "best person" who should be followed as king. The philosophers generally taught that the king was in fact the best person, and that he could claim divine rights and divine kinship. Stoic concepts contributed the idea that the exercise of the royal office on earth corresponded to Zeus's royal office in heaven. In any case, the philosophers of the Hellenistic period went to great lengths to demonstrate that the absolute monarchy was the best form of government.

Nonetheless, the Greeks did not consider the state to be the personal property of the ruler. At the same time, it was understood that private interests were subject to the interests of the state, and that everyone had to serve the state whenever necessary with sacrifice of time, possessions, or life. In saying that, however, the Greeks would not have used the word "state"—a concept missing in Greek thought and language—they would have spoken about the "polis" or the "commonwealth" (τὸ κοινόν). An identification of the state (as distinct from polis and commonwealth) with the ruler is only conceivable where the land is the property of the king. Indeed this was exactly the case in the Hellenistic empires of the east: the new countries were "lands conquered by the spear," over which the king possessed unlimited sovereign rights. Here, his will was law. The inhabitants of these countries were simply subjects. The position of the Greek cities in these areas was somewhat different because their citizens possessed certain rights and privileges. Even these cities, however, could not act in opposition to the will of the king. In addition, it served their own best interest to render him special honors and thus express their recognition of him as absolute sovereign.

In Macedonia itself the situation was quite different. The office of the king, even in the Hellenistic period, continued to be understood as something legitimized by the people. Once the Antigonids had been recognized by the Macedonians as their rightful kings, they could count on the people's allegiance to the very end. Thus there was no basis in Macedonia for the development of a ruler cult (and only Greek cities outside of Macedonia extended divine honors to the Macedonian kings).

(b) Origin and Beginnings of the Ruler Cult

Scholars have attempted to explain the origin of the Hellenistic ruler cult from oriental concepts, but this is not possible. To be sure, in Egypt the divinity of the Pharaoh had been the unquestioned foundation of royal ideology for centuries. The Pharaoh, however, was divine simply because he was the Pharaoh, while "the divinity of the Hellenistic ruler was based on his excellence" (A. D. Nock). A derivation of the Hellenistic ruler cult from Persian concepts is even less plausible. Even though the Achaemenid kings practiced the oriental court ceremony, which demonstrated that the king was elevated above all his subjects, the Persian kings were not considered gods. The concept of the divine king had long since disappeared in the east by the time of Alexander's conquests. In considering the possible Greek background, one could refer to the hero cult. But hero worship was rendered to someone who had already died, not to a person still living. Thus there is no direct connection between the ruler cult and the hero cult; it is necessary to consider a different development of Greek thought in order to explain the origin of the worship of the living king.

At the time of the crisis and failure of the Greek polis at the end of v bce and the beginning of iv bce, the philosophers were the first to advertise the idea that only a divinely gifted individual would be able to reestablish peace, order, and prosperity. Plato, Xenophon, and Aristotle expressed this idea quite clearly, though each in his own way. In their thought education, charisma, and divine authorization were intimately related. In accordance with such sentiments, significant rulers and generals on occasion received divine honors during their lifetime, even before the rise of Alexander the Great. In Syracuse, such honors were accorded to the dead ruler in v and iv bce, and later also to the living ruler, who was worshiped as benefactor. The Spartan general Lysander received divine honors after his victory over the Athenians in the Peloponnesian War, and Philip II of Macedonia was hailed as a god by the Athenian rhetor Isocrates.

Alexander at first understood himself as an imitator of his "hero" Hercules. It is not known when and how his self-conception changed. When

---

Bibliography to §1.5b–d: Texts
Grant, *Hellenistic Religions,* 64–70.

Bibliography to §1.5b–d: Studies
Nilsson, *Griechische Religion,* 2. 132–85.
L. Cerfaux and J. Tondriau, *Le culte des souverains* (BT.B 5; Tournai: Desclée, 1957).
Fritz Taeger, *CHARISMA: Studien zur Geschichte des antiken Herrscherkultes,* vol. 1: *Hellas* (Stuttgart: Kohlhammer, 1957).
Christian Habicht, *Gottmenschentum und griechische Städte* (Zet. 14; München: Beck, 1970).
Heinrich Dörrie, *Der Königskult des Antiochos von Kommagene im Lichte neuer Inschriften-Funde* (Göttingen: Vandenhoeck & Ruprecht, 1964).
Nock, "Notes on Ruler-Cult I–IV," in: idem, *Essays,* 1. 134–59.
Idem, "Deification and Julian," in: idem, *Essays,* 2. 833–46.

he visited the oracle of Ammon in the Egyptian desert, the priest greeted
him in front of the temple as the son of the god Re. But this was nothing
extraordinary for Egypt, because after its conquest, Alexander became the
legitimate Pharaoh, and thus also the legitimate son of this god because of
his office. Nobody knows what happened inside the temple. It is quite
possible that at the time Alexander understood that he was indeed the son
of the god Ammon Re (= Zeus). In any case, it seems that it was on the
basis of this new self-conception that he began to solicit tokens and signs of
divine veneration of his own person (§1.2b). Nevertheless, ruler worship
did not become an institution during his lifetime. The abortive attempt
(327 BCE in Bactria) to introduce the customary oriental adoration of the
ruler is no proof to the contrary, because this was simply an eastern court
ceremony, not an act of divine worship. The letter of Alexander to the
Greek cities of 324 BCE, in which he demanded the return of the exiles,
cannot be used as evidence, because only later sources report that in this
letter Alexander requested to be worshiped as a god. One must mention,
however, that divine worship of Alexander by some Greek cities seems to
have taken place already during his lifetime, though only sporadically.

The Diadochi did not make any requests that implied divine worship of
their own persons. Perhaps they were still too close to the overwhelming
impact of the personality of Alexander. Nevertheless, they received such
honors by Greek cities, even before they assumed royal titles. It seems that
these honors were actually forced upon them, most obviously in the case of
Demetrius Poliorcetes with Athens. The cult of the dead Alexander was
energetically promoted by the Diadochi. Eumenes placed the throne of
Alexander in the tent which served as a council chamber. The corpse of
Alexander, which Arrhidaeus wanted to transport to Macedonia, was
seized by Ptolemy I, who brought it to Memphis. Alexander's remains
were later transferred to Alexandria, where a permanent cult for the dead
king was established with all expenses paid by the government. Temples
and sanctuaries dedicated to Alexander's worship are known to have existed, especially in the Ionian cities of Asia Minor; some of these may go
back to his own time. But this worship of the divine Alexander, which
continued in many places for several centuries, is not directly responsible
for the institution of the Hellenistic ruler cult.

(c) The Ruler Cult in Egypt

The divine veneration of the Greek king by the native population of
Egypt was a matter of course from the very beginning. Since the king was
the successor of the Pharaoh, such worship was due to him by virtue of his
office. Thus the traditional Egyptian ruler cult was simply transferred to
the Ptolemies and later to the Roman emperor.

For the Macedonians and Greeks in Egypt, the first step towards the institution of a ruler cult was the worship of Ptolemy I and his wife Berenice as Savior Gods organized by the second Ptolemy after their death. In this way other members of the royal family (including even a mistress) were also deified after their deaths. According to Greek custom the building of a temple and the institution of a festival were regular parts of the establishment of a new deity (Ptolemy II decreed that the winners of the games for these Savior Gods should receive the same honors as the winners at the Olympic games).

But at a later date Ptolemy II also included himself and his sister-wife Arsinoë II as "Divine Brother and Sister" in the worship of the divine members of the royal house. Such worship of the ruling king and queen during their lifetime clearly transcended the limits of the traditional hero cult, but can be understood as a Greek development on the basis of Greek presuppositions. The worship of the Pharaoh's successor as god already present in Egypt probably contributed to the strong institutional development of the Greek ruler cult under the Ptolemies. It is also quite possible that Ptolemy II intended the cult of the living king and queen as gods, which was now an authorized institution for both the Egyptian and the Greek populations, to be a unifying bond for his Greek and non-Greek subjects. But in its basic character, this ruler cult remained a Greek institution and did not differ from the ruler cult practiced in the Seleucid realm or occasionally elsewhere in Hellenistic kingdoms.

A special development of the ruler cult in Egypt occurred under Ptolemy IV Philopator (222–204). He claimed to be a descendant of Dionysus and had that god's ivy leaf tattooed on his body. According to a legend preserved in *3 Macc.* 2.28ff., he attempted to force the Jews of Alexandria to be tattooed in the same way. The expansion of the cult of Dionysus is clearly reflected in these traditions (§4.3f). Ptolemy IV appears on coins wearing the insignia of Helios, Zeus, and Poseidon. There is also evidence of syncretism: in a dedication of a temple for queen Berenice II (III BCE) she is called "Isis, Mother of the Gods, Berenice." If "Mother of the Gods" is a reference to the Phrygian Magna Mater (§4.4b), this appearance of an Asian deity in combination with Isis demonstrates the spread of syncretism at a comparatively early time in the Hellenistic period. This identification of a royal person with particular traditional deities became a typical phenomenon of the further development of the ruler cult, a tendency which found its continuation in the imperial cult of the Roman period (§6.5b).

During II BCE, especially after the loss of the Greek parts of the Ptolemaic realm in Asia Minor and the Aegean, the religious policies of the Alexandrian court closely exhibit features which are more and more

Egyptian. The state also took over the supervision of the synods of Egyptian priests. Cleopatra III (who died in 101 BCE) and later queens of Egypt appeared in official proclamations under the name of the goddess Isis. The sacred marriage of Marc Antony as a New Dionysus with Cleopatra VII as New Isis was the natural culmination—as well as the termination—of the development of the Egyptian ruler cult.

(d) Ruler Cult in the Seleucid Empire

Analogously with the deification of the first Ptolemy after his death, the second Seleucid decreed that his father Seleucus I be worshiped as "Zeus Nicator." It can be assumed that very soon the cult of the living king was also introduced. However, there is·scanty evidence for such a state cult from the Seleucid empire, because direct testimonies are on the whole much rarer for the Seleucid realm than they are for Egypt, which is so rich in papyrus finds. In any case, for Antiochus III there is proof of the worship of the king as a god while still living. This ruler cult was closely related to the worship of Zeus and Apollo, the primary state deities of the Seleucid empire (cf. the famous sanctuary of Apollo in Daphne, near Antioch on the Orontes).

In addition, the Seleucids energetically promoted existing local cults. This was especially important for political reasons; the Seleucid empire included a large number of temple territories which (like some of the Greek cities) possessed certain privileges of autonomy and were thus not subject to the satrapies' administration. Usually they were ruled by a high priest (as was the case for the Jewish temple state of Jerusalem, which came under Seleucid rule in II BCE). Such temples could normally regulate their own affairs. Conflicts might arise if an attempt was made to introduce the state cult into these temples (for the conflict of the Jewish temple state with Antiochus IV Epiphanes, see §5.1c).

Silver Tetradrachma of Lysimachus
The obverse (above) shows the head of Alexander the
Great with the horn of Zeus-Ammon above his ear.
The reverse (a cast) shows the goddess Athena,
seated, with shield and snake, and holding winged Vic-
tory (*Nike*) in her hand, flanked by the inscription
ΒΑΣΙΛΕΩΣ ΛΥΣΙΜΑΧΟΥ ("of king Lysimachus").

Warehouses on Delos

These warehouses, lining the shore near the ancient harbor of the island of Delos in the Aegean Sea, were built in III and II B.C.E. Because of its central position, Delos was used as a primary place for the reshipment of goods transported from the eastern parts of the Mediterranean to Rome. Awaiting reshipment, goods could be stored safely in these warehouses.

SOCIETY AND ECONOMICS

1. HELLENISM AND HELLENIZATION

(a) The Concept of Hellenism

Ever since J. G. Droysen, the term "Hellenism," contrary to its original sense, was understood to mean the amalgamation of Greek and oriental culture. Recent scholarship, however, is more cautious. On the one hand, there was lively exchange between Greece and the east already during the centuries before Alexander, i.e., before the Hellenistic period. Greek colonization, the expansion of Greek economic power, and close cultural contacts, especially among the Greeks of Ionia, had long since led to many combinations of Greek and non-Greek elements, especially outside the Greek homeland. If this process is called "Hellenism," then the term is not well suited as the designation of a particular period of time which begins in the latter part of IV BCE. On the other hand, it is not possible to describe the results of the encounter of Greece with the orient with such terms as "combination" or "amalgamation." Alexander's attempt to unite the Greeks and the Persians into a new nation remained an unfulfilled dream. Alexander's successors insisted that they were first of all Macedonians and Greeks, and they made great efforts to promote and to maintain the Greek element in their countries.

It is advisable, therefore, to use the term Hellenism primarily as a designation of the historical period which begins with Alexander the Great and ends with the final conquest of the east by the Romans, at which point the Roman imperial period begins. The most characteristic phenomenon of the Hellenistic period is "Hellenization," namely, the expansion of the Greek language and culture and, most of all, the establishment of the Greeks' political dominion over other nations of the east. Never was there any question as to which element would predominate: even the successor states of the Hellenistic empires claimed to represent the Greek inheritance. Even when Greek culture encountered the Roman, the Greek element prevailed: the whole eastern part of the Roman empire remained essentially Greek, and the Greek language and culture as well as Greek religion gained considerable ground even in the Latin west.

Thus, Hellenism continued to be effective throughout the Roman imperial period, and insofar as the Roman empire was Hellenized, it found its
natural continuation in the Byzantine period. Indeed, Christianity, which
had its beginnings in the early Roman imperial period, was rapidly Hellenized and appeared in the Roman world as a Hellenistic religion, specifically as the heir to an already Hellenized Jewish religion.

(b) The Greeks and the Nations of the Hellenistic Empires

The nature and extent of the influence of the Greeks and Macedonians
upon the nations they governed differed from country to country, and was
subject to changes in the course of time. There were also changes in the
policies of Hellenization from one ruler to the next. In the beginning the
Greek influence was slight, especially since the Diadochi did not continue
Alexander's policies in this respect. Greeks, the ruling class, occupied all
important positions in the administration and in the army. The Greek

Bibliography to §2

W. W. Tarn, *Hellenistic Civilization* (3d ed.; rev. by author and G. T. Griffith;
    London: Arnold, 1952). A very useful introduction.
Michael I. Rostovtzeff, *The Social and Economic History of the Hellenistic World* (3
    vols.; Oxford: Clarendon, 1941). The fundamental and comprehensive study with
    rich documentation.
Jean-Philippe Levy, *The Economic Life of the Ancient World* (Chicago and London:
    University of Chicago, 1967). An instructive brief survey.
M. I. Finley, *The Ancient Economy* (Berkeley: University of California, 1973).
Horst Braunert, *Das Mittelmeer in Politik und Wirtschaft der hellenistischen Zeit*
    (Kiel: Hirt, 1967).
Ulrich von Wilamowitz-Möllendorf and B. Niese, *Staat und Gesellschaft der
    Griechen und Römer* (Die Kultur der Gegenwart 2,4; Berlin and Leipzig:
    Teubner, 1910).

Bibliography to §2.1

Joh. Gust. Droysen, *Geschichte des Hellenismus* (2 vols.; Hamburg: Perthes, 1836–
    43). The classic treatment of Hellenism.
Moses Hadas, *Hellenistic Culture: Fusion and Diffusion* (New York: Columbia
    University, 1959).
Richard Laqueur, *Hellenismus* (Giessen: Töpelmann, 1925).
John Pentland Mahaffy, *The Progress of Hellenism in Alexander's Empire*
    (Chicago: University of Chicago, 1905).
Paul Cloché, *Alexandre le grand et les essais de fusion entre l'Occident Gréco-
    Macédonien et l'Orient* (Neuchâtel: Messeiller, 1947).

Bibliography to §2.1b

Arnaldo Momigliano, *Alien Wisdom: The Limits of Hellenization* (Cambridge and
    New York: Cambridge University, 1975).
Samuel K. Eddy, *The King is Dead: Studies in the Near Eastern Resistance 334–31
    B.C.* (Lincoln: University of Nebraska, 1961).
Eduard Meyer, *Blüte und Niedergang des Hellenismus in Asien* (Kunst und
    Altertum: Alte Kulturen im Lichte neuer Forschung 5; Berlin: Curtius, 1925).

populations of the cities and the military colonies were more or less set apart from the native populations. The Greek cities enjoyed a certain degree of autonomy in their administration: they had their own gymnasia to which only Greeks were admitted (§3.1), their own temples in which primarily traditional Greek deities were worshiped, and their own social life, which was expressed in the typical Greek system of associations. With all these institutions the native populations at first had very little contact. For them Greek influence appeared in the predominance of the Greek tongue as the official language of the administration and in their relationship to Greek trade and the rapidly expanding Greek commerce and industry.

An encounter in the areas of culture, literature, morality, and religion evolved only gradually. "Syncretism," a substantial mixture of Greek and oriental elements, can be observed first in the area of religious history. This is especially true in the domain of the Egyptian rulers, where oriental deities and traditions appear in Greek dress as early as the III BCE. The initiative of the Ptolemies is clear in the case of the creation of the Greco-Egyptian cult of Sarapis, and with regard to the Greek translation of the Hebrew Bible, royal initiative is claimed by the legend about the origin of the Septuagint (§5.3b). Both events belong to III BCE. But despite such examples, it is still better in general to speak of Hellenistic culture as characterized by the antithesis of east and west, of barbarian custom and Greek education, although its antithesis appeared in different ways among the peoples living together in the various Hellenistic domains.

The antithesis was neither an irreconcilable opposition nor a stimulus for amalgamation; rather, a mutual fascination and mutual stimulation prevailed in the political, economic, cultural, and religious realms. In each sector the Greek element determined the shape of the antithesis. Political actions as designed by Macedonians and Greeks were strongly influenced by the desire to maintain some relationship to their homeland. Economy and trade followed Greek standards (the Attic standard of coinage was almost universally accepted; banks were usually in Greek hands), although the centers of business and trade shifted to places outside of the Greek homeland. The Greek language and Greek methods of education dominated culturally, but the centers of education shifted to Alexandria, Pergamum, and Rhodes. The non-Greek contribution was present from the beginning, but was not always immediately recognizable, since it made its appearance by means of the Greek language and Greek forms and structures of organization. Non-Greeks played an even larger role in the cultural life of Hellenism (e.g., Zeno, the founder of Stoic philosophy, was the son of a Phoenician merchant from Cyprus) and it also became a matter of course for barbarians to organize their social structures according to patterns they learned from the Greeks (e.g., an establishment of Syrian merchants from Berytus/Beirut on Delos is styled a *thiasos* of Poseidon).

The most important element of Hellenization in the Seleucid empire was the founding of numerous cities of Greeks and Macedonians. Some of these cities were military colonies, but they did not serve only military purposes; they also had an important function for the internal stabilization of the empire. The new cities became home for the immigrants (cf. the Greek and Macedonian names of such cities as, e.g., Larissa and Edessa), who were quite willing to work and fight for their own prosperity and security. The Seleucids did not consciously pursue a policy of Hellenization, nor did they intend to create a national state of Greeks and Hellenized barbarians. Rather, they accepted the pluralism of the different nations, cultures, and religions in their realm as natural. But they wanted to maintain their control, the most effective support for which was a strong Greco-Macedonian presence as a counterbalance to the considerable centrifugal powers present in their multinational kingdom. In this situation it happened that the Greeks became orientalized and that the orientals became Hellenized—a result of the Seleucid policies which came about more by chance than by design.

The situation in Egypt was quite different. Egypt had only two Greek cities, Alexandria and Naucratis, and the Ptolemies founded no new cities there. Thus, there was no instrument which could serve to break down the differences between the Greek urban population (the Jews of Alexandria in this respect belonged to the Hellenes) and the native population of the country. The native Egyptians did not even learn Greek, although all official documents had to be written in the Greek language. Egyptian remained the country's spoken vernacular, which was to reappear soon as a literary language in the "Coptic" documents of the early Christian church. The frequent insurrections of the native Egyptian population which characterized II BCE are due to the failure of Hellenization in this country's vast rural areas outside the city of Alexandria.

2. THE BASIC STRUCTURES
OF ADMINISTRATION AND ECONOMY

The Hellenistic states were composed of countries stretching over large areas, having millions of inhabitants of various nationalities. This made possible a completely new concept of the state for the Greeks, whose traditional image of a political community was the city-state or the petty kingdom; it also suggested new tasks and presented new opportunities previously outside the horizon of Greek experience. It was necessary to set up an adequate system for the administration and pacification of the vast areas conquered by Alexander. In doing this, the Hellenistic empires relied largely on the existing Persian (or Egyptian) administrations. But this did not mean simply a transfer of power, as had happened when the Babylonians took over from the Assyrians, or the Persians from the Babylonians. The Greeks brought an advantage which no other conquerer before them possessed: a highly developed economy which could be immediately utilized to stimulate the economic growth of the new realms. The economic horizon was further expanded by expeditions and voyages of discovery (e.g., the sea route to India, or an expedition into the Sudan). Furthermore, the conquerers introduced and developed a new entity of social and political life: the Greek city. With the exception of Egypt, the founding of numerous new cities and the reconstitution of older cities created cultural and economic centers everywhere, to an extent that was unknown in the east heretofore.

(a) Greece and Macedonia

All major powers tried repeatedly to gain a foothold in Greece and thus carried their wars onto Greek soil. As a consequence, Greece sank more and more deeply into poverty. With respect to agriculture and mineral resources Greece was already disadvantaged. But even the demand for manufactured products from Greece, which had increased in the beginning of the Hellenistic period, sank to new lows.

The gradual economic recession was not felt in the same way everywhere. Athens, in spite of some difficulties, maintained a moderate prosperity for a long period. Under Macedonian rule it was the major trade center and clearing house of the Macedonian kingdom. The cultural level of Athens also remained relatively high. Delphi continued to flourish as a wealthy center of religious and cultural life and lost only some of its significance as the diplomatic capital of Greece. The economic decline caused

Bibliography to §2.2

Michael I. Rostovtzeff, "The Hellenistic World and its Economic Development," *AHR* 41 (1935–36) 231–52.

Fritz M. Heichelheim, *An Ancient Economic History: From the Palaeolithic Age to the Migrations of the Germanic, Slavic, and Arabic Peoples,* vol. 3 (Leiden: Sijthuff, 1970).

Bibliography to §2.2a

Ulrich Kahrstedt, *Das wirtschaftliche Gesicht Griechenlands in der Kaiserzeit: Kleinstadt, Villa und Domäne* (Bern: Franke, 1954).

the greatest difficulties in those cities which traditionally had only a small share of industrial production and trade. That is most evident in the case of Sparta. The original number of eight thousand full citizens had sunk to only seven hundred in III BCE, and most of the land was in the hands of no more than a hundred citizens. Attempted reforms by the kings Agis and Cleomenes III were frustrated by the resistance of the oligarchs and were wrecked by the military interference of the major powers. It remains an open question whether Sparta actually had a strong enough economic base to have sustained these social reforms.

The islands of the Aegean suffered least from the continued warfare, but they were harassed by pirates and weighed down by the financial burdens of foreign occupation. Financial and economic troubles were most strongly felt here. Rhodes, however, enjoyed a special position. It was able to maintain its independence and served as a clearing house and as host to many international trade agencies, since it was the most important port of reshipment in the eastern Mediterranean (shipments from Tyre and from Egypt usually passed through Rhodes). In order to protect its trading interests Rhodes maintained a strong navy, which had considerable success in controlling piracy. In the interests of its trade Rhodes was quite willing to support other cities or to use its military power. The Rhodian maritime law, which epitomized the traditions and experience of Greek seafaring, remained valid even into the Roman imperial period. After an earthquake of 227 BCE which ruined the city, Rhodes received aid for its rebuilding from many countries, although the motives of the donors were not altogether altruistic. The wealth of this island and its well-balanced system of social and political structures meant that Rhodes was one of the few Greek states which never experienced any social unrest in this period. In spite of some setbacks at the beginning of Roman dominance in the east, Rhodes preserved its economic prosperity in the Roman imperial period as well.

Like Rhodes, the small Cycladic island Delos also enjoyed the status of an international banking and trade center, at first dependent upon Rhodes, later under a Roman protectorate. Trade relationships with Syria were especially important. The island continued to prosper until its destruction by Mithridates VI of Pontus in the year 88 BCE. Other islands (Cos, Chios) were able to manage fairly well as long as they had a substantial agricultural production and a share of the manufacturing industries (as, e.g., Cos with its silk production). In these instances, the property-owning middle class citizens had a better chance to survive than they would have had in the cities of the Greek mainland. But even here, declining wages, an increase in slave labor in farming and industry, and heavy tax burdens were strong indicators of economic recession.

(b) The Greek Cities of Asia Minor

The Ionian cities of the west coast of Asia Minor (Ephesus, Miletus, and others) remained independent in their internal administration, but were under the military and political rule of Egypt during III BCE. Tax burdens were heavy during this period. Military personnel were quartered in the houses of citizens, and the cities also suffered other obligations to the Egyptian army (such as maintaining their horses) and navy (the building of ships). The economic power of these cities could be rebuilt only after the end of Egyptian rule, but even the subsequent Seleucid rule was troublesome. "The Seleucids could not exist without these cities, and they were unable to live with them" (Rostovtzeff). Although the cities preserved their own internal administration, they were politically dependent and had to pay tribute. In addition, each citizen had to pay the usual royal taxes. In spite of occasional royal donations and favors such as exemption from tributes, the cities waited in vain for the "freedom" which had been promised ever since Alexander liberated them from Persian rule. Nevertheless, the surviving documents and the evidence for building activity during this period demonstrate that their agriculture, industry, and trade brought the cities a good deal of prosperity, which continued during the period of Pergamum's rule in Asia Minor. Their economic ruin, aggravated through the wars of Mithridates, came ultimately from Rome's mismanagement and exploitation during the first century of its administration. Later on, the Roman emperors had to intervene personally in order to restore the prosperity that these cities had enjoyed during the Hellenistic period.

The cities on the coast of the Black Sea (Cyzicus, Byzantium, Heraclea, Sinope, Trapezus) remained independent for some time; some were later incorporated into the kingdom of Pontus. They were small territorial states with an agricultural base (farming was done by the citizens or by serfs). Trade, fishing, and manufacturing were the basis of a relative prosperity.

(c) The Kingdoms of Asia Minor

In Pergamum the plan of the city, its citadel, and its buildings are still a visible document of the Greek spirit. The inspiration and models were

Bibliography to §2.2b

David Magie, "Rome and the City-States of Western Asia Minor from 200 to 113 B.C.," in: Calder and Keil, *Anatolian Studies,* 161–85.

A. H. M. Jones, "Civitates liberae et immunes in the East," in: Calder and Keil, *Anatolian Studies,* 103–17.

provided partly by Alexandria, partly by Greece (Athens, or Epidaurus, as in the rebuilding of the Asclepieion of Pergamum). In every respect, the buildings demonstrated increasing wealth. The expansion and consolidation of the kingdom, only a small territorial state at the beginning, quickly secured its almost complete economic independence. Pergamum had its own ports, a rich agriculture (wine and olives) and numerous raw materials (wood, silver, and copper from the Ida Mountains). The administration was fashioned according to the Egyptian model (§2.2d). The capital was the only significant city. The country, with its villages, was divided into districts, remained the king's property, and was farmed by indigenous farmers or tenants (*klerouchoi*), who paid rent or tithes to the king. In addition, as elsewhere in Asia Minor, there seemed to have been a number of major agricultural estates. The industry received royal subventions and was partly concentrated in manufacturing plants owned by the king (especially textiles and parchment).

Bithynia, richly endowed by nature, could boast of a productive agriculture, many forests, and quarries of precious stones and crystal. On the Propontis and the Black Sea were free Greek cities (Cyzicus, Heraclea) which made the Thracian inhabitants of the country dependent on Greek trade. The Thracian kings of Bithynia, able to maintain their independence (partly with the help of the Celts whom they called into the region), competed with other Hellenistic kings in their founding of cities (Nicomedia, Prusa). They also entered into trade agreements with the Ptolemies and with the Macedonians and appeared as patrons of Greek culture in Delos and Delphi. Bithynia remained independent until 74 BCE, while its neighboring kingdom of Pergamum became a Roman territory much earlier; thus, Bithynia was able to compete with the Romans in banking and the slave trade. Its wealth and prosperity continued into the Roman period.

Pontus, situated inland from the central and eastern coast of the Black Sea, possessed productive agricultural areas in its river valleys. In its eastern districts it controlled the most important mining area of the ancient world, which produced iron, copper, and silver. Exports went not only to Mesopotamia and Syria, but after the founding of the Greek cities on the coast (Sinope, Trapezus), also to Greece. Pontus and Cappadocia had been the centers of the ancient Hittite empire, and in the period before

Bibliography to §2.2c

M. Rostovtzeff, "Pergamum," in *CambAncHist* 8. 590–618.

Idem, "Some Remarks on the Monetary and Commercial Policy of the Seleucids and Attalids," in: Calder and Keil, *Anatolian Studies,* 277–98.

Esther V. Hansen, *The Attalids of Pergamum* (2d ed.; Ithaca: Cornell University, 1947).

Alexander the Great they were the mainstay of the Iranians of Anatolia. This is reflected in the social and economic organization of the country: large estates with villages controlled either by feudal lords or by temples (in which Iranian deities were often worshiped). There were no major cities and thus no urban culture. The royal family was originally Iranian, but had been Hellenized, and the kings made great efforts to give their country its due share of the Hellenistic economy and trade. An important step in this direction was the conquest of the Greek cities Sinope and Amisus. Sinope became the new capital and reaped increasing profits from the growing wealth of the kings, who now controlled the export of ores and levied transit duties on the goods which arrived on the caravan roads from Asia to be shipped west. Merchants from Sinope were well known figures in Greece, and later also in the western Mediterranean, wherever metals and ores were traded. At the end of II BCE, Mithridates V of Pontus was the wealthiest king in Asia Minor. His successor, Mithridates VI, made use of these rich resources to equip his army and navy for war with Rome.

The Celtic Galatians had been settled in the regions of ancient Phrygian culture with its cities and temples (Gordion, Ancyra, Pessinus—the home of the Magna Mater; §4.4b), and their princes had established themselves as masters of large estates and robber knights. The Galatians had their own tribal organization, whose princes and nobility were known for their wealth; contact with the ancient Phrygian cities was minimal in the beginning. Neither the indigenous population nor the Galatian lords were initially much influenced by the process of Hellenization. In II BCE the Galatians made some attempts to share in the culture and economy of the Hellenistic world and to gain access to the Black Sea by conquest of the Greek city Heraclea. But Pergamum and Rome brought this to naught. The Romans devastated the country, triggering a terrible insurrection by the Galatians (168 BCE), which had to be quelled by Eumenes II of Pergamum. Only after these events did the slow Hellenization of the central districts of Asia Minor begin, especially under the Roman vassal kings of I BCE. Like Galatia, Cappadocia also remained economically and culturally on the margins of the Hellenistic world. There is scarcely any evidence from Cappadocia for Hellenization and urbanization during this period.

(d) Egypt and Cyprus

The major part of the Greek and Macedonian population of Egypt was concentrated in Alexandria. Outside of this city, the older Greek city of Naucratis, the city of Ptolemais founded by Ptolemy I in upper Egypt, and new settlements such as those in the Fayyum, Greeks and Macedonians could be found only insofar as they were employed in the royal administration. The wealth of the country was almost exclusively controlled by the Alexandrian population. The navy and private shipping were stationed there and nearly all transfer of goods in the import-export trade took place in Alexandria.

Egypt was administered by the Ptolemies according to the principles of a capitalistic state monopoly, which they took over from the Pharaonic government. The greater economic expertise of the Greeks enabled them to introduce Greek patterns of administration and to apply this system with more consistency, thus intensifying production. Most of the agricultural land belonged to the king and was managed according to directions from the central government. Stock farming, insofar as it was still in private hands and not carried on in the royal ranches, was strictly supervised by the state; statistics were collected annually. Bee-keeping and fishing were in private hands, but a share of the proceeds had to be paid. All rights of hunting, mining, and lumbering were vested with the royal administration. Most manufactured goods were produced by the royal industries—since the state owned the raw materials. In addition, there were some factories owned by the temples, from which the kings may have originally learned the methods of monopolistic industrial production and its organization. Private production was restricted to the manufacturing of simple consumer goods.

The most important monopolies of the state were the production of oil (several different types of vegetable oil), together with price controls for its sale; textiles, especially linen, whereas wool was manufactured privately; beer; salt; leather; and paper. Paper (papyrus) was produced in great quantities for domestic use (the administration consumed immense quantities) and to satisfy the brisk demand for export to other countries. Whether this monopoly existed from the beginning and how it was organized is uncertain.

Bibliography to §2.2d

Michael I. Rostovtzeff, "The Foundations of Social and Economic Life in Egypt in Hellenistic Times," *JEA* 6 (1920) 161–78.

Fraser, *Alexandria.*

André Bernard, *Alexandrie la Grande* (Paris: Arthaud, 1966).

Hugh MacLennan, *Oxyrhynchus: An Economic and Social Study* (Princeton: Princeton University, 1935).

Claire Préaux, *Les Grecs en Egypt d'après les archives de Zénon* (Bruxelles: Lebègue, 1947).

Wilhelm Schubart, *Verfassung und Verwaltung des Ptolemäerreichs* (Leipzig: Hinrichs, 1937).

William Linn Westermann, "The Ptolemies and the Welfare of Their Subjects," *AHR* 43 (1937/38) 270–87.

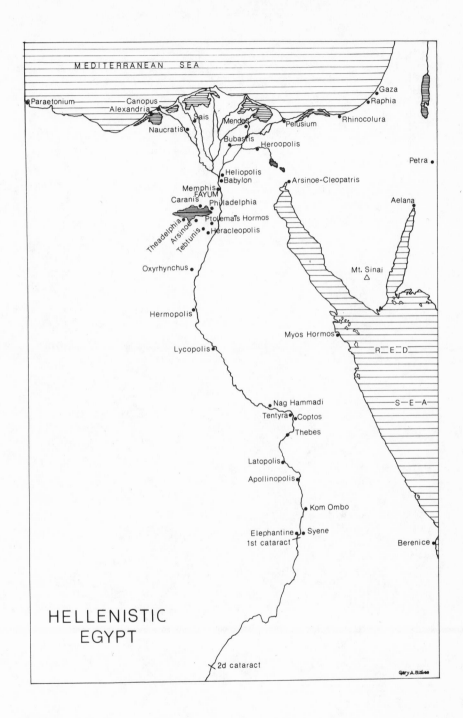

MEDITERRANEAN SEA

Paraetonium

Canopus
Alexandria
Sais
Naucratis
Mendes
Bubastis
Heroopolis
Pelusium
Rhinocolura
Gaza
Raphia

Petra

Heliopolis
Babylon
Memphis
FAYUM
Caranis
Theadelphia
Arsinoe
Tebtunis
Philadelphia
Ptolemaïs Hormos
Heracleopolis
Arsinoe-Cleopatris

Aelana

Oxyrhynchus

Hermopolis

Mt. Sinai
△

Lycopolis
Myos Hormos

R E D

Nag Hammadi
Tentyra
Coptos
Thebes

S E A

Latopolis

Apollinopolis

Kom Ombo

Elephantine
1st cataract
Syene

Berenice

HELLENISTIC
EGYPT

2d cataract

Gary A. Bisbee

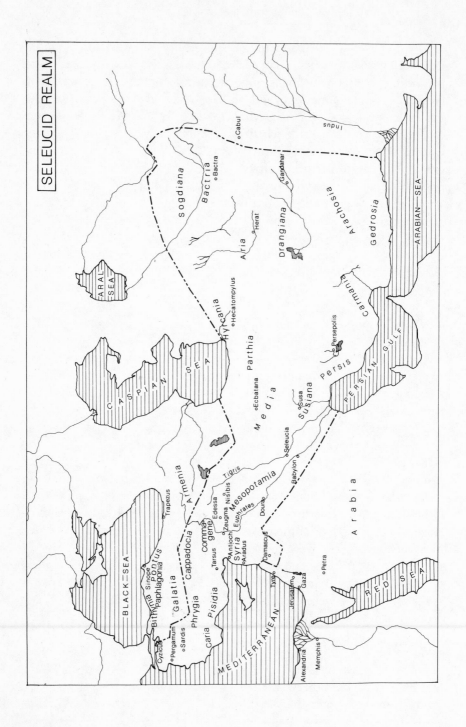

SELEUCID REALM

ARAL
SEA

Cabul
snpul

Sogdiana
Bactria
Bactra

Aria
Herat
Drangiana
Gandahar
Arachosia
Gedrosia

ARABIAN—SEA

Hyrcania
Hecatompylus

Parthia

CASPIAN SEA

Carmania

Persis
Persepolis

Media
Ecbatana

Susa
Susiana

PERSIAN GULF

Seleucia

Mesopotamia

Tigris

Armenia
Nisibis
Edessa
Zeugma

Euphrates
Doura

Babylon

Arabia

BLACK—SEA

Trapezus

Commagene

Antioch
Syria
Aradus

Damascus

Galatia
Cappadocia
Pontus
Bithynia Sinope
Paphlagonia

Phrygia
Pisidia
Caria
Tarsus

Tyre
Jerusalem
Gaza

Petra

RED SEA

Pergamum
Sardis
Cyzicus

MEDITERRANEAN

Alexandria
Memphis

Egypt actively participated in the trade of the eastern Mediterranean, first of all with its possessions in Africa, southern and western Asia Minor (including Cyprus, which was ruled by the Ptolemies until the beginning of the Roman domination), and on the Greek islands. But while the Ptolemaic possessions in Asia Minor and in the Aegean retained their economic independence, the partly Greek and partly Phoenician island of Cyprus was to some degree incorporated into the system of state monopoly. The copper mines were directly managed by the kings; Egypt itself possessed few mineral resources. Under the Ptolemies, Egypt made a strong effort to become economically independent. The wealth of the kings was largely due to the vigorous promotion of exports and the rigorous restriction of imports (only lumber and ores had to be imported regularly). Southern Syria, Phoenicia, and Palestine, under Egyptian domination during III BCE, will be discussed below.

(e) The Seleucid Empire

It was impossible to enforce a unified economic system in the vast Seleucid realm, with its many nationalities and diverse traditional economic structures. But the Seleucids instituted a uniform administrative structure which was founded on their claim to be the legitimate heirs of Alexander and of the Achaemenids. There was a centralized fiscal administration, but no centralized system of levies and taxes; the central government also controlled the mints and monetary policies and made decisions about the export of such goods and manufactured products which were by right due to the king from the several satrapies. But otherwise, only those properties which were directly owned by the king were managed by the royal administration. Such lands and estates belonged to his "house." It is difficult to assess the actual size of these lands, but they may have comprised as much as half of the entire area ruled by the Seleucids. All other parts of the country were owned and managed by the various subject nations, vassal princes, and cities. Since the king could not normally rely on the indigenous populations to administer the royal estates, Macedonians and Greeks were brought into the country as administrators. The numerous new cities founded by the Seleucids, settled mostly by Greeks, also served this purpose and were instrumental in the strengthening of royal power.

Some information is preserved about the royal estates in Asia Minor and Babylonia, but otherwise our information about the Seleucid empire is much more meager than about Egypt. There were numerous older

Bibliography to §2.2e
See Rostovtzeff under §2.2c.

temple territories, especially in Asia Minor. Their land was considered part of the royal estates, yet the priests usually continued to serve as administrators. The inhabitants of the villages were serfs or, in many instances, temple slaves. There were also large estates owned by Persian noblemen or indigenous families. Some of these remained with their former owners; others were transferred to Macedonian noblemen, or became the king's property and were administered in his name. In the villages connected with these large estates the people were serfs or bondsmen, but rarely slaves. In Mesopotamia even the inhabitants of the temple territories remained free and retained their tribal organizations. While the kings interfered little with the existing structures of Babylonia and Persia, they still used their power of disposition over the lands they owned in order to found cities and military colonies.

Southern Syria, Palestine, and Phoenicia, though governed by the Ptolemies for a century, had an administrative system not unlike that of the Seleucids and quite differenct from Ptolemaic Egypt. To be sure, the country was divided into hipparchies (corresponding to the Egyptian *nomoi*), through which the kings exercised their control, and there were tax farmers everywhere who looked after the royal interests (not only the collection of revenues, but also such matters as the registration of cattle). But various forms of limited self-government continued to exist, since the country was much less uniform than Egypt itself. Several nations existed side by side with the partially Hellenized cities on the Syrian and Phoenician coast. Among these cities Sidon was preeminent and became the center of a far-reaching Hellenization: there were colonies of Greek Sidonians even in Palestine. The Ptolemies also granted a measure of self-government to temple states like Jerusalem and to sheikdoms like that of the Tobiads in Transjordan. Here the people remained free and preserved their ethnic traditions; the high priest or the sheik was required to pay a fixed sum for annual tribute. Similar arrangements were made with respect to the coastal cities.

The Ptolemies also founded Greek cities in this region, and thus promoted the process of Hellenization. Among these cities were Gaza and Ptolemais-Ake on the coast, Philoteria, Philadelphia, and Pella in Transjordan, and several cities in Idumea. These cities were founded mainly for political and military reasons. The primary aim was to prevent foreign invaders from building a base for attack upon Egypt, and therefore these new cities, as well as existing urban settlements, were equipped with fortifications. As the Zeno correspondence demonstrates, Greek merchants from Egypt traded not only with the coastal cities but also with the interior (Palestine and Transjordan), where Zeno, travelling through the country on behalf of his master Apollonius in the year 260/59, bought slaves and merchandise from the Nabatean caravan trade.

Not much change came with the Seleucid rule over this region, although the new subjects now had direct experience of the difficulties which beset the Seleucid realm, especially its financial problems. The Seleucids reinforced the process of Hellenization as part of their effort to stabilize their increasingly shaky control. That these efforts would actually mobilize the resistance of the Jewish people against the foreign rulers was an unintentional result of these policies.

(f) Taxes

Taxes were an important element of the administration and economic policies of the Hellenistic empires. Direct taxes levied on the whole population, customary in the empires of the east, were unknown in classical Greece, with the exception of tyrannic rule. Direct taxes were usually levied only upon those inhabitants of the cities who were not full citizens. Citizens could be requested to make special contributions in exceptional circumstances, and wealthy individuals were expected to make voluntary payments on special occasions. All other taxes were indirect: customs duties, sales taxes, market taxes, and fees for the use of public facilities, such as port taxes. The Hellenistic kings continued and further refined this system of indirect taxation, but the huge expenditures of these empires, especially for the maintenance of the army and navy, required new and different sources of income. Since all the conquered lands were legally owned by the king, rents from land leases and real estate taxes imposed by the king by virtue of his office became the most important sources of revenue. But some direct taxes were also used: head taxes, property taxes, including such property as slaves, cattle, buildings, and commercial license fees.

Similar systems of taxation were used throughout the Hellenistic kingdoms. Egypt had a central financial administration which collected taxes through employees in the area of Egypt proper. But for the Egyptian possessions in southern Syria, Asia Minor, and the Aegean islands, the system of tax farming was used. Wealthy people applying for a job as tax farmer went to Alexandria in person every year to submit their bids to the

Bibliography to §2.2f

A. M. Andreades, *A History of Greek Public Finance* (Cambridge, MA: Harvard University, 1933).

Henri Francotte, *Les finances des cités grecques* (Paris: Champion, 1909).

A. H. M. Jones, "Taxation in Antiquity," in: P. A. Brunt (ed.), *The Roman Economy* (Oxford: Blackwell, 1974) 151–85.

king. The highest bidder usually received the franchise. The story of the
Tobiad Joseph, reported by Josephus (*Ant.* 12.169ff.), is a good example
of this procedure. This sytem of tax farming was taken over by the
Seleucids in Syria and later by the Romans. Surviving source materials
from Egypt give repeated evidence for the heavy tax burdens under
Ptolemaic rule. It seems that the oppressiveness of the tax burden was due
not so much to the high level of taxes but rather to the perfection of the
system, which left no loopholes. Taxation under the Seleucids was much
less rigid. Established traditions and individual agreements usually determined the amount of real estate taxes and revenues which the cities,
temple states, and tenants of royal lands were required to pay. There were
also considerable differences among the several satrapies; even within one
particular satrapy the taxation was anything but uniform. It is difficult to
determine how oppressive the taxes actually were. Tax levies do not seem
to have been exorbitant even in the case of the Jews (see 1 Maccabees 10
and 14), who did not object to the high level of taxes imposed upon them as
such, but to the principle of imposing taxes at all.

3. The Society

(a) The Situation of the Indigenous Populations

The Egyptians in the Ptolemaic Kingdom were a social class strictly
separated from the Macedonians, Greeks, and other immigrants (including many Jews). Nevertheless, native Egyptians did not become bondsmen of the king, but retained their independence and were permitted to
move freely within the district (*nomos*) in which they lived, and under
certain conditions also elsewhere in Egypt. They had their own courts,
which adjudicated according to traditional Egyptian law. Moreover, they
were neither unemployed nor penniless. Yet the Egyptians were a class
without privileges, totally dependent upon their Macedonian and Greek
masters, whose wealth they did not share. Employment opportunities and
income were determined solely by the foreign rulers of the country. The
Egyptian workers were strictly supervised, and their income was subject
to rigid taxations. In the case of default in the payment of debts, sale into
slavery was a continuous threat. Egyptians employed in the lower ranks of

Bibliography to §2.3a

Horst Braunert, *Die Binnenwanderung: Studien zur Sozialgeschichte Ägyptens in
der Ptolemäer- und Kaiserzeit* (Bonn: Habelt, 1964).

W. Peremans, "Ethnies et classes dans l'Égypte ptolemaique," in: *Recherches sur les
structures sociales dans l'antiquité classique, Caen 25–26 avril 1969* (Paris:
Centre National de la recherche scientifique, 1970) 213–23.

the royal administration (e.g., as the mayor or scribe of a village) were completely at the mercy of the royal administration.

The Greeks always remained foreigners to the Egyptian population, and not simply because they spoke a foreign language and worshiped foreign gods. The Greeks also confronted the native Egyptians as officials of a civil administration much more efficient and demanding than that to which the native population was accustomed. At the end of III BCE and at the beginning of II BCE the pressure of the bureaucracy increased still more. Further restrictions on the possession of private property were imposed (even among Greeks), and higher levels of service from the Egyptian population were demanded. The riots and insurrections which resulted from such demands were intensified by the general deterioration of the economic situation. The administration was unable to control the unrest, despite bloody suppression and attempts of the kings to lend support to the cause of the indigenous Egyptians.

The repeated outbreak of these insurrections cannot be explained by pointing to the incompetency of the later Ptolemies and the decline of their rule, nor through the increasing political pressure of Rome. It is, furthermore, quite unlikely that the insurrections arose from the Egyptians' desire to shake off the despised foreign rule. The primary cause can rather be found in the system of state monopoly, which continuously confronted the native working class with oppressive rules and regulations, but never granted a share in the proceeds of their labor and in the general wealth of the country. Not even in the later Hellenistic period, when many Egyptians had advanced to higher positions in the administration and had become members of the ruling class, and when many Greeks had become "Egyptianized," would the unrest abate. The organization of the whole economy under the system of state monopoly finally led to the depopulation of the villages, a decrease in cultivated farmland, and a national economic crisis. It was this system which finally resulted in nearly complete impoverishment of the indigenous population at the end of the Hellenistic period—with the exception of those lucky few who had managed to rise to the upper classes.

The situation in the Seleucid empire was completely different, because the Seleucid kings never tried to impose any unified economic system, nor did they attempt to assign a clearly defined social and economic status to the indigenous populations. On the contrary, the newly inaugurated social structures, especially the Greek city, offered opportunities for social advancement which were imcomparably better than the inherited structures. To be sure, for a large portion of the rural population there was little change, because the Greek language and culture had little effect outside of the cities. Things also remained much the same, at least in the early period, in the tributary states and those temple territories which had an autonomous internal administration. The Seleucids made no attempt to change the social and economic structures of such territories, which thus experienced foreign rule primarily through military occupation and through taxes and tributes imposed upon them. In the older cities which had escaped destruction and had not been reconstituted as Hellenistic cities, the inhabitants continued in their inherited vocations and occupations. These city populations were nevertheless Hellenized to some degree, more deeply in the west, at least superficially in the east.

The new cities, especially the large cities of Seleucia on the Tigris and Antioch on the Orontes, had mixed Greek and non-Greek populations. But no one hindered the non-Greeks who wished to move into new occupations. In this way, these cities made innummerable people into Greeks during the following centuries. It was primarily for this reason that the Seleucid empire did not create a social contrast between Greeks and non-Greeks. Other contributing factors included increased mobility and the manifold economic opportunities. Even larger groups of the population could migrate and settle elsewhere, as is evident from the formation of large Jewish diaspora communities in the east as well as in the west. In all these cases the Greek culture and language provided the means by which such groups could establish themselves in their new homes. Therefore, the new institution of the Greek city proved to be particularly beneficial for the native population.

(b) The Position of the Greeks and the Foreigners

In Egypt the foreigners (Greeks and non-Greeks) were constituted as a separate ethnic group. They were subject to the same taxes and revenues as the native Egyptians and also had to respect the state monopolies. But the foreigner had more rights than the native. The immigrants enjoyed a certain degree of self-governance, were permitted to organize (e.g., in gymnasium associations), and had the right to own real estate. It is only to be expected that most of these foreigners had employments related to the service of the king. Service in the army, in the administration, and in the supervision of the economy (in agriculture as well as factories managed by the state monopolistic system) offered the best opportunities. In the beginning, all higher positions in the civilian administration and in the army were occupied by Greeks and Macedonians. Later on members of the Egyptian upper classes also advanced in the king's service, but only after they had been Hellenized. Some Greeks also had other occupations, such as craftsmen, farmers, or tax collectors. But most of the Greeks and other foreigners were employed in positions in which they relied completely on the good graces of the king. This dependence was visible even among the philosophers, scientists, and artists whom the king had called to the Museum and whom he could remove at will (which actually happened in II BCE). The foreigners were separately organized in national *politeumata*, which comprised a number of various associations (cultic, professional, and gymnasium associations; see §2.3e). They had their own courts which were allowed to use either the Greek laws or the laws of any other people (e.g., the Jewish law) as long as this did not create any conflicts with royal ordinances. All privileges were personally granted by the king and could be annulled at any time. The associations were exclusive, and admission was strictly supervised; for example, to become a member of a Greek gymnasium association, one had to pass a Greek language examination. Thus, children of Greek parents as well as children of the Egyptian upper class eagerly studied Greek grammar books, available everywhere, in order to pass these examinations.

Of course, Greeks and Macedonians also initially constituted the upper class in the Seleucid empire. The aristocracy included the following groups: (1) the "house" of the king, i.e., his family, friends, and closest advisors; (2) the highest administrative officers and other members of the king's court, each having his own "house," which included subordinates, servants, and slaves; (3) independent Greeks, such as wealthy landed proprietors or wholesale merchants. From the beginning there were non-Greeks who belonged to the second and third groups (Phoenician merchants, Iranian landed gentry and high administrative officers), but they were never very numerous. All members of these groups had various privileges and were likely very rich.

Greeks and Macedonians were also predominant in the following classes in the Seleucid empire: officers and soldiers; lower-ranking public servants, especially those employed in the financial administration and the internal revenue service; owners of estates, farmers, and colonists; people employed in occupations typical for the Greek bourgeoisie, such as scholars, physicians, merchants, and craftsmen. These groups also had privileged positions. Non-Greeks could be found among them, even in the early Hellenistic period, and as time went on, their ranks were filled more and more by non-Greeks. The kings were vitally interested in strengthening these groups and preserving them as a "Greek" middle class. This was not due to any belief in the ethnic superiority of the Greek race, but rather was based on their knowledge of the superiority of the Greek culture. It is a conviction typical for Greek culture that only education, training, and instruction enable a human being to make an appropriate contribution to the functioning of society. This was exactly what was needed for the large realms of the east: a large number of trained specialists (*technitai*) for numerous professions. Of course, there had always been specialists for particular occupations; but they had usually been recruited from restricted segments of the population, and entrance into such professions was a carefully guarded tradition. Only the Greeks had developed a concept of citizenship which included education and professional training as a general requirement. It is thus quite natural that the kings would admit to these privileged classes only those people who were willing to accept the Greek culture (i.e., language, education, and professional training) as their own.

The demand of the Hellenistic kingdoms for trained specialists was considerable. Army and navy needed not only soldiers and sailors, but also craftsmen and technicians for the building of ships and for the construction and operation of war machines. The royal administrations employed thousands of public servants, accountants, financial experts, lawyers, scribes, and secretaries, who were required to have a high degree of specialized training. These complex, but usually well-functioning administrations of the Hellenistic empires, which bore little resemblance to their oriental predecessors, were constantly concerned with the training of new generations of qualified professionals.

In addition, there were many independent occupations which had reached a high degree of professionalization in the Hellenistic period: physicians and lawyers; actors, dancers, musicians, and others whose jobs were directly related to the theater (who were organized in the professional association of the Dionysiac *technitai*); professional athletes; and finally writers, philosophers, scientists, and poets. The last group was sometimes in the employment of the kings (as in the Alexandrian Museum), sometimes supported by private patrons; otherwise they had to earn their living as orators, teachers, and wandering preachers. In addition to lawyers, physicians could also find employment in the service of the king; it seems that Egypt had a public health service (this is less certain with respect to the Seleucid empire). Teaching became a widely known profession. The cities employed teachers (at low pay) for their schools, and wealthy people often hired private teachers. All these professions generally presupposed education and training in school and gymnasium. Professional schools did not exist; the philosophical and rhetorical schools and the libraries did not educate people for particular professions. The schools for physicians were the only exception. Otherwise, professional education took place by apprenticeship in the particular job which one wanted to practice. Thus, the theaters were at the same time schools for actors and dancers. Admission and training for a particular job was supervised by the guilds and professional associations, which therefore played a significant role in the Hellenistic cities and in the life of the Greek populations in general.

(c) Slaves and Slavery

Various forms of personal dependence, servitude, and diminished legal status were by no means rare in the older cultures of antiquity. In the Hellenistic and Roman periods, it was commonplace that slaves were offered for sale in large numbers and were bought like any other goods. Certain types of agriculture and industrial production were dependent upon slave labor. Slavery of this sort was introduced into Greece during VI BCE, and to Rome during IV BCE. Since slavery in the Roman imperial period resembles that of the Hellenistic period in many ways, it will also be treated in this chapter.

The slaves of classical Greece were usually barbarians. During the wars of the Hellenistic period, the supply of new slaves grew considerably. Many prisoners were taken in the wars of the Diadochi, the Hellenistic kings, and the Greek cities and leagues, and as a consequence, large numbers of Greeks and Hellenized orientals were sold into slavery. Another source for the supply of new slaves was piracy; pirates were very successful over a long period of time, systematically kidnapping people and selling them in the major slave markets. Often whole towns were attacked and the entire population sold into slavery. Piracy particularly haunted the Greek homeland, less the new Greek areas in the east. Finally, when the Romans conquered Greece and Macedonia and subjected the former Hellenistic empires in numerous eastern campaigns, immense numbers of prisoners fell into their hands, including many Greeks. Thus slavery reached its largest extension during the time of the later Roman republic. There were few wars of conquest during the Roman imperial period, and thus the supply of new slaves dropped noticeably. At the same time, manumissions of slaves increased in the imperial period, which also led to a marked decrease in the number of slaves. In late antiquity slavery was not altogether outlawed, but at least severely restricted, so that it had almost disappeared by the beginning of the

Bibliography to §2.3c: Texts

Thomas Wiedemann, *Greek and Roman Slavery* (Baltimore: Johns Hopkins, 1981). Extensive collection of sources in English translation.

Bibliography to §2.3c: Studies

M. I. Finley (ed.), *Slavery in Classical Antiquity* (Cambridge: Heffer, and New York: Barnes and Noble, 1968).

Joseph Vogt, *Ancient Slavery and the Ideal of Man* (Cambridge, MA: Harvard University, 1975).

William L. Westermann, *The Slave Systems of Greek and Roman Antiquity* (Philadelphia: The American Philosophical Society, 1955).

Joseph Vogt, *Struktur der antiken Sklavenkriege* (Wiesbaden: Steiner, 1957).

Middle Ages. Many factors contributed to the diminution of slavery (see below), particularly changes in the economic structures which no longer favored employment of slaves.

The economic, social, and legal status of slaves in antiquity was far better than, for example, the status of African slaves in the southern states of the United States in the eighteenth and nineteenth centuries. In antiquity slaves were by no means deprived of all legal rights; rather, they retained a number of privileges, such as the right to marry and certain property rights. Slaves were also admitted as witnesses in court under certain conditions. With the Roman emperors the legal status of the slaves was further improved and humanized: abuse and killing of slaves became a punishable crime.

The economic situation of slaves spanned a wide scale of possibilities and often depended on their education, professional training, and abilities. Many slaves were employed in households and charged with the numerous jobs and services which an ancient household required. It must be remembered here that the better-situated households were much more independent economically in antiquity than today. Grinding corn, baking bread, sewing of clothes, pressing of oil, boiling of soap, and many other activities were carried out within the home itself. The slaves who performed these jobs were members of the household and would eat together with the families of their masters; this changed only if the number of slaves increased considerably in well-situated households.

Otherwise slaves were employed in farming, especially in the large landed estates of the Romans, in manufacturing and industry, and in the mines. While the major factories might employ as many as a few dozen slaves, the owners of mines and estates often owned hundreds or thousands of slaves, especially when such establishments belonged to the state and were managed by the royal administration, or in the case of estates owned by the Roman emperor. To be sure, in these instances important management and leadership positions were also open to slaves. When employed as managers and supervisors, slaves often acquired knowledge and skills which would prove extremely useful after their eventual manumission. Leading positions were also occupied by slaves who served in the "house" of a king or emperor, or in the household of wealthy merchants and businessmen. As the number of educated Greeks increased among the prisoners of war, there were also more slaves who could use their scientific, literary, or rhetorical training in employment as teachers, court poets, librarians, and high-ranking administrators.

That the ancient economy was able to function only because of the institution of slavery is nonsense. One must remember that in the Seleucid empire and in Egypt, slavery played only a minor role. Egypt knew, of course, the indigenous form of temple slavery (*hierodoulia*). Slaves performed the more humble duties in the temples and were employed in factories and agricultural lands owned by the temples; but these were only of minor economic significance. Among the Greeks and other foreigners in Egypt, only the king and a few wealthy citizens were rich enough to own slaves. The kings did not favor slavery and tried to restrict it as much as possible through the imposition of high taxes upon slave owners. An edict is known from Syria which forbids serfs to be considered and treated as slaves. The Seleucid kings had no interest in reducing the subjects of their realm into the status of slaves. The institution of temple slavery continued to exist in some areas of Asia Minor, and the Seleucid kings themselves and some wealthy people employed slaves, but the larger economy, and especially the agriculture of the Seleucid empire, did not depend on the institution of slavery. The only Hellenistic kingdom in which slavery played a major role was Pergamum. In the farming of their estates and in their industrialized factories the kings of Pergamum primarily employed slaves, and such royal enterprises as major buildings and the library indeed relied heavily upon slave labor.

In comparison, Rome was much more dependent upon slaves during II and I BCE. This was less the case for manufacturing and industry, where the slaves, in Rome as well as in the east, were usually owned by private contractors and had to be paid wages (of which the owner collected a certain proportion). Such slave labor was expensive. Thus the employment of slaves competed with the free labor force only when the owner of a plant also owned the slaves he employed. But this was rarely the case. Yet it is difficult to imagine how the huge Roman estates could function without the use of whole armies of slaves.

It is no accident that it was here, primarily in southern Italy and Sicily, that the major slaves insurrections took place, namely those of Eunus of Apamea (136–132 BCE) and Spartacus (73–71 BCE). During that period the Romans indeed employed a multitude of slaves, in Rome itself and on the estates—the number of slaves in the city of Rome alone has been estimated at between 200,000 and 300,000—one-third of the total population! How much these slave insurrections were caused by social problems is difficult to determine. Religious and nationalistic motivations also seem to have played a major role.

The insurrection of Aristonicus of Pergamum (133–130 BCE) should probably also be counted among these slave insurrections. It was a revolt against Rome, which had just inherited Pergamum through the testament of its last king. Aristonicus disputed the legitimacy of the testament, claimed to be the legal heir of the last king, and organized the rural population for the struggle against Rome. He proclaimed an end to all slavery and called his followers "citizens of the state of the sun," thus drawing upon some of the utopian and social-revolutionary ideas of his time (see §3.4e, on the Hellenistic romance). In any case, the relative significance of slave labor decreased after the beginning of the Roman imperial period, even though it continued to be an important economic factor for some time.

Public opinion about slavery vacillated between rejection and indifference. The institution of slavery was never positively justified, nor does one find any revolutionary demands to abolish slavery at any cost, though condemnations of slavery occur repeatedly. The Sophists were the first to deny the right to own slaves. Stoic and Cynic philosophers emphasized again and again that slaves were human beings just as everybody else, that they possessed the same natural abilities and rights, and that the true freedom of humanity was independent of social status. Accordingly, antiquity did not treat slaves as beings of less than human status. In comedy and in literature in general, slaves were presented as having the same weaknesses and the same virtues as other human beings. The actual intercourse between masters and slaves usually implied that they had the same rights and obligations. This was especially true with the household slaves, whereas the slaves working on the large estates and in the mines were excluded from normal interaction with free citizens.

There is little doubt about the position of the religious associations on the question of slaves: differences in social position were irrelevant. The Eleusinian mysteries accepted Athenian slaves as well as full citizens and initiated them into the secret rites. But the oriental religions in particular, which were often brought into the west by the slaves themselves, acknowledged no differences in class and social status. Christianity was one of these religions. But it would have been too much to expect these religions to have advocated the abolition of slavery as an institution (although some of the church fathers indeed demanded just that). Genuine social-critical ideas did not appear in antiquity. Slave insurrections had already failed with much blood and tears, and the social position of the slaves was not seen as a human disqualification. But when the new religions insisted on the equality of the slaves within their own ranks, they assumed the noblest traditions of Greek thought. There was never any question: among the Christians, the manumission of a slave was considered to be a good work.

(d) Wealth and Poverty

In the Hellenistic period, especially in the countries of the east, agriculture remained the primary basis of economic prosperity and one of the most important sources of income, not only for the villages, but also for the cities. Rural areas with villages of free farmers or with serfs working on large estates or in temple territories accounted for some of the agricultural lands; one could find various types of land use, from intensive grain production to semi-nomadic cattle raising. Other agricultural lands were controlled by the cities. This land was originally owned by a broad segment of the citizens and formed the basis of the economic prosperity of all inhabitants. While people in the rural areas were usually poor and often bound in servitude, they were not an impoverished proletariat. In the cities, however, the possibility of poverty was a social problem. Whenever a large segment of the city population had no share in the possession of land and real estate, the formation of a proletariat was a necessary consequence.

In the cities the wealthy upper class was relatively small. All cities of the Hellenistic and Roman periods had a proletariat of wage earners, petty farmers, tenants on small parcels of land, and slaves. More variable was the size of the propertied middle class of farmers, craftsmen, merchants, and the various other groups of *technitai* (§2.3b). The social stability of a city largely depended on this class.

In Greece, and perhaps to a certain degree also in the older Greek cities of western Asia Minor, most of the land passed into the hands of a small upper class; the middle class all but disappeared, and the proletariat grew considerably. After an initial upturn at the beginnng of the period, wages fell throughout Hellenistic times, while prices rose. Although population numbers did not fall, the number of available jobs decreased. This was caused both by increasing economic difficulties and by the competition of slave labor in the households, in agriculture, and in industry. As a consequence the contrast between rich and poor became increasingly pronounced. Among the poor, free workers and indebted farmers were even worse off than many slaves. At least slaves had to be fed whether or not they could be employed profitably. (In the Roman imperial period, slaveholders experiencing economic problems sometimes freed large numbers of their slaves; this was later prohibited by law, since it led to increased misery for the working class.) But nobody was obliged to care for the unemployed proletariat of the cities. Unrest, revolts, and insurrections of the urban working classes became a regular part of city life during the Hellenistic period.

All these revolts, aimed at the redistribution of the land, were doomed to failure, not only because of the resistance of the rich, but ultimately because of Greece's natural poverty and its continual ravishment by wars until the Roman conquest. The methods of warfare were both cruel and economically devastating. Half of the vanquished soldiers were often killed in battle. Not only the military prisoners, but also the inhabitants of a conquered city were sold into slavery; there was no other booty which could be used to pay for war expenses. Whole cities were razed to the ground, Mantineia by the Achaeans and Macedonians, and Corinth by the Romans. To profit by plunder was often seen as the primary purpose of war; the vanquished country was completely despoiled, and its fields devastated. Moreover, piracy, freebooting, and kidnapping were commonplace. Not only the islands and coastal cities, but also the interior country suffered under this scourge. More than once it seems that a thousand or more people were captured in a single raid. Surviving sources from this period leave the impression that sacrilege, desecration of temples, and violation of the rights of asylum had become everyday occurrences. Those at war often used pirates for their own purposes; Crete and the Aetolians were especially closely allied with the pirates.

The situation, however, was totally different in the countries of the east, in Macedonia, and, once the wars of the early period were over, in the cities of Asia Minor. In III BCE, Egypt was the wealthiest nation of the Mediterranean world—an initial success of its monopolistic state capitalism. But most of the wealth was in the hands of the king or was directly under his control. The property of the top administrators could be confiscated by the king at any time. The Greeks and other foreigners, especially those living in Alexandria, seem to have been quite well situated. Among the native Egyptians, only the few who had become Hellenized shared this prosperity. But the rest of the Egyptian population was not what one could call "poor," certainly not in the early period of the Ptolemaic rule, since wages were high and jobs were plenty. But this would change in the later Ptolemaic period. The Ptolemaic administration respected existing rights of property and even encouraged private ownership to a certain degree because it was hoped that Egypt would thus become more attractive for immigrants. The contributions that resulted from private initiatives were needed and it was desirable to have a class of citizens from which administrative personnel could be recruited. Last but not least, such a propertied class was also a source of revenue. But the economic and taxation policies of the Ptolemaic administration prevented the native Egyptians from gaining much of a share in the country's wealth. Once the economic situation worsened, with prices rising while wages fell, this part of the population was hit the hardest. Alexandria, on the other hand, preserved its broad propertied class of Greek, Jewish, and Hellenized Egyptian citizens into the beginning of the Roman period.

There was no uniformity in the Seleucid empire with respect to the distribution of wealth. Asia Minor suffered considerably during III BCE because of continual wars, dynastic quarrels, and the Galatian invasion. The pirates raided coastal districts repeatedly, especially during the wars of the Seleucids with Egypt in the Aegean Sea and in the eastern Mediterranean. The cities suffered most and were ruined financially—a major cause for the increasing impoverishment of the middle class. The few sources which are preserved from this period speak only about troubles and misery. But the following centuries brought a return to some prosperity. In spite of subsequent exploitation at the beginning of Roman rule, a comparatively broad class of propertied citizens survived and during the early imperial period enjoyed considerable wealth, which was shared by a large segment of the population of these cities. Syria, Mesopotamia, and Babylonia were less affected by the Syrian wars. The rich agricultural production of these regions, which was not subject to the vicissitudes of a centralized system, and a flourishing commerce in the ancient centers of international trade enabled the native populations to share in the general prosperity. The Seleucid kings did not interfere with the existing rights of private property except in the case of the founding of new cities. But even those transactions actually gave more private property to individual citizens, as these new cities were largely settled by Greek and Macedonian immigrants and soldiers who drew their livelihood from the allotted parcels of land. Even if one could soon find both rich and poor people in these new cities, their general wealth was usually much higher than that of the cities in Greece, and their middle class had a better chance to survive for a long time.

(e) The Associations

The Hellenistic period was the time of the greatest flourishing of the system of associations, though they were still an important social institution during the Roman period. Next to the political administration of the states and cities, the associations were the most important structural element of the life of the society. A vast number and variety of associations existed. Many of the associations of the Hellenistic cities were continuations of the older Greek associations. But there was also a native tradition of associations in Egypt and the Seleucid countries, some of which became partially Hellenized and others of which mixed with the Greek system in various ways.

Because of the great variety of associations and the considerable differences from place to place, it is difficult to classify them satisfactorily. But a simplified survey must be tried here. It is useful to distinguish: (1) associations which fulfilled tasks for the whole community (especially the

Bibliography to §2.3e

Erich Ziebarth, *Das griechische Vereinswesen* (Leipzig: Hirzel, 1896).

Franz Poland, *Geschichte des griechischen Vereinswesens* (Leipzig: Teubner, 1909).

Mariano San Nicoló, *Ägyptisches Vereinswesen zur Zeit der Ptolemäer und Römer* (MBPF 2; München: Beck, 1913–15).

Nock, "The Gild of Zeus Hypsistus," in: idem, *Essays*, 2. 414–43.

gymnasium associations); (2) professional associations, guilds, and unions; (3) clubs serving purely sociable purposes; and (4) religious associations (*thiasoi*). Almost all associations served multiple purposes; for instance, gymnasium associations also intended to promote social contact. Furthermore, even in their organizations and external appearance, different types of associations had many things in common. Not only religious types of associations but also social clubs or professional associations could have religious features and be dedicated to, or named after, a certain deity. Sometimes this seems purely an external formality, at other times it may imply a serious religious commitment. The character of our sources does not always permit us to make clear distinctions. Musical clubs preferred Apollo as their patron deity, social clubs Aphrodite and, later on, Dionysus, who became the most popular patron of associations of any sort.

The most important associations of communal life were the gymnasium societies. They appear everywhere, not only in the cities, but in many other places, wherever Greeks were settled. They were officially recognized by the authorities of the city, received subsidies, and possessed certain privileges, including the right to own real estate, buildings, and other property. Their presiding officer was the gymnasiarch, whose office was a "service" (*leitourgia*), i.e., he received no salary, and it was expected that he would finance festivals and athletic competitions on special occasions out of his own pocket. The primary purpose of the gymnasium associations was to build, maintain, and equip the gymnasia, and thus to advance Greek education for the young people. At the same time, the gymnasia were available for various social events for which they functioned as the "clubhouse." Life in a Greek city would have been inconceivable without a gymnasium.

There was a great variety of professional associations. Not all of them were supervised by the cities or by the kings. Some were Hellenized guilds or unions formed by a part of the population that was not Greek. The associations of the royal officials in Egypt are a continuation of an older Egyptian institution. Associations of craftsmen and of merchants are in evidence in large numbers from Asia Minor, especially in sources from the Roman period. Most likely they existed already in the Hellenistic period and were the successors to the native guilds from the time before the Greek conquest. Professional associations were particularly important in view of the great mobility of the population; they were able to offer accommodations and lodging to travelling colleagues and could help them find work and settle in a foreign city. A typical example for such an association is the establishment of the wealthy merchants from Berytus in Syria on the island of Delos: they were organized as a religious association of Poseidon and owned a large house on this Aegean island, where Syrian merchants could stay while conducting their business. The house also contained rooms for worship and social gatherings. Most widely distributed were the associations of the Dionysiac *technitai,* which included in their membership all those whose profession was related to the theater. These associations occupied privileged positions and were organized under royal supervision in some places (certainly in Egypt). Their members were also active as teachers, so that these associations also functioned as schools for actors, dancers, and musicians. It can be assumed that other professional associations exercised a similar control over vocational training, perhaps as part of the admission into such organizations.

Clubs serving primarily to encourage social fellowship existed in great numbers. They appear under such names as "club of the young men" or "club of the seniors" and similar designations. Their sole purpose was to make all sorts of social gatherings possible, e.g., for people who came from the same country or who had attended the same school. Such associations were most likely to be especially popular among non-citizens and foreigners, who were excluded from the regular duties and opportunities of full citizens.

Religious associations were primarily founded for those gods and cults which were not sponsored by the political community, and which did not have publicly recognized temples. Such associations, therefore, often became the primary instrument for the dissemination of the new oriental religions (Sarapis, Isis, Attis, Men Tyrannos, and others). Many Dionysus associations were not purely social clubs, but rather serious cult associations, particularly since it must be assumed that private Dionysus mysteries were celebrated in houses unconnected with the temples of Dionysus, usually found in close proximity to the theater. These religious associations usually admitted men regardless of their social class, especially slaves and foreigners, and often also women. All these people were allowed to occupy positions of leadership in associations. This reveals a new sense of community for which differences in social status had become irrelevant.

4. THE HELLENISTIC CITY

(a) The Founding of New Cities (including Military Colonies)

There was only one truly ancient Greek city in Egypt: the merchant city of Naucratis, founded by Miletus ca. 650 BCE. The Ptolemaic kings did not found cities in Egypt, except Ptolemais in upper Egypt, which became the center for the Greeks in that part of the country. Otherwise the Ptolemies restricted their activity to the establishment of new settlements attached to the major royal estates, which were held by higher officials of the king in fee. Many Greek immigrants came to these settlements and formed their upper class (administrators, soldiers, and craftsmen); all services in these places were provided by native Egyptians. These settlements cannot be called "cities" in the Greek sense of the word; they were merely living quarters for technocrats and soldiers. Nor did they function as places in which indigenous Egyptians could grow in Greek culture and thus become Hellenized.

Alexandria in Egypt, however, founded by Alexander, and residence of the kings of the Ptolemaic realm, became the symbol of the Hellenistic city for the whole Mediterranean world. Alexandria could not be compared with any other Greek city, because it did not develop independently and under its own administration. From the beginning, it was the king's city. It quickly grew to a size larger than the cities of Greece and Ionia, and in this respect Alexandria was probably second only to the large capitals of the Seleucid empire, Antioch (on the Orontes) and Seleucia (on the Tigris). The city was equipped with splendid buildings. One-third of its area was occupied by a complex of royal buildings: the palace, the library, the Museum, the zoological garden, and the tomb of Alexander the Great. There were two magnificent boulevards, grandiose squares, lovely fountains, and great temples, of which that of Sarapis was the most eminent. The people lived in several distinct quarters, which were primarily reserved either for the Greeks or for the Jews. Total population of the city is estimated to have been at least half a million, possibly as much as a million, during the Hellenistic and Roman period; a little more than half were free inhabitants, the others slaves. The number of full (Greek) citizens was much smaller; the other free inhabitants (including the Jews) were organized according to their own constitutions (*politeumata*), but disadvantaged in various ways, especially during the Roman period. This was the cause of much social unrest which sometimes led to bloody controversies. As a major trade center, Alexandria was the equal of the other large cities of the eastern Mediterranean. As a city of the arts, sciences, and literature, it had no rivals during the period of the flowering of Hellenism and it still excelled in this respect in the Roman period.

Bibliography to §2.4

A. H. M. Jones, *The Greek City from Alexander to Justinian* (Oxford: Clarendon, 1971).

Ernst Kirsten, *Die griechische Polis als historisch-geographisches Problem des Mittelmeerraumes* (Bonn: Dümmler, 1956).

Roland Martin, *L'urbanisme dans la Grèce antique* (Paris: Picard, 1956).

Victor Tcherikower, *Die hellenistischen Städtegründungen von Alexander dem Grossen bis auf die Römerzeit* (Ph.S 19,1; Leipzig: Dieterich, 1927).

R. E. Wycherley, *How the Greeks Built Cities* (London: Macmillan, 1967).

Fraser, *Alexandria*, 1. 3–92.

The Seleucids resumed Alexander's policies in their founding of new cities and made this an important part of their political program. The founding of cities began under Seleucus I and continued under his two successors, Antiochus I and Antiochus II. The cities became the most important element in the process of Hellenization, although this was not the original purpose of their foundation. Rather, the Seleucids established these cities to protect their most important trade routes and military supply lines, to restrain the mountain tribes in the north and the Arabic tribes in the south, and to defend their realm against the Galatians in Asia Minor.

Quite a few of these cities were founded not as "polis," but rather as military colonies. The founding of a new polis was an expensive undertaking in which the king had to invest much time and effort. Military colonies (*klerouchiai*) had already been founded by Alexander in Bactria, and offered many advantages. (The Ptolemies also settled their soldiers, not in fortified towns, but in smaller settlements scattered over their whole country. Therefore these Ptolemaic settlements did not become effective in the process of Hellenization.) The advantages of the creation of settlements for the soldiers were obvious. To maintain a standing army of paid mercenaries could become very expensive over a period of time. But once soldiers were settled on royal lands which they could farm, they would possess a source of independent income, and a new bond would be established to the country which they would have to defend in the case of war. This policy also offered an attractive opportunity for Greek immigrants, since service in the Seleucid army could eventually give them a new home and a farm of their own. Finally, more effective agricultural methods, well known to the Greeks, could be introduced in this way, and new areas opened up for agriculture. Even if these military colonies did not have the same privileges as the new "cities," they eventually fulfilled similar functions.

Among the new foundations of the Seleucids were the following cities: in Syria, Antioch on the Orontes, the political capital of the realm; Seleucia in Pieria and Laodicea on the Sea, the two most important port cities; in Asia Minor, Thyatira in Lydia, Apamea Kibotos in Phrygia, Seleucia and Antioch in Cilicia; in Mesopotamia, Edessa, Dura Europos, Antioch in Mygdonia, and, most important of all, Seleucia on the Tigris, the eastern capital. In addition to these better known examples, there were hundreds of other new cities and colonies founded by the Seleucid kings. Much rarer was the establishment of a colony in Persia and Media, because these areas lay outside the realm of Greek colonization. But several fortresses were built, some as reconstitutions of older Persian cities, for example, Seleucia on the Elaios, the site of the ancient Persian Susa.

Once some time had passed, all these new foundations had become "cities." In the manner of their founding there remained some legal differences. In a newly founded "city" (*polis*) the land became property of the city and was then transferred to citizens as their personal property. But in military colonies the land allotted to the individual settlers remained the legal property of the king, although it could be passed on through inheritance. It reverted to the king only when there was no heir. Some colonies were laid out like a polis and were fortified (*katoikiai*), but they did not possess the legal rights of a city. Other differences relate to the people who settled in these new foundations. In the case of a military colony, the inhabitants were as a rule Greek and Macedonian soldiers. In other cases, civilian immigrants founded daughter-cities of their home city. Others were created through a *synoikismos*, that is, several smaller villages and towns were united into a new city; in this case the non-Greek population would be predominant. This was also the case when the king transferred whole groups of people to another place of his realm for resettlement; in this way many Jews from Mesopotamia were settled in Asia Minor (see the report in Josephus, *Ant.* 12.148). Finally, there were instances in which an older city was reorganized as a Greek polis, provided with new privileges, and given a new name, though often the old name reemerged at a later time. In this way Edessa was refounded as Antioch, Nisibis as another Antioch, Ecbatana as Epiphania. Other older cities were Hellenized to a certain degree: Uruk-Warka became Orchoi; although it included in its walls a sizeable Greek population, the administration remained in the hands of its original population.

Seleucia on the Tigris (not far from modern Baghdad) was founded by Seleucus I as the capital of his kingdom. As a new center for banking and the east–west trade, it took the place of the ancient city of Babylon, and this became the basis of its wealth. The city's population is estimated to have been about 600,000. Even when Seleucia came under Parthian rule, it maintained some of its independence as a Greek city. Seleucia was finally destroyed during the campaigns of the Romans against Parthia, first by Trajan, and finally in 164 CE. Seleucus I also founded the city of Antioch on the Orontes, which became the capital of the country after his death. (Antioch experienced its first flowering under Antiochus IV, was conquered by the Romans in 64 BCE, and became a splendid city and cultural center as the capital of Syria under Roman rule. This was the place of the establishment of the first Hellenistic Christian church. Though badly damaged through an earthquake and frequently embattled in the wars between Rome and Sassanian Persians, and in later conflicts between the Byzantine empire and the Muslims, Antioch remained an important city into the Middle Ages.)

(b) City Plans and Buildings

The plan and buildings of the Hellenistic city were a direct continuation of those in the classical Greek city. The powerful city walls enclosed the private homes, a central agora with temples and government buildings (*bouleuterion, prytaneion,* city archives), a theater and odeum, a gymnasium, and a fountain house. The city plan named for the architect Hippodamus had been used in Ionia as early as v BCE. The streets of the city were laid at right angles, dividing the whole city into rectangular blocks of the same size. Hippodamus had used this plan for the building of Piraeus (Athen's port city) and Thurii (in southern Italy), and it was now used as the basic pattern for the new cities of the Hellenistic colonization. Typical examples include Alexandria, Europos, Damascus, and Aleppo. The plan was also used for the rebuilding of cities in the older Greek areas of Asia Minor, e.g., in Miletus, the home of Hippodamus, and in Priene. The last city is a good example for the rigorous application of this pattern, because no adjustments were permitted, even though the city was situated on the slopes of a steep hill.

The new Hellenistic cities, when compared with the cities of classical Greece, received a number of modifications which, though partly dictated by the Hippodamian plan, also reflected the changed social and economic situation. The older cities usually had an acropolis, originally the fortified castle of the king, which a later democratic spirit adorned with temples. Such an acropolis is frequently missing in the Hellenistic cities. A special fortified place within the city itself, to which one could withdraw if an attacker were to take the city walls, but which could also serve as a tyrant's stronghold against the citizens, was at variance with the concept the citizens had of their city. Thus, the acropolis disappeared, or was only superficially fortified (acropolis fortifications were reintroduced in the Byzantine period), while the defense of the city was entrusted completely to the city walls. These walls enclosed the area of the city in an irregular circle, and could include large vacant spaces if this was advisable for purposes of better defense. (This differs markedly from Roman foundations, where the walls of cities follow the pattern of the rectangular Roman army camp.) The walls, often of enormous dimensions, had gates and bastions built with hewn natural stone, with an interior filled with earth and rubble. The walls had to be strong, since they were expected to withstand the onslaught of highly developed war machines; their building therefore constituted a considerable challenge to the energy and initiative of the citizens.

In the classical period, the agora tended to be of irregular shape. Since it served as the center of political and economic life, it was surrounded by market halls, shops, administrative and government buildings, courts, and temples, while still providing sufficient room for access to the major streets of the city. In the Hellenistic period, the agora was built in a strictly rectangular form, surrounded by buildings and stoas (porticos) on all four sides and thus closed off from the rest of the city; usually only two entrances were left open, which invited the building of impressive gates during the Roman period. Often a second agora was built and reserved for public and administrative buildings and temples. Thus major cities had two or more agoras. The agora used for trade and shopping assumed the character of a mall. New stoas were built in all public places, and older stoas were enlarged, sometimes with two inner colonnades. These stoas served as the center of the city's life and were open to all its people, for varied purposes: trade and relaxation, entertainment and talk, private or public debates, or as picture galleries or for exhibitions. It was here that philosophers and missionaries would hold forth with their message and teachings.

Temples and public buildings had to fit the rectangular layout of the city streets. The most important temples were, of course, situated directly at the agora, as well as the *bouleuterion* (meeting place of the city council) and the *prytaneion* (the magistrates' hall with the sacred hearth). Other major buildings could encompass two or three city blocks, and larger sanctuaries might be situated outside the city walls, especially if ancient traditions demanded that they be built on a specific hallowed site, as was the case with the famous temple of the Ephesian Artemis (see Acts 19:23ff).

Whenever possible, the theater was also adjusted to the Hippodamian layout of the city. If the city walls enclosed a mountain or hill, that could be used for the auditorium. But there were also theaters, especially from the Roman period, in which the seats of the auditorium rose to an immense height, supported by terraces and huge vaults. A stage building with a *proskenion* (raised stage) became a regular part of the theater during the Hellenistic period. The actors would play on this stage, although the circular (later semi-circular) orchestra could still be used in addition to the stage. It was left to the quite different tastes of the later Roman period to rebuild the orchestra into an arena that could be filled with water for the performance of small-scale naval battles.

The gymnasia belong to those ancient structures which have left impressive ruins, still to be admired today. There were originally gymnastic fields irregularly surrounded by a few buildings, but in the Hellenistic period the gymnasia were constructed as well-designed architectural units. There was a large peristyle court with colonnades on all sides of the rectangular field, giving access to a number of larger and smaller rooms serving various purposes. There were rooms for dressing, bathing, and annointing, rooms for social gatherings and for lectures and instruction, small chapels, and later even libraries. Some of the gymnasia were of immense proportions. The harbor gymnasium of Ephesus, built in the Roman period, included a gymnastic field of 200 by 240 meters. Each city also possessed a stadium, usually situated outside of the city walls. The cities began to equip the stadiums with rows of stone seats (originally spectators sat on the grass of the sloped enclosure) and with semi-circular rows at one end, which could be used as a small theater.

The houses of the Hellenistic cities were built according to a number of traditional types, which cannot be discussed in detail. The Hippodamian layout of the city with its standard-sized city blocks determined the size of the houses. One could find two, four, and sometimes even more houses within a single block, but within one city the number of houses in each block was originally the same throughout. Each citizen thus received a lot of the same size for the building of his home. This principle was, however, often violated in the course of time. Wealthy citizens could eventually acquire an entire block for their spacious homes, and sometimes large houses could even close a side street in order to use the space of the adjacent block. In cities which did not use the Hippodamian plan, the dwellings of the rich and poor, spacious houses and small buildings, could be found side by side in various mixtures (Delos is the best known example). Among the various types, the peristyle house was preferred by affluent citizens: an open court, often covering an elaborate system of cisterns, was surrounded by columns and by rooms of different size on all four sides. While there were rarely any windows to the street, all the rooms opened to the central court for light and fresh air. Houses with two stories were not rare. The peristyle court could be covered by beautiful mosaics, which along with frescoes decorated many rooms as well.

Further developments of the cities in the Roman period preserved most of the basic features of the Hellenistic city, but also brought some characteristic changes. One or two main boulevards, intersecting with each other if possible, displayed the city's wealth with splendid buildings and colonnades. The agora took on the features of the Roman forum and was closed off by monumental gate structures. Aqueducts helped answer the increasing demand for fresh water, and artistic fountain houses replaced the simpler wells of an older period. Such city renewal began at exactly the time at which Christianity was attempting to establish itself as a new missionary religion in the major cities of the eastern part of the Roman empire. This renewal brought new jobs and a renewed prosperity to the older Hellenistic cities.

5. AGRICULTURE

(a) Agricultural Production and its Setting

All countries of the Hellenistic empires included areas of rich agricultural production. Only Greece, though possessing a highly developed agriculture, was unable to produce enough to provide for its own population. The Greeks therefore always needed to import grain, most of which came from southern Russia and Thrace. The Celtic invasion in III BCE cut off most of these supplies. The other sources of grain imports, namely Cyprus, Phoenicia, and the Cyrenaica, were in the hands of the Ptolemies during the early Hellenistic period, and thus the Ptolemies controlled the Greek market. At the same time, they increased grain production, making Egypt one of the primary grain exporters in antiquity, a role it continued in the Roman period. Control of the Egyptian grain market thus became vital for control over the whole Mediterranean realm. Egypt itself was independent in its entire food production, but the fertility of its fields depended upon the Nile, its most important source of irrigation. The Seleucid empire included areas of the most diverse agricultural products and had to adjust differences through trade within its own borders. Difficulties arose as many important agricultural areas were lost in the gradual dissolution of the Seleucid empire.

(b) Innovations in Agriculture

The land used for agriculture increased considerably during the Hellenistic period. Several attempts were made in Greece to drain swamps, which is also attested for the Fayyum in Egypt; it can be assumed that the Seleucids made similar attempts in Mesopotamia. Technicians and engineers for such projects were supplied by the king. Vacant and fallow areas were also opened up for agricultural usage through the founding of new cities and settlements. In other cases land owned by the king was sold, rented, or given to new settlers to establish farms and estates.

Bibliography to §2.5

John Scarborough, "The Plow and the Mind," and "Who Bought What, and Why," in: idem, *Facets of Hellenic Life* (Boston: Houghton Mifflin, 1976) 31–69.

Auguste Jardé, *Les céréales dans l'antiquité grecque I: La production* (Paris: Boccard, 1925).

Michael Schnebel, *Die Landwirtschaft im hellenistischen Ägypten* (MBPF 7; München: Beck, 1925).

K. D. White, *Roman Farming* (London: Thames and Hudson, and Ithaca: Cornell University, 1970).

Nothing is known from the Seleucid empire about the improvement of agricultural methods and the introduction of better machinery. The Seleucid kings did not attempt to plan their economy as the Ptolemies did. It is certain, however, that many innovations were introduced—analogous to the introduction of new methods in Ptolemaic Egypt—especially on those farms which were cultivated by Greek settlers. But there was little change for the native farmers, the temple territories, and the estates which remained in the hands of their former owners. The Persians had already begun to acclimatize oriental fruit trees in Asia Minor, and the Seleucids probably continued those efforts. But the Persian fruit trees, apricot, peach, and cherry, did not become established in the Mediterranean world until the Roman period, when they were introduced first of all to Italy. The same applies to the introduction of most of the citrus fruits.

Much more is known about Egypt. The Greeks brought iron implements to replace the wooden tools used in Egypt (plowshares, hoes, and shovels). The wheel for raising water (for which the Arab word *sakieh* is used today in Egypt) was introduced by the Ptolemies, which permitted much more effective irrigation than the traditional use of human water carriers. Machines for the processing of harvested fruits were either Greek inventions or Greek improvements of older tools. Several new kinds of produce were brought into the country by the Ptolemies; production already established was improved or expanded. Among the new fruits and vegetables were apples, nuts, garlic, and several improved varieties of traditional vegetables. Egypt had few vineyards during the time of the Pharoahs, for the national drink of the Egyptians was beer. The Ptolemies expanded the vineyard regions and introduced grape varieties from Greece and Asia Minor. Egypt grew olives, but primarily for consumption as a fruit. The Ptolemies encouraged oil production in order to meet the demand for vegetable oil (import duties of up to 50 percent were charged for olive oil produced elsewhere). Sheep were brought from Asia Minor and Arabia to produce a better wool, since the Greeks, accustomed to wool from their home country, did not want to give up their traditional clothing. For the raising of pigs, horses, and donkeys, breeding animals were brought to Egypt from other countries. At the same time, the kings introduced Egyptian produce into other countries of their domain. Typical Egyptian plants such as beans, lentils, mustard, and pumpkins were in this way established in southern Syria and Palestine.

The kings of Pergamum followed the Ptolemaic-Egyptian example and actively engaged in the planning and execution of agricultural production. They attempted to simplify the cultivation and increase the harvests. The kings of Pergamum were especially concerned to improve cattle breeds, and their stud-farms became famous.

6. MANUFACTURING AND INDUSTRY

(a) Mining and Metal Industry

The Hellenistic states had an enormous demand for metals, especially gold, silver, and copper (for the production of bronze). The known mines yielded only a limited supply; it was therefore extremely important to find new sources. Alexander the Great included prospectors in his army, who were charged with the task of investigating new sources of ore in the eastern countries. All the known iron ore deposits of Greece had already been exhausted by that time, so that the Greek cities of the classical period were forced to import what they needed. Only Macedonia had access to some reserves (including gold) in its Thracian mines and could supply most of its needs. Egypt had a rich supply of ores so long as it was able to keep its possessions in southern Syria and Asia Minor. Iron and copper were mined in Cyprus and in Palestine, but the copper mines of the Sinai peninsula were soon abandoned because of the greater productivity of the mines of Cyprus. Gold for the Ptolemies came from mines in southern Egypt and Nubia. The Seleucid empire possessed numerous sources for ores and metals, which were scattered over their vast realm. Gold had to be imported from Siberia, although these imports went no further than Bactria after the rise of the Parthians. The Seleucids were also cut off from their supplies of silver from Asia Minor once they lost their western provinces. The kings of Asia Minor also controlled the mining of iron ore; thus the Seleucids were finally left with nothing but the copper and iron mines of their possessions in southern Syria, formerly Egyptian.

The techniques of Greek mining are well known from the mines of Laurion in Attica, which have been thoroughly explored. These procedures did not change throughout the Hellenistic and Roman periods. Very little was provided for the miners, so free workers would normally not

Bibliography to §2.6

R. J. Forbes, *Studies in Ancient Technology* (9 vols.; Leiden: Brill, 1955–64).

Albert Neuburger, *Technical Arts and Sciences of the Ancients* (London: Methuen, 1930).

J. G. Landels, *Engineering in the Ancient World* (Berkeley and Los Angeles: University of California, 1978).

T. R. Glover, "Metallurgy and Democracy," in: idem, *Greek Byways* (Cambridge: Cambridge University, 1932) 58–77.

M. I. Finley, "Technical Innovation and Economic Progress in the Ancient World," *Economic History Review* 2,18 (1966) 29–44.

Hermann Diels, *Antike Technik: Sieben Vorträge* (Leipzig and Berlin: Teubner, 1920).

Carl Roebuck (ed.), *The Muses at Work: Arts, Crafts and Professions in Ancient Greece and Rome* (Cambridge, MA: MIT, 1969).

want to work in the mines. Slaves, prisoners, and convicts were employed instead. Sometimes the local population would be forced to work in the mines.

The methods of metalwork had become highly developed even before the Hellenistic period. Manufacturing was not industrialized, but remained in the hands of small family businesses. Some of these workshops specialized in the production of only a few items. Because of the great demand for war equipment, the production of weapons was the most important branch of the iron industry. Weapons were continuously manufactured in mass production and bought by the kings for storage in their large arsenals. Household goods were also manufactured in mass production. The best steel was produced in Asia Minor but throughout antiquity India remained famous for the best manufacturers of hard steel products. (What became known in the Middle Ages as damask steel was actually Indian steel imported via Damascus.) Egypt's production of gold, silver, and bronze vessels continued to flourish throughout this period, supplying both domestic and external demand. These exports, however, had to compete with centers of production in Syria, eastern Asia Minor, and Armenia, especially the famous workshops of the Chalybians on the southeastern shores of the Black Sea. The Persian toreutic art also continued to flourish and had a strong influence on the Hellenistic toreutic style.

(b) Textiles

Textiles were mostly manufactured in individual households. Small family workshops supplied local demand. Only the more precious textiles and luxury items were produced in factories and exported. The manufacture of textiles relied upon unchanging traditional methods. The only exception was the vertical loom, an innovation which originated in Egypt and came into use in Italy and Greece at the beginning of the Roman period. The books of the philosopher Bolos of Mendes (II BCE) about dyeing, with instructions for the imitation of precious dyes and textiles, demonstrate that there was intense interest in the dyeing of clothes. These books were frequently copied and excerpted, and some of their material reappeared later in the pseudoscientific literature of alchemy.

The countries of the east were the leading producers of textiles, as was true in the pre-Hellenistic period. The Greek contribution was the improvement and wider distribution of wool production to satisfy the demands of Greeks in the eastern countries. Flax was grown in Egypt, but was rare in other countries. Fine-textured linen, known as byssus, was produced in the royal weaving-mills and, as in former times, in the weaving mills of the temples. Byssus was in great demand and famous worldwide. Its decorative motifs, however, were no longer Egyptian but

Greek. Other export articles in wide demand included Egyptian and Babylonian carpets. Silk was imported regularly from China from the time of Alexander the Great; it was processed in Phoenician factories before being shipped for sale to western countries. Silk production on a small scale was developed on the island of Cos. Silk products manufactured here (not identical with the genuine Chinese silk) were known as "Coan fabrics." Coan silk was produced in large factories where female slaves did most of the work. The kings of Pergamum promoted methods for the refinement and strengthening of textile production. Several smaller cities of the realm produced carpets for export. Pergamum was especially renowned for its production of curtains and brocades interwoven with gold. These were manufactured in royal factories which also employed mostly female slaves.

(c) Ceramics and Glass

Ceramic articles for daily use were produced and sold at local potters' shops. Artistically designed ceramic products were a speciality of several of the older Greek cities. The export of such pottery was still important during III BCE. From Greece they were shipped into all countries of the east, and from Sicily primarily to Egypt. But before long, pottery imitating Greek forms and decoration was produced in eastern countries. Egyptianized Greek forms were exported by Egypt with great success. Red-figured Attic ware, predominant in the classical period, was replaced by black-glazed pottery without figurative design. Light-colored vessels with various decorations were also made in the Hellenistic period. Expensive ceramic vessels were in less demand, because toreutic products had become much more fashionable. Gold, silver, and bronze vessels with artistic reliefs began to decorate the houses of the rich everywhere. In imitation of such popular toreutic products, ceramic vessels with decorations in high relief began to appear about 250 BCE. Oriental influence inspired the production of faience vessels (painted pottery with a glossy glaze).

Glass was rarely manufactured in Greece, though it was not unknown there. Most glass products came from Phoenicia and Egypt. Egypt had been a center of glass manufacturing from very ancient times. The Ptolemies strengthened and promoted this industry, particularly the production of luxury items (vases and bowls) and decorative pearls (as a substitute for precious stones), all designed for export. In the Seleucid empire

Bibliography to §2.6c

Anita Engle (ed.), *Readings in Glass History* (4 vols.; Jerusalem: Phoenix Productions, 1973–74).

the Persian tradition of manufacturing glass vessels with gold decoration was continued by the Syrians. All these products were made with molten glass, worked and shaped as it congealed. Glass-blowing was invented in the beginning of the Roman period and quickly revolutionized the manufacturing of glass products. The new centers of production in Italy, Egypt, and Syria thus could make large quantities of inexpensive glass articles for everyday use and export these successfully.

(d) Writing Materials and Books

All sorts of materials were used for writing in ancient times: wood, stone, tablets of wax or clay, pieces of pottery (ostraca), and various metals (note the copper scroll found in Qumran). But only leather (vellum) and papyrus were widely used in the Hellenistic and Roman period and commercially produced. Whether to use leather or papyrus often depended on the economic policies of the Hellenistic kings. Egypt possessed an industrial monopoly in papyrus, which it produced in large quantities and various degrees of quality, ranging from delicate luxury paper to rough packing material. Egyptian policies insured that papyrus was exported at a good price. Sometimes other countries placed an embargo on the importation of papyrus. Syria did so for a while and Pergamum followed later,

Bibliography to §2.6d: Texts

Barrett, *Background,* 23–29.

Jenö Plettky, *Sources on the Earliest Greek Libraries (with the Testimonia)* (Amsterdam: Hakkert, 1968).

Bibliography to §2.6d: Studies

Mohammed A. Hussein, *Origins of the Book: Egypt's Contribution to the Development of the Book from Papyrus to Codex* (Greenwich, CT: New York Graphic Society, 1972).

David Diringer, *The Hand-Produced Book* (New York: Philosophical Library, 1953) 228–74.

C. H. Roberts, "The Codex," *PBA* 40 (1954) 169–204.

Idem, "Books in the Greco-Roman World and in the New Testament," in *Cambridge History of the Bible* 1. 48–66.

Wilhelm Schubart, *Das Buch bei den Griechen und Römern* (Handbücher der Staatlichen Museen zu Berlin; Berlin: De Gruyter, 1921).

Frederic G. Kenyon, *Books and Readers in Ancient Greece and Rome* (2d ed.; Oxford: Clarendon, 1951).

C. Wendel and W. Gröber, "Das griechisch-römische Altertum," in *Handbuch der Bibliothekswissenschaft* 3,1 (2d ed.; Wiesbaden: Harrassowitz, 1955) 51–145.

Hans Widmann, *Buchformen, Buchherstellung und Buchvertrieb im alten Griechenland und Rom* (München: Münchner Arbeitsgemeinschaft der Verlagshersteller, 1966).

Clarence Eugene Boyd, *Public Libraries and Literary Culture in Ancient Rome* (Chicago: University of Chicago, 1916).

Tönnes Kleberg, *Buchhandel und Verlagswesen in der Antike* (Darmstadt: Wissenschaftliche Buchgesellschaft, 1969).

thus forcing the use of leather as the writing material (also called "parchment"; see below). The Seleucid empire was self-sufficient in the production of this widely used writing material; therefore, the kings wanted to make their country independent of Egyptian papyrus imports.

Papyrus was produced from the papyrus plant, found in the shallow waters and swamps of the Nile delta, growing as high as four or five meters. Its stem, which had a diameter of about 5 cm, was divided into pieces of about 30 to 50 cm. These were cut open lengthwise, and the soft pith was then cut into thin strips laid out side by side upon a firm support. A second layer was laid crosswise upon the first. Pressing and hammering produced a firm papyrus sheet; the juice of the plant acted as a glue. On the upper side the papyrus strips ran from right to left; this side is called *recto*. It was possible to write on the other side, called *verso*, but this was more troublesome, since here the papyrus strips ran from top to bottom. Because of this difference, papyrus was better suited for the production of scrolls, where only one side was used for writing, than for a codex, where the leaves were used on both sides.

Vellum (or parchment) as writing material is the specially processed skin of cattle, donkeys, horses, sheep, or goats. The most delicate parchment was made from the skin of newborn animals. The skin was not tanned, as in the production of leather, but treated with chalk and water, cleaned of all hair, stretched, dried, and smoothed with pumice. As in the case of papyrus, there was a great variety in quality. The introduction of special methods of preparation of the skins was ascribed to Eumenes II of Pergamum. The name "parchment" is derived from Latin *pergamina* (*charta*), i.e., "the paper from Pergamum." The older Pliny reports in his *Natural History* (*Hist. Nat.* 13.21f) that Eumenes intended to buy large quantities of papyrus from Egypt in order to produce books for his new library; however, King Ptolemy V of Egypt, jealous of this competition for his own library, imposed an embargo on the export of papyrus. Thus Eumenes was forced to look for a different writing material for his books and invented parchment, to be made from animal skins. This story is probably merely a legend, but there is no doubt that the kings of Pergamum had a vital interest in establishing their economic independence. It is also well known that the Attalids contributed substantially to the improvement of industrial production in general. Parchment, in any case, was produced by the kings of Pergamum not only for their own library, but also for export.

The book format most widely used in antiquity was the scroll (Latin *volumen*, from *volvere* "to roll"). Several papyrus sheets were glued together until the customary length was achieved. In the case of parchment, the individual pieces were sewn togethr. The normal length of a scroll was

6 to 10 meters, its average height 25 to 30 cm. One wrote on scrolls in individual columns of the same width with an identical number of lines; margins were left at the top and bottom, as well as between the columns, where corrections and other *marginalia* could be written. Since there was a maximum limit to the length of a scroll—to prevent it from becoming too unwieldy—the works of ancient authors were divided into books ("volumes"). Each of the larger books of the New Testament, provided a standard size was used for lettering, would fit on a scroll of average length. Only Luke had to divide his work into two volumes, the Gospel and the Acts of the Apostles.

In the early Christian period the codex began to replace the scroll. A codex was much less cumbersome than a scroll, and one of normal size could contain more than a single "volume." To produce a codex, several sheets of papyrus were laid on top of each other and folded in the middle. The individual units were then stitched together and bound, usually in leather. Ancient codices are described according to the number of sheets in each unit, e.g., " a four-ply codex." Papyrus was not well suited for the production of codices, because it would tend to break at the fold (the fold was therefore sometimes reinforced with parchment). In a codex, the back of the papyrus (*verso*) would also have to be used, which was usually left blank in scrolls (there are, however, some scrolls with writing on the back, called "opistographs"). It is not impossible that the Christians were the first to produce and use codices, for practical and liturgical reasons. Among the papyrus books which have been found from II CE, most of the codices are Christian writings, and all of the scrolls are pagan texts. It is striking that copies of New Testament books from II to IV CE are always codices, even when papyrus is used as writing material, while the non-Christian literary papyri are usually scrolls. Although Christians relied mostly on papyrus codices, and pagans continued to consider the papyrus scroll as the more distinguished form of a book, the parchment codex finally prevailed. It had clear advantages over papyrus (and especially over the papyrus scroll): the parchment codex was more durable and more serviceable, and one could write on both sides without difficulty. The economic policies of the Ptolemies were the most important reason for the long-lasting popularity of papyrus in the Mediterranean world. Traditionally grown and used in Egypt anyway, papyrus was the most inexpensive writing material for the immense demand of the Ptolemies' own administration (for official correspondence, revenue lists, statistical materials, documents, and contracts), and it also paid to promote the export of papyrus, because it substantially improved Egypt's foreign trade balance. Once papyrus had become fashionable in other countries, its predominant position lasted for many centuries. It was probably the introduction of the codex, mostly by the Christians, as the more useful form of the book which made parchment the most frequently used writing material, until it in turn was slowly replaced by paper after its introduction from China in the high Middle Ages.

Commercial production of books was known as early as the classical period of Greece. Writing shops (*scriptoria*) employed a number of professional scribes, who wrote from dictation (resulting in a number of mistakes and textual corruptions, well known to text critics) and were paid according to the number of lines they wrote. In the later period slaves were often used for such work. Uncial letters were used for the production of books, i.e., stylized capitals written separately without ligature, but still without separation between words. In everyday correspondence a cursive script was used, in which groups of letters were written together. The autographs of ancient works (which are no longer preserved) were certainly written in cursive script. The price of a book varied according to the quality of the writing material, the number of illustrations, and expenses for the binding. Illustrations in books are attested for the first time in I CE and were widely used in late antiquity. It is quite certain that illustrations were used as early as the Hellenistic period, e.g., in textbooks for craftsmen. A picture of the author was provided in some books of this period. The Roman period can be called the time of the flowering of ancient book production, and it is here that the beginning of Christian book production belongs.

7. TRADE, MONETARY SYSTEMS, AND BANKING

(a) The Most Important Trading Interests

Trade over long distances and monetary systems of payment were developed in the Mediterranean world by VII BCE, and the Greek monetary system spread over the entire area during IV BCE. The trade of the Phoenicians, Carthaginians, Etruscans, and Greeks stretched from the Atlantic Ocean in the west to India in the east. The conquests of Alexander brought fundamental changes by making vast areas, which had previously been partners in foreign trade, now part of the same inland trade area. Trade among the different Hellenistic kingdoms had the character of domestic trade, for which partially independent cities such as Athens, Miletus, Delos, and Rhodes served as the primary commercial centers. This large inland trade area, to which Rome would also soon belong, and

Bibliography to §2.7
Fraser, *Alexandria,* 1. 132–88.

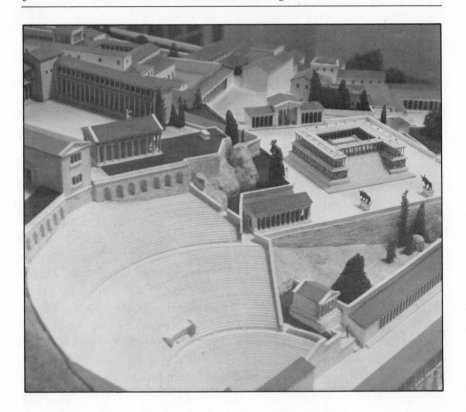

Reconstruction of Pergamum

This reconstruction shows the theater of the city, carved out of the rock of the mountain, above it the temple of Athena, behind the temple and to the left the famous library. On the right is the altar of Zeus in the center of a peristyle court and accessible by a large staircase. On the lower right a stoa flanking the entrance way to the theater.

which thus included all the countries from the western Mediterranean to the Euphrates, had foreign trade partners of a completely different culture and economic structure, even though some Hellenistic influences may have reached them at times. Foreign trade was carried out in the east with India (later also Parthia); in the south, the people of the Arabian Peninsula and the Libyans, Nubians, and Ethiopians in Africa; in the west and north, the people of central and western Europe (Illyrians and Celts, later also the Germanic tribes); in the northeast, the Scythians and the Sarmatians. Within the inland trading area, Rome ultimately became the dominant political and military power and played an increasingly significant role as a Hellenized commercial power. In the foreign trade, luxury articles predominated: precious stones and pearls, expensive textiles (silk and cotton), frankincense, ointments and cosmetic articles, rare wood and ivory. Food staples and other goods for mass consumption, however, were traded for export only close by and were otherwise restricted to the inland trading area.

Trading with foodstuffs and mass consumption goods among the Hellenistic kingdoms was very important in the beginning. The Greek cities needed grain and in turn the Seleucid empire and Egypt bought large quantities of manufactured goods from Greece. But this soon changed; the kings were eager to make their countries independent, not only in food production, but also in the supply of other widely used goods. Therefore, trade within each of the major kingdoms flourished, but the striving for economic independence became an obstacle for trade between these countries. Complete independence, however, was never achieved. Egypt always needed to import wood and metals, and the decline of the Seleucid empire brought an increasing demand for the import of many goods necessary for everyday life. But, in general, trade among the various countries of the Mediterranean world tended to favor items of special value and quality: expensive wine, fine olive oil, ceramic and toreutic products of particular beauty, etc. At the end of the Hellenistic period this commerce was strengthened by the slave trade.

The cities of Greece continued to require imports of grain, wood, and metals. At the same time, they experienced difficulties in increasing the volume of their exported goods. Thus, Greece's shortage in raw materials and foodstuffs became chronic. To be sure, some cities and islands were successful in securing for themselves a share in the trade passing through the Aegean Sea, which was the center of international trade during iii and ii BCE and lost little of its significance during the Roman period. The attempt of Ptolemaic Egypt to gain control of the Aegean trade succeeded only partially and not for long. Athens maintained its position as an important commercial center; Rhodes always played a leading role; and

Delos, supported by Rome, gained great importance for a certain time. Ephesus and Miletus, temporarily under Egyptian domination, soon regained their traditional position.

Egypt's trade is well known through the discoveries of countless documentary papyri. Egypt imported metals, lumber (especially for its fleet), horses, and elephants (for the army). Gold, ivory, and elephants were imported by sea from East Africa through the ports on the Red Sea, occasionally also via Nubia and the Nile. Sometimes slaves were imported from Arabia, while tortoise shells, dyes (Indigo), rice, spices, cotton, and silk came from India (see below on the trade routes). In order to import wood and metal, Egypt had to rely on other Mediterranean countries. Products such as fine olive oil were also imported, despite high protective tariffs for inland production. Egypt's main exports were grain and papyrus. Some of the goods imported from India into the western Mediterranean passed through Egypt. Much less is known about the trade of the Seleucid kingdom. Luxury items must have been as much in demand there as in Egypt. The Seleucids would naturally profit from the trade in luxury items for sale in the west which passed through their realm, even though they had strong competitors in Egypt and in the cities on the Black Sea. In the Roman period the only shift came from Rome's immense demand for luxury items from the east, which brought considerable profits to the commercial cities in the eastern Mediterranean.

(b) The Important Trade Routes

The most significant trade routes were those of the sea, namely through the Mediterranean, the Black Sea, and the newly opened passage to India. Nearly as important were the land routes, all of which were caravan roads. River traffic played only a minor role, with the exception of the Nile, the Euphrates, and the Tigris, the only rivers which were used by traders to any large extent. All trade routes were beset by numerous perils. Warfare threatened the security of trade repeatedly. Caravans, forced to traverse large deserts, were exposed to brigands and so needed military protection, which at times they had to procure for themselves. The sea routes from the east terminated at different points on the eastern Mediterranean and the Black Sea. From there the imported goods were transported by sea, and often reshipped several times before they reached their final destination. The northernmost caravan road ran north of the Caspian Sea to the Black Sea (this was later one of the Chinese silk roads). This road was not controlled by the Seleucids, and it gained in significance

Bibliography to §2.7b
Lionel Casson, *Travel in the Ancient World* (London: Allen & Unwin, 1974).

once the worsening troubles which beset the Seleucid realm made the southern routes more risky. Another northern road, running south of the Caspian Sea, had to pass through countries controlled by the Parthians, the Seleucids, and the kings of Pontus, and was much less used. To the south were the ancient roads connecting India and Babylonia, a northern route through Bactria, and a southern route through Gedrosia and the Persis. In the Hellenistic period both roads terminated in Seleucia on the Tigris, the most significant commercial city and point of reshipment in the east. As long as the Seleucids ruled the east, they maintained and secured both roads for military purposes. Reshipment to the Mediterranean Sea was difficult from here, since Egypt controlled the port city of Seleucia in Pieria for some time. Later on one would follow either the route which paralleled the upper course of the Euphrates and terminated in Antioch (the way along which Christianity later moved in its eastward expansion) or the road via Palmyra and Damascus to the cities on the Phoenician coast. The southernmost route used the sea passage from India to the Persian Gulf.

Further transport westward to the Mediterranean varied with the political situation. Merchants preferred the road which led from the Persian Gulf and across the Arabian Peninsula to the Red Sea through the country of the Nabateans, or to Egypt via the Sinai Peninsula. As long as Egypt had good relations with the Nabateans and controlled the Phoenician cities on the Mediterranean coast, it could profit considerably from this transit trade. The Seleucids tried to detour the goods arriving at the Persian Gulf via Seleucia, and later on the Parthians were able to intercept this route on the Persian Gulf. The wars of the Romans with Parthia for possession of Mesopotamia involved in part the attempt to control this important trade route. Furthermore, the Ptolemies and later the Romans had a vital interest in maintaining the direct sea route to India. Using the monsoon winds, Egyptian sailors could sail from the Red Sea to India around the Arabian Peninsula. Once the canal from the Red Sea to the Nile had been reopened, goods from India could be transported by sea from India all the way to Alexandria.

For trade in the western Mediterranean sea routes were used almost exclusively. Among the Greek cities, Corinth led in trading with the west; when Caesar rebuilt Corinth, it became the most important point of transfer. There were, of course, ancient commercial ties between Carthage and its mother city Tyre on the Phoenician coast. This connection became significant during the Hellenistic period by creating new markets for the sale of luxury goods from India and Arabia in the west and supplying raw materials for the Hellenistic empires. Sulfur was thus exported from Italy, silver from Spain, and tin came from as far away as Brittany. These

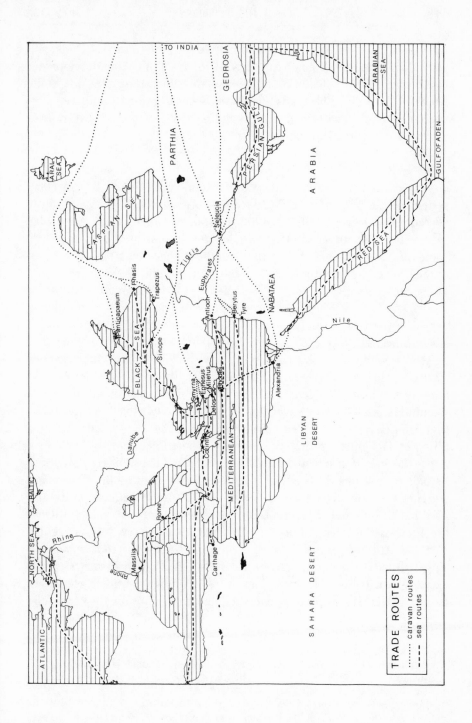

TRADE ROUTES
.... caravan routes
– – – – sea routes

sea routes, however, came more and more under the control of Rome and were dominated by Roman commercial interests. Yet this development also brought an expansion of the Mediterranean trading area due to the Roman conquests. The roads which the Romans built for military purposes very soon also served the expanding trade of the Mediterranean world with western Europe.

(c) Coins and Monetary Systems

In the time before the conquest of Alexander the Great, the monetary system of the ancient world was chaotic. A variety of gold and silver currencies was used, with no uniform standard of coinage. Alexander made silver the currency of his whole empire and introduced the Attic standard for all mints. From the beginning there was no shortage of minted silver and, with the exception of the time of the wars of the Diadochi, the supply of silver remained stable throughout most of the Hellenistic period. Shortages were experienced towards the end of this period, caused by a combination of factors: a decrease in the output of silver mines, and increase in hoarding, and a drain of money to Rome.

Money was minted by each state, city, and league, as soon as they claimed political independence. But monetary policies were determined only by the large kingdoms and the independent and commercially influential cities. The Attic silver standard was always used, the only exception being Egypt. In the beginning Egypt used the Attic standard just as all other Hellenistic states. But as early as the later years of Ptolemy I Soter, the weight of silver coins was decreased and the standard reduced to become almost identical with the one previously used by the Phoenician states. This new silver money was minted in the Phoenician cities and used in all Ptolemaic possessions outside Egypt. For use in Egypt itself, the Ptolemies minted copper, not as emergency money, but as regular currency (the Egyptians, to be sure, were accustomed to copper money). Egypt thus had in fact a currency system based on three metals: gold, exclusively used for the export/import trade, foreign subsidies, etc.; silver for the Ptolemaic possessions overseas; and copper for Egypt itself. The

Bibliography to §2.7c

Colin M. Kraay and Max Hirmer, *Greek Coins* (New York: Abrams, 1966).

Edward Allen Sydenham, *The Coinage of the Roman Republic* (rev. G. C. Haines; New York: Arno, 1975).

Harold Mattingly, *Roman Coins* (2d ed.; London: Methuen, 1960).

C. H. V. Sutherland, *Ancient Numismatics: A Brief Introduction* (New York: American Numismatic Society, 1958).

Karl Christ, *Antike Numismatik: Einführung und Bibliographie* (Darmstadt: Wissenschaftliche Buchgesellschaft, 1967).

Ptolemies also enforced the exclusive use of their own currency within their realm. Other currencies, especially gold, were rigorously excluded from the inland market.

The monetary arrangements decreed by Alexander remained unchanged in the Seleucid empire. The Attic standard was retained. Gold, silver, and copper coins were minted and circulated freely. This, however, does not mean that the Seleucids had a three-metal system like the Ptolemies. Rather, gold and silver coins were produced in royal mints all over the country in the early period, but gold coinage was halted, soon to be resumed only on special occasions. Copper was used in the local markets, and a number of cities, certainly the Greek cities of Asia Minor, were granted the privilege to mint their own copper coins, though other rights to strike coinage were not given until the time of Antiochus IV Epiphanes. Antiochus delegated the royal rights to strike coinage to several cities, and later on even independent issues were permitted. Foreign currencies were by policy not legal tender within the Seleucid realm, but more and more exceptions were made in this respect. In addition, there was a kind of international currency existing side by side with the Seleucid gold and silver coins: the posthumous coins of Philip II, Alexander, and Lysimachus, which were minted following the same standard everywhere in the Hellenistic world outside of Egypt.

Roman coinage appeared relatively late in the commerce of the Mediterranean world. In addition to the pieces of cast bronze which had been used as money in central Italy for centuries, Rome began to strike its own silver coins in the beginning of III BCE, imitating the standard of the drachma of Magna Graecia. During the Second Punic War, Rome issued a silver denarius roughly equivalent to the Sicilian drachma and the Punic half-shekel. This coinage became standard for all of Italy and Sicily, and local coinages were discontinued. Augustus finally established a three-metal monetary system which remained in effect as the currency for the whole empire into III CE. While gold coins were issued during the republic only as special strikings, Augustus made the *aureus*, valued at 25 silver denarii, a standard part of the currency. One silver denarius was valued at sixteen *asses; asses* were minted from copper, the intermediate values *sestertius* (= 4 *asses*) and *dupondius* (= 2 *asses*) from an alloy of copper and tin. Side by side with this imperial currency there existed provincial currencies supervised by the emperor and—especially in the Greek East—local coinages of copper money, and occasionally even silver drachmas. The imperial issues of the Roman period were totally in the sevice of state propaganda. The coins announced government programs, significant political events (e.g., the conquest of a new province), the virtues of the emperor, and his benefactions. The numerous representations of deities and of temples on Roman coins are extremely important for the history of religions in the Roman period.

MONETARY SYSTEMS

Greek coins	*Roman coins*
1 talent = 60 mines	1 aureus (gold) = 25 denarii (silver)
1 mine = 50 staters (gold)	1 denarius = 4 sestercia
1 stater = 2 drachmas (silver)	1 sestertius = 2 dupondii
1 drachma = 6 obols (bronze)	1 dupondius = 2 asses
	1 ass = 4 quadrants

Relation of Greek and Roman coins: 1 drachma = 1 denarius

(d) Banking

The treasuries of the temples and the kings were once the only existing banking facilities. The Hellenistic period saw new banks owned by those cities which had the right to strike coins, as well as private banking institutions. The latter, evolved from the trade of money-changing, became the most important banks next to the treasuries of the kings. Their activities were highly diversified. Continuing their original business of money-changing, the private banks became international monetary clearing-houses. In addition they kept the accounts of their customers and their deposits (short- and long-term deposits with or without interest), made transfers and handled remittances, and gave loans and mortgages.

There were banks in all commercial cities, but Athens was always the leading banking center of the ancient world. In some places temple treasuries functioned as banking facilities; the temple of Apollo on the island of Delos is the best known example. The wealth of the Delian temple attracted the attention of the Ptolemies, who used it as one of their central banks and made Delos the capital of the island league which they controlled. Later on, Rhodes, Macedonia, and Rome also used the Delian temple treasury. Temple banks were usually not concerned with commercial transactions, but were used as repositories and safe deposits of large sums of money. The function of temples as banks did not result from their interest in commerce but from the notion that everything owned by a temple was inviolate. There were banks not only in the major commercial places and reshipment centers for trade that used the Mediterranean sea routes, but also in the major cities situated on the caravan routes. Since caravans normally transported their goods only over a limited distance, such banks were responsible for equipping and financing new caravans in order to allow the further transport of such goods.

The Ptolemies developed a unique banking system in Egypt. The banking system was as centralized as the rest of the economy. The royal treasury functioned as the central state bank, with branches everywhere in the country. Perhaps these branches were not clearly differentiated from the local offices of the royal administration. This banking system used exclusively written documentation instead of oral agreements. Since the local banks were all members of one centralized system, which in turn was part of the central royal administration, payment by check or transfer through remittance were the regular forms of money transactions. Some of these elements were taken over by the Roman banking system. The most important Roman contribution to banking, however, was the introduction of fully developed double-entry bookkeeping.

Inscription from Library of Pantaenus in Athens

The marble fragment with this inscription was apparently a part of a herm that was standing at the entrance to the Library of Pantaenus, built ca. 100 c.e. in the southeast corner of the Athenian Agora:

"No book shall be carried out, because we have sworn it. (The library) shall be open from the first hour to the sixth hour."

EDUCATION, LANGUAGE, AND LITERATURE

1. Basic Features of Cultural and Intellectual Life

(a) The Public Character of Cultural and Intellectual Life

The foundation of the public character of cultural and intellectual life was the institution of the schools. Primary schools were normally the responsibility of the administration of the Hellenistic cities, and gymnasia, even if they were in fact sponsored by private associations, were viewed as a public and communal responsibility. The Ionic cities were the first to develop a three-tiered school system. In the primary schools (whose teachers were paid by the city in the more progressive cities), children were instructed in reading, writing, music, and athletics from the age of seven to fourteen. In a number of cases there were also schools for girls, and co-education of boys and girls is occasionally attested. The methods of instruction were simple: one started by learning the alphabet and proceeded to the reading and writing of words and sentences. Rote learning played a significant role. Not much changed in this elementary instruction in the Roman period; it was certainly no advantage when teachers on this level came to be paid privately in the later period.

The next stage of schooling was instruction by a grammarian paid by the parents. In addition to instruction in grammar, he introduced students to the poets, reading primarily Homer and Euripides. That tradition did not change for many centuries. The predominant position of the poets in school teaching was critically discussed by Plutarch in I CE (*Quomodo adolescens poetas audire debeat*). In their fifteenth (or seventeenth) year the young men went to the gymnasium for a one- or two-year period (the so-called *ephebia*, where athletics and preliminary military training predominated).

There were no universities or professional schools, except medical schools. The major cities (Rhodes, Pergamum, Alexandria, Athens, and others) did have schools of rhetoric which were financed either through public funds or private foundations. Usually, however, instruction in rhetoric was private and had to be paid for by the student or his parents.

Therefore, education in rhetoric (as also philosophy) was open to only a small number of the young men who had completed their training in the gymnasium. Schools of philosophy were strong competitors to those of rhetoric, but the latter were more popular. An education in rhetoric, which might last as long as five years, would lead to a career in politics, law, or public administration. It is remarkable that the teaching of rhetoric included no specific preparation for these professions, but consisted of rhetorical theory, study of the famous classical orators, and practical exercises in public speaking. After completing this education, students would receive their professional training in the form of an apprenticeship in a lawyer's office or an administrative agency.

As early as the end of iii bce Greek teachers of rhetoric began to settle in Rome. At the beginning of the imperial period, education in rhetoric had become the accepted form of higher education in Roman society; the language of instruction was Greek; Greek or bilingual (Greek and Latin) instruction was still used in the imperial period. The result of the establishment of this rhetorical education in Rome was that the same educational standards applied for all higher public offices and other vocations requiring an academic education. At the same time, certain moral standards for such professions found general acceptance (due to the strong influence of Stoic philosophy; see §4.1d). Christian theology later established the same criteria for ecclesiastical officers: certain oral qualifications and rhetorical (or philosophical) training were presupposed as a matter of course.

With the production and sale of books in larger quantities (§2.6d), literary works were increasingly available to the general public. Hand in hand with this development went the establishment of public libraries.

Bibliography to §3

François Chenoux, *The Civilization of Greece* (London: Allen & Unwin, 1965).

Werner Jaeger, *PAIDEIA: The Ideals of Greek Culture,* vol. 3 (Oxford: Blackwell, 1944).

Paul Wendland, *Die hellenistisch-römische Kultur in ihren Beziehungen zum Judentum und Christentum* (4th ed. with bibliography by Heinrich Dörrie; HNT 1,2–3; Tübingen: Mohr/Siebeck, 1972). Since its 3d ed. of 1912, a classic in the study of Hellenistic culture and Christianity.

Bibliography to §3.1

M. L. Clarke, *Higher Education in the Ancient World* (London: Routledge and Kegan Paul, 1971).

H. I. Marrou, *A History of Education in Antiquity* (London: Sheed and Ward, 1956).

H.-I. Marrou, "Education and Rhetoric," in: M. I. Finley, *The Legacy of Greece: A New Appraisal* (Oxford: Clarendon, 1981) 185–201.

Martin P. Nilsson, *Die hellenistische Schule* (München: Beck, 1955).

Originally the only libraries had been the private property of the rich, because the acquisition of large numbers of books presupposed considerable wealth. The first public libraries were established by the kings, in Pella, Alexandria, and Pergamum. The Roman emperors followed this example, as in the founding of the Palatine library by Augustus in Rome. More important for the literate public were the city libraries, which could be financed through public or private funds. Smaller libraries were found in the gymnasia and schools. In both east and west the same works constituted the standard holdings, with the smaller libraries having only a limited selection: the classical Greek authors, with the poets (especially Homer and Euripides) being more fully represented than prose writers and philosophers; and handbooks, textbooks, and compendia (which were not always of high quality).

The classical poets were available for reading everywhere, but they could also be heard: in the theaters poetry became accessible to the illiterate public as well as to the educated reader. Every city possessed a theater. The tradition of the Dionysiac theater, with fixed annual dates for the competitive presentation of tragedies and comedies, had long been a typical institution of classical Athens. Though Alexandria still arranged for such competitions at certain dates every year, the theaters of the Hellenistic cities did not continue this tradition. Instead there were irregular, yet frequent performances of the classical plays. Euripides' tragedies must especially have been performed again and again. New tragedies and comedies were performed on occasion, and also mimes; in the Roman period pantomimes were especially popular in the theaters. Greek tragedies in Latin translation were performed in Rome as early as III BCE. Theaters built for these performances reproduced the classical Greek architecture. Comedies written by Roman poets at first were nothing but adaptations of plays from the New Comedy of Athens, published in Latin translation with the addition of some typically Roman features. Roman tragedies were also closely tied to their Greek predecessors, especially Euripides (§3.4b; 6.4b).

In addition to the theaters, many cities had an odeum and auditoriums which were sometimes built as independent structures, at other times as part of other buildings, such as the auditorium of the large gymnasium in Pergamum. These halls were used for public lectures and for competitions of poets, orators, and singers. But most of all, the stoa, the covered colonnade, was the place for public lectures and discussions. It is characteristic that the most important philosophical movement of this period, Stoicism, was founded not in a private house or in the sacred district of a temple, but in the Stoa Poikile in Athens, where the Phoenician Zeno presented his teachings in public (§4.1d). When he died, Athens mourned not merely the death of the head of a philosophical school, but a citizen who was well known to the general public, who was respected and highly esteemed, and whose moral integrity was admired by all. This must be remembered if one is to understand the spirit from which the Christian missionaries inherited their insistence on the public character of their message and on the moral integrity of the messenger (cf. 2 Cor 4:1–4). Sectarian seclusion was at variance with the principles of educational policy of the Hellenistic city, which insisted upon the public character of education and instruction. Christian sectarians violated this principle as much as the emperor Domitian, who drove the philosophers out of Rome.

The role of the plastic and graphic arts in the life of the Hellenistic city also follows this principle. The original place of painting and sculpture was in the realm of sacred places, especially the temples and tombs. The classical period had already secularized these arts, although sacred art, of course, continued to exist. Art in the Hellenistic period was first of all and fundamentally public. The prerogative of the commonwealth over the private sphere is striking. Theaters, agoras, public buildings, gymnasia and, naturally, the sacred districts of the temples, were the places where works of art could be found. Hundreds, sometimes thousands of statues and numerous pictures were displayed in the picture galleries and stoas. Rarely did the cities have to pay for works of art, most of which were donated by the rulers, by private associations, or by wealthy individuals. It is characteristic of the spirit of the city that people financially able to maintain a private art collection instead donated large sums of money to their city for buildings, athletic games, or grain supplies, and even paid generously for the statues erected in recognition of their benefactions. The flowering of architecture in the Hellenistic cities of the east during iii and ii BCE also testifies to the public spirit of the time. With few exceptions, private houses remained comparatively modest. Building activity was concentrated instead on the erection of temples, administrative buildings, public places, and theaters.

Even the modern viewer is impressed by the way in which Hellenistic sculpture presents human beings in their own peculiar individualities. The classical tendency towards idealization receded and gave place to a much more clearly expressed individualism. A merchant from Delos, the priest of an oriental cult, a bearded philosopher, a dying Celtic warrior, kings and rulers on their coins—all appear before our eyes in their own individual personality. To be sure, this is not the same as the often brutal realism of the Roman period. What is presented is the individual instance in which character, conviction, and life experience become transparent in the features of a face, challenging even the modern viewer to engage in a dialogue about the meaning and limitations of human life. Together with these sculptures one must also read the inscriptions, both honorary and funerary in nature. In spite of many stereotyped clichés, both inscriptions and sculptures speak of the works and virtues, not only of the great and mighty, but also of untold numbers of private citizens. Whatever these people had done and experienced, their faith, their fate, and the power of the gods who determined their lives, all this was visibly present for each inhabitant of a Hellenistic city in hundreds of examples.

Much of this continued into the Roman period, along with some profound changes. In competition with public treasures of art, private art collections grew quickly in the luxurious villas of the rich. After a renewed tendency toward idealization in the early imperial period, interest in individualistic expression grew again in the plastic arts, often expressed in an almost brutal realism. At the same time, the Roman period brought a revival in the mass production of copies of famous works of classical art, a practice which had already flourished in the Hellenistic period. Large works of architecture often testify to the power of an individual rather than to the public spirit of the citizens. Nonetheless, certain aspects of the obligation of art to the general public can still be found in the Roman period.

(b) The International Character of Cultural Life

Although the Hellenistic world was divided into several independent kingdoms and a number of semi-independent city-states, its cultural life was nevertheless a unity, i.e., it was international. Once the whole realm became politically united under Roman rule, Hellenistic culture became the culture of the world. Greek education had already begun to extend its influence beyond the Hellenistic kingdoms and cities, and even Rome came under its influence as early as III BCE. Individual national elements by no means disappeared, but they assumed a new role as contributions to the dominant Greek culture. Native cultural traditions within the realm of Hellenistic influence often maintained their own strength and vitality, but they lost their ideological justification. To be sure, there were circles which resisted the influence of Hellenism. A good example for such resistance is the Maccabean revolt against the Seleucids. But even there, only a small portion of the Jewish people offered resistance to the further spread of Hellenism, while the majority of the Jewish people became thoroughly Hellenized. Christianity, after all, became a Hellenistic movement

Bibliography to §3.1b

Edward Alexander Parsons, *The Alexandrian Library, Glory of the Hellenic World: Its Rise, Antiquities, and Destructions* (New York: American Elsevier, 1952).
Fraser, *Alexandria*, 1. 305–35.

through and through, largely because Judaism had already marked the path into Hellenistic culture.

Whatever individual nations could claim as their own peculiar tradition was transformed into a contribution to the world culture of Hellenism. This is true for all areas of cultural and intellectual activity, for craftsmanship as well as for the fine arts, literature, and religion. This process was encouraged by the natural curiosity and fascination of the Greeks for foreign cultures and their peculiarities. Often the kings encouraged the process by their energetic promotion of native cultural traditions and religions, advisable for internal political reasons, with the result that such traditions were revived in Greek dress and thus contributed even more readily to the international culture of Hellenism. Books written in Greek were published on such subjects as Babylonian, Egyptian, or Jewish history, religion, wisdom, and science. Mosaics of Syrian artists were found on the island of Delos in the Aegean Sea; paintings of Greek artists were introduced to Rome; and artistically decorated glazed vases with Parthian motifs were exported from Syria into all parts of the Mediterranean world.

The Stoic philosophy expressed these new horizons of a world culture most appropriately. The Stoics taught that the world was but one large polis in which people from all nations were citizens of equal rights, that all the gods of different nations represented one and the same divine providence, and that the moral obligations of all people should not recognize any distinction of race or social status. Wandering philosophers proclaiming such teachings everywhere were soon joined by wandering missionaries preaching religious messages addressed to all people. The milieu of Hellenism provided a fertile ground in which religions once rooted in the tradition of individual nations and bound to particular holy places could be transformed into missionary movements claiming to be world religions.

Hellenistic literature no longer saw human beings as members of a particular state or city; rather city and nation became accidental environments in which people happened to live. To be sure, people were still obligated to serve the community in which they resided, and the community spirit of the citizens of the Hellenistic cities is documented in many impressive monuments and testimonies. But one might just as well contribute to the community life of another city or a foreign country, because the powers ruling the lives of people and demanding their loyalty were no longer identical with the rulers of a particular city or country.

The Hellenistic rulers of course promoted first of all the interests of their own countries and capital cities where they made considerable efforts to support literature, the arts, and science. But it was not rare for great sums of money to be spent to support a foreign city, particularly certain Greek cities which had become symbols of cultural unity for the entire Hellenistic-Roman world. Antiochus IV Epiphanes donated funds for the resumption of the building of the monumental temple of Zeus Olympius in Athens. The Pergamene kings, jealously concerned to further the fame of their own realm and of their capital city Pergamum as an international center of cultural and intellectual life, donated several buildings in Athens (the Stoa of Attalus and the Stoa of Eumenes). Roman emperors emulated these examples, and private donations of wealthy individuals were often made for the benefit of the cities and sanctuaries of Greece (e.g., the Leonidaeum in Olympia, which was donated and built by the architect Leonidas of Naxos). Yet no one could compare with Herodes Atticus. Magnificient buildings in Athens, Corinth, Delphi, Olympia and other cities of Greece testify to the generosity of this famous rhetorician of II CE, who is said to have been the most wealthy person in antiquity. The report that his contemporary, the Christian merchant Marcion of Sinope, donated 200,000 sesterces to the Roman church is probably authentic; such actions were typical of the spirit of Hellenism.

Athens was the symbol of cultural and intellectual life. Even in the Roman period, it was still considered the cultural capital of the world, even though this no longer corresponded to its actual significance. Paul, who had preached in Athens only briefly and without much success, recognized this more clearly than Luke, who could not imagine the activity of the famous apostle without a speech presented in Athens, the renowned Areopagus speech (Acts 17). Hellenistic rulers had contributed to the beauty of Athens through the donation of several buildings. Roman emperors spent large sums of money to enhance the city's splendor and fame. Nero renovated the theater of Dionysus Eleutherius; Hadrian completed the immense temple of Zeus Olympius and donated a large library building; Augustus' friend Agrippa gave a new odeum, which was built in the center of the agora; and the rhetorician Herodes Atticus built another odeum on the slopes of the Acropolis. In the Roman imperial period Athens was nearly a museum, but it retained its significance as the seat of the philosophical schools. In addition to the Stoic school, founded at the beginning of the Hellenistic period, this city was the home of the "academic" school of Plato in the garden of the hero Academus; of the Lyceum, the school of Aristotle; and of the Garden of the Epicureans. For the study of philosophy students would flock to Athens from all parts of the ancient world, even as late as the beginning of the Byzantine period.

Rivaling Athens was Alexandria, the capital of the Ptolemaic kingdom. Its fame as a center of culture and scholarship was renewed under Augustus, and it is remembered as the birthplace of Christian theology and as the place where Plotinus, the founder of Neoplatonism, received his education. The Museum of Alexandria was founded before 280 BCE by Ptolemy I Soter. It was the first institution in the history of humankind specifically dedicated to scientific research. Scholars, poets, and artists who were called to the Museum by the Ptolemies lived in a community organized as a religious association under the direction of a priest appointed by the king. Since the king provided their full support, the members were free to devote all their time to study and research. There were very significant productions of poetic works in III BCE, and equally important achievements in textual interpretation, and also geography, astronomy, medicine, and other sciences. Attached to the Museum was the Alexandrian library, magnificently built and richly endowed, and with its 400,000 volumes the most famous library of antiquity. (The Museum was destroyed in 269/70 CE or 273 by Zenobia or Aurelian; afterwards the scholars apparently moved to the Sarapeum, using its library which was burned by the Christian Patriarch Theophilus in 389 CE.)

In the second half of III BCE, Pergamum began to compete with Alexandria as a cultural capital, though it never achieved the same significance. More important for the cultural and intellectual life of the Hellenistic and Roman period was Rhodes. Freed from Persian rule by Alexander the Great, the island republic remained independent, and though conquered and destroyed by Cassius in 42 BCE, it became a free ally of Rome in the imperial period. Rhodes was the home of an important school of sculpture which, among other works, produced the famous sculpture of Laocoon, now in the Vatican. Beginning in II BCE it could boast of one of the most famous schools of rhetoric. Rhodes was also the residence of many renowned scholars and philosophers, such as Apollonius, poet and scholar and previously the librarian at Alexandria, and the Stoic philosophers Panaetius and Posidonius. Many Romans came to study in Rhodes in I BCE (including Cicero, Lucretius, Caesar, and Tiberius); thus Rhodes played an important part in the mediation of the Hellenistic cultural inheritance to Rome.

The international character of education is documented not only in the tendency for students to enroll in schools of philosophy and rhetoric far away from their home cities, but also in the fact that so many leading philosophers and scholars came from countries which had only recently been incorporated into the realm of Greek cultural influence. Among the heads of the philosophical schools in Athens, there were many who were not born and raised in Athens or Greece, but came from Greek families residing in Asia Minor or in the east, or from oriental families which had become Hellenized (whether the former or the latter was the case is often difficult to determine). A foreign origin is most striking among the leading Stoic philosophers: the founder of Stoicism, Zeno, was a Phoenician from

Cyprus; his successor, Cleanthes, a Greek from Assus in the Troad (Asia Minor); the next head of the school, Chrysippus, came from Soloi in Cilicia; then came Zeno from Tarsus, and Diogenes from Seleucia on the Tigris; Panaetius was the offspring of a rich Rhodian family; and Posidonius' home was Apamea in Syria. The situation was not much different in other schools: the academician Carneades, for example, was a North African from Cyrene, and Antiochus came from the Phoenician port city of Ascalon. It would be entirely wrong, however, to search for any "foreign" elements which these men might have introduced into the philosophical schools. On the contrary, they were all "Greeks" who had no other interests than to develop further the *one* Greek culture which had become the culture of the world.

2. THE LANGUAGE

(a) The Development of the Greek Language into the Koine

In v BCE Greeks spoke a number of dialects; some of these were limited to certain localities and no longer appear in extant literature, though occasionally they are attested through local inscriptions. The most important dialects or groups of dialects were the following: Ionic, spoken in the central section of the west coast of Asia Minor and in the northern part of the Aegean Sea; Attic, the dialect of Athens and Attica, which is closely related to Ionic; Aeolic, spoken in the northern part of the west coast of Asia Minor, on Lesbos, and in Thessaly and Boeotia; Doric, spoken in the southern and western parts of the Peloponnesus, in the southwestern sections of Asia Minor, on Crete, Rhodes, and Cos; the closely related Doric dialects of Elis, Achaea, and of central and western Greece; and finally the Arcado-Cyprian dialect of the interior of the Peloponnesus and of the island of Cyprus. Macedonian is not a Greek dialect, but a different branch of the family of Greek languages.

Bibliography to §3.2

Eduard Schwyzer, *Griechische Grammatik* (HAW 2,1; München: Beck, 1953) 1. 45–137.

F. Blass and A. Debrunner, *A Greek Grammar of the New Testament and Other Early Christian Literature* (trans. and rev. Robert W. Funk; Chicago: University of Chicago, 1961).

Bibliography to §3.2a

B. F. C. Atkinson, *The Greek Language* (London: Faber and Faber, 1931).

A. Meillet, *Aperçu d'une histoire de la langue grecque* (7th ed.; Paris: Klincksieck, 1965).

In extant Greek literature only Ionic, Aeolic, Doric, and Attic occur. Ionic is the language of the older Greek epic literature (Homer), lyric poetry, and in part the older prose works from Asia Minor (Herodotus, Hippocrates). Aeolic is limited to the lyric poetry of Lesbos (Sappho). The lyric of the tragic chorus is written in Doric. The development of Attic prose began in v BCE; it soon became dominant in literary writing, and also as the most important commercial and diplomatic language, due to Athens' leading position in economy and politics. This Greek dialect, which had meanwhile assimilated some elements from the closely related Ionic dialect (e.g., -σσ- for -ττ- in Attic, as in τάσσειν; ρσ for σσ, as in ἄρσεν; also ναός for νεώς), was used by Alexander the Great and by his successors as the official language of administration, and thus became the *lingua franca* of the Hellenistic world. In the east, it soon rivalled and partly replaced Aramaic, which had been the administrative and commercial language of the Achaemenid Persian empire.

It was this "Ionicised Attic" which became the Koine, i.e., the "common" language of the Hellenistic and Roman period. In its further development after the classical period, a number of peculiar features emerged which distinguished the Koine more and more from classical Attic prose:

1) *Phonetics:* The diphthongs disappeared by the beginning of Christian literature; they survived only in writing and are often missing in inscriptions and papyri, sometimes also in early Christian writings; ει became ē, ου became ū (later αι changed to ä, οι to ē, and ευ and αυ became *ef* and *af*), αι, ηι, and ωι became α, η, and ω (while the ι was normally retained as an iota subscript). η became identical in sound with ι (as ει and later also οι). Among the consonants φ = p^h became *f*, θ = t^h changed to voiceless *th*, and χ = k^h to *ch* (later β became *v*, δ a voiced *th*, and γ became g^h or *y*).

2) *Morphology:* The so-called second Attic declension disappeared (ἵλεως became ἵλεος—both forms are still found in the New Testament). The vocative was largely replaced by the nominative (θεός for θεέ). The ending of the accusative plural of the consonantal stems of the third declension invaded the vocalic stems of this declension (ἰχθύας for ἰχθύς). The superlative of the adjectives became rare. In the conjugation of the verbs, the optative fell into disuse and periphrastic constructions were more frequent. The verbs ending in -μι were used only rarely.

3) *Vocabulary:* Numerous changes took place as the composite forms became more frequent, and new technical terms were formulated in the various areas of specialized scientific, philosophical, religious, and administrative language. Some neologisms emerged on the basis of older Greek words; other terms were borrowed from other languages. Thus there were

occasional loanwords from the Semitic languages and from Latin, more rarely from Persian and Egyptian.

4) *Syntax:* the departures from classical Attic usage were considerable. However, insofar as typical features of Koine syntax appear most frequently in nonliterary texts, or in writers untrained in the writing of literary prose, they simply reflect the fact that the vernacular language in any case prefers a paratactic style, brevity, anacoluthon, and solecisms. Other features typical of the style of New Testament writers will be discussed below.

(b) The Language of Literature

Koine Greek as a common language of discourse, commerce and administration developed according to its own laws and dynamics. It was a complex phenomenon, comprising the actually spoken vernacular as well as the technical languages of law, science, economy, and administration, the language of school and rhetoric, and various degrees of influence from classical literary conventions. There were also a number of writers who wrote in an "elevated Koine," i.e., in a kind of cultivated common language. The character of the sources which are preserved gives rather rich information about the common language of the Hellenistic and Roman period, while the materials for the literary language, especially for the Koine as a literary language, are few and far between. Evidence is somewhat more plentiful for the Roman imperial period. Much of Hellenistic literature has not been preserved because the study of the classical Greek authors was preferred in the later period. Furthermore, the archaizing movement of the imperial period, the so-called Atticism, established standards for written Greek works which the written Koine was unable to meet—another reason for the disappearance of most of the earlier Greek Koine literature. It is necessary, therefore, to discuss this Atticistic movement briefly.

While the common spoken language naturally became more and more distant from the classical Attic prose, the Atticistic revival, which became increasingly dominant in Greek literature, returned to the ideals of the classical language and sought to establish the style of Attic literary prose as the standard for all literary writing. To be sure, even in the Hellenistic period certain writers chose to adopt Attic prose as the ideal for their own writing. But as a conscious movement of literature, Atticism began in I BCE as a reaction against "Asianism." Asianism was a rhetorical style developed in Asia Minor in III BCE which deliberately used uncommon syntactical constructions and phrases, overloaded sentences with resounding words, and employed sequences of abridged clauses for rhetorical effectiveness. The reaction to Asianism made recourse to classical Greek prose and its lucid, rational style in order to overcome the bombastic pomposity of the Asian rhetoricians. To be sure, Asianism survived: it occurs in a number of inscriptions (e.g., those of Antiochus of Commagene), was taught in many second-rate rhetorical schools (Petronius in his *Satyricon* attacks the bombastic phrases which students of rhetoric had to learn), and was preferred by a number of authors (among Christian writers, Ignatius of Antioch has been cited as an example). Asianism also to some degree affected the style of the later Atticistic rhetoricians. But, on the whole, beginning with Cicero's polemic against the Asianists, Atticism became the predominant literary style of the period of late antiquity.

The rhetor and historian Dionysius of Halicarnassus, who taught in Rome after 30 BCE, emulated Demosthenes as his example and, especially in his work *On the Arrangement of Words,* made imitation of the classical authors the criterion of educated speech. In II CE, Herodes Atticus, vastly wealthy and a patron of the arts, a leading representative of the Second Sophistic (§6.4e), became the most accomplished master of the Attic style. The text of one of his speeches is preserved, which shows such a perfect mastery of early classical Attic prose style that some modern scholars have argued for a V BCE date for its composition. Aelius Dionysius of Halicarnassus and a certain Pausanias from Syria (ca. 100 CE) composed dictionaries designed to ensure that literary vocabulary was identical to that of the classical Attic authors. Ingenious craftsmanship and scientific precision combined in a successful archaizing movement which perpetuated a bilingualism within the Greek language, which has not yet been overcome even today. The leading proponents of rhetoric and literature of ancient Atticism were unable to comprehend that the principal task of literature is the cultivation of the living, spoken language.

Some examples of a literary Koine, however, have survived. Most closely related to the vernacular is the language of the Hellenistic historians. Though most of their works have been lost, extensive fragments and several complete books of the historians Polybius (ca. 200–120 BCE) and Diodorus Siculus (I BCE) are preserved. Plutarch (45–125 CE) and the Jewish writers Philo and Josephus show some influence from the vernacular Koine. The sophist and satirist Lucian of Samosata (120–180 CE), though an admirer of classical literature who would recognize no other authorities for his own style, was not afraid of making extensive use of the language of his own time and to ridicule the excesses of Atticism. Other exceptions include the astrologer Vettius Valens, who did not hesitate to use the vernacular language, and the philosopher Epictetus, whose lectures, as recorded by his student Arrian, are a direct and uncorrupted testimony for the vernacular language of the early Christian period.

(c) Evidence for the Vernacular Koine

The most abundant evidence for the vernacular Greek language of the Hellenistic and Roman periods comes from non-literary papyri (nearly all of which have been found in Egypt) and from private inscriptions. In addition to papyri of literary texts, Egypt has yielded thousands from the beginning of the Ptolemaic period to the Islamic invasion, which are either official documents or private correspondence. The precise relationship of these papyri to the actual spoken vernacular is a matter of debate. Technical language is reflected in various ways. Writers of letters sometimes tried to emulate a more literary style. Barbarisms occur in documents produced by people whose native language was Egyptian. Thus not all the peculiar features of these papyri are direct witnesses of the vernacular Koine. Official documents that give evidence for administrative terminology include governmental edicts, administrative files, court records, reports of officials and of governmental agencies, and also petitions of citizens of all classes, requests, complaints, and private contracts of marriage and divorce, sales, rental of property, loans, securities, and testaments (often written by official scribes). The last group of documents reflects the spoken language more directly than do official records.

The vernacular language is most clearly visible in private correspondence. Letters are preserved which were written by people from all walks of life: husbands away on business write to their wives at home; a son who had become a soldier writes to his parents; a father admonishes his children who are away from home; slaves and free citizens, rich and poor speak in these letters. A number of magical papyri have also been discovered. They may be of limited value for the history of religions, since religious thought and rites appear here only in the shadow of magic, but as a source for the religious language of the time, the magical papyri are of inestimable value. They also demonstrate the degree to which terms from non-Greek religions (including Judaism), transcribed or translated, had invaded the language of the Greek Koine.

During the decades following the first great discoveries of papyri at the end of the nineteenth century, much of this material was shifted and collected by philologians and New Testament scholars in order to elucidate the language of early Christian literature, and has also been absorbed by New Testament dictionaries (such as that of Walter Bauer) and grammars (such as Blass-Debrunner). But the rich materials discovered in

Bibliography to §3.2c

E. G. Turner, *Greek Papyri: An Introduction* (Oxford: Clarendon, 1968).

more recent decades have not yet been explored systematically from the perspective of the language of early Christianity.

While almost all of the papyri have been found in Egypt, thus providing a geographically limited picture of the vernacular language of that time, private inscriptions are preserved from almost all parts of the Hellenistic world, most abundantly from Greece, and Greek isles, western Anatolia, and Italy. Most of these inscriptions are on stone, but a few appear on wood, metal, ostraca, and in mosaics. Like the official inscriptions, many of the private inscriptions are publications of originals, written on papyrus, which were kept in archives. These comprise primarily contracts, business documents, bills, and testaments. Of particular interest for the language of early Christian literature are inscriptions which contain dedications, curses, votives, reports of miraculous healings, dreams, and visions, and which speak of pilgrimages and generally about the life and death of human beings. Though many of these inscriptions no doubt use traditional formulas and clichés, and do not always tell us what the individual thoughts and beliefs of people were, they nonetheless testify to the conventions of language describing such special events as birth, death, consecration, or healing. Often such conventions will reflect the common usage and terminology. What has been said with respect to the papyri is even more applicable to these inscriptions: a systematic collection and investigation from the perspective of the history of early Christian language, with particular attention to local differences, is still needed.

While the nonliterary papyri and inscriptions are primary witnesses for the conventions of the spoken language, evidence for the literary Koine exists not only in the writers mentioned above (Polybius, Epictetus), but also in the extensive corpus of Jewish writings in the Greek language from the Hellenistic and Roman periods. Many of these writings are Greek translations of Hebrew (or Aramaic) originals, such as most of the books of the Greek Bible of Judaism and some of the so-called pseudepigrapha of the Old Testament (e.g., the *Testaments of the Twelve Patriarchs* and the *Psalms of Solomon*). Such translations frequently follow the Hebrew original very closely; thus their Greek contains numerous Semitisms in syntax and vocabulary. These writings nevertheless strongly influenced the religious language of Hellenistic Judaism and Christianity. More important for understanding the literary Koine are those translations of Hebrew books which less slavishly follow the original and, of course, Jewish literature originally written in Greek. The latter group includes the Wisdom of Solomon, the 2nd, 3rd, and 4th Books of the Maccabees, and, outside the Septuagint, the Jewish *Sibylline Books, Joseph and Asenath,* the *Letter of Aristeas,* and others (§5.3b, d). Of particular importance are the fragments of Jewish writers which were collected by Alexander Polyhistor in I BCE (preserved in Eusebius *Praep. Ev.* 9.17–39) and the poetic version of Jewish sayings preserved under the pseudonym Phocylides. Thus there is an extensive corpus of Hellenistic literature written in the vernacular language of the Koine. Some of these writings reflect a higher Koine, influenced by the conventions of Attic prose—varying with the author's literary education—but taken as a whole, these writings are witnesses for the vernacular language as it was spoken and written by those people who knew very little about the conventions of refined literary style.

(d) The Language of Early Christian Writings and the Koine

Early Christian writers without exception wrote the language of their time, the Greek Koine. Until the beginning of this century scholars called this language "Biblical Greek." The differences between New Testament (and Septuagint) Greek on the one hand and classical Greek on the other have been well known for some time. There are, as a matter of fact, some peculiarities which arise from the close relationship of the New Testament to the Old Testament and to the language and literature of Jews who did not use Greek (this will be discussed in §3.2e below). But there can be no doubt about the place of the Greek of early Christian literature within the historical development of the Greek language: it belongs to the ongoing development of Greek as a living language, which extends from the beginning of the Hellenistic period to the language of the Greek people today, the "Demotic." The New Testament has very little relationship to the artificial representation of the language of Attic prose in the literature and rhetoric of the Roman imperial period.

Within this general framework, however, the language of the various authors of the New Testament writings exhibits considerable differences. In various degrees the early Christian writings show some elements of the vernacular, of the technical language of popular philosophy, rhetoric, history writing, and the occasional influence of Attic prose. The Epistle to the Hebrews has more affinities to Attic prose than any other writing of the New Testament. The skillful periodization and hypotactic construction of its sentences reveal that the author of this writing had enjoyed a good literary education. This is also apparent in the vocabulary of the Epistle, although the author does not hesitate to use words which a strict Atticist would not permit. The other books of the New Testament, how-

Bibliography to §3.2d

Walter Bauer, "An Introduction to the Lexicon of the New Testament," in: idem, *A Greek-English Lexicon of the New Testament and Other Early Christian Literature* (2d ed.; Chicago: University of Chicago, 1979) xi–xxviii.

ever, as well as other early Christian writings, are dominated by the vernacular language. To be sure, neither Paul, nor Luke, nor the authors of
the Pastoral Epistles and 2 Peter were people without an education. The
author of 2 Peter, for example, attempts to write a more elevated Greek—
though his style is less refined than that of the author of Hebrews—and
his vocabulary reveals that he is at home in the language of a well-educated Greek writer.

Luke, the author of the Third Gospel and of the Acts of the Apostles,
relies more heavily on literary models than the authors of other New
Testament books. He is also quite familiar with the higher Koine style,
the conversational and literary language of the educated Greeks. The
prologue to his books (Luke 1:1–4) reveals his knowledge of literary conventions. Aramaic and Latin loan words, wherever they appeared in
Luke's source (the Gospel of Mark), were replaced by appropriate Greek
terms because good literary taste considered such loan words to be barbaric. Thus Luke writes διάβολος for σατανᾶς, διδάσκαλος for ῥαββί/
ῥαββουνί, φόρος for κῆνσος/census, ἑκατοντάρχης for κεντυρίων/
centurio. In his Gospel, Luke restyles Mark's simple paratactic sentence
structure into participial and relative clauses that are more in keeping
with the higher literary language. Furthermore, in the Acts of the
Apostles, Luke demonstrates in the composition of the speeches and also
in his choice of language and grammatical style that he is conscious of the
level of education of the speaker: an educated speaker uses the optative, a
mood which was no longer used in the vernacular language.

The author of *1 Clement* makes abundant use of terms and phrases
which derive from the literary language. The same is true of the Pastoral
Epistles. In the writings of the apologist Justin Martyr in the middle of II
CE, and shortly afterwards in the *Apology* of Athenagoras, the use of a
higher Koine style influenced by Atticism has become a matter of course.
The *Epistle to Diognetus,* an apology written ca. 200 CE, shows a higher
than average standard in its employment of literary prose. Clement of
Alexandria, writing at about the same time, is a master of literary prose
style. His command of literary language is so perfect that he can afford to
disregard the strict rules of Atticism. In his writings the expressive power
of Greek prose once more reaches heights which the rigid stringency of
Atticism was unable to achieve. Henceforth Christian authors employed a
prose style in which the strict rules of Atticism are somewhat relaxed; in a
number of writers, a greater proximity to the spoken vernacular Greek
language repeatedly appears, probably due to influence from the Christian sermon, which was designed to address the common people.

These examples, however, only mark the end of a long development
which began with Luke and the Epistle to the Hebrews. The majority of

the New Testament writings, unlike Luke, did not cross the threshold
between vernacular and literary language. Paul dwells wholly in the
world of the vernacular, although he uses the common language of his
time in a masterly and skillful way. He is quite capable of employing
dependent clauses and has access to a comparatively large vocabulary,
which he uses with conscious purpose. He also controls a variety of stylistic techniques, such as play on words and paronomasia. These skills derive from Paul's rhetorical education, his training in the debating style of
the Cynic-Stoic diatribe and the preaching style of the Hellenistic synagogue. It would be quite mistaken to ascribe the peculiarities of Paul's
language to his temperament and to the depths of his religious experience.
Rather, he deliberately uses such features as ellipsis and anacoluthon as
stylistic devices.

   Like the Pauline letters, the Gospels of Matthew, Mark, and John, the
Revelation of John, and the Catholic Epistles (with the exception of 2
Peter) also use the vernacular. This is the case as well in the writings of
the Apostolic Fathers (with the exception of the *Epistle of Diognetus*) and
in the apocryphal writings of the early Christian period which are preserved in Greek. Most closely related to the unartistic language of the
uneducated common people are the Gospel of Mark, the Revelation of
John, the *Shepherd of Hermas,* and the *Teaching of the Twelve Apostles*
(the so-called *Didache*). Paratactic syntax prevails (i.e., the simple connection of sentences by "and" is the rule); there are no optatives; and periphrastic forms of the verb are frequent (e.g., Mark 13:25 ἔσονται
πίπτοντες, appropriately corrected to πεσοῦνται in Matt 24:29. To be
sure, examples of perphrastic verbs also occur in the Lukan writings, but
this is due to Semitic or "biblicistic" influence; see below). Loan words
from Semitic languages and from Latin are used as naturally as in the
contemporary vernacular Greek. In the Gospel of Mark, the signs of vulgar Koine are so flagrant that its language could not appeal to the semi-
educated middle classes: Matthew, even though himself writing in an
unpretentious Koine style, had to correct numerous expressions and sentences of the Gospel of Mark in order to produce tolerable and intelligible
Greek sentences. Not unlike Paul, Matthew also succeeds in writing a
literary style which stays as close as possible to the spoken language, but
avoids the awkwardness and clumsiness of an uneducated style. This
achievement may have been one reason for the popularity which this
Gospel enjoyed as the most frequently quoted book of the church.

   The Gospel of John occupies a special position. The language of this
Gospel is no doubt simple and normal Koine Greek. All the peculiarities
of this book, as E. C. Colwell has demonstrated, also occur in other writers
who use Koine Greek, such as Epictetus. If the language and style of the

Fourth Gospel still appear to differ from other books of the New Testament, this may be due to the fact that the author's stylistic devices are simple and limited, and are used time and time again. Perhaps there is also a greater proximity to the world of Semitic languages, but the question of the relationship of the New Testament writings to the Semitic language is not easily answered and deserves special treatment.

(e) The New Testament and the Semitic Languages

All the books of the New Testament without exception were originally written in Greek; there is no early Christian Greek writing which can be shown to have been translated from Hebrew or Aramaic. It is necessary to keep this in mind when discussing the difficult and much disputed problem of Semitisms in the New Testament. We cannot doubt that there are Semitisms in the New Testament, in the writings of the Apostolic Fathers, and in the Apocrypha. Some writings contain more Semitisms than others, but on the whole their number is relatively high; this is indisputable. Difficulties arise when one wants to determine specific instances of Semitisms, as well as their type and origin, because a number of different causes can explain their occurrence, and the conclusions which should be drawn from such instances are much debated. It is therefore necessary to clarify the character and type of the different Semitisms which occur in the New Testament writings.

1) *Hebraisms.* Semitisms can be caused by the fact that the text has been translated from Hebrew into Greek. These must properly be called Hebraisms, and in the New Testament they occur only in quotations from a Greek translation of the Hebrew Bible. Christian authors normally quote from the Septuagint, sometimes from other sources, and occasionally from the translation efforts of certain scribal traditions (which is the case for most Old Testament quotations in the Gospel of Matthew). Such Hebraisms may occur in explicit quotations, but they are also found in clauses and phrases derived from the Old Testament which the author has

Bibliography to §3.2e

Joseph A. Fitzmyer, *A Wandering Aramean: Collected Aramaic Essays* (SBLMS 25: Missoula: Scholars Press, 1977).

Matthew Black, *An Aramaic Approach to the Gospels and Acts* (3d ed.; Oxford: Clarendon, 1967).

Idem, "The Biblical Languages," in *Cambridge History of the Bible* 1. 1–11.

Raymond A. Martin, *Syntactical Evidence of Semitic Sources in Greek Documents* (SBLSCS 3; Missoula: Scholars Press, 1979).

Klaus Beyer, *Semitische Syntax im Neuen Testament,* vol. 1,1: *Satzlehre* (SUNT 1: Göttingen: Vandenhoeck & Ruprecht, 1962 and 1968).

Moisés Silva, "Semantic Borrowing in the New Testament," *NTS* 22 (1976) 104–10.

included in his own sentences without quoting explicitly. Such Hebraisms can also quite naturally occur in writers who write a good literate Greek style. The occurrence of such Hebraisms proves only that the author knew, quoted, and used the Old Testament.

2) *Aramaisms.* Semitisms can be caused by the fact that a particular text has been translated into Greek from Aramaic, that is, from the vernacular language of the non-Hellenized populations of Syria and Palestine. Such Semitisms must be called Aramaisms. They are most frequent in the Gospels, because Jesus as well as the early Palestinian church spoke Aramaic. All materials which derive from Jesus or from the tradition of the earliest Christian community, or even from later Christian churches in Syria which spoke Aramaic, must have been translated into Greek at some time, before they were incorporated into an early Christian writing. As a rule, such translation occurred at a stage of the tradition which is much older than the period when the Greek sources of the extant Gospels were composed. Translations were made already as early as the oral tradition, and certainly as early as the first collections of oral materials in bilingual Christian communities. As this must have occurred several decades before the writing of the Gospels now extant, it is likely that many of the original Aramaisms were worn away and replaced by more appropriate Greek terms and phrases in the oral and written transmission of such materials in Greek-speaking Christian communities. Only the Gospel of Mark seems to have used Greek sources which were straightforward translations of Aramaic originals, the most obvious of which are found in Mark 4, the parable chapter. It is also possible that the source for the miracle stories of the Gospel of John was directly translated from an Aramaic writing. Aramaisms, furthermore, are found in those liturgical traditions which were fixed at an early date, and we find them, for example, in the Greek version of the Lord's Prayer.

3) *Biblicisms.* Early Christianity inherited not only the Bible from Judaism, but also a religious language which had been deeply influenced by the Bible. Within the Greek-speaking world this inheritance was mediated to Christianity primarily by Hellenistic Judaism, because Greek is the language of the Septuagint (one can therefore speak of "Septuagintisms"), and of the Hellenistic synagogue as it was influenced by the Greek Bible of Judaism. Such biblicisms—ultimately usually Hebraisms, since they derive from the Hebrew Bible—can still be found in the later products of early Christian literature, so long as the Greek Bible of Hellenistic Judaism was also the Bible of the Christians; modern speech abounds with such "biblical" language as well, often phrases taken from the KJV. Among the early Christian writings, Paul's letters are remarkably free of biblicisms. But in the Lukan writings, composed sev-

eral decades after the letters of Paul, biblicisms occur frequently, especially in the Acts of the Apostles. Because it is very difficult to distinguish Luke's biblicisms from Semitisms that derive from the use of a source translated from Aramaic, it is debated whether the author used such a source for Acts 1–12. Nonetheless, the biblicisms of the second half of the book of Acts are very similar to those of the first part. Biblicisms are especially frequent in those Christian authors which are influenced by the preaching style of the synagogue, such as 1 Peter and *1 Clement*. They also occur wherever the Jewish methods of exegesis of the Greek Bible were adopted and continued. Both elements, closely related to each other in any case, are visible in *1 Clement* and in the *Epistle of Barnabas*.

4) *Bilingualism*. Many Semitisms seem to derive from a Greek vernacular which was formed in a bilingual milieu. Pagans and Christians, as well as Jews who spoke either Greek or Aramaic, or were able to use both languages, were living closely together in many cities of Syria and Palestine. It is well known that in such environments influences from another language are more quickly absorbed in colloquial and commercial speech than in the literary conventions of language. Some of these Semitisms are semantic borrowings deriving from the general language milieu, such as the use of θάλασσα not only for "sea," "ocean," but also for "lake," since the Aramaic ימא is used for both. Others are ultimately derived from the Hebrew Bible. To these belong such expressions as πρόσωπον λαμβάνειν = "to be partial" and πρόσωπον θαυμάζειν = "to flatter," and especially a number of theological terms which are often perfectly good Greek words, but are used more frequently and with different meanings due to the significance of their Hebrew equivalents, e.g., ἄγγελος "angel" (not "messenger"), δόξα "glory" (not "opinion"), σπλάγχνα "love," "mercy" (not "bowels," "guts"). Here we encounter the phenomenon of an "in-group" language. Semitisms of this kind may have arisen in Christian communities in which many members spoke Greek as well as Aramaic, whether or not they were of Jewish origin. The earliest Christian church in Antioch certainly was such a bilingual community, and even in Jerusalem there were not only the Aramaic-speaking community of the followers of Jesus, but also the "Hellenists," that is, Greek-speaking Jewish-Christians. Many Semitisms in the Gospel of John can be explained on the same basis: the Gospel or its sources may have been composed in a bilingual community of Syria. It is not easy to establish a clear borderline between common colloquial Greek on the one hand, and features which derive from Aramaic influences on the other. Some peculiarities which are quite possible in Greek, though normally rare, occur more frequently when analogous features in Aramaic (or Hebrew) favor such usage. This is no doubt the reason for the striking increase in the Greek instrumental dative

with the preposition ἐν =ב) and for the preference for the paratactic καί (= ו) in early Christian writings.

5) *Loan words* from Hebrew and Aramaic appear for various reasons. Semitic words like βύσσος = the fine linen called "Byssos," and μνᾶ = "Mine," a monetary unit of 100 drachmas, had long been widely used terms in Greek commercial language. Other foreign words probably derived from the direct contact of the two languages in bilingual communities as, for instance, the address ῥαββί = "Rabbi" for a teacher. Liturgy always tends to preserve special terms and phrases of a foreign language, such as the well known μαράνα θά = מרנא תא = "Lord, come!" (1 Cor 16:22; *Did.* 10.6) or "Hosanna" and "Amen," which have been preserved from their original Hebrew via Greek and Latin in the liturgical usage of modern languages. It is also important to note the preservation of foreign phrases as magical formulas. The Gospel of Mark quotes the term ἐφφαθά (transcription of the Aramaic אתפתח = "be open!"; Mark 7:34) and the phrase ταλιθὰ κοῦμ (transcription of טליתא קום = "Maiden, arise!"; Mark 5:41). Numerous parallels can be found in the magical papyri and in gnostic writings.

3. The Sciences

(a) Presuppositions and Beginnings

In the countries and cities settled by the Greeks, the beginnings of scientific thinking date back into VI BCE. The Greek colonization widened the horizons of their experience, although Babylonian and Egyptian influences had already been felt in the early classical period and made a substantial contribution. The Greeks of the Ionian cities of Asia Minor and of the Aegean islands opened the doors for a more scientific view of the world in almost all areas of thought; philosophical endeavors played an important role as well. The views of the pre-Socratics had been largely speculative, but ever since Plato's criticism of myth there was a growing interest in a view of the world which was mathematically exact.

Ethnography began very early. The Greeks explored the whole expanse of the Black Sea and the Mediterranean, an endeavor which is reflected in literature, as in the *Odyssey* and the legend of the Argonauts. The countries to the east became accessible through the caravan routes. Phoenician and before long Greek explorers began to sail into the Atlantic Ocean. Carthaginian ships reached the British Isles in V BCE. Some time between 322 and 313 BCE, the Greek Pytheas of Massilia (Marseilles) sailed into the North Sea and perhaps to the island "Thule" six days north of Great Britain. (It has been debated whether this was Iceland, the

Shetland Isles, or Norway; in any case, Pytheas brought back the report that in those northern regions the sun never sets during the summer solstice.) Euthymenes, also from Massilia, sailed down the west coast of Africa and reached the mouth of the Senegal or Niger river as early as VI BCE. Scylax (from Caria in Asia Minor), under the commission of the Persian king, took his ship down the Cabul and Indus rivers and continued his journey along the shores of Persia and Arabia into the Red Sea (519–516 BCE).

Such sea travels formed the background for the development of a literary genre called *periploi* ("circumnavigations"), which described foreign countries from the perspective of ships sailing along their coasts. These books contained information about directions and distances, and sailors even used them as handbooks. They were also used by geographers as sources for their own writings. The oldest known ethnographer is Hecataeus of Miletus (ca. 560–480), who is reported to have already used a schematic division of zones for his maps of the world. But beginning with Herodotus (ca. 484–430), interest turned to the description of foreign peoples and their customs and habits (= νόμοι) as well as the character of their land (φύσις τῆς χώρας). As ethnography prevailed in historical scholarship, geography proper had to take a temporary back seat. The beginnings of medical science are closely related to the interest in ethnography. In V BCE Hippocrates and other members of the Coan school of

Bibliography to §3.3: Texts

Morris R. Cohen and I. E. Drabkin, *A Source Book in Greek Science* (New York: McGraw-Hill, 1948; reprint: Cambridge, MA: Harvard University, 1958).

Bibliography to §3.3: Studies

Rudolf Pfeiffer, *History of Classical Scholarship from the Beginnings to the End of the Hellenistic Age* (Oxford: Clarendon, 1968).

O. Neugebauer, *The Exact Sciences in Antiquity* (Acta Historica Scientiarum Naturalium et Medicinalium 9; Copenhagen: Munksgaard, 1951; 2d ed.; Providence, RI: Brown University, 1957).

I. L. Heiberg, *Geschichte der Mathematik und Naturwissenschaften im Altertum* (HAW 5,1,2; München: Beck, 1925).

George Sarton, *A History of Science: Hellenistic Science and Culture in the Last Three Centuries B.C.* (Cambridge, MA: Harvard University, 1959).

Bibliography to §3.3a

M. Cary and E. H. Warmington, *The Ancient Explorers* (London: Methuen, 1929).

Lionel Casson, *The Ancient Mariners: Sea Farers and Sea Fighters in Ancient Times* (New York: Macmillan, 1959).

Walter Woodburn Hyde, *Ancient Greek Mariners* (New York: Oxford University, 1947).

S. Sambursky, *The Physical World of the Greeks* (London: Routledge and Kegan Paul, 1956).

medicine tried to connect the physical features of particular countries with the characteristic features of the populations.

Scientific astronomy began in IV BCE. The spherical form of the earth had already been discovered in the preceding century. Heraclides of Pontus, a student of Plato and contemporary of Aristotle, suggested in his dialogues that the earth turns around its axis; he also discussed the possibility that some planets circle around the sun. Eudoxus of Cnidos (ca. 391–338), another student of Plato's Academy and head of a school in Cyzicus and later in Athens, was, next to Aristotle, the most important scholar with universal interests in IV BCE. A tractate *Eudoxi Ars Astronomica* was not written by him, but uses many of his insights, though it also reinforced the widespread opinion that the sun, moon, and planets travel around the earth in concentric spheres. Eudoxos made a systematic assessment of the insights of the Eleatic school and the Pythagoreans in the field of mathematics and developed theories which enabled Euclid (in Alexandria from 306–283) to write his *Elements*, which became the standard textbook of mathematics and geometry in antiquity. Practical insights of mathematics and physics, as, e.g., the law of leverage, were also beginning to be applied to the building of simple machines and military equipment.

This scientific work reached its climax with the natural scientist and philosopher Aristotle, the son of a physician from Stageira on the Chalcidice. Aristotle studied, like so many other important scholars of his time, at the Academy of Plato. For several years he taught in Mysia, in Mytilene on Lesbos and at the Macedonian court of Philip II in Pella. In the year 335 he moved to Athens and founded his own school in a gymnasium known as the Lyceum. He organized and supervised an extensive research program covering a large number of fields. In addition to most of the natural sciences, his research included the fields of politics and history, for which his school collected extensive source materials; 158 different constitutions of cities and states were collected and compared. Aristotle's own contributions were most significant in the fields of meteorology, botany, and zoology. In the last field he supplemented existing collections of materials, added many valuable observations, and created a system of classification; his insights remained unequalled until the beginnings of modern natural science. In the field of botany, all the ancient world had known were occasional descriptions of plants useful for the pharmacological interests of medicine. Nothing is preserved of Aristotle's own works in botany; but the accomplishments of his student Theophrastus became authoritative for the ancient world. Theophrastus set up a system of classification for all plants, described their structures, and collected the materials which physicians, travelers, and authors of agricultural books had brought together. With these works, scholarship in the field of biology had already reached its apex at the beginning of the Hellenistic period.

(b) The Golden Age of Scholarship in the Hellenistic Period

The flowering of Greek scholarship occurred in the two centuries after Alexander. The widening of the horizon of human experience through the conquests of Alexander had its fullest impact in this period. Oriental influences had lasting and deep effects. The Hellenistic kings, especially the Ptolemies, and also several cities (e.g., Rhodes) proved to be generous supporters of scholarly projects.

In the school of Aristotle (the so-called Peripatetics), the research that had been undertaken earlier was continued. Next to Theophrastus, Eudemus of Rhodes was the most distinguished scholar of this school. In addition to the fields already mentioned, research was devoted to anthropology, hydrology, minerology, and also to musical theory (Aristoxenus being the first known musicologist), and the history of science (natural philosophy, geometry, and astronomy). An important result of this interest in the history of various disciplines was the creation of biographies of important and famous people from the past (§3.4d). Although the decline of this school soon became visible, it remained an important center for studies in political science, history of science, biography, and natural sciences.

The high point of ancient mathematics was reached through the work of Archimedes of Syracuse, born in 287 BCE and slain in 212 by Roman soldiers conquering Syracuse. A large number of the mathematical calculations and geometrical discoveries which modern science owes to antiquity were made by Archimedes. He calculated that the relationship between the circumference and the diameter of the circle, designated by the Greek letter π, was a number between 3 10/70 and 3 10/71, i.e., between 3.1428 and 3.1408; the number assumed today is 3.1416. He discovered the relation between the contents of a sphere and the corresponding cylinder. The insight that a body of water loses as much of its weight as the weight of the water it replaces is still known today as the "Archimedean Principle." He also experimented with practical applications of mathematical and physical scientific results, constructed the differential pulley,

Bibliography to §3.3b

Fraser, *Alexandria,* 1. 336–479, 520–53.

O. Neugebauer, *A History of Ancient Mathematical Astronomy* (3 vols.; Berlin/ Heidelberg/New York: Springer, 1975).

G. E. R. Lloyd, "Science and Mathematics," in: M. I. Finley, *The Legacy of Greece: A New Appraisal* (Oxford: Clarendon, 1981) 256–300.

Thomas L. Heath, *Greek Astronomy* (London: Dent, and New York: Dutton, 1932).

and the "Archimedean Screw," which could be used for water pumps on boats and for irrigation. Archimedes also constructed the defense machinery which Syracuse used successfully for a number of years in order to withstand the Roman siege.

The most ingenious astronomical discovery of the Hellenistic period was made at its very inception: the anticipation of the Copernican universe in the heliocentric system of Aristarchos of Samos (first half of III BCE). He taught that the sun was about three hundred times the size of the earth, that the earth and the planets move in circles around the sun, and that the earth rotates on its own axis. He thus satisfied Plato's demand to demonstrate that the apparent loops in the courses of the planets were actually circles. But inasmuch as Aristarchus' theories did not prevail (the Stoic Cleanthes even accused him of blaspheming the gods) antiquity did not make a breakthrough here to a new view of the universe. Nevertheless, significant astronomical discoveries were made in the Hellenistic period, and Babylonian astronomy made an essential contribution. Copious Babylonian materials were published in Greek translation during III BCE, but it is not quite clear to what degree the most important astronomer of antiquity, Hipparchus of Nicea (who taught mostly in Rhodes, 160–125 BCE), depended on Babylonian calculations. His most significant discovery was that of the precession of the equinoxes. He also calculated the exact length of the year (which differs from modern calculations by only 6 minutes and 26 seconds), and determined that the lunar revolution lasts 29 days, 12 hours, 44 minutes, and 2½ seconds (differing by less than a second from the modern calculations!). Hipparchus also created a catalogue of eight hundred fixed stars, arranged according to three different degrees of brightness. According to Posidonius, the diameter of the sun was assumed to be 39½ times that of the earth—earlier calculations concluded that the sun was much smaller (today's value is about 109 times the diameter of the earth). For the distance of the sun from the earth, Posidonius calculated that it was 6545 times the earth's diameter (the actual distance is 11,741 times the earth's diameter).

The discovery of the spherical shape of the earth created the necessary presuppositions for a new scientific geography. Significant incentives came from the conquests of Alexander the Great, who had employed a staff of geodetic surveyors immediately after his conquests. This established a purely geographical interest distinctly different from the older science of ethnography, which was primarily concerned with the description of peoples, climate, plants, and animals. The new goal became the drawing of maps of the various countries and of the earth. Eratosthenes, the leading geographer of antiquity (who also wrote philosophical and mathematical works and a history of comedy), librarian in Alexandria from 246 BCE, designed a system for the cartographical survey of all known countries. He also recognized that all the oceans of the world are connected with each other and, therefore, that the inhabited earth—Europe, Asia, and Africa—must be one huge island. In his calculation of the circumference of the earth, Eratosthenes erred by only 300 km. The astronomer Hipparchus, mentioned above, later criticized the cartographical endeavors of Eratosthenes and demanded that collaboration of observers at various places should first establish the longitude and latitude of as many places as possible. Only a small part of these grand designs was actually accomplished, but quite a few determinations were actually achieved as can be seen from the materials collected by Ptolemy (3.3c).

In the field of medicine, progress was made primarily in anatomy, especially by the physicians Herophilus and Erasistratus, who worked in Alexandria during III BCE and were able to use human corpses for dissection. (A later report says that they also made vivisections of criminals who had been condemned to death.) Herophilus discovered the nervous system of the human body, and perhaps also the system of blood circulation; the traditional assumption was that the arteries transported air, an error which again prevailed in later times.

Philology became a scientific discipline for the first time during the Hellenistic period, especially in the consolidation of grammar and the edition of texts. Several generations of scholars in Alexandria participated in this process. The leading mind was Aristarchus of Samothrace (ca. 216–144 BCE). Incentives for the codification of grammar came from Stoic philosophy, which undertook the first division of letters into vowels and consonants and suggested a doctrine of inflections and tenses. Aristarchus systematically elaborated the patterns of inflections, established paradigms for the various conjugations and declensions, and prepared a list of irregular words. His student Dionysius Thrax collected the results of these efforts and edited a handbook which remained definitive throughout antiquity.

The second major task of the Alexandrian philologists was the systematic revision and edition of classical texts: collection and comparison of manuscripts, emendation, and new publication. In order to facilitate this work, commentaries, monographs, and concordances were produced. Alexandria played a leading role in these scholarly pursuits from the beginnings of scientific philology in III and II BCE until III CE, when it began to see a decline. Christian scholars like Origen, Lucian of Antioch, and Eusebius of Caesarea, who produced learned works on the Christian Bible, were still able to take their starting point from this philological tradition of scholarship. On the other hand a different branch of philological scholarship, namely etymology, though eagerly pursued by many, never reached the level of scientific clarification. From the time of Homer, attempts had been made to explain certain words etymologically. Poets, sophists, and Homeric interpreters vied with each other in this art. But in spite of Plato's criticism of those etymologists who tried by this means to define the true essence of the things, these efforts continued unabated among grammarians and philosophers, especially the Stoics. Philoxenus of Alexandria, of I BCE, tried to establish a scientific base for etymology in grammatical scholarship: he claimed that monosyllabic verbs were the roots of all other words. However, not only in this field, but also in its methods of interpretation (Aristarchus, e.g., established the principle of analogy, according to which Homeric texts should be interpreted solely through other Homeric texts) ancient philology never advanced beyond the first beginnings of scholarly work.

(c) The Later Developments in the Roman Period

Even a careful and unbiased observer cannot help but see the developments in the Roman period and beyond as a decline of scholarship and science. Creative research came to an end in I BCE. Its place was taken by encyclopedias and collections of the results of scholarly work of former generations, but also by uncritical popularizations written solely for entertainment. At the same time, superstitious opinions became more widespread, and views were revived again which had already been shown to be inaccurate by the scholars of the Hellenistic period.

In mathematics no new discoveries were made during the Roman imperial period, but the achievements of previous mathematical scholarship were preserved and passed on in the form of compendiums. In the field of astronomy the Alexandrian scholar Ptolemy (ca. 100–170 CE) wrote a comprehensive compendium of all astronomical achievements of antiquity, which is preserved under the title "Almagest" ("Al" is the Arabic article, "magest" is derived from the Greek title "Megist[e Syntaxis]"). This work also contains some of Ptolemy's own insights, which are, however, often inferior to those of his predecessors. Even during the Hellenistic period zoology had shown an increasing interest in the strange and curious phenomena of the animal kingdom. There were also studies of the intelligence of such subjects as poisonous animals. But on the whole, anecdotes prevailed over scientific inquiry. All this was collected in the encyclopedic works of the later period. Even geography and ethnography were partly dominated by such interests. There was a prevalent curiosity about the peculiarities and oddities of other nations, countries, and cities. Such works, therefore, contain historical information and paradoxography rather than ethnographic scholarship. There must have been voluminous collections of these materials. Historians (Polybius) and geographers

(Strabo) used such collections and also contributed new materials, but did not always evaluate their information critically. Some of these writings had no other aim but to entertain the reader. This led to the production of books which indiscriminately collected whatever was available about foreign nations and countries, serious information as well as amusing stories, authentic reports along with completely unreliable tales. The Hellenistic romance derived much of its material from such sources.

Medical scholarship reached new heights during the Roman imperial period, although there were signs of decline in the position of the physician in society. The major cult and healing establishments of the god Asclepius (§4.3d) from the classical and Hellenistic periods continued to flourish. Yet the public health services that had employed scientifically trained physicians declined. The period of late Hellenism saw a division of medicine into several schools, whose endless quarrels resemble those of the philosophical schools. Dogmatism often prevailed over the results of scientific investigation. At the beginning of the Roman imperial period, medical handbooks collecting the insights and knowledge of the older period were replaced by uncritical popularizations about medicine, pharmacology, and diet. Closely related phenomena were the rapid growth in quackery and magic and an increase of specialists among practicing physicians who catered to the tastes of a spoiled urban upper class. In view of this general deterioration in medical services, the achievements of the great physicians of the imperial period are all the more remarkable. Their medical observations and scholarly works enriched medical science considerably. Rufus of Ephesus (beginning of II CE) collected and clarified the anatomical insights of his predecessors, and his careful descriptions of pathological symptoms contributed considerably to the progress of internal medicine. His contemporary, Soranus of Ephesus, published works on gynecology and baby care which were the best that antiquity achieved in this field. From his other proliferous literary productions, Soranus' lost book "On the Soul" became the source for Tertullian's *De anima*. The most important physician from the imperial period was Galen of Pergamum (129–199 CE). His numerous medical books were based upon his wide experience as a practicing physician and upon his own endeavors in medical research, and they summarize the medical knowledge of antiquity for most areas of medical science. In every instance he uses his own judgment, which often surpasses that of his predecessors. Galen's books are not only the last truly great medical works from ancient times, they also constitute the final climax of ancient scholarship in the natural sciences, and continued to be authoritative for medical praxis and theory until the end of the Middle Ages.

4. LITERATURE

(a) Presuppositions

In the writing of literary works, new subjects, forms, and traditions which were generated by the wider horizons of the understanding of the world became predominant. The relationship of the Greek literary inheritance to the world of the orient and its people became visible in many ways. Materials from the east could appear in the forms of classical Greek literature as, e.g., the drama "Moses" of the Jewish tragedian Ezekiel. Equally characteristic is the fact that Greeks in turn included in their literary works not so much the forms, but many narratives, topics, and subjects that genuinely reflected the experience and views of other people. Very soon Hellenized barbarians also began to contribute to the further development of Greek literary forms: Iambulus, the author of one of the oldest Hellenistic romances, came from Syria; Lucian of Samosata was also a Syrian and one of the most productive Greek writers of the Roman period; Babrius, a Roman by birth, became the court poet of a certain king Alexander in Cetis of Cilicia, a grandson of Alexander, son of Herod the Great. Babrius put the fables of Aesop into Greek verse. In addition, there were numerous writers, such as the Babylonian priest Berossus, the Egyptian priest Manetho, and the Jewish author Josephus, who wrote in Greek about the history and traditions of their own peoples.

As Greek and oriental elements became inextricably mixed in literary works, the quantity and variety of the writings also increased. The strict

Bibliography to §3.4

Albin Lesky, *A History of Greek Literature* (New York: Crowell, 1966). The most useful comprehensive treatment.

E. Vogt (ed.), *Griechische Literatur* (Neues Handbuch der Literaturwissenschaft 2; Wiesbaden: Athenaion, 1981).

Bibliography to 3.4a: Texts

Euripides: Greek texts and English translations by A. S. Way in LCL.

E. R. Dodds (ed.), *Euripides Bacchae* (with introduction and commentary; Oxford, 1960).

Greek texts and German translations with notes by Gustav Adolf Seeck and Ernst Buschor (6 vols.; Tusculum; München: Heimeran, and Darmstadt: Wissenschaftliche Buchgesellschaft, 1972–81).

Bibliography to §3.4a: Studies

Gilbert Murray, *Euripides and His Age* (13th ed.; Oxford: Oxford University, 1955).

G. M. A. Grube, *The Drama of Euripides* (2d ed.; New York: Barnes and Noble, 1961).

forms of classical Greek literature were dissolved. But there is no question that the Greek literature of the Hellenistic and Roman periods surpassed in its variety, quantity, and influence anything known to preceding centuries or even in the subsequent period up to the invention of the printing press. An enormous number of people wrote a great deal about a vast number of topics, much of which is lost. There were, of course, educated readers, who would usually restrict their reading to philosophical and scientific literature; but there also was a broader public, able to read and hungry to be entertained. It is therefore not surprising to find writers not only at the courts of the great kings, but also as the poets and historians of every petty prince; even authors living in remote Hellenistic towns could hope to find a public which would honor them and perhaps even read their books.

A by-product of book production in the Hellenistic and Roman periods was the writing and distribution of books designed for private use. Philosophical schools and the Museum in Alexandria produced collections of materials which were primarily designed to be used by scholars, and religious communities also cultivated their own literatures as is seen in so many examples from Jewish and Christian writings. Some of these works were written for particular occasions, e.g., letters which were only published at a later date; other writings were intended for distribution among community members, although some of these books might also be written for a broader public. The forms and genres of such literature sometimes vary with the peculiar traditions of a religion or sect. But the history of this sort of literature should not be separated from the general history of Hellenistic literature. As these religions became Hellenized, the literary culture of Hellenism strongly influenced the formation of the specific literatures of various religious communities and movements.

In view of the diversity and multiformity of Hellenistic literature, it is simply not possible to describe comprehensively all its important features. Even so, this literature does exhibit a certain coherence, since it is basically connected to the tradition of classical Greece. The literature of Hellenism, moreover, expresses fundamental cultural insights and currents which gave it some cohesiveness. As Hellenism also came to shape decisively the culture of the Roman period, one can observe a continuous development of literature extending into areas where Greek was not the primary spoken language. In any case, our review must be limited to those features which are significant for the understanding of early Christianity. From this perspective especially it is advisable to begin by discussing one particular presupposition of Hellenistic literature, namely, the work of the last great dramatist of the classical period, Euripides.

Although Euripides wrote his plays in the second half of v BCE (he died in 407/6), Hellenistic literature as well as the spirit of Hellenism as a whole can hardly be discussed without him. The subjects, motifs, and problems of Hellenistic literature were more decisively influenced by Euripides than by anyone else. As the last of the great dramatists of classical Greece, living in a period in which the first signs of cultural disintegration were becoming visible, Euripides was the first to see the fateful predicament of human existence, which was to become such a strong factor in the human sensibility of the following centuries. With this insight Euripides marks the threshold of a new epoch, and his influence upon the literature of the following centuries cannot be overestimated.

It would be quite wrong, however, to understand Euripides as an advocate of reason in the fight against superstition, or as an innovator or revolutionary. Although he was influenced by the Sophists, his insights do not belong to any particular philosophical school. His influence is based rather upon his radically new characterization of human life; human beings with all their judicious thoughts and with all their passions are, as individuals, ultimately left isolated and helpless. Euripides describes a human predicament which does not permit the reconciliation of opposites, and in which the existing political and religious institutions (which for him, of course, are the institutions of the Greek polis) are no longer able to provide a solution. The greatness and impotence of humanity are equally fraught with fate—again Euripides anticipates a basic insight of Hellenism—but not because there are no longer any gods and mysterious powers in the world. On the contrary, human beings in the midst of their conflicts are subject to such powers, whether they be called gods, or chance, or fate, or by a particular name, such as Dionysus. One can recognize these powers, but to encounter them can be one's doom, for it is impossible to predict or calculate their actions. Humans may even be willing to acknowledge and worship such powers, but they cannot claim to be their equals; harmony with the powers is not allotted to the human race. A deity may even force someone into its realm of sovereignty, though this can lead to destruction, as when Dionysus destroys Pentheus, the king of Thebes (the *Bacchae*). This view of human existence points to some of the most important questions which occupied Hellenistic literature for many centuries, and became its theme in innumerable variations.

(b) Drama, Comedy, and Poetry

The tradition of classical Greek tragedy was continued in the Hellenistic period. The Ptolemaic kings of Egypt especially sponsored the cultivation of this genre. Philadelphus, the second of the Ptolemies, arranged dramatic contests in Alexandria. But this dramatic poetry had little influence, and almost nothing of the rich acomplishment in playwriting from this period has been preserved. Of the works of more than fifty known dramatists from III BCE, only a few fragments, totalling just a few dozen lines, have survived. From the following century only two fragments are known; one of these is from the Exodus drama of the Jewish tragedian Ezekiel. In Latin, however, there appeared a remarkable revival of Greek tragedy among the great playwrights of III BCE in Rome (§6.4b). In the early imperial period it still was fashionable among the educated to try one's hand at writing a tragedy; even Caesar and Augustus made the attempt. Yet public performances of tragedies became less frequent. One would more likely prefer to listen to the reading of favorite sections and excerpts from classical Greek tragedies. Performances of pantomimes were liked best anyway: thus, in the Roman imperial period classical Greek tragedies were rarely performed as such, but one could see a pantomime show which presented a complete tragedy of Euripides with dance and music, but without words.

More directly than in the later developments in tragedy, the spirit of Hellenism is mirrored in the New Comedy of Athens. During the time of the successors of Alexander the Great, the revival of comedy grew out of

Bibliography to §3.4b: Texts

E. W. Handley, *The Dyskolos of Menander* (Cambridge, MA: Harvard University, 1965).

Fragments of Menander: Greek text with English translation by F. G. Allenson in LCL.

Rudolf Pfeiffer (ed.), *Callimachus* (2 vols.; Oxford: Clarendon, 1949–53).

Callimachus: Greek text and English translation of hymns and epigrams by A. W. Main, of fragments by C. A. Trypanis in LCL.

Hermann Fränkel, *Apollonius Rhodius: Argonautica* (Oxford: Clarendon, 1961).

E. V. Rieu, *Apollonius* (Baltimore: Penguin, 1959).

A. S. F. Gow (ed.), *Bucolici Graeci* (Oxford: Clarendon, 1952).

A. S. F. Gow, *Greek Bucolic Poets: Translation with Brief Notes* (Cambridge, 1953).

W. Headlam and A. D. Knox, *Herondas: The Mimes and Fragments* (Cambridge: Cambridge University, 1922).

Herondas: Greek text and English translation by A. D. Knox in LCL (Choliambics).

Anthologia Palatina: Text and English translation by W. R. Paton in LCL (5 vols.).

F. L. Lucas, *A Greek Garland: A Selection from the Anthologia Palatina* (2d ed.; London, 1949).

Bibliography to §3.4b: Studies

T. B. L. Webster, *Hellenistic Poetry and Art* (New York: Barnes and Noble, 1964).

Fraser, *Alexandria*, 1. 553–674, 717–93.

Alfred Körte, *Die hellenistische Dichtung* (2d ed.; rev. P. Händerl; Stuttgart: Kröner, 1960).

Ulrich von Wilamowitz-Möllendorf, *Hellenistische Dichtung in der Zeit von Kallimachos* (2 vols.; Berlin: Weidman, 1924).

Ph.-E. Legrand, *La poésie alexandrine* (Paris: Payot, 1924).

K. Ziegler, *Das hellenistische Epos* (Leipzig: Teubner, 1934).

E. A. Barber, "Alexandrian Literature," in *CambAncHist* 7. 249–83.

The Stoic Philosopher Chrysippus

The leading systematician of the Stoic philosophy.
Roman copy of a statue from III B.C.E.

the atmosphere of this city, once the foremost political power in Greece. The most important poet, and the only one whose work is at least partially preserved, was Menander (342/41–293/92). It is probably due to his view of the political situation that the New Comedy does not share the concerns of Aristophanes' comedies. Menander presupposes that the individual no longer possesses political power. His comedy focusses upon the particulars of the human situation. The persons who appear in his comedy are no longer types, as in the old comedy, but individual characters. The topics and cast of his plays are derived from the milieu of the middle and lower classes: citizens, their wives and daughters, craftsmen, farmers, slaves, and travelers, all seen with their personal and social problems. They are presented as individuals who in their own way try to cope with the adversities of their social situation, which is threatened by poverty and malice as well as by an unpredictable fate. Greed and desire for money, or at least a few material possessions which would secure one's existence, often seem to be the only impulses in the lives of the characters appearing in these plays. But in the midst of all this, Menander tries to discover the last vestiges of genuine and true humanity, visible in the ability to forgive and to be reconciled. Humaneness becomes real in these virtues, which Menander insists is a general human possibility, open equally to Greeks and to barbarians, to free and to slaves.

The New Comedy certainly extended its influence beyond Athens, but it is difficult to judge how broadly it affected other areas. Many writers were not Athenians. The names of more than seventy authors of comedies are known, some of whom are said to have written more than a hundred comedies. But at the beginning of the Roman imperial period, the New Comedy together with its Roman successor was pushed aside by the mimes and the pantomimes. Paul quotes a sentence ("Bad company destroys good morals") from one of Menander's comedies in 1 Cor 15:33, but this does not prove that the comedies were still popular because the sentence had become a familiar phrase that is also cited elsewhere.

Neither the continuation of classical tragedy nor the New Comedy could satisfy the demand for entertainment. This need was filled by the mimes, which dominated the theater everywhere in the later Hellenistic and Roman periods. Developed out of some ancient forms of dance, probably connected with cultic rites, and strongly influenced by the New Comedy, the mime became the most popular form of dramatic performance. Troupes of mimes went from town to town, giving solo or group performances on quickly improvised stages in the marketplace. They spoke the language of the people while presenting ancient subjects and modern improvisations, along with dance, music, acrobatic performances, and juggling tricks in farcical skits. Occasionally kings would hire groups of mimes, and rich people invited them into their houses. Naturally very little is preserved from their rich repertory. But the fragments of the *mimiambi* of the Coan poet Herondas (III BCE) give a taste of the content and subjects of these theatrical performances. Characteristic titles of these plays include "The Bawd," "The Pimp," "The Schoolmaster," "The Women Worshippers," "The Jealous Mistress," "The Private Conversation," and others. Like the New Comedy the mimes also put the individual from the middle and lower classes who lacks political ambitions on center stage. Daily life and the all too ordinary predicaments of common people are presented to the audience in all their licit and illicit variety. Right and wrong might be illustrated in situations not normally discussed in polite society. True and false friendships are discussed in relationships which do not accord with one's social class. The mimes mirror the realities of everyday life: one could find a reflection of one's true self, in which to commiserate or laugh at oneself. But the mimes do not permit their audience to transcend the limitations of banal everyday experience and recognize their true identity in experiences of the realm of unique and extraordinary events.

Poetry had its golden age under the patronage of the second Ptolemy in Alexandria. The most important poet was Callimachus who was born shortly before 300 BCE, author of the Alexandrian library catalogue, of the first known encyclopedia, and of geographical, mythological and polemical writings. Epigrams and hymns are preserved from his poetic works (the quotation in Tit 1:12 is adapted from his hymn to Zeus) as well as large fragments of his primary work *Aitia*. Mythological traditions are used in these works in a manner characteristic of the spirit of Hellenism. Callimachus' poetry divorces religious customs and festivals as well as their legends and stories from their original cultic setting; however, rationalistic criticism of mythology is equally absent. Rather, this poetry represents mythology positively in refined and elegant pieces of art. Occasionally one finds references to the Ptolemaic king, whose divinity is acknowledged. This is not an expression of faith in royal divinity, but simply a piece of court poetry, though without flattery. Neither the ancient religion with its cult nor the criticism of myth by Plato and the Sophists seems to be a live issue. Mythology, instead, was rejuvenated by resumption of the poetic tradition of Hesiod and the *Homeric Hymns*. Callimachus' poetry deeply influenced Roman poets such as Ovid and Virgil.

The most significant bucolic poet of Hellenism was Theocritus, a contemporary and colleague of Callimachus in Alexandria who later moved to Cos. For the celebration of the victory of Ptolemy Philadelphus in the First Syrian War, he wrote a hymn praising the king and his sister/wife as "savior gods." Theocritus' *Eidyllia* (not "idylls" in the modern sense) describe pastoral topics and scenes, whereas some of his poems are in fact "Mimes" which depict city life with characters that are mostly borrowed from a lower class milieu, like the *mimiambi* of Herondas. Also typical of Hellenistic writing is the "Argonautica" of Apollonius of Rhodes (who lived in Alexandria, but moved to Rhodes after 246/45 BCE). This is the only Greek epic work still preserved after Homer and before the "Dionysiaca" of Nonnus from v CE, and was written by Apollonius after intensive source studies. As a typical Hellenistic writer he demonstrates a pronounced interest in etiologies, psychological descriptions of the actors, and descriptions of nature; there are also a number of rather dry travel narratives. Several of the elements which became important and constitutive parts of the Greek romance were already present in this epic.

The epigram, which was widely practiced by these poets, is a true mirror of the soul of Hellenism. Its original place in life was as a lament for the dead and as a votive inscription. But it had long since become detached from its original cultic setting and become a short elegy which could be read at all sorts of occasions, e.g., at a symposium. Themes emphasizing heroic greatness had almost completely disappeared; instead one emphasizes individual joy or love. There also are elegiac descriptions of a craft or profession, of artistic works or impressions of nature.

Along with other forms of poetry the didactic poem was very popular. The Hellenistic world considered it great art to treat of the most eccentric subjects in verse form. Special scientific literature from the areas of medicine, zoology, astronomy and others became subjects of poetic works. The less the poet understood of his subject matter, the more he could be sure the public would admire his work.

(c) Historiography

The Hellenistic period was unusually productive in the field of historiography. This richness contrasts sharply with the poor state of preservation of this literature. Although hundreds of small fragments have survived from the universal histories, local histories, autobiographies, and historical monographs, major portions are extant only from the works of

Bibliography to §3.4c: Texts

F. Jacoby, *Die Fragmente der griechischen Historiker* (15 vols.; reprint: Leiden: Brill, 1954–64).

M. I. Finley (ed.), *The Greek Historians: The Essence of Herodotus, Thucydides, Xenophon, Polybius* (New York, 1959). Selections with introductions and notes.

Polybius: Greek text and English translation by W. T. Paton in LCL (5 vols.).

Diodorus Siculus: Greek text and English translation by C. H. Oldfather et al. in LCL (12 vols.).

Polybius and Diodorus Siculus. Somewhat better preserved are the works of the Greek historians from the Roman imperial period: almost all the books written by the Jewish historian Josephus are extant, and large parts of the histories of Dionysius of Halicarnassus, Arrian, Dio Cassius, and Herodian (§6.4d).

The beginning of the Hellenistic period marks a decisive point of innovation for historiography. The generation which had personally known Alexander the Great produced—not without designs of political propaganda!—well-informed reports based upon personal experience or upon reliable sources such as diaries and original documents. Among these works was a history of Alexander written by king Ptolemy I of Egypt, the report of Alexander's admiral Nearchus about his sailing expedition from India to the Euphrates (both works preserved in part by Arrian), and the history of the Diadochi by Hieronymus of Cardia (friend and associate of the Diadoch Eumenes), a work now lost, but widely used and quoted by later historians. All these historians occupied important political positions, a phenomenon which continued into the Roman imperial period, even among Latin historians (Livy is probably the only exception): Polybius, Arrian, Dio Cassius, as well as Caesar and Tacitus, and to a certain degree also Josephus, played significant roles in the political events of their time.

Bibliography to §3.4c: Studies

Felix Jacoby, *Abhandlungen zur griechischen Geschichtsschreibung* (Zu seinem achtzigsten Geburstag . . . ed. Herbert Bloch; Leiden: Brill, 1956).

Kurt von Fritz, *Die griechische Geschichtsschreibung* (vol. 1,1-2; Berlin: De Gruyter, 1967).

Idem, "Aristotle's Contribution to the Practice and Theory of Historiography," *University of California Publications in Philosophy* 28 (Berkeley and Los Angeles: University of California, 1958) 113–38.

Arnaldo Momigliano, "Die Geschichtsschreibung," in: E. Vogt, *Griechische Literatur* (Neues Handbuch der Literaturwissenschaft 2; Wiesbaden: Athenaion, 1981) 303–36.

Idem, "History and Biography," in: M. I. Finley (ed.), *The Legacy of Greece: A New Appraisal* (Oxford: Clarendon, 1981) 155–84.

Eduard Schwartz, *Griechische Geschichtsschreiber* (Leipzig: Koehler und Amelang, 1957).

Fritz Wehrli, "Die Geschichtsschreibung im Lichte der antiken Theorie," in: idem, *Theoria und Humanitas* (Zürich and München: Artemis, 1972) 132–44.

Hermann Strasburger, *Die Wesensbestimmung der Geschichte durch die antike Geschichtsschreibung* (Sitzungsberichte, Wissenschaftliche Gesellschaft an der Wolfgang-Goethe-Universität Frankfurt am Main 5; Wiesbaden: Steiner, 1966).

F. W. Walbank, "History and Tragedy," *Hist* 9 (1960) 216–34.

Fraser, *Alexandria*, 1. 495–519.

Martin Dibelius, "The Speeches in Acts and Ancient Historiography," in: idem, *Studies in the Acts of the Apostles* (London: SCM, 1956; and reprints) 138–91.

T. R. Glover, "Polybius," in *CambAncHist* 8. 1–24.

Polybius (born before 200 BCE, died in 129 or after 120 BCE) was the scion of an aristocratic family from Megalopolis in western Arcadia. As one of the leading officials of the Achaean League, he was deported to Rome in 167 BCE, together with a thousand other members of the leading Achaean families. During the subsequent seventeen years, which he spent in Rome, Polybius had much contact with the influential political circles of Rome. His friendship with the younger Scipio dates from this period. After a brief return to Greece in the year 150, he participated in the African campaign of Scipio against Carthage and joined a naval expedition westward along the coast of North Africa. After the disastrous defeat of the Achaean League at the hands of the Romans in 146 (after which Corinth was razed to the ground), Polybius negotiated successfully with the Romans on behalf of his fellow countrymen in order to ease their lot. It seems that he participated later in Scipio's Numantian war in Iberia (134–133 BCE). He also travelled extensively outside of his home country of Greece.

Polybius' historical work is intimately related to his activity as a politician. When he wrote that only those who participate actively in the events of their time are capable of writing history (12.25), he accurately described the reason for the high quality of this political historiography. The goal of universal history for him is the critical search for truth through "pragmatic historiography." The writing of history must be universal in order to understand the goal toward which all historical events move—which for Polybius was the Roman mission to rule the world (1.3–5). Miracle stories and *paradoxa* have no place in the writing of history. They only obscure the quest for the causes of historical events, which is the most eminent and most important task of the historian. In order to accomplish this task, one must inquire into the presuppositions of the political situation, and of the leading political figures, which Polybius finds through the investigation of countries and nations. Three disciplines are therefore of utmost importance for the work of the historian: ethnography, the study of state constitutions, and biography. At the same time, Polybius also knows the power of *tyche*—whether this be chance, luck, or fate—and he is wise enough to grant a considerable margin to this most incalculable of all causes. Polybius also seeks to teach morality in his historical writing, but he explicitly rejects the notion that historiography should provide entertainment (2.56). The sources that Polybius uses are in keeping with his view that the historian must be a person who has participated actively in the events described: these sources include his own experiences; the questioning of other participants; written statements, letters, and speeches of politicians; and documents and information from older historians which have been evaluated according to these criteria.

There is no other historian of the Hellenistic period who can be compared with Polybius, with respect to either his accomplishments or his methodical treatment of sources. It is debated whether the "pragmatic" writing of history advocated by Polybius was rivalled by another school of "tragic-pathetic" historiography. Although Polybius (2.56) attacks the third-century historian Phylarchus because of his attempts to affect the feelings of his readers by vivid descriptions of terrible and tragic events, it is quite unlikely that there was indeed such a program of historiography. Most Hellenistic historians at least knew and subscribed to the principle of objective historiography. Whether and to what degree they were successful is another matter. Rhetorical devices were often used, even by Polybius himself. Sources were not always critically evaluated. Hearsay and legendary materials were presented as facts.

As Polybius had continued the work of the third-century historian Timaeus (whom he attacks in book 12), Posidonius endeavored to continue Polybius' universal history. Of the fifty-two books of his historical work, which may have extended to the wars of Pompey, only very little is preserved. For Posidonius, history is seen as guided by divine providence (this Stoic concept replaces Polybius' *tyche* as the ultimate cause for history), but is, on the other hand, still evidence for the continuing decadence of culture and morality. In this context Posidonius used quite uncritically stories about slaves from Sicily to express his social concerns, though in his evaluation of the reforms of the Gracchi (§6.1d) he condemns their motivations and lack of psychological control.

While Posidonius was writing "history" and tried to evaluate its causes, other historians of the Hellenistic period were primarily collectors and compilers. This, of course, suggests that they therefore preserved many pieces of valuable information. Nicolaus of Damascus, the court historian of Herod the Great, wrote a world history in 144 books which was used by Josephus; this material provides us with rich and detailed information about this Jewish king. The compiler Alexander Polyhistor from Miletus (ca. 100–40 BCE) collected materials about the peoples of the east, including many fragments of Jewish writers (some of which are preserved by the church historian Eusebius). More extensive are the sections preserved from a part of the universal history of Diodorus Siculus (I BCE); important older source materials have thus survived, although Diodorus' own accomplishments as a historian are negligible. More able as a historian was Dionysius of Halicarnassus (in Rome 30–80 BCE) though his history of Rome, full of admiration for Roman greatness, sometimes reveals a lack of knowledge of subject matter and of critical judgment. These later historians wrote at the very end of the Hellenistic period (the historians of the Roman imperial period will be discussed below in §6.4d).

Side by side with the major historical works which have a relatively high value as historical sources stood an extensive literary activity dealing with historical subjects which cannot satisfy the modern standards of historiography, neither in its mastery of its subject matter nor in its intentions. The panegyric glorification of Alexander the Great which began during Alexander's life deeply influenced the literary composition of the Alexander legend and romance and thus, indirectly, also the image of Alexander in later antiquity. There were other works about rulers of the Hellenistic period in which panegyrics, rhetoric, legendary imagination, and entertainment of the reader were the leading motifs. Such materials were often included in the history of Diodorus Siculus. As ethnographic interests were widespread in antiquity, uncritical reception of such information led to the inclusion of untrustworthy accounts about foreign countries and peoples into historical works, and also promoted an emphasis upon anything that was curious and peculiar. This corresponds to developments in other genres of literature during this time, a development which continued well into the Roman imperial period.

(d) Biography and Aretalogy

In the countries of the east, the cultural medium for the formation of the biography was the monarchic form of government. Egypt had developed the biography of the ruler, as well as the biography of leading officials and dignitaries, according to fixed and detailed schemata which had been firmly established since the ancient times. Biographical sections of the Old

Bibliography to §3.4d: Texts

Philo, *Life of Moses:* Greek text and English translation by F. H. Colson in LCL (Philo, vol. 6).

Suetonius, *Lives of the Caesars:* Latin text and English translation by J. C. Rolfe in LCL (2 vols.).

Philostratus, *Life of Apollonius of Tyana:* Greek text and English translation by F. C. Conybeare in LCL (2 vols.).

Bibliography to §3.4d: Studies

Arnaldo Momigliano, *The Development of Greek Biography* (Cambridge, MA: Harvard University, 1971).

Albrecht Dihle, *Studien zur griechischen Biographie* (AAWG.PH 3,37; Göttingen: Vandenhoeck & Ruprecht, 1956).

Duane Reed Stuart, *Epochs of Greek and Roman Biography* (Sather Classical Lectures 4; Berkeley: University of California, 1928).

Ludwig Bieler, ΘΕΙΟΣ ANHP: *Das Bild des "göttlichen Menschen" in Spätantike und Frühchristentum* (Darmstadt: Wissenschaftliche Buchgesellschaft, 1976).

Moses Hadas and Morton Smith, *Heroes and Gods: Spiritual Biography in Antiquity* (RPS 13; New York: Harper, 1965).

David Tiede, *The Charismatic Figure as Miracle Worker* (SBLDS 1; Missoula: University of Montana, 1972).

Testament, found in the story of Moses, in the prophetical books (especially Jeremiah), and in Nehemiah, make use of the same schemata. In classical Greece, however, the biography was not used as a genre of literature. Of course, the Homeric epic already shows a certain interest in the primary data of the life of its heroes, and books like Xenophon's *Cyropaedia* and Plato's *Apology of Socrates* contain biographical elements. But they are not biographies in the strict sense of the term. The political and social structures of the Greek society at that time did not favor an interest in the single individual who surpassed all others, and for this reason the literary genre of the biography entered Greek literature at a relatively late time, namely, at the beginning of the Hellenistic period. The causes for this development were very different from the cultural matrix which formed the oriental biography of the ruler. The beginnings of Greek biography grew out of an increasing interest in the lives of famous poets and philosophers. Greek biography was born when one began to inquire into the relationship between the works and the life (*bios*) of such persons, and when one began to search for examples for the right conduct of the wise man.

The systematic development of these interests into a systematic literary activity is the achievement of the students of Aristotle, especially of Aristoxenus, who is otherwise known as the first scholar of music. He wrote biographies of Pythagoras, Socrates, Plato, and others, of which unfortunately nothing is preserved. We can assume, however, that Aristotle's philosophical views about the differentiation of the virtues and about the relationship between conduct (*ethos*) and character (*pathos*) were applied in these works. It was thus the purpose of these biographies to present the principles of philosophical doctrines, conduct of life, and formation of character in the form of a *bios*. As was customary in the school of Aristotle, collections of relevant materials were made first, in preparation for the writings of biographies. Such materials were not only used in the biographies of individuals, but also in series of *vitae* presenting the lives of poets and philosophers, and also in the brief *vitae* which were later put at the head of editions of the classical authors. From the few fragments which are preserved of this literary activity, it is striking to find a completely uncritical attitude: anecdotes, legends, and romantic glorifications predominate.

At the beginning of the Hellenistic period the personalities of several rulers made strong impressions upon many people. It is therefore not surprising that biographies of these rulers were written, especially about Alexander the Great and several rulers of Syracuse and Macedonia. With the exception of some serious works from the hands of such historians as Ptolemy I and Polybius, these biographies show a tendency toward the genre of panegyric and romance. The later Alexander romance has its roots in such biographies. A politically interested ruler-biography did not develop until I CE. Even autobiographies of rulers seem to have been rare. It is reported that such autobiographies were written by Demetrius of Phalerum, for ten years governor of Athens at the end of IV BCE, Pyrrhus king of Epirus, the Achaean politician Aratus of Sikyon, and the Egyptian king Ptolemy VIII Euergetes II.

The Hellenistic biography became a characteristic expression of its culture. The impetus for the formation of this genre was the Hellenistic discovery of the significance of the human individual. With Polybius, the biography also became a standard feature of the writing of history. Polybius recognized that one of the important causes for historical developments was the individual as he was shaped by the factors of his *vita*. This insight was still valid for the historiography of the Roman imperial period. Numerous biographies have been preserved in both Greek and Latin from this later period. They continue the tradition of the biographies of poets and philosophers (as, e.g., the collections of *vitae* by Diogenes Laertius), and also deal more frequently with the biography of important political figures (cf. the parallel biographies of Plutarch and Suetonius' *Lives of the Emperors*). Furthermore, biographies of the philosophical founders of religious movements were also written (see Philo's *Vita Mosis* and Philostratus' *Vita Apollonii*).

In order to understand this literary genre, especially in its extant examples from the Roman imperial period (which nevertheless depend upon Hellenistic prototypes), it is necessary to consider yet one more important genre: the aretalogy. The aretalogy did not develop on the basis of biographical interests, but it is nonetheless closely related to the Hellenistic view of the individual person. The origins of the aretalogy must be sought in the cultic hymns which enumerated the great acts of a particular deity. Beginning in the Hellenistic period, such hymns were recorded on stone and publicly displayed in temples, soon to be joined by prose narratives of the god's miraculous acts down to the present time—thus going beyond the divine acts from the mythical past! In several cults, especially those of Asclepius and of Sarapis and Isis (§4.3d), such records were used in religious propaganda and recited in public.

For the Greek mind, however, special and extraordinary human gifts were not fundamentally different from divine powers manifested in present events (see §1.5b on the ruler cult). It was therefore quite possible to praise the divine gifts and wonderful deeds of human beings in the same form in which one praised the acts of god. For this reason, aretalogy and biography became closely related in the Hellenistic period, and with respect to the aretalogy of a divine human being, aretalogy and biography could become identical in the common understanding. The typical Hellenistic belief, that divine powers are manifested in the great poets, philosophers, and rulers, can be traced back to the end of iv bce. The Euhemeristic form of the criticism of myth (§4.2b) had already tried to demonstrate that some of the gods were originally human benefactors of humankind, who for that reason had received divine honors. In the case of the claims of divinity for Homer or Socrates, it is possible to ask whether this is not simply a hyperbolic expression for great poetic or philosophical gifts. As for Pythagoras and Epicurus it must be admitted that the borderline between the divinely gifted philosopher and the divine founder of a religion has been obliterated.

No wonder, therefore, that the biographies of the Hellenistic period already include miracle stories in a strikingly uncritical manner. The biography thus contained aretalogical elements at a very early date. Indeed, had some of these biographies survived, we would probably come to the conclusion that it as hard to determine whether they were in fact biographies or aretalogies. That is altogether clear in the case of several biographies from the Roman period, especially in the presentations of the life of the divine founder of a religion. In the case of the *Vita Mosis* of Philo of Alexandria, the materials used by the author were already aretalogical, namely the well known Old Testament stories of the miracles which were connected with the figure of Moses and the Exodus. For the biography of Apollonius of Tyana, Philostratus used a collection of miracle stories which was nothing but an aretalogy. And even though Plutarch designed his biographies in order to describe the close relationship between *bios* and character, his works nevertheless demonstrate that many of the materials used by him were strongly aretalogical.

The Roman biography owes its origin entirely to Greek influences. The Roman interest in the life and fate of the extraordinary individual has no other source; in ancient Roman political thought such interest would have found as little room as in the Greek democracy. The development of the Roman biography begins with the presentation of the lives of Sulla, Pompey, and Caesar, continues with the lives of the emperors (Suetonius) and the collections of *vitae* of famous persons (*De viris illustribus*), and ends with the Christian lives of martyrs and saints. Aretalogical elements are clearly present, although the Roman mind was hesitant to view the great human deed as a direct manifestation of the divine or of a god. But in the lives of the emperors, stories of political and military achievements stand side by side with narrations of prodigies and supernatural appearances, which point to the greatness and significance of the events and of the person acting. In praise of the extraordinary abilities of individual human beings, panegyric features frequently appear. Moreover, in the later period, and especially in the legends of Christian saints, even Latin literature is entirely dominated by miracle stories.

(e) The Romance

Relatively recent discoveries of papyri have demonstrated that the beginnings of the Greek romance, formerly dated in the later Roman imperial period, belong into II BCE. This has made it possible to understand the romance as the typical literary expression of the late-Hellenistic view

Bibliography to §3.4e: Texts

Pierre Grimal (ed. and trans.), *Romans grecs et latins: Textes présentes, traduits et annotés* (Paris: Gallimard, 1958).

Moses Hadas (ed.), *Three Greek Romances, Translated with an Introduction* (Indianapolis: Bobbs-Merrill, 1964).

Achilles Tatius: Greek text and English translation by S. Gaselee in LCL.

Longus: Greek text and English translation by J. M. Edmunds in LCL.

Otto Schönberger (ed.), *Longos: Hirtengeschichten von Daphnis und Chloe: Griechisch und deutsch* (SQAW 6; Berlin: Akademie-Verlag, 1960).

Helmut van Thiel (ed.), *Leben und Taten Alexanders von Makedonien* (TF 13; Darmstadt: Wissenschaftliche Buchgesellschaft, 1974). Greek text of manuscript L and German translation.

Bibliography to §3.4e: Studies

Erwin Rohde, *Der griechische Roman und seine Vorläufer* (4th ed.; Hildesheim: Olm, 1966). The classic study of the Greek romance, first published 1876.

Elizabeth H. Haight, *Essays on the Greek Romances* (New York: Longmans, Green, 1943).

Eduard Schwartz, *Fünf Vorträge über den griechischen Roman* (Berlin: De Gruyter, 1943).

Rudolf Helm, *Der antike Roman* (Studien zur Altertumswissenschaft 4; 2d ed.; Göttingen: Vandenhoeck & Ruprecht, 1956).

Martin Braun, *Griechischer Roman und hellenistische Geschichtsschreibung* (Frankfurt a.M.: Klostermann, 1934).

Ben Edwin Perry, *The Ancient Romances. A Literary-Historical Account of Their Origins* (Sather Classical Lectures 37; Berkeley and Los Angeles: University of California, 1967).

Tomas Hägg, *Narrative Technique in Ancient Greek Romances: Studies of Chariton, Xenophon Ephesius, and Achilles Tatius* (Uppsala: Almquist & Wiksells, 1971).

Fritz Wehrli, "Einheit und Vorgeschichte der griechischen Romanliteratur," *MH* 22 (1965) 133–54.

Alexander Scobie, *Aspects of the Ancient Romance and its Heritage: Essays on Apuleius, Petronius, and the Greek Romances* (BKP 30; Meisenheim am Glan: Hair, 1969).

Reinhold Merkelbach, *Die Quellen des griechischen Alexanderromans* (München: Beck, 1954).

Otto Weinreich, *Der griechische Liebesroman* (Zürich: Artemis, 1962).

Karl Kerenyi, *Die griechisch-orientalische Romanliteratur in religionsgeschichtlicher Beleuchtung* (2d ed.; Darmstadt: Wissenschaftliche Buchgesellschaft, 1962).

Reinhold Merkelbach, *Roman und Mysterium in der Antike* (München: Beck, 1962).

of human existence. All essential elements of human experience and of the conquest of its limitations, as they found expression in the various genres of Hellenistic literature, were joined together by the romance into a new literary concept. The romance takes account of the larger geographical horizons which were opened up through the conquests of Alexander, but it places the human individual in the center of the plot, and it reconciles this human being with the powers of fate which often seem to render life meaningless; because at least the romance knows a happy end. All the genres which Greek literature had created reappear in the Hellenistic romance. Its interest in travel and foreign countries is derived from geography and ethnography. The frequent reports of sea travel are drawn from the old *periploi,* but such an interest in travel to foreign countries is, of course, as old as Homer's *Odyssey,* and a description of a shipwreck is rarely missing. The erotic motif is borrowed from Greek tragedy; although it also appears in the comedy, the romance elevates this motif: the lovers preserve their chastity to the very end; Euripides had already used the same feature. Sexual excesses and erotic aberrations are reserved for the secondary figures of the narrative; only the later parodies of romances (Petronius, Apuleius) ascribe such actions to the heroes of the story. From biography the romance drew the description of the wonderful birth or origin of the hero and heroine and of their exemplary moral conduct. How virtue and character are to be related to the conduct of life and to the acts of providence, the romance learned from the philosophical biography. Many elements are borrowed from aretalogy, paradoxography, and from the popularizations of ethnography, zoology, and pharmacology which so strongly emphasized whatever was curious and peculiar: thus we find miracles and *paradoxa,* demons and magic, appearances of dead people, animals which are able to speak, miraculously fast travel by ship, strange countries and peoples, crevasses in the earth opening up unexpectedly, and finally the salutation of hero and heroine as god and goddess. Religious and moralizing speeches by the hero, the overcoming of dangers and persecutions, divine commands, oracles and dreams—all these features can also be found in inferior historiography. There are, finally numerous motifs and considerable materials which the romance drew from popular story-telling. Such story-telling is rarely extant in literary works; it is therefore difficult to characterize it more accurately. But there is no question that such narrative oral traditions were widespread; legends, fables, riddles, and anecdotes in literature are repeatedly drawn from this source. A particularly rich tradition of story-telling existed in Ionia, and its influence can be seen in Herodotus' writings. A collection of such stories from the Hellenistic period, entitled *Milesiaca,* mostly of somewhat dubious erotic character, was made by Aristides of Miletus. The collection was translated into Latin by Sisenna, and according to Plutarch (*Crassus* 32), many Roman officers would always carry a copy in their luggage. In any case, the writers of romance could and frequently did avail themselves of a large treasure of popular stories.

In the two oldest known romances, *Ninus and Semiramis* and Iambulus' *Commonwealth of the Sun*—both written in II BCE, though perhaps Iambulus' romance might be dated in III BCE—the two primary features of novelistic literature were already fully developed: in *Ninus* the erotic motif, and in the *Commonwealth of the Sun* the motif of adventurous travel. The fragment of the *Ninus* romance which is preserved does not permit a reconstruction of the whole story. But the surviving portions of Iambulus' romance tell enough of the story: after adventurous travels via Ethiopia, the hero arrives at mysterious islands in the southern ocean; later he returns via India. The central portion of the narrative concerns a utopia. For several years the hero is permitted to participate in the life of the ideal commonwealth of the happy inhabitants of the islands in the southern ocean; they worship the sun, have their women in common, and all citizens share equally in the honorable and the less desirable jobs. Both basic motifs, the travel adventure and the erotic motif, are found together for the first time in *Chaereas and Callirhoe* of Chariton, from Aphrodisians in Asia Minor. The date of this romance is not certain; papyrus fragments from II and III CE show that is was written no later than I CE. The action is located in Miletus and in Persia. Various novelistic motifs appear in colorful sequence: drama, comedy, aretalogy; even historiography made its contribution. Hermocrates, the general of Syracuse from the Peloponnesian War, appears, and also the Persian king Artaxerxes II, who falls in love with the heroine, and whose court provides the setting for the climax. Tyche finally provides the resolution and joins the lovers together.

All other romances which are still preserved were written in II or III CE. This genre seems to have been very popular during this period, because a number of fragments of otherwise unknown romances are preserved in the papyrus finds from that period. It is therefore no accident that most of the Christian romances (the apocryphal acts of apostles) were written during the same period. In the *Ephesiaca* of Xenophon of Ephesus, the action leads the reader to Egypt and includes the Potiphar motif (cf. the Joseph story in Genesis), as well as the motif of chastity in the marriage of the heroine with a poor shepherd—both of which motifs had been used by Euripides. The *Babyloniaca* of the Syrian Iamblichus does not include the otherwise obligatory travel by ship, but miraculous stories, ghosts, magic, and gruesome entanglements appear in abundance; a number of short stories are also included here. The *Ethiopiaca* of Heliodorus of Emesa (III

CE) is the last great romance from antiquity, distinguished by a highly artistic narrative. This work also transcends that basic presupposition of the Hellenistic understanding of human existence which had been the foundation of the romance literature, namely, the view that human beings are exposed to a hostile world whose powers and gods they cannot comprehend, though a favorable fate might be able to save them. In Heliodorus' work, new religious concepts derived from Neoplatonic or Neopythagorean beliefs replaced this view. The heroine, for whom chastity is a religious requirement, learns that the cause of all adversities as well as the final resolution is a higher divine justice. The romance *Daphnis and Chloe* of Longus (II CE) is of a special character, and has enjoyed popularity since the time of the Renaissance. The travel motif is completely missing. Instead, the erotic theme predominates in the form of a shepherd's idyll located on the island of Lesbos and glorifying the rustic life.

An attempt has been made somewhat recently to understand the Hellenistic romance as a disguised mystery narrative (Reinhold Merkelbach). The content of the erotic romances is itself seen as religious, and it is suggested that these works were written in the service of oriental mystery religions. Iamblichus' romance would present the mysteries of Mithras, Longus the mysteries of Dionysus, Xenophon those of Isis, Heliodorus the religion of Sol Invictus, the romance of a certain Antonius Diogenes, of which only a fragment is preserved, the doctrine of the Pythagoreans. It is indeed indisputable that the Latin romance *Metamorphoses* of Apuleius (born in 125 CE), in which the hero is ultimately initiated into the mysteries of Isis, was indeed written as propaganda for the Isis religion. One must also admit that certain portions of the Christian romance of the Apostle Thomas (*Acts of Thomas*) are symbolic narratives of the ascent of the soul into heaven. But in both cases one is dealing with a secondary religious adaptation of older novelistic materials in the interests of the propaganda of a missionary religion. But it is out of the question to believe that the romance was intended to convey a religious message symbolically at any time before this literary genre was employed for such purposes by Apuleius and by the *Acts of Thomas*.

If one wants to use the term "religious"—the term is by no means necessary—the romance can indeed be said to convey a religious message in a different sense: it reflects the longing of human beings for an experience which transcends the experiences of everyday life. It is the longing of people for whom the future of the nation and political communities has ceased to be the object of their hopes and aspirations. As a positive value, the community appears in the romance only as a utopia or as an idyll (the romances of Iambulus and Longus). Such views are not prophetic political messages. It is not such a salvation that the romance promises, and the reader could scarcely have expected to find a message of this sort. The fulfillment of a longing for a transcendent experience is offered in the description of the extraordinary fate of individual human beings. Historical and political events are nothing but a backdrop. But the descriptions of foreign countries and peoples are still important, because the imagination of the reader looks for something wonderful and extraordinary which lies outside the horizon of everyday life. Once the fated ordeal of the central figures of the romance reaches its climax, it is not as a symbolically described religious experience—religious elements and materials are nothing but accessories—but as the fulfillment of love; in all its nobility, purity, and faithful endurance, love is presented as the true goal and ultimate meaning of human experience. It is by no means rare in the history of literature that the intrinsic import of a literary genre is most clearly understood in its contemporary parodies. What has been said above with respect to the genre of the romance can be verified in considering the romance parody of Petronius (died in 66 CE): his *Satiricon* features as its central theme the hero's infatuation with the beautiful boy Giton, and Petronius describes in a masterly way the often risqué adversities which thwart the fulfillment of this love.

PHILOSOPHY AND RELIGION

1. THE PHILOSOPHICAL SCHOOLS AND PHILOSOPHIC RELIGION

(a) The Academy and Platonism

After Plato's death (348/47 BCE) the older Academy was primarily interested in rounding out the cosmological and theological teachings of its master. Plato's students Xenocrates and Speusippus created the "Platonic" system which is reflected in the popular Platonism of the subsequent centuries. Of the teachings of the older Academy, only its demonology would become very influential. Plato had already suggested various understandings of the *daimones*. He thought that they were intermediate beings who were able to communicate with human beings on behalf of the gods. He also distinguished between different classes of demons, which were active either in the realm of the heavens, or in the air, or in the realm of the spirit, or in the human soul. Xenocrates (who died ca. 315 BCE) added to these concepts the distinction between good and evil demons; the latter, he thought, haunted the sublunar realms. This provided philosophical legitimacy for beliefs which were already widespread in popular thought and thus contributed to their later propagation in philosophical and theological literature. Platonists of the Roman period, like Plutarch and the Neopythagoreans, gave a central place in their thought to this concept. But the Christians also employed these concepts and used them repeatedly. Justin Martyr elaborated them in his apologetic arguments against paganism: he claimed that the pagan cults had been invented by evil demons in order to create the delusion that they were the fulfillment of the prophecies from the Old Testament. In constructing such arguments, the Christians were able to take their starting-point from the teachings of Xenocrates, who had already relativized the distinction between demons and gods.

The so-called "Middle Academy" of III and II BCE was locked into a battle with the Stoics and increasingly also with other philosophical schools. These controversies began with Arcesilaus, who became head of the academy in 268 BCE, and they continued in the next century under

Carneades. In such disputes, the Platonists made recourse to the older Platonic dialogues and to the Socrates of these dialogues. As Socrates had demonstrated to the Sophists that knowledge through sense perception was impossible, the Academy now argued against Stoic epistemology, which ascribed truth value only to those concepts which had been developed on the basis of experience, observation, and scientific insight (Epicurus had made knowledge dependent upon experience in a similar way). The Academicians opposed this viewpoint with their dialectic, which

Bibliography to §4.1: Texts

Cornelia Johanna De Vogel, *Greek Philosophy: A Collection of Texts* (3d ed.; 3 vols.; Leiden: Brill, 1963–67).

Bibliography to §4.1: Introductions and Surveys

A. H. Armstrong, *An Introduction to Ancient Philosophy* (3d ed.; London: Methuen, 1957) 114–40.

P. Merlan, "Greek Philosophy from Plato to Plotinus," in: A. H. Armstrong, *The Cambridge History of Later Greek and Early Medieval Philosophy* (Cambridge: Cambridge University, 1967) 11–132.

Edwyn Bevan, "Hellenistic Popular Philosophy," in: T. D. Bury (ed.), *The Hellenistic Age* (Cambridge: Cambridge University, 1923) 79–107.

Nilsson, *Griechische Religion*, 2. 395–466.

Bibliography to §4.1: Comprehensive Treatments

Eduard Zeller, *Die Philosophie der Griechen in ihrer geschichtlichen Entwicklung*, 3,1: *Die nacharistotelische Philosophie* (2 vols.; 6th ed.; Darmstadt: Wissenschaftliche Buchgesellschaft, 1963). Most comprehensive and detailed presentation, reprint of 5th ed. of 1923; now often surpassed by more recent works.

Frederick Copleston, *A History of Philosophy*, vol. 1: *Greece and Rome* (Westminster, MD: Newner, 1960).

W. K. C. Guthrie, *A History of Greek Philosophy* (Cambridge: Cambridge University, 1962–75).

A. A. Long, *Hellenistic Philosophy: Stoics, Epicureans, Sceptics* (New York: Scribner's, 1974).

Bibliography to §4.1a

Philip Merlan, *From Platonism to Neoplatonism* (2d ed.; The Hague: Nijhoff, 1960).

Hans Joachim Krämer, *Platonismus und hellenistische Philosophie* (Berlin: De Gruyter, 1971).

Paul Shorey, *Platonism Ancient and Modern* (Berkeley: University of California, 1938).

J. Glucker, *Antiochus and the Late Academy* (Hyp. 56; Göttingen: Vandenhoeck & Ruprecht, 1978).

Mary Mills Patrick, *The Greek Sceptics* (New York: Columbia University, 1929).

Charlotte L. Stough, *Greek Skepticism: A Study in Epistemology* (Berkeley and Los Angeles, University of California, 1969).

J. Dillon, *The Middle Platonists: 80 B.C. to A.D. 220* (Ithaca, NY: Cornell University, 1977).

Kurt Flasch (ed.), *Parusia: Studien zur Philosophie Platons und zur Problemgeschichte des Platonismus: Festgabe für Johannes Hirschberger* (Frankfurt a.M.: Minerva, 1965).

demonstrated that each argument could be countered with another argument and that judgment should therefore be suspended (ἐποχή or, in Sextus Empiricus, σκέψις). The Academy thus was accused of having fallen into the skepticism of Pyrrho of Elis. But, in any case, this skepticism regarding the derivation of truth from the world as it is perceptible through the senses became very influential in the late Hellenistic and Roman periods. Not until Philon of Larissa (first half of I BCE) did the Academy begin to move beyond skepticism to overcome its radical opposition to the other philosophical schools. In Rome, Philon was the teacher of Cicero, who still shared a moderate skepticism. Philon's successor, Antiochus of Ascalon, broke decisively with the skepticism of his predecessors and abandoned opposition to the Stoa. This corresponds on the side of the Stoa to an increasing acceptance of Platonic concepts. A new epoch thus began for the Academy with Antiochus. The philosophers of this tradition no longer called themselves Academicians, but Platonists, and the Athenian Academy lost its significance as the primary center for the philosophy which was indebted to Plato. This went hand in hand with the wide dissemination beginning in I BCE of Platonic thoughts and concepts, which was by no means the success story of a particular philosophical school, namely, of the Academy, but a cultural development. Platonism determined the general thoughts and world view of the entire subsequent period.

Closely associated with this dissemination of Platonism was the development of dualistic anthropological and cosmological concepts. In his demonology, Plato's student Xenocrates had already taken up Plato's statements about the two world souls: a good and an evil world soul are in turn responsible for the actions of the good and evil demons. The Stoic philosopher Posidonius—however controversial the interpretation of his philosophy may be—certainly adopted essential parts of this Platonic dualism for his own system. He distinguished two worlds in his cosmology: the celestial world above the moon, which is imperishable and immutable, and the sublunar world, which is transitory and subject to change. It was possibly also Posidonius who developed the trichotomic anthropology which later became widely disseminated: the human *spirit* has its origin in the sun, but from the intermediate world (the moon) it receives the *soul* which animates and maintains the *body* provided by the sublunar world. At the point of death, the whole process is reversed; once the spirit has freed itself from the soul, it returns to its solar origin. These concepts, once introduced into Stoic philosophy, reappear among later Stoic and other philosophers, including the Romans Cicero and Seneca (§6.4c, f), perhaps in direct dependence upon Posidonius.

A Platonizing Stoicism became the basis of philosophical and religious reflection at the close of the Hellenistic period, especially outside of the philosophical schools, a fact which is most clearly demonstrated by the Jewish philosopher Philo of Alexandria. His allegorical method of exegesis is Stoic, as is his interpretation of Old Testament figures whom he sees as virtues. His concept of God, too, has Stoic features: God is immutable and eternal, more the basic power of the cosmos than a person (of course, Philo cannot completely eliminate the individualized features of the Old Testament concept of God). God and Nature are identical in Philo, and the Logos, as in Stoic philosophy, is the power permeating all things. But despite all this, Philo's world view, and especially his anthropology, is Platonic. The visible world as perceived through the senses is not only transitory, it is also characterized with negative predicates. The soul or the spirit had its origin in the world of God. As long as it dwells in the body, it is caught in the snares of earthly existence from which it must free itself. True insight into the essence of reality is not possible through sense perception. Only the human spirit can recognize God and the Logos in order to become free from the visible world through the knowledge of wisdom and through exercise in virtue; only thus will the spirit overcome the body and its passions and be able to return to its home, the celestial world. Philo does not simply see the material world as the cause of evil and vice, he conceives of the body as an absolutely foreign place in contrast to the celestial home, and as an unsuitable garment for the divine soul. Philo's cosmology also contains a clearly Platonic element: God has created the world of ideas first, as the prototype of the visible world. Only the former is permanent and imperishable, whereas the latter is nothing but its changing and mortal copy. The Logos is seen by Philo in both Stoic and Platonic terms. According to the Stoic concept, it is the power governing the whole universe; but in the Platonic sense, it is also the image of God according to which the human being has been created. For this reason, human beings belong to God in their true essence and are fundamentally different from the visible world. It is irrelevant whether or not we call this dualism "gnostic," because the beginnings of Gnosticism overlap and intersect with the victory of Platonism in many ways (§6.5f; on the Platonism of the Epistle to the Hebrews, see §12.2b).

(b) The Peripatetic Philosophy

Aristotle himself and his philosophy cannot be discussed here. For several centuries very little effect of Aristotle's philosophy can be detected. Hellenistic cosmology had no use for Aristotle's concept of the "first mover" and his mechanistic picture of the course of the world. His ethics were not appreciated because they were too closely associated with the political unit of the *polis* and not easily applicable to a radically changed political environment. Though it is not unlikely that several major schools (Skepsis, Alexandria, Rhodes, Athens) possessed copies of Aristotle's didactic writings, he was best known during the Hellenistic period, and indeed in the Peripatetic school itself, as a biologist and natural scientist. There is a famous story that Aristotle's didactic writings were hidden in a basement of a house in Skepsis in northwestern Asia Minor for two hundred years, and that their rediscovery brought a momentous renewal of interest in Aristotle's logic. In any case, Andronicus of Rhodes (middle of i BCE), head of the Peripatetic school, was responsible for a new edition of these didactic writings which established Aristotle's significance as a logician for the imperial period.

After Aristotle's death, the Peripatetic school in Athens was directed by his friend and associate Theophrastus (371–287 BCE). Some of Theophrastus' numerous writings are preserved: his famous *Inquiry into Plants*, the *Aetiology of Plants* (§3.3b), *Characters* (a description of thirty typical characters), and, among other writings, extensive fragments of his work *On Religion*. The primary interests of the Peripatetics are well mirrored in these works: studies in natural science, along with the composition of character studies and biographies, especially of poets and philosophers (§3.4d).

(c) Epicurus and the Epicureans

While the Academy and the Peripatetic school were established before the beginning of the Hellenistic period, the Epicureans and the Stoics first appeared in the early decades of that time. Their founders, Epicurus and Zeno, were contemporaries, and both taught in Athens. However opposite their opinions and teachings were, both produced typical Hellenistic philosophies. This includes the fact that both schools were strongly dependent upon the personal conduct of life of their founders—a factor which played only a minor role in the Academy and in the Peripatetic school.

Epicurus (341–270 BCE) was the son of an Athenian colonist from Samos, who finally settled in Athens in 306 BCE and established his school in a garden (thus it is often referred to as "the Garden"). It is difficult to reconstruct Epicurus' teachings because all his writings are lost, with the exception of three didactic letters. In addition, the writings of his students and successors are only scantily preserved. The epistemology of Epicurus (who held that all sense perceptions are true) and his atomism need not be

Bibliography to §4.1b

Paul Moraux, *Der Aristotelismus bei den Griechen von Andronikos bis Alexander von Aphrodisias* (Peripatoi: Philologisch-Historische Studien zum Aristotelismus 5: Berlin and New York: De Gruyter, 1973).

discussed here. More significant for the intellectual world of Hellenism was the so-called atheism of the Epicureans, their teaching of true happiness (*eudaimonia*), and the organization of the "Garden" as a religious association of friends. Epicurus' philosophy sought to be a substitute religion. This implies that the Epicureans were neither irreligious nor atheistic, although both accusations were leveled against them by their ancient opponents. They did in fact deny that the gods (whose existence Epicurus never doubted) were in any way involved in the lives of human beings. Thus it was meaningless to worship the gods, pointless to call upon them in distress, and useless to offer sacrifices to them. These beliefs of the Epicureans were actually not much different from the ideals of life propagated by some other philosophical schools, which also taught that one should make oneself independent of all other beings and all things. The Stoics and the Peripatetics would also have declared it disgraceful for the truly wise man to be dependent upon divine intervention in his personal affairs. But while the Stoics, despite their materialistic world view, admired the working of the divine power in the realities and movements of the world and of nature, the Epicureans drew the consequences from their atomistic materialism: the course of natural events is determined by laws which derive from the movements of the atoms; hence, there is no need for the gods. There are also no spiritual realities outside of the material world as constituted by the atoms, and even the soul is nothing but a part of this world. It was therefore impossible for Epicurus to associate his notions of religion and deity with any transcendent powers. He radicalized the concept of piety and consistently directed it toward the idea of the independence and imperturbability of the wise man.

This was accomplished in the Epicurean teaching of true happiness and in the development of the ideal of friendship. Both concepts assume a deeply religious meaning among the Epicureans—without doubt demanding too much of these human ideals! To be sure, other philosophical schools were also structured like religious associations. But among the

Bibliography to §4.1c: Texts

Barrett, *Background*, 72–75.

Grant, *Hellenistic Religions*, 156–60.

Bibliography to §4.1c: Studies

Wolfgang Schmid, "Epikur," *RAC* 5 (1961) 681–819. The best comprehensive discussion.

Eduard Zeller, *The Stoics, Epicureans, and Sceptics* (2d ed.; London: Longmans, Green, 1892; reprint: New York: Russell, 1962).

A. J. Festugière, *Epicurus and His Gods* (Cambridge, MA: Harvard University, 1956).

G. Rodis-Lewis, *Épicure et son école* (Collection Idées 342; Paris: Gallimard, 1975).

Epicureans, this form of organization was expected to provide the basis for the realization of the life of true happiness and friendship. Thus the school became a kind of mystery club, because it provided the environment of religious fulfillment for its members, and its founder was seen as a divine figure. Friendship, community, and mutual pastoral care were understood as religious duties, while the regular common meals of the members and the memorial festivals on the birthdays of the founder and of other distinguished members were liturgical celebrations. These performances and duties, however, were not designed to build up the community because the community was there to serve the individual: the only goal was to establish the true happiness and imperturbability of the individual soul. Like all other philosophical schools of the Hellenistic period, the Epicureans subordinated all other matters of common interest to that of the individual. We can see an obvious parallel to the mysteries here (§4.3e). The mysteries were also institutions into which individual human beings could be initiated in order to obtain personal salvation. But whereas the mysteries promised a salvation which included guarantees for a life after death, the religious goal of true happiness among the Epicureans was limited strictly to the experiences of earthly life: independence from all affections and experiences, from luck and misfortune, even an existence beyond all desire and pleasure—in short, a kind of nihilistic harmony. In this way the wise man could prove to himself the nonexistence of all affections and experiences in his own life. This also explains the peculiar Epicurean way of overcoming even death: since death is nothing but dissolution, in fact dissolution of the soul, which simply dissolves into the atoms by which it was constituted, it is impossible to experience death and, therefore, there is no reason to fear it.

Epicureanism was quite influential for a time, but probably only in the educated upper classes. It played a considerable role in Rome during I BCE; the long didactic poem of Lucretius is one of our most important witnesses (§6.4b). Seneca still imitated the Epicurean custom of writing pastoral letters. But Epicurean influence declined during the imperial period, and in later antiquity the Epicurean teachings were little more than the target of pagan and Christian polemics against atheism.

(d) The Stoa

The Stoa was founded by Zeno of Citium on Cyprus. He was born in the year 333/32 as the son of the Phoenician merchant Mnaseas (= Manasseh or Menahem). In 300 BCE he came to Athens and taught regularly for many years in the *Stoa Piokile* on the Athenian agora—the terms "Stoa" and "Stoicism" are derived from his place of teaching. Zeno died in ca. 264 in Athens, highly respected by all Athenians. His successor

Cleanthes (ca. 331–232 BCE), who consolidated Zeno's teachings, came from Assos in Asia Minor; his famous hymn to Zeus is preserved. After Cleanthes, Chrysippus from Soli in Cilicia was the head of the Stoic school; he is known as the systematizer of the Stoic doctrine (he died ca. 205 BCE).

From its inception, Stoic philosophy was cosmopolitan and pantheistic. The problem of the polis, dominant in Aristotle's philosophy, did not exist for the Stoics; local gods were understood in universal terms from the beginning. At the same time, the Stoics understood themselves as the heirs of Socrates (as mediated through the Cynics; see §4.2a). This explains the preeminence of ethics in Stoic teaching: virtue is the only good that exists. All other goals and motivations for human action of whatever kind— material goods, political ambitions, and especially human affections—are seen as falsifications and perversions of the moral destiny of human beings. This meant that Stoic ethics dissociated itself from all the external and empirical motivations which were present in the social structures of the world, or in the affections and desires of human beings. Rather, the only goal (*telos*) of moral action is "to live in agreement (with the Logos)," as Zeno said, or as formulated by Chrysippus: "to live in agreement with nature (*physis*)." Further modifications of this *telos* formula provide an interesting index for the historical development of Stoic philosophy.

Bibliography to §4.1d: Texts

Johannes von Arnim (ed.), *Stoicorum Veterum Fragmenta* (4 vols.; Leipzig: Teubner, 1903–24).
Barrett, *Background,* 61–72.
Grant, *Hellenistic Religions,* 152–56.
Max Pohlenz (ed. and trans.), *Stoa und Stoiker: Die Gründer, Panaitios, Poseidonios* (Zürich: Artemis, 1950). Selections in German translation.

Bibliography to §4.1d: Studies

J. M. Rist, *Stoic Philosophy* (Cambridge: Cambridge University, 1969).
Edwyn Bevan, *Stoics and Sceptics* (Oxford: Clarendon, 1913).
Max Pohlenz, *Die Stoa: Geschichte einer geistigen Bewegung* (2 vols.; 4th ed.; Göttingen: Vandenhoeck & Ruprecht, 1970).
Ludwig Edelstein, *The Meaning of Stoicism* (Cambridge, MA: Harvard University, 1966).
Samuel Sambursky, *Physics of the Stoics* (London: Routledge and Kegan Paul, 1959).
André Bridoux, *Le Stoicisme et son influence* (Paris: Librairie philosophique J. Vrin, 1966).
R. D. Hicks, *Stoic and Epicurean* (New York: Russell & Russell, 1962; originally published 1910).
Nock, "Posidonius," in: idem, *Essays,* 2. 853–76.
A. Dihle, "Posidonius' System of Moral Philosophy," *JHS* 93 (1973) 50–57.
Albert Henrichs, "Die Kritik der stoischen Theologie in PHerc. 1428," *Cronache Ercolanesi* 4 (1974) 5–32.

"Nature" does not refer to the external physical world (although much can be learned from it), but to the true "nature" of human beings, i.e., the *logos* which is rational discernment. Human reason is seen as identical with that reason which governs the whole cosmos. "According to nature" is therefore in Stoic philosophy the same as "according to reason," while the normal, natural experiences of human existence, like one's physical body, health, and all those things which are necessary for daily life, are no more than a preliminary stage of "the life according to nature."

This view of the nature of human beings and of their moral destiny demanded two things from Stoic philosophy: the development of a cosmology and the elaboration of a psychology. The cosmology clarifies the unity of the world reason and the cosmos. "Cosmos" includes all things which can be experienced, including material things and political and social circumstances, as well as the natural world and the extraterrestial universe. The Stoics drew upon two different sources in the development of their cosmology: the belief in destiny as amplified by astrology—fate (*heimarmenē;* §4.2c) was understood as the compelling force of the stars—and the insights of the natural sciences, which had made great progress in the early Hellenistic period (§3.3b). The result was a strictly materialistic and deterministic view of the course of all things. Even the world reason which governs all things is seen as "the fire," that is, as if it were some form of matter, since ultimately matter and its ruling rational principle are seen as a unity. Only in perception do they seem to be two different things, while in reality they are one. The return of the universe into itself in the world conflagration concluding each cycle of the world's time is also a thoroughly materialistic view of destruction and renewal. To be sure, the Stoics did not see the order of the world as arranged by meaningless determinism, but rather as the result of a most perfect legislation in which everything has been perfectly arranged. It was therefore possible to identify the world reason with Zeus, who predetermines and rules everything through his law. Cleanthes expressed this in his *Hymn to Zeus,* in which he names the impressiveness of the starry firmament as well as the perfect order of heaven, sea, and earth as proofs for the beneficial actions of the deity.

Stoic psychology is a doctrine of affections (πάθος; Latin: *perturbatio, passio,* or *affectus*). All affections, including not only desire, fear, and pleasure, but also regret and compassion, are, according to Stoic doctrine, pathological states of the soul from which the wise man must free himself in order to reach the goal of imperturbability (*apatheia;* later, in Epictetus, also *ataraxia*). In their description of the affections, Stoic philosophers borrowed many terms and concepts from the medical sciences. Their view of the affections as diseases of the soul is modeled on pathological insights of the diseases of the body. The philosopher becomes the physician of the soul.

Stoic parallels to Epicurean doctrines are obvious, both in the description of the task of the philosopher and in the materialistic cosmology. The close affinity of the two bitterly feuding schools is most clearly evident in their view of the ideal of the wise man, which rests upon the elucidation of the appropriate moral values. Formally defined, these values are seen as the understanding of all those things that truly concern the individual, as distinct from those things which are a matter of indifference. Only those things which are truly of concern must be mastered, if one wants to live in agreement with the order of nature. As far as the content of moral values is concerned, the Stoics rejected the Aristotelian distinction between inner, physical, and external values, and did not recognize any hierarchy of virtues. But they accepted the Platonic cardinal virtues of prudence, fortitude, temperance, and justice. Usually, however, the Stoic definition of moral criteria returns to the formal standard of "that which is according to nature." This encouraged the rise of general aphoristic rules for moral behavior, for instance, "that which is considered good at all places and at all times." In this way Stoic ethics naturally presented itself as the basis for popular moral teaching.

In addition to the Epicureans, the Stoics were primarily responsible for the formation of the ideal of the wise man which was typical for the Hellenistic period. According to classical philosophy, the wise man gave evidence for his full possession of virtue through his actions in the world and in society, his fortitude in battle, his prudence in political decisions, and so on. Cynicism (§4.2a), however, developed a new image of Socrates, in which the wise man is distinguished through his independence and frugality, and thus also through his withdrawal from the obligations of society. This image became determinative for the Epicureans and the Stoics. Both schools pursued the same goal: to attain to the true happiness (*eudaimonia*) of the individual, who is in full harmony with himself and has therefore overcome the bondage of fate. But for the Epicurean, withdrawal from society is a necessary presupposition for attaining true happiness, while for the Stoic the relationship to world and society remains paradoxical. He can prove his imperturbability, that is, his possession of true happiness, even in the midst of worldly endeavors, in whatever activity his origin, education, or political position has assigned to him, whether it be that of the emperor or that of a slave. This view is expressed in the famous "as if not"—a formula which also occurs in Paul's letters, although within a Christian perspective. Thus the wise man can be actively involved in the affairs of his society, but his position and his share in it—whether he is actively working or passively suffering—do not affect his true goal and his real being, since true happiness does not depend upon the external circumstances of life.

It is peculiar that Stoicism, a philosophy with a strictly materialistic view of the world, became the main support for the Hellenistic renewal of the belief in the gods and thus the basis for Hellenistic theology. The primary reason for this alliance between Stoicism and religion was the fact that the materialistic doctrine of the all-governing fire or Logos was at the same time a pantheistic theology, because God and the world were one and the same. In contrast to the equally materialistic doctrine of the Epicureans, the Stoics did not understand the course of the world as a mechanistic process, but assumed that there was a rational principle, the Logos, which ruled all things. It was therefore possible to combine the old beliefs in the gods with the new philosophical insights, even though the purely external cultic performances were rejected. The gods became the symbols for the wise government of world reason, Zeus for the heavens, Hera for the air, Poseidon for the water; the stars were seen as rational beings. The different gods worshiped by the various nations were only diverse names for one and the same divine reason. This Stoic view matched the syncretistic tendencies of the time very well and provided the desired philosophical rationale.

In order to present their new view of the world as one which represented the truth contained in ancient traditions, the Stoics adopted and developed the allegorical method. Its primary purpose was to reinterpret the old myths and rituals in order to relate the old beliefs in the gods to the insights of philosophy. For the founders of Stoic philosophy, the motivation for this sort of interpretation was a genuine reverence for the traditional religions. This explains their efforts to discover the religious meanings of the writings of the classical authors, especially Homer. It was in these endeavors that the allegorical method was further elaborated and refined. This is the origin of the standard hermeneutical method of antiquity which Hellenistic-Jewish and Christian theologians readily used later on for the interpretation of biblical texts. The *Homeric Problems* of Heraclitus (Pseudo-Heraclitus, I BCE), though not exclusively committed to Stoic philosophy, is the best surviving example of this religious allegorical interpretation of Homer as it was practiced in the schools of the time. Heraclitus explicitly defends the necessity of understanding Homer in this way. A synopsis of the Stoic theology which was developed on the basis of allegorical interpretation of ancient myths was written by Cornutus in I CE.

The so-called Middle Stoa began with Panaetius of Rhodes (ca. 180–110 BCE). His philosophy was characterized by a "return to the old philosophers," namely, the classical philosophy of Socrates, Plato, and Aristotle.

In his physics and cosmology Panaetius departed from the older Stoic dogmatism and rejected the contradictions in the system of Chrysippus. Instead, he emphasized the ethical teachings directed to the practical conduct of life, which were heavily indebted to Plato and Aristotle. His thought strongly influenced Roman authors: his work *On Right Conduct* was used extensively in Cicero's *De officiis*.

Decisive for the further development of Stoicism was a man who has been much disputed in modern scholarship: the historian, geographer, astronomer, and philosopher Posidonius of Apamea, who taught in Rhodes during the first half of I BCE. He ingeniously assimilated Stoic doctrines with the general thought of late Hellenism to such a degree that his philosophy became unacceptable to the later Stoics. But at the same time he reshaped Stoic thought into a more general philosophical system that greatly influenced not only the later philosophical developments but especially the world view of the larger educated class of the Roman imperial period. Posidonius adopted many elements from the Pre-Socratics and from Platonic and Aristotelian philosophy, while he drew a sharp line of demarcation against the Epicureans. As a consequence, Epicurean philosophy became more isolated, while the amalgamation of concepts from all other philosophical traditions was greatly encouraged. The effects are clearly visible in many pagan (Plutarch), Jewish (Philo of Alexandria), and Christian (Justin) thinkers of the following centuries, and the new philosophical synthesis of late antiquity, namely Neo-platonism, owes much to this development.

The reconstruction of Posidonius' philosophy is highly problematic, since scholarship must rely completely upon indirect and secondary sources and witnesses. Nevertheless, it is necessary to reconstruct, however tentatively, some of his cosmological teachings because of their decisive influence in the subsequent period. His view of the sun as the pure fire and the source of the human spirit, to which the moon contributes the soul and the earth the body, recurs in the cosmic anthropology of Gnosticism. Here, as well as in the Hermetic writings, the celestial journey of the soul or spirit is understood in a very similar way: when a human being dies, the body decays, while the soul remains for some time in the sublunar realm, until it too wastes away in order to liberate the spirit, which returns to the sun. With these concepts, Posidonius at the same time created a schema which could be used to describe the ascent of the human spirit in mystical experience. But Posidonius also went at least halfway in accommodating the dualistic concepts which more and more dominated the thought of the late Hellenistic period. Despite all his efforts to maintain a Stoic monism in his cosmology, the sublunar world is clearly the realm of a lower and inferior order. While the sun and the celestial world are identical to the pure realm of the divine, the relationship of the sublunar realm to divine power is ambiguous; in other words, the human beings living in this realm stand in need of redemption. Naturally, the all-governing divine power also becomes differentiated into energies of various degrees, into either—in mythological terms—gods, heroes, and demons, or—in astrological terms—astral powers of different ranks. However influential these thoughts may have been, the Stoics of the imperial period turned away from Posidonius. For them, Chrysippus remained the authoritative systematician of Stoic teachings, to whom one could refer whenever necessary. While there was little interest left in cosmology among the Stoics of the Roman times, Stoic ethics was now ready to conquer the world (§6.4f).

2. THE SPIRIT OF THE HELLENISTIC AGE

(a) The Cynics

Socrates was famous for going into the streets and public places to contend with all sorts of people and to challenge them to reflect about themselves. It is this pattern of doing philosophy, not any specific Socratic teaching, which Cynicism took over from Socrates. The founder of Cynic philosophy, Diogenes of Sinope (400/390–328/323 BCE), who was called "the dog" (*kyon*) because of his impudence, hesitated at nothing when he wanted to demonstrate his rejection of cultural values and bourgeois conventions. Diogenes proclaimed no specific philosophical doctrine, nor did his successors; but later Cynics were often influenced by Stoic philosophy. Their frugality and impudence were chiefly expressions of their repudia-

Bibliography to §4.2

Nilsson, *Griechische Religion* 2.

E. R. Dodds, *The Greeks and the Irrational* (Berkeley and Los Angeles: University of California, 1951).

Bibliography to §4.2a: Texts

Abraham J. Malherbe, *The Cynic Epistles: A Study Edition* (SBLSBS 12; Missoula, MT: Scholars Press, 1977).

Harold W. Attridge, *First-Century Cynicism in the Epistles of Heraclitus* (HTS 29; Missoula, MT: Scholars Press, 1976).

Bibliography to §4.2a: Studies

Farraud Sayre, *The Greek Cynics* (Baltimore: Furst, 1948).

Ragnar Höistad, *Cynic Hero and King* (Uppsala: Bloms, 1948).

Rudolf Bultmann, *Der Stil der paulinischen Predigt und die kynisch-stoische Diatribe* (FRLANT 13; Göttingen: Vandenhoeck & Ruprecht, 1910).

Abraham J. Malherbe, "'Gentle as a Nurse': The Cynic Background to 1 Thess ii," *NovT* 12 (1970) 201–17.

tion of the conventions of society. On the positive side, they stressed following only natural standards of behavior, acted as pastoral counselors, and volunteered to work for the welfare of others. Cynic philosophy was not based upon the formulation and handing down of doctrines, but upon the creation and transmission of striking examples for behavior. Cynic propaganda fixed such examples in the form of philosophical apophthegms, usually about the person of its founder Diogenes.

The preaching and teaching of the mendicant Cynics developed the *diatribē*. The original meaning of this word is "pastime," and in IV BCE it was used, together with *scholē* ("leisure," "school"), as a designation of a philosophical school. During III BCE, diatribe as a method of philosophical disputation replaced the (Platonic) dialogue. Whereas the dialogue addressed the philosophical colleague or student, the diatribe sought to engage the layman. The diatribe scorned technical language and used for its images and examples the vernacular language of the common people, even to the point of rudeness. Objections by a fictitious opponent, rhetorical questions, extreme examples, anecdotes, and striking quotations are typical of this style of popular oratory. What finally emerged as the "Cynic diatribe" was not purely Cynic; elements from other philosophical schools were also absorbed, and the diatribe style affected other circles, especially the Stoics. The popular philosopher Dion of Borysthenes, considered the founder of the diatribe style (III BCE), was strongly influenced by Platonic and Aristotelian philosophy. The first tangible evidence of this style appears in the fragments of an otherwise unknown philosopher named Teles, which have been preserved by Stobaeus. The diatribe also influenced literary style in the period of early Christianity, in writers such as Philo of Alexandria, Seneca, Musonius, Epictetus, Maximus of Tyre, Lucian, and, among Christian writers, especially Paul.

(b) Euhemerism

The Hellenistic period was not lacking in theories seeking to explain the origin of belief in gods. Some of these explanations derived from earlier allegorizing of Homer's writings and from Sophistic opinions. Plato's criticism of myth, which had identified the gods with astronomical powers, became especially significant in the Hellenistic and Roman period. An alternative explanation was offered by the Stoics, according to which the gods are identical with the forces that permeate the whole

Bibliography to §4.2b

K. Thraede, "Euhemerismus," *RAC* 6. 887–890.

H. F. van der Meer, *Euhemerus van Messene* (Amsterdam; Vrije Universiteit te Amsterdam, 1949).

cosmos. Human beings are intimately related to the gods because reason is the essence of their natures. Side by side with this pseudoscientific explanation, one finds the much more popular theory which views the gods as various classes of demons (§4.1a).

The theory about the origins of belief in the gods which was to find the widest reception in antiquity, though it was at the same time considered by many to be the epitome of atheism, is known as Euhemerism. Its founder, the writer Euhemerus of Messene (340–260 BCE), was widely disparaged as a notorious atheist. The Euhemeristic explanation of myth belongs to a tradition of interpretation of myth that began with Homer. The gods and their behavior, actions, and feelings came more and more to be understood in anthropomorphic terms. This interpretation of myth was rationalistic from the beginning. Shortly before Euhemerus, Hecataeus of Abdera (350–290 BCE) had appropriated Egyptian concepts, in which the gods of Egypt, partially identified with Greek gods, were seen as kings from primordial times. These kings had founded states, promulgated laws, and taught people everything that is necessary for civilization and that distinguishes human culture. Euhemerus drew upon Hecataeus, but went beyond him: in his utopian political romance, the Greek gods Ouranos, Kronos, and Zeus (with their wives Hestia, Rhea, and Hera) are depicted as primordial kings. The Greeks had spoken ever since Homer about the love affairs of the gods as if they were moral or immoral amorous adventures of human beings; but Euhemerus now wrote about the mythical battles of the gods against the Titans as if they were court intrigues and dynastic struggles in the families of kings and potentates. Zeus is described in the image of Alexander the Great: he marches through all countries from west to east, founding kingdoms and appointing his friends as rulers; he also gives laws and establishes cults for his own worship—a clear reflection of the ruler cult in the decades after Alexander.

Euhemerus may have done nothing more than draw the consequences from a long tradition of critical interpretation of myth; but it was he who finally dethroned the gods. They no longer ruled in those areas of experience which could not be controlled by human powers. Euhemerus reduced the gods to heroes; they were to be worshiped like heroes or like divine rulers. Such worship would not serve any other purpose than to secure their benefactions in the same way in which one would seek similar rewards through the observance of the ruler cult. The world which lay outside this limited political theology lost its divine parents and was handed over to the powers of the stars and to the demons. Astrology, demonology, and magical rites were only too eager to fill the place once held by the old belief in the gods.

(c) Astrology and Fate

Plato had already stated that the stars are divine beings. Perhaps even before Plato, the Pythagoreans had accepted similar astrological beliefs from the east. But such opinions were unusual in the tradition of Greek religious thought. The gods of Greece had nothing in common with the stars; worship of the sun was not practiced; and Helios, the sun god, was not personalized in the same way as the other gods. The notion that the stars, sun, moon, and planets were powerful deities which determine the fate of cities and nations, war and peace, the growth of the fruits of the field and the health and fertility of domestic animals has its origin in Mesopotamia. The horoscope for human individuals was found there for the first time at the end of v BCE, whereas the horoscope for a city or a nation is much older.

The Greeks began to learn about these astrological beliefs in IV BCE. Eudoxus of Cnidus and Theophrastus, Aristotle's student and successor, explicitly rejected such beliefs. But in the course of the following century, Babylonian beliefs in the power of the stars, together with advances in astronomical science, spread quickly in the Greek-speaking world of the eastern Mediterranean. Zeno, the founder of Stoic philosophy, seems to have been influenced by Babylonian astrology. Berossus, a Babylonian priest, gave an extensive description of astrology in his history of Babylon, which was written in Greek and dedicated to Antiochus I of Syria; these peculiar eastern concepts thus became accessible to the Greek reading public. As a consequence of these successful advances, astrology became so firmly established that the protest of Carneades, head of the Academy in II

Bibliography to §4.2c: Text

Grant, *Hellenistic Religions,* 60–63.

Bibliography to §4.2c: Studies

Erwin Pfeiffer, *Studien zum antiken Sternglauben* (Στοιχεῖα: Studien zur Geschichte des antiken Weltbildes und der griechischen Wissenschaft 11; Leipzig: Teubner, 1916).

Franz Cumont, *Astrology and Religion among the Greeks and Romans* (New York and London: Putnam's, 1912).

Franz Boll, Karl Bezold, and Wilhelm Gundel, *Sternglaube und Sterndeutung: Die Geschichte und das Wesen der Astrologie* (5th ed.; Darmstadt: Wissenschaftliche Buchgesellschaft, 1966).

O. Neugebauer and H. B. van Hoesen, *Greek Horoscopes* (MAPS 48; Philadelphia: American Philosophical Society, 1959).

Hans Georg Gundel, *Weltbild und Astrologie in den griechischen Zauberpapyri* (München: Beck, 1968).

Franz Boll, "Der Sternglaube in seiner historischen Entwicklung," in: idem, *Kleine Schriften zur Sternkunde des Altertums* (ed. V. Stegemann; Leipzig: Koehler und Amelang, 1950).

BCE, came too late, and the Stoic Panaetius sought in vain to liberate his philosophical tradition from entanglement with astrology. The new belief in the stars could no longer be rooted out.

The victory was not won by Babylonian astrology alone, but in concert with its allies, Greek science and the new philosophical religion of Hellenism. Alexandria was, of course, the city in which Greek science made its most spectacular advances, and astronomy was the science in which Greek erudition celebrated its greatest triumphs. Nevertheless Alexandria was also the birthplace of systematic and scientific astrological endeavors. New systems for the determination of astrological fate were developed with the aid of the most modern insights and the most advanced mathematical methods because the scientific discoveries of the Hellenistic astronomers were far superior to those of their Babylonian predecessors. It seems that there was no awareness of a possible conflict between astronomy and astrology. The leading ancient astronomer, Hipparchus of Nicaea (§3.3b), who also worked in Alexandria for a brief period during ii BCE, was apparently firmly persuaded of the truth of astrological ideas. Mathematics and mysticism were by no means mutually exclusive. The second century also produced the best-known handbook of astrology, under the pseudonyms "Nechepso and Petosiris," and a similar work claiming to be written by Hermes Trismegistus, a name which would become significant later as the authority for Hermetic literature (§6.5f). These works, of course, have no relation to Egyptian traditions; they are books which Greek scientists wrote on the basis of Babylonian astrology.

Astrology, appearing from the beginning as a consistent scientific system, was successful because it provided the framework for a new philosophico-religious interpretation of the world. The old Greek religion was a religion of city gods, and traditional beliefs could survive in this form only so long as those gods were acknowledged as effective patrons and protectors of their cities. The mobility of the population, the widening of geographical horizons, and the universalization of economics, politics, and science, however, could no longer be satisfied with "local" gods. Even though the rulers of the new Hellenistic kingdoms used the ancient city cults in the service of their more universal policies, this did not result in a new understanding of the old gods as universal deities (the religion of Isis and Sarapis is no proof to the contrary; see §4.4a). Instead, it would be philosophy which pointed in new directions.

Stoicism, the most important universalistic philosophy, quite appropriately made recourse to the universally valid astrological concepts in formulating its cosmology. Astrology provided the framework in which the old gods could make their reappearance in the garments of universal power. Zeus, once the ruler on Mount Olympus, was transformed into the planet "Jupiter," the radiant lord of heaven, as soon as he was identified with the Babylonian healer god Marduk and rediscovered as the brightest planet. Thus Aphrodite became "Venus" (= Ishtar), Ares was "Mars" (= Nergal, the Babylonian god of death), Kronos was "Saturn" (= Ninurtu, the Babylonian god of war), and Hermes became "Mercury" (= Nebo, the Babylonian god of wisdom). The days of the week were now determined by these five planets and the sun and the moon. That this was a product of the Greek spirit is demonstrated by the dominant position of the sun: this agrees with the opinion of advanced Greek science, whereas in Babylon the moon was a more significant power of fate. This universalization of the Greek gods, which, contrary to the ancient Greek tradition, gave the sun a central place, was the basis for the later Roman development which made the "Invincible Sun" (*Sol invictus*) the most powerful symbol of paganism in its fight against Christianity. It was the philosopher Posidonius who declared that the sun as pure fire was also the origin of all reason and all "spirits," and that ultimately all power derived from the sun. The popularization of such ideas, however, took place during the Roman period.

The astrological world view, with its concepts of universal law and power, ably provided an image of the new, larger world in which human beings had to learn to live, and gave some idea of the powers with which they had to reckon. But this world view also had a negative side, which conjured up a ghost which could not be exorcised: *heimarmenē*. The term is derived from the Greek word μείρομαι ("to receive one's portion") which is also the root of the Homeric term μοῖρα ("lot" or "fate"). Classical tragedy had instead spoken about *anankē*, the incalculable "necessity." *Anankē* was the powerful mystery of human life which appeared in love, guilt, calamity, and death in order to demand its due. Aristotle had defined *anankē* as "that which is contrary to the movement of free choice" (*Metaphysics* 4.5; p. 1015a, 20ff.). But "necessity" does not render human life meaningless or absurd; it only prevents human beings from calculating their lives in advance. Thus it provides the opportunity for true experiences of life, which are full of mystery; it demands that one remain true to one's humanity, without its revealing whether success or despair will determine the end.

In Hellenism, however, Heimarmene (sometimes also called *anankē*) became a power which predetermined human life like a mathematical calculation. Heimarmene was the highest god, with final power over everything, the fate written in the stars and running its course as inevitably as the heavenly courses themselves. There is a characteristic description of Babylonian astrology and of the concept of Heimarmene in Philo of Alexandria (*Migr. Abr.* 179):

These men imagined that the visible universe [i.e., the earth and the stars] was the only thing which existed and that it was either itself god or contained god in itself as the soul of the universe. And they made fate [*heimarmenē*] and necessity [*anankē*] into gods, thus filling human life with much impiety; because they teach that outside of the visible phenomena [of the cosmos] there is no agent causative of anything whatsoever, but the sun and moon and the other bodies of heaven determine by their circuits the good as well as its opposite for every being.

There is no room for individual freedom, because the astrological view of the world delivers every human being into the hands of fate. The powers and relationships of the social structures of human life were not even discussed as a possible realm of freedom. Human beings had been taken out of their inherited social structures, and Hellenistic philosophy was unable to determine either the realm of human freedom or moral responsibility with respect to their political and social dimensions. The new view of the world under the sign of Heimarmene did not reckon with political structures, but only with sidereal and physical laws. Coins of the emperors and military standards later exhibited astrological symbols, thus persuading everyone that even the ruling political power was subject to the law of the stars. The direct confrontation of the human individual with the sidereal powers, which were unchangeable and merciless though at least calculable, favored the spreading of astrological determinism. Because one had to contend with powers of material and physical character, magic that could influence such powers invaded all realms of life. One needed a magician to be successful in a love affair, one chose the most opportune hour for a banquet according to an astrological handbook, and one made important political decisions only after consulting an astrologer. It was futile to argue with fate, but at least one could arrange one's plans accordingly. As the belief in astrology and Heimarmene reached its climax only in the Roman period, the new religions of salvation were compelled to come to terms with it.

(d) Orphism and Concepts of the Afterlife

The origins of Orphism and the figure of the Thracian singer Orpheus, whose life his followers dated in the time before Homer, remain uncertain and enigmatic. Orphism becomes clearly visible for the first time in the context of the production of mythical writings in the archaic period of Greece. Following the example of the mythical poems of Hesiod, Greek authors produced a number of theogonies in poetic language. All these works were written between 600 and 500 BCE. They were by no means homogenous, and they appropriated large amounts of oriental mythical traditions, as Hesiod had already done earlier. As far as Hesiod is concerned, the close relationship of his *Theogony* to Anatolian myths about the god Kumarbi and the monster Ullikummi (preserved through Hittite texts) and with the Babylonian creation myth *Enuma Elish* (1500 BCE) is clearly evident. In the later period, these myths were made known once more in the Greek world, the latter through the Babylonian priest Berossus (III BCE), the former through the Phoenician Philo of Byblus (46–141 CE). These cases of the appropriation of oriental mythic material are those clearly attested in literary works, but other, similar contacts with the east cannot be excluded. Such contacts seem to have inspired the mythic poetry of the VI BCE, and they were renewed in the Hellenistic period.

Orphic circles apparently had a considerable share in such mythopoeism, though we should not overestimate their role. Several theogonies of VI BCE were Orphic works. At least that early there must have been Orphic conventicles, which largely included members of the lower classes. Orphic priests offered religiously edifying books for sale and invited others to participate in the Orphic rites ("mysteries"). Orphic myths and Orphic mysticism also seem to have had considerable influence upon the development of the Greek mysteries (§4.3e, f). Fully established mysteries are first attested for III BCE. The heartland of Orphism was southern Italy, the ancient seat of the Pythagorean school (which, however, no longer existed in the early Hellenistic period; see §6.5d). Perhaps the remnants of the Pythagorean sect were absorbed into Orphic circles. Orphic hymns are also attested for the eastern Greek world. The older Orphic theogonies lived on in these hymns during the Hellenistic period.

The tendency toward monotheism is characteristic for the theology of

Bibliography to §4.2d: Texts

Apostolos N. Athanassakis (ed.), *The Orphic Hymns* (SBLTT 12; Missoula: Scholars Press, 1977).

Grant, *Hellenistic Religions*, 105–11.

Bibliography to §4.2d: Studies

W. K. C. Guthrie, *Orpheus and Greek Religion: A Study of the Orphic Movement* (2d ed.; London: Methuen, 1952).

Martin P. Nilsson, "Early Orphism and Kindred Religious Movements," *HTR* 28 (1935) 181–230.

Nock, "Orphism or Popular Philosophy?" in: idem, *Essays,* 1. 503–15.

Vittorio D. Macchioro, *From Orpheus to Paul: A History of Orphism* (New York: Holt, 1930).

Lewis Richard Farnell, *Greek Hero Cults and Ideas of Immortality* (Oxford: Clarendon, 1921).

Ernst Maass, *Orpheus: Untersuchungen zur griechischen, römischen, altchristlichen Jenseitsdichtung und Religion* (München: Beck, 1895; reprint: Aalen: Scientia Verlag, 1974).

Orphism. The formula "there is *one* god," which appeared in a famous quotation from Xenophanes, was very widespread in the later centuries and appears in an Orphic text from III BCE. On the other hand, the polytheistic speculations of the older Orphic theogonies were maintained in a modified form. Kronos occupies the first position, as he comes into being out of the primordial principles, water and mud. Kronos creates Aither and Chaos, and in them the world egg, out of which rises Phanes, the typically Orphic creator god. Phanes is a winged androgynous figure with animal heads, who is sometimes identified with Dionysus and is called Protogonos. Other divine entities come into being in the following course of creation; some of these are identified with traditional deities, others are designated as powers like Heimarmene and Ananke. The question whether these Orphic myths directly influenced gnostic mythology, or whether the latter derived from an analogous appropriation of oriental myths, deserves further investigation.

Orphism had its most profound influence through its doctrine of the transmigration of souls and through its conceptions of the underworld and of punishment after death, which were developed in close connection with popular beliefs. The common opinion of the Hellenistic period was that after death the souls would find themselves in a shadow life, in which they would have no true consciousness. At the same time, various ancient beliefs lived on with respect to the cult of the dead, to rites of burial, and to magical practices, several of which came to a new flowering in late antiquity. Meals for the dead were a widespread custom, which was continued in the Christian meals at the graves of martyrs. The belief is closely associated that the dead, if they had received a good lot, would be able to enjoy an everlasting banquet of food and wine. It was also customary to bring food and wine repeatedly for the dead, to be poured out over the grave or into pipes stuck into the ground. Curse tablets were laid upon the grave, and the dead person was thus charged to carry out the curse. It was assumed that the souls of persons who had died a violent death, or were left unburied, were still haunting the neighborhood of their corpses: through magic they could be summoned and made serviceable. Cases of necromancy are also reported. Sometimes one would speak about the sad fate of the souls after death as drinking from the well of forgetting (*lēthē*). This Hellenistic concept is new as compared to the classical equivalent, which knew about the "House of Lethe," to which the drinking from the well of remembrance (*mnēmosynē*) also belonged. Whoever drank from it was transferred to live among the gods and heroes. It seems that it was particularly the Orphics who used this classical concept. They put small gold sheets into the graves, with inscriptions admonishing the dead person to avoid the well of Lethe and to drink from the well of Mnemosyne.

All this mirrors an increasingly widespread belief that the souls of the dead would live on in order to receive punishment for their evil deeds or to go to a place of lasting bliss and joy, or even to become a hero and commune with the gods. Funerary inscriptions, to be sure, only rarely give evidence for such beliefs: we find only meaningless clichés in most instances. Such belief is more clearly present in the vase paintings from southern Italy, in the wall paintings of Macedonian tombs with pictures of the judges of the dead, and, continuing into the Roman period, in the numerous buildings and donations which promote and maintain the cult of heroized dead people. The teachings of the Orphics, and later of the Neopythagoreans, were apparently the catalysts for the formation and expansion of such belief in immortality.

Conceptions of the underworld are closely related. In spite of the astrological world view, the Orphics kept to their old conception of a place of punishment in the depths of the earth (Tartarus) and of the fields of bliss in the far west. This was also the belief which lived on among most of the common people. Occasional attempts to adjust such beliefs to the more modern astrological world view, which transferred the place of punishment to the southernmost sky on the other side of the earth, never found general acceptance. In agreement with the original Orphic doctrine, the punishment of souls was believed to take place in the interior of the earth. This doctrine is the foundation of the descriptions of hell which were perhaps widespread already in the Hellenistic period and are abundantly attested in the Roman period among pagans (Virgil, Plutarch, Lucian), Jews (1 Enoch), and Christians (Apocalypse of Peter, Acts of Thomas). Plato had been the first to use the Orphic doctrine of punishment in the afterlife in the context of a discussion of justice and retribution. It is thus a thoroughly Greek phenomenon when in ii CE the pagan mocker Lucian competes with Christian preachers in highly gruesome descriptions of punishment in hell. Both, of course, also demonstrate that those centuries were unable to establish the idea of justice in the political order, and, thus, had to rely almost completely on the concept of just reward and punishment for the individual in the afterlife. It is for this reason that parts of an older mythical view of the world were preserved, regardless of advances toward more adequate scientific insights. The idea of justice could not be abandoned. There was no place for it in the scientific view of the world, which was materialistic; the world view of astrology could speak about powers and forces, but it was dominated by the concept of fate. Therefore, there was no choice but to cling to the old mythic descriptions of hellfire and punishment, which provided an asylum for the idea of justice—though only in a gruesome fashion.

Gilded Bronze Crater from Derveni (Macedonia)
This large crater from the early Hellenistic period was
used as a funerary urn. It shows Dionysus and Ariadne
and various scenes with Maenads and Satyrs (III B.C.E).

3. The Development of Greek Religion

(a) "Syncretism"

The Hellenistic period has been called the time of syncretism. It is necessary, however, to clarify the meaning of this term. Recourse to the original meaning of the word yields little: "syncretism" (συγκρητισμός) was first used to designate a federation of Cretan cities which had earlier lived in enmity with each other. In modern times the term was misunderstood as a derivative of the Greek verb κεράννυμι "to mix" and thus was used to describe the "mixing" of religions, especially Greek and oriental religions. "Mixture," however, is a misleading description of the encounter of these two religious traditions and its result. That encounter began with the increased mobility of the population at the beginning of the Hellenistic period, with the result that Greeks and barbarians came to live in much closer proximity with each other. The immediate consequence was a religious pluralism in which Greeks and other peoples lived side by side, all with their own religious traditions. Actual mixture of religions occurred only gradually. The mere mixing of populations apparently did not cause religious syncretism. The real causes were spiritual and psychological because the dominant position of the Greeks necessarily led to an expansion of Greek culture. The fascination of the Greek mind with everything new and foreign nevertheless led to a reception of oriental elements, especially in the religious realm. This resulted in a number of quite different developments, all in their own way syncretistic phenomena.

Originally the religions of the Greeks as well as of oriental peoples were local cults, firmly established as religions of the state, city, or people. None

Bibliography to §4.3

Nilsson, *Griechische Religion* 2.

Martin P. Nilsson, *Greek Piety* (Oxford: Clarendon, 1948).

B. C. Dietrich, *The Origins of Greek Religion* (Berlin and New York: De Gruyter, 1974).

Ulrich von Wilamowitz-Möllendorf, *Der Glaube der Hellenen* (Berlin: Weidmannsche Buchhandlung, 1931–32; reprint: Darmstadt: Wissenschaftliche Buchgesellschaft, 1955).

A. J. Festugière, *Personal Religion among the Greeks* (Sather Classical Lectures 26; Berkeley and Los Angeles: University of California, 1954).

Walter F. Otto, *Die Götter Griechenlands: Das Bild des Göttlichen im Spiegel des griechischen Geistes* (3d ed.; Frankfurt/Main: Schulte-Bulmke, 1947).

Bibliography to §4.3a

Nock, "ΣΥΝΝΑΟΣ ΘΕΟΣ," in: idem, *Essays*, 1. 202–51.

Richard Reitzenstein and Hans Heinrich Schaeder, *Studien zum antiken Synkretismus* (Leipzig and Berlin: Teubner, 1926).

of these cults would ever claim to be a world religion since the belief that deities were bound to particular holy places was still very much alive. But this view was changing, due both to the influence of philosophy and the new intellectual enlightenment, and to the mobility of the population. Greek gods were brought to the east to be the gods of the new Greek cities. As the kings sought to maintain and strengthen the Greek element in their countries, this development was encouraged. On the other hand, eastern deities and their cults were brought to the west by slaves, merchants, sailors, and soldiers. Such immigrants established these gods at first through the founding of religious associations which gave their ancient gods recognition and a new home. In this way the Greeks who went east founded such sanctuaries as the famous temple of Apollo in Daphne near Antioch. Even before this, however, eastern gods became established in the west; for example, the slaves from Asia who worked in the Lavrian mines in Attica had already brought the Asian god Men to Greece in pre-Hellenistic times. Thus, such a transplantation of deities was not really something new, and there is no reason to call it syncretistic. In the centuries prior to this period, the Thracian Dionysus and the Asian Great Mother had been brought to Greece and were officially recognized by most Greek cities. Some other elements, then, must be present in the transplantation of a cult in order to make it a syncretistic process.

One such element is the identification or combination of deities of different origins, although even this was nothing new in the history of Greek religion. Artemis of the Ephesians was an Asian fertility goddess whose many-breasted cult statue has little in common with the Greek Artemis. Many other examples of a similar syncretism from an earlier period could be cited. But the Hellenistic period witnessed a veritable explosion of such combinations of different deities, a process which would begin with the adoption of a Greek name for the newly imported deity. Thus cultic associations of foreign gods with Greek names were established in Greek-speaking areas. On Delos, for example, one finds an association of merchants and shipowners from Berytus (Beirut) in Syria who call themselves Poseidoniasts; here Poseidon is certainly the Greek designation of a Phoenician sea god. Greek gods were also associated with eastern deities: from the island of Cos there is evidence for an association of Zeus and (the Syrian) Astarte. Finally, Greek gods would receive oriental surnames; this was particuary frequent in the case of Zeus, and usually is the sign of the presence of an oriental cult which had been officially recognized by a Hellenistic king (e.g., Zeus Keraunius, Zeus Sabazius). Ethnography and philosophy had already prepared this identification of Greek and oriental deities. But Greek and Roman gods were also identified quite early (Zeus = Jupiter, Aphrodite = Venus, and so on). As a result, the Roman gods assumed features that Greek beliefs and mythology had ascribed to them, although they had originally been divinities of different types.

Another important factor in the syncretistic process was the mutual permeation of various elements of the different religions and cultures. Here one can observe the following phenomena: first, oriental religions were hellenized. The rites and cultic practices of the oriental deities were usually preserved, but their myths and cult legends were translated into the Greek language, which also supplied Greek ideas and concepts along with the linguistic expressions. Second, concepts growing out of the general Hellenistic religious experience invaded all religions, whether of Greek or oriental origin (e.g., the notion of the one god of heaven who rules over the all); or elements of the new world view were accepted everywhere (e.g., astrology, popular Platonism, demonology, belief in miracles, and an emphasis upon the salvation of the individual human being). Third, inherited ancient concepts that had been separated from original local tradition had to be reinterpreted to fit the new world culture. Many rites had originally been connected with the fertility of the land. Once such cults migrated into the cities, their peculiar rites required explanations, which were often presented in the framework of a spiritualized understanding of salvation. In this context in particular, the popularization of the enlightenment, criticism of myth, and Stoic theology became very effective because their allegorical interpretation of myths, rites, and customs as spiritual and moral statements of universal significance had already prepared the way.

A final syncretistic phenomenon was the actual creation of a new religion out of Greek and non-Greek elements of older religions. This much was clearly the case in the formation of the cult of Sarapis (§4.4a), but this example only appears to be typical, since syncretism is in its very essence not the result of artificial manipulations, but a process of historical development. It is a response to the encounter of two opposing historical forces: first, the constraints which arise from inherited traditions, dignified by a long history; and second, the need to enter into discourse with a new culture and its spirit. The artificial creation of a new religion seeks to harmonize these opposing forces and hence avoids any creative conflict. Indeed, the history of the Sarapis cult in the following centuries demonstrates that it still needed to go through the process of syncretistic development. No single religion of the Hellenistic and Roman period was spared. Christianity became deeply enmeshed in the syncretistic process, and this may very well have been its particular strength. Christianity began as a Jewish sect with missionary ambitions, but it did not simply arise out of Judaism, nor directly out of the ministry of Jesus. On the basis of these beginnings, however, Christianity, probably more than the other religions of its time, was able to adapt itself to a variety of cultural and religious currents and to appropriate numerous foreign elements until it was ready to succeed as a world religion—thoroughly syncretistic in every way.

(b) The Old Gods and Their Cults

At the beginning of the Hellenistic period the old established cults were generally thought to be continuing with undiminished strength, and it contributed to their final demise that this fiction was maintained until late antiquity. Not only the old Greek cultic places, but also the cults of the Asian, Syrian, and Egyptian gods which were firmly rooted in their local traditions, enjoyed recognition among large parts of the local populations. The cults could also count on the support and protection of the new rulers, who made no deliberate attempts to Hellenize oriental cults. Insofar as such Hellenization took place, the initiative usually came from the cults' actual followers, and only in exceptional cases from the kings. To be sure, the worship of these deities in Greece was no longer naively taken as a matter of course, thanks to the criticism of myth during the classical period. From the time of Alexander the Great, the gods of the once independent cities and states had also lost any political significance in foreign affairs. The political power of the central sanctuaries of the political leagues (amphictyonies) had come to an end in the west as well as in the east. The superpower politics of the oriental empires from the time of the Assyrians to the Persians had long since led to the result that, for example, the Yahweh sanctuary of the Israelite amphictyony was first transformed into a royal sanctuary in Jerusalem and later, under priestly leadership, into the reorganized cult of a client state of no political significance. The numerous temple states of Syria and Asia Minor, often with large estates, owed their existence to similar developments. Only rarely was such a state able to achieve political independence; in such a case, the existing cult would then assume new political functions. The well known history of the Jewish temple state demonstrates this well. But it also exemplifies that it was impossible to reverse the direction of religious developments which

Bibliography to §4.3b: Texts

Grant, *Hellenistic Religions,* 3–32.

Franciszek Sokolowski, *Lois sacrées des cités grecques* (Paris: Boccard, 1969).

Bibliography to §4.3b: Studies

Lewis Richard Farnell, *The Cults of the Greek States* (Oxford: Clarendon, 1896–1907).

W. K. C. Guthrie, *The Greeks and Their Gods* (London: Methuen, 1950; Boston: Beacon, 1951).

Martin P. Nilsson, *Greek Popular Religion* (LHR NS 1; New York: Columbia University, 1940).

had taken place in the meantime and to reestablish the traditional religion as a state cult. The defenders of the Jewish tradition who had fought for political and religious freedom seceded from the temple cult at the very moment when it regained its old position as the state cult of Israel (§5.1c, d), and large portions of diaspora Judaism maintained only formal ties with the temple in Jerusalem.

This loss of function as a state religion demanded religious and liturgical reforms, and such reforms of the cults of the old gods were frequent in the early Hellenistic period. Typical features appear in the reform of the Yahweh cult in Jerusalem under Nehemiah and Ezra; it can, therefore, serve as an example, even though these events actually took place before the Hellenistic period. Attempts to adjust to the situation of a small client state had been made in the east earlier than in the Greek countries. It appears that two problems required special attention: first, the regulation and sanctioning of religious rites needed a new basis in order to retain continuity with very ancient tradition, since it was now impossible to appeal to the more recent past in which the temple had been a royal sanctuary imitating the royal cults of the great empires. Second, the sacral revenues needed to be established, since the changed political situation required new regulations to determine the relationship of public revenue to the income of the temple. Once largely independent temples could no longer count on a regular income, neither could they rely on regular payments from the government. On the other hand, even cities and petty states were quite capable of extorting rather large sums of money from a well-functioning temple cult. Nor did the kings of the Hellenistic empires consider it beneath their dignity to avail themselves of the opportunity to plunder a temple treasury (Antiochus III was slain when he attempted to rob a temple). Along these lines, then, the cultic law which Ezra introduced (the Priestly Codex) gives first place to describing the procedures to be followed in the temple sacrifices, and painstakingly detailed rules and regulations for participating in certain rites and religious festivals. Ezra's law also pays attention to the fact that the Jewish authorities in Jerusalem did not have the right to collect taxes and duties (see Ezra 4:13, 20; 7:24). The Persian king donated some capital for new equipment in the temple (Ezra 7:15ff.), and the heads of the families pledged large sums of money (Ezra 2:68f.; cf. Neh 5:14ff.; 7:70ff.). But such steps could not serve as a lasting financial basis for the maintenance of the temple cult. Regular income was therefore fixed in the form of payment for ritual services, first fruits, tithes, and revenue from the temple estates; officials were appointed whose special duty was to collect these funds (Neh 12:44). It was also determined with great precision which persons should benefit from these revenues (Neh 11:19ff.; 12:1ff.).

It is striking to find in the reforms of many Greek temples at the beginning of the Hellenistic period the same recourse to ancient laws in the regulations for the sacrificial procedures and in the fixing of calendars for festivals and sacrifices (*fasti*). Special attention is also given to securing the financial base for the various activities of the temple. The reforms of Lycurgus, who was the secretary for financial and cultic affairs in the city of Athens from 338–326 BCE, are well known. He initiated financial reforms not only for the temples within Athens, but in addition for other sanctuaries under its control, such as the temple of the healer Amphiaraus in Oropus and the mystery sanctuary at Eleusis; new equipment was bought and festivals were reorganized. Similar reforms are known in other Greek cities. New rules were also issued for ritual purity and fasts during the preparation of sacrifices, entering of temples, and participation in festivals.

Renewed activity in the building of temples also demonstrates that the old cults of the Greek gods continued to flourish in the Hellenistic period. In addition to some major architectural projects in Greece, several monumental building programs were initiated in Asia Minor and on the Greek islands, where the economic situation was better than in Greece itself. The temple of the Ephesian Artemis was completely rebuilt, and also the Apollo temple in Didyma, both of which had immense proportions; in Pergamum the huge altar of Zeus was built; on the island of Cos the Asclepieium was redesigned as a large complex erected on four terraces— to give only a few characteristic examples. In addition, building activities were financed by the Hellenistic kings, such as the large temple of Zeus Olympius in Athens, for which building activities were resumed, after an interval of more than four hundred years, on the basis of donations from the Syrian king Antiochus IV Epiphanes. The Roman emperors resumed this policy; thus, from I BCE, impressive sanctuaries of the old gods were again constructed in new splendor, not only in the Greek countries, but also elsewhere, such as the great temple of Jupiter in Baalbek (Lebanon). The magnificent reconstruction of the temple in Jerusalem by Herod the Great also witnesses to this interest in the cult of the old gods.

The continuing life and vitality of the old cults are also seen in the numerous festivals and games which were multiplied and reorganized in this time. The occasions for such festivals were numerous: the annual celebration of the anniversary of a sanctuary's dedication (cf. the Christian celebrations of the dedication of a church), the honoring of a king or the emperor, or the resumption of an old religious tradition which had fallen into disuse. These festivals may have lacked religious depth and pious seriousness, but they nevertheless demonstrate the continuing acceptance of the old cults by large portions of the population. Whenever there was a special procession, or the anniversary of a temple dedication with sacrificial meals and special markets (for these were part of such celebrations, as were a school vacation for children and a free day for slaves), visitors would come both from the surrounding country and at times from far away. Popular piety, fun for the masses, religious devotion expressed in hymns and prayers, and political propaganda were insepa- rably mixed at such occasions, whether it was the festival of Apollo of Didyma in Miletus or the Feast of Tabernacles in Jerusalem.

The Roman imperial period brought some basic changes. Augustus began an era of imperial support for the Greek cults which reached its climax under the philhellene emperor Hadrian. But there should be no doubt that this period also reflects a decline for the old religions. The number of sacral inscriptions drastically decreases during the Roman period. Especially in Athens, the city in which the most magnificent cultic buildings were erected, the visible presence of splendid temples did little but create the impression that this city was only a museum of classical greatness. The more the old traditions received support and were sub- sidized by the government, the more the cultic activities of the temples were estranged from the religious consciousness of the majority of the population. Not much was changed by the occasional reforms and the increasing acceptance of oriental rites and concepts (i.e., the stronger syncretistic development of the old cults) nor by the introduction of rites borrowed from the mysteries. Among these innovations was the introduc- tion of lamps, which were customary in oriental cults, to take the place of the traditional Greek torches, first as votive offerings, later also as cultic implements. The burning of incense was introduced everywhere as a special form of sacrifice. Following the example of Egyptian and other oriental cults, daily worship became customary in the Greek cults, espe- cially in the much visited temples and healing sanctuaries, such as those of Asclepius. In this context, blood sacrifices were restricted to special festive occasions and had almost completely disappeared from the daily service and liturgy; by the beginning of the Roman period, hymns, prayers, incense, and lamps came to constitute the daily ritual. On special occa- sions sermons were preached. Thus, in its last phase, the cult of the old gods of Greece was not much different from the forms of worship that had developed in Judaism (in the diaspora synagogue) and in Christianity.

There are only three areas in which the early Roman imperial period cannot be characterized as a time of decline for the worship of the old gods. In the rural areas the cults of the established local deities continued with their traditional strength; the sanctuaries of the healing deities, especially Asclepius, reached the height of their popularity only in the first and second Christian centuries; and those Greek gods which had "mysteries," in particular Demeter and Dionysus, continued to receive popular support. Side by side with the new deities from the east, whose worship had spread from the beginning of the Hellenistic period—Sarapis and Isis, the Great Mother and Attis, Mithras and Sol Invictus, Judaism and Christianity—three Greek gods thus remained among the most widely worshiped deities: Asclepius, Dionysius, and Demeter.

(c) The Oracles

The political significance of the oracles, which were mostly sanctuaries of Apollo, diminished in the Hellenistic period. Delphi alone was able to maintain some of its political influence until the beginning of Roman rule in Greece. In Asia Minor, the oracle of Apollo at Didyma occasionally assumed a certain significance. In general, however, the role of these oracles was limited to the area of sacral regulations. One would inquire from oracles about the proper time for religious festivals, about votive offerings, donations, and all sorts of other matters which were significant in those communities specifically under the jurisdiction of the oracle. Oracles also played a role as guarantors of legal transactions, as is demonstrated by the numerous documents about the manumission of slaves which were publicly exhibited in inscriptions at Delphi.

Although there was little room in the Hellenistic period for a political role for the oracles, a different kind of prophecy developed to new heights of significance: the Sibyl. In their ancient form, the Sibylline oracles were prophetic women who resided in several places and who would utter ecstatic predictions, mostly of doom, whether or not any prophecy had been requested. (The oracle sanctuaries, on the other hand, usually required a specific request, and their answers were given only at predetermined times.) In the later period, "Sibylline oracles" usually meant prophecies found in books that were published and circulated under the name of one of the famous ancient Sibyls (as, e.g., the Sibyl of Erythrai in Asia Minor and the Sibyl of Cumae in Italy). Such books usually pred-

Bibliography to §4.3c: Texts
Grant, *Hellenistic Religions,* 33–43.

Bibliography to §4.3c: Studies
Peter Hoyle, *Delphi* (London: Cassell, 1967).
H. W. Parke and D. E. W. Wormell, *The Delphic Oracle* (2 vols.; Oxford: Blackwell, 1956).
Georges Roux, *Delphes: Son oracle et ses deux* (Paris: Les Belles Lettres, 1976).
Idem, *Delphes au IIe et au Ier siècle depuis l'abaissement de l'Étolie jusqu'à le paix romaine, 191–31 av. J.-C.* (Paris: Boccard, 1936).
H. W. Parker, *The Oracles of Zeus: Dodona, Olympia, Ammon* (Cambridge, MA: Harvard University, 1967).

icted a fatal turn in the history of the world and of humankind. In general, the Sibylline books maintained a negative and critical position over against the dominant Greek and Roman culture. The Sibylline books which are still preserved, though written in Greek, thus reflect the critical undercurrent of the anti-Greek and anti-Roman sentiments of the eastern countries, and also include many traditions of oriental origin. Therefore, in addition to the Greek Sibyls, a so-called Chaldaean (= Babylonian) Sibyl also claimed authority. Jews and Christians appropriated such books and used this form of prophecy to propagate their own apocalyptic predictions of doom, as well as their image of a better world to come, all in the dress of an established Greek genre of religious literature.

In the beginning of the Roman period, the oracles experienced an increased popularity, which led to renewed prosperity for several of the older oracle sanctuaries. Delphi, to be sure, became more and more a mere tourist center; Plutarch complains that in Delphi many requests for oracles were motivated by frivolity, curiosity, or ignoble and selfish interests. In general, however, the success of an oracle was dependent to a large degree upon its ability to respond to the demands and tastes of its time. One of the handicaps of Delphi was its awareness of its dignified ancient tradition. The only oracle which is known to have adapted itself to the demands of a new time, both in its formal manipulations, and in its theological attitude, is the oracle of Apollo in Claros (near Colophon, between Smyrna and Ephesus in Asia Minor). Several traditions indicate that Claros appropriated the monotheistic concepts of the philosophers along with other more modern ideas, that it was not opposed to syncretism—according to an oracle from Claros, IAO (= Yahweh?) is the highest god—and that it initiated visiting delegations or their leaders into a mystery cult. Such innovations, even more than the fact that some of Claros' published predictions have been found to be correct, seem to have been the primary basis for Claros' popularity throughout the Greco-Roman world. Not only from all of Asia Minor, but also from Macedonia, Dalmatia, Sardinia, and as far away as Britain, requests were sent to Claros, as numerous inscriptions demonstrate.

Other oracles tried to meet the demands of the beliefs in mysteries and miracles halfway by adapting their procedures for oracular requests. Complicated rites of initiation are known from the Roman period for the oracle of the ancient chthonic deity Trophonius near Lebadeia in Boeotia. After several days of purification, the sacrifice of a ram, drinking from the well of forgetting and remembering (in order to forget the past and remember what was to be experienced in the adyton), the client descended into the adyton, the innermost cave sanctuary. The initiate was dragged down into the cave through a small opening, through which he was to be pushed out afterwards; then he was set upon the throne of remembrance, and priests would question him about his experience. Everything that the initiate reported was recorded and interpreted by the priests. It seems that similar procedures were also used in other oracles, since adytons have been found in several temples of Apollo. The report of Lucian of Samosata tells us more about the manipulations of the prophet Alexander of Abonuteichus, who established in his oracle sanctuary a flourishing business with prophecies, healings, and advice in religious guise. Whoever wanted could also be initiated into a mystery cult. The story of Alexander makes clear that, in II CE, there was little interest in oracles for the serious concerns of the political affairs of states and cities; rather, people wanted to secure the aid of supernatural powers for their personal endeavors. Alexander was successful because there were enough people around who were willing to entrust their needs and anxieties to any promising institution or person claiming to control divine and otherworldly powers. The oracles of the Roman imperial period, insofar as they were now or again functioning successfully, were as different from the ancient oracles as the Θεῖος Ἀνήρ, the "divine man," differed from the Cynic or Stoic wandering philosopher of previous centuries. What mattered was a representation of divine power on the religious market in order to satisfy the desires and needs of human beings who no longer had a secure home in this world. Like the "divine man," the oracles also moved closer to magic and occultism.

(d) Asclepius

The cult of Asclepius had its origin in Thessaly, where he was a local healing deity (like, e.g., Amphiaraus, whose sanctuary was situated in Oropos near Athens). But the center for the expansion of the cult of Asclepius, a growth which began in early V BCE, came to be Epidaurus, in the Peloponnesus. It was from Epidaurus that many new sanctuaries of Asclepius were founded. Among these were the Asclepius sanctuary in Athens, on the south slope of the Acropolis, and the Asclepieium in Pergamum, which achieved great fame in the Roman period. Perhaps we

Bibliography to §4.3d: Texts

E. J. and L. Edelstein, *Asclepius: A Collection and Interpretation of the Testimonies* (2 vols.; Baltimore: Johns Hopkins, 1945).
Grant, *Hellenistic Religions,* 49–59.

Bibliography to §4.3d: Studies

Rudolf Herzog, *Die Wunderheilungen von Epidauros: Ein Beitrag zur Geschichte der Medizin und der Religion* (Leipzig: Dieterich, 1931).
Lewis R. Farnell, *Greek Hero Cults and Ideas of Immortality* (Oxford: Clarendon, 1921).

should also include the sanctuary in Cos, the home of Hippocrates, unless this Asclepieium was founded directly by the city of Tricca in Thessaly in VI BCE. There is evidence for more than three hundred Asclepius sanctuaries, striking proof for the successful and systematic propaganda of Epidaurus and other leading Asclepieia. There is no question that the great expansion of this cult during the Hellenistic and Roman periods was not accidental, but rather the result of methodical propaganda aided, no doubt, by other favorable circumstances rooted in the general religious mood of the time.

It is difficult to overestimate the significance of the Asclepius sanctuaries for the religious expectations of broad segments of the population. Many factors contributed to their popularity. First of all, the Asclepieia continued the old religious tradition of local healing deities, to whom one brought sacrifices either regularly or on special occasions, and who were consulted by people in the event of sickness or calamity. Another element was the claim by some of these temples that they had accomplished some spectacular healings; records of such cures, originally preserved on wooden votive tablets, were later "published" in the form of stone inscriptions. The larger sanctuaries employed aretalogists to tell the great deeds of the god on special occasions. Such accounts of miracles ("aretalogies") were widely distributed and very popular. Finally, the larger Asclepius sanctuaries organized extensive clinical and health-spa services, which must have been considerable in sanctuaries such as Cos, Epidaurus, and Pergamum; this development was certainly closely related to the ancient beginnings of scientific medicine.

These Asclepieia were usually situated outside of a major city and, within their sacred districts, they maintained all facilities which were required for a longer stay in a health spa. In addition to one or often two Asclepius temples, as well as temples for Apollo, Artemis, and the daughter of Asclepius, Hygieia, there were baths—including hot baths, of course, in the Roman period—a library, a theater, often a gymnasium and a stadium, rooms for medical treatment, an *abaton* (the sacred room in which the god appeared to the patient in a healing dream), and a guest house (the *katagogion;* in Epidaurus it had 160 rooms!). No doubt, the healings which were accomplished would range from dream and miracle healings to quite believable and successful psychosomatic cures (with baths, exercise, lectures, and readings) and methodical medical treatments. Surgical instruments have repeatedly been found in the excavation of Asclepius sanctuaries, and medical schools were connected to several of these healing establishments (Cos, Pergamum). Obviously there were not always and everywhere the same conditions and practices, and among the priests there seems to have been the feeling that one should rather trust the

Votive Monument with a Healing Scene

On the right, a patient enters making a vow. The next scene (center right) shows the same patient dreaming that the god appears in the form of a snake healing his wounded shoulder. On the left the god appears as the physician applying medical treatment. The votive is offered by Archimos to the god Amphiaraus, a healer god who is much like Asclepius.

healing powers of the god than the methods of modern medicine. But for the thousands of people who visited these sanctuaries, the difference between scientific medicine and miraculous healings, methodical cures and quackery was rarely obvious. They were quite willing to praise the god for any kind of healing and contribute to his glory with votive offerings and donations.

The cult of Asclepius was particularly concerned with the individual human being, in medical treatment as well as in its ritual preparation. It is, of course, also to the individual that the god appeared in his healing dream. This involved a personal relationship with the god, which may have been further deepened by a mystery initiation. However, about that our knowledge is very limited; the designation and use of certain rooms or chambers in the sanctuaries also remains unknown. The Asclepius cult parallels the mysteries also in one other respect: it demanded of those who sought healing that they should be "pure," which, in the Hellenistic period, was understood partially as a moral requirement. Cases are reported in which certain persons were rejected because their conduct of life did not meet this requirement.

Among all the gods of Greece, Asclepius was the most humane god. He was the "Savior" ($\sigma\omega\tau\acute{\eta}\rho$), benefactor, and friend of human beings. The humane features of this god are clearly expressed in several statues of Asclepius: his loving care, his compassion, and his knowledge of human suffering. Last but not least, many of the stories of his healing miracles not only demonstrate his miraculous powers, but also his sympathy, forbearance, and good will, especially for the poor and socially disadvantaged. One must, of course, be careful in ascribing features of the Christian image of God to pagan deities, but it is obvious that the humaneness in the divine image, which Asclepius reflects more than any other god, expresses a deep desire of that time, to which Christianity also eagerly responded, and which did not remain without influence upon the Christian image of God and Jesus.

(e) The Greek Mysteries (Eleusis and Samothrace)

The term "mysteries" ($\mu\upsilon\sigma\tau\acute{\eta}\rho\iota\alpha$) was used from v BCE for sacred rites in the cult of Demeter, of the Cabiri, and of some other deities. The word $\acute{o}\rho\gamma\iota\alpha$ ("orgies" = ritual actions) was also used, especially in the cult of Dionysus. Finally, one finds the more general term $\tau\epsilon\lambda\epsilon\tau\acute{\eta}$, which means simply "initiation." For the development of the Greek and Hellenistic concept of the "mysteries," the Demeter cult in Eleusis was the most significant.

The sanctuary of Demeter in Eleusis, situated thirty kilometers west of Athens, had a remarkable central building. Instead of the normal Greek temple, in which the "cella" is still a relatively small room, even in the case of very large temples, the Demeter temple in Eleusis had the dimensions of a large assembly hall as early as the archaic period. Later periods of building expanded the cella even further, so that it could provide enough room for several thousand people. Demeter, though of Minoan origin, was the most Greek of all deities, deeply rooted in the religious beliefs of the people. Demeter sanctuaries and festivals were known everywhere in Greece (though not quite so well in the Greek parts of Asia Minor). Demeter was the "Mother of Grain," not—as is sometimes assumed— "Mother Earth." Her primary festival was the feast of sowing in the spring, the *thesmophoria,* to which in most cases only women were admitted. In Eleusis, however, men and women participated in the cult.

The cult legend (*hieros logos*) of Demeter is the only archaic Greek cult legend which is preserved in one of the *Homeric Hymns* from VII BCE. It contains an etiological section, which mentions some of the elements of the *thesmophoria* (fasting, drinking of barley water, the so-called *kykeon*) and reports the myth of the cult: the daughter of Demeter, Kore-Persephone, had been carried off by the god of the underworld, Hades-Pluton, who wanted to marry her. Demeter searches for her daughter everywhere, but is unable to find her and withdraws in sorrow to fast. As a result, the grain will no longer grow, and all the people fear death by starvation, until Zeus intervenes and forces Hades to release Demeter's daughter. Now Kore spends two-thirds of the year with her mother and one-third in the underworld. The actual ritual and cult actions of the celebration of the mysteries in Eleusis and their significance in relation to the cult legend are, however, insufficiently known. Among the descriptions of the church fathers, the oldest is found in Clement of Alexandria (*Protr.* 2.29). Yet, although Clement was born in Athens and might have been acquainted with some elements of the cult in Eleusis, one must treat his report with caution. The repeated accusation of the church fathers that obscenities were part of the ritual is not altogether convincing; nor is it likely that the rite in Eleusis presented a performance of a "sacred marriage" (*hieros gamos*). We must therefore be content with a few general statements

Bibliography to §4.3e

George E. Mylonas, *Eleusis and the Eleusinian Mysteries* (Princeton, NJ: Princeton University, 1961).

Apostolos N. Athanassakis, "Music and Ritual in Primitive Eleusis," *Platon* (Athens) 28 (1976) 86–105.

Karl Lehmann, *Samothrace: A Guide to the Excavations and Museum* (2d ed.; Locust Valley, NY: Augustin, 1960).

Hans Gsänger, *Samothrake* (Mysterienstätten der Menschheit; Freiburg i. Br.: Verlag die Kommenden, 1960).

about the ritual of the Eleusian mysteries. There were three stages: initiation, consecration, and a higher consecration. Each stage consisted of "demonstrations," "actions," and "words," although we do not know with certainty what was shown, done, and said. Fasting was certainly practiced as part of the ritual, and the *hierophantēs*, the priest who shows a holy object, was the highest ranking cult official in Eleusis. Quite likely it was the sacred ear of wheat which was shown here, as it was illuminated by the rising sun shining through a hole in the ceiling of the room. But this does not tell us how the cult legend of Demeter was enacted in the mystery celebration which took place during the night. We may only say that these mystery rites must have been related to the sorrow of Demeter because of her lost daughter, and her joy at the reunion. The initiate thus participated in the divine mysteries of nature which caused the fruit of the field to grow again every year. It seems that in Hellenistic times interpretations of these rituals were related to the concepts of death and immortality. Although many other sanctuaries were celebrating secret or public rites connected with the growth of the fruits of the field and used various cult legends of Indo-European or Mediterranean origin, Eleusis appears to have been distinguished by its understanding of these rites as symbols of death and its conquest.

In the course of time Eleusis deeply influenced other Greek mystery cults and became their epitome. Its influence remained strong during the Roman imperial period, at which time it came to assume worldwide significance. Many Romans were initiated into the Eleusinian mysteries; Cicero after his initiation told Atticus that in Eleusis we recognize "the true foundations of life" and receive the conviction that "we can live with joy . . . and die with a better hope" (*De leg.* 2.38). Several emperors were consecrated at Eleusis: Augustus was initiated together with the Indian Zarmaros, who later burned himself publicly in Athens; Hadrian was consecrated twice; also initiated were Antonius Pius, Lucius Verus, Marcus Aurelius, and Commodus. It is interesting that Nero never went to the Eleusis—he knew that he was not welcome there—and that Apollonius of Tyana, the Neopythagorean miracle worker, had difficulties with Eleusis, because he was a magician. Eleusis also resisted syncretistic tendencies for a long time. Iakchus-Dionysus was not received among the Eleusinian gods until IV CE and only at that time could a Mithraic priest become *hierophantes* of Eleusis. These events, therefore, only happened at the end of the history of this celebrated mystery cult. It was finally destroyed in V CE.

There were other ancient Greek mystery sanctuaries in addition to Eleusis. Phyla, near Athens, had a mystery sanctuary, and there were several in the Peloponnesus: the mysteries of the Great Goddesses of

Telesterion at Eleusis

Seats of the western part of the Telesterion, the large assembly hall for the Eleusinian Mysteries; in its largest form, it measured 180 by 170 feet, and its ceiling was supported by 42 columns.

Megalopolis, of Despoina in Lycosoura, and the mysteries of Andania. The institution or reform of these mystery cults in the Hellenistic period was accomplished in the first two instances under the auspices of Eleusis, in the latter case with the help of Phyla. In the regulations that were preserved, rules regarding order and the police are surprisingly predominant. Indeed, the mysteries were celebrations in which a large number of people participated, just as the great proportion of the Athenian population had been initiated into the Eleusinian mysteries. (Dionysus mysteries will be discussed in §4.3f.)

Among other Greek mysteries the most famous was the sanctuary of the Cabiri in Samothrace. The cult had its origins in the period before the Greek settlement. The female deity may have been of Phrygian origin, related to Cybele; she and her male consorts were worshiped as "the Great Gods of Samothrace" and sometimes identified with Greek deities, especially after 700 BCE, when the island was occupied by Greek settlers from Samos. The mysteries of the Cabiri enjoyed wide recognition during the Hellenistic and Roman periods. The sanctuary in Samothrace also engaged in systematic propaganda and missionary activity. In this respect it was clearly different from Eleusis, which could not be exported. Its influence extended beyond the sanctuary in Eleusis only insofar as priests and theologians from Eleusis served as advisors in the institution and reform of cults elsewhere, as the Eumolpid Timothy assisted in the organization of the Sarapis cult in Alexandria. But through the missionary activity of the Samothracian priests the cult of the Cabiri was transplanted to other cities, especially to Ionia and the islands of the Aegean Sea. On the whole, and especially with respect to the general problem of the Hellenistic mystery religions which must be discussed later, it is important to state here that "mysteries" are a thoroughly Greek phenomenon, since mystery sanctuaries were widely distributed over the Greek countries already in the Hellenistic period.

(f) Dionysus

However dignified, respected, and influential the mysteries of Eleusis and Samothrace may have been, the most important Greek mystery religion was always that of Dionysus. This god, also called Bakchos (Bacchus in Latin), was not Greek in origin, but had become naturalized in Greece already in the preclassical period. He probably came from Thrace, meaning that he belonged to the Indo-European immigrants who had settled in the southeast of the Balkans and in the northwest of Asia Minor. His name can be interpreted as "Son of Zeus," and his mother was the Thracian-Phrygian goddess of the earth, Semele. This corresponds with the oldest understanding of Dionysus as the god of fertility and of the fruits of the field. His cult had many unusual features. Originally only women participated (as also in many cults of Demeter in Greece). His orgiastic feasts were celebrated in the middle of winter, when women in large groups went into the forests and the wooded mountains. The so-called *omophagia* was a rite in which wild animals were torn to pieces alive and eaten raw—doubtlessly a sacramental meal in which one sought to become one with the god, who was believed to appear as a wild animal. Because of its savagery and its ecstatic rites, this form of the cult of Dionysus found as much rejection as interest in Greece, but was nevertheless successful. Its triumphal progress has found an impressive and lasting monument in the *Bacchae* of Euripides.

But in addition to the Thracian Dionysus, there was a related deity (to whom belongs the Lydian name Bakchos) who came from Phrygia and who was the god of the fruit trees and therefore also of the vine. In his myth he appears as a child born into the spring, when nature begins its cycle of growth once again. His primary festival was the *anthestēria*, the feast of the spring; his most striking symbol was the phallus, which was carried in the festal procession. Dionysus himself, however, is never presented as an ithyphallic deity; only the satyrs and Silenus who accompany him appear in this way. This particular cult of Dionysus had also migrated to Greece in the preclassical period and was combined with the Thracian Dionysus. Therefore, with respect to Greece, one must speak of one single Dionysus religion, although the cultic practices differed from place to place and often defy explanation, as, for example, in the ritual of a *hieros gamos* of the god with the wife of a high official in Athens.

Next to Asclepius, Dionysus was most widely accepted among all Greek gods in the Hellenistic period. Both gods, and especially Dionysus, were much more significant than the Olympian gods for the religious life of the people in Greece itself and elsewhere. But the means and manner of his worship are difficult to evaluate because he appears in so many different forms and sometimes seems to be little more than a fashion, so that it becomes doubtful whether the widespread representations in pictures and mosaics of Dionysus, his symbols, and his company can be taken as

Bibliography to §4.3f

Martin P. Nilsson, *The Dionysiac Mysteries of the Hellenistic and Roman Age* (Lund: Gleerup, 1957; New York: Arno, 1975).

Albert Henrichs, "Greek and Roman Glimpses of Dionysos," in: Caroline Houser (ed.), *Dionysos and His Circle: Ancient through Modern* (Cambridge, MA: Fogg Art Museum, Harvard, 1979) 1–11.

Walter F. Otto, *Dionysos: Mythos and Kultus* (3d ed.; Darmstadt: Wissenschaftliche Buchgesellschaft, 1960).

Susan Guettel Cole, "New Evidence for Mysteries of Dionysos," *GRBS* 21 (1980) 223–38.

serious witnesses of a religion of Dionysus or of his mystery cult. Actual mysteries of Dionysus, however, are frequently attested in the Hellenistic period for the cities of Asia Minor and for the islands. We learn that men were also admitted and could participate in the wild orgies of Bacchantian women. One also finds men in the offices of priest, *hierophantēs*, and *dadouchos*. Priests and priestesses are the leaders of the *thiasoi* of the participants in the mysteries. In Egypt the expansion of the cult of Dionysus is clear through the religious policies of Ptolemy IV Philometer (later III and II BCE; see §1.5c). In the Attalid kingdom of Pergamum, from the middle of III BCE, Dionysus was worshiped as the official god of the realm under the title *kathēgemōn* (= "the founder"; later this designation was understood as "founder and creator of the whole universe"). He also assumed the features of Sabazius, whose cult had been introduced into Pergamum by the wife of Attalus I. On the silver coins which were minted in Pergamum (called *kistophoroi*) one can see a snake creeping out of a basket, surrounded by a wreath of ivy. This seems to be a combination of the cult symbols of both gods.

In those cases where the cult of Dionysus was accepted by the state and publicly promoted one cannot assume that it was still primarily a mystery cult; but neither does it appear as a strictly regulated state religion, not even when Roman leaders or emperors identified themselves with Dionysus (the first one was Marc Antony, who demanded to be worshiped as Dionysus, together with Cleopatra, the new Isis). Public celebration clearly exhibited the typical "Dionysiac" features: processions with sileni and dancers, mimes and jugglers, women as Bacchae, young men as satyrs and Pans, public performances of pantomimes, bacchantic dances, and theatrical presentations. All these things were part of Dionysiac festivals, which could last several days, and in which men and women, young and old, and people of all classes participated. At least in this respect the cult associations of the Dionysiac initiates were public associations and not mystery clubs.

This, however, seems to have been chiefly the form of Dionysus religion that appears especially in Asia Minor. The other important manifestation was that of a mystery cult, pregnant with profound religious concepts, which comes into view in Italy as early as V BCE. The religion of Dionysus was there connected with Orphic ideas, which were at home among the Greeks of southern Italy and stressed a religious orientation towards a better afterlife. What terrified the Romans so much in the beginning of II BCE was a mystery cult of Dionysus (Bacchus) of considerable missionary strength. The famous *Senatus consultum de Bacchanalibus* from the year 186 BCE gives evidence for the severe measures taken against these mysteries; this decree formed for centuries the judgment of Roman officialdom about foreign religions of salvation which held secret meetings not accessible to the public.

The rites and religious concepts of these mysteries of Dionysus are not fully known. They were probably not the same everywhere and may have been influenced by other mystery cults. Although temples of Dionysus existed everywhere, usually in the neighborhood of the theaters, the mysteries were apparently celebrated in private homes. It is possible that the Villa Item in Pompey and the House of the Masks on Delos were such house sanctuaries. The celebrations certainly included a common meal and the drinking of wine—Dionysus was, after all, the god of the vine. The myth of Dionysus' dying and revivification was widely known and may have served as the basis for the hope of achieving immortality. This is not simply the spiritualization of an older cult of vegetation, but a representation of Orphic concepts which served to interpret myths and rites of Dionysiac origin. Specifically eastern influences cannot be presupposed. The explanation of the wall frescoes in the Villa Item is difficult: a naked boy who reads something (Orphic texts?); the *liknon* (a kind of winnowing fan with a phallus on it); a dark winged figure with a scourge (a representation of the horrors of the underworld?—on a mosaic from Delos; Dionysus himself is depicted with wings); the view into the mirror (recognition of the immortal self?); and other objects such as thyrsus and torches. There also seem to have been observances of ritual purity and rules of abstention. The assumption that these mysteries were essentially a preoccupation of the upper classes is certainly false, at least for the Hellenistic period. The people against whom Rome intervened in the *Senatus consultum* mentioned above did not belong to the upper classes. But it seems that in the Roman period the Dionysus mysteries were also popular among the affluent population; poor people could not afford frescoes and mosaics, and therefore much less is known about them. It is difficult to estimate how serious was the belief in immortality which the mysteries mediated. No doubt the cult had great significance. One should hesitate to assume, however, that it was a movement that had such religious impact that it successfully contributed to the renewal of spiritual life—in spite of the great popularity of the god Dionysus and of his festivals and mystery celebrations.

4. THE NEW RELIGIONS

(a) Sarapis and Isis

The cult of the Egyptian gods was the most Hellenized oriental religion of the Hellenistic period. Its basis was a complex development of Egyptian cults and myths which had by no means come to an end at the time of the Greek conquest. A number of Egyptian gods were involved: Isis, Osiris, Apis, Horus, Anubis, and Seth. It is impossible to describe in a brief space the significance of these deities in the pre-Ptolemaic period of Egypt, because each of these divine figures had different functions in the various Egyptian cultic places. But one can at least begin by describing some of the presuppositions which illuminate the myth of Isis and Osiris, even though its final form was not an Egyptian, but a Hellenistic product. Isis was the goddess of the royal throne and thus the mother of Horus, the mythical representation of the living Pharaoh. Osiris, probably in his origin the god of the shepherds of the Nile's eastern delta, became the mythical embodiment of its fertile lands, which flooded every year and were thus restored to new life. His enemy, therefore, was Seth, the god of the desert. At the same time, Osiris was the god of the dead, and in this function he was identified with the dead Pharaoh: he represents the life of the deceased king in the world of the dead. In this function he is closely associated with Anubis, the protector of the graveyard who defends the Pharoah's corpse

Bibliography to §4.4

Nilsson, *Griechische Religion* 2. 622–67.

A. J. Festugière, *Études de religion grecque et hellénistique* (Paris: Vrin, 1972).

Arthur Darby Nock, *Conversion* (London: Oxford University, 1933). A very instructive introduction.

Richard Reitzenstein, *Hellenistic Mystery Religions: Their Basic Ideas and Significance* (Pittsburgh Theological Monograph Series 15; Pittsburgh: Pickwick, 1978). Translation of a most provocative and controversial monograph, 3d German ed., 1927.

Franz Cumont, *The Oriental Religions in Roman Paganism* (New York: Dover, 1956).

Edwyn Bevan, *Later Greek Religion* (London: Dent; New York: Dutton, 1927).

Ph. Derchein, F. de Cenival et al., *Religions en Egypt hellénistique et romaine: Colloque des Strasbourg, 16–18 mai 1967* (Paris: Presses universitaires de France, 1969).

Bibliography to §4.4a: Texts

Ladislav Vidman, *Sylloge inscriptionum religionis Isiacae et Sarapiacae* (Berlin: De Gruyter, 1969).

Grant, *Hellenistic Religions,* 124–44.

Y. Grandjean, *Une nouvelle arétalogie d'Isis à Maronnée* (EPRO 49; Leiden: Brill, 1975).

Helmut Engelmann, *The Delian Aretalogy of Sarapis* (EPRO 44; Leiden: Brill, 1975).

J. Gwyn Griffiths, *Apuleius of Madauros: The Isis-Book (Metamorphoses, Book XI): Introduction, Translation and Commentary* (EPRO 39; Leiden: Brill, 1975).

Theodor Hopfner (ed.), *Plutarch über Isis und Osiris,* part 1: *Die Sage: Text, Übersetzung und Kommentar* (Darmstadt: Wissenschaftliche Buchgesellschaft, 1967).

Bust of Sarapis

The God wears the "calathus" (a basket for fruits) as a symbol of fertility. The "globe" supporting the bust has been interpreted as the universe, thus signifying Sarapis's rule over the whole world. Roman copy of a Hellenistic work (ultimately, all known statues of Sarapis are copies of the famous cult statue of Sarapis in Alexandria).

(i.e., Osiris) against Seth. That Osiris was also connected with Isis is apparently the result of royal and throne mythology: because Isis was the mother of Horus, now the living king, Osiris, the dead king, became her husband and the father of Horus.

In its classical form, the Isis myth relates the battle in which Seth kills his twin brother Osiris, cuts his corpse into pieces, and throws them into the Nile; in a later Greek version, the dragon Typhon finds the corpse, dismembers it, and persecutes Isis and her child. Together with Nephthys, the wife of Seth, Isis mourns for Osiris; both women together search for him, and upon finding the pieces of his corpse they fit them together again. Isis revives his phallus, becomes pregnant and gives birth to Horus or Harpocrates (= Horus as a child, often represented sitting on the lap of his mother). Anubis buries Osiris, who becomes king of the realm of the dead as Horus rules over the living.

Isis was already known to Herodotus and was at first identified with Demeter. But she began her triumphal procession through the Hellenistic world only in the entourage of Sarapis—the syncretistic creation of early Hellenism. The sacred Apis bull was worshiped in Memphis long before the Ptolemies came to Egypt. The dead bull was believed to become

Bibliography to §4.4a: Studies

Ladislav Vidman, *Isis und Sarapis bei den Griechen und Römern. Epigraphische Studien zu den Trägern des ägyptischen Kultes* (Berlin: De Gruyter, 1970).

Friedrich Solmsen, *Isis among the Greeks and Romans* (Martin Classical Lectures 25; Cambridge, MA: Harvard University, 1979).

F. Le Corsu, *Isis: Mythe et Mystère* (Collection d'Études Mythologiques; Paris: Les belles Lettres, 1977).

R. E. Witt, *Isis in the Graeco-Roman World* (Ithaca, NY: Cornell University, 1971).

Wilhelm Hornbostel, *Sarapis: Studien zur Überlieferungsgeschichte, den Erscheinungsformen und Wandlungen der Gestalt eines Gottes* (EPRO 32; Leiden: Brill, 1973).

Regina Salditt-Trapmann, *Tempel der ägyptischen Götter in Griechenland und an der Westküste Kleinasiens* (EPRO 15; Leiden: Brill, 1970).

Françoise Dunand, *Le culte d'Isis dans le bassin oriental de la Méditerranée* (EPRO 26; 3 vols.; Leiden: Brill, 1973).

Pierre Roussel, *Les cultes égyptiens à Délos du IIIe au Ier siècle avant J.-C.* (Nancy: Berger-Levrault, 1916).

John E. Stambaugh, *Sarapis under the Early Ptolemies* (EPRO 25; Leiden: Brill, 1972).

Thomas Allen Brady, *The Reception of the Egyptian Cults by the Greeks (330-30 B.C.)* (University of Missouri Studies 10,1; Columbia, MO: University of Missouri, 1935).

Theodor Hopfner, *Über Isis und Osiris,* part 2: *Die Deutungen der Sage* (Darmstadt: Wissenschaftliche Buchgesellschaft, 1967).

Martin Dibelius, "Die Isisweihe bei Apuleius und verwandte Initiationsriten," in: idem, *Botschaft und Geschichte* (Tübingen: Siebeck/Mohr, 1956) 2. 30–79.

Osiris, while the soul of the dying Osiris, on the other hand, was united with the living Apis. From this close connection of Osiris and Apis resulted the divine name Oserapis. Ptolemy I not only brought the corpse of Alexander the Great from Memphis to Alexandria, he also transferred the Oserapis cult into the new capital and transformed it into the central cult of his realm. He also gave Greek features to this Egyptian god. The statue of the god which is said to have been made by he Greek sculptor Bryaxis (one of the leading sculptors who worked on the famous Mausoleum, the tomb of king Mausolus of Halicarnassus), though it may have been made earlier for a different purpose, has the features of Zeus and Hades and has no similarity with the traditional images of Egyptian gods. Timothy, a well-known priest from Eleusis and author of numerous theological books, advised the king about how to institute the new cult. The name Oserapis was Hellenized to Sarapis. The cult and ritual were arranged according to Greek patterns, though they also contained some Egyptian elements. It seems that the latter assumed renewed significance in later centuries.

There is much discussion among scholars about the motivations and intentions which determined the creation of this new cult. Did Ptolemy intend to create a new religion that would appeal to Greeks and Egyptians alike and thus unite the two peoples of the kingdom? That is unlikely, because there is no evidence that the first Ptolemies ever pursued such policies. The Egyptians did not accept Sarapis anyway, and instead continued the traditional forms of the cult of the Apis bull. It is more likely that the first Ptolemy created Sarapis as the god of the Greek populations of his realm, which at that time also included Cyprus, parts of western and southern Anatolia, and several Greek islands. The political significance of a god of the whole empire with its most important sanctuary in Alexandria might have played some role. We know of no attempts by the Ptolemies, however, to establish the Sarapis cult as the central religion of their kingdom, even though they supported this cult generously. The most important motivation for the cult's creation may have been somewhat different: the Ptolemies had to legitimate themselves as the true heirs of the Pharaohs by adopting an Egyptian god as their own deity. The establishment of a relationship to the cult of Osiris-Apis at the old capital of Memphis and the official transfer of the god to the new capital would prove this point. Obviously, the Ptolemies could not simply accept any Egyptian god without substantial modifications, because they were, after all, too closely identified with the Greek inheritance. Thus the Hellenization of an Egyptian god was the only alternative.

The lasting significance of this Greco-Egyptian cult lies outside of the political aims that led to its creation, since it belongs rather to the realm of religious history. It was not in fact primarily the figure of Sarapis which led to its final triumph, although his cult spread quickly. Rather, it was the overwhelming impact of the Hellenized Isis, who came with Sarapis' entourage, that finally carried away the victory. Sarapis as well as other Egyptian gods (Anubis, Horus) had to yield first place to her. If ever any deity of that time was on the way to becoming the central divine figure of a world religion, it was Isis. Not, however, the Isis who was the goddess of the throne of the Pharaoh and wife of Osiris, but Isis as the goddess of heaven and mother of the All, who united in her person everything that was significant for the religious expectations of her time. Egyptian elements aided Isis' development into a universal deity. As the Egyptian Hathor, Isis was the goddess of heaven in the shape of a cow (whence the image of a cow which is, according to Apuleius, carried in front of the image of Isis in her procession); also Egyptian are many of the attributes of the goddess: the dress and headdress, the sistrum (a metal rattle used as a musical instrument), and her constant companion Anubis with the head of a jackal. But her overall appearance and essence are Greek. Greek artists created her image, which expresses beauty, dignity, harmony, and benevolence. Sometimes she also takes on the features of Aphrodite. Particularly effective was her representation as a mother goddess, affectionately holding the child Harpocrates in her lap or to her breast. Mary, the mother and goddess of heaven in Christianity, is little more artistically than a copy of Isis. Features of Isis also appear in the birth story of the Messiah in Rev 12:1ff.: the woman who is dressed with the sun and stands on the moon with the zodiac on her head, who is pregnant and must flee the dragon (Typhon) with her newborn child.

The most characteristic descriptions of Isis, however, can be found in the Isis aretalogies which have been preserved in different versions and which can be called the genuine creed of the Isis religion. Here Isis presents herself with the formula "I am Isis" (ἐγώ εἰμι Ἶσις) and, in the short sentences which follow, describes her position and her power, identifies herself with other deities, and claims their works and accomplishments for herself. The aretalogies show the influence of cosmological and astrological concepts as well as a strong tendency toward universality and monotheism. A typical example is the Isis aretalogy from the eleventh book of Apuleius' *Metamorphoses* (11.5.1–3):

> I am with you, Lucius, I who am the mother of the universe,
> The mistress of all the elements,
> The first offspring of time,
> The highest of deities,
> The queen of the dead,

Foremost of heavenly beings,
The single form that fuses all gods and goddesses;
I who order by my will the starry heights of heaven, the health-giving
breezes of the sea, and the awful silences of those in the underworld:
My single godhead is adored by the whole world in varied forms, in
differing rites and with many diverse names.
Thus the Phrygians, earliest of races, called me Pessinuntia, Mother of
the Gods;
Thus the Athenians, sprung from their own soil, call me Cecropeian
Minerva;
And the sea-tossed Cyprians call me Paphian Venus,
The archer Cretans Diana Dictynna, and the trilingual Sicilians Orty-
gian Proserpine;
To the Eleusinians I am Ceres, the ancient goddess, to others Juno, to
others Bellona and Hecate and Rhamnusia.
But the Ethiopians, who are illumined by the first rays of the sun-god
as he is born every day, together with the Africans and the Egyptians
who excel through having the original doctrine, honor me with my
distinctive rites and give me my true name of Queen Isis.

Not only the names of the other deities, but also their works become the
works of the one and only god, Isis, the ruler of the universe. She has
promulgated the laws of all people, given them speech and taught them
the art of writing, but also instructed them in the cultivation of the land.
She protects marriage, gives safety to the sailors on the high sea, gives the
laws for the proper circuit of the stars and, as the sun, illumines the whole
world. She even has power over fate.

We have good information about the processions and public services of
the cult of Isis. Egyptian cultic vessels and Egyptian rites predominate,
though there is no uniformity from place to place. As for initiation into the
Isis mysteries, Apuleius (*Metamorphoses* 11) gives a number of details,
but does not tell us what actually happened in the sanctuary during the
initiation itself. Apuleius speaks about the preparations, instructions
about the date of the initiation, which was given through a dream, the
purchase of the various vessels and garments which were required—the
initiation was by no means inexpensive!—and about a period of fasting
and a bath for purification. The initiation itself is described only by allu-
sion: the initiate came to the limits of death and to the threshold of
Proserpina, he was led through all elements, saw the sun shine in the
middle of the night, and beheld the gods above and below and worshiped
them. On the morning after the initiation the initiate is presented to the
people dressed with special garments and insignia: twelve stoles symbol-

izing the zodiac; a precious dress, the garment of the highest god; a crown of palm leaves arranged so as to indicate the rays of the sun. Having overcome all the powers, the initiate has thus attained identity with the highest heavenly deity; being no longer a part of the transitory earthly domain, he appears as the sun, surrounded by his rays, i.e., he is now one with the eternal world of pure spirit.

A number of questions pertaining to the process of initiation remain unanswered. It is, of course, not of great consequence to find out what was actually seen in the adyton of the temple. Preparatory fasting and the skill of the priests, who were quite able to manipulate images, symbols, torches, and lamps, could easily produce the desired effects. Rather, it is the interpretation that concerns us: the rite obviously meant the experience of death and rebirth. But this does not take place as a participation in the fate of the deity; the myth of Isis and Osiris does not suit such an understanding. To be sure, Osiris died and became lord of the realm of the dead, but it is never said that he rose. Moreover, Osiris does not play a role here anyway: the text speaks about Proserpina (i.e., Isis) as the mistress of Hades. What are the benefactions of Isis for the one who came to her threshold on a journey that symbolizes not just death, but the cosmic journey of the soul (*Himmelsreise* and *Descensus ad inferos*)? The one who has thus undergone, as it were, "a voluntary death" (*Metam.* 11.21) and was reborn is set by Isis on a new course of life and salvation ("quodam modo renatos ad novae reponere rursus salutis curricula"). This seems to be neither immortality nor resurrection from the dead, but a dying to one's former life and the possibility of a new life in the service of the goddess. This new life is an experience of existence in which the initiate is conscious of his being united with the deity who rules the whole world. This is expressed by the heavenly garments and the crown of the sun which he wears, and which sets him apart from the uninitiated. The symbolic experience of death is not identical with the attainment of immortality, but it signifies a new life that is radically different from the past. Hellenistic concepts of rebirth were understood in a very similar fashion in early Christianity (cf. Romans 6). The Isis initiate, of course, knows just as well as Paul that earthly human life has a natural limit. And as Paul can point to the expectation that Christ will raise from the dead all those who have believed in him, so also the devotee of Isis receives the assurance: "Once you have measured out the span of your earthly life and descend to those who are in the realm below, . . . and living in the Elysian fields you will worship me as your gracious protector" (*Metam.* 11.6). Since Isis rules over everything, including Hades, those who have been initiated into her mysteries are protected even after death. The new life which has been attained in the initiation has its counterpart in a life after death.

Parallels with Christian statements abound in this narration of an initiation into a mystery religion. One should not deny that the New Testament and the mysteries often speak the same language. When Paul says that those who have been baptized have died with Christ and should, therefore, walk in a new life, his words closely resemble those of the initiation into the Isis mysteries. That the Christians can also expect eternal life after they have been raised from the dead does not constitute a difference from the Isis mystery, because the devotees of Isis also know that they are not condemned to become unconscious shadows after death. The differences lie elsewhere: the initiation into the mysteries of Isis—and this is also true of other mystery religions—was reserved for only a few elect persons, i.e., to those who were able to pay the rather high expenses associated with the initiation. In the case of Apuleius, even more initiations were required elsewhere in order to validate the original and to obtain higher stages of the mysteries which were restricted to a small circle of the truly elect. Christianity, on the other hand, democratized the mysteries and liberated the process from financial requirements. Paul's fight against several opposing groups indicates that the formation of an elitist consciousness was one of the greatest dangers facing the early Christian churches. The success of Christianity as a religion for all people would depend upon the result of this fight, to which Paul and other early Christian missionaries committed themselves for fundamental theological reasons.

Sanctuaries of Sarapis from the Roman imperial period have been discovered in a number of cities. It is striking that some of these sanctuaries were not regular temples with a small inner room (cella) but assembly halls which provided room for a large number of people. The so-called "Red Basilica" in Pergamum, a Sarapis sanctuary built in the first half of II CE, was large enough to accommodate more than a thousand people. The Sarapeia in Ephesus and Miletus were not quite as big, but could still serve as assembly rooms for a whole congregation. Thus it seems that these sanctuaries were actually "churches" which could provide the opportunity for a congregation to participate regularly in services and perhaps also in mystery initiations. That would contradict the picture of the initiation into the Isis mysteries that is suggested by the report of Apuleius; the cult of Sarapis may have had a structure which closely resembled the service of a Jewish synagogue or a Christian church.

(b) The Magna Mater and Attis

Cybele, the Great Mother (*Magna Mater*) of life, the mighty and fierce fertility deity of the Phrygians, had her primary sanctuary in Phrygian Pessinus. Her cult was accompanied by orgiastic rites leading to a climax at which servants of the deity would castrate themselves in ecstatic frenzy. Cybele had been known in Greece since the archaic period and possessed temples in many Greek cities, serving as the depository for state archives (e.g., in Athens). But the ecstatic features of her cult were eliminated in the process of the acceptance of the Great Mother in Greece; in particular, the castration rite disappeared—Attis, the lover of Cybele (also called Agdistis in her myth), who castrates himself in his sorrow about his infidelity, does not appear in classical Greece. This feature may also have been introduced into the cult of Cybele from Syria at a later date. Instead of Attis, the Greeks worshiped Adonis, the lover of Aphrodite (who is here identical with the Syrian Ishtar). The cult of Adonis was widespread as a symbol of the quickly-passing springtime. But among the Greeks, Adonis did not usually have temples; he was worshiped in private rituals. The only Greek city in which Cybele was the leading public deity in the classical period was Smyrna on the west coast of Asia Minor.

The early Hellenistic period witnessed a renewed expansion of the cult of the Great Mother. But this time the Great Mother, coming out of her home city, the Phrygian Pessinus, brought with her the wild and primitive features of her cult, and also the myth of her unfortunate lover Attis. In the east there were powerful competitors: Atargatis/Ishtar in Syria, Isis in Egypt. Greece proved unreceptive to the cult and its propaganda, but the west accepted her quickly: the cult of the Great Mother was officially recognized in Rome as early as 204 BCE—the first, and for a long time the only oriental cult to find such recognition. Restrictions for participating in the cult of Cybele were finally removed under the Emperor Claudius, and the spring festival of the Great Mother became one of the most popular festivals celebrated in Rome. This is the public side of this religion, the part which is well known.

The great spring festival lasted two weeks, March 15 to 27. On the first day, reeds were carried to the sanctuary of the goddess, whose significance in the rite is not clear. On March 22, a pine tree was cut, carried to the

---

Bibliography to §4.4b: Texts
Grant, *Hellenistic Religions,* 116–23.

Bibliography to §4.4b: Studies
M. J. Vermaseren, *The Legend of Attis in Greek and Roman Art* (EPRO 9; Leiden: Brill, 1966).
Idem, *Cybele and Attis: The Myth and the Cult* (London and New York: Thames and Hudson, 1977).
Hugo Hepding, *Attis, seine Mythen und sein Kult* (RVV 1; Giessen: Töpelmann, 1903; reprint: Berlin: Töpelmann, 1967).
Robert Duthoy, *The Taurobolium: Its Evolution and Terminology* (EPRO 10; Leiden: Brill, 1969).

sanctuary, erected there and decorated: this is the symbol of Attis, and it reveals an ancient tree cult. The following days were for fasting to express sorrow for the death of Attis. March 24 was the *dies sanguinis:* the *galli,* a lower class of priests, cut their skins in a frenzied, ecstatic dance and sprinkled their blood upon the image of the goddess while the novices castrated themselves in ecstasy. A quiet day, called *hilaria,* followed. On March 27, the statue of the deity was brought to the river and washed. Nothing is known about the actual initiation rite of the *galli* after their castration, but one can assume that it was a "mystery." It is doubtful, however, that this was the normal or regular means for initiation for the devotees of the Great Mother. The higher class of priests was not castrated, and it is quite probable that only the initiation of the *galli* took place during the spring festival, whereas other rites of initiation were celebrated at other times. Many have speculated about the interpretation of the Attis mysteries, but we do not know whether they were related to the ideas of death and resurrection, or were somehow connected with the idea of a holy marriage (*hieros gamos*). The myth never speaks about a resurrection of Attis, and the features of Cybele (or Agdistis) in the myth do not suggest the idea of a *hieros gamos* in order to explain the relationship of the initiate to the goddess. It is also quite possible that the repulsive rite of self-castration of the *galli* during the spring festival has led interpreters astray. This rite may not have been an initiation into a mystery after all, but a rite of sacrifice in which the testicles were offered to the goddess, for there are reports that the testicles were cleaned and anointed and deposited in the temple. If this is the case, the actual mystery initiation of the cult must have had a different character and remains unknown. The well-known taurobolium also cannot have been this initiation rite. Originally this act was a bullfight, but as early as the beginning of the Roman period it was practiced as part of the ritual of the Great Mother and Attis. The evidence for taurobolia is most widespread in II and III CE. They were usually offered on behalf of the emperor or a special private citizen. The high priest would climb into a pit, over which a bull was slaughtered; when he reemerged, the participants would worship him. The testicles of the sacrificial bull were consecrated with certain ceremonies and offered to the goddess, perhaps as a vicarious offering for those who did not want to castrate themselves. The essential significance of the taurobolium, however, must be seen in the symbolic power of blood: it accomplished expiation for sin and granted rebirth to the initiate, normally for the period of twenty years (in one case it is said "in all eternity"); after this period the rite had to be repeated. In IV CE there is also evidence that the taurobolium was understood as initiation into a mystery cult.

The cult of the Great Mother and of Attis produced some peculiar effects. The cult and its myth were subjected to theological and mystical interpretations in which Attis played a more significant role than the Great Mother. Together with the god Men, who was worshiped in Asia Minor, Attis became a god of heaven, and his castration was understood as an act of creation. Christian Gnostics also claimed the Attis myth and used it for their own purposes. This is evident from a report of Hippolytus about the Naassenes in which a portion of an Attis hymn is quoted:

> Be it the race of Kronos, or the blessed child of Zeus or great Rhea [=
>   Cybele];
> Hail to thee, Attis, sad message of Rhea;
> Assyrians call the thrice-desired Adonis, all Egypt, Osiris, . . .
> I will sing of Attis, the son of Rhea, . . .
> All hail! All hail!—as Pan, as Bacchus,
> As shepherd of the shining stars.

But one should not be misled by these syncretistic and gnostic concepts: they were not the reason for the great popularity of the cult of Cybele and Attis. Rather, one must consider the impression that the rites, festivals, and cultic celebrations of the Great Mother and of Attis made upon the minds and feelings of many people. The religious fervor of the cult of the *Magna Mater* was radical and extreme. The festivals were colorful, filled with wild music of percussion instruments and raptured dance; the rites primitive, cruel, and fascinating, although in extremely bad taste by Greek standards. It is known that the moral demands of the religion of the Great Mother were severe and rigorous. Consciousness of sin and guilt played a significant role in addressing a level of religious experience and a psychological dimension which the speculative theories of the religiously interested philosophers never touched.

(c) Sabazius, Men, and Others

Sabazius was a Phrygian (and Thracian) god from Asia Minor. He is related to Dionysus, and the identification of Sabazius and Dionysus which is occasionally found has ancient roots. Some of the orgiastic elements in the cult of Sabazius also recall the cult of Dionysus. Though Sabazius was known in Greece during the classical period, his worship found widespread acceptance in the Roman west only in the Hellenistic period. This popularity is evident from the many Sabazius hands which have been found, i.e., raised hands in the form of the *benedictio Latina*, decorated with pine cones, snakes, and other symbols. Like the cult of Dionysus, the ancient worship of Sabazius had features of mystery cults. There apparently were common cultic meals which—judging from the painting on the Vincentius tomb in Rome—seemed to symbolize one's acquittal before the judge of the dead and reception into the everlasting meal of the blessed. Syncretistic tendencies appear to have been particularly strong.

In addition to the old identification of Sabazius with Dionysus in Asia Minor, we find a frequent connection with Zeus and with *Hypsistos* ("The Highest God"), occasionally also with the Great Mother, and later with Mithras. Strange, and not yet explained, is the identification with Yahweh, the god of Israel. In 139 BCE Jews were expelled from Rome, "who had tried to corrupt the Roman customs with the cult of Sabazius Jupiter" ("Ioudaeos qui Sabazi Iovis cultu Romanos inficere mores conati erant," Valerius Maximus 1.3.2). From the interior of Asia Minor several documents speak of a monotheistic mystery cult of the "God the Highest," and it is said that the members observed the Sabbath and certain dietary laws. There are also inscriptions of cult associations called the "Sabbathists" with reliefs of banquet scenes. It is not clear what the cult of these "Sabbathists" of "Hypsistarians" was, nor how they relate to Sabazius on the one hand and to Judaism on the other. It is quite possible that those Jews of Asia Minor who were Hellenized to a large degree had, in the organization of their congregation and in the understanding of their services as mysteries, accepted religious forms that were characteristic for the period. Jewish features are clearly present in the testimonies referred to above: the designation of God as "The Highest" appears in the Septuagint and frequently in the Hellenistic literature of Judaism (Philo and Josephus), where Christians borrowed the term; the Sabbath celebration—a festive meal with wine—is typically Jewish; the *angelus bonus* on the tomb of Vincentius in Rome mentioned above is certainly of Jewish origin. But it is not possible to decide whether the Sabazius/Hypsistus Sabbathists were a Jewish-syncretistic mystery cult, or a pagan religion which had borrowed from Judaism, or whether we are confronted with a simple confusion of names (Sabazius-Sabbath-Sabaoth). The hypothesis of a simple confusion of names is not satisfactory, however, in view of the

Bibliography to §4.4c: Texts

Harold W. Attridge and R. A. Oden (eds.), *The Syrian Goddess (De Dea Syria) Attributed to Lucian* (SBLTT 9, Greco-Roman Series 1; Missoula, MT: Scholars Press, 1976).

Bibliography to §4.4e: Studies

Sherman E. Johnson, "A Sabazios Inscription From Sardis," in: Neusner, *Religions in Antiquity,* 542–50.

Paul John Morin, "The Cult of the Dea Syria in the Greek World" (Ph.D. diss., Ohio State University, 1960).

W. O. E. Oesterly, "The Cult of Sabazios," in: S. H. Hooke (ed.), *The Labyrinth* (New York: Macmillan, 1935) 113–58.

explicit mention of "Jews" in the report about the expulsion of Sabazius worshipers from Rome. Thus, one must assume that there was a syncretistic group of some kind or other which was at home in Asia Minor. In the later controversies of early Christianity with heretical groups it seems that Christian congregations were also influenced by the same Jewish syncretistic mystery cults (see §12.2a on the Epistle to the Colossians).

Another Phrygian deity whose cult appeared as a mystery religion in the Hellenistic period was Men, frequently called Men Tyrannus. Slaves working in the Lavrian mines of Attica had introduced Men to Greece as early as IV BCE. Later on Men is found also in Italy in the entourage of Attis. Men is a god of the moon, usually presented with the crescent moon. Together with Attis, Men was worshiped as a universal god of heaven.

The *Dea Syria*, Atargatis, was not very widely worshiped in the Greek-speaking world, though a temple of the Syrian goddess with a theater has been excavated on the island of Delos. Lucian (who came from Samosata in Assyria; see §6.4g) wrote an entire book about the *Dea Syria*.

(d) The Problem of the Mystery Religions

The question of the so-called "Hellenistic mystery religions" is much debated in scholarship. Richard Reitzenstein's thesis of an oriental-Iranian origin of the mystery religions, brought forward more than half a century ago, proved to be an extremely productive point of departure, calling attention to several neglected areas and opening up new perspectives. Since he ascribed to the mystery religions as a whole a specific mystery theology and mystery terminology, more detailed consideration was given to the peculiar history-of-religions development of the Hellenistic and Roman periods. At the same time, the close relationship of early Christianity with these developments came into view.

Criticism of Reitzenstein's hypothesis proceeds from the argument that the term "mystery religions" falsely suggests that one is dealing with a homogeneous phenomenon. In particular, the following objections have been raised:

1) There were, to be sure, "mysteries." But in many specific instances it would be inappropriate to call them "religions."

2) Not only the rites, but also the religious concepts of the mysteries are so diverse that it is impossible to reconstruct a theology and a terminology

Bibliography to §4.4d: Texts
Barrett, *Background*, 92–104.

Bibliography to §4.4d: Studies
Nock, "Hellenistic Mysteries and Christian Sacraments," in: idem, *Essays* 2. 791–820.

which would apply to all of them. Insofar as concepts common to all mysteries can be found, they belong to the general language of Hellenism; in other words, they are not limited to the mysteries and thus not specifically characteristic of them.

3) The thesis of an oriental origin of the mystery religions, specifically a Persian origin, is extremely questionable. For one thing, there is insufficient Persian source material to support this hypothesis. On the other hand, it is quite probable that it was Hellenistic concepts that were brought to the east. Finally, the only truly Iranian mystery religion, the mysteries of Mithras, was not propagated until the Roman period.

4) The oldest mysteries which are known are those of Eleusis and Samothrace, and are in fact Greek, not oriental. To be sure, ultimately both seem to have had non-Greek origins and were Hellenized in the preclassical period. Demeter's connection with the lower world (her daughter, Kore, was the goddess of Hades as Persephone) is not typically Greek. The Samothracian gods, as well as Dionysus, are Thracian and Phrygian respectively. But these considerations do not advance Reitzenstein's cause because whatever they contributed to the concept of mystery religions in the Hellenistic and Roman periods was a Greek contribution.

Indeed, one must begin with the observation that Greek concepts are at the root of any cult or religion practicing special initiation rites and services that were not generally open to everyone. To be sure, at least in the Roman imperial period, the use of the term "mystery" had become so diversified that it is useless as a point of orientation—not to speak about its general and literary use. Several cults of the old gods instituted "mysteries" and founded religious associations organized as *thiasoi* with presidents and priests, fixed membership and regular meetings. Sometimes these mystery associations had no other purpose than to provide organization for public festivals and processions. In analogy with the old Greek and newer oriental mysteries, they were intended to provide existing cults with a deeper meaning and a more mysterious aura. Mysteries were even attached to the emperor cult, occasionally also to oracles, as has already been pointed out. The term "mystery" is, therefore, of little use in determining the essential features of a mystery religion. On the other hand, when oriental religions boasted that they possessed secret rituals and that they were in essence and name "mysteries," they claimed equality with something that had always existed in Greece and which had become popular and widespread in the recent past. Such mystery religions, thus, are actually Hellenized oriental cults in which the understanding of special secret rites as "mysteries" is a Greek component of their Hellenization.

But this points only to one of several characteristic features of the formation and transformation of religions in the Hellenistic and Roman periods. In a number of oriental cults which became Hellenized mystery cults, the denotations of the Greek word *mystērion* are insufficient to describe their peculiar character. This is already the case for the Greek cult of Dionysus, and probably also for the cultic establishments of the Cabiri in the Aegean and Asia Minor, which were founded through the missionary activities of Samothrace. Therefore, one of the marks of a Greek mystery, i.e., that it was restricted to a single location, cannot be applied to mysteries of the Hellenistic period. Rather, characteristic features such as the following must be employed in order to describe mystery religions adequately, although not all these features are always present in each individual instance: (1) a firm organization in each congregation to which all members are subject; (2) membership obtained through rites of initiation; (3) participation in regular meetings, in which sacramental ceremonies (such as meals) are celebrated according to fixed rites; (4) obligation to observe certain moral, sometimes also ascetic precepts; (5) mutual support of all members; (6) obedience to the leader of the cult or community; (7) cultivation of traditions which were subject to arcane discipline. In many instances we do not possess much information about such religious communities. The reasons are manifold. Secret disciplines were often observed. The traditions were frequently transmitted in oral form, which was also the case in the early period of Christianity. The social niveau was predominantly middle class and included members of the lower classes, only rarely noble and rich people (see 1 Cor 1:26); therefore votive offerings and inscriptions were rare, where they were not already ruled out on religious grounds. Meetings took place in private houses. Lack of information, therefore, does not prove that such religions were not widely disseminated. On the contrary, there is good reason to believe that the mystery religions were well established in many places, especially in Asia Minor and Italy.

Using the criteria enumerated above, it is still not an easy task to assign any one of the known religions to the "mystery religions." This lack of information is unfortunate because we are dealing with a long period of time in which various changes may have taken place in each of the religions concerned. Rites as well as the interpretation of cult symbols and traditions were not dogmatically fixed. Differences within each of these religions were also due to differing regional conditions. All of this can be observed very well in the case of the history of early Christianity: there were various forms of the words of institution for the Lord's Supper, which only a long development shaped into one formula used everywhere; some congregations observed dietary laws, and others did not; some churches had "apostles" and "prophets" as their leaders, and other had

presbyters or a bishop; there was certainly no uniform interpretation of
the tradition, for indeed a generally accepted tradition did not even exist in
the early period. Whereas some Christians celebrated the eucharist as a
mystery that guaranteed immortality for each participant, others understood the common meal as a messianic banquet in expectation of the
coming of the savior. One must take account of such differences, if one
wants to understand the Hellenistic mystery religions as a history-of-
religions phenomenon. Very important also is the fact that a worldwide
organization for a mystery religion was an exception and probably always
lacking in the early stages of development. Sometimes older cult centers
may have exerted a certain influence, as, for example, Pessinus in Phrygia
for the religion of the Great Mother, and Jerusalem for the Jews and the
Christians. But such centers could have only symbolic significance in the
long run. When Jerusalem was destroyed, the Christian churches had
long since become independent of Jerusalem in their organization. The
development of Judaism and of Christianity in the Roman imperial
period demonstrates the way in which worldwide organizations came
about, insofar as there was any such interest. One or several centers would
first establish control on the regional level. For Judaism this center was
Jamnia; for the Christians such centers developed in Antioch, Ephesus,
Carthage, and Rome. At the next stage, agreements between such centers
were worked out, albeit not without conflicts. Decades, if not centuries,
were necessary for such worldwide organizations to come into being, and
even then they always meant the exclusion of "heretical" groups which an
outsider might not always be able to distinguish from "orthodox" congregations.

In view of these presuppositions and caveats, and using the criteria
established above, it is possible to state that among the mystery religions
were the worship of Dionysus, of Men Tyrannus, Sabazius, Hypsistus,
and Mithras, to a certain degree also the cults of the Great Mother, of Isis,
and of the Syrian Goddess. Of course, Christianity with its many groups
and sects, some parts of diaspora Judaism, and even rabbinic Judaism
must also be mentioned here. As Judaism was reconstituted in Jamnia
after the destruction of Jerusalem, it was characterized by the cultivation
of an oral tradition, the exact determination of moral and ritual rules for
all members, an obligation for mutual support, and a sharp delineation
over against outsiders—all typical features of a mystery religion. Thus it
is not surprising that initiation rites were emphasized (circumcision, proselyte baptism), through which one pledged allegiance to the community.
Pensive mystical interpretations of the tradition—G. Sholem has demonstrated this convincingly—were flourishing in Judaism as much as in
Christianity and in other mystery religions.

On the basis of everything that has been said so far, it seems unwise to tie the term "mystery religions" theologically to the concept of "mystery." In that case it would be necessary to demonstrate not only that mystery rites of a similar structure were present, but also that there were certain theological interpretations which understood such rites as providing salvation or the appropriation of immortality for the individual. This would lead us astray, because such language and ideas are found very widely in Hellenistic and Roman times, and not only in circles that were directly connected with a mystery religion. Seen theologically, such language and ideas are not a specific phenomenon of the mystery religions, but of the Hellenistic history of religions in general which came to its flowering in the Roman imperial period. Judaism and Christianity shared fully in this language, but that says nothing about their specific character as mystery religions. Of course, the ideas of salvation and immortality are also part of the theology of the mystery religions—indeed they cannot be imagined without them. These ideas are, incidentally, not typically "oriental"; they are part of the theology and world view of Hellenism to which the east contributed. Oriental features, however, are frequently present in rites, cult myths, traditions, and names, i.e., in those features which characterize each mystery religion individually.

Ritual actions through which individuals were accepted as members of religious communities and which provided the central focus for the religious experience of the community were widespread. They are found likewise in Greek and oriental religions and also infiltrated the cults of the old gods and even the emperor cult. Common and solemn meals were also practiced in semireligious associations and in philosophical communities, and of course also in Judaism and Christianity. Symbolic content and theological significance varied widely in these communities, but all interpretations had a number of Hellenistic concepts in common. Cosmology and belief in fate, ideas of the soul and its immortality, demonology and concepts of power were the same everywhere, in popular philosophy as well as in mystery religions, in magic as well as among those people who were faithful to the old gods. Jews and Christians were no exception. The language in which one spoke of these things was the general religio-philosophical language of Hellenism, not the special language of the mystery religions; the latter appeared rather in the specific terminology of ritual and liturgy and was different in each case. It was the general religious language of the time which was given to the religious mystification of philosophical and scientific insights and had an almost eccentric interest in the profound and enigmatic. Once a religion like Christianity employed such language, it immediately came under the suspicion of being a mystery religion. Indeed, the Christians called their central cultic

rite, the Lord's Supper, a *mystērion* (Latin: *sacramentum*), and sometimes used the same word to designate their message. All this, of course,
was nothing else but an external sign of the fact that Christianity was
deeply engaged in a process through which it became one with the Hellenistic world and its religious concepts.

One might ask whether the mystery religions were distinguished from
other religions and philosophical circles by an appeal to the specific religious expectations of a particular class of the population. But we do not
know enough about the social stratification of the members of the different
religious groups. It is difficult to advance our knowledge substantially
beyond the general insight that the religious disposition of the fluctuating
populations of the big cities differed considerably from those of the small
towns and villages. On the other hand, it can be said with great certainty
that belief in mysteries and hope of immortality, occultism, and magic,
were at home in all social classes of the urban population. There were
exceptions like the incorrigible mocker Lucian, people who thought that
they were thorough skeptics; but otherwise, educated and literate people
were just as susceptible as the middle class and the slaves. Well-educated
people used magic; Cicero found courage to live and hope for (life after)
death in Eleusis; and the highly sophisticated Neoplatonic philosophers
practiced theurgy with great seriousness. Writers who were committed to
a mystery religion could be quite snobbish with respect to uneducated
people who would be no match for them in respect to their insight into
secret subjects. By no means does this imply that mysteries were only for
the educated upper classes. The ideas and hopes propagated by the mystery religions were fundamentally unrelated to class distinctions, even if a
particular religious community might appeal more specifically to only one
class. It is well known that the Mithras religion was most widespread
among soldiers. If emperors were eager to be initiated into the Eleusinian
mysteries, this reflects only the international fame of this ancient Greek
mystery cult: an emperor was not just like anybody in this case. To claim,
therefore, that Christianity was specifically the religion of the poor and
underprivileged is nonsense and can be easily refuted.

As for the means of propaganda, there were certain differences, but
they were not significant. The practices of the wandering philosophers
and missionaries were the same everywhere, and the active demonstration
of divine power was widespread. One's choice of the instruments of propaganda was mostly a question of individual integrity and had little relation to the philosophical or religious content of the message. The philosopher Dio Chrysostom was as much aware of the danger of falsifying his
message through sordid means as was the apostle Paul. Of course, the
intent of the propaganda would vary. One could either try to win some

individuals for a strictly limited circle of initiates or one could invite the masses for an all-inclusive community. But even if this distinction seems quite clear, it cannot be used to distinguish mystery religions from other religious movements. The Mithras religion seemed to address everybody, but it had a strictly structured hierarchy of adherents who to a greater or lesser degree were counted among the elect. The initiation into the mysteries of Isis reported in Apuleius seems to presuppose that only chosen (and wealthy) individuals could be initiated; but from Asia Minor we know Sarapis temples from the same period which offered room for numbers of people as participants in religious services. In Christianity, the conflict between the gnostic concept of the elect few and Christian universalism lasted a long time.

It should be clear that the Hellenistic and Roman period may be rightly called the age of the mystery religions. In spite of the difficulties in precise definition, there is sufficient material to prove the widespread existence of phenomena germane to the mystery religions and to the milieus in which they could thrive. Mystery religions must be seen as part of this milieu because they are intimately linked to the typical Hellenistic view of human beings and their world. The cosmos has its divine order, but human beings are not granted their full share in this divine universe because they are caught in the realm of sense perception and matter, disorder and mortality, and are subject to Heimarmene, the power of fate. However, in their soul humans have a share in the divine world; various forces, powers, and demons are ready to aid in the act of salvation because humans are ultimately related to them. But salvation cannot take place within the realm of the visible world which is, by definition, the cause of the dilemma. This also explains the lack of initiative for responsible political action—apart from the fact that such opportunities were rare and institutions for such action nonexistent. Whoever wanted to seek fulfillment there would either have to be a member of the leading Roman aristocracy—where the concept of political action as the destiny of human beings was still alive—or plunge into such hopeless political adventures as a slave insurrection or the Jewish rebellion. Salvation could only come through faith in those invisible powers which existed in a realm beyond the visible world, and which belonged to a greater and more harmonious order unthreatened by transitoriness, although these powers were quite capable of extending their influence into this earthly, human world.

The mastery of life, therefore, depended on whether one could secure the favor of those otherworldly powers and share in their benefits. The belief in the power was primary, whether one saw the whole universe pervaded by the power of the Logos, with which one had to be in agreement (the Stoic view), or whether one saw good and evil demons and gods at work everywhere and tried to secure their aid through magic and secret knowledge. In the same way, divine power was present in the spirit as opposed to matter, or in the world of the stars as opposed to the sublunar realm, and last but not least in the demonstrable power of new gods which represented a new and hitherto unknown force, and which constituted the attraction of the new religions from the east. The aim was still the mastery of earthly life with the help of otherworldly powers and guarantees which extended into the life beyond death. Only Gnosticism was more radical (§6.5f), since life in this world had become entirely irrelevant in its view; knowledge and power were completely directed toward the goal of liberation from this world, no longer toward its mastery through the aid of higher forces. Of course, it was easy for Gnosticism to invade the mystery religions; gnostic and non-gnostic writings stand side by side in the Hermetic mystery literature, and gnostics and non-gnostics existed side by side in Christianity.

The visualization, concretization, and representation of the overcoming of matter, death, and fate, as well as of the participation in divine power, as it was offered by the mystery religions, quickly proved to be superior to abstract philosophical doctrines. The rite of initiation had two advantages: first, it was able to symbolize the guarantees for the work of supernatural powers (divine images, lightning effects, symbolic garments, allegories); and second, it provided the opportunity to be accepted into a community of friends who possessed the same secret, i.e., saving knowledge. To be sure, this community had only secondary significance, because it was not the community but the power that the individual would share, which was the goal of the initiation. The purpose of the mystery rites, therefore, must not be understood as the creation of the community of a new and better world. What mattered was the appropriation of power and the securing of the protection of higher authorities in the adversities of life and for the passage of the soul into a better world after death—ideas which also found widespread acceptance in Christianity. It was possible, of course, to reach the same goal without the aid of an organized cult or religion, through philosophical contemplation, for example, or in mysticism, or by submersion into a mystery book (e.g., the Hermetic literature); even magic and astrology might provide access to the realm of otherworldly powers. The mystery religions, however, offered maximal opportunities and were able to institutionalize access to these divine powers. Thus, the mystery religions, and not least Christianity, were ultimately more successful.

Hand of Sabazius

Numerous hands of the god Sabazius, made of bronze or terra cotta, have been found. Decorated with snake, frog, lizard, and pine cone, they were believed to possess magical powers.

JUDAISM IN THE
HELLENISTIC PERIOD

1. THE HISTORY OF ISRAEL TO THE ROMAN CONQUEST

(a) From the Exile to Alexander the Great

After the destruction of Jerusalem in 597 and 585 BCE by Nebuchadnezzar, the king of the Neobabylonian empire, the upper class of the Jewish people was exiled in Babylon and settled there. In 521 Babylon was conquered by the Persians, and many of the exiles received permission from the Persian king to return to Jerusalem. The rebuilding of the religious commonwealth of Jerusalem in the following decades was accomplished with the aid and under the influence of those Jews who stayed behind in Babylon. The temple was rebuilt from 520 to 515. The reconstruction of the walls began in v BCE, but was soon interrupted. Jerusalem was initially subject to the Persian satrap at Samaria. Soon after the middle of v BCE, Nehemiah came to Jerusalem with royal authorization to become the satrap of a province at Jerusalem, now independent of Samaria; he completed the building of the city's walls and successfully defended its claim of independence against the resistance of the Persian administrators in Transjordan and Samaria. This period witnessed the beginnings of the rivalry of Jerusalem with the powerful (Jewish!) families of Samaria related to the Samarian satrap and with the Tobiads, a wealthy Jewish family which governed Transjordan for the Persians.

A generation after Nehemiah, in about 400 BCE, Ezra came to Jerusalem from Babylon (contrary to the sequence of Chronicles, many scholars argue that Nehemiah should be dated *before* Ezra). Ezra inaugurated a new law which had been authorized by the Persian state. This law was not identical with the later Pentateuch, but only with some of its parts relating to ritual and cultic purity. Ezra also reorganized the administration of the Jewish state. The Persian governor was replaced by a council of elders which was directly accountable to the Persian king, closely allied with the leading priestly families, and hence the highest authority for the execution of justice and the supervision of cult and ritual. Jerusalem was thus reorganized into a typical temple state like many others in

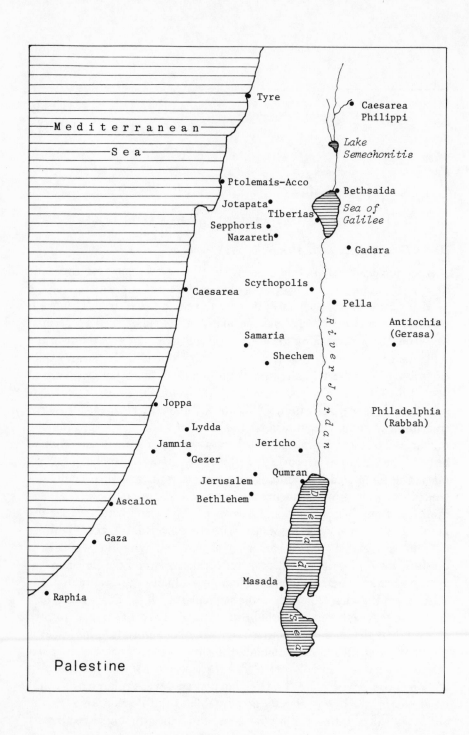

Palestine

Syria and Asia Minor. Although this state consisted primarily of the city of Jerusalem and a number of townships in Judea, its constitution was entirely different from that of a Greek city-state: it was not authorized by the free citizens of the city and its magistrates, but derived its authority from a temple, sanctioned by divine presence. The law of this state was not a civil law (even one with divine legitimization), but the religious law given by God, and the high priest was therefore the highest official of the commonwealth ("theocracy"; see §4.3b).

Bibliography to §5

Emil Schürer, *The History of the Jewish People in the Age of Jesus Christ (175 B.C.–A.D. 135)* (rev. and ed. Geza Vermes, Fergus Millar, and Matthew Black; vols. 1–2; Edinburgh: Clark, 1973–79).

W. O. E. Oesterley, *The Jews and Judaism during the Greek Period: The Background of Christianity* (London: SPCK, and New York: Macmillan, 1941).

Adolf Schlatter, *Geschichte Israels von Alexander dem Grossen bis Hadrian* (3d ed.; Stuttgart: Calwer Verlag, 1925; reprint, 1972).

Arnaldo Momigliano, "Greek Culture and the Jews," in: M. I. Finley, *The Legacy of Greece: A New Appraisal* (Oxford: Clarendon, 1981) 325–46.

S. Safrai and M. Stern (eds.), *The Jewish People in the First Century* (vol. 1; CRI 1; Philadelphia: Fortress, 1974).

Gerhard von Rad, *Old Testament Theology* (2 vols.; New York: Harper & Row, 1965) 2. 263–315.

Martin Hengel, *Judaism and Hellenism: Studies in Their Encounter in Palestine during the Hellenistic Period* (2 vols.; Philadelphia: Fortress, 1974).

Michael Edward Stone, *Scriptures, Sects, and Visions* (Philadelphia: Fortress, 1980).

S. Freyne, *Galilee from Alexander the Great to Hadrian, 323 B.C.E. to 135 C.E.: A Study of Second Temple Judaism* (University of Notre Dame Center for the Study of Judaism and Christianity in Antiquity 5; Notre Dame, IN: University of Notre Dame, 1980).

Bibliography to §5.1

Siegfried Herrmann, *A History of Israel in Old Testament Times* (London: SCM, 1975).

John Bright, *A History of Israel* (2d ed.; Philadelphia: Westminster, 1972).

Martin Noth, *The History of Israel* (2d ed.; New York: Harper & Row, 1960).

Elias Bickerman, *From Ezra to the Last of the Maccabees* (New York: Schocken, 1962).

Victor Tcherikover, *Hellenistic Civilization and the Jews* (New York: Atheneum, 1970).

Martin Hengel, *Judaism and Hellenism: Studies in Their Encounter in Palestine during the Early Hellenistic Period* (Philadelphia: Fortress, 1974).

Idem, *Jews, Greeks and Barbarians* (Philadelphia: Fortress, 1980).

Max Weber, *Ancient Judaism* (London: Collier-Macmillan, and New York: The Free Press, 1952; reprint, 1967).

William R. Farmer, *Maccabees, Zealots, and Josephus: An Inquiry into Jewish Nationalism in the Greco-Roman Period* (New York: Columbia University, 1956).

A. Reifenberg, *Israel's History on Coins from the Maccabees to the Roman Conquest* (London: East and West Library, 1953).

As in other western provinces of the Persian empire, Greek influences also increased in Palestine during this period. Greek imports reached both the coastal cities of Phoenicia and the inland areas such as Judea. Jewish coins imitated the Attic drachma and might bear the image of Zeus or the Athenian owl. But the substance of the religious and cultural life of Jerusalem continued for the time being without any essentially Greek influences.

(b) Palestine under the Hellenistic Rulers

After the battle of Issus (333 BCE; see §1.2b), Palestine came under the control of Alexander the Great. His general Permenion occupied the land, resisted only by Samaria, the seat of the Persian satrap. When Samaria rose up once again while Alexander was in Egypt (331), Alexander's army (probably under Perdiccas) conquered the city and destroyed it. Samaria was subsequently refounded as a Greek colony. It was apparently at this time that the ancient city of Shechem was rebuilt by Jewish people who had been expelled from Samaria; they also erected their own temple near Shechem on Mount Gerizim, thus laying the foundation for the Samaritan schism. The final break, however, between the Jews and Samaritans did not occur until the time of the Hasmoneans. After the death of Alexander, Palestine, along with Samaria and Judea, came under the rule of the Egyptian Ptolemies as part of southern Syria (it changed hands only temporarily during the wars of the Diadochi). Ptolemaic rule lasted an entire century; although the Seleucid kings made repeated attempts to conquer southern Syria, they were not successful in several wars. Finally, the most powerful of the Seleucid kings, Antiochus III the Great (223–187 BCE; see §1.4d), although beaten at first by Ptolemy IV Philopator at Raphia (in southwestern Palestine) in 217, defeated Ptolemy V Epiphanes near the sources of the Jordan (at the site of the later city Caesarea Philippi) in 198 and made Phoenicia and Palestine part of the Seleucid empire. Jerusalem supported Antiochus in this war, held the Egyptian garrison of the city captive, and greeted the Seleucid

Bibliography to §5.1a

Peter R. Ackroyd, *Israel under Babylon and Persia* (London: Oxford University, 1970).

Frank Moore Cross, "A Reconstruction of the Jewish Restoration," *JBL* 94 (1975) 4–18.

Jacob Neusner, *A History of the Jews in Babylonia*, vol. 1: *The Parthian Period* (StPB 9; Leiden: Brill, 1965).

Bibliography to §5.1b

R. Koebner (ed.), *Studies in Classics and Jewish Hellenism* (Jerusalem: Magnes, 1954).

king jubilantly. In turn, Antiochus renewed all the old privileges of the Jewish temple state and granted new favors (the decree is preserved in Josephus *Ant.* 12.138–44). Good relationships continued between Jerusalem and the Seleucid administration during the following years, but a crisis developed under Antiochus IV Epiphanes.

Neither the Ptolemies nor the Seleucids interfered in the internal cultural and religious affairs of Jerusalem. But a process of Hellenization began in the early Hellenistic period which affected the whole country and eventually also Jerusalem itself. Here as elsewhere the cities were the primary agents of Hellenization. The Ptolemies, though they did not sponsor the founding of new cities in Egypt, actively supported the creation of Greek cities in Syria and Palestine. Samaria had been reconstituted as a Greek city already during the time of Alexander the Great. More Greek cities were founded in both the east and west of Palestine during the Ptolemaic and Seleucid periods, most of which were reconstitutions of older cities: on the Phoenician coast, Ptolemais (formerly Acco), Jamnia, Ascalon, and Gaza; to the south and east of the Sea of Galilee, the cities which later belonged to the "Decapolis": Pella, Philadelphia (Rabbath-Ammon, today Aman), Gadara, Scythopolis (Beth-Shean), Seleucia in Bashan, and especially Gerasa, reconstituted by Antiochus IV as Antiochia—until the late Roman empire one of the most magnificent and most important cities of western Syria. Some of the inhabitants of these cities were Macedonians and Greeks, but Hellenized Semites, Syrians, Phoenicians, Arabs, and of course also Jews, predominated. An unavoidable consequence was that Greek or Hellenized oriental cultural elements, a new style of life, and foreign cults were imported. The gods worshiped in those cities were oriental deities under Greek names (e.g., Ashtoreth as Aphrodite in Ascalon) or Greek gods introduced by the Greek founders of the city (e.g., Dionysus in Scythopolis; coins display the name Nysa, the mythological birth place of Dionysus, as the official name of the city).

Syria and Palestine had not been fully subject to the strictly centralized administration of the Ptolemies. The estates owned by the king were managed by royal officials who were directly responsible to the king. But large parts of the country remained under the semi-autonomous governance of cities, temples, and princes. Jerusalem and parts of Judea made up one of these temple states; among the princes, the wealthy Tobiads of Transjordan, the traditional enemies of Jerusalem since the Persian period, were most conspicuous. The Tobiad Joseph (second half of III BCE), whose father had been the Ptolemaic army commander for Transjordan, and whose mother was a daughter of the high priest at Jerusalem, held the office of Egyptian finance minister for all of southern Syria for twenty-two years. Although Joseph was an Israelite, he seems to have been a typical

Hellenistic tycoon who had accepted, along with political and economic power, also the Greek style of life. Among the upper class of the Jews, Joseph may not have been an exception. The leading priestly families of Jerusalem, closely related to the Tobiads through marriage and financial interests, were apparently also Hellenized to a large degree. Seleucid rule, which began in early II BCE, brought no basic changes in this respect. It only implied a shifting of power from the pro-Ptolemaic party to the pro-Seleucid party in Jerusalem. Nevertheless, a crisis was soon to develop which was closely connected with the question of Hellenization.

(c) The Maccabean Revolt

The origin and causes of the Maccabean revolt are not completely clear; a multiplicity of factors was probably involved. Jerusalem must have had a Seleucid party already before the conquest of Palestine by Antiochus III. Among its leaders was the high priest Simon (perhaps Simon the Just), as well as the older sons of the Tobiad Joseph, in other words, the most powerful Jewish families of the country. Thus, it is not surprising that the new king, Antiochus III, found a cordial welcome and that he was eager to confirm "the laws of the fathers" which were the basis of the theocratic administration and the religious life of the Jewish people. But it must be remembered that the leading Jewish circles whose "laws of the fathers" were thus guaranteed were already Hellenized, especially the wealthy and influential Tobiads. It seems obvious that these circles would find themselves in a growing opposition to those who held on to the traditional forms of religious life and culture. However, the contrast between traditional forms of religion on the one hand and accelerating Hellenization on the other would not in itself provide sufficient cause and political motivation for a bloody revolution and a protracted war of liberation. To be sure, the only (and not always reliable) source for developments before the outbreak of open hostilities, the Second Book of Maccabees, indicates that the political infighting of the leading (priestly) families of Jerusalem played a considerable role in the events preceding the revolution. But the eruption of hostilities also coincides with the humiliation of the Syrian king Antiochus IV Epiphanes by the Romans (§1.4d) and is closely related to the increasing financial difficulties of the Seleucid empire. Furthermore, ele-

Bibliography to §5.1c

Elias Bickerman, *The God of the Maccabees: Studies on the Meaning and Origin of the Maccabean Revolt* (SJLA 32; Leiden: Brill, 1979).

Thérèse Libmann-Frankfurt, "Rome et le conflit judéo-syrien (164–161 avant notre ère)," *L'Antiquité classique* 38 (1969) 101–20.

A. Giovanni and H. Müller, "Die Beziehungen zwischen Rom und den Juden im 2. Jh. v. Chr.," *MH* 28 (1971) 156–71.

ments of utopian apocalypticism, developing since the time of the exile, seem to have found a rather wide acceptance (§5.2b). The second century of the Hellenistic epoch is especially characterized by a number of revolutionary movements in which utopian concepts play a significant role (cf. the insurrection of the adherents of "the Commonwealth of the Sun" in Pergamum; see §1.4b).

Insofar as it is possible to reconstruct the course of events which led to the Maccabean revolt, its beginnings appear in a controversy of the pro-Syrian and the pro-Egyptian parties over the high-priestly office and control of the financial interests and power of the temple. After the death of the high priest Simon (after 200 BCE), who belonged to the Zadokite family, his son Onias III became his successor. But Onias leaned toward Egypt and supported the youngest son of the Tobiad Joseph; the latter had had a falling out with his older brothers, who had been friends and partisans of the late pro-Seleucid high priest Simon. The younger Tobiad, as a friend of the new high priest, was able to use the banking services of the temple to his advantage. The assassination of the Syrian king Seleucus IV in 175 gave the older Tobiads and their Hellenistic followers the opportunity to expel Onias and appoint Onias' brother Jason (the Greek form of the Hebrew name Joshua) as high priest in his stead. All of this happened with the knowledge and support of the new king Antiochus IV Epiphanes, from whom Jason actually had bought the office of high priest. At the same time, Jason received permission from the king to reconstitute Jerusalem as a Greek city to be named Antioch, in other words, to appoint a city council instead of the traditional council of elders (*gerousia*), to organize an assembly of the citizens who were entitled to vote, to build a gymnasium, and to make arrangements for the education of *epheboi*. It is not clear from our sources whether this new legislation also included a religious reform. Jason is never accused of having set aside the "laws of the fathers," but judging from analogies it would seem natural that in such a program of the Hellenization of a city, the traditional oriental deity (in this case Yahweh, though for the Greeks he had no name) would be identified with a Greek god (most likely Zeus Olympius). But even if this were the case, neither Antiochus IV nor any of his predecessors would have interfered with established ritual or religious conventions. Had the Hellenization of the Jewish religion been nothing but the identification of Yahweh with Zeus Olympius, a religious revolt would have been quite unlikely.

The turning point was the expulsion of Jason, who, though a member of the reform party, was still a legitimate Zadokite and thus even for the conservatives a guarantor of the "laws of the fathers." However, in 172 BCE, Menelaus, the brother of an officer of the temple named Simon, took

Jason's place. Apparently he was more suitable in the eyes of the reformers, had the support of the Tobiads, and had offered the king an even bigger sum of money than what Jason had paid for the high-priestly office. Only now did the situation reach a crisis point. It became evident that the office of the high priest must not be abused with impunity in the interests of the leading aristocracy. More was at stake: the high priest was the guarantor of religious law for all the people, and an illegitimate high priest was a threat to the constitution of the whole commonwealth. As the resistance of the people grew, Menelaus was barely able to hold on to his office. While he was in Antioch, his brother Lysimachus, whom Menelaus had appointed as his deputy, was slain in Jerusalem. The external political situation also provided an opportunity for the "pious" to organize themselves. Thus the "pious," the Hasidim (the family of the Maccabees belonged to this group, and their later offspring included both the Pharisees and the Essenes), formed a new political movement which no longer permitted the aristocracy to treat the whole affair as if nothing was at stake but their rivaling claims to power.

In 169–168 Antiochus Epiphanes led two campaigns against Egypt. Returning from the first campaign, he visited his friends, the citizens of the new Greek polis Antioch-Jerusalem; it turned out, however, that he was primarily interested in the treasury of the temple: the financial crisis of the Seleucids had become so severe that the kings repeatedly resorted to such measures. This naturally enraged the people, and when the king had left the city—and after an apparently abortive attempt of Jason to occupy Jerusalem—the conservative party took possession of the city and locked up Menelaus and the partisans of the reform in the Acra, the fortified Hellenistic quarter. This action signaled the beginning of the revolt. Antiochus, who had just been humiliated in Egypt by the Romans—an ultimatum of the Roman Senate had forced him to relinquish all his Egyptian conquests—reacted promptly. He captured Jerusalem (probably through his official Apollonius), murdered or expelled the Jewish inhabitants, and made Jerusalem a *katoikia,* that is, a city in which soldiers, veterans, and other colonists (mostly Syrians) formed the citizenry. Only now did Apollonius, Antiochus' governor, begin a persecution of the faithful Jews, not for religious reasons, but in order to subdue a rebellious people; it is not possible to maintain the traditional view, according to which the rebellion was a reaction to the religious persecution. Only now was the temple cult of Yahweh (called Zeus Olympius since the reform) transformed into the cult of a superficially Hellenized Syrian god, Zeus Baal Shamayin, whose sacred rock was brought into the temple; there he was worshiped together with his consorts "Athena" and "Dionysus."

Only at this time were the "laws of the fathers" annulled, because they were useless as the constitution of the Syrian-Greek citizenry of the *katoikia* Antioch-Jerusalem. The political and religious reorganization was completed with the decrees of Antiochus from the year 167, which legitimized the new cult and outlawed the practice of the Jewish religion in Jerusalem and Judea (not, however, in Jewish communities elsewhere). The persecution of the faithful Jews was a necessary consequence. It is difficult to estimate the severity of the persecution, because the information about this persecution provided by the Books of the Maccabees is mostly legendary. Antiochus was correct in seeing the core of the resistance among those people who adhered to the Jewish religion most faithfully. He therefore forced the population to participate in the new pagan cult and he outlawed circumcision. The eating of pork became the test of loyalty: whoever refused demonstrated, in the view of the royal officials, that he belonged to the rebellion. It cannot be doubted that many Jews who were unwilling to deny their faith were cruelly executed and martyred.

But other Jews chose to flee into the mountains of Judea to join the guerillas commanded by a certain Judas with the surname Maccabeus (= "the Hammer")—this is reported by 2 Macc 5:28 and 8:1. However, the First Book of Maccabees, written by the official court historian of the Hasmoneans, gives a different account because the later Hasmoneans descended not from Judas, but from his elder brother Simon: not Judas, but his and Simon's father Mattathias is said to have founded the resistance movement. There is no doubt, however, that this newly organized resistance would appeal directly to the traditional values which the Hasidim had defended against the Hellenistic reformers, and thus the rebellion developed into a powerful national religious movement enjoying wide support. Because of the persecution, leadership would naturally fall to someone who knew how to fight a guerilla war. While all Hasidim seem to have supported Judas during the revolt, it is understandable that certain groups of Hasidim, such as the Essenes and the Pharisees, would later break with the heirs of this guerilla leader when they aspired to, and actually achieved, political power. The government of Antiochus IV, on the other hand, was also quite successful in rallying to its support all vested powers and interest groups, namely, the Greek cities, the non-Jewish population of the neighboring areas, the Samaritans, and finally those Jews who had favored Hellenization and wanted to establish a peaceful coexistence of all people in the country. To this final group belonged, of course, the Hellenized aristocracy of Jerusalem under the leadership of the high priest Menelaus, whom Antiochus had appointed.

After four years of war, in which the guerillas under Judas were repeatedly successful (168–164 BCE), the Hellenized Jews of Jerusalem made a final attempt at reconciliation and succeeded in persuading Antiochus to repeal the edicts against the Jewish religion (the new decrees are preserved in 2 Macc 11:16–21, 27–32). Within a specified period all those who fled because of the persecution were permitted to return and their right to the free exercise of their religion was guaranteed. But it was too late: shortly after the publication of these edicts, Judas conquered Jerusalem, and the Hellenists had to retreat once more to the fortified Acra. Antiochus Epiphanes was in the east, fighting against the Parthians, where he died in 163. His deputy Lysias, governor of the western part of the kingdom, and thus responsible for Judea, was unable to intervene because the problem of the royal succession forced him to stay in Antioch. This gave Judas the opportunity not only to consolidate his power, and even to humiliate his enemies beyond the borders of Judea, but also to reach a compromise agreement with the new king, Antiochus V Eupator, in which Jerusalem's temple was officially returned to the traditional Jewish cult (162 BCE; see the document in 2 Macc 11:22–26). Menelaus was executed; the new high priest Alcimus, probably from the house of Onias and therefore a legitimate Zadokite, was however not recognized by Judas because of his sympathy for Hellenism.

Shortly afterwards, Antiochus V was assassinated by his cousin, who became king as Demetrius I Soter (162–150). Fortune now turned against Judas, because the new king supported Alcimus against Judas, and the Hasidim in Jerusalem were now willing to accept Alcimus as high priest. Demetrius' general Bacchides defeated Judas' army, in part because it was no longer strengthened by the Hasidim, who now seemed content with the reestablishment of the Jerusalem cult. Judas died in battle in 160. Soon thereafter Alcimus also died, and the Syrian commander Bacchides offered a new compromise treaty. It was finally agreed that Judas' brother Jonathan should be established as a "judge" in the town of Michmash (near Jerusalem), but he had to promise not to interfere in the affairs of Jerusalem (157). Thus ended the revolt of the Maccabees; the Syrian sovereignty was established once more, and freedom of religion was guaranteed for the Jews; the office of high priest, however, was left vacant.

After several years of peace (157–153), renewed fighting among the pretenders to the Syrian throne opened another period of instability and war. Jonathan, and later his brother Simon, were able to use the internal difficulties of the Syrian empire to their advantage and, in spite of some setbacks, finally achieved their goal of political independence. In 153 BCE Alexander Balas tried to gain the Syrian throne. To defend himself against this pretender, King Demetrius I sought the support of Jonathan and, in return, gave Jonathan permission to occupy Jerusalem. But soon thereafter Jonathan switched his allegiance to Alexander Balas, who rewarded him by appointing him high priest: in 152 Jonathan appeared for the first time in public in that office. After his victory over Demetrius I, Alexander Balas honored Jonathan by making him a "friend of the king," and appointed him as *strategos* and governor of Judea. The foundation stone was thus laid for the Hasmonean state.

(d) The Time of the Hasmoneans

In order to achieve their goal of becoming the rulers of an independent country and to bring all of Palestine under their control, the Hasmoneans had to take advantage of the continuing dynastic wars in Syria and the shift of power on the international scene from the Greek kingdoms to Rome. Jonathan was apparently quite successful in this respect. Even when the young son of Demetrius I, Demetrius II Nicator, overthrew Alexander Balas in 145 BCE, Jonathan was able to strenghten his position: Demetrius II awarded him with the southern districts of Samaria. Another change of allegiance, however, proved to be his undoing. When Diodotus Trypho rose against Demetrius II in order to gain the throne for Antiochus VI, the son of Alexander Balas, he received Jonathan's support, confirmed Jonathan in his office and appointed Jonathan's brother *strategos* of the coastal district of Palestine. These two brothers were now able to conquer the whole area from the Philistine coast to Galilee and Damascus. When Trypho imprisoned Antiochus VI in order to occupy the throne himself, however, he also captured Jonathan and executed him for unclear reasons. Simon, the last of the five sons of Mattathias, now made a treaty with Demetrius II against Trypho, in which Demetrius recognized Simon as independent ruler of Judea, gave freedom from taxation to the Jews, and permitted Simon to expel the Syrian garrison from the Acra in Jerusalem (142–141 BCE).

This confirmed Simon's *de facto* independence, which he now used to conquer Gezer (west of Jerusalem) and Jaffa, thus gaining free access to the Mediterranean coast. Simon also established diplomatic ties with Sparta and Rome and began to date official documents according to his regnal years. While Jonathan, like all his predecessors, had been appointed high priest by the Syrian king, Simon was confirmed by a great assembly of the priests, the leaders of the Jews, and the elders of the country as "regent" and as "high priest forever, until a faithful prophet should arise" (140 BCE). This event seemed to be the fulfillment of all the hopes and expectations which thirty years earlier had united the conservatives, the Hasidim, and the political rebels in their fight against Antiochus IV Epiphanes; indeed, this is exactly what the author of the First Book of Maccabees tries to communicate to his readers in the fourteenth chapter of his book.

Maccabees and Hasmoneans

(all dates are BCE)

Rulers	Events
after 200 high priest Simon dies; Onias III successor	195 Jerusalem welcomes Antiochus III
175 Jason high Priest	175 Seleucus IV assassinated; Jerusalem reconstituted as Greek polis
172 Menelaus high priest	169 Antiochus IV takes temple treasury
168–160 Judas leader of revolt	168–164 Maccabean revolt
	167 Jerusalem becomes "Antiochia"
	164 Antiochus IV dies
	160 Temple returned to Jewish worship
152–143 Jonathan high priest	
143–134 Simon high priest	142 Expulsion of Syrian garrison from Jerusalem
	Exile of "Teacher of Righteousness"
134–104 John Hyrcanus	128 Destruction of Samaritan temple on Mt. Garizim
104 Aristobolus	
104–78 Alexander Janneus	94 Revolt of Pharisees
76–67 Alexandra	
67–65 Hyrcanus II & Aristobulus II	65 Pompey enters Jerusalem temple

But the political and religious problems of this step cannot be overlooked. Even though the title "king" was consciously avoided in Simon's proclamation of his office, it was nevertheless a declaration of independence and authority in the typical style of a Hellenistic ruler. His position was based upon military power; he alone had the right to be clothed in purple and wear a gold buckle; any resistance or disobedience was explicitly threatened with severe punishment. The *res gestae* of Simon (all the other members of his family who had in fact fought most of the battles for independence are scarcely mentioned in this document) were finally inscribed on bronze tablets and publicly displayed in the precinct of the temple as a sign of his power and authority.

The illegitimacy of Jonathan's and Simon's high priesthoods, because they were not Zadokites, is of course not mentioned in 1 Maccabees, the official court history of the Hasmoneans. But at least one faction of the Hasidim, namely, the Essenes, who have now become quite well known through the discovery of the texts from Qumran, apparently went into exile at this time. Under the leadership of the "Teacher of Righteousness," who was a Zadokite priest, they founded their own religious center in the desert on the shores of the Dead Sea. For them Simon (and perhaps already his brother Jonathan?) was the "evil priest" who persecuted the Teacher of Righteousness without mercy (§5.2c). No wonder the decree of 1 Macc 14:44 explicitly threatens punishment for priests who disobey Simon's rule. Another faction of the Hasidim, the Pharisees, were persecuted by Simon's successors half a century later. Even though the Hasmoneans attempted in the following years to make the Jewish state as powerful as it had been in the time of David and Solomon, and with some success, nonetheless the pious people remained unwilling to accept this state and its rulers as the fulfillment of their religious hopes.

In the year 139 the throne of the Seleucid kingdom was occupied for the last time in its history by an able ruler, Antiochus VIII Sidites. The new king, although willing to recognize Simon's independence, demanded that Simon withdraw from Gezer and Jaffa and accept a Syrian garrison in the Acra. Simon refused, and his sons Judas and John (Hyrcanus) were able to defeat Antiochus' general in battle. But shortly thereafter, in 135, Simon fell prey to a conspiracy of his son-in-law Ptolemy during a drinking bout. Ptolemy also murdered Simon's wife and two of his sons, but John Hyrcanus escaped. Meanwhile, Antiochus Sidites was preparing to invade Judea with a new army. Although John Hyrcanus had prevailed over his rival Ptolemy and was recognized as his father's successor, he could not defend himself against Antiochus and had to withdraw behind the walls of Jerusalem. Antiochus and John Hyrcanus reached a compromise settlement, in which the latter agreed to give up all new conquests made by his father and to pay a substantial tribute. In return, Antiochus recognized John Hyrcanus' independence and left the Acra in Jewish hands. When Antiochus Sidites was killed in battle against the Parthians (129), a campaign in which John Hyrcanus was obliged to participate, the danger of Syrian interference in the affairs of the Jewish state ended, since the Seleucid empire never regained its military power and political influence.

The following decades were characterized by a systematic conquest of the whole area of Palestine by the Hasmoneans, including the coastal area and the Greek cities. Most of these conquests were accomplished during the long reign of John Hyrcanus (135–104 BCE), some under his sons (Judas) Aristobulus (104) and Alexander Janneus (104–78). Among the cultural and religious problems which followed upon these conquests, the fate of the Greek cities had the most momentous consequences. Hellenization of the country had once been closely linked to the founding of Greek cities. Their citizens, to be sure, were not actually Greeks in most cases, but Hellenized Phoenicians, Syrians, and others. But the concept of the free city—"free" because of its constitution and self-government—as a center of cultural and commercial life was itself Greek. The right to education (gymnasia were among the most important institutions of these cities) and the free exercise of religion as soon as the official deities had received their due recognition were also fundamentally Greek concepts.

But the understanding of a Jewish state which was propagated by the Hasmoneans could not be reconciled with the idea of the Greek city. The Maccabean revolt had been ignited by an attempt to reconstitute Jerusalem as a Greek city. Even the notion of cultural and religious pluralism was necessarily repulsive when applied to Jerusalem. From the perspective of the traditional Jewish religion, the only consistent continuation of the revolt was the return of the whole country to faith in the god of Israel. This religious view was in natural agreement with the political insight that the existence of independent cities occupying positions of economic power was irreconcilable with the interests of a relatively small nation state. Therefore the Hasmoneans proceeded to conquer nearly all Greek cities in their region of power (only Acco-Ptolemais on the coast and Ammon-Philadelphia in Transjordan were able to remain independent). The inhabitants of these cities were forced to emigrate or to convert to Judaism, and those who remained were deprived of their privileges and became subject to Hasmonean rule. This removed from the process of Hellenization its most important sociological institution, although Greek elements, customs, and language continued to exist in many places. On the other hand, the influence of Hellenism was still very evident in the political conduct and external manifestations of the ruling house of the Hasmoneans. John Hyrcanus changed the names of his sons Judas, Mattathias, and Jonathan to Aristobulus, Antigonus, and Alexander. Aristobulus called himself "Philhellenos" and assumed the title "king," though only for his relations with other countries—his coins still read "John the High Priest." It appears that John Hyrcanus had already employed foreign mercenaries. Only two goals were consistently pursued by the Hasmonean rulers: to enlarge the power of the Jewish state, and to make all inhabitants of the country Jewish subjects, even if force was necessary to accomplish this goal.

At the beginning of the Maccabean war of independence, the religious goal was predominant: to liberate the temple, the city of Jerusalem, and the land from pagan abominations. But in the hands of the Hasmoneans, religion became a tool through which all inhabitants of the country could be made loyal to Jerusalem, where the ruler was at the same time the high priest. After the conquest of Idumea, all male inhabitants were compelled to be circumcised. This was even the case in the conquest of Greek cities, unless the non-Jewish inhabitants were killed or expelled instead. The Samaritan capital of Shechem was also conquered, the temple on Mt.

Gerizim destroyed, and the Samaritan population forced to acknowledge the religious jurisdiction of Jerusalem. The Essene literature reveals that for some the idea of the elect people of God could no longer be reconciled with the political reality of the religious community under the jurisdiction of the Jerusalem temple. The party of the Pharisees (on its beginnings, see §5.2d), apparently a continuation of the politically engaged section of the older Hasidim, also seems to have viewed this religious policy of the Hasmoneans with ever-growing reservations. Open conflict came during the reign of Alexander Janneus, who became high priest after the short rule of his brother Aristobulus I (104 BCE) and who continued the imperialistic policies of his father until 78 BCE. In 94 a revolt began, apparently instigated by the Pharisees, a revolt which led to six years of civil war and the intervention of the Syrian king Demetrius III on behalf of the revolutionaries. Janneus, finally victorious, had eight hundred leaders of the rebels publicly crucified. But in the reign of Janneus' widow Alexandra, the Pharisees appear to have been the ruling party of the country; they made use of their new power by recalling those who had been exiled under Janneus and by punishing his advisers.

After the death of Alexandra, the power of the Hasmoneans disintegrated in the intrigues and fighting of her sons. Hyrcanus, who had assumed the office of high priest, was forced by his brother Aristobulus (II) to seek refuge with the Nabateans in Petra. Together with the Nabateans, and with the help of the most formidable politician of the country, the Idumean Antipater (son of the governor of Idumea and father of Herod the Great), Hyrcanus was able to defeat Aristobulus, who was forced to barricade himself in the Jerusalem temple (65 BCE). In this situation, both sides appealed to the Roman general Pompey, who controlled most of the eastern Mediterranean and had just begun to reorganize the area of the former Seleucid empire on Rome's behalf. With the conquest of Jerusalem by Pompey came the end of Hasmonean rule over Palestine, although several members of the Hasmonean house were still to play a subordinate role in the political events and intrigues of the following decades (§6.6a, d).

(e) The Jewish Diaspora

The history of the Jews in Palestine is but a small segment of the history of the Jewish people in the Hellenistic period. Beginning with the Babylonian exile, a large part of the Jewish people, or at least of its upper class, lived outside of Palestine. There was little change in this situation when some of the exiled were permitted to return to Jerusalem. During the Hellenistic period, which involved substantial migrations of peoples from many nations, the proportion of Jews living in the dispersion grew even further, so that the Jewish diaspora became increasingly important and began an independent religious and cultural development.

The Babylonian diaspora began with the exile to Babylon. Only a small portion of the Jewish population in Babylon seems to have taken advantage of the first opportunity to return to Jerusalem, and even those who returned later with Nehemiah and Ezra still left a substantial Jewish population behind in Babylon. The most important cities with large Jewish populations during the Hellenistic period were Babylon, refounded by Alexander, and Seleucia on the Tigris, founded by Seleucus I (312 BCE), which became the capital, economic center, and most populous city of the whole east. The Hellenization of the mostly oriental inhabitants of these cities also affected the Jewish diaspora, though not to the same degree as in Alexandria. Since the Babylonian Jews had a considerable influence upon the Jewry of Palestine, even in the beginnings of the Roman period (during which the most influential teacher of Pharisaic Judaism, Hillel, came to Palestine from Babylon), Hellenistic influences reached the Jews of the home country even from the east. The bond between Babylon and Palestine was particularly intimate, since in both places the majority of the Jews spoke Aramaic, while the diaspora in Egypt, Asia Minor, and the west used Greek as their common language. The Babylonian Jews were, as a whole, not hostile to the Seleucid and Parthian rulers. They seem to have been much less positive, however, in their feelings regarding Rome. The learned tradition of Sacred Scripture in Babylon was remarkable. In the reorganization of Judaism after the destruction of Jerusalem by the Romans in 70 CE, the Babylonian text of the Hebrew Bible became the accepted text among the rabbis of Jamnia (now the basis of modern editions of the Masoretic text) and replaced the Palestinian text which had been in use until this time; the latter is preserved only in the Greek translation of the Septuagint, the Pentateuch of the Samaritans, and the newly discovered biblical manuscripts of Qum-

Bibliography to §5.1e: Texts

V. A. Tcherikover, *Corpus Papyrorum Judaicarum* (Cambridge, MA: Harvard University, 1957–64).

Bibliography to §5.1e: Studies

J. Gutmann (ed.), *The Synagogue: Studies in Origins, Archeology and Architecture* (Library of Biblical Studies; New York: Ktav, 1975).

Erwin R. Goodenough, *The Jurisprudence of Jewish Courts in Egypt: Legal Administration by the Jews under the Early Roman Empire as Described by Philo Judaeus* (New Haven: Yale University, 1929).

Jean Juster, *Les Juifs dans l'Empire romain: leur condition juridique, économique et sociale* (Paris: Geuthner, 1914).

J. N. Sevenster, *The Roots of Pagan Anti-Semitism in the Ancient World* (NovTSup 41; Leiden: Brill, 1975).

Synagogue of Sardis

Built in II c.e. in one of the wings of the gymnasium in a choice location of the city, and remodeled in V c.e., the synogogue was excavated recently and restored by a Harvard-Cornell team under George M. A. Hanfmann. The entrance was at the far left through a peristyle court; between the three doors are two shrines (for the book of the Torah). On the right a monumental table, supported by two eagles, in front of an apse with rows of seats. The building measured about 200 feet (= 60 m.) in length (without the court) and rose to a height of over 70 feet.

ran. Later the Babylonian Talmud became the authoritative codification of the rabbinic traditions. There were also Jewish communities in other cities of the east, for example, in Edessa, Nisibis, and Dura Europus. In most of these cities the Jewish communities were not very large. Adiabene is a special case, a district at the upper Tigris river (the ancient Assyria) which was ruled by Parthian princes. It had a strong Jewish population, perhaps remnants of the exiles from the northern kingdom of Israel who had been brought there by the Assyrians at the end of III BCE. At the beginning of the Christian era, even the ruling prince and his mother converted to Judaism (described in detail by Josephus, *Ant.* 20.17ff).

The Egyptian diaspora, however, would soon surpass Babylon in significance. Already in the Persian period there were several large colonies of Jews in Egypt. A group of Jews migrated to Egypt after the conquest of Jerusalem by the Babylonians and forced the prophet Jeremiah to go with them, where he died. A Jewish military colony with a temple existed, as papyrus finds have revealed, in Elephantine in upper Egypt from VI BCE. More Jewish immigrants came to Egypt after the Persian conquest. After Alexander the Great had founded Alexandria, many Jews settled there making this city the home of a large Jewish diaspora community as early as III BCE. Apparently many of these immigrants had previously lived elsewhere in Lower Egypt, while others came from Palestine, which was an Egyptian province during the early Hellenistic period. No doubt Ptolemaic rule over southern Syria and Palestine strenghthened the Jewish diaspora of Alexandria and its economic and social position. But even when Seleucid control of Palestine began in the early II BCE, Jewish immigration to Egypt did not end. There was still a pro-Egyptian party in Jerusalem, and Egypt remained a convenient place of refuge for its members. The story of Onias (IV), son of the high priest Onias III who was overthrown during the Hellenistic reforms in Jerusalem, is very revealing in this respect. This Onias was apparently a mercenary leader in Egyptian service during the reign of Ptolemy VI Philometor (180–145 BCE). A *katoikia* (military colony) was founded for him and his soldiers in Leontopolis, and a Jewish temple was built there. The strong position of the Jews during the reign of Philometor, and the fact that they had supported him as well as his widow, may have been the reason for the persecution of the Jews under Philometor's rival Ptolemy VIII Euergetes (145–116 BCE). This persecution apparently formed the historical background for the attempted pogrom which *3 Maccabees* mistakenly ascribes to Ptolemy IV. Around the year 100 BCE, two sons of Onias IV are reported to have been Egyptian generals. All this shows that the Jewish diaspora in Egypt enjoyed a relatively favored position during most of the Hellenistic period.

The Jews of Alexandria by no means lived in a ghetto, but settled in various quarters of the city, although most of them were concentrated in two of the five sections. They were not without political influence and participated in the cultural life of the city. While the Jews of Babylon and of other cities in the east spoke Aramaic, the language of the Alexandrian diaspora was Greek. Alexandria was the place where the Greek translation of the Hebrew Bible began in III BCE (the translation which later became authoritative for the Christians; see §5.3f). But Jews from Egypt also migrated to other parts of the Mediterranean world. The important communities in the Cyrenaica were founded by Egyptian Jews no later than III BCE. Jewish diaspora communities were also found on those Aegean islands which were ruled by Egypt during III BCE, especially on Crete, and, not least, on Cyprus, which also belonged to the Ptolemaic empire. Since Alexandria was a significant port of transfer for exports to the western Mediterranean, it is quite possible that the Roman diaspora owed its beginnings to Alexandrian Jews.

Not much is known about the Jewish diaspora in western Syria. There was certainly a Jewish community as early as II BCE in the Seleucid capital of Antioch, which later became the seat of the Roman governor. We have evidence for Jewish communities in other major cities like Apamea and Damascus, and many Jews lived in the areas of Syria bordering on Palestine.

Next to the Babylonian and Egyptian communities, the diaspora of Asia Minor assumed the greatest importance. The earliest reliable information comes from around the year 200 BCE: Antiochus III settled two thousand Jewish families from Babylonia in western Asia Minor, probably in military colonies. Beginning with the Roman conquest (at the end of II BCE), one finds reports about Jews and Jewish communities from all districts of southern and western Asia Minor, especially in the most important cities. But there was also a Jewish diaspora in the Greek cities along the Black Sea. It is striking that almost all Jewish inscriptions from Asia Minor use the Greek language. Among the synagogues which have been excavated, that of Sardis has attracted the most attention in recent times. It is a large basilica, a building which testifies eloquently to the size and social position of the Jewish community in Sardis. (However, this building did not serve as a synagogue until II CE. See photo p. 204.)

Nothing is known about the beginnings of the Jewish diaspora in Greece. At the beginning of the Roman imperial period there were Jewish communities in all major cities, such as Thessalonica, Athens, Corinth, and Argos. But it seems that the Jews of Greece were less numerous than those of Asia Minor and the Greek islands. Very little is known about Jews in the western Mediterranean during the Hellenistic period, and there is no doubt that the Jewish diaspora grew much more slowly there than in the east. The earliest Jewish communities in the west were founded in the Greek colonies of southern Italy and Sicily. The wars during the expansion of Rome into the eastern Mediterranean in II and I BCE meant that Jews were brought to Rome and Italy as prisoners of war; many stayed after their release. In the imperial period, Rome became the center of Judaism in the western part of the empire; as many as thirteen synagogues have been discovered through excavations in various quarters of the city (there was no Jewish ghetto in Rome) as well as many catacombs and inscriptions.

As a development of cultural history, Hellenization affected all Jews, not only those of the diaspora, but also the Jews of Palestine. But in the diaspora especially in the Greek cities, the results of Hellenization were much more profound. In Palestine, the Grecizing of Hebrew proper names was limited to the ruling house and to the upper classes, whereas in the diaspora it was a widespread phenomenon. The Greek language was known in Palestine, but it did not replace Aramaic as the commonly spoken language; religious literature continued to be written in Hebrew, while the Bible was still copied in Hebrew and translated into Aramaic for use in the synagogue services. On the other hand, the language of the Jews in Alexandria, Asia Minor, and Rome was Greek. The translation of the Hebrew Bible into Greek began as early as III BCE, and Greek readings from the Bible as well as the use of Greek as the language of liturgy became the rule in the synagogue services. This seems to have been the case everywhere except in Babylon and in the eastern provinces. The literature which the Jewish diaspora produced in the Greek language was apparently very rich and diversified, although most of these writings are lost or preserved only in fragments. Even in the Hellenistic period, many Jews of the diaspora could no longer understand Hebrew, and for all those who had come to the west from Babylon and from other eastern provinces it was rather a question of changing from Aramaic to Greek.

As Greek became the language of the Bible, of liturgy, preaching, and literature, so did Hellenistic concepts and ideas invade Jewish thinking and bring fundamental changes in the tradition and reception of Israel's literary inheritance. Theological statements now became "philosophy." The books of the Bible were understood as writings containing deep philosophical and religious insights and were interpreted allegorically, just as the writings of Homer in the Greek tradition. The story of the creation was seen as a cosmogony; religious observances like circumcision and the Sabbath were understood as symbols and reinterpreted spiritually. Traditional Jewish prayers used Stoic formulations in their translated Greek form. Hellenistic Jews utilized the forms of Greek literature for their writings and sometimes published their books under the pseudonym of a famous Greek author from the classical period (§5.3d, e). In its missionary activities in the Greek-speaking world, Christianity was able to take its starting point from this Hellenization of the Old Testament inheritance.

In its external appearance and organization, Hellenistic diaspora Judaism also adopted Greek forms. In their institutional organization, Jewish diaspora communities were "associations." As in the case of other ethnic or religious groups, these were either associations of resident aliens, who had received certain privileges pertaining to incorporation and the practice of their trade or profession, or cultic associations, like those organized by adherents of other cults. The titles for the officers of these Jewish communities were borrowed from the Greek associations. Legal or business contracts, even among Jews, were made according to Greek or Roman law, and relevant documents were always written in Greek. Thus the forms of relationship among Jews did not differ from the forms of relationships between Jews and gentiles. It is therefore very probable that the hierarchical structures of authority which were typical for the Jerusalem temple and its theocracy were replaced in the Jewish diaspora communities by the democratic procedures which were typical for the Greek associations (all decisions were made by the assembly of all voting members or by an elected council).

There was certainly no institutionalized central authority that was recognized everywhere. Insofar as Jerusalem possessed any authority in the diaspora, it was ideal and not institutional. The fact that the diaspora communities sent an annual temple tax to Jerusalem cannot be construed as evidence for a juridical authority of Jerusalem; nor does it permit the conclusion that the jurisdiction of Jerusalem was universally recognized. (The attempt of the rabbis of Jamnia after 70 CE to establish such a universal jurisdiction of the *Beth Din*—and even this did not yet become a fact during the early rabbinic period—cannot be read back into the situation before the Jewish War.) The temple tax was rather a symbol of a religious relationship to Jerusalem as the center of Israel's history of salvation. At no time did the officials of the temple have any juridical or police power over Jews living outside the political boundaries of the Jewish state of which the temple was the center. Locally, each Jewish diaspora community had the right to decide disputes and quarrels among its members before its own court of arbitration—a right that other religious associations also exercised (cf. the constitution of the Bacchists in Athens and 1 Corinthians 5–6). The Jewish diaspora tried as a rule to steer clear of the political affairs of Palestine—interest in self-preservation alone would make this necessary—and to show obedience to whichever political authority exercised power over them. This fundamental attitude was later adopted by many Christian churches (cf. Rom 13:1ff; 1 Pet 2:13ff). This stance is quite understandable; the relationship of these communities to the world in which they lived was already full of problems anyway.

The Jewish religion could be exercised without disturbance and interference only so long as the responsible authorities were willing to grant certain privileges, either silently or explicitly: the observance of the Sabbath (only in the Roman period did the Jews try to be excused from military service in order to observe the Sabbath; in the Hellenistic period Jews were frequently employed in the military and also settled in military colonies), the right to assemble, and the privilege to send money to Jerusalem. Such privileges were usually granted by the cities or by the kings, or in the imperial period by the Roman authorities. But the members of the Jewish diaspora communities had the rights of full citizenship only in exceptional cases, and they were never officially exempted from participation in the public cults of the city or state. The idea that Judaism was a *religio licita,* an officially licensed religion, is a modern construction, because this concept did not exist in antiquity, neither in the Hellenistic nor in the Roman period. On the one hand, all could practice the religion of their tradition or their choice; the procedures to achieve recognition of a religious cult were open to everyone, whether in the form of a religious association, or in the form of a cult which was accepted into the civic cults and supervised accordingly. On the other hand, no one could possibly receive official permission to scorn the deities of the city—or even the gods of the Roman people. It is no accident that no document is preserved which grants such a right, and the claims of Jewish authors in this respect are purely apologetic. In actual practice, it was simply ignored when Jews failed to show up at official religious celebrations. Such nonobservance was noticed only when there were other reasons for a rise in anti-Jewish feelings among the residents of a city. The Roman authorities took the same attitude later in respect to the Christians (§12.3d).

If it was necessary for a citizen to acknowledge the public gods of his city, there were obvious problems for a Jew in exercising the full rights of citizenship if he wanted to remain faithful to the exclusive monotheism of his religion. In all Greek cities, however, a considerable proportion of the resident population did not possess the rights of citizenship anyway, but could nevertheless be an important part of the cities' economic and cultural life. Among the many occupations that were open to noncitizens, military service was not unkown to Jews, at least in the Hellenistic period. Such Jews usually lived in military colonies, owning a piece of land and working as farmers during times of peace. Others were merchants or bankers. Craftsmen are rarely mentioned; perhaps the established associations of craftsmen would defend their privileged membership against foreigners. Of course, much less is known about the professions of lower social status. Be that as it may, the apostle Paul and Aquila, a Jewish-Christian from Rome, appear in Acts 18:3 as tent-makers. Emancipated Jews are known to have occupied high positions in the public service. In the Roman period, Tiberius Alexander, a nephew of the Jewish philosopher Philo, was governor of Palestine for several years and later prefect of Egypt.

In spite of its considerable degree of assimilation and its generally positive attitude towards the political authorities, the Jewish diaspora was repeatedly subjected to "anti-Semitic" (better: "anti-Jewish") actions and persecutions which found their literary expression as early as the Hellenistic period. This anti-Judaism had its origin in the diaspora and is closely connected to the contrast of different cultural and religious traditions existing side by side. But it did not arise primarily on the basis of the conflict between the Jewish religion and the dominant Greek culture; more significant were the tensions that arose in the competition of several older cultural traditions within the process of Hellenization. This is already indicated in the oldest known testimony of anti-Judaism, the writing of an Egyptian priest Manetho from III BCE, a work still known and read three hundred years later during the time of the Jewish historian Josephus, who quoted from Manetho's writing and refuted it (*Contra Apionem* 1.227ff). Manetho understood the tradition about Israel in Egypt and about the exodus in a pro-Egyptian sense; in his writing there is no end to slander of the Jews as lepers and as barbaric desecrators of cultural and religious values. He does it, however, in a writing which is addressed to the Greeks in an attempt to commend the Egyptian culture and religion with all its wisdom, piety, and justice by appealing to ancient records. The Jewish apologists soon began to respond in kind, and later the Christian apologists did not hesitate to compete with their Jewish predecessors, using the same methods.

This competition of different cultures, however, was only the historical framework for the rise of anti-Judaism. The immediate occasions were different in each instance and cannot be subsumed under one common denominator. Political and economic factors seem to have played a role alongside religious differences. Anti-Jewish polemic indicates what was offensive: strange rites such as circumcision and the observance of the Sabbath, or the Jewish refusal to worship other gods. The lack of a cult statue in the temple of Jerusalem gave rise to the accusation of atheism and to the malicious calumny that the head of an ass was worshiped there. The Jews insisted upon their special status, permitting the practice of their religion and granting them privileges like exemptions from taxation and the right to send a temple tax to Jerusalem. At the same time, the Jews in the diaspora wanted to be citizens of the cities in which they lived, but without giving due honor to the gods of those cities. It is not unlikely that in such a situation an already-existing anti-Judaism could be intensified through the Hasmonean expulsion and forced Judaization of the non-Jewish populations of the Palestinian cities. Such actions violated the ethnic and religious pluralism which was an essential foundation of the idea of the Hellenistic city. Jews living outside of Palestine wanted to take advantage of this pluralism, but their own religious loyalty limited their participation in the life of these cities because they were critical of many things which constituted the life of the city: temples, gymnasium, and public religious festivals. Therefore, the situation of diaspora Judaism necessarily remained somewhat precarious; the underlying conflict was such that a real solution was impossible. The Hellenistic kings, and later the Roman emperors, had to intervene repeatedly to establish a modus vivendi, something which cities with large Jewish communities were either unable or unwilling to establish themselves.

2. The History of the Jewish Religion

(a) Temple, Law, and Priests (Sadducees)

The final redaction of the Pentateuch was completed in the decades before the Hellenistic conquest and incorporated the law that Ezra had introduced. The rebuilding of the temple had instituted its cult as the center of the officially established religion; the law primarily involved ritual and was thus closely associated with the temple cult. The highest political authority, to be sure, was invested in the Persian administration, but in the Jewish temple state there was no higher political authority than the temple and its priestly hierarchy. Jerusalem and the Judean districts subject to its jurisdiction were first of all a cultic community ruled by priestly interests. The development and enforcement of laws of cultic purity were identical with the maintaining of social norms; one example is the prohibition of marriage with residents of the country who did not belong to the Jewish temple community. Such legislation was the beginning of the particularistic development of Jerusalem, something which led to increasing tensions with those Israelites who were not subject to its jurisdiction; those most affected were the Tobiads in Transjordan and the Samaritans. The Pentateuch had nonetheless been accepted everywhere, and the Palestinian recension of the Pentateuch was the accepted holy book in Jerusalem as well as in Samaria until the end of the Hellenistic period. In order to understand the religious development of Judaism during this period, it is necessary to remember the continued existence of the priestly theocratic ideals and the close association of the law with these ideals.

The guardians of the temple and its cult and the interpreters of the law were the priests. They constituted the aristocracy of the country; the ruling priestly families were at the same time the wealthiest families of the land, although there also seem to have been families of priests which had only a small share of power and money. It would be wrong to picture the priests of the early Hellenistic period as old-fashioned conservatives. There can be no doubt that the better-situated families of the priestly class were quite open to Hellenistic influences. The high degree of Hellenization of the Zadokite family of the Oniads was one of the factors which led to the Maccabean revolt. Those priests, however, who became the primary support of the Hasmoneans after the revolt show a different theological orientation: after the disaster of the reformers' party, no one would have dared even to think about the possible Hellenization of the temple cult in Jerusalem! Certainly in this respect, but also in others, the priestly aristocracy of the Hasmonean period, known as the "Sadducees," was clearly conservative. The name "Sadducees" is probably identical with "Zadokites" and thus reveals their claim to be the legitimate successor of Zadok. (Ezekiel and Ezra had demanded that the descendents of Zadok, the high priest of David, should always provide the high priest; cf. Ezra 7:2; Ezek 40:45f; 43:19 etc.; this explanation of the term "Sadducees" is, however, only one of several possible interpretations.) The Sadducees wanted to guarantee the exact fulfillment of the temple and cult legislation

Bibliography to §5.2

Salo Wittmeyer Baron, *A Social and Religious History of the Jews,* vols. 1–2 (2d ed.; New York and London: Columbia University, 1952).

Johann Maier, *Geschichte der jüdischen Religion von der Zeit Alexanders des Großen bis zur Aufklärung* (GLB; Berlin: De Gruyter, 1972).

Wilhelm Bousset, *Die Religion des Judentums im späthellenistischen Zeitalter* (3d ed. of 1926 rev. by Hugo Gressmann; HNT 21; 4th ed.; Tübingen: Mohr/-Siebeck, 1966).

Hans G. Kippenberg, *Religion und Klassenbildung im antiken Judäa* (StUNT 14; Göttingen: Vandenhoeck & Ruprecht, 1978).

Morton Smith, *Palestinian Parties and Politics* (New York: Columbia University, 1971).

Marcel Simon, *Jewish Sects at the Time of Jesus* (Philadelphia: Fortress, 1967).

Kurt Schubert, *Die jüdischen Religionsparteien im neutestamentlichen Zeitalter* (SBS 43; Stuttgart: Katholisches Bibelwerk, 1970).

Bibliography to §5.2a

Th. A. Busink, *Der Tempel von Jerusalem von Salomo bis Herodes* (2 vols.; Leiden: Brill, 1970–80).

Jean Le Moyne, *Les Sadducéens* (EtBib; Paris: Gabalda, 1972).

which was codified in the written law. It was their duty to interpret the law, and they insisted that only the literal application of this law was proper. The Prophets and the Hagiographa (Writings) were not rejected, but neither were they recognized as authoritative. The Sadducees also rejected the oral tradition and refused to accept any theological ideas which could not be explicitly documented in the written law (Josephus *Ant.* 13.297, etc.). It is no accident that they appear in the New Testament as the opponents of the Pharisaic teaching of the future resurrection (Mark 12:18ff). Josephus confirms this when he says that the Sadducees believe that the soul perishes together with the body at death (*Ant.* 18.16). Hence, rewards and punishments are explained only with regard to life on earth. They are the immediate result of human actions, and there is no such thing as fate (*Ant.* 13.173). This is in keeping with the statement of the Acts of the Apostles that the Sadducees denied the existence of angels and spirits (Acts 23:8).

What is preserved in these few and meager reports about the Sadducees—always as negative judgments of opponents—leads to the conclusion that these priestly circles, who were entrusted with the preservation of the temple, cult, and law, resisted without compromise any renewal born out of the spirit of Hellenism. On the other hand, it is not difficult to see that they had been assimilated to the culture of Hellenism in their personal style of life. But they were successful in their determination to exclude any reformist experiments from the established cult of the Jerusalem temple. As the guardians of the law of Moses they maintained the traditional integrity of the temple, where one of the "established deities" was worshiped and which had the high reputation of many other temples of its kind. This enabled the Sadducees to maintain their leading position in the religious policies of Israel into the Roman period, until the fall of Jerusalem in the Jewish War. They were scarcely aware of the fact, however, that the religious development of the Jews in Palestine as well as in the diaspora had long since passed them by and had gone in directions which were clearly determined by the sort of foreign influences which they so meticulously tried to exclude.

(b) Apocalypticism

The apocalyptic movement became the most important theological movement in Judaism during the Hellenistic period, and it was also to play a decisive role in the formation of Christianity. It was apocalypticism that mediated the essential inheritance of Israel and its prophetic tradition to Jesus and his followers, although in a characteristic transformation. Thus, apocalypticism is the real bridge between the Old and New Testaments; but it also decisively influenced the later development of Judaism.

The beginnings of apocalyptic thought predate the Hellenistic period: its origins are closely related to a fundamental change in the theological thought of Israel which took place during the time of the exile. It is not impossible that the fall of the kingdom of Israel and the destruction of Jerusalem in VI BCE was the cause of fundamental doubts about the concept of historical theodicy. It is nevertheless problematic to seek the origin of new beginnings in negative historical experiences. As is well known, the Deuteronomistic history, which was written during the exile, did not reject the concept of divine theodicy in history: God is justified by historical events; it was always the guilt of Israel which led to repeated setbacks and subsequently to the final catastrophe of the nation; if Israel would only repent, God would provide new historical opportunities for its people. But in addition to the author of this historical work which is mostly concerned with the past, there were others who refused to conceive of God's actions solely within the limited horizons of the nation's historical experience. Rather, history had become a conundrum. The Book of Job (which may perhaps be dated as early as VI BCE) envisaged the revelation of God's power completely outside the realm of history and politics. God appears in the powers of creation and nature, and triumphs over the powers of chaos. Human beings are nothing compared to the power and wisdom of God, who has accomplished the miracle of creation, and who commands Behemoth and Leviathan as well as the storm and the weather. At the same time, the prophecy of Israel turned its back upon an imma-

Bibliography to §52.b

H. H. Rowley, *The Relevance of Apocalyptic: A Study of Jewish and Christian Apocalypses from Daniel to Revelation* (3d ed.; New York: Association, 1963). Together with Volz's book, a classic treatment of this topic.

Paul Volz, *Die Eschatologie der jüdischen Gemeinde im neutestamentlichen Zeitalter* (2d ed.; Tübingen: Mohr/Siebeck, 1934; reprint: Hildesheim: Olms, 1966).

Paul D. Hanson, *The Dawn of Apocalyptic: The Historical and Sociological Roots of Jewish Apocalyptic Eschatology* (rev. ed.; Philadelphia: Fortress, 1979). Deals especially with the beginnings in the Exilic and post-Exilic periods.

Walter Schmithals, *The Apocalyptic Movement: Introduction and Interpretation* (Nashville: Abingdon, 1975).

Frank M. Cross, "New Directions in the Study of Apocalyptic," *JTC* 6 (1969) 157–65.

Hans Dieter Betz, "On the Problem of the Religio-Historical Understanding of Apocalypticism," *JTC* 6 (1969) 134–56.

David Noel Freedman, "The Flowering of Apocalyptic," *JTC* 6 (1969) 166–74.

Joshua Bloch, *On the Apocalyptic in Judaism* (JQR.MS 2; Philadelphia: Dropsie College, 1952).

Peter von der Osten-Sacken, *Die Apokalyptik in ihrem Verhältnis zu Prophetie und Weisheit* (TEH 157; München: Kaiser, 1969).

Johann Michael Schmidt, *Die jüdische Apokalyptik: Die Geschichte ihrer Erforschung von den Anfängen bis zu den Textfunden von Qumran* (2d ed.; Neukirchen-Vluyn: Neukirchener Verlag, 1976).

nent and historical view of the future. To be sure, the prophet known as Deutero-Isaiah was still able to point to the Persian king Cyrus, i.e., to a historically identifiable person as the bringer of salvation appointed by God. But even here the dimensions of thought have been transformed, since Israel, the servant of God, no longer endures its sufferings because of the guilt incurred in historical actions, but in behalf of a new order of the world, an order which can only be described by mythological allusions. Ezekiel depicts the new temple in the measurements of mythological and cosmological speculations. Finally, the so-called apocalypses of Isaiah and Zechariah (Isaiah 24–27; Zechariah 9–14), written in v BCE, or not much later, and the book of Trito-Isaiah present a mythological view of the future in the fully developed form which was to become typical for apocalyptic theology.

The history-of-religions background for this new discovery of mythic traditions is complex. Old Canaanite myths as well as influences from the east (Babylonian and perhaps Iranian mythology) must have played a role. Most important is the fundamental change in theological thought which made it possible to absorb and assimilate these myths in a syncretistic process, and thus open the way for a theological reorientation which determined Jewish thought in the Hellenistic period. The Hellenization of Jewish thought brought an additional element into apocalypticism, insofar as the contact with Hellenistic mythology introduced theological structures which have many parallels in Hellenism.

The most important features of apocalypticism in the Hellenistic period can be characterized as follows:

1) The concepts of chaos and creation are increasingly dominated by elements stemming from oriental mythology. Creation is at the same time a battle with chaotic powers and their vanquishment; Greek mythologies reveal a similar understanding of creation.

2) In accordance with this view of creation, the future is expected to bring a new creation of cosmological dimensions; renewal will not come from a turn in historical events, but from a dramatic and catastrophic revolution, to take place in the heavenly realms as well as on earth. In the later Hellenistic and Roman periods, astrological speculations are closely associated with the concept of eschatological catastrophe.

3) A dualistic view of the cosmos and of the human sphere is commonly found. Both realms are determined by the battle of two diametrically opposed powers: God and Satan; heavenly hosts of divine and satanic angels; on earth, the elect of God and the men of Belial; good and evil spirits in the human heart.

4) The view of the present time is pessimistic. In the ancient version of the myth of the coming of the sons of God to the daughters of men, as it

appears in Gen 6:1ff, the story is historically domesticated: it was an event before the Flood which increased the evil in the world, so that the subsequent destruction necessarily appeared as a just punishment. But in apocalypticism this myth becomes a symbol of the rule of evil powers in the present time, a symbol which repeatedly appears in apocalyptic literature in numerous forms.

5) In comparison with God, human beings are not seen simply as weaker and less powerful, but are viewed as fundamentally defective: they are bound to a physical body and subject to the vicissitudes of history. Salvation cannot be expected to result from the fulfillment of human aspirations within the realm of these bonds, but only from their ultimate dissolution.

6) The idea of prophetic mission is democratized: the servant of God, the prophet who represents God in the world, is no longer a single individual, but Israel as the elect people. The tasks and the promises originally attached to the prophetic office are transferred to Israel. This involved a decisive modification of the consciousness of election; if, as in Deutero-Isaiah and the Book of Daniel, the elect people are destined to become the judges and rulers of the world, the fulfillment of this expectation is necessarily transferred to a new age, which will come after the expected historical experiences have concluded.

7) The nation and the elect people are no longer identical. The prophetic mission can only be accomplished by those members of the nation who remain faithful and observe the divine commandments, while those in Israel who are disobedient and faithless will receive their due punishment.

8) Beliefs in individual resurrection or immortality become widespread, and, closely related, conceptions of hell and eternal punishment are taken over from the Greek world (§4.2d). All these notions are missing in the older tradition of Israel.

9) The theology of history is replaced by "wisdom." It is no longer possible to derive knowledge of one's own situation from the political experiences of the nation's history; rather, insight into the human situation and the knowledge of right conduct in a world dominated by evil can be derived only from an understanding of the larger cosmic realities. "Philosophy" and "gnosis" are therefore the consistent conclusions of apocalyptic thought; both of these make their appearance in Judaism at the beginning of the Roman period (§5.3e; 6.5f).

Very little is known in the early Hellenistic period about the religious groups which were the bearers of this apocalyptic theology. The writings in which such ideas appear for the first time (Deutero- and Trito-Isaiah, Ezekiel, and the apocalypses of Isaiah 24–27 and Zechariah 9–14) were all generally recognized books and belonged to the literary tradition of all

Jews, whether they lived in Jerusalem, Babylon, or Alexandria. The Book of Ezekiel had considerable influence upon the reorganization of the temple cult after the exile. It is therefore quite possible that many even among the priestly circles had accepted the apocalyptic ideas which were rejected later by the Sadducees after the Maccabean revolt. But it is characteristic that most of the older apocalyptic literature was transmitted within prophetic books. The bearers of apocalyptic concepts, therefore, must have been those circles which appealed to the prophetic tradition of Israel and continued it. Although we know nothing about those circles with respect to institutional structures, the result of their activity—prophetic books with apocalyptic expansions—give tangible evidence for their existence.

The Hasidim, who were the backbone of the revolt against the Hellenists, obviously did not come into existence simply at the occasion of the attempted Hellenization of the cult, but must have had a previous history. This history, however, was not one of a firmly organized group. Apocalyptic concepts were certainly cultivated in these circles, as is shown by the Book of Daniel, which (at least in its most substantial portions) was written during the Maccabean revolt and can be understood as a presentation of the hopes and experiences of the revolutionaries. The author, however, does not call for a political solution, but expects that an act of God will usher in a new period of the world in which the elect people (symbolized by the figure of the "Son of Man") will become the just rulers of the nations. It does not take much imagination to realize that the establishment of the rule of the Hasmoneans could scarcely be accepted as the fulfillment of these hopes by those who were associated with the author of Daniel. Apocalypticism turned away from history, because what was claimed as the fulfillment of history could not measure up to the demands of that expectation. If the movement of the Hasidim was to survive, it had to be reconstituted in opposition to the official temple cult, that is, as a sect. Henceforth, apocalyptic concepts were kept alive only in sectarian movements: among the Essenes, the Pharisees, and the Christians, and in a more radical form in Gnosticism, in which the rejection of history became a metaphysical principle.

(c) The Essenes

The sect of the Essenes has long been known through the reports of Philo (*Quod omn. prob. lib.* 75–91), Josephus (*Bell.* 2.119–61, etc.) and Hippolytus (*Refutatio* 9. 18–28), as well as through occasional remarks in Pliny and Dio Chrysostom. But only since the discovery of the manuscripts from the Dead Sea, and the excavations of the ruins of the Essenic settlement at Kirbet Qumran during recent decades, has it been possible to reach a better understanding of that ancient information. There is no question that the Jewish sect of Qumran was indeed identical with the sect mentioned in the ancient reports about the Essenes. The history of the sect can now be reconstructed with relative certainty, and the views and concepts of the Essenes, because of the rich finds of original documents, are now better known than the views of any other Jewish sect of that period.

The Essenes developed out of the circles of Hasidim, whose protest against the Hellenization of the cult in Jerusalem led to the Maccabean insurrection and lent to it the power of a religious movement (§5.1c). It is quite possible that those priestly circles of the Hasidim who later went into exile, forming the sect of the Essenes, supported the insurrection out of protest against the appointment of the non-Zadokite high priest (Menelaus); their adherence to the Zadokite's legitimate claim upon the office of the high priest led to their breach with the new Hasmonean rulers in Jerusalem. This apparently happened when the Hasmonean Simon usurped the high-priestly office for himself and his descendants (140 BCE; see §5.1d). What the texts of Qumran say about the "Wicked Priest" is best understood as referring to Simon (or less probably to Jonathan). It is apparently Simon who is accused (especially in the *Habakkuk Commentary*) of usurping authority through violence and wickedness, or perse-

Bibliography to §5.2c: Texts

Geza Vermes, *The Dead Sea Scrolls in English* (2d ed.; Harmondsworth: Penguin, 1975).

Eduard Lohse, *Die Texte aus Qumran, hebräisch und deutsch* (2d ed.; München: Kösel, 1971).

Alfred Adam and Christoph Buchard (eds.), *Antike Berichte über die Essener* (KlT 182; Berlin: De Gruyter, 1972).

Bibliography to §5.2c: Studies

Frank Moore Cross, *The Ancient Library of Qumran and Modern Biblical Studies* (rev. ed.; Garden City: Doubleday, 1961).

Joseph A. Fitzmyer, *Essays on the Semitic Background of the New Testament* (London: Chapman, 1971).

Geza Vermes, *The Dead Sea Scrolls: Qumran in Perspective* (rev. ed.; Philadelphia: Fortress, 1981).

Kurt Schubert, *The Dead Sea Community: Its Origins and Teachings* (New York: Harper, 1959).

Helmer Ringgren, *The Faith of Qumran* (Philadelphia: Fortress, 1963).

Bertil Gärtner, *The Temple and the Community in Qumran and the New Testament* (SNTSMS 1; Cambridge: Cambridge University, 1965).

Doron Mendels, "Hellenistic Utopia and the Essenes," *HTR* 72 (1979) 207–22.

Roland de Vaux, *Archaeology and the Dead Sea Scrolls* (New York: Oxford University, 1973).

Joseph A. Fitzmyer, *The Dead Sea Scrolls: Major Publications and Tools for Study* (SBLSBS 8; Missoula, MT: Scholars Press, 1975).

cuting the Teacher of Righteousness (or, better: "the Righteous Teacher")
who had founded the sect, of amassing riches for himself through unlaw-
ful acts, and seducing the people into basing the commonwealth on blood
and lies. Even the end of Simon, his assassination during a drinking-bout,
is mentioned with a certain sense of satisfaction.

A building complex bearing some similarity to a monastery has been
excavated at the northwest corner of the Dead Sea. It was erected by the
Essenes as the place of their exile "in the desert," on the site of an older but
long-since ruined Israelite fortress; according to the archeological find-
ings, the time of the first Essenic building period must have been soon
after the middle of II BCE. The establishment existed for more than two
centuries (the buildings were damaged by an earthquake in 31 BCE and
only repaired several decades later), until it was finally conquered and
destroyed by Romans during the Jewish War (68 CE). It comprised a
central building (37.5 meters square) with common rooms, a scriptorium,
and next to it a large banquet and assembly hall (4.5 by 22 meters). Near
the main building and in the immediate surroundings were a number of
cisterns with channels and reservoirs which could be used for irrigation,
and which were large enough to provide several hundred people with
sufficient water during the dry season. Near the main building, remnants
of several other structures were found: agricultural buildings, storehouses,
workshops, two mills, and one large and two smaller cemeteries with
about twelve hundred graves and, oddly, carefully buried bones of animals. The manuscripts were found in several caves nearby. They doubtlessly constitute the sect's library, which must have been hidden in the
caves at the beginning of the Jewish war.

The Essenic community of Qumran understood itself as the true people
of God, the people of the renewed covenant of the last days. The establishment at the Dead Sea was designed to make it possible for the members of the community to conduct their lives according to this eschatological concept. The preservation of the cultic purity of the community was a
central concern. The authority for this was interpretation of the law, for
which the community appealed to its founder, the Righteous Teacher. He
was a priest and as such possessed a legitimate authority to interpret the
law. New members of the community were explicitly requested upon admission to pledge to observe everything that had been revealed to the
Zadokites, the priests. (After the death of the Righteous Teacher the
leadership of the community remained in the hands of the Priests.) The
cultic purity included the observation of the ritual commands of the law.
There were a number of related Essenic peculiarities, such as the introduction of a solar calendar, which was arranged in such a way that the
major festivals of the liturgical year would never fall on a Sabbath. Of

equal rank, however, was the promise of absolute truthfulness and sincerity in one's moral conduct. All the regulations and obligations were compiled in the *Rule of the Community,* which has been preserved (1QS); this writing concerns the full members of the sect who lived permanently at Qumran, namely celibate men only. Another work, which also contains rules for the community, the *Damascus Document* (previously known through medieval manuscripts) seems to have been written for members who lived in various places of the country, were married, and lived more like ordinary citizens.

The meaning of these regulations for the maintenance of purity becomes clear when one considers the basic eschatological orientation of the Essenic community. Their adherence to the law did not arise simply from religious conservatism. Rather, the Essenes understood themselves as the true people of the elect, who were destined to play a decisive role in the battles of the end time. They had to live in constant preparedness for the war of the sons of light against the sons of darkness. Old Testament concepts of the holy war obviously influenced this idea of the ritual purity of the community's members: the members are all soldiers in the holy war of God and must therefore observe all the relevant biblical commandments, including abstinence from sexual intercourse. In one of the writings from Qumran, the *War Scroll* (1QM), the formation for the last, decisive eschatological battle is described in detail. The eschatological orientation of the community can be detected in all aspects of its life. The Essenes anticipate in their present lives the promised future of the true people of God; indeed, they are already the true people of God, and God's temple. Community of goods and personal poverty for full members—every new member had to give all his possessions to the community—represent the fulfillment of the messianic times, which knows no difference between rich and poor. The common meals, regularly celebrated every day, are mirrors of the order and liturgy of the messianic banquet. The scriptural interpretation of the Essenes was also eschatological; examples are preserved in the commentaries from Qumran (cf. the *Commentary on Habakkuk,* 1 QpHab, and the *Commentary on Nahum,* 4QpNah). Their hermeneutical method is not allegorical, but rather relates each scriptural passage to a particular event in the recent past, the present, or the future.

The theological concepts of the writings from the Dead Sea are apocalyptic throughout. No doubt they continue the older apocalyptic theology of the postexilic period, and especially of the Hasidim (Daniel is one of the books which was read and copied several times by the Essenes). This apocalyptic theology was developed in a way which is characteristic for the late Hellenistic period. The theological schemata are strictly dualistic, though this is not a dualism of the material and immaterial worlds. One finds instead a dualism of powers which rule the earthly as well as the heavenly realm. Light and darkness, God and Belial, the spirit of truth and the spirit of wickedness, confront each other on earth as well as in the heavens. Irreconcilable enmity exists between the two, because their opposition is described in mythical terms, as grounded in the primordial past. A strict determinism is closely linked with these dualistic views. The generations of the sons of light and the sons of darkness have been predetermined by God. When one enters the community, one is not converted from darkness to light, but instead one is instructed about one's destiny, namely, that one belongs to the sons of light on the basis of one's origin. This insight belongs to the secret knowledge (the "mysteries") of the wise men of the community in which all members are instructed.

Another part of the special knowledge of the community is insight into the future because the future directly illuminates the organization of life in the present time. The messianic concepts are especially striking. The community expects several "messianic" (divinely authorized) figures: the eschatological prophet, the messianic king from the house of David, and the messianic priest from the house of Aaron. It must be noted that the Righteous Teacher, the founder of the community, is not found among the messianic figures (the texts from Qumran do not contain any parallel to the Christian expectation of the second coming of Jesus). Among the several messianic figures, the highest rank belongs to the priestly messiah. But even this does not prove that the concept of "*the* Messiah" can be found in these texts. In any case, the center of the apocalyptic expectation is not occupied by any single messianic figure, but by the people of the elect. Closely associated with special insight into the future is the knowledge of angels, spirits, and demons; their acitivity is directly related to the designs and deeds of human beings, those of the elect as well as those of the wicked. The writings of Qumran show knowledge of an entire host of divine and evil spirits and angels. But they are not mediators between God and the human world; they are rather powers at work in the heavenly and earthly realms, whose actions are analogous to the eschatological events taking place in the human realm. Insofar as the term "spirit" appears in such contexts, it is not always possible to determine whether it refers to the thought of God, to an angelic figure, or the human mind. The angels are divided into two hostile armies. On one side we find the hosts of the angels led by the "prince of light," or the "spirit of truth." Individual angels are often named, such as Michael, and it is assumed that the angelic army is hierarchically structured. Their tasks involve heavenly worship as well as the battle against the angels of darkness. The community of the elect participates in both of these angelic activities. Opposed to these angels is the "angel of darkness" (generally called Belial, but also the angel of "enmity" = Hebrew *mastema*) and his host. Belial is both the enemy of God and tempter of the human race. His angels or spirits (the fallen angels of Genesis 6) are called the "spirits of wickedness" or the "spirits of error." They cause people to sin, and they inspire evil actions among those who belong to the realm of Belial. Sometimes Belial and his angels also appear as angels of punishment.

Especially in their angelology and demonology, the texts from Qumran remain peculiarly suspended between mythology and psychology. In keeping with the eschatological consciousness of the community, the angels are mythological cosmic powers locked into battle with each other. But they also appear in statements of individualized piety, where they are seen as helpful or seductive powers, or inclinations in the human heart. This indicates that the Essenes not only strove to preserve the purity of their community as the elect, eschatological people of God, but also that they strongly emphasized problems of individual piety as these arose in the context of their religious experience. The sect's book of hymns (*Hodayot*, 1QH) is a lively witness. These hymns speak about the experience of transitoriness in human life, and about its dependence upon God's mercy; they know of the human being whose heart is but stone until God "engraves upon it events of eternity." They emphasize confidence in God's everlasting faithfulness to the pious people, which might be understood as an expression of belief in immortality. At any rate, Josephus ascribes this belief to the Essenes.

The Essenes disappeared from history after the destruction of Qumran by the Romans. The Pharisaic school, which led in the rebuilding of the Jewish community after the destruction of Jerusalem, did not share the special teachings of the Essenes. But Pharisaic Judaism, and Christianity to an even greater degree, took over many elements of the apocalyptic expectation which the Essenes, in the tradition of the Hasidim, had cultivated and further developed during the Hellenistic period.

(d) The Pharisees

Our knowledge of the sect of the Pharisees (the interpretation of the word is not certain; it may mean "those who are separated") and of their development during the pre-Christian and early Christian period is limited. Since no single surviving writing can be assigned to the Pharisees with certainty (though some scholars see the *Psalms of Solomon* as a Pharisaic writing), we are totally dependent upon sources which come from the last decades of I CE: the Gospels of the New Testament, the reports of the Jewish historian Josephus, and the information which is preserved in the rabbinic tradition, especially in the Mishnah. All three sources are strongly biased, though in different ways. The gospels preserve traditions which originated with the sect of Jesus' followers, whose attitudes over against the Pharisees were by no means friendly. Josephus sought to demonstrate that the Pharisees, as the predecessors of the reorganization of Judaism after the Jewish War, had always been a religious movement that possessed the full support of the people, and had had no part in the radical political movements that had led to the Jewish insurrection against the Romans. The rabbinic traditions, fixed in written form at a much later date, contain many older Pharisaic traditions, but tradition- and form-critical analysis of these materials has barely begun; furthermore, the rabbinic movement cultivated primarily only one segment of the older Pharisaic traditions, namely the materials from the school of Hillel.

The Pharisees seem to have been descendents of the movement of the Hasidim, the primary supporters of the Maccabean insurrection in II BCE. Thus, with respect to their origin, they were closely related to the Essenes. But unlike the Essenes, they did not withdraw from the political life of the Jewish people during the period of the Hasmoneans. They apparently tried instead to consolidate their position and to expand their influence. They also were not priests like the Essenes, but laypeople—a priest could not become a rabbi—and they did not share the Essenic protest against the illegitimate usurpation of the high-priestly office by the Hasmoneans. Thus they did not find themselves in fundamental opposition to the new political establishment. We cannot be certain whether the Pharisees had already clashed with the Hasmonean John Hyrcanus during the last decades of II BCE because the relevant information in Josephus (*Ant.* 13.288ff) is questionable. The rabbinic tradition connects the same information with Alexander Janneus. Josephus indeed presupposes (*Bell.* 1.113; *Ant.* 13.403ff) that the Pharisees were among those people who were persecuted by Alexander Janneus. He never says, however, that the eight hundred Jews who were crucified by Janneus were Pharisees. It is therefore not possible to get a clear picture of the relationship of the

Bibliography to §5.2d

Jacob Neusner, *From Politics to Piety: The Emergence of Pharisaic Judaism* (Englewood Cliffs: Prentice Hall, 1973).

Idem, *The Rabbinic Tradition about the Pharisees before 70* (3 vols.; Leiden: Brill, 1971).

Leo Baeck, *The Pharisees and Other Essays* (reprint with introduction by Krister Stendahl; New York: Schocken, 1960).

Louis Finkelstein, *The Pharisees: The Sociological Background of Their Faith* (2 vols.; 3d ed.; Philadelphia: Jewish Publication Society of America, 1962).

R. Travers Herford, *The Pharisees* (Boston: Beacon, 1962).

Leo Baeck, *Paulus, die Pharisäer und das Neue Testament* (Frankfurt: Ner-Tanid, 1961).

Pharisees to the first Hasmonean rulers. Still, the few pieces of information we have are best explained by the assumption that the Pharisees were indeed a rather well-organized political movement. This is altogether obvious in the reports about the role which the Pharisees played during the reign of Janneus' widow Alexandra, who ruled the Jewish state from 78 to 69 BCE. During those years, the Pharisees determined the policies of the state, and they apparently dealt mercilessly with the advisors of Janneus and with other enemies (Josephus *Bell.* 1.107–15; *Ant.* 13.399–418). Herod the Great had an adequate arrangement with the Pharisees for some time. But there were conflicts later, since the Pharisees seem to have played some role in the court intrigues which were directed against the king: Herod executed several of their leaders. This seems, however, to be the termination of the period in the Pharisaic movement during which this politico-religious association of laypeople, lawyers, and scribes played a role as a group wielding political power.

At the time of Jesus and of the first Christian communities in Palestine—this is the picture conveyed by the older source materials preserved in the Gospels and in the general reports of Josephus about the character of the Pharisaic movement (*Bell.* 2.162–64, 166; *Ant.* 13.12–17, 171f)—the Pharisees appear as a group whose sole purpose was the realization of purely religious goals. It is most likely correct to assume that this transformation of Pharisaism was essentially due to the influence of Hillel, whose student and successor took over the leadership of Judaism from the students of Hillel's opponent Shammai after the catastrophe of the Jewish War. Hillel (ca. 50 BCE–20 CE) was a Jewish lawyer from Babylonia, who founded a school in Palestine which became the rival of the school of Shammai. In the numerous rabbinic traditions which contrast Hillel and Shammai, Hillel appears as the more liberal, patient, and popular teacher, whereas Shammai, strict and irascible, insists upon an elitist interpretation of the law. It is significant that Hillel's method of interpretation made it possible to detach the observance of the law from the realm of the cult and hence to transfer it into the realm of everyday life; that is, he laid the foundations for a democratization of the law (§6.6f).

Hillel came from the diaspora, and this apparently contributed considerably to a development within Pharisaism which enabled it to become a religious movement that could exist *de facto* without the temple cult, became thoroughly Hellenized, and was quite open to popular religious ideas. The apocalyptic and messianic expectations of the Pharisees, however, are not due simply to the influx of popular concepts, but are an inheritance from the older Hasidic movement. But in contrast to the Hasidic revolution and to the earlier, political phase of the Pharisaic sect, Hillel no longer tied the fulfillment of apocalyptic expectations to the realization of political goals. To be sure, messianic expectations were very much alive among the Pharisees of Jesus' time, and also in later rabbinic Judaism, but they were then closely bound up with Israel's fulfillment of the law. The idea that the fate and future of human beings and a nation should depend upon the moral and ritual fulfillment of a legal code is as much a Hellenistic concept as the presumption that such conduct be taught at all. Accordingly, the "school" and the traditions of interpretation which were handed down from teacher to student became the central religious institution of Pharisaic Judaism, analogous to the function of the school in the philosophical development of the Hellenistic and Roman periods. Josephus was not entirely wrong, then, when he described the Pharisees as a philosophical sect. The establishment of chains of traditions connected with particular teachers, the cultivation of the teacher-student relationship, the designation of the teaching as wisdom or philosophy—all this is typically Hellenistic. As the rabbinic writings show, the terminology of the Pharisaic schools had also adopted many Greek philosophical terms.

The so-called liberalism of Hillel is nothing else than the successful teaching that one can observe the ancient law of Moses even under the changed conditions of a new time. By no means did the Pharisees intend to make the fulfillment of the law more difficult; their interpretation in fact wanted to make fulfillment possible—for the sake of the rule of God! Their method of interpretation is called *Halacha* ("how one should walk"), namely, the discussion of arguments and counter-arguments about the meaningful fulfillment of each commandment under the conditions of a new time. This hermeneutical method indeed presupposes that everything that was written in ancient times was written in order to be valid for a new time. This presupposition is fully in keeping with the spirit of Hellenism; Stoic exegesis of Homer rests on very similar presuppositions. In both cases, eccentricities and sophistries in interpretation were a natural consequence: it was not possible to admit that the written record of a tradition from the past could not be applied to the problems of conduct in the present, whether as a whole, or in detail. Jesus' antitheses from the Sermon on the Mount ("You have heard that is was said to those of old, . . . but I say to you") contrast sharply with this hermeneutical method.

Another Hellenistic element of religious Pharisaism is its individualism. The separation of the observance of the law from the temple cult and from the immediate context of the cult community enabled the individual to fulfil the law even when living within a non-Jewish society, because he could learn to distinguish between clean and unclean for himself. Such conduct thus became his own accomplishment, through which he received his own personal share in the righteousness of God, something originally promised to Israel as a whole. It goes without saying that the individual can, therefore, also boast of his fulfillment of the law. Accordingly the concepts of reward and punishment, as well as the expectation of resurrection and last judgment, were understood by the Pharisees as applying to the individual, and thus paralleled the Greek concepts of immortality and judgment of the dead. A final Hellenistic feature of piety for which the Pharisees developed a Jewish analogy is mysticism. At the present state of research, it is difficult to determine how much later rabbinic mysticism (*kabbala*) as well as Gnosticism are indebted to origins which lie in Pharisaic Judaism. In any case, Paul, a former Pharisee, is able to refer to his own experience of the "celestial ascent of the soul."

As for the organization of the Pharisees, the term "sect" would be ill-chosen. Pharisees seem to have met for common meals, but nothing is known about the liturgy of such meals, nor did they have rites of initiation or rules for a common life. This clearly distinguishes them from the Essenes. The Pharisees were instead an association informally bound by common interests; their only institutional tie was the school house, which just like a philosophical school provided instruction for the young men. After the catastrophe of the Jewish War, the reorganization of Judaism in the spirit and tradition of Pharisaism was to use the institution of the school as its basis, and this remained characteristic for rabbinic Judaism (§6.6f).

(e) Wisdom Theology

The predecessor of the wisdom theology of the Hellenistic period was the experiential wisdom of Israel. In the preexilic period such wisdom traditions existed in Israel just as among other people of antiquity. Thus one must recognize this as an international phenomenon. The treasure of such traditions grew in the experience of many generations in various walks of life: family, occupations, social position, and political activity, but also through the observation of nature. Traditionally, gods or mythic

Bibliography to §5.2e

Gerhard von Rad, *Wisdom in Israel* (Nashville: Abingdon, 1972).

Hartmut Gese, *Lehre und Wirklichkeit in der alten Weisheit: Studien zu den Sprüchen Salomos und dem Buche Hiob* (Tübingen: Mohr/Siebeck, 1958).

Burton L. Mack, *Logos und Sophia: Untersuchungen zur Weisheitstheologie im hellenistischen Judentum* (SUNT 10; Göttingen: Vandenhoeck & Ruprecht, 1973).

Felix Christ, *Jesus Sophia* (AThANT 57; Zürich: Zwingli, 1970).

Robert L. Wilken (ed.), *Aspects of Wisdom in Judaism and Early Christianity* (University of Notre Dame Center for the Study of Judaism and Christianity in Antiquity 1; Notre Dame: University of Notre Dame, 1975).

figures, or human beings and rulers of ancient times, were considered to have been the originators and transmitters of wisdom; in Israel we think of Enoch and Solomon. Because of their attachment to such figures, wisdom traditions often carried with them the claim of having sprung from divine relevation, whether in primordial times, or from a historical person (e.g., Solomon) who was credited with extraordinary, even divine gifts. The transmission of wisdom required firmly fixed traditions and relied upon the office of the wisdom teacher. In Israel, the institutionalization of the wisdom tradition goes in all likelihood back to the time of Solomon. An accumulated wealth of observation was arranged in lists, series, and onomastica. Such lists often survived for centuries and reappeared in later apocalyptic and gnostic texts, now in the context of cosmological speculations and eschatological timetables. In their original life situation, the codification of the material took place for very practical interests: it was designed as instruction for officials, as professional information, and as general advice for human beings, in order to provide assistance for the mastery of the problems of individual and communal life. As in Greece, the emphasis in Israel was also placed upon learning the right measure.

After the collapse of the inherited social and political structures in the Babylonian exile, a completely new task fell to wisdom. Until the time of the Deuteronomistic writing of history, it had been the task of the prophets, and of the move to reconsider the people's history under the perspective of the history of salvation, to defend the understanding of the political and social order against the threat of the powers of calamity. The increasing conviction of the futility of such efforts demanded a new answer from the tradition of wisdom. Wisdom had not simply confirmed things everybody already knew. Rather, its task had always been to make the world intelligible, to make it possible to discern its order, and to defend it against the powers of chaos. The rationale for the order of the world was not found in a reconsideration of historical experience, but in the contemplation of creation, of the phenomena of nature, and of the primordially determined structures of generally valid human experience. Wisdom could thus make recourse to foundations of knowledge which were not subject to the contingencies of history. Human beings could find a point of orientation in wisdom, even if the history of salvation did not hold what it had promised. Like apocalypticism, its twin sister, wisdom was able to invoke primordial time and creation. The beginnings of wisdom theology are, therefore, closely linked with the rise of apocalypticism. It was only later that their paths separated, though connections continued to exist for a long time. In apocalypticism, the appeal to creation and to primordial time was related to the new historical experiences and expectations of an elect remnant of the people of Israel. Wisdom theology, however, consistently directed its message to the experience of the individual, and, by relating this to a typically Hellenistic universalistic view of the world, thus developed the ideal of the religious human being—that is, of the wise man or philosopher.

But "wisdom" as such did not remain simply a method of insight into creation; personified Wisdom became herself the plan of that creation, and finally, as a mythical figure, the mediator of creation. It is ultimately unimportant whether this transformation happened through the recrudescence of mythical undercurrents or through the hypostatization of an idea. Attempts to prove that the figure of celestial Wisdom mirrors an oriental deity (e.g., Anat or Astarte) have not been successful because in each instance only a few parallel features exist. Analogies to the late Egyptian-Hellenistic Isis are more convincing; she is more closely associated with wisdom and creation than other oriental deities. Wisdom was not created by God, but she came out of the mouth of God and existed before the beginning of creation. She also appears as consort (*syzygos*) of Yahweh. Since all things were created and are sustained by her, she also bears the features of the queen of heaven. She guarantees the order of the world and defends it against chaos.

If human beings want to find their way about in the world, they must do more than pay attention to Wisdom's instruction and listen to her voice. They also must recognize themselves and learn about their destiny, something which is to be discerned from the created order rather than from history. The divine claim no longer relates to human membership in an elect nation, but results from the creation of human beings according to the image of God, that is, it is ultimately based in the divine essence of humanity. Thus, Wisdom addresses human beings regarding their ultimate destiny, which is as divine as their origin (cf. the Wisdom of Solomon and Philo; §5.3e, f). In this way the wise and righteous persons are fundamentally, and even metaphysically, distinguished from the unrighteous. Knowing their divine origin, the wise recognize the true meaning of the course of the world, which will lead them to final justification and vindication, in spite of the contempt and the persecutions which they may now have to endure.

The skeptical wisdom of Judaism resisted this message of wisdom theology and instead emphasized the absurdity of the course of the world and the transitoriness of human existence. The Book of Ecclesiastes (Qoheleth; §5.3e) is the clearest witness for the skeptical attitude. It is possible, of course, to observe and to describe the course of natural events, but no meaning can be found in the empty cycle of continuous return. And once one looks to the end of life to learn about the decline of human faculties which people have to endure during old age, it is absurd to assign to humans a divine destiny. According to this skepticism, it is impossible to relate the idea of God to the individual's experience of life. God can only be understood as the general power of the course of the world and of the general fate of all human creatures.

The defense of wisdom theology against skepticism, and against its resulting consequences for human morality, was the uniting of wisdom with the law. What wisdom teaches became identical with that which the law demands. Thus fulfillment of the law was seen as the only path to the fulfillment of the divine destiny of human beings. The teachings of wisdom are those things which the ancient legislation of Israel always intended. In this context the figures from Israel's history of salvation gain new significance. They become prototypes and examples for a life in the service of wisdom. Their imperturbable adherence to their destiny, despite the long delay in the confirmation of their faithfulness, is especially stressed because this corresponds to the understanding of the existence of the righteous in the present time. The experience of the wise people in the world is presented as a timeless and generally valid experience; this is accomplished, for example, by the elimination of individual names in the recitation of these examples from history (see the Wisdom of Solomon). When Philo of Alexandria portrays the patriarchs of Israel as prototypes of the true philosopher, he is in continuity with the tradition of wisdom theology. But the motif of the divine origin of the wise and of the obscurity of their true being in the world—expressed in the myth of Wisdom who comes into the world and finds no place in it—leads directly into gnostic thought (§6.5f).

Wisdom also played a significant role within apocalyptic theology, though the accents are set quite differently. Wisdom comes only through revelation; it is a secret that visions, dreams, and raptures (celestial journeys) unveil. From this concept of wisdom there is no link to philosophy, because that would presuppose that wisdom can be taught. Apocalyptic wisdom is couched in the language of mythology; older, scientific wisdom lists are often translated into mythological narratives. The earthly and celestial "geography" of this wisdom is therefore thoroughly mythological; from such an inheritance the early Christian world view received its mythological features. Knowledge of the world no longer rests upon experience and observation of nature, but derives from inspired visions of those things in heaven and on earth which are not accessible to normal human observation. The wise man is the inspired possessor of secrets, on which basis he can reveal the future, instruct others about the past, and about how both determine the present. A typical phenomenon of this concept of the wise man is pseudepigraphy: such writings appear under the name of a wise man of ancient times, such as Enoch or Daniel.

(f) The Samaritans

Before its conquest by Alexander the Great, the province of Samaria (named for its capital city), the area of the tribes of Ephraim and Manasseh, was as much an Israelite country as Judea and the Transjordan. The city of Samaria had been founded by Omri (878/7–871/70 BCE) as the capital of the northern kingdom of Israel. Conquered by the Assyrians in 721 BCE, it became the capital of a province which, however, did not comprise the entire former northern kingdom, but only the mountains of Ephraim and the land to the north as far as the valley of Jezreel. No substantial changes were made under the Babylonian and Persian administrations. After the return of the exiles from Babylon, Jerusalem and Judea were at first subject to the governor of Samaria; only under Nehemiah did Judea receive the status of an independent province. During the Persian period there was no doubt some rivalry between the two provinces of Samaria and Judea. But this seems to have had no significance for the religious situation. In spite of the Assyrians' deportation of part of the population of the northern kingdom, most of the inhabitants of Samaria were Israelites, who fully accepted the legal reforms of Ezra, as is shown by the Samaritan Pentateuch. In this respect, the inhabitants of Samaria must be called "Jewish." There are also other indications for a positive relationship between the two parts of the country during this period; there were, for example, repeated marriages between the houses of the Samaritan satraps and the Jerusalem high priests.

After the conquest by Alexander, the history of Samaria began to take a course that differed from Jerusalem's history. In contrast to Jerusalem, Samaria rebelled against Alexander's government during his stay in Egypt. One of Alexander's generals conquered the city, expelled the population, and founded a Macedonian military colony on the site of the old royal city of Israel. The population of Samaria fled to Shechem and re-

Bibliography to §5.2f

Frank Moore Cross, "Aspects of Samaritan and Jewish History in the Late Persian Period," *HTR* 59 (1966) 201–11.

R. J. Coggins, *Samaritans and Jews: The Origin of Samaritanism Reconsidered* (Atlanta: Knox, 1975).

J. Bowman, *The Samaritan Problem: Studies in the Relationship of Samaritanism, Judaism, and Early Christianity* (Pittsburgh Theological Monograph Series 4: Pittsburgh, PA: Pickwick, 1975).

John MacDonald, *The Theology of the Samaritans* (London: SCM, 1964).

Hans Gerhard Kippenberg, *Garizim und Synagoge: Traditionsgeschichtliche Untersuchungen zur samaritanischen Religion der aramäischen Periode* (RVV 30; Berlin: De Gruyter, 1971).

Moses Gaster, *The Samaritans: Their History, Doctrines and Literature* (London: The British Academy, 1925).

built that city, which had lain waste for four hundred years; excavations have shown that after hundreds of years of desolation a new building era began in Shechem at the beginning of the Hellenistic period. On Mt. Gerizim, near Shechem, the Shechemite Samaritans constructed their temple. This, however, would have provided in itself no necessary disruption of the religious communion with Jerusalem, because similar Jewish temples are in evidence elsewhere: the Tobiads in Transjordan had their own temple, and later the high priest Onias IV, when he was driven out of Jerusalem, founded his own temple in Leontopolis in Egypt. There is indeed no indication that the building of the Samaritan temple on Mt. Gerizim was the cause for the Samaritan schism. On the contrary, there are a number of suggestions that the events which led to the final breach between Samaritans and Jews occurred only during the Hasmonean period. In the year 128 BCE, John Hyrcanus destroyed the temple on Mt. Gerizim. Twenty years later he conquered and destroyed the city of Samaria and annexed the whole province to the Hasmonean kingdom. At the same time, he tried to subject Samaria as well as other parts of his new Palestinian empire to the religious policies of Jerusalem. The Samaritans resisted this brutal method of religious unification; only after the conquest of Palestine by the Romans, however, were they able to gain recognition as an independent religious unit. The separate development of a Samaritan religious literature (Samaritan targums, and later also midrashim) began in the Hasmonean period.

The reasons for this late dating of the Samaritan schism have become clear only through recent advances in scholarship. The Samaritan Pentateuch is identical with the codification of the Jewish law which incorporated the reforms of Ezra. Its text is related more closely than was formerly assumed to that which Jerusalem used during the Hellenistic period. Former scholarship had only been able to compare the Samaritan Pentateuch with the Masoretic text which rests upon the Babylonian recension of the Pentateuch. But many of the variants of the Samaritan text which have emerged from this comparison disappear when one considers the Palestinian form of the Pentateuch text, a form better known now through the discoveries from Qumran. The close relationship of the Samaritan and the Palestinian texts is also apparent in their orthography: both forms show orthographical peculiarities which agree with the usage that was established during II BCE and which are largely attested also in the writings from Qumran. Therefore the separation of the Samaritan tradition cannot be dated before the end of II BCE. This is confirmed by the Samaritan script: its special development does not begin until I BCE, as can be shown on the basis of the ancient Hebrew script used in the Pentateuch manuscripts from Qumran and also found on Hasmonean coins. Finally, essential elements of Samaritan apocalypticism are closely related to the Maccabean phase of Jewish apocalyptic thought. The expectation of the coming of Moses as the prophet of the last time and of the *Taheb,* the Samaritan Messiah who is expected to restore all things, as well as the Samaritan angelology and belief in the last judgment and the resurrection of the dead, are closely analogous to contemporary Jewish apocalyptic concepts. However, most of these concepts are preserved only in the rich medieval literature of the Samaritans, and are often so much overgrown by later elaborations that it is not easy to determine their time of origin with certainty.

There is no doubt that at the time of Jesus and early Christianity the Samaritans were rejected and despised by the most influential circles in Jerusalem. But the insinuation that the Samaritans were semi-pagan, schismatic Jews deeply mired in syncretism is certainly unjustified. Indeed, there are no syncretistic elements in Samaritanism which are not found at the same time in Jewish sources. It was not the fault of the Samaritan religious community that Herod the Great magnificently rebuilt the city of Samaria, called it *Sebaste* in honor of Augustus (who had awarded Samaria to him in 30 BCE), and erected in it a large temple for Augustus; nor are the Samaritans responsible for the Christian archheretic Simon Magus of Samaria. The Gospel of John (John 4) knows quite well that the religious center of the Samaritans was not Samaria, but Mt. Gerizim near Shechem, and that just like the Jews the Samaritans expected the coming of a Messiah. If one searches for the true cause of the Jews' rejection of the Samaritans in the beginning of i CE, one must take into account the separate development of the Samaritan cult community, which had already begun more than a century before the religious renewal of Judaism took shape under the Pharisee's influence. It is no wonder that in the eyes of those who shared the Pharisaic view of the observance of the Jewish law, the Samaritans appeared as schismatic and "unclean." On the other hand, this did not prevent the early Christian missionaries from carrying their message to Samaria (Acts 8:1ff). Only some parts of early Christianity shared the Pharisaic prejudice against the Samaritans (Matt 19:5), and Jesus himself did not accept it at all (Luke 19:33).

3. THE LITERATURE OF JUDAISM IN THE HELLENISTIC PERIOD

(a) The Languages of Judaism in Hellenistic Times

Hebrew, the language of Israel, continued as the language of religious literature even after the exile. The older books were still copied and read in Hebrew, and new writings were composed in this language as late as the end of the Hellenistic period. Many of these books have come to light recently in their original Hebrew through the discoveries of the Dead Sea Scrolls. In the Hellenistic period, Hebrew was the language of scholars (and occasionally also used as the official language, as on Hasmonean coins and later in the letters of Bar Kochba). This restricted use found its continuation in the Mishnaic Hebrew of rabbinic Judaism.

The colloquial and business language of Syria and Mesopotamia was Aramaic, which was also spoken by most Jews in Palestine in their daily life. Like Hebrew, Aramaic belongs to the Northwest Semitic languages, and was spoken by the Semitic people who had settled in northern Syria and along the Euphrates from the latter half of the second millenium BCE; together with Phoenician and Ugaritic, it formed a separate branch of these languages. An official form of the Aramaic language had developed in the chancelleries of the Assyrian empire as the language of adminis-

Bibliography to §5.3: Text

R. H. Charles, *The Apocrypha and Pseudepigrapha of the Old Testament* (2 vols; Oxford: Clarendon, 1912).

Bibliography to §5.3: Introductions and Surveys

George W. E. Nickelsburg, *Jewish Literature between the Bible and the Mishnah* (Philadelphia: Fortress, 1981). Indispensible introduction, handbook, and reference work with good bibliographies.

Robert A. Pfeiffer, *History of New Testament Times, With an Introduction to the Apocrypha* (New York: Harper, 1949).

Leonhard Rost, *Judaism Outside the Hebrew Canon: An Introduction to the Documents* (Nashville: Abingdon, 1976).

Johann Maier and Josef Schreiner, *Literatur und Religion des Frühjudentums: Eine Einführung* (Würzburg: Echter, 1973).

Otto Stählin, "Die hellenistisch-jüdische Literatur," in: Wilhelm von Christ and Wilhelm Schmid (eds.), *Geschichte der griechischen Literatur* (HAW 1,2,1; 6th ed.; München: Beck, 1920) 535-656.

Peter Dalbert, *Die Theologie der hellenistisch-jüdischen Missions-Literatur unter Ausschluss von Philo und Josephus* (Hamburg-Volksdorf: Reich/Evangelischer Verlag, 1954).

Gerhard Delling and Malwin Maser, *Bibliographie zur jüdisch-hellenistischen und intertestamentarischen Literatur: 1900-1970* (2d ed.; TU 106; Berlin: Akademie-Verlag, 1975).

James H. Charlesworth, *The Pseudepigrapha and Modern Research* (SBLSCS 7; Missoula: Scholars Press, 1976).

Daniel J. Harrington, "Research on the Jewish Pseudepigrapha during the 1970s," *CBQ* 42 (1980) 147-59.

Bibliography to §5.3a

Joseph A. Fitzmyer, *A Wandering Aramean: Collected Aramaic Essays* (SBLMS 25; Missoula: Scholars Press, 1979) 29-56.

Matthew Black, *An Aramaic Approach to the Gospels and Acts* (3d ed.; Oxford: Clarendon, 1967).

Idem and David Diringer, "Language and Script," *Cambridge History of the Bible* 1. 1-29.

tration and business. This *lingua franca* was taken over by the Babylonians and Persians. Known as "Imperial Aramaic," it was used and understood in the entire Persian empire, from the far eastern provinces to Egypt. After the conquest of the Persian empire by Alexander the Great, Aramaic took second place to Greek for use in the administration, but continued to be used as a business and colloquial language even during the Roman imperial period. Blending with many local dialects, Aramaic formed a number of derivative languages which were spoken in the later Christian period, and in some cases even today. The western Aramaic languages include the dialects which were spoken by the Israelites in Palestine, such as Galilean (which is the language of Jesus, and closely related to the Aramaic of the Palestinian Talmud and the later Targums), Samaritan, and the Christian Aramaic of the Melchites in Syria and Egypt. On the other hand, the language of the Babylonian Talmud as well as Mandean and Syriac (which became the most important Christian literary language of the east) belong to the eastern branch of Aramaic. In the Jewish writings of the Hellenistic period Aramaic was occasionally used instead of Hebrew, and a number of Jewish writings are preserved in translations which stem from an Aramaic original.

With the beginning of the Hellenistic period, however, the Greek language quickly gained ground in the successor states of Alexander's empire, especially as the language of administration, in the form of the "Koine" (§3.2a–c). Greek also became more influential as a colloquial and business language, despite the survival of Aramaic, which was due to two different factors. The first was the Greek colonization documented in the many new foundations of Greek cities in the provinces of the east, including Palestine; the second was the significance of Greek as the language of culture, which made its study the first step in the education of all people who wanted to participate in the new ecumenical civilization. Thus, contact with the Greek language came to the Jews of Palestine first of all through the country's new cities, in which it was the normal language. But they also saw themselves confronted with a new ecumenical culture in which they could not gain recognition for the faith of their fathers unless they learned to speak and write in Greek. This was true not only for the Jewish diaspora; even in Palestine itself, Jewish writings were composed in Greek, and original Aramaic and Hebrew writings were translated into Greek, although a real mastery of Greek was limited to a relatively small portion of Palestinian Jews. Yet, not only the diaspora of Alexandria, but also several other Jewish diaspora communities, as well as the Jews of Palestine, shared in the translation of the Jewish religious inheritance into Greek—a process of far-reaching consequences for the later development of Christianity.

(b) The Septuagint

The term "Septuagint" (LXX) designates the Greek translation of the Old Testament. The word is derived from the legend about the origin of this translation, which is preserved in the *Epistle of Aristeas* (§5.3e): Ptolemy II Philadelphus (284–247 BCE) invited seventy-two scholars from Jerusalem to translate the Jewish book of laws for his library in Alexandria, which they did in seventy-two days. A later version of this legend says that through divine inspiration all the scholars produced the same Greek text independently of each other. Originally the story spoke only about the translation of the Pentateuch, which reflects the fact that its Greek version came into being in Alexandria during III BCE. The basis of this translation was the Alexandrian form of the Hebrew text, a branch of the Palestinian text of the Hebrew Bible; the text transmitted by rabbinic Judaism rests on the Babylonian text, which is often inferior to the Palestinian Hebrew basis of the Septuagint.

During II and I BCE other books of the Old Testament (the Prophets and Writings) were translated into Greek, and that legend of wonderful origin was extended to cover all the books of these Greek collections of Old Testament writings. Several later books which were originally written in Greek (*3* and *4 Maccabees,* Wisdom of Solomon) were eventually added. This, as well as the inclusion of books which failed to be accepted in the later Hebrew canon of rabbinic Judaism (1 Maccabees, Tobit, Judith, Baruch, Sirach), made the Greek collections of Old Testament writings larger than the Hebrew canon, which was fixed by rabbinic Judaism around 100 CE. Martin Luther, however, used for his German translation the Hebrew canon which was in use among the Jews of medieval Europe. Those Septuagintal books which were missing in the Hebrew canon, but were still in part included in the Latin Vulgate, he relegated into an appendix as "Apocrypha," i.e., "books which are not equal to Holy Scrip-

Bibliography to §5.3b: Texts

Alfred Rahlfs (ed.), *Septuaginta* (2 vols.; 2d ed.; Stuttgart: Privilegierte Württembergische Bibelanstalt, 1935).

Göttingen Septuagint = Septuaginta auctoritate Societatis Litterarum Gottingensis editum: for individual volumes, see bibliographies in the following sections.

Bibliography to §5.3b: Studies

Peter Walters (Peter Katz), *The Text of the Septuagint: Its Corruptions and Their Emendation* (ed. by D. W. Gooding; London: Cambridge University, 1973).

Peter Katz, "Septuagintal Studies in the Mid-Century," in: W. D. Davies and D. Daube, *The Background of the New Testament and Its Eschatology . . . in Honor of C. H. Dodd* (Cambridge: Cambridge University, 1964) 176–208.

Sidney Jellicoe, *The Septuagint and Modern Study* (LBS; New York: Ktav, 1968).

ture, but still useful and good for reading." In the biblical translations of the Reformed tradition, the "Aprocrypha" were left out completely. The judgment of the Reformation is only partially justified. To be sure, neither Hellenistic Judaism nor the ancient church ever made a final judgment about the canon of the Old Testament. But the Old Testament of the ancient church, following the usage of the Hellenistic synagogue, was always the LXX, a collection of book which is older than the canon of rabbinic Judaism and which included Luther's "Apocrypha" as well as other ancient Jewish writings.

It is difficult to overestimate the significance of the LXX for Hellenistic Judaism. The translations were originally made for the synagogue services in the Greek diaspora. They are, thus, an indirect testimony to the fact that as early as III BCE a knowledge of Hebrew could no longer be generally assumed among diaspora Jews. But the translation of the Hebrew Old Testament into Greek created more than a book that was useful for Jewish services of worship; it also provided a basis for a new departure of Jewish theology in a new cultural environment, and made it possible that the ferment for renewal, already present in the tradition of Israel and in postexilic theology, could further develop within the horizons of Hellenistic culture and religion. Thus, the LXX became the most significant factor in the process of the Hellenization of Judaism. To be sure, some of the Greek translations are barely readable, slavish renderings of the Hebrew phrases and expressions. In other instances the translators followed their Hebrew texts less closely, as in the Book of Job (though the Hebrew prototype of LXX-Job was not identical with the preserved Hebrew text, being about one-sixth shorter) or in the Book of Proverbs, where the LXX differs markedly from the Hebrew original. In Prov 8:22–31, Wisdom is present more clearly than in the Hebrew text as a divine figure, issuing from God, the guarantor of a perfect creation. In exceptional cases, Greek philosophical terms played some role in the translation. But whether the translations were more literal or more independent, the LXX became the source for the theological language of Judaism and thus also of early Christianity.

This Greek Bible influenced religious thought and religious and philosophical literature in various ways. Very early one finds the LXX used as a basis for new written versions of the Old Testament history, especially the stories of the creation and the patriarchs as well as those of Moses and the exodus (§5.3d). Prototypes and parallels can be found in Hebrew and Aramaic literature. The Greek literary genres which were used for such writings include romance and epic, as well as drama and history. Apologetic and allegorical commentaries appear somewhat later and are fully developed in the writings of Philo of Alexandria; they became the prototype for Christian biblical commentaries. The influence of the LXX is also clearly visible in those writings which do not deal with biblical subjects. The translation of the Bible into Greek made it a generally accessible, divine and inspired book containing ancient wisdom, deep religious truths, and political insights. It could be used as instruction for right conduct, but also as a source for magic. Jewish apologetics and propaganda could proudly claim that the Bible was a book of the Hellenistic world culture, in no way inferior to Homer and the Greek philosophers, and equal, if not superior, to the ancient wisdom of even Babylon and Egypt.

The history of the recensions of the Greek Bible demonstrates that the relationship between the Greek and Hebrew texts remained alive for many centuries; the revisions of the Greek text are closely tied to the development of the Hebrew text. The later recensions of the LXX show the increasing influence of the Babylonian text of the Hebrew Bible. The older revisions, those up to the beginning of the Christian period, are only partially known. The oldest seems to be the proto-Lucianic recension, which seeks to approximate the Greek text more closely with the Palestinian Hebrew text. It appears in some manuscripts of the LXX, in the quotations of Josephus, and in the books of Samuel and Kings in the column of Origen's *Hexapla* which is designated as "Theodotion." The proto-Theodotionic recension (also called the "*kai-ge*" [καί γε] recension) was made in I CE. It follows the Babylonian Hebrew text, which had just gained recognition at that time and become very influential. A fragmentary manuscript of the twelve Minor Prophets, found in Palestine and dating from I CE, belongs to this recension; it is also visible in quotations from Daniel in the New Testament; in the writings of Justin Martyr, who used it for several books of the Old Testament; and in Origen's *Hexapla* it appears under the designation "Quinta." The precise description of this edition is closely bound up with the evaluation of new manuscript discoveries and is still incomplete. Following upon these early recensions, further developments of the Greek text are visible in what are generally known as the three Jewish "translators," Theodotion, Aquila, and Symmachus. They were actually revisers, dependent upon older recensions and each other. Theodotion continued the tradition of the proto-Theodotionic recension during II CE and made it very popular. Aquila, a proselyte from Pontus, published his "translation" in 128 CE. Taking up older revisions he tried to obtain greater accuracy and consistency (by constant use of the same Greek equivalents for the same Hebrew words), with the result that his Greek sentences are often nearly unintelligible. The translation of Symmachus, who is said to have been an Ebionite, is quite different and distinguished by its more elegant Greek style.

The climax of these editions of the Bible's Greek text is the *Hexapla* of Origen. This is a colossal work, in which various versions of the Old Testament were put side by side in six different columns: the Hebrew text; the Greek transcription of the Hebrew; the translations of Aquila and Symmachus; Origen's own revised text, in which the deviations from the Hebrew original were marked according to Alexandrian text-critical methods with an asterisk (*) or obelus (÷); and the sixth column which contained the text of Theodotion. In additional columns (called Quinta, Sexta, and Septima, since they follow upon the other four translations) Origen occasionally quoted further translations known to him. Only a few remnants of this work are preserved, and its influence was limited. Origen's successors in the school of Caesarea, Pamphilus and Eusebius attempted to put Origen's text into wider circulation. But meanwhile, Lucian (who died in 312 CE), the founder of the Antiochian school, had published a new text of the LXX which relied on an earlier recension (the proto-Lucianic text) and was mostly concerned to smooth out passages which were linguistically rough. This Lucianic edition was widely disseminated and became the official text of the Greek Old Testament in the Byzantine church.

(c) The Literature of the Apocalyptic Movement

1) *Daniel:* The oldest, and at the same time most influential apocalypse of the Hellenistic period was the Book of Daniel, preserved in the Jewish Canon of the Old Testament among the Writings (not among the prophetical books). Its text appears partly in Hebrew (Dan 1:1–2:4a; 8:1–12:13), and partly in Aramaic (Dan 2:4b–7:28). It was written in the years after the desecration of the Jewish temple by Antiochus IV (167 BCE) and before his death (164 BCE). The "kings of the north" are the Seleucids, the "kings of the south" the Ptolemies (Dan 11:5ff). Thus, "Daniel," the Jewish sage at the court of the Babylonian king, was certainly not the author of the book, although some portions of Daniel 1–7 may preserve older materials which stem from the Persian period. It is part of the style of apocalyptic literature to recount the events of past

Bibliography to §5.3c (1): Text

Joseph Ziegler (ed.), *Susanna: Daniel: Bel et Draco* (Göttingen Septuagint 16,2).

Bibliography to §5.3c (1): Studies

John J. Collins, *The Apocalyptic Vision of the Book of Daniel* (HSM 16; Missoula: Scholars Press, 1977).

C. Brekelmans, "The Sons of the Most High and Their Kingdom," *OTS* 14 (1965) 305–29.

Ferdinand Dexinger, *Das Buch Daniel und seine Probleme* (SBS 35; Stuttgart: Katholisches Bibelwerk, 1969).

history up to the actual time of writing in the form of an ancient prophecy. In this way the Old Testament formula of the covenant is altered in characteristic fashion: the apocalypse replaces the historical introduction with a "prophetic" presentation of past history, and the place of the announcement of curses and blessing is occupied by a visionary prediction of future events. Another distinctive mark of apocalyptic writing can be seen in Daniel's assimilation of mythological materials of Babylonian (such as the astrological names of the nations and the myth of chaos) and Canaanite origin (the "Ancient of Days" is *El;* the one who is "like a son of man" is *Baal* from Canaanite mythology). Such material is then applied to the present situation: the one "like a son of man" becomes a symbol for Israel ("the people of the holy ones of the Most High"; Dan 7:27) in its expected role as the ruler over the nations. This image expresses the eschatological expectation of the Hasidic movement. It is no accident that a number of fragments of the Book of Daniel have been found among the manuscripts of the Essenes, who, in contrast to the Hasmoneans, held on to this expectation. Daniel became extremely influential for later Jewish and Christian apocalyptic literature.

2) *1 Enoch:* Next to Daniel, the apocalypse of Enoch (*1 Enoch*) is the most important apocalyptic writing of the Hellenistic period. It is preserved in complete form only in an Ethiopic translation. This "Ethiopic Enoch" is a compilation made in I or II CE. Its original was written in Aramaic, with the conclusion in Hebrew (this part is based upon an older "Apocalypse of Noah"). A number of fragments of *1 Enoch* have been found in Qumran. The older parts which were incorporated into *1 Enoch* certainly include the "Apocalypse of Weeks" (*1 Enoch* 91:12–17; 93) and the "Apocalypse of Animals" (*1 Enoch* 85–90), which parallels a *Daniel Apocryphon* found in Cave 4 of Qumran. These as well as other sections were written no later than I BCE. *1 Enoch* 1:9 is already quoted in the New Testament (Jude 14f). No trace of the "Similitudes of Enoch" (37–71) has been found in Qumran; but this does not necessarily imply that they were

Bibliography to §5.3c (2): Text

Michael A. Knibb, *The Ethiopic Book of Enoch; A New Edition in the Light of the Aramaic Dead Sea Fragments* (text and English translation in 2 vols.; Oxford: Oxford University, 1978).

Bibliography to §5.3c (2): Studies

Michael E. Stone, "The Book of Enoch and Judaism in the Third Century BCE," *CBQ* (1978) 479–92.
Jonas C. Greenfield and Michael E. Stone, "The Enochic Pentateuch and the Date of the Similitudes," *HTR* 70 (1977) 51–65.
Erik Sjöberg, *Der Menschensohn im äthiopischen Henochbuch* (Acta Reg. Societatis Humaniorum Literarum Lundensis 41; Lund: Gleerup, 1946).

written at a later time. Very striking in *1 Enoch* are the repeated interpretations of Gen 6:1-4, which seem to use mythological materials which could be much older than the "domesticated" version of the myth of the intercourse of the sons of the gods with the daughters of men in Genesis 6. Older materials are used abundantly throughout the whole book, e.g., wisdom speeches and astrological lists. Some concepts in the book are related to the apocalyptic thought of the Essenes, who certainly knew some of the writings which were included in this compilation; but the Essenic origin of these materials is not certain.

3) The *Ascension of Moses* is preserved only in a Latin translation, which depends on a Greek version that was in turn translated from a Hebrew or Aramaic original. The book is usually dated in I CE, but the traditions used for its composition are probably much older (from II BCE). This apocalypse reports the last words of Moses before his ascension (which itself is not described). As in Daniel and *1 Enoch,* a sage from ancient times, Moses, predicts the events of the last times. Taxo (a Greek term meaning "the organizer"), from the tribe of Levi, is expected to prepare all things for the coming of the eschatological prophet. The emphasis upon the role of Levi, as well as the polemic against Hasmoneans, Herodians, and Pharisees, demonstrates the affinity of this work with the writings from Qumran.

4) The *War Scroll* from Qumran (*Milhama,* 1QM) is a peculiar apocalyptic writing. Nineteen columns of this Hebrew scroll are preserved; a few lines are missing at the end of each column, and the conclusion of the book is lost. The version of this work preserved in this, the most complete scroll, was composed in I CE, because the formation of the army of the sons of light for the final conflict contains parallels with the battle formation of the Roman army. In Caves 1 and 4 of Qumran, however, additional fragments of the writing have been found, of which one may be from an earlier version. The book, an eschatological elaboration of the topic of the holy war, describes in detail (including even the weapons!) the formation of the army of the sons of light for the battle against the sons of darkness led by Belial. Inserted into this description are prayers, hymns, and speeches of the priests.

5) In the Jewish *Sibylline Oracles* apocalyptic expectation used a Hellenistic genre of literature for its purposes. The name is derived from the

Bibliography to §5.3c (5): Text
Johannes Geffcken, *Die Oracula Sibyllina* (GCS 8; Leipzig: Hinrichs, 1902).

Bibliography to §5.3c (5): Studies
John J. Collins, *The Sibylline Oracles of Egyptian Judaism* (SBLDS 13; Missoula: Scholars Press, 1974).

Greek Sibyls: inspired prophetic women whose oracles were recorded in hexameters and collected in extensive writings (§4.3c). Three books of oracles of the Cumean Sibyl were kept in Rome, in a vault under the temple of capitoline Jupiter. After the fire of 83 BCE, they were carefully replaced, and a purified version was entrusted by Augustus to the temple of Apollo on the Palatine in 12 BCE. Only on the most important occasions was it permitted to consult these books, and then only officially, in the interest of the state. These procedures demonstrate the reputation of Sibylline books, as well as the fear of falsification and abuse. Books of oriental Sibyls written in the Hellenistic period tried to compete with the older and officially recognized Greek Sibyls. Among the new competitors was the work of a Jewish Sibyl composed during II BCE in Greek hexameters; it was later revised by Christians and finally grew to a total of fourteen books. The third book of this collection, with more than eight hundred verses, seems to be a Jewish writing; a Jewish origin can also be assumed for parts of the fourth and fifth books. At the same time, older materials of non-Jewish origin were incorporated. In addition to apologetic motifs and propaganda for monotheism, apocalyptic predictions are the most important theme. The history of the world is seen from the perspective of a divine plan. God is the master of all history and also rules the powers of nature (the worship of idols is accordingly criticized). The course of history runs towards the final judgment and punishment of the unrighteous, while the righteous can expect to receive in the end the reward for their deeds.

6) *Testaments of the Twelve Patriarchs:* The testamentary literature constitutes a Hellenistic development of an older Israelite genre of literature, the Old Testament formula of covenant. The historical introduction was replaced by the personal biography of an individual, while the blessings and curses of the covenant formula were supplanted by apocalyptic

Bibliography to §5.3c (6): Text

M. de Jonge (ed.), *The Testaments of the Twelve Patriarchs: A Critical Edition of the Greek Text* (PVTG 1,2; Leiden: Brill, 1978).

Bibliography to §5.3c (6): Studies

M. de Jonge, "Recent Studies on the Testaments of the Twelve Patriarchs," *SEA* 36 (1971) 77–96.

Christoph Burchard, Jacob Jervell, and J. Thomas, *Studien zu den Testamenten der Zwölf Patriarchen* (BZNW 36; Berlin: De Gruyter, 1969).

M. de Jonge, *The Testaments of the Twelve Patriarchs: A Study of Their Text, Composition and Origin* (2d ed.; GTB 25; Assen: van Gorcum, 1975).

M. de Jonge (ed.), *Studies on the Testaments of the Twelve Patriarchs: Text and Interpretation* (SVTP 3; Leiden: Brill, 1975).

H. Dixon Slingerland, *The Testaments of the Twelve Patriarchs: A Critical History of Research* (SBLMS 21; Missoula: Scholars Press, 1977).

predictions. The most significant document of this genre is the *Testaments of the Twelve Patriarchs*. It is fully preserved only in Greek translation (the Armenian and Church-Slavonic translations depend upon the Greek version); in this form it shows signs of a superficial Christian recension from II CE. But several fragments of the *Testament of Levi* in Aramaic and the *Testament of Naphthali* in Hebrew have been found in Qumran. It is certain, therefore, that the Greek version of the full *Testaments of the Twelve Patriarchs* is largely a translation of Hebrew (and Aramaic) originals from the pre-Christian period. In these testaments, each of the sons of Jacob gives admonitions to his children. In each case these admonitions are introduced by an autobiographical review and treat one particular vice (fornication, envy, etc.). Much traditional parenetic and wisdom material is employed in the composition of the speeches. The eschatological concepts include the expectation of a royal messiah from Judah, who is subordinated to the priestly messiah from Levi; this agrees with the Essenic expectation.

7) *Manual of Discipline and Damascus Document:* The organization of an apocalyptic sect as the people of the renewal of the covenant led to the creation of several Essenic documents which use the covenant formula that characterizes the covenantal legislation of the Old Testament. Among these writings is the *Manual of Discipline (Serek hayyahad,* also called the *Rule of the Community;* 1 QS) from Qumran. It consists of eleven columns, written in Hebrew, which are almost completely preserved. Numerous additional fragments have been discovered. Though the writing contains varied materials, it is presented as the basic legislation for the community of the new covenant. In addition to liturgical instructions for the admission of new members, it contains regulations for the festival of covenant renewal, instruction about the two spirits, the spirit of truth to whom the sons of light belong, and the spirit of wickedness from whom the sons of darkness descend, and regulations for the community and an order of discipline; the document concludes with a hymn. The *Rule of the Congregation* (1QSa), recorded on the back of the *Manual of Discipline,* is a closely related document. It contains additional regulations and, most important, instructions for the convocation of all Israel, including women and children, for the messianic banquet. It is possible that these instructions were written down for use in the eschatological time of salvation.

The *Damascus Document* (CD) is a very similar writing. It was discovered in the year 1896 in three fragmentary manuscripts from X and XII CE in the Cairo Geniza, and has been known since its publication by Solomon Schechter in 1910. But it has been only through the manuscript discoveries at the Dead Sea since 1945 and the discovery of several fragments of the *Damascus Document* in Caves 4, 5, and 6 of Qumran, that it has become possible to determine the origin of this book. The "People of the New Covenant in the Land of Damascus," for whom this writing was composed as a community regulation, must have been Essenes or a closely related group, perhaps Essenes living outside of the establishment at Qumran, who included married people in their ranks. Like the writings from Qumran, the document emphasizes that only the Zadokites faithfully adhered to the covenant of God. Regulations for the religious calendar, purity, oaths, and the somewhat moderated prohibition of property resemble those from Qumran. But in addition, the *Damascus Document* contains legislation for marriage, which is, of course, missing in the Qumran documents.

8) *Commentaries (Peshers)*. In the interpretation of the Bible, the Essenes developed a special form of biblical commentary which is called *pesher*. Several examples of such commentaries have been found in Qumran, although they are in a fragmentary state of preservation. The most important and most extensive commentary is the *Pesher on Habakkuk* (1QpHab). Thirteen columns of a continuous interpretation of Habakkuk are preserved on a scroll which is partially damaged on the bottom. The commentary first quotes one or two sentences from the text of Habakkuk; then follows a comment, usually short, introduced by: "The interpretation refers to . . ." The interpretations relate all the prophet's statements to events of the present or the recent past, e.g., to the Wicked Priest in Jerusalem and his outrageous deeds, the desecration of the sanctuary, the persecution of the Righteous Teacher, and the latter's ability to interpret the Scriptures and to announce the secrets of God. Prophetical words are frequently understood as references to political and military events, such as the allusions to the "Kittim" (i.e., either the Seleucids or the Romans). Even more explicit is the contemporary interpretation in the fragment of the *Pesher on Nahum* (4QpNah, which preserves only the commentary on Nah 2:12–3:12). References are made to events from the time of Demetrius III, one of the last Seleucid kings (96–88 BCE), to the coming of the Romans. It is noteworthy that Demetrius and Antiochus (IV Epiphanes?) are referred to by name. The "lion of wrath" who hangs people alive is apparently Alexander Janneus. On the other hand, the *Pesher of Psalm 37* (4QpPs 37) restricts its comments to the experiences of the community and the Righteous Teacher, and the persecutions which they suffered.

This type of scriptural interpretation, however, was not necessarily restricted to a verse-by-verse commentary on a particular biblical book. The library of Qumran also preserved a *Florilegium* (4QFlor), which exegetes in sequence 2 Sam 7:10–11; Ps 1:1 and Ps 2:1–2; additional biblical passages are quoted with the formula "as it is written in the book of . . ." Here the interpretation is eschatological and speaks about the erection of the sanctuary in Israel at the end of the days, and about protection from Belial and his wickedness. Evidence which is important for the hypothesis that later Christian authors used florilegia of scriptural passages is the Qumran book called *Testimonia* (4QTest). Deut 5:28–29; 18:18–19; Num 24:15–17; Deut 33:1–8, and Jos 6:26 are quoted in sequence, without explicit reference to their interpretation (the intended topic is apparently the coming of the messiahs from Aaron and from Israel). Only the last quotation is unexpectedly explained as a reference to Belial.

9) *Hymns (Hodayot):* The several hymns which are quoted in the *Manual of Discipline* and in the *War Scroll* demonstrate that the composition of hymns also had its life situation in the apocalyptic movement. Cave 1 of Qumran yielded a large scroll with a number of hymns, the *Thanksgiving Hymns* (*Hodayot,* 1QH). The manuscript is badly damaged and a complete reconstruction is no longer possible, although additional fragments were found in Caves 1 and 4. All these hymns, usually introduced by the formula "I praise you Lord," are written in the first-person singular, some of which, it has been suggested, were composed by the Righteous Teacher. Despite frequent allusions to the psalms of the Old Testament and use of traditional phrases, the hymns clearly express personal and religious experiences. They speak repeatedly of persecution by the men of wickedness, and of divine assistance and salvation. New insights appear in the reflections about the complete emptiness of human existence, not only in view of the human bondage to sin, but also because of human transitoriness; life and righteousness can only be obtained through the grace of God.

10) Another collection of hymns, not found at Qumran, is preserved under the title *Psalms of Solomon* in a number of Greek manuscripts (the Syriac manuscripts derive from a Greek original). But these hymns must have been composed first in Hebrew, probably in Palestine. The time of composition is the period from 60 to 30 BCE, since they contain statements which are best understood as allusions to Pompey and Herod the Great. It is not possible to be certain about the religious circles which produced these psalms, which throughout imitate the style of the Old Testament psalter. The authors were certainly not Essenes because they neither share the expectation of a priestly messiah nor reject the ongoing temple cult. From this it appears that their opponents were not the Sadducees who controlled the temple cult at that time. Attempts have been made to show that the Pharisees produced the *Psalms of Solomon.* Although this hypothesis is very appealing, it is impossible to find conclusive evidence for it. The hymns in this collection may have several different authors, but

they express one and the same religious orientation, namely pietism, with the strongly expressed self-confidence of the righteous person, and sharp criticism of sinners who include foreign and native rulers as well as the impious among the people. Messianic and apocalyptic views are frequently expressed, especially in *Ps. Sol.* 17 and 18. These expectations include the coming of a messiah from David and the judgment over all sinners and ungodly people.

(d) The History of Israel as Reflected in the Jewish Literature of the Hellenistic Period

Among the Jewish writings dealing with the history which is recorded in the books of the Bible, adaptations of the stories of the creation and the patriarchs predominate, as well as books about Moses. The only comprehensive historical works that are preserved were written just before and after the period under consideration: the Books of Chronicles, composed in Hebrew during IV BCE and definitively revised in III BCE, and the *Antiquities* of the Jewish historian Josephus (§6.4d). From the Hellenistic period only a few fragments of such works have survived. Works which deal with the more recent past are better preserved; they include both historical presentations and legendary glorifications of individual events.

1) The book of *Jubilees* is partially preserved in Latin, and is complete in a Ethiopic translation; both derive from a Greek version translated from a Hebrew original. Fragments of nine Hebrew manuscripts have been found in Qumran. Jubilees is a reproduction of Genesis 1–Exodus 12 in the style of a midrash, cast in the form of a revelation by the "Angel of the Presence." The framework is derived from Exodus 24. The entire course of history, beginning with the creation, is strictly arranged in periods of 49 years = 1 "jubilee." There are 49 such jubilees from Adam to the legislation through Moses. Each jubilee is subdivided into 7 year-weeks, i.e., periods of 7 years. A solar calendar of 364 days = 52 weeks determines the length of the year. The book consistently emphasizes the cultic and ritual legislation, which is ascribed already to Noah and Abraham. It stresses the observance of the Sabbath, and the law of circumcision is explicitly based in the covenant with Abraham. The large number of fragments of this book which were found in Qumran and the use of the solar calendar justify an assumption of Essenic origin for the book of *Jubilees*. It was thus probably written in I BCE.

Bibliography to §5.3d (1)

James C. Vanderkam, *Textual and Historical Studies in the Book of Jubilees* (HSM 14; Missoula: Scholars Press, 1977).

2) The *Genesis Apocryphon* (1QapGen), though also found at Qumran and in its genre comparable to the book of *Jubilees,* does not contain any typically Essenic features. Unknown before its discovery at the Dead Sea, it was written between 50 BCE and 50 CE, and is preserved in a badly damaged Aramaic manuscript of twenty-two columns containing an expanded retelling of Gen 5:28–15:4; there are also several fragments of the first part of the book. The *Genesis Apocryphon* is an apologetic and edifying expansion of the first book of the Bible. The patriarchs themselves appear as the narrators; thus the first person singular prevails (cf. the *Testaments of the Twelve Patriarchs* above). A similar apologetic and edifying interest dominates Pseudo-Philo's *Biblical Antiquities* (*Libri Philonis Judaei de initio mundi*), which was probably edited shortly after 70 CE, but uses materials of an earlier date. It is preserved only in Latin, deriving from a Greek version which was translated from a Hebrew original. The book retells the biblical history from Adam to Saul with many interpolations of legendary materials, hymns, long speeches, and homiletical pieces. It shares belief in the resurrection, has a strongly developed angelology, and stresses the election of Israel. But the theological position of the author cannot be identified with any particular Jewish group.

3) *Fragments of Alexander Polyhistor.* Excerpts of works of Greco-Jewish authors who wrote about the figures of the book of Genesis and of the history of Israel are almost exclusively preserved in the works of Alexander Polyhistor. Though his works are lost, Josephus, Clement of Alexandria, and more extensively, Eusebius have quoted a number of passages. Alexander Polyhistor came from Miletus; he was taken prisoner in the war with Mithridates and brought to Rome, where he remained after his manumission by Sulla until his death (ca. 50 BCE). His historical works, among them a book "On the Jews," were primarily uncritical collections of materials and excerpts, but they thus preserved valuable portions of the works of other authors. Among these is a fragment of a comprehensive historical work by a certain Demetrius (from Alexandria?), "About the Kings of Judea," which Josephus quotes. It must have

Bibliography to §5.3d (2): Text

Joseph A. Fitzmyer, *The Genesis Apocryphon of Qumran Cave I* (BibOr 18a; 2d ed.; Rome: Biblical Institute, 1971).

Daniel J. Harrington, Jacques Cazeaux, Charles Perrot, and Pierre-Maurice Bogaert, *Pseudo-Philon: Les Antiquités Bibliques* (SC 229–30; Paris: Cerf, 1976).

Bibliography to §5.3d (3)

John J. Collins, "The Epic of Theodotus and the Hellenism of the Hasmoneans," *HTR* 73 (1980) 91–104. Contains extensive bibliographies.

been written ca. 200 BCE and follows the Old Testament in chronographical fashion.

In other Jewish historians whose works were partially preserved by Alexander Polyhistor, the apologetic element is more strongly present. Typical for such reinterpretations of the biblical tradition is the work of the so-called Samaritan Anonymous (also known as Pseudo-Eupolemus; fragments in Eusebius). That this was the work of a Samaritan seems clear from his identification of Mt. Gerizim, the holy mountain of the Samaritans, with the "Mountain of the Most High." This book, written after 200 BCE, but before the Maccabean revolt (i.e., still before the Samaritan schism), is an attempt to recast the primeval history and the story of the patriarchs. Biblical persons are identified with Greek gods and heroes: Enoch is Atlas; Noah (= Nimrod) is the Babylonian Bel as well as the Greek Kronos. Abraham appears as a teacher of astrology in Egypt and as the mediator of oriental wisdom to the west. Thus the tradition of Israel is seen as the cultural link between Babylon on the one hand and Egypt and Greece on the other. Another writer, Eupolemus, wrote in Palestine in the second half of II BCE, from whom fragments about Moses, David, Solomon, the destruction of the temple, and chronographic information are found in Eusebius and Clement. For him, Moses is the "first wise man," the inventor of the alphabet, and the founder of the sciences. Solomon appears as the "Great King" who erected the temple in Jerusalem, with the aid of the Egyptian and Phoenician kings, to be the cultural center of an international empire. These typically Hellenistic apologetic motifs Eupolemus employed in the service of the political propaganda of the Hasmoneans. Of Artapanus, who wrote before the middle of I BCE, smaller fragments about Abraham and Joseph, and a larger fragment about Moses, are preserved in Eusebius. Here Moses is presented as a typically Hellenistic "divine man" (*theios anēr*), a wise Egyptian prince who invents ships as well as machines for agriculture and irrigation, and who gives instruction about philosophy and correct religious worship. The presentation of history has been transformed into aretalogy (§3.4d).

Even genres of Greek poetry were used by Greco-Jewish writers in order to present anew the tradition of Israel and its legacy. From the drama *Exodus* of the tragedian Ezekiel, six fragments totalling 269 lines have been preserved in Eusebius. The material of this drama is taken from the biblical account of the exodus, but legendary features have been added. This work from II (or III) BCE is completely in keeping with the fashion of the Alexandrian writing of tragedy (§3.4b) and is the only tragedy of that time of which at least a major fragment has survived. In the same century the epic poet Philon composed a poem in hexameters about

Jerusalem, comprising four (or fourteen?) books, of which a few fragments about Abraham, Joseph, and the water conduits of Jerusalem are
quoted in Eusebius. It is likely that much more literature of this kind
existed, but it is difficult to say anything about its distribution and effects.

4) *Joseph and Asenath*. A unique employment of the stories of the
patriarchs appears in the book *Joseph and Asenath*. It is extant in sixteen
Greek manuscripts and in a number of translations (Latin, Syriac, Armenian, Church-Slavonic, and others). This writing was probably composed during I BCE, presumably in Egypt. Christian elements cannot be
detected. *Joseph and Asenath* is best called an allegorical romance (§3.4e)
for which the erotic motif is constitutive, although the travel motif is
missing from the work at hand. The primary characters of the romance
must be understood allegorically: Asenath is the representation of the
community of the believers, not just of the proselytes, but perhaps of those
who have been converted from within Judaism to become members of the
true community (or mystery community) of God. Joseph represents the
celestial messenger. Bread, cup, and ointment are symbols of the sacraments of the true community which understands its sacramental food as
the bread from heaven (Manna).

5) *Hecateus*. Almost nothing is preserved of Jewish writers from the
early Hellenistic period whose works deal with the more recent past. The
quotations preserved by Josephus (*Con. Ap.* 1.183–204) under the name
of Hecateus could be assigned to this period. Hecateus of Abdera was a
Greek writer of the period around 300 BCE who lived in Egypt under
Ptolemy I, and, among other works wrote a book called *Aegyptiaca*. This
work contained a long excursus about the Jews from which Diodorus
Siculus quotes some passages. Some scholars believe that Josephus' quotations from an alleged book of Hecateus, *About the Jews,* are also genuine, but there are good reasons for doubt. The reports about the Jewish
migration to Egypt, about the size of the country and its population, about
Jerusalem and the temple, the Jewish observance of the law, and finally
the anecdote about the Jewish archer Mosollamus, are more likely the
work of a Jewish apologetic author from the later years of the Egyptian
rule over Palestine who wrote under the name of Hecateus.

Bibliography to §5.3d (4): Text
Marc Philonenko, *Joseph et Aséneth* (SPB 13; Leiden: Brill, 1968).

Bibliography to §5.3d (4): Studies
Dieter Sänger, *Antikes Judentum und die Mysterien: Religionsgeschichtliche Untersuchungen zu Joseph und Asenath* (WUNT 2,5; Tübingen: Mohr/Siebeck,
1980).
Christoph Burchard, *Untersuchungen zu Joseph und Asenath* (WUNT 8; Tübingen: Mohr/Siebeck, 1965).

6) *1 and 2 Maccabees*. The time of the Maccabees produced several historical works. The most significant work on the history of the Maccabean revolt was written by Jason of Cyrene. Unfortunately it is lost; only some parts of it are preserved through excerpts in 2 Maccabees (see below). Jason was a Hellenized Jew from the diaspora, but he had a good geographical knowledge of Palestine and made use of reliable sources and materials. Among these were a biography of Judas Maccabeus, a chronology for the Seleucid kings, priestly yearbooks for Onias, Menelaus, and Jason, and documents from the temple archives in Jerusalem. Jason's history was written in five books shortly after the middle of II BCE. The book called 2 Maccabees is an epitome of Jason's work. Like Jason's history, it was written in Greek, probably about 100 BCE or a little later. 2 Maccabees treats the years 175–161 BCE, but also contains a report about the events of the preceding period under Seleucus IV (187–175 BCE), which form the backdrop for the revolt. The central figure in the revolt is Judas the Maccabee. But 2 Maccabees also included many legendary materials, such as the narrative about the martyrdom of the aged scribe Eleazar and the seven brothers and their mother (8:18–31), a story which was later used by *4 Maccabees* (§5.3e), and especially the reports about the miraculous divine interventions in behalf of the temple, usually through an angel. The primary interest of the author is the glorification of the temple and an emphasis on the faithful observance of the law by the Jewish people. Another important element is the description of the events which form the background for the feast of the reconsecration of the temple (10:1–8 *Hanukkah;* however, the two letters in 2 Macc 1:1–2:18, written to inculcate this festival, are later additions) and the memorial festival for the victory over Nicanor (15:36–37). 1 Maccabees in part treats the same events which are the subject of 2 Maccabees, and, on the whole, it uses the same source materials which formed the basis of the historical work of Jason of Cyrene. However, it deals with a longer period, from 175 to 134 BCE, i.e., from the accession of Antiochus IV to the death of the Hasmonean high priest and prince Simon. Written originally in Hebrew, but preserved only in Greek translation, this book is extremely valuable as a historical source. Its obviously tendentious character

Bibliography to §5.3d (6): Text

Werner Kappler (ed.), *Maccabaeorum Liber I* (Göttingen Septuagint 9,1).
Robert Hanhart (ed.), *Maccabaeorum Liber II* (Göttingen Septuagint 9,2).

Bibliography to §5.3d (6): Commentaries

Jonathan A. Goldstein, *1 Maccabees* (AB 41; Garden City: Doubleday, 1976).
Idem, *2 Maccabees* (AB 41a; Garden City: Doubleday, forthcoming).
Klaus D. Schunck, *1. Makkabäerbuch* (JSHRZ 1,4; Gütersloh: Mohn, 1980).

should not be overlooked, however, because it represents those political circles which supported the Hasmoneans. Therefore, Judas Maccabeus is described as somewhat less significant in comparison with his father and his brothers. The author's intentions are those of an official court historian writing on behalf of the Hasmonean dynasty.

7) *Esther.* All other Jewish writings which deal with the events and persons from the time after the Babylonian exile are either legends concerning the temple or religious festivals, or narratives in the style of the Hellenistic romance. The Book of Esther, which is preserved in its original Hebrew as a part of the Jewish canon, uses various legends and fairy tale motifs: the heroine (Esther), wife of the (Persian) king, who saves her people using her beauty as well as her intelligence; the member of a suppressed people (Mordecai) who rises to high public office; and the villain (Haman) who finally becomes a victim of his own intrigues. It has been conjectured that the names Mordecai and Esther were derived from the Babylonian gods Marduk and Ishtar, but this similarity probably has no other purpose than to localize the story in the east. If there are any allusions to actual historical situations, they are nothing but stylistic devices used to create a suitable backdrop, just as in Hellenistic romance. The LXX translation of Esther has added further legendary features (the so-called "Additions to Esther"). The purpose of the book is to propagate the festival of Purim, perhaps to introduce this festival, which was originally celebrated in the diaspora, to Palestine during the Hasmonean period. This would also suggest the date for the composition of the book.

8) The Book of *Judith* is closely related to Esther. Like Esther, it was originally written in Hebrew; but it is preserved only in a Greek translation as part of the LXX. Judith also tells the story of the salvation of the people through the deed of a beautiful woman. There is again no basis in any particular historical events. Its religious intention appears in the general emphasis upon faithfulness to law, especially through the observation of ritual purity, even under the most adverse circumstances. Both Judith and Esther are influenced by Hasidic piety and have much in common with 2 Maccabees. But they do not represent any particular religious group, but rather reflect a more widespread current within the Jewish

Bibliography to §5.3d (7): Text
Robert Hanhart (ed.), *Esther* (Göttingen Septuagint 8,5).

Bibliography to §5.3d (8): Text
Robert Hanhart (ed.), *Iudith* (Göttingen Septuagint 8,4).

Bibliography to §5.3d (8): Studies
Morton S. Enslin and Solomon Zeitlin, *The Book of Judith* (JAL; Leiden: Brill, 1972).

people after the Maccabean revolt, in which the temple, ritual observance, and popular festivals like Hanukkah and Purim played an important role.

9) *Other Hellenistic Jewish Legends.* The new edition of the books of Ezra and Nehemiah which is preserved under the name of *3 Ezra* (1 Esdras of the LXX), and which must have been composed at the same time as Judith and Esther, reveals a very similar attitude towards the temple. It is no more than typical that a narrative developed from a fairy tale motif, i.e., the story of the competition of the pages at the court of Darius has been added (3 Ezr 3:1–4:63). Another legendary motif, the salvation of the righteous from great distress, appears in the Additions to Daniel in the LXX: the narratives of Susanna and of Daniel, Bel and the Dragon (it is possible that the Greek text derives from a Hebrew original that was lost very early). In all these cases an interest in edification predominates. This is also obvious in *3 Maccabees,* though this book was originally written in Greek and takes its historical framework from the Hellenistic period. This work relates the miraculous salvation of the Jews of Egypt from a persecution by Ptolemy IV (221–204 BCE). The story is either pure fiction or a legendary narrative of events which occurred under Ptolemy VIII (after 145 BCE; see §5.1e). This book may have been written ca. 40 CE, or perhaps already at the end of I BCE, probably in the context of the attempts of Alexandrian Jews to obtain full rights as citizens. *3 Maccabees* opposes these efforts, and instead refers to the ancient vested privileges which had belonged to the Jews of that city for generations. It is not impossible that this writing is the cult legend of an otherwise unknown festival of the Jews in Alexandria.

10) An even closer relationship to the Greek romance appears in the Book of *Tobit* (Tobias), which was composed ca. 200 BCE. It is transmitted in Greek in the LXX, but one Hebrew and three Aramaic fragments found in Cave 4 of Qumran prove that the Greek text derives from a Semitic original (probably Aramaic, if the book was written in the east). The literary genre of Tobit can be defined as the Hellenistic romance, or the oriental-Jewish wisdom novel, or the fairy tale as all three elements are equally present. As in the romance, the travel motif with the backdrop of a fictitious historical scene (Nineveh at the time of Salmanassar V and Sanherib) plays a significant role. Its didactic intent agrees with the wisdom novel. But the fairy tale motif of the grateful dead man is constitutive for the story.

Bibliography to §5.3d (9): Text
Robert Hanhart (ed.), *Maccabaeorum Liber III* (Göttingen Septuagint 9,3).

(e) From Wisdom to Philosophical Apologetics

1) *The Wisdom of Jesus the Son of Sirach* (Ecclesiasticus in the LXX) is the most extensive Jewish wisdom book from the Hellenistic period. In 130 BCE the grandson of the author translated the book into Greek in Alexandria, and for a long time it was known only in this form and in other translations. However, at the end of the last century, Hebrew fragments of about two-thirds of the book were discovered in the Cairo Geniza, and smaller fragments appeared in Qumran; most recently a complete scroll of the Hebrew text was found in Masada. The Hebrew original was probably written during the first decades of II BCE. The high priest Simon, extolled in Sirach 50, can be identified with Simon the Just, who held that office around 200 BCE. This writing is actually a large collection of wisdom traditions; in addition to five groups of sayings arranged according to particular topics, it contains didactic poems, wisdom hymns, and psalms of thanksgiving and lament, as well as many other pieces which were composed by the author. These sections identify the author as a member of the educated aristocracy of Jerusalem, who was the head of a school and also active as an advisor and a diplomat, rather like a Greek philosopher. On the whole he occupies a conservative position, but is nevertheless critical of wealth and intercedes in favor of the righteous poor; he also emphasizes the wisdom inherited from the fathers and identifies it with the law. Skepticism regarding the perfection of the world is rejected: everything has been arranged with meaning and purpose for the human race. Interest in the preservation of the tradition is thus combined with a relative openness towards the world, just as in the ideal of citizenship propagated in the Hellenistic world by popular philosophy.

Bibliography to §5.3e

Walter Baumgartner, "The Wisdom Literature," in: H. H. Rowley (ed.), *The Old Testament and Modern Study* (Oxford: Clarendon, 1951) 210–37.

James M. Reese, *Hellenistic Influence on the Books of Wisdom and Its Consequences* (AnBib 41; Rome: Biblical Institute, 1970).

James L. Crenshaw, *Old Testament Wisdom: An Introduction* (Atlanta: John Knox, 1981).

Bibliography to §5.3e (1): Text

Joseph Ziegler (ed.), *Sapientia Jesu Filii Sirach* (Göttingen Septuagint 12,2).

Yigael Yadin, *The Ben Sira Scroll from Masada* (Jerusalem: Israel Exploration Society, 1965).

Bibliography to §5.3e (1): Studies

Gerhard von Rad, "The Wisdom of Jesus Sirach," in: idem, *Wisdom in Israel* (Nashville: Abingdon, 1972) 240–62.

Th. Middendorp, *Die Stellung Jesu ben Siras zwischen Judentum und Hellenismus* (Leiden: Brill, 1973).

2) The book *Qoheleth* (the Ecclesiastes of the LXX), written in Palestine (Jerusalem?) in Hebrew with many Aramaisms, was apparently composed shortly before the time of Sirach. It was accepted into the Hebrew canon while the book of Sirach was excluded from it; nonetheless Qoheleth is the product of a much more critical impact of the Hellenistic spirit upon Jewish wisdom. This, of course, excludes the two epilogues, 12:9–11 and 12:11–14; together with numerous "orthodox" interpolations of a later editor, they are written in order to soften the book's skeptical attitude. The original author expresses radical doubts about justice in the natural order, emphasizing the inevitability of the human predicament of death. This is quite in keeping with sentiments of early Hellenistic thought which are in evidence in Euripides, in the New Comedy, and in funerary inscriptions of that time. The Book of Qoheleth seems to demonstrate that such ideas had also invaded the educated aristocracy of Israel during the Ptolemaic period.

3) *1 Baruch*. But in the continuation of the Palestinian (and to a certain degree also the Alexandrian) tradition of Jewish wisdom, it was not the skepticism of Qoheleth which succeeded, but the new alliance between wisdom and law propagated by Sirach. This is evident in the Book of Baruch (1 Baruch in the LXX), which used the name of the scribe of the prophet Jeremiah as a pseudonym. It is preserved only in Greek, and was probably composed in this form towards the end of the Hasmonean period. But at least some sections of the book go back to Hebrew originals. The first and third parts (1:15–2:10; 4:5–5:9) contain prayers and psalms, while the middle part is a wisdom speech in poetic form inviting Israel to return to wisdom, i.e., to the law. In the form of the Jewish law, wisdom appears as the exclusive possession of Israel.

4) *Epistle of Aristeas and Pseudo-Phocylides*. But those wisdom books which were originally composed in Greek do not simply identify wisdom and law; rather, in an apologetic manner, they try to demonstrate that the biblical law is the source of all true philosophy. The *Epistle of Aristeas* attempts to provide the underpinnings for the authority of the biblical law

Bibliography to §5.3e (2)

H. L. Ginsberg, "The Structure and Content of the Book of Kohelet," in: M. Noth and D. Winton Thomas (eds.), *Wisdom in Israel and the Ancient Near East, Presented to Harold Henry Rowley* (VTSup 3; Leiden: Brill, 1955) 138–49.

Bibliography to §5.3e (3): Text

Emmanuel Tov, *The Book of Baruch also Called 1 Baruch* (SBLTT 8; Missoula: Scholars Press, 1975).

Bibliography to §5.3e (4)

Moses Hadas, *Aristeas to Philocrates* (JAL; New York: Harper, 1953).

in its Greek version, mostly in the interest of propaganda, only to a lesser degree with a view to the Greek-speaking Jews of the diaspora. This writing addresses the gentiles, since the Alexandrian Jews had long been accustomed to the Greek translation of the law at the time at which the *Epistles of Aristeas* was composed. Indeed, the writing itself is already strongly influenced by the well-established language of the LXX. There are also a number of historical inconsistencies which demonstrate that the epistle was not written, as it claims, during the time of Ptolemy II Philadelphus (284–247 BCE), but at least a century earlier. That the work is addressed to the gentiles is shown in its pseudonym, a pagan court official of Philadelphus with the name of Aristeas; in its description of Jerusalem (83–120); the philosophical apology for the Jewish law (121–71); and finally in the presentation of the wisdom of the Jewish sages in the form of a symposium. Some elements from the Jewish wisdom tradition are blended with numerous, and sometimes rather trivial, Greek proverbs and generalities as well as borrowings from philosophical ethics, all to create the impression that Jewish sages dining at the king's table do not have to take second place to their Greek philosophical colleagues.

The didactic poem of Pseudo-Phocylides belongs to a somewhat higher level of intellectual achievement. It was written during II or I BCE by a Jewish poet who used the pseudonym of the Greek gnomic poet Phocylides of Miletus (VI BCE). In 230 hexameters the poem offers Jewish wisdom sayings and moral teachings from Greek gnomic poetry and popular philosophy. No proof is needed that Jewish wisdom teachers and interpreters of Scripture also appeared and wrote in the garment of Greek philosophers, but only very little is preserved of the writings of the predecessors of the Alexandrian Jewish philosopher Philo (§5.3f). A few fragments from the Jewish philosopher Aristobolus are preserved by Eusebius. Aristobolus seems to have lived in Alexandria in II BCE. In his description of the creation, he used, just as Philo after him, Greek concepts of cosmogony and speculations with numbers. His allegorical interpretations of the Pentateuch reject a literal and anthropomorphic understanding of the statements about God, as well as mythological interpretation. In this respect Aristobolus also anticipates Philo. Moses is a teacher of wisdom and at the same time a prophet, thus uniting philosophy and piety in his person; Plato and Pythagoras, Homer, and Hesiod are said to have borrowed many things from Moses. Essential elements of later Christian apologetic arguments are anticipated here.

5) In *4 Maccabees* a Jewish philosopher from the first half of I CE (from Antioch?) presents a diatribe about the power of reason. Even though reason is identical with obedience to the law, it is understood in typically Greek fashion as the confirmation of the cardinal virtues, namely, right-

eousness, prudence, mercy, and fortitude. The author uses the example of the Maccabean martyrs, Eleazar and the seven brothers and their mother (cf. 2 Maccabees; §5.3d) in order to show how these virtues can overcome sufferings, pain, and death. Other Greek concepts in this martyrological account illustrate an understanding of vicarious expiation for the sins of the people through suffering, and the conviction of the immortality of the soul. In writings like *4 Maccabees* Jewish wisdom is dissolved into Greek popular philosophy; only the examples from Jewish history still demonstrate that one is dealing with the book of a Jewish author.

6) The *Wisdom of Solomon* (Sapientia) is an original Greek writing from I BCE, which has been included in the LXX (the writing surprisingly appears in the oldest canon list of the New Testament, in the *Canon Muratori*, between the Letters of John and the Book of Revelation). The Wisdom of Solomon occupies a special place within the Jewish wisdom literature. On the one hand, Jewish wisdom poetry appears less Hellenized here than in the other writings of this kind discussed above, although its author knew some Greek literature. But the first part of the book essentially continues the tradition of the theological wisdom of Israel (1–5), and its interpretation of the history of Israel does not employ the typically Hellenistic method of allegory (10–12; 16–19). In the controversy with skepticism, the writer directly attacks the book Qoheleth. The discussion of pagan idol worship is typically apologetic (13–15), yet it exhibits sharp rejection without any empathy, but still without any recourse to the Jewish cult and ritual. The "Royal Speech," an invitation to wisdom, is strongly under the influence of philosophical concepts (6–9), but the author of *4 Maccabees* would have made a better philosopher. On the other hand, the Wisdom of Solomon presents the concept of wisdom in a theologically radicalized form, which is more intimately related to the basic tendencies of Hellenistic thought than any other Jewish writing discussed so far. The Wisdom of Solomon does not discuss wisdom as a possibility for the pious Israelite alone, but presents it as a fundamental

Bibliography to §5.3e (5)

Moses Hadas, *The Third and Fourth Books of Maccabees* (JAL; New York: Harper, 1953).

Bibliography to §5.3e (6): Text

Joseph Ziegler (ed), *Sapientia Salomonis* (Göttingen Septuagint 12,1).

Bibliography to §5.3e (6): Studies

Dieter Georgi, *Weisheit Salomos* (JSHRZ 3,4; Gütersloh: Mohn, 1980).
Idem, "Der vorpaulinische Hymnus Phil. 2,6–11," in: *Zeit und Geschichte* (Dankesgabe an Rudolf Bultmann zum 80. Geburtstag; Tübingen: Mohr/-Siebeck, 1964) 262–93.

human path. The experience of Israel has become anonymous (all proper names have been deleted), because wisdom as a possibility of existence has been taken out of its historical framework and has received its only foundation in its divine origin. Belief in immortality is, therefore, no longer an alien Greek element in a Jewish writing. Injustice, foolishness, and paganism are rejected not in favor of a Jewish concept of righteousness, but in the service of a universalistic concept of the oneness of the deity with righteousness in which the true being of the righteous person (his "soul") is concealed. With these thoughts, Jewish wisdom seems to flow directly into Gnosticism.

(f) Philo of Alexandria

The Alexandrian philosopher Philo was the most learned and most productive author of Hellenistic Judaism. His writings are also highly significant for the history of ancient philosophy, because after Aristotle they represent the first extensive corpus of philosophical writings that is preserved, both in medieval manuscripts, which derive from the library of Caesarea, and in numerous quotations by the church fathers. Philo, strictly speaking, belongs to the Roman imperial period; but actually he

Bibliography to §5.3f: Text

Leopold Cohn and Paul Wendland, *Philonis Alexandrini opera quae supersunt* (vols. 1–6; Berlin: De Gruyter, 1962).
F. H. Colson et al. in LCL (10 vols. and 2 supplementary vols.).
Cartlidge and Dungan, *Documents*, 253–92.

Bibliography to §5.3f: Studies

Erwin R. Goodenough, *An Introduction to Philo Judaeus* (2d ed.; New York: Barnes & Noble, 1963).
Samuel Sandmel, *Philo of Alexandria: An Introduction* (New York: Oxford University, 1979).
Isaak Heinemann, *Philons griechische und jüdische Bildung* (Breslau: Marcus, 1932; reprint: Hildesheim: Olms, 1962). The works of Heinemann, Goodenough and Wolfson are the three classic studies of Philo.
Erwin R. Goodenough, *By Light, Light: The Mystic Gospel of Hellenistic Judaism* (New Haven: Yale University, 1935; reprint: Amsterdam: Philo, 1969).
Harry Austryn Wolfson, *Philo* (4th ed.; 2 vols.; Cambridge, MA; Harvard University, 1968).
Wilhelm Bousset, *Jüdisch-christlicher Schulbetrieb in Alexandria und Rom* (Göttingen: Vandenhoeck & Ruprecht, 1915).
Ekkehard Mühlenberg, "Das Problem der Offenbarung in Philo von Alexandrien," *ZNW* 64 (1973) 1–18.
Willy Theiler, "Philo von Alexandria und der Beginn des kaiserzeitlichen Platonismus," in: idem, *Untersuchungen zur antiken Literatur* (Berlin: De Gruyter, 1970) 484–501.
Helmut Koester, "ΝΟΜΟΣ ΦΥΣΕΩΣ: The Concept of Natural Law in Greek Thought," in: Neusner, *Religions in Antiquity*, 521–41.

marks the endpoint of Hellenistic philosophy as well as of the development of Hellenistic Judaism.

The few scattered pieces of information about Philo's life permit the
reconstruction of at least a rough outline of his biography. Philo must
have been born about ca. 20 BCE in a Hellenized Jewish family of Alexandria. His education followed the normal patterns of Greek schooling
and, since his parents were wealthy, was under the best teachers. Philo
had an excellent command of the Greek language, was well educated in
Greek philosophy and history, and was able to cite poets and tragedians
without effort. We know much less about his Jewish education. He certainly did not know much Hebrew; one finds in his writings only a few
Hebrew words and terms, and a scanty knowledge of the etymology of
some Hebrew names. To suggest that Philo had the sort of Jewish education which could be compared to the training in the later rabbinic schools
is out of the question, despite occasional parallels in his writings with
rabbinic exegesis. On the other hand, one must assume that he became
thoroughly acquainted in the Jewish synagogue not only with the regular
services of the religious community but also with Hellenistic-Jewish
scriptural interpretation and apologetics. The question of whether or not
the synagogue offered some regular school instruction can remain undecided. In any case, much that is found in Philo's writings is not original
with him but an elaboration of older sources and traditions.

In keeping with the position of his family, which possessed the right of
Roman citizenship, Philo occupied leading positions in the Jewish community of Alexandria, a population perhaps in excess of 100,000 members. Philo's brother Alexander, whom Josephus gives the title *alabarch*
(probably a high-ranking revenue officer), was known to have been one of
the wealthiest men of his time. A son of Alexander, Alexander Tiberius,
was the Roman procurator of Palestine from 46 to 48 CE; under Nero he
became prefect of Egypt and played a decisive role in the events which led
to Vespasian's proclamation as emperor. Another son, Marcus, was
married to the daughter of the Jewish king Agrippa I. In 40 CE, Philo
himself, then already an old man, became the leader of a Jewish delegation which traveled to Rome to appeal to the emperor Gaius (Caligula)
on behalf of the Jews in Alexandria. The Roman prefect Flaccus had
exposed them to the frenzy of the urban lower class when the Jews refused
to worship the cult images of the divine emperor. Philo has described these
events in his writings *Ad Flaccum* and *Legatio ad Gaium*.

These two writings belong to one of the two different genres which
characterize his literary production. They are apologies—unique insofar
as they were occasioned by a specific historical event which demanded a
literary defense of the Jewish position. It is clear in these writings that

such apologetics did not arise from the mentality of a despised minority which had no share in the general affairs of the society. On the contrary, the Jewish community had a right to expect that the vast majority of all educated people would welcome and support the concerns of a philosophical world religion, which had been wronged by an emperor who was obviously crazy. The same basic attitude also appears in the other apologetic writings of Philo—an optimism which may cause some amazement today. Philo also wrote a voluminous *Apology* which is now lost. But two writings are preserved which were originally closely connected with this *Apology: De vita contemplativa* and a book about the Essenes, of which a fragment is found in Eusebius. The significance of these works lies not only in the historical information they provide—neither the existence of the Therapeutae, described in the writing on the contemplative life, nor that of the Essenes can any longer be doubted—but also in the attraction of the ideals which they propagate. The idea of a common religious life that overcomes the senselessness of life in the existing social structures would fulfill the yearnings of many people in antiquity, something like that expressed in the *State of the Sun* of Iambulus (§3.4e) as also in the later Neopythagorean communities, the mysteries, and Christianity.

A second category of Philo's writings demonstrates his close association with Jewish religious life in Alexandria: the *Quaestiones in Genesin* and *in Exodum*. Unfortunately only a secondary translation of these writings into Armenian is preserved, in addition to a few Greek fragments. Further fragments show that Philo had written similar commentaries about the Book of Leviticus and Numbers. These writings briefly sketch the literal as well as the allegorical sense of each successive passage and are best understood as exegetical and homiletical lectures designed for use in the synagogue. They indicate that Philo's official position in the worship of the Alexandrian Jewish community was that of a homilist. The interpretations reveal a congenial understanding of the mindset of the average members of a congregation.

Philo's apologetic commentaries on the Bible are well preserved. They are not systematic theological treatments, but interpretations of the law for the educated gentile (or even Jewish) reader. Though belonging to the category of propagandistic literature, they are at the same time a large-scale reinterpretation of the Pentateuch for Hellenistic Judaism. It is no accident that they follow the structure of the Old Testament formula of the covenant: (1) Previous history; this includes the books about creation, the patriarchs, and Moses. (2) Basic statement; the book about the decalogue. (3) Legal stipulations; these are presented in the books about the individual laws. (4) Call for repentance; the book about virtues. (5) Curses and blessings; the two books now combined in *De praemiis et poeniis.* An eschatological orientation is missing, to be sure (it appears only in the last section). In addition, the concern is no longer with the people of Israel, but only with the salvation of the individual.

The first book of the apologetic commentary is *De opificio mundi,* a complex philosophical interpretation of Genesis 1–2. It often follows Plato's *Timaeus* and also uses Pythagorean speculations with numbers. The first creation is not seen as an event within time and space, but as immaterial and taking place in the realm of reason, that is, within the Logos. Part of this first creation is the first Adam, the rational archetype of empirical humanity. The second creation takes place in the application of the archetypes to matter. Thus human beings become a race mixed with both reason and body. The fall into sin is caused by the woman, who expresses the material aspect of humanity through her desire.

The subsequent books deal with Abraham, Isaac, Jacob, and Joseph; only the first and the last of these books are extant. *De Abrahamo* describes the successful striving for salvation which still exists as an ideal possibility even after the fall. It consists of the right use of the law of nature, which is identical with the Logos-self of the human being. Sarah symbolizes wisdom and virtue; as Abraham marries her, he is no longer human but becomes a friend of God. *De Josepho* describes the ideal ruler who always follows divine guidance, and who declares the law of nature to be the universal law of the world and the constitution of the ideal state. This writing very plainly contains advice for the Roman administration. It also became an important source for the later development of doctrines of natural law for the constitutions of states and their legislation.

The climax of these biographical works is found in the two books *De vita Mosis.* Corresponding to the Greek biographies of that time, and following earlier Jewish aretalogies of Moses (Artapanus; see §5.3d), Moses is not only prophet and priest, but also miracle worker, mystic, and mediator of divine wisdom, that is, a "divine man." His activity culminates in his legislation, which is seen as the actual translation and concretization of the natural law, which Moses applies to specific situations. The accomplishment of this task fulfills the royal mission of the greatest divine man of all times.

The treatment of the law itself begins with an explication of the basic principles in *De decalogo.* The decalogue is the central formulation of the law, issuing from God himself. The first five commandments (including the commandment to love one's parents) contain duties having to do with God, the other five duties with other human beings. Philo uses this division as the basic principle of his entire interpretation of the law. *De specialibus legibus* explains the individual regulations of the law. The first book begins with a long-winded treatment of the first commandment (including, for the first time, a hygienic explanation of circumcision) and then treats the regulations for cult, ritual, priests, and sacrifices (second commandment). The second book deals with the prohibition of oaths (third commandment), the regulations for festivals (fourth commandment; sanctification of the Sabbath), and explains the festivals as sacraments. The third and fourth books arrange all stipulations of the law which relate to civil and criminal law according to the sixth through the tenth commandments, and explain these stipulations in great detail, with numerous references to Greek and Roman law.

De virtutibus lays the foundation for ethics, as distinct from legislation. This writing treats in sequence the four cardinal virtues of Philo, first, fortitude (ἀνδρεία); second, in great detail, kindheartedness (φιλανθρωπία); third, conversion (μετάνοια); and fourth, nobility of thought (εὐγένεια), namely, true dignity, which rests not on one's birthright but on wisdom. *De praemiis et poeniis* is not completely preserved; of the tractate preserved under this title, only chapters 1–78 survive. Philo begins with examples of the reward one receives for genuine striving after perfection (Enoch, Noah, Abraham, etc.). This reward is mystical contemplation, the vision of God—not immortality. On the other hand, the punishment for immorality is continuous fear, along with exclusion from the joyful life and communion with God. The text breaks off after the treatment of the examples of Cain and of the Korahites. What follows in chapters 79–172 is a different writing: *De benedictionibus*. This is a popularized synagogue sermon speaking about the blessings for those who do the law (peace or victory in war, prosperity, long life, and health) and the curses for transgressors (famine, slavery, ill fortune, war, disease, etc.). The conclusion is eschatological: when the people convert, they will receive the blessings, whereas their persecutors will fall under the curse.

Philo's allegorical commentary on the Book of Genesis represents his deepest searching and also his most extensive work. It is only partially preserved, in a total of twenty-one books, not all of which are complete; at least nine books are completely lost. This is Philo's *magnum opus*. The commentary begins with the second chapter of Genesis and ends with its last chapter. A clear organizational principle cannot be found, neither for the work as a whole, nor for the individual books. The thought progresses according to the principle of association, which often arises from allegorical interpretations of biblical sentences and words, whose literal meaning is categorically presented as insufficient. In the course of the commentary, philosophical, ethical, political, scientific, and theological questions are discussed in varied sequence, and often with reference to other biblical passages. As for its literary genre, this writing resembles the *Stromata* of Clement of Alexandria or the *Enneads* of Plotinus. Such a lack of clear organization is characteristic of a certain Hellenistic fashion in literature dealing with matters of religious philosophy. In these books Philo addresses the initiated, whether a Jew or gentile—all those who had a right to call themselves "philosophers" according to the standards of that time. The sheer enjoyment of speculating, reflecting, and philosophizing inspired him just as much as did his true concern: the liberation of the spirit in contemplation, which leads to the mystical vision of God. Because of the disorganized variety of the content of these writings, only a few essential points can be mentioned with respect to each of this work's books.

The commentary begins with three books called *Legum allegoriae*. The first book begins with Gen 2:1–7, treating the difference between reason and sense perception, and between the heavenly and earthly humanity. The garden, the trees, and the rivers of paradise are interpreted as virtues. The second book also contains allegorical interpretations of the "serpent" and about "nakedness," as well as a large number of allegorical explanations of individual terms. The third book (on Gen 3:8–19) speculates about the human being who is called by God, and understands the curse as a judgment upon various forms of craving for pleasure. The books of the allegorical commentary which follow have individual titles. *De Cherubim* (Gen 3:24 and 4:1) considers in its first part a possible explanation of the flaming sword as planetary and astral spheres, but decides that what is really meant are divine attributes and powers. The second part explains Adam as pure reason, Eve as sense perception, and Cain as the evil intent which is born by the two. *De sacrificiis Abelis et Caini* contains among other things, an elaborate juxtaposition of the beloved harlot, vice, and the hated lawful wife, virtue; in this context Philo offers the longest catalogue of vices ever written, containing 146 vices. The last part treats at length the sacrifice of the first fruits. *Quod deterius potiori insidiari soleat* (Gen 4:2–4) understands Cain and Abel as the opposite principles of self-love and love. *De posteritate Caini* offers a symbolic interpretation of the names of the offspring of Cain from Gen 4:16–25.

De gigantibus (Gen 6:1–4a) is a short, but very important tractate. In the discussion of Gen 6:2 about angels, demons, and the human soul, Philo offers a Platonic description of the descent of the soul into the human body (chaps. 12–15). With reference to Gen 6:4 he discusses the distinction between the three classes of souls, namely, the earthly, the heavenly, and the divine-born. *Quod Deus immutabilis sit* (Gen 6:4b–12) explains, among other things, the Stoic distinction of all things in nature according to ἕξις (inorganic materials), φύσις (plants), ψυχή (animals), and νοῦς (human beings). *De agricultura* and *De plantatione* use as their text Gen 9:20. The first tractate speaks about the gardener of the soul, which is the shepherdess of the body, and about the relationship of reason and the desires; the second presents God as the planter of the world, the soul, and so on, and adds a moral-philosophical treatment about the drinking of wine and drunkenness. *De ebrietate* continues this discussion (because of Noah's drunkenness in Gen 9:21) and gives an allegorial interpretation to the five things which are characterized by Moses as wine: foolishness, loss of control over one's senses, gluttony, hilarity, and nakedness. Only his discussion of the first three is still preserved. *De sobrietate* explains the curses of Noah for his descendants, which he pronounced when he awoke from his drunkenness (Gen 9:24–27).

The next tractate seems to begin a new section; thus some inner connection may exist from this point to *De fuga et inventione*. *De confusione linguarum* contains several basic controversies with the literal and mythological interpretations of Gen 11:1–9. *De migratione Abrahami,* in a verse-by-verse exegesis of Gen 12:1–4 and 6, presents Abraham as the archetype of the souls that follow the divine call. *Quis rerum divinarum heres* interprets Gen 15:2–18, following the text very closely. It is the most extensive tractate of the entire allegorical commentary. Its primary theme continues the discussion of the truly wise person on a pilgrimage to the country of wisdom. *De congressu quaerendae eruditionis gratia* comments on Gen 16:1–6a, understanding Hagar allegorically as the encyclopedic sciences, and Sarah as the superior true wisdom. *De fuga et inventione,* in an interpretation of Gen 16:6b–9 and 11–12, adduces many examples from the Pentateuch about flight and about seeking and finding.

De mutatione nominum (Gen 17:1–5 and 15–22) uses the story of the changing of names to show that a literal understanding is meaningless and therefore an allegorical interpretation is mandatory. The conclusion of the allegorical commentary is formed by the two books *De somniis*. A preceding book on dreams is lost. The first of the two preserved books interprets Jacob's dreams of the heavenly ladder (Gen 28:12–15) and of the different markings of the herd (Gen 31:11–13). The second book is poorly preserved and incomplete. It deals with two dreams each of Joseph, of the court baker and the cupbearer of Pharaoh, and of Pharaoh himself. Both books on dreams are largely obscure collections of various allegories and expositions.

The remainder of Philo's writings is made up of philosophical books. *De aeternitate mundi* critically discusses the Stoic doctrine of the periodic destruction of the universe. *Quod omnis probus liber sit* is also directed against the Stoics, and argues against Stoic determinism on behalf of the freedom of the wise man. As examples Philo quotes Moses, the Essenes, the Indian gymnosophist Calanus, as well as numerous figures from the Greek tradition. *De providentia* (two books) is preserved in an Armenian translation, and it has been translated only into Latin to this day. The authenticity of this work has been questioned, but it is in any case an important document for the history of post-Aristotelian philosophy. Also preserved in an Armenian version is the dialogue *Alexander*, in which Philo discusses with his nephew Alexander whether or not animals possess reason.

It was Philo's intention through his extensive literary activity to transform the sacred book of the Jewish worshiping community, the Pentateuch, into a Hellenic book. By means of his apologetic and allegorical interpretation, he was able to associate the mystical meaning of this book, translated into Greek philosophical language, with the ultimate goal of Greek education; but he also translated the moral and legal content of the Pentateuch into Greek categories. He thus perfected what Jewish wisdom theology had intended to accomplish. The concept of the figure of heavenly wisdom merged with the philosophic and religious idea of the Logos, who was both creator of the world and human reason. The legislation of Moses was identified with the Stoic concept of a rational order in the universe ($\lambda\acute{o}\gamma o\varsigma\ \phi\acute{v}\sigma\epsilon\omega\varsigma$) and thus became the divinely authorized law of nature. From this, Philo could derive the design for a universal legislation, as well as the notion of human morality that could be described with internalized and psychological categories. World citizenship and moral striving after inner perfection in mystical contemplation are not mutually exclusive. To be sure, the negative world view of Jewish wisdom also made its reappearance in a new form in Philo; but Philo connected this view with the philosophical cosmology of Middle Platonism. This resulted in a fundamental subordination of the earthly to the heavenly world, of the visible to the invisible, of matter to reason, and of the body to the soul. Even if Moses, as the royal legislator, fulfilled most perfectly the role of the "divine man," the real Moses for Philo was the mystagogue, the leader into divine mysteries, and the wise man who was able to direct the soul on its way out of the earthly prison.

To be sure, these Philonic thoughts had no direct relationship to the very earliest beginnings of Christianity. But already in the writings of the second generation, for example, in the Epistle to the Hebrews, the influence of such ideas began to show. Through the continuation of his allegorical method of scriptural interpretation and of his Hellenistic-Jewish religious philosophy among the great Alexandrian theologians Clement and Origen, Philo became one of the most significant factors in the development of Christian theology and for the Christian world view as a whole.

THE ROMAN EMPIRE
AS THE HEIR OF HELLENISM

1. THE DEVELOPMENT OF ROME INTO A WORLD POWER

(a) The Western Mediterranean and Its Peoples

Beginning around 1000 BCE several groups of peoples migrated into the western Mediterranean realm and began to found major states. This happened centuries before Rome even became an independent city-state. The Phoenicians had been established on the Syrian coast from the beginning of the second millenium BCE, as part of the migrations of the Aramaic people. Powerful city-states, independent of each other, had been founded there by the Phoenicians as trade centers (Tyre, Sidon, Ugarit, and others) and had prospered for many centuries. Trade interests had also brought Phoenician merchants and settlers to the western Mediterranean as early as the end of the second millennium BCE. The oldest Phoenician centers of commerce included Gades (today Cádiz) and Tarshish (Tartessus; the exact location is not known) in Southern Spain. Trade centers on Sardinia, Sicily, and on the coast of North Africa were added later. Because of pressure from the Assyrians, larger groups of the population then began to migrate west. The most important colony that was established as a result of such migrations was Carthage (founded ca. 850–800 BCE). By V BCE Carthage had become the undisputed leading commercial power of the whole western Mediterranean realm, and counted the southern and eastern coasts of Spain among its possessions, as well as the western part of the Mediterranean coast of Africa. Its trade interests also controlled the inland areas of northwest Africa.

The people ruled by the Phoenicians in southern and eastern Spain belonged to the older Mediterranean population; its cities had developed a comparatively high culture, which revealed a lively exchange with the east and showed Greek influence. The northern and western parts of Spain were occupied by Celtic tribes. In northern Spain and southwestern France the ancient nation of the Vascones (Basques) was firmly established; they maintained their own language, which has no relationship to any other known Indo-European people. The Ligurians, an ancient Indo-European people, were living along the northern coast of the western Mediterranean from the Pyrenees to the Po valley in northern Italy. Beginning in the middle of the first millenium BCE they came under increasing pressure from Celtic tribes. On the coast, the Greek-Phocian colony of Massilia (today Marseilles) was founded ca. 600 BCE. The Greeks used this city as a base for their attempts to gain control over part of the western Mediterranean trade, to found additional colonies, and to extend their influence into southern Gaul.

Indo-European tribes had migrated to Italy from about 1000 BCE. They came from the areas of the Danube and Illyria and primarily settled in the central areas of Italy. These tribes, which included the ancestors of the Romans, spoke several closely related dialects, collectively called the Italic dialects. Beginning in IX BCE, the Etruscans migrated to Italy. The question of their origin is a conundrum, though it is often assumed that they came from Asia Minor. Their language, attested in hundreds of inscriptions written in Greek letters, has not yet been deciphered. The Etruscans, organized in several leagues of tribes and cities, ruled central Italy for many centuries. They had a highly developed culture, dominated at first by oriental, and later by Greek influences. Contact with Greece remained significant for the later development of Etruscan culture, and many Greek elements were to be mediated to the Romans by the Etruscans. Greek immigrants came to southern Italy and Sicily beginning in VIII BCE; they founded several colonies along the coastline and extended their influence

Bibliography to §6.1

Hermann Bengtson, *Grundriss der römischen Geschichte mit Quellenkunde:* vol. 1: *Republik und Kaiserzeit bis 284 n. Chr.* (2d ed.; HAW 3,5,1; München: Beck, 1970).

Moses Hadas, *A History of Rome from its Origins to 529 A.D. as Told by the Roman Historians* (Garden City, NY: Doubleday, 1956).

Alfred Heuss, *Römische Geschichte* (3d ed.; Braunschweig: Westermann, 1971).

Karl Christ, *Römische Geschichte: Einführung, Quellenkunde, Bibliographie* (Darmstadt: Wissenschaftliche Buchgesellschaft, 1973).

Bibliography to §6.1a

B. H. Warmington, *Carthage* (2d ed.; New York and Washington: Praeger, 1969).

Arthur Geoffrey Woodhead, *The Greeks in the West* (Ancient Peoples and Places 28; London: Thames and Hudson, 1962).

Raymond Bloch, *The Ancient Civilization of the Etruscans* (New York: Cowles, 1969).

H. H. Scullard, *The Etruscan Cities and Rome* (Ithaca, NY: Cornell University, 1967).

David Trump, *Central and Southern Italy before Rome* (New York: Praeger, 1966).

E. T. Salmon, *Samnium and the Samnites* (Cambridge: Cambridge University, 1967).

into the inland areas. The Corinthians founded Syracuse, the Euboeans Cumae and Naples, the Spartans Tarentum; most other Greek cities of southern Italy were Achaean colonies (Sybaris, Croton). Thus southern Italy and Sicily became a realm that was completely dominated by Greek culture (Magna Graecia). The Greek expansion in Italy led to an increasing rivalry with the Etruscans involving never-ending wars, although the close cultural connection of the Etruscans to Greece remained. To make things worse for the Etruscans, in v BCE Celtic tribes began to threaten their northern frontiers. This dilemma of the Etruscans gave Rome, situated between Etruscan and the Greek spheres of influence, an opportunity to shake off the Etruscan yoke.

(b) The Roman Republic

The beginnings of Rome belong in the legendary past. The Romans were a tribe of the Latini, speaking one of the Italic dialects, who settled in the immediate neighborhood of other tribes of the Latini (Sabini, Samniti) in central Italy at the lower course of the Tiber. The city of Rome was built and fortified under Etruscan rule. The famous tradition about the expulsion of the last king, Tarquinius Superbus, probably in ca. 510 BCE, apparently refers to the liberation of Rome from Etruscan domination. The rejection of the institution of royalty remained an important element in the political attitudes of the Roman people.

Rome's primary concern in its external policies during v and IV BCE was the preservation of its independence, which it secured through a steady expansion of its territory. Its internal development was marked by persistent struggles among its classes, which moved toward the establishment of the political equilibrium of a semi-democratic corporate state. After the expulsion of the Etruscan kings, Rome was dominated by a few hundred families of patricians, who held unceasing control of most of the agricultural land. The heads of the patrician families formed the Senate, which had the power to appoint all the priests and to fill most of the public offices. The state was governed by two consuls, elected by the Senate, who held office for one year at a time. The majority of the population belonged

Bibliography to §6.1b

H. H. Scullard, *A History of the Roman World from 753–146 B.C.* (Methuen's History of the Greek and Roman World 4; 3d ed.; London: Methuen, 1961).

Raymond Bloch, *The Origins of Rome* (Ancient People and Places 15; London: Thames and Hudson, 1960).

Arnaldo Momigliano, "An Interim Report on the Origins of Rome," *JRomS* 53 (1963) 95–121.

Pierre Grimal (ed.), *Der Hellenismus und der Aufstieg Roms* (Fischer Weltgeschichte 6; Frankfurt: Fischer, 1965).

to the class of the plebeians. In the course of the drawn-out battles with the patricians, the plebeians were able to establish a religiously sanctioned organization of their own, and in the course of time gained access to most of the public offices—but not without having threatened several times to emigrate en masse.

In 367 BCE a new statute went into effect that one of the two consuls should normally be a plebeian. Plebeians could also become praetors (who were equal in rank to the consuls and functioned as their deputies, later as provincial governors, and had certain functions in the administration of justice), quaestors (officials who served under the consuls administering the several departments; they became chief financial officers in the provinces), and censors (who administered the citizenship and revenue files). Two aediles had always been elected from among the plebeians. They supervised certain temples and controlled the police for the streets of Rome as well as public places and buildings. Later, two additional aediles were appointed, the so-called curulian aediles, elected by an assembly of all classes (the *comitia centuriata*); plebeians and patricians alternated in this office. The two tribunes had always been plebeian officials, elected by the assembly of the plebeians (*comitia tributa*). These offices represented a considerable part of the plebeian power, because the tribunes possessed immunity and could propose laws which became effective as soon as they were approved by the *comitia*. Even more important was the fact that a plebeian holding office received the right to become a member of the patrician class. Thus the patriciate was continuously renewed, and an upper class developed which did not depend exclusively on the rights of birth.

The unstable equilibrium of the corporate Roman state was made even more complex in II BCE, when the equestrians were established as an additional class with rights of their own, a third class between the patricians and plebeians. The equestrians became a broad and wealthy social class that soon lost its original military function. Since the senators were forbidden to enter into trade and commerce (their wealth rested on their lands), business and commercial enterprise became the domain of the equestrians. Entrance into the equestrian class was also made possible to an increasing degree for the provincial nobility, who thus gained an opportunity to participate in Roman-dominated business and commerce, and ultimately also in public office. In the expansion of the Roman empire, the equestrians played an important role as leaseholders administering public lands and as officials in the juridical processes.

For their fight against the Etruscans, the Romans had established an alliance with the neighboring tribes of the Latini. Shortly after the conquest of the powerful Etruscan city of Veii, with which Rome had been at war for decades, the Celts invaded central Italy (387 BCE). They defeated the Roman army and burned the city of Rome after the Romans had withdrawn to the Capitol. Only by paying an enormous ransom were the Romans able to buy their freedom and induce the Celts to withdraw. A century of continuous war followed. In addition to the repeated wars with the Etruscans and the Celts, the Romans had to fight the Samniti (343–341, 327–304, 298–290 BCE) and to suppress a revolt of their Latin confederates. These circumstances forced Rome to change its relationship to these allies, resulting in a new constitution of the Roman state: some of the Latin cities received both the right of citizenship and the right to vote, others only the right of citizenship; still others remained dependent upon Rome as allies. After the final victory over the Samniti, and the last arduous battles with the Celts (285–282 BCE), the Romans emerged as the masters of a confederate state which dominated all of central Italy. Immediately afterwards, the ambitious plans of the Epirot king Pyrrhus forced the Romans, for the first time, into a serious encounter with the Greek world (§1.4e). Although beaten twice by Pyrrhus, Rome emerged from the war in full control of southern Italy. Until then Rome had fought for its own independence and security, and was finally successful despite difficult wars and severe setbacks. But now Rome saw itself confronted with a completely new situation. It controlled a large area with several million inhabitants, experienced an economic upturn, and had become wealthy through its wars. By 270 BCE Rome had begun to issue its own silver coins. The traditional provincial policies had to give way to a new world-political orientation. However, the question of why this new policy became an endeavor to conquer the whole Mediterranean world has not found a sufficient explanation, in spite of the appeal to many possible causes (e.g., hunger for power and military supremacy, economic interests, consciousness of a political mission).

(c) The Conquest of the Empire

For the wars against Pyrrhus Rome had sought the support of Carthage and had entered into an alliance with the Phoenicians. After the withdrawal of Pyrrhus, Rome inherited his protectorate over the Greek cities of southern Italy. Prepared for this encounter through their contact with the Hellenized culture of the Etruscans, the Romans had begun to be fascinated with Greek culture already before the beginning of III BCE. On the other hand, Carthage necessarily became more and more the primary enemy of Rome in the western Mediterranean. Carthage controlled all of the southern and western coast of the western Mediterranean; nor were the Carthaginians modest in their choice of methods by which to maintain their control of the western Mediterranean trade. It was therefore not simply the ultimate result of somewhat aimless policies that Rome—after its entirely unnecessary intervention in Messina, into which the plebeians had forced the Senate against the better judgment of its majority—finally found itself engaged in a war in which Carthage was its deadly enemy and Syracuse its ally. This First Punic War lasted from 264–241 BCE. Rome had to build its own navy for this war, and its ships remained an important instrument for maintaining newly won acquisitions. The war ended with a division of the western Mediterranean into Roman and Carthaginian sections. Sicily, with the exception of the area of Syracuse and of other allied Greek cities, became a Roman province. This meant that, for the first time in the course of the expansion of its power, Rome used an instrument of imperialistic policy instead of its traditional policies of federation. This set the pattern for Rome's future policies in consolidating newly acquired realms.

The establishment of provinces, which was the result of these new imperialistic policies, implied the exploitation of the conquered lands. The administration of the province was entrusted to a governor appointed by the Senate (praetor; later a proconsul or propraetor), assisted by a quaestor. The local administration and the lower courts remained in the control of the traditional native authorities. But all higher courts, the administration of taxes and duties, and the military came into the hands of the Roman governor; each new governor had the privilege of determining the basic principles and details of his administrative policies and would publish them in an edict upon taking office. Whenever a governor might intend to feather his nest through exploitation and extortion, he would not have to fear the protests of a colleague nor any restraints from local authorities. Yet things would become even worse if a governor tried to prevent the exploitation of his province by Roman businessmen or leaseholders; he had to reckon that this would create powerful enemies in Rome, and that since the days of his administration were limited, his

Bibliography to §6.1c

A. H. J. Greenidge and A. M. Clay, *Sources for Roman History 133–70 B.C.* (2d ed.; revised by E. W. Gray; Oxford: Clarendon, 1960).

F. B. Marsh and H. H. Scullard, *A History of the Roman World from 146–30 B. C.* (Methuen's History of the Greek and Roman World 5; 3d ed.; London: Methuen, 1961).

Pierre Grimal (ed.), *Der Aufbau des römischen Reiches* (Fischer Weltgeschichte 7; Frankfurt: Fischer, 1966).

E. Badian, *Roman Imperialism in the Late Republic* (Oxford: Blackwell, and Ithaca, NY: Cornell University, 1968).

P. A. Brunt, *Italian Manpower 225 B.C.–A.D. 14* (Oxford: Clarendon, 1971).

Stewart Irvin Oost, *Roman Policy in Epirus and Acarnania in the Age of the Roman Conquest of Greece* (Dallas: Southern Methodist University, 1954).

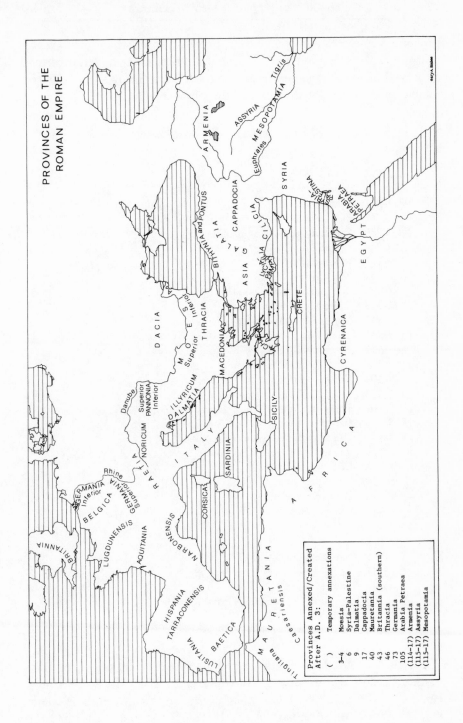

PROVINCES OF THE
ROMAN EMPIRE

Provinces Annexed/Created
After A.D. 3:

( ) Temporary annexations

3-4   Moesia
6   Syria-Palestine
9   Dalmatia
17   Cappadocia
40   Mauretania
43   Britannia (southern)
46   Thracia
73   Germania
105   Arabia Petraea
(114-17) Armenia
(115-17) Assyria
(115-17) Mesopotamia

province would certainly end up with a new governor who was willing to conspire with the exploiters. Until the beginning of the imperial period, even well-meaning laws and repeated court suits (*De repetundis*) were unable to cope with abusive, exploitative practices.

CONQUESTS OF THE ROMÁN EMPIRE

BCE

280–275	Pyrrhic War
since 275	Domination of central and southern Italy
264–241	First Punic War
241	Sicily province
238	Sardinia and Corsica province
218–201	Second Punic War
200–197	Macedonian War
195	2 Spanish provinces
191–190	War against Antiochus III of Syria
171–168	Third Macedonian War
148	Macedonia and Achaia provinces
149–146	Third Punic War (province Africa Proconsularis)
133	Kingdom of Pergamum bequeathed to Rome (province Asia)
121	Gallia Narbonensis province
102	Cilicia province
74	Cyrene and Bithynia provinces
66–64	Conquest of the East by Pompey (province Syria)
58–50	Caesar conquers Gallia
55–54	Caesar begins conquest of Britannia
46	Numidia province (Africa Nova)
34–33 & 14–12	Conquest of Illyria
30	Egypt province
29–28	Conquest of Moesia
25	Galatia province

CE

5	Germania province
17	Cappadocia
41/42	Mauretania
105	Arabia Felix (formerly Nabataea)
106	Dacia province
116	Mesopotamia province (never secured)

Shortly after the First Punic War, Rome successfully pressured Carthage to cede Sardinia and Corsica and organized these islands as a Roman province (238 BCE). On behalf of the Greek cities on the Adriatic sea, Rome conquered a part of the Illyrian coast and established the province of Dyrrhachium in 229 BCE (what is today called Albania). In order to create a firmly established bulwark against further Celtic invasions, Rome conquered northern Italy, which became the province of Gallia Cisalpina (222 BCE). In a second Illyrian war the Romans also occupied the Dalmatian coast (province of Dalmatia, 219 BCE), and thus became the unchallenged master of the Adriatic Sea. The Greeks rewarded Rome for these wars—conducted for the protection of Greece—by admitting Rome to the Olympic games.

But during these decades Carthage by no means became reconciled to the defeat it had suffered at the hands of the Romans. The Carthaginian general Hamilkar, with the surname "Barkas" (= "Lightning"), had been able to crush an insurrection by mercenaries, and then began to reconquer Spain, which had slipped from Carthaginian control during its war with Rome. His successful operations established a new power base for Carthage in southern Spain and thus also a source of wealth. This meant that Hamilkar's party (the "Barkides"), which was quite eager for war with Rome, once more was in a position to assume power in Carthage. After the death of Hamilkar (229 BCE), his son-in-law Hasdrubal, however, prevented a new war with Rome through diplomatic negotiations. A treaty with Rome determined that the river Ebro (perhaps a river in central Spain south of Saguntum, not the river which is today called Ebro) should be the dividing-line between the Carthaginian and Roman spheres of interest (226 BCE). Five years later Hasdrubal was assassinated, and his brother-in-law Hannibal, the twenty-five year old son of Hamilkar, was made commander-in-chief by the army. He attempted to conquer all of Spain. But when he besieged the Greco-Iberian city of Saguntum, north of the "Ebro," the city appealed to Rome. The Second Punic War began, as Roman expostulations to Carthage were of no avail; both sides had wanted war anyway. This became the most wearisome and dangerous war of Roman history, especially since Rome had to fight against the greatest military genius ever produced by the Semitic world.

Hannibal's famous crossing of the Alps after the beginning of hostilities (218 BCE) is well known. All Roman resistance proved to be in vain. The Celts in northern Italy defected, and finally even the Italian confederates deserted their cause when Hannibal dealt the Romans a crushing defeat in one of the most famous battles of world history, at Cannae (216 BCE). Even Syracuse made an alliance with Hannibal, who induced all of Magna Graecia to revolt against Rome and concluded a treaty with Philip V of Macedonia. To be sure, the Romans managed to gain some ground, holding on tenaciously to their last resources, desperately appealing to their own and to the Etruscan gods with the promise of splendid games in their honor, consulting the Sibylline books, and sending a delegation to the Delphic Apollo. Capua, which had defected to Hannibal, was reconquered, and the population severely punished; Syracuse fell after a long siege, during which Archimedes, who had assisted the defenders of the city with various inventions of war machinery, found his death. But in the following year (211 BCE), two Roman expeditionary armies which had operated successfully in Spain under P. Cornelius Scipio and his brother Gnaeus Scipio were reduced by Hannibal's brother Hasdrubal; both Scipios were killed.

The course of the war took a decisive turn only when the twenty-four year old Cornelius Scipio (known as Scipio Africanus Maior) declared his willingness in 210 BCE to accept the seemingly desperate assignment of commanding the battered expeditionary force in Spain as the successor of his father. Scipio Africanus Maior has been called the greatest Roman military genius before Caesar; nonetheless, his strategic ingenuity, as well as the confidence, hope, and enthusiasm which he was able to inspire among his men from the beginning, are not enough to explain his success. An ancient Roman belief appeared in a new garment for the first time in Roman history: the *felicitas* of the gifted leader and savior in a situation of greatest need. *Felicitas* was for the Romans the almost supernatural ability to lead a project to a happy and successful conclusion through insight, courage, and dexterity. But the Romans saw even more in Scipio. They recognized his *felicitas* as a manifestation of divine intervention in the deeds of an individual. The Scipio legend, which was formed already during his lifetime, demonstrates that the Roman idea of *felicitas* had begun to merge with the Greek concept of the "divine man." This legend was later, at the time of Caesar, developed further for propagandistic purposes under the influence of the Alexander legend—a consistent continuation of these beginnings. The further course of the war justified the hopes of all those who had seen more than the appointment of just another magistrate in the mission of Scipio. 209 BCE saw the legendary conquest of the Punic headquarters Carthago Nova (Cartagena) in Spain, and then came the victory over Hasdrubal at Baecula. Hasdrubal escaped to the north in order to join his brother's army in northern Italy, but was defeated by a Roman army (207 BCE). In 206 BCE came the completion of the conquest of Spain, and in 205 BCE, Scipio's election as consul in Rome. Scipio went to Africa in 204 in spite of the reluctance of the Senate; successful campaigns in Africa followed with the help of the Numidian prince Massinissa. Hannibal was forced to leave Italy and return to Spain, and in 202 BCE was defeated by Scipio at Zama. Finally, in 201, Carthage accepted the conditions of peace dictated by Scipio, and had to be satisfied with the status of a North African petty state which could no longer pose any danger to Rome.

But the Second Punic War was much more than a contest with Carthage. Rome made alliances with Pergamum and Rhodes, which had been at war at the same time with Carthage's ally Macedonia. Rome had also cultivated its relationship with Macedonia's sworn enemy in Greece, the Aetolians. This meant that Rome could not disentangle itself from the further affairs of Greece. Indeed, Rome never seems to have contemplated such a step, partly out of consciousness of newly gained power—partly out of a feeling of fear, since the victories of Pyrrhus had never been forgotten in Rome. Thus the Second Punic War was the beginning of about 150 years of invited and uninvited interventions by Rome into the affairs of the Hellenistic states, which always ended with the annexation of the state in question, unless that territory fell to Rome by testament. The individual stages in this historical process have already been discussed above (§1.4a–d). The war with Macedònia of 200–197 BCE gave no additional territories to the Romans. Rome restricted the power of Philip V to Macedonia itself, declared the freedom of the Greek states, and then retreated from Greek territory. But when the Seleucid king Antiochus III (the Great) landed in Greece, the Romans intervened once more, defeated and repelled him, and deprived him of all his possessions in Asia Minor. Again, the Romans made no annexations, but instead distributed the conquered lands to their allies Rhodes and Pergamum (190 BCE). Even in 167 BCE, victorious in the war with the last Macedonian king Perseus—a war which was started without any real reason—Rome hesitated to annex Macedonia. Rather, it divided that kingdom into four independent states. In the same way, Rome had forced the victorious Seleucid king Antiochus IV Epiphanes to withdraw from Egypt in 168 BCE through a diplomatic ultimatum, without any attempt to gain a foothold in Egypt for itself.

This policy of restraint changed after the middle of II BCE. Perhaps there were people in Rome who seriously believed that there was no other way to get rid of the continuous unrest in the Mediterranean world, and with respect to Greece, they may have been right. But it is difficult to allow the same explanation in the case of Carthage. Long-standing hate and irrational fear triggered a third war against Carthage. Hostilities were officially declared in 149 BCE because of a negligible violation of a treaty and despite Carthage's desperate last minute efforts to preserve the peace; Carthage was conquered in 146 BCE, and the country became a Roman province. As the province of "Africa," it became an important pillar of Latin culture in later antiquity and the native land of western "Roman" Christianity. During those same years, the Romans finally subdued restless and rebellious Greece and organized the provinces of Macedonia (147 BCE) and Achaea (146 BCE). In 133 BCE the kingdom of Pergamum was bequeathed to Rome through the testament of the last Pergamene king, which led to the establishment of the province of Asia. The first phase of world conquest was thus concluded. Further acquisitions were directly related to the Roman civil war, which began immediately after these events and lasted over a century.

(d) The Civil War of 133–30 BCE

The reasons for the beginning of the century-long Roman civil war are highly complex. Only a few items can be mentioned in brief fashion. One important factor was Rome's inability to adjust its social structures to the changing economic situation. This was especially the case in Italy itself. Here viticulture and olives had largely supplanted grain production; at the same time, more and more land had passed into the hands of the small upper class, which was now confronted with a growing number of dispossessed citizens and a vast army of people who had become slaves through the numerous wars. Another factor, particularly evident in Rome, was the rapid progress of Hellenization; after the conquest of Greece, Rome seemed to be left without any protection against the influx of Greek culture. The ancient moral and cultural values were not well suited for the ideals of world citizenship, while the new universalistic values of Hellenism were to a certain extent considered threatening by the champions of traditional Rome; they could therefore succeed only after difficult controversies. Finally, it soon became obvious that the established Roman administration was not capable of responding to the demands of governing an empire. Rome's wars of conquest had been designed for profit; the subsequent exploitation of the provinces by the Roman administration became a notorious problem and was a substantial obstacle to the establishment of peace. Dissatisfaction with the Roman administration and outbreaks of violence were an everyday occurrence. In addition, there were threats from the outside (e.g., the invasions of Germanic tribes) which reinforced the Roman belief that a strong army was all that was needed to solve any problems. It took several generations before Rome began to understand that the establishment of peace required a new attitude toward the conquered peoples and a fundamental reorganization of the Roman administration. Until then the people ruled by Rome had to go through unspeakable sufferings, because Rome fought out its own problems at their expense. Only the general outlines can be indicated here, as

Bibliography to §6.1d

H. H. Scullard, *From the Gracchi to Nero* (4th ed.; London: Methuen, 1976).

Ronald Syme, *The Roman Revolution* (Oxford: Oxford University, 1939).

Robin Seager (ed.), *The Crisis of the Roman Republic* (Cambridge: Heffer, and New York: Barnes and Noble, 1969).

P. A. Brunt, *Social Conflicts in the Roman Empire* (New York: Norton, 1971).

Ch. Wirszubski, *Libertas as a Political Idea at Rome during the Late Republic and Early Empire* (Cambridge: Cambridge University, 1950).

well as some particular instances which are significant for social, cultural, and religious developments.

EVENTS OF THE CIVIL WAR
(all dates are BCE)

133	Tiberius Sempronius Gracchus elected tribune
123	Gaius Sempronius Gracchus tribune
107	Marius consul
104	Marius defeats Jugurtha of Numidia
102 & 101	Marius defeats the Cimbers and Teutones
91–87	"Social War" against Italian allies
88–87	War against Mithridates of Pontus
88–79	Sulla consul and dictator
77	Pompey receives command in Spain
67	Pompey vanquishes the pirates
66–64	Pompey conquers the East
60	First triumvirate between Pompey, Crassus, and Caesar
58–50	Caesar in Gaul
49	Caesar marches upon Rome
48	Pompey killed in Egypt
48–44	Caesar dictator
43	Second triumvirate between Lepidus, Marc Antony, and Octavian
31	Octavian victorious over Marc Antony at Actium
30	Marc Antony and Cleopatra commit suicide
27	Octavian accepts title "Augustus"

1) The single event which highlighted the social grievances of Italy for the first time was the attempted *agrarian reform of the Gracchi*. Several slave insurrections in Italy and in Greece had preceded the year 133 BCE, when Tiberius Sempronius Gracchus was elected tribune. He was a scion of an old patrician family: his father had been consul twice, and his sister was married to Scipio Aemilianus, the victor in the Third Punic War. The thoughts which inspired his agrarian reform bills derived from ancient Roman ideals, which received fresh stimulus from Stoic philosophical concepts. The large landed estates owned by the Roman patricians would be replaced by smaller farms, on which a broad agrarian middle class could be firmly rooted in its own soil. The agrarian laws demanded that no senator should cultivate more than 125 hectares (500 *iugera*) of publicly owned lands; in addition, each was allowed half of this area for each of his two oldest sons. All other public lands were to be distributed to

Bibligrahy to §6.1d (1)
Hugh Last, "Tiberius Gracchus," and "Gaius Gracchus," in *CambAncHist* 9. 1–101.

a new class of yeoman farmers. The majority of the Senate used every conceivable legal and illegal device to circumvent this reform, and finally, when all else failed, did not shrink from assassinating the tribune.

His brother Gaius Sempronius Gracchus was elected tribune ten years later and resumed the reform legislation. He succeeded with at least some parts of the more comprehensive legislation: a grain bill, which gave to every head of a household the right to buy each year a limited amount of grain at reduced prices; a bill which gave equestrians the right to staff the courts charged with the investigation of incompetent or corrupt provincial governors (this law survived and had ill consequences, since senatorial governors no longer dared to take measures against the exploitation of tax farmers and businessmen who were of equestrian rank); finally a law which was designed to grant full citizenship to the Latin confederates and the status of Latin rights to the Italian allies. But this reform legislation was also wrecked by the cynical selfishness with which the majority of the Senate defended its personal interests. Three thousand followers of Gaius Gracchus were killed; Gaius himself, seeing no other way out, requested one of his slaves to kill him (122 BCE).

2) *Marius.* Outwardly the Senate had reestablished its control over the state. But it had now become clear how powerful the people could be as soon as they found a leader capable of organizing the people and of retaining their favor. In practical terms, the Senate grew to depend upon those who could count on the favor of the plebeians, be they true leaders or demagogues—and persons of the latter type were often encouraged by the Senate. After the fall of the Gracchi, the Senate tried to gain the favors of the people through imperialistic policies, establishing a new province in the large Hellenized area of southern Gaul. Precisely this area as well as northern Italy was invaded soon thereafter by the Germanic Cimbers and Teutones, who demolished the two Roman armies which tried to stop them in 113 and 105 BCE. At the same time, Rome was involved in drawn-out warfare with the Numidian king Jugurtha. In this situation, the people forced the Senate to accept as a savior in time of need the popular general Marius, a farmer's son who had risen through the ranks of the army. Marius was elected consul in 107 BCE and—against all tradition—reelected six times in the following years. Marius immediately began to establish an army of his own: in place of the army drafted from the higher classes of Roman society, Marius created a professional army recruited from the lowest classes, for a sixteen- to twenty-year period of military

Bibliography to §6.1d (2)

Hugh Last, "The Wars of the Age of Marius," and "The Enfranchisement of Italy," in *CambAncHist* 9. 102–210.

service. Henceforth the soldiers became "clients" of their general; they were no longer "citizens in uniform." Marius defeated Jugurtha, for which he celebrated a triumph in Rome in 104 BCE, and vanquished the Cimbers and Teutones in 102 and 101 at Aquae Sextiae and Vercellae. But in the following years Marius fell into political trouble in his attempts to find land on which to settle his veterans, and had to retire from the political scene for the time being.

3) *Mithridates VI and Sulla.* Gaius Gracchus' attempt to secure a better legal status for the Italian allies had been frustrated. The consequences were now brought home to Rome in the revolt of the allies, the so-called Social War (91–87), which severely threatened the very existence of the Roman state. What the Senate was unwilling to give of its own free will, it was now forced to grant after grievous battles. The war did not end until Rome granted Roman citizenship to almost all of Italy south of the Po.

In the year 88 BCE, the king of Pontus Mithridates VI Eupator, apparently overestimating Rome's internal difficulties, attempted to rescue Asia Minor and Greece from Roman domination. After swift victories over a Roman army and the Roman ally Bithynia, he went to Greece, where he was celebrated as the liberator of the Hellenes (§1.4b). Sulla, a fifty-year-old politician, and one of the consuls for that year who had as yet not distinguished himself, was charged with the war against Mithridates. While Sulla was in Capua gathering his troops, his opponents transferred the command to Marius by popular referendum. But Sulla marched upon Rome with his troops, entered the city, pushed through a suspension of all resolutions which had been made against him, and drove his opponent out of the city. This done, he finally moved to Greece, where he defeated Mithridates in several decisive battles.

But meanwhile the tide had turned again in Rome. Marius had come back from his refuge in Africa and had been elected consul for the year 86 BCE. As a result of this political change, two Roman armies appeared unexpectedly in Greece, sent by the second consul Cinna (Marius had died suddenly) against Sulla, now outlawed. Most of the soldiers, however, refused to fight against Sulla and deserted to him. Sulla was also successful in Asia Minor. Mithridates capitulated and had to give up all his conquests. Sulla returned to Rome as a victor and within a short time was able to overcome his opponents (who even tried to revive the Social War) and to assume absolute power, being appointed "dictator for the reconstitution of the state." His regimen began with a reign of terror. His political

Bibliography to §6.1d (3)

David Magie, *Roman Rule in Asia Minor* (2 vols; Princeton: Princeton University, 1950).

opponents, forty senators and sixteen hundred equestrians, were put on the proscription lists, which meant that they were outlawed and their property confiscated. Subsequently the Senate was reorganized (raising the number of senators from three hundred to six hundred), as were also the administration and the courts, while many other reforms were inaugurated. All this was done with the intention of restoring the power of the Senate. But in reality, the senatorial administration could only function as long as a strong leader like Sulla ruled with practically regal authority. When Sulla retired voluntarily in 79 BCE (the year before his death), it became apparent that not a single problem had been solved. But as Sulla had already been honored in the east as a divine man (hence he issued coins bearing his own image), there was no question after his retirement that only a new "divine" leader would be able to address the real problems energetically.

4) *Pompey*. This leader appeared in the person of Pompey (Gnaeus Pompeius), who came from a family which had entered the ranks of the patricians only recently. Under Sulla, who married him to his stepdaughter, Pompey had distinguished himself as an able army commander, and his soldiers had given him the honorary name "Magnus." Three pressing tasks existed after Sulla's death which the Senate was unable to solve. In Spain, Sertorius, a partisan of Marius, had created a practically independent, romanized Iberian state; the pirates had become so strong that they seriously imperiled all the Mediterranean trade; in the east, Mithridates threatened to go to war with Rome once more. In 77 BCE the Senate, though not without hesitation, gave the command for the war in Spain to Pompey, who succeeded in subjugating that country in 71 BCE. In his reorganization of Iberia, Pompey demonstrated that he was following a new ideal, which suggested to the leader of the Roman empire that his actions should fulfill the expectations of the conquered people. Instead of cruel punishment of his enemies, suppression, and exploitation, Pompey advocated clemency and the distribution of benefactions. He was the first Roman general who tried to realize in his own actions these qualities of the Hellenistic ideal of the divine ruler. These qualities were also visible in his subjugation of the pirates, a task with which he was charged in 67 BCE. Piracy was not a new phenomenon: it had flourished since III BCE in the eastern Mediterranean. After the collapse of the eastern empires, Rhodes had some success for a while in controlling the pirates. But once the countries of the eastern Mediterranean were either ruled by Rome or had lost all their military power, no effective control over piracy existed

Bibliography to §6.1d (4)
Matthias Gelzer, *Pompeius* (2d ed.; München: Bruckmann, 1959).

any longer. And, in fact, Rome's hunger for slaves was one of the strongest economic foundations for the pirates. King Mithridates of Pontus had even strengthened their organization in order to gain an ally in his fight against Rome. Protected by their rocky fastnesses on the barely accessible coasts of Crete and Cilicia, they could be rooted out only with great difficulty. Pompey, however, organized a navy with which he overcame the pirates in the western Mediterranean in only forty days; in the eastern Mediterranean it took him only forty-nine days. He captured more than a thousand vessels, followed them into their hiding-places, and took about twenty thousand prisoners. But again the generosity of Pompey provided an example of the new ideal of the Roman statesman. Instead of severely punishing the pirates and selling them into slavery, he settled them in various sections of Greece, Asia Minor, and Italy.

The war against Mithridates led Pompey to the height of his fame. In 75 BCE, the last king of Bithynia, following the example of the last ruler of neighboring Pergamum, had bequeathed his land to the Romans. Mithridates had used this as an opportunity to invade Bithynia and to resume his plans for further expansion at Rome's expense. The Roman general Lucullus who had been sent against him was able to drive Mithridates out of Bithynia and Pontus, and also defeated the Armenian king Tigranes, to whom Mithridates had fled. However, Lucullus made a tactical error when he ordered a remission of part of the debts of the province Asia in order to help its people recover economically. He thus enraged the whole Roman equestrian class, whose economic interests he had severely hurt. When his fortunes of war also turned, Lucullus' soldiers mutinied and forced him to retreat. In this situation the Senate transferred the command to Pompey. From Crete, where he stayed after his victory over the pirates, Pompey immediately went to Asia Minor. Meanwhile Mithridates had tried to organize his forces again, but he was beaten by Pompey.

Cicero made a speech in support of Pompey's appointment, in which he recommended Pompey as a man whom the people of the east looked upon not as a man sent by Rome, but as a god. Pompey fulfilled these expectations. He was not content with his victory over Mithridates and with the appointment of the king's son as a Roman ally; he proceeded to attempt a political reorganization of all the countries of the eastern Mediterranean world. He turned first against Tigranes, the king of Armenia, who had incorporated Syria into his empire after the collapse of the Seleucids. Having forced Tigranes to capitulate, Pompey advanced to the east as far as Colchis (on the southeastern coast of the Black Sea), then marched into Syria and Palestine, where the two Hasmonean brothers Hyrcanus and Aristobulus were quarrelling with each other about the office of high priest. After his conquest of Jerusalem, Pompey even entered into the

Holy of Holies of the temple. While he appointed and confirmed vassal princes, including Hyrcanus as high priest in Jerusalem, the people of the east celebrated him as their savior and benefactor. Upon his return to Rome, he was granted a splendid triumph, though only half-heartedly. At that moment Rome considered not Pompey but rather Cicero to be the savior of the fatherland. Cicero had just succeeded in uncovering and thwarting the Catiline conspiracy, and he played a major role in the bloody suppression of Catiline's final desperate attempt to usurp power. Pompey was forced to seek new allies if he wanted to find recognition for his claims. Such a new alliance was realized in the so-called First Triumvirate of Pompey with Crassus, then the wealthiest man in Rome, and Caesar, a younger politician who had played an increasingly important role in Roman politics. As the consul for the year 59 BCE, Caesar saw to it that Pompey's veterans were properly provided for.

5) *Gaius Julius Caesar,* born in 100 BCE, belonged to an ancient Roman patrician family. Nevertheless, according to his origin and his personal attitude, he belonged to the *populares,* that is, the political alignment which had its power base in the popular assembly (like the Gracchi and Marius and Cinna at the time of Sulla). Marius had been related by marriage to Caesar's parents, and Cinna's daughter became Caesar's wife; despite the threats of Sulla, Caesar had steadfastly refused to divorce her. Unlike his somewhat older contemporary, Pompey, who had skipped all the regular offices in his rise to power, Caesar followed the normal course, after serving as an officer in the army and studying for three years with the famous rhetor Molon in Rhodes. Although he was still a young politician, who was said to have been involved in some dubious machinations (e.g., in the Catiline conspiracy), and whose conduct of life was considered as less than moral, Caesar managed to be appointed *pontifex maximus* in 64 BCE. He thus came to occupy a life-long office (in which all later Roman emperors were invested) which was highly respected and which entrusted to him the supervision of all aspects of the religion of the Roman state.

The secret pact between Pompey, Crassus, and Caesar, the Triumvirate, reveals that these three men had recognized the ineffectiveness of the existing political institutions. They expected that this pact would allow each of them to pursue his own aims without hindrance, as long as

Bibliography to §6.1d (5)

Matthias Gelzer, *Caesar: Politician and Statesman* (Cambridge, MA: Harvard University, 1968).

J. P. V. D. Balsdon, *Julius Caesar and Rome* (New York: Atheneum, 1967).

F. E. Adcock, "From the Conference of Luca to the Rubicon," "The Civil War," and "Caesar's Dictatorship," in *CambAncHist* 9. 614–740.

each could count on the others' support and did not do anything that would frustrate the others' pursuits. Caesar profited from the Triumvirate in two ways: he received the consulate for the year 59, as well as the administration of the province Gallia Cisalpina—to which Gallia Transalpina was added—for the five succeeding years. Caesar's consulate was filled with feverish activity. He attacked the two most pressing problems of internal Roman politics: the distribution of agricultural land in Italy, and the exploitation of the provinces. It seems that his legislation regarding settlements succeeded, since forty thousand veterans and a hundred thousand citizens were in fact settled on public lands during the next few years. Caesar simply ignored the growing opposition of the Senate and had no scruples about using illegal means. But when he went to Gaul in 58 BCE, he left Rome in a state of anarchy. There was continuous fighting between the *populares,* supported by the somewhat dubious character of Clodius, first tribune, and then leader of a gang (acting by arrangement with Caesar), and the conservative circles of the Senate, with spokesmen like the venerable Cicero and Cato, who for their part also employed street gangs. But as long as he was absent, the growing chaos in Rome was in Caesar's best interests.

From 58 to 51 BCE Caesar was busy with the conquest and pacification of Gaul. As late as 52 he had to suppress an insurrection led by Vercingetorix, who was supported by many Gallic tribes. The Triumvirate had been renewed for another five years in 56 BCE: Caesar received another five years in Gaul, Pompey was given the administration of Spain, while Crassus was given free rein in the east. But the situation changed rapidly, for in 53 BCE Crassus was killed fighting against the Parthians, his army suffering a crushing defeat. A year earlier, Caesar's daughter Julia, who was married to Pompey, had died in childbirth; this hastened the alienation between Caesar and Pompey. In Rome, Caesar's enemies openly pushed for his removal from office. The increasing gravity of the political situation reached a crisis in the legal debate as to whether Caesar could become consul immediately after the termination of his tenure as governor of Gaul. When the Senate declared a state of emergency in order to prevent Caesar's election as consul, Caesar decided to march upon Rome with his army (his famous crossing of the Rubicon, the border between the province Gallia Cisalpina and Italy). The civil war had thus become an open military conflict between the two most powerful men in Rome. Caesar had the better-trained army and was sure of the sympathy of large parts of the population. Pompey, acting on behalf of the Senate, could claim legal sanction for his cause and had at his disposal the immense military and economic resources of the empire as a whole. But Caesar moved so swiftly that Pompey had no chance to build up any resistance in

Italy and had to withdraw to the east. Pompey had been victorious there before, and was hence respected and even venerated. But despite some initial setbacks, Caesar not only gained control of the entire west (Spain and Italy)—Pompey's delay of grain supplies from the east for Italy did not enhance his popularity in Rome—he also forced Pompey to give battle at Pharsalus in Thessaly, where he vanquished him. Pompey fled to Egypt, yet was slain when he had arrived there. When Caesar came to Egypt and was shown Pompey's head, he wept—the expression of an honest sentiment which well fit the man who had now become master of the world.

But the civil war was not yet finished. Until the beginning of 45 BCE Caesar had to contend with both internal enemies, partisans of Pompey, and with threats from the outside, especially from the Parthians and the kingdom of Pontus, which had once more risen against Rome. After mastering the difficulties with Egypt—Caesar's liaison with Cleopatra, who bore him a son, is well known—and reorganizing the east (for the events in Palestine, see §6.6a), Caesar turned to the west, where the partisans of Pompey had gathered in Africa, and later in Spain, to offer their last resistance. In the treatment of his vanquished enemies, Caesar, like Pompey before him, followed the ideal of the Hellenistic divine king: the generosity and pardon offered to his defeated enemies were rooted in this ideal, as well as in his personality. However, true reconciliation and lasting peace were not to be achieved through these actions. The traditional Roman society was not willing to accept these new ideals of the ruler, and the repeated attempts to establish something that resembled the cultic veneration of the ruler (§6.5b) were seen as a betrayal of the concept of the Roman republic. Although leading circles of the Senate were quite willing to appoint Caesar as dictator for life, Caesar was denied the status of a divine king, even though all the power was his. This also implied that it was not possible to reconstitute the Roman state as the ideal international commonwealth, though many of the concessions which Caesar made to other nations (including the Jews) indicate that he had this in mind. This same direction in his thoughts is manifest in his plans for an ambitious military campaign into the east, through which he hoped to unite the Roman empire with the ancient centers of culture in Mesopotamia, Persia, and India; on his return he apparently wanted to pass through southern Russia and central Europe in order to include also the Slavic and Germanic peoples in this one large commonwealth of nations. If such plans appear to be fantastic to us, it should not be forgotten that for Caesar's republican opponents they were real threats. They knew that after the accomplishment of such a campaign Caesar would be thought an invincible king and god. Caesar's assassination on the Ides of March, 44

BCE, ended not only his life, but also put an end to this magnificent dream of a peaceful, united world.

What remained were Caesar's numerous reforms. In addition to his restructuring of the administration, the settlement of veterans and destitute citizens, and the alleviation of debts, the calendar reform which bears his name ("Julian") is the most significant. The introduction of a solar year of 365 days, with the intercalation of an additional day every four years, ended the complex tangle of conflicting national calendars. But the new calendar also gave an unexpected boost to the spread of astrology, since the alignment of human life with the power of the stars seems to have become "official" (§4.2c). Caesar's death, however, also meant that the advocates of the old republic, Brutus and Cassius, had opened the doors for the return of civil war once again.

(e) Augustus

In his testament, Caesar had adopted his nephew Octavius (usually called Octavian, from the diminutive of his name) and made him his heir. Although just nineteen years old at that time, Octavian managed through his skillful tactics to find recognition as Caesar's heir in the Senate as well as among Caesar's powerful generals, Marcus Antonius (= Antony) and Lepidus. As a consequence, he was elected consul for the year 42 BCE, and with Antony and Lepidus he formed a Triumvirate, in which all three men together received a mandate, limited to a period of five years, for the reconstitution of the republic (43 BCE). Brutus and Cassius, Caesar's murderers, had managed to gather an army in the east, but they were beaten by Antony at Philippi in 42 BCE. After several revisions of the distribution of the spheres of power, Antony emerged as the ruler of the entire eastern

Bibliography to §6.1e: Texts
Barrett, *Background,* 1–10.

Bibliography to §6.1e: Studies
A. H. M. Jones, *Augustus* (London: Chatto and Windus, 1970; New York: Norton, 1971).
Walter Schmitthenner (ed.), *Augustus* (WdF 128; Darmstadt: Wissenschaftliche Buchgesellschaft, 1969).
Mason Hammond, *The Augustan Principate* (2d ed.; New York: Russell and Russell, 1968).
Glen W. Bowersock, *Augustus and the Greek World* (Oxford: Clarendon, 1965).
Michael Grant, *From Imperium to Auctoritas: A Historical Study of Aes Coinage in the Roman Empire, 49 B.C.–A.D. 14* (Cambridge: Cambridge University, 1946; reprinted, 1969).
G. E. F. Chilver, "Augustus and the Roman Constitution 1939–1950," *Hist* 1 (1950) 408–35.
F. E. Adcock, "The Achievement of Augustus," in *CambAncHist* 10. 583–606.

half of the empire, and Octavian received Italy, Spain, Africa, and Sardinia. But after his victory over Sextus Pompeius (the youngest son of Pompey) and the elimination of Lepidus, Octavian was in control of the entire west. The triumvirate, after expiring in 38 BCE, was renewed for another five years, at first without the consent of the Senate. But Octavian, who now called himself *Imperator Caesar divi filius*, seems to have secured the approval of the Senate retroactively.

Antony resided primarily in the east. In 41 BCE he met Cleopatra for the first time, when—summoned to give account for her actions—she appeared before him adorned as Isis. In the following years his relationship with Cleopatra led to an increasing estrangement between Antony and Octavia, Octavian's sister, to whom he had been married since 40 BCE, and subsequently to an aggravation of the differences between him and Octavian. His liaison with Cleopatra also inspired Antony to propagate an image of himself as a ruler, which Rome found simply unacceptable. Soon after his victory over Caesar's murderers at Philippi, he had entered Ephesus as the "New Dionysus" at the head of the Thiasus. Together with Cleopatra he later travelled through the empire's eastern provinces as the New Dionysus who had been united with the New Isis (or Aphrodite). The twins who were born from his marriage to Cleopatra, Alexander and Cleopatra, were worshiped as Helios and Selene. Thus Antony fully accepted the Hellenistic concept of the ruler as the divine man or the manifestation of a deity. Moreover, he made no attempt to relate this Hellenistic concept to any traditional Roman ideas. To be sure, even Caesar seems to have planned to introduce the concept of the divine king into the future development of Roman rule. But for him it would have been the symbol of a united new world, which would bring together the east of the Persians and Indians with the west of the Greeks and Romans. Antony, however, could not claim any success other than the conquest of Armenia, and he had not been very fortunate in his campaigns against the Parthians. His claim to divinity was therefore not based upon the successful and fortunate accomplishments of great deeds. In such a case, as the example of the elder Scipio demonstrates, the Romans would not have found it difficult to accept the Hellenistic concept of the divine man by connecting it with the Roman idea of *felicitas;* but as it was, the divine worship of this pair of rulers could only appear as a histrionic gesture.

Rome, of course, was used to the fact that its generals received divine honors in the east. This fact alone would not have held any danger for Antony. In order to proceed against him, Octavian had to prove that these claims to divinity were a part of a political design aimed at the division of the empire. He was able to do this in the last year of the Triumvirate (32

BCE), when Antony requested from the Senate a confirmation of his donations of territories to Cleopatra and his children. Both consuls for that year were Antony's partisans. When one of these consuls, Sossius, assaulted Octavian (and apparently also requested his removal from office), Octavian announced in a dramatic Senate meeting that in a short time he would submit documentation of Antony's treason. As a result of this announcement both consuls fled to join Antony, together with a substantial minority of the Senate, a flight which Octavian made no attempt to prevent. But the remaining part of the Senate, faithfully committed to Octavian, deprived Antony of his power as a member of the Triumvirate and took away the consulate to which he had been elected for the following year. The Senate formally declared war with Cleopatra, and gave Octavian the *imperium* for this war, authority which was even confirmed by an oath of the Roman people and the western provinces. In contrast to Antony, two aspects of Octavian's actions were highly significant: first, for the confirmation of his new position, he had strictly observed the existing laws and the constitution; second, Octavian's position was confirmed by the will of the people, expressed through a legal referendum and vote, not only of the urban lower classes, but of all the inhabitants of Italy, who were Roman citizens and whose will had the support of the western provinces. It seems that Octavian also resigned as a *triumvir* when Antony was deprived of his authority; after all, this had been a power which ultimately rested upon the suspect office of the dictatorship. Octavian's new *imperium,* which was later continued in the new institution of the principate and which was designed to reestablish peace and justice after a hundred years of civil war, should be understood as based upon the rights and the will of the people. Thus Octavian was able to advertise the differences between his own position and that of Antony, who had ventured to express his claim to power by means of the Hellenistic concept of the divine king, without being able to relate this to any legitimately transferred Roman *imperium.* Worse, Antony shared this divine kingship with a foreigner, and he had tried to secure future world rulership for the children whom both Caesar and he himself had begotten with this Egyptian woman.

The war of Octavian against Antony thus became a war of national patriotism, in which Octavian had the better fortune. His enemy's power was shattered through the naval victory at Actium (31 BCE) which Agrippa won for him. When the victorious armies moved into Egypt from the east and west, Antony and Cleopatra committed suicide (30 BCE). In the following year, Octavian celebrated a splendid triumph in Rome, and after having set everything in order, he surrendered his *imperium* to the Senate at the beginning of the year 27 BCE. Actually, Octavian did not

intend simply to restore the old republican structures. Whatever his motives and intentions may have been at that moment, the following years
saw the basic development of the monarchic form of government, known
as the principate. It began with a resumption of older republican institutions and incorporated special honors which the Senate conferred upon
Octavian. Chief among these, conferred already at the beginning of 27
BCE, was the title "Augustus," an ancient sacral title which had not been
compromised by the events of the civil war, and which was designed to
express the foundation of Octavian's position in divine law as well as his
felicitas. Henceforth the victorious heir of Caesar was known by the name
of *Imperator Caesar divi filius Augustus*. For the next few years he was
invested each year with the office of consul and received the authority *pro
consule* for those provinces in which the major parts of the Roman army
were stationed (Egypt, Syria, Gaul, and Spain).

A substantial reorganization came only from the steps which were tak-
en after a crisis in the year 23 BCE. During a long and serious illness of
Augustus, a plot of his fellow-consul was uncovered. After his recovery,
Augustus decided that he would no longer exercise his power by means of
the annual office of consul. Thus he resigned his consular office during
that year, but expanded his authority *pro consule* over the whole empire,
including the city of Rome, which gave him the right to maintain an army
detachment (the praetorians) even within the capital. In addition he assumed the authority of the tribune, which gave him the power to initiate
legislation in behalf of the people and brought with it his personal inviola-
bility. Beginning in 12 BCE, he also occupied the office of *pontifex
maximus*. Thus the actual authority of the princeps rested upon the
imperium proconsulare and the *imperium tribunicium;* both *imperia*
were separated from the ancient republican institutions and were specifically connected with the new principate. At the same time, Augustus
began to create his own administrative instruments, which functioned
alongside the Senate and its administrative organs. These were instituted
step by step, according to the specific tasks and requirements which
occurred. Among these were the supervision of the grain supply, the
supervision of the imperial roads, and the establishment of an imperial
financial administration (*fiscus* = "basket"), which existed alongside the
senatorial state treasury and received the income due from the imperial
provinces and estates. This imperial administration was not a separate
government, but consisted of a staff which was directly dependent upon
the household of the princeps. It also offered opportunities to the equestrians for a new series of offices, opening up service in behalf of the state to
this class, which so far had been interested exlusively in its own personal
enrichment (for the structures of administration, see §6.3a).

Statue of Augustus

This well-preserved statue was found in Thessaloniki. It shows Augustus with the gesture of an orator. His naked upper body, an iconographic peculiarity of Zeus, indicates his divine status.

As for his policies concerning the frontiers of the Roman empire, Augustus abandoned Caesar's far-reaching designs of conquest. This conformed with the mentality of a ruler whose primary concern was the preservation of peace. To be sure, the Roman empire was at war during most of the years of Augustus' rule, but these wars had in fact no other purpose than to create more secure borders. In the north, the border was advanced as far as the Danube through the conquest of the trans-Alpine territories. The border was also moved forward in the areas of the Thracians and Illyrians to the Danube. But the attempt to secure a better frontier along the Elbe river by the conquest of Germany was quickly abandoned after the defeat suffered by Varus (9 BCE), and the Roman legions were stationed on the west banks of the Rhine. Augustus created new provinces in Asia Minor: Galatia, Lycaonia, Paphlagonia, and Pontus. On the eastern frontier he established a number of petty vassal kingdoms (one of which was the Palestinian kingdom of Herod the Great, which later became a Roman province; see §6.6a–b). Egypt was taken under direct imperial administration and secured on its southern frontier. On the western African frontier, Juba II of Numidia became a reliable Roman vassal. Within these regions peace was securely established; for the people living in this realm, who had been haunted by never-ending unrest and civil war, this must have seemed a true gift from the gods, and many inscriptions honored Augustus as a benefactor whose coming had surpassed all hopes, and whose deeds had made it impossible for any future benefactors of humankind to boast of any greater accomplishments.

The problem of succession in the office of the princeps turned out to be unusually difficult for Augustus, who enjoyed a very long rule (27 BCE–14 CE). The principate he had created was not precisely a monarchical institution, but even a monarchic succession would have been made difficult by the fact that Augustus had no son of his own, only a daughter, Julia, from his short second marriage. His third and last marriage to Livia Drusilla (who had to divorce her first husband Tiberius Claudius Nero while already pregnant) remained childless. But Livia brought two sons into her marriage with Augustus: Tiberius (the later emperor) and Drusus, who was born only after Livia had become Augustus' wife. Augustus married his daughter Julia first to his nephew Marcellus; but Marcellus died young. Then Augustus' old comrade-in-arms and faithful friend, Agrippa, had to marry Julia, and Augustus adopted the two sons who came from this marriage. But both of them died before him. Finally Augustus adopted Livia's son from her first marriage, Tiberius, who in turn married Augustus' daughter Julia, again a widow since Agrippa had died. Tiberius left Julia after a few years, and Augustus was later forced to sentence his daughter to exile because of immorality. All subsequent emperors down to Nero descended from the Julio-Claudian house, that is, they were either descendents of Augustus through his daughter Julia, or of his wife Livia and her first husband Tiberius Claudius Nero. But a direct succession from father to son never occurred.

2. THE ROMAN EMPIRE TO THE END OF THE "GOLDEN AGE"

(a) The Emperors of the Julio-Claudian House

The four emperors who followed upon Augustus, since they were members of the families of the Julians and Claudians, belonged to the ancient Roman nobility. But while Augustus possessed enough skill to surmount the tensions between the new institution of the principate and the ancient republican institutions, friction frequently occurred under his successors. The princeps, however, was always able to prevail, thanks to the powers with which Augustus had endowed the office. The new order proved to be stable and capable of preserving peace, although the emperors of this house were hardly extraordinary personalities.

1) *Tiberius* (14–37 CE), son of Livia and stepson of Augustus, fifty-six years old when he became emperor, had been entrusted with numerous tasks and proven to be a successful general and an experienced administrator. Tiberius once and for all abandoned the plans for conquering

Bibliography to §6.2

E. T. Salmon, *A History of the Roman World from 30 B.C. to 138 A.D.* (Methuen's History of the Greek and Roman World 6; 6th ed.; London: Methuen, 1968).
Harold Mattingly, *Roman Imperial Civilization* (New York: St. Martin's, 1957).
J. P. V. D. Balsdon, *Rome: The Story of an Empire* (London: Weidenfield and Nicolson, 1970).
Fergus Millar (ed.), *The Roman Empire and its Neighbors* (London: Weidenfield and Nicolson, 1967; New York: Delacorte, 1968).
Ch. G. Starr, "The History of the Roman Empire 1911–1960," *JRomS* 50 (1960) 149–60.

Bibliography to §6.2a: Texts
Barrett, *Background,* 10–17.

Bibliography to §6.2a: Studies

Eckhard Meise, *Untersuchungen zur Geschichte der julisch-claudischen Dynastie* (Vestigia 10; München: Beck, 1969).

Bibliography to §6.2a (1)

Ernst Kornemann, *Tiberius* (Stuttgart: Kohlhammer, 1960).
Frank Burr Marsh, *The Reign of Tiberius* (London: Oxford University, N. Milford, 1931).
M. P. Charlesworth, "Tiberius," in *CambAncHist* 10. 607–52.

Germany, and through treaties with Armenia and Parthia secured a peace on the eastern frontier which was to last for a century. He consciously deemphasized the power and dignity of the princeps and tried to transfer major responsibilities to the Senate—though not with much success. He also did not permit divine honors to be given to him, and insisted that the person of the emperor should be subordinated to the office of the princeps. Nevertheless, history has not thought well of Tiberius. One of the reasons for this can be found in the lawsuits for lese majesty (*crimen laesae maiestatis*) through which a few actual and many imaginary opponents of Tiberius were condemned. Furthermore, Tiberius had very little knowledge of human nature and was thus unable to draw responsible and faithful friends into his circle, as Augustus had done in the case particularly of Agrippa. The affairs of the state were instead in the hands of power-hungry sycophants. Particularly disastrous was the power which Tiberius gave to the ambitious praetorian prefect Sejanus. Sejanus persuaded the emperor to transfer his residence to Capri, so that he himself could establish his reign of terror undisturbed in Rome—even members of the imperial family were no longer secure! Sejanus was overthrown and executed in 31 CE, and although his successor, the praetorian prefect Macro, may have been less ambitious, he certainly was no less cruel. The emperor did not even put in an appearance in Rome, communicated with the outside world only through letters, and in the company of his astrologer Thrasyllus devoted himself exclusively to his studies of occult subjects. Tiberius' death was generally welcomed as a great relief.

2) *Caligula.* The question of the succession was difficult. Tiberius' own son Drusus had been poisoned (by Sejanus?). Of the five children of Agrippa and Augustus' daughter Julia, Tiberius' second wife, none was still alive. Two greatnephews had also become victims of Sejanus' terror. His nephew Claudius, a sickly scholar, had been kept away from all public offices and was out of the question as a successor. This left only Gaius, greatnephew of Tiberius, son of Germanicus, and great-grandson of Augustus, who had received the nickname "Caligula" from the soldiers while he stayed in his father's army camp. He was proclaimed emperor by the praetorian prefect Macro and recognized as such by the Senate (37 CE). After the oppressive final years of Tiberius' reign, the young emperor was greeted with hopeful anticipation. But his reign very quickly turned into a nightmare. The divinization of the late emperor, and in the east, the

Bibliography to §6.2a (2)

J. P. V. D. Balsdon, *The Emperor Gaius (Caligula)* (Oxford: Clarendon, 1934; reprint, 1966).

M. P. Charlesworth, "Gaius and Claudius," in *CambAncHist* 10. 653–701.

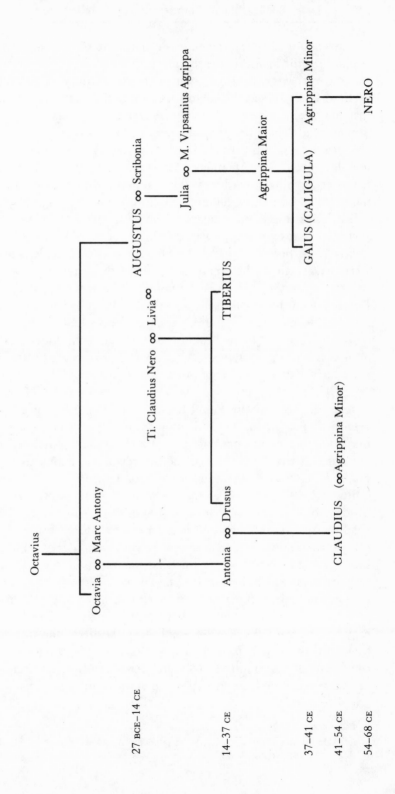

The Julio-Claudian House

Octavius

Octavia ∞ Marc Antony

AUGUSTUS ∞ Scribonia   27 BCE–14 CE

Ti. Claudius Nero ∞ Livia∞

Julia ∞ M. Vipsanius Agrippa

TIBERIUS   14–37 CE

Antonia ∞ Drusus

Agrippina Maior

GAIUS (CALIGULA)   37–41 CE

Agrippina Minor

CLAUDIUS (∞Agrippina Minor)   41–54 CE

NERO   54–68 CE

divine worship of the ruling emperor, had no doubt become an important support for the institution of the principate. But it was a catastrophe that an emperor was seriously convinced of his divinity already during his lifetime. Caligula soon began to appear in public in the dress and with the insignia of one god or the other, believing that he was an incarnation of Jupiter, and demanding that his statues be put up everywhere in order to receive divine worship—even in the synagogues of Alexandria and in the temple of Jerusalem! He intended to live in a brother-sister marriage with his sister Drusilla, according to the example of the divine Pharaohs. In his political behavior Caligula imitated the oriental "great kings," appointing vassal kings in several Roman provinces in the east (among these was Herod's grandson Agrippa I in Palestine; see §6.6d). The Jews of Alexandria, who fiercely resisted the blasphemous insanity of the emperor, were persecuted by the fanaticized plebs of that city, and a delegation of protest, which they sent to Rome under the leadership of the philosopher Philo, did not have much success. But at the end, not only the leading circles of Roman society, but also the army had had enough of this emperor who claimed to be Jupiter, but nervously hid under a table at the approach of a thunderstorm. After several unsuccessful attempts on his life he was slain by officers of the imperial guard (41 CE).

3) *Claudius.* It is reported that after the assassination of Caligula the praetorians accidentally found his 49-year-old sickly uncle Claudius, a grandson of Augustus' wife Livia, in the imperial palace and proclaimed him emperor. He has been accused of lacking dignity and depending too much on his wives and his freedmen; nevertheless, supported by a highly qualified staff of civil servants, he conducted the affairs of the government quite well. Claudius was a learned historian, who wrote comprehensive histories of Augustus, of Carthage, and of the Etruscans. He had studied legal matters thoroughly, and was an expert administrator. In order to carry through several of his projects, he restructured the "imperial house" into an administration with different departments: a chancellory for military and political affairs, a treasury department, an archival administration, and a department for petitions. As heads of these departments he appointed imperial freedmen, who were mostly of Greek or oriental origin. This gave the Roman empire for the first time in its history a "government" which proved to have considerable stability in years to come. Claudius also introduced a number of reforms; a reorganization of the financial administation, expansion of the right to citizenship, appoint-

Bibliography to §6.2a (3)

Arnaldo Momigliano, *Claudius* (translated by W. D. Hogarth; 2d ed.; New York: Barnes and Noble, 1962).

ment of nobility from the provinces as members of the Senate, and also a number of religious reforms, in both the established Roman cults as well as the more recently introduced religions (e.g., the cult of Attis). In his building activity, Claudius concentrated the use of imperial money upon projects which would benefit general commerce: the enlargement of Ostia to become Rome's primary commercial seaport, new aqueducts, regulation of the Tiber, and road construction (e.g., a new road from the Adriatic Sea along the Etsch to the Danube). Among the new cities which he founded was Colonia Agrippina (Cologne in Germany), which the emperor named after his last wife, the mother of Nero. In external politics he accepted Augustus' goal of securing the frontiers, but in his conquest of a part of Britain he went beyond it. Provinces which Caligula had given away to vassal kings were returned to direct Roman administration (including Palestine; see §6.6d–e).

But what also remained in the memory of history are the scandals associated with Claudius' rule. He was married to Messalina, a great-granddaughter of Augustus' sister Octavia. It is reported that Messalina publicly prostituted herself with imperial permission. When she married the consul-designate of that year during the emperor's absence, she was done away with by Narcissus, the head of the imperial chancellory. This murder improved nothing, since Claudius afterwards married his niece Agrippina (a sister of Caligula) upon the advice of his treasury secretary. Agrippina was ambitious and hungry for power. Once persecuted, mistreated, and exiled by Tiberius, she had determined that she would never again be one of those members of the imperial house who could be considered as a danger to the state. Claudius had to adopt her son Tiberius Claudius Nero, and to promise him his daughter Octavia in marriage. Thus she secured first rank in the succession for Nero, and Claudius' own son Britannicus, four years younger than Nero, had to take second place. In order to obviate any unexpected turn of fate, it seems that Agrippina, together with her personal physician, poisoned the emperor, whose longevity might have threatened her designs.

4) The new emperor *Nero* (54–68 CE) was greeted with enthusiasm. He gave the funerary oration for his stepfather Claudius (the philosopher Seneca, Nero's educator, had actually written the speech), while the Senate deified Claudius and appointed Agrippina as the priestess of the cult. The reign of this emperor, who would become the first to persecute

Bibliography to §6.2a (4)

A. Momigliano, "Nero," in *CambAncHist* 10. 702–42.

B. H. Warmington, *Nero: Reality and Legend* (London: Chatto and Windus, 1969).

Michael Grant, *Nero* (London: Weidenfield and Nicolson, 1970).

G. E. F. Chilver, "The Army in Politics A.D. 68–70," *JRomS* 47 (1957) 29–35.

the Christians, and who brought the Jews the most catastrophic war of
their history, began in great splendor. The office of the princeps had been
created by Augustus because he had recognized that the immense Roman
empire could only survive if the military leadership and administrative
supervision were under the control of one and the same person. Thus the
princeps had to be a military leader as well as an expert administrator.
Tiberius and Claudius had been quite equal to this task, but Nero had no
inclination whatsoever to prove his gifts in these endeavors. The consequences of this failure were not immediately apparent, because Nero left
the business of government in the hands of his advisors Seneca and
Burrus. The Gaul Burrus, praetorian prefect from 51 CE, was an excellent financial expert, and it was due to his efforts that the affairs of the
government ran smoothly during the first years of Nero's reign. The poet
and philosopher Seneca (§6.4f), a Roman nobleman from Spain, immensely rich but personally frugal as a Stoic philosopher, had been recalled from exile by Agrippina (the cause for his exile was probably a
personal intrigue of Messalina) in order to assume the rhetorical education of her son Nero. When Nero became emperor, he wrote a treatise on
generosity which was designed as the governmental program for the
young emperor. An ideal seemed to become reality: the greatest philosopher of his time as the guide of a young ruler had the opportunity to
determine the fortunes of an empire, a state in which the generosity and
magnanimity of the ruler preserved the peace within the land and with its
neighbors.

Although Nero was quite open to such ideals, he had no intention to
make his personal tastes for pleasure subject to the demands of morality
and fulfillment of duty. The moral corruption of the Roman nobility had
finally reached the emperor himself. Nero was convinced that neither
moral considerations nor natural inhibitions should stand in the way of
the fulfillment of normal and perverse sexual desires, and he felt that it
was perfectly justifiable when he murdered even the closest members of
his family as soon as he suspected that they might stand in his way.
Already in the second year of his government he had his stepbrother
Britannicus (Claudius' son) poisoned. His mother Agrippina, whose
image appeared together with Nero on coins from his first year of government, was soon forced to withdraw from political life, and in 59 CE Nero
determined that his mother also had to die; he probably feared for his own
security as long as she was still alive. When Burrus died in 62 CE, Seneca
had to retire from political life. Nero also repudiated his wife, Claudius'
daughter Octavia, and married Poppaea, the wife of his friend Otho (who
became emperor for a brief time after Nero's death). When Poppaea was
pregnant for the second time, Nero killed her by kicking her in the

stomach (accidentally or in a drunken stupor?). In 65 CE a conspiracy was discovered, at whose head was a senator with the name of Piso. This gave Nero an opportunity to murder all the members of the imperial family who were still alive and to force several of his old friends and advisors to commit suicide: Seneca, whom the conspirators might have designated as the new emperor; the writer Petronius, who had been for many years Nero's closest advisor in his unbecoming amusements; and the poet Lucan, who had once been a flatterer of Nero, but now had to pay with his life, because he had quoted a line from one of Nero's poems in an indecent context in a public toilet.

In his public appearances Nero by no means presented himself as a sinister tyrant. His enthusiasm for everything Greek combined in a peculiar way with his desire to find public approval. Beginning in 59 CE, first in private, and then also in public, he gave performances as a poet, singer, and athlete. In order to enhance his popularity among the people, he arranged the most magnificent and refined but most outlandish public games. In the midst of this activity a catastrophe almost ended his career. A terrible fire broke out in Rome, raged for an entire week, and destroyed the major part of the old city. Since the rumor began to circulate that the emperor himself was the arsonist, Nero looked about for a scapegoat, and he chanced to hit upon the Christians. They were driven together and martyred in most ingenious ways; some were covered with pitch and burned at night as torches in the imperial gardens. If there was any protest against such cruelties, a well-functioning system of informers was capable of discouraging any public debate. For the masses, however, Nero's government continued to be a splendid show, although the state's finances were ruined. In 66 CE the Parthian-appointed Armenian king Tiridates appeared in Rome in order to receive his crown in great pomp from the hands of the Roman emperor. Nero spent huge amounts of money for the appropriate celebration of this, allegedly the greatest result of his policies of peace. Nor did he spare any funds in the rebuilding of Rome, for it was Nero who gave "Eternal Rome" its architectural shape. His tour of Greece became an equally costly venture. Since the emperor wanted to compete personally in all Greek games and contests, many had to be shifted so that all of them would take place within the same year. While in Greece, the Hellenophile emperor proclaimed the "freedom" of this country that he admired so much, and exempted it from the payment of taxes. Nero returned to Rome with 1,008 victory crowns for a magnificent triumph of peace. At the same time he began to gather an army, which he wanted to lead personally in a campaign as far as the Caucasus. But the governors of the western provinces protested. Nero, completely at a loss in this political crisis, lost his nerve. When even the two praetorian prefects turned against him, he fled from the city and committed suicide in the most undignified manner in a villa near Rome.

There was no possible successor left among the descendents of Augustus. The Senate had deposed Nero one day before his suicide, but was not able to solve the problem of his succession because all power lay in the hands of the troops. Heading the rebellion against Nero was Galba, the governor of Spain; thus the Senate appointed him as emperor. Galba, who was then seventy-two years old, belonged to the Roman nobility. He was just and austere, but did not possess enough political skill to master the problems facing the state. As soon as six months later, the army stationed on the Rhine revolted and proclaimed their general Vitellius emperor. Meanwhile Galba was slain in Rome by Otho and his people, and the Senate recognized this former friend of Nero, first husband of Poppaea, and the people's favorite. But Vitellius invaded Italy with his army; for the first time after a century of peace a battle was fought on Italian soil. Otho lost and committed suicide. But Vitellius also quickly gambled away whatever authority he had. He was fond of good living and much too lazy to tackle any problems. There was, however, still another Roman army which had so far not intervened in the fight for Nero's succession: the army of Vespasian, occupied with the suppression of the Jewish revolt of 66 CE. On 1 July 69 the Roman prefect of Egypt, Tiberius Alexander (a nephew of the Jewish philosopher Philo of Alexandria; see §5.3f), proclaimed Vespasian emperor. The Syrian legate Mucianus joined him two days later.

(b) The Flavian Emperors

1) *T. Flavius Vespasianus* was almost sixty years old when he became emperor. He descended from an equestrian family which had only recently been elevated to senatorial rank; his father had been a tax collector in Asia Minor. As a general, Vespasian had served with success in Britain and Germany, and had been a competent administrator as proconsul of Africa. Vespasian was intelligent enough not to meddle with the problems of Nero's succession, and he hesitated to accept the summons to become emperor. But once he had made up his mind, he planned his moves care-

Bibliography to §6.2b: Texts
Barrett, *Background*, 18–21.

Bibliography to §6.2b: Studies
Hermann Bengtson, *Die Flavier: Vespasian, Titus, Domitian: Geschichte eines römischen Kaiserhauses* (München: Beck, 1979).

Bibliography to §6.2b (1)
Léon Homo, *Vespasian, l'empereur du bon sens* (Paris, Michel, 1949).

fully and with circumspection. First he went to Egypt, transferred the command in the Jewish War to his son Titus, and shut off the grain supply for Rome. While he negotiated with the Parthians in Syria to make sure that he was not attacked from the rear, he left to his supporters the organization of the army and navy, as well as the actual fighting in Italy, the conquest of Rome, and the overthrow of Vitellius. Not until the following year (70 CE) did Vespasian himself go to Rome. Once there, however, he undertook to solve the many pressing problems energetically. Because of the mismanagement during Nero's last years and the subsequent wars among the successors, the state's finances were ruined. Italy had suffered severely through the civil war, and parts of Rome were demolished, with the Capitol a heap of rubble and the state archives destroyed. Insurrections in Gaul and at the lower course of the Rhine had to be crushed, and the Jewish War ended only during this year through the conquest of Jerusalem (the fortress of Massada was not taken until three years later). In 70, Vespasian's son Titus celebrated a splendid triumph, which is depicted on the Arch of Titus, still preserved in Rome. The rebuilding of the city was supervised personally by the emperor, and the regulation of the Tiber was completed. Extreme thriftiness, tight revenue policies, and sobriety in the conduct of the administration distinguished the years of Vespasian's rule. He was more interested in the reorganization of the patrician class and the strengthening of the Senate than in titles of honor for his own person. The same Vespasian who is said to have worked miracles like a divine man while staying in Alexandria, when he felt that his death was approaching—since emperors were often declared gods after their death—joked: "Woe is me. I think I'm turning into a god."

2) *Titus and Domitian.* Vespasian was followed by Titus, who, however, ruled for only two years (79–81). He continued the work of his father, but several catastrophes occurred during his reign. In 79 Mt. Vesuvius erupted and buried the cities of Pompeii and Herculaneum; a year later, a major fire destroyed parts of the city of Rome; finally a plague decimated the population of the capital. Posterity has not forgotten Titus' personal efforts as he worked for the relief of the victims, nor his integrity and clemency (*Clementia Titi*). Thus he left the memory of an exemplary ruler. This stands in sharp contrast to the judgment about his brother Domitian, who had been appointed coregent by Titus. The years of Domitian's rule (81–96 CE), however, also produced a number of positive results. The rebuilding of the city of Rome after the fire in the year 80 was

Bibliography to §6.2b (2)

John A. Crook, "Titus and Berenice," *ASP* 72 (1951) 162–75.

continued; the administration was strengthened through a consolidation
of the civil service; Roman rule in Germany was secured (Upper and
Lower Germany were established as provinces and the erection of the
German *limes* was initiated); and the conquest of Britain was completed.
But the arrogance of the emperor who demanded to be addressed as "Lord
and God" called forth the Senate's opposition. His severe paranoia led to a
large number of death sentences for real and alleged enemies; he did not
even exclude members of his own family, as in the case of his cousin
Flavius Clemens. The "philosophers" were expelled from the city—probably mostly the Stoics and some astrologers.

ROMAN EMPERORS
FROM VESPASIAN TO COMMODUS
(all dates are CE)

Rulers		Events	
69–79	Vespasian	70	Fall of Jerusalem
79–81	Titus	79	Eruption of Vesuvius
81–96	Domitian		Conquest of Britain completed
			Beginning of German Limes
		95	"philosophers" expelled
97–98	Nerva		
98–117	Trajan	101–102	
		& 105–106	Dacian Wars
		115–117	Parthian War
		116	Jewish diaspora insurrection
118–138	Hadrian	132–35	Bar Kochba insurrection
138–161	Antoninus Pius		
161–180	Marcus Aurelius	162–66	Parthian War
		167	Beginnings of plague
		170–174	
		& 175–180	Wars with Marcomanni
180–192	Commodus		

Some historians doubt that the Christians were also persecuted. But it
cannot be denied that under this emperor, for whose divine worship temples were built already during his lifetime, many Christians suffered martyrdom, that the apocalyptic mood was intensified, so that Christians
spoke about the coming of the Antichrist (see §12.1c, on the Revelation of
John), and that the Christian community in Rome was indeed persecuted
(see §12.2d on *1 Clement*). Domitian's last years became a reign of terror,
and his assassination by his friends and freedmen was a great relief to
everyone. That fact is demonstrated by the *damnatio memoriae* which was

thoroughly executed after Domitian's death: his name was erased on all inscriptions and all his statues were removed. Thus the Flavian dynasty ended in a widespread pessimistic mood, which was intensified by the economic problems of the last years of Domitian's reign. This mood is found not only among Christians, but also in the didactic lectures of Epictetus and in the works of the historian Tacitus (§6.4d). In spite of all this, however, the time of the Flavian emperors, Domitian included, laid the foundations for the "golden age" of the "five good emperors." The economic upturn under Vespasian and Titus had shown that the existing economic order was viable, and that revolutionary interventions were not needed. The decline under Domitian was not as catastrophic as it may have seemed to many contemporaries. The peace, especially with the Parthians in the east, had been maintained. To be sure, the "Lord and God" Domitian had been an unbearable tyrant, but a more authentic occupant of the position of the divine Caesar by all means would have the opportunity to bring peace and prosperity to large parts of the population of the Roman empire.

(c) The "Golden Age"

The decades following upon the death of Domitian saw the rule of emperors who in each case adopted their successors. This indeed became a period of internal peace and widespread prosperity. The emperors promoted the welfare of the cities, encouraged building activity and supported it generously, and reorganized the financial and legal administrations; science, rhetoric, and philosophy enjoyed imperial favor. It is no accident that this period also became a time of consolidation for Christianity, which is visible in the formation of an ecclesiastical organization, the foundation of a Christian morality of the good citizen, and the beginnings of the institution of schools of philosophical theology.

1) *Nerva.* No plans had been made for the time after Domitian's assassination, and so when it happened nobody quite knew what to do. This is demonstrated in the choice of his successor: Nerva (96–98 CE), a respected senator in his sixties who had no political following. He did his

Bibliography to §6.2c

Léon Homo, *Le siècle d'or de l'Empire romain: Les Antonins (96–192 ap. J.C.)* (rev. ed. by Ch. Piétri; Paris: Fayard, 1969).

Mason Hammond, *The Antonine Monarchy* (Papers and Monographs of the American Academy in Rome 19; Rome: American Academy, 1959).

Wilhelm Weber, *Rom, Herrschertum und Reich im 2. Jahrhundert* (Stuttgart and Berlin: Kohlhammer, 1937).

Roberto Paribeni, *Optimus Princeps* (2 vols.; Biblioteca storica Principato 5–6; Messina: Principato, 1926–27; reprint: New York: Arno, 1975).

best to repair the damage of the last years of Domitian's rule: the exiles were recalled; the memory of Domitian was wiped out. Nerva began by rebuilding the state treasury, distributing land to the poor, and purchasing grain for the population of Rome. He tried to encourage building construction and gave support to the cities. But his political position remained insecure. In order to strengthen it, he adopted the governor of Upper Germany as his son, M. Ulpius Traianus, and made him co-regent. When Nerva died shortly thereafter, Trajan became his successor.

2) *Trajan* (98–117 CE) came from an equestrian Roman family of southern Spain. Thus he was the first Roman provincial to become emperor. For two decades Trajan had been the legate of a legion and an army general, and had distinguished himself in wars in Syria, Spain, and Germany. Circumspect and experienced in administrative matters, he personally concerned himself with a large number of diverse problems, for which the extant correspondence of Trajan with the younger Pliny is very instructive. His building activity in Rome and in the provinces promoted the economic upturn which had begun under Nerva. But contrary to his predecessors, Trajan returned once more to a policy of territorial expansion. His first target was the prosperous region of Dacia, north of the lower Danube, and adjacent to the Roman province of Moesia. In two wars (101–102 CE and 105–106) the inhabitants were subjugated; Dacia became a Roman province and was rather thoroughly Romanized in a very short time (today's Rumanian language is one of the Romance languages). In this case, Trajan's policies of expansion were successful, and Dacian gold as well as the new economic opportunities proved to be beneficial to the whole Roman realm.

Trajan's expansionary policy in the east was more questionable. He first conquered the kingdom of the Nabateans, east and south of the Dead Sea, which had remained independent for many centuries. In its place he founded the Roman province of Arabia Felix with Bostra and Petra, and expanded Roman rule to the Gulf of Akabah. A Roman fleet was stationed in the gulf, which gave Rome control of all the sea trade between east and west which used the routes between the Persian Gulf and Egypt, as well as the land trade routes through Nabatea. At the same time, Trajan had thus fortified his base for an attack upon the Parthian empire. There had been peace on the frontier with the Parthians since the time of Augustus: Armenia was a Roman vassal state, Commagene (south of Cappadocia), first ruled by kings of partly Parthian and partly Seleucid origin, had later (72 CE) become part of the Roman province of Syria; since that time northern Armenia (Armenia Minor) had been joined with the province of Cappadocia. But meanwhile, the southern part of Armenia (Armenia Maior), with its capital Tigranocerta, had come under

Parthian influence. This was the signal for Trajan to declare war against the Parthian empire (115–117 CE). His army conquered Armenia and marched on Mesopotamia. Osrhoëne, with Edessa and Nisibis, became Roman territory; Babylon, Seleucia, and the Parthian winter residence Ctesiphon fell into Roman hands. With an advance to the Persian Gulf and the conquest of Adiabene, east of the Tigris, Rome achieved its greatest territorial expansion. But before Trajan was able to secure these newly conquered realms, he fell ill and died. In consequence Armenia, the Osrhoëne, and Mesopotamia remained embattled areas for centuries, frequently afflicted by wars between Rome and its eastern enemies (the Parthians and later the Sassanian Persians). The development of Christianity in these areas was not unaffected by this political situation. It is not impossible that Trajan's policy of conquest in the east was one of the causes of the Jewish diaspora insurrection which began during the Parthian campaign. The revolt started in the Cyrenaica and quickly spread to Egypt and Cyprus, but was cruelly suppressed. It may be that the insurrection speeded up the separation of Christianity from Judaism, although this process had begun much earlier (§6.6f).

3) *Hadrian* (117–138 CE), Trajan's ward, distant relative, and adopted son, also came from Spain. In the Dacian and Parthian campaigns he had been entrusted with important military assignments. But he did not continue the policies of conquest of his predecessor: Mesopotamia was abandoned as a Roman province, Armenia became a vassal state, and further conflicts with the Parthians were solved through diplomatic negotiations. In the north, Hadrian sought to stabilize the Roman frontiers, as can still be seen by the Wall of Hadrian, which was designed to protect Britain from the invasions of the Scots and Picts. In his domestic policies, Hadrian continued to sponsor building projects. The administration was further developed in the direction of a professional civil service: the imperial freedmen were replaced by men from the equestrian class who administered the several departments. On the basis of a reform designed by the African Salvius Julianus, Hadrian reorganized the legal system and made it more directly responsible to imperial supervision. Like Trajan, Hadrian respected the Senate and tried to maintain good relations with it, though he was never able to overcome its hostility.

Hadrian was an enthusiastic friend of the Greeks and spent a large part of his reign travelling (121–127 and 128–134 CE), especially in the eastern

Bibliography to §6.2c (3)

Stewart Perowne, *Hadrian* (London: Hodder and Stoughton, 1960).

T. D. Barnes, "Hadrian and Lucius Verus," *JRomS* 57 (1967) 65–79.

Bernard d'Orgeval, *L'empereur Hadrien* (Paris: Domat Montchrestien, 1950).

eastern part of the empire. He involved himself in the promotion of the welfare and beauty of the Greek cities, as well as the furthering of scholarship and education. The emperor himself was a man of wide reading in Greek literature, completely at home in the Greek language, and inspired by the scientific and religious thirst for knowledge. He renewed the university in Athens, built a magnificent library, and completed the temple of Olympian Zeus, which had stood partly finished for centuries: it became the largest temple ever built in Greece. Inscriptions demonstrate that Hadrian himself was worshiped there as an Olympian god. In Eleusis Hadrian was initiated into the mysteries. In northern Greece his most important foundation of a new city was Hadrianopolis (which is today Edirne in European Turkey). During a journey on the Nile, Hadrian's lover, a twenty-year-old Bithynian named Antinous, drowned (the statues of this beautiful young man are preserved in numerous copies and versions). Hadrian founded a new city at that site, Antinoöpolis, in whose temple Antinous was worshiped as a god.

Hadrian also made preparations to build a temple for the Capitoline Jupiter on the site of the temple of Yahweh in Jerusalem, which was destroyed in the Jewish War, and he reconstituted Jerusalem as the city of Aelia Capitolina. This, however, caused the Jewish insurrection of Bar Kochba, a revolt which also spread to other provinces. It took several years of war (132–135 CE), conducted with the utmost ferocity on both sides, to crush this insurrection. The result was the virtual annihilation of Palestinian Judaism. Hadrian died only a few years later in his villa near Rome (138 CE). L. Aelius, who had been adopted by Hadrian and designated as his successor, had died before him. Thereupon Hadrian adopted the civil servant and lawyer Antoninus, under the condition that Antoninus would adopt L. Aelius' son (the later emperor Verus) and his wife's nephew (the later emperor Marcus Aurelius). The Senate at first refused to grant Hadrian divine consecration, but his successor in the end prevailed and finished the mausoleum (the Hadrianeum in Rome).

4) *Antoninus Pius* (138–161 CE) belonged to a Roman family from southern Gaul. The time of his reign has been remembered as a period of uninterrupted peace and prosperity. Actually some wars along the frontiers did take place during his rule: a war against the Brigantes in Britain (erection of the Wall of Antoninus), and campaigns against the Dacians and Parthians. Antoninus adopted the surname "Pius" early in his reign. He cultivated a good relationship to the Senate and supported the devel-

Bibliography to §6.2c (4)

Willy Hüttel, *Antoninus Pius* (2 vols.; Prague: Calve, 1933–36; reprint: New York: Arno, 1975).

opment of religions and cults. Personally concerned with the details of
administration, he oversaw its smooth operation, strengthening the treasury department and the supervision of the legal system. Extreme
thriftiness went hand in hand with generous support of the cities
(Ephesus, destroyed by an earthquake, received financial aid for its
reconstruction). Principate and succession by adoption, instead of election
by the Senate or proclamation by the army, seemed to have become an
established institution, and the Pax Augusta for the whole empire appeared to be a lasting reality. But this would change rapidly with his successor.

5) *Marcus Aurelius* (161–180 CE), adopted by Antoninus Pius as instructed by Hadrian, the philosopher on the imperial throne, possessed a
comprehensive education. In addition to grammar and painting, he had
studied rhetoric (Fronto was his teacher in Latin rhetoric, Herodes
Atticus in Greek rhetoric). Since 146 he had been a convert to philosophy,
namely, to the Stoa which two generations before had still suffered imperial disfavor. Marcus Aurelius' philosophical thoughts are preserved in
his *Meditations*. He was married to the younger Faustina, daughter of
Antoninus Pius, in 145 and was co-regent of his father-in-law from 146.
After Antoninus' death he immediately promoted his adoptive brother L.
Verus to be co-emperor (but Verus proved to be incompetent; he died in
169 CE). War began in the first year of Marcus Aurelius' reign. The
Caledonians rose in Britain, while the Chatti invaded Raetia. One year
later the Parthian king Vologeses III started a major offensive. The
Roman legate for Syria, Avidius Cassius (himself of Syrian origin),
received the command for the Parthian campaign. He was able to take
Seleucia and Ctesiphon, and after a campaign into Media a peace treaty
was signed (166 CE): at least Armenia and the Osrhoëne remained in
Roman hands. But the soldiers who returned from the war against the
Parthians brought the plague, which raged among the population of the
Roman empire for many years. In 165 the Marcomanni, who had
founded a strong Germanic state north of the Danube (what is today
Czechoslovakia), had begun to invade the area of the empire. After some
initial Roman success, the war spread to the whole northern frontier, so
that at times Germanic and Celtic tribes from Gaul to Illyria were in-

Bibliography to §6.2c (5)

Anthony Birley, *Marcus Aurelius* (Boston: Little, Brown, 1966).

Richard Klein (ed.), *Marc Aurel* (WdF 550; Darmstadt: Wissenschaftliche Buchgesellschaft, 1979).

J. H. Oliver, *Marcus Aurelius: Aspects of Civic and Cultural Policy in the East*
(Hesp.S. 13; Princeton: American School of Classical Studies at Athens, 1970).

J. F. Gillam, "The Plague under Marcus Aurelius," *AJP* 82 (1961) 225–51.

volved. The Germanic tribes overran Moesia and Dacia, and even invaded Greece, sacking Eleusis. The repulsion of this invasion demanded many years of full effort from the emperor. In 175, shortly before a victorious conclusion of the war, the Syrian legate Avidius Cassius, to whom Marcus Aurelius had entrusted the administration of the entire east, revolted and had himself proclaimed emperor. Marcus Aurelius went to Syria immediately; but Avidius Cassius was assassinated by his own partisans before the emperor arrived in Antioch. A new invasion of the Marcomanni forced Marcus Aurelius to return to the German frontier, where he died of the plague in Vindobona (Vienna) in 180 CE.

6) *Commodus.* With the death of Marcus Aurelius, the "golden age" of the Roman empire was definitely finished. His continual wars had consumed considerable money; the plague had taken countless human lives and had accelerated the economic decline. Marcus Aurelius' son Commodus, his co-regent and successor, proved to be unworthy and incompetent. What is reported about him has disgusted both ancient and modern historians. Commodus was incapable of bringing any of the many border wars of his reign to a successful conclusion. He was governed by the praetorian prefects and chamberlains, spend unconscionable amounts of money on games and athletic competitions, in which he loved to compete himself, and had those who opposed him quickly executed (including his own wife for adultery), supported the oriental cults, and towards the end of his life received divine worship as Hercules. In 192 conspirators had Commodus strangled in the baths by an athlete. The subsequent 120 years, which saw the struggle of the Roman state with Christianity, belong to a new period of Roman history. Traditional historiography considers that period as the time of the decline of Rome. The image of the Roman emperor no doubt changed as much as the economic situation. The pessimistic experience of the world, which became more common during the reign of Marcus Aurelius and was to dominate the following century, found its counterpart in the renewal of apocalyptic movements (Montanism), the expansion of Gnosticism, and in the beginnings of a speculative philosophical theology; reactions to such developments include the creation of the canon of the New Testament scriptures, the codification of the early rabbinic traditions in the Mishnah, and the conclusion of ancient philosophy in Neoplatonism.

3. Administration and Economy

(a) Government and Administration

Augustus' new institution of the principate, in which a large part of the actual power was transferred to the emperor, became the basis for the structures of government and administration during the first two centuries of the imperial period. This form of government would be misunderstood if thought of as a monarchy. The republican institutions continued to exist, still retaining certain limited authorities and carrying a symbolic significance which should not be underestimated. These ancient institutions—not the emperor—represented the state, whose legal sovereign was the Roman people (*populus Romanus*). Despotic rule by an emperor was relatively rare during these two centuries, and in each instance only of short duration. Both in the army and also in the various areas of civil service, all classes of the Roman people shared in the actual execution of power, to such a degree that an emperor could disregard the will of the people and their representatives only to his detriment. Most of the emperors, in spite of their seemingly monarchic power, attached great im-

Bibliography to §6.3

Michael Rostovtzeff, *The Social and Economic History of the Roman Empire* (2d ed. by P. M. Fraser; 2 vols.; Oxford: Clarendon, 1957).

Ludwig Friedländer, *Roman Life and Manners under the Early Empire* (4 vols.; New York: Barnes and Noble, 1968).

Pierre Grimal, *The Civilization of Rome* (New York: Simon and Schuster, 1963).

Jerome Carcopino, *Daily Life in Ancient Rome* (New Haven: Yale University, 1940).

Donald O. R. Dudley, *The Civilization of Rome* (New American Library, 1960).

Michael Grant, *The World of Rome* (Cleveland: World, 1960).

Samuel Dill, *Roman Society from Nero to Marcus Aurelius* (London: Macmillan, 1904; reprint: New York: Meridian, 1956).

F. Millar, *The Emperor in the Roman World (31 B.C.–A.D. 337* (Ithaca, NY: Cornell University, 1977).

Ramsay MacMullen, *Soldier and Civilian in the Later Roman Empire* (Cambridge, MA: Harvard University, 1963).

Bibliography to §6.3a

A. H. M. Jones, *Studies in Roman Government and Law* (Oxford: Blackwell, 1960).

F. H. Lawson, "Roman Law," in: J. P. V. D. Balsdon (ed.), *The Romans* (New York: Basic Books, 1965).

H. F. Jolowicz, *Historical Introduction to the Study of Roman Law* (Cambridge: Cambridge University, 1952).

Ernst Meyer, *Römischer Staat und Staatsgedanke* (2d ed.; Zürich: Artemis, and Darmstadt: Wissenschaftliche Buchgesellschaft, 1961).

G. H. Stevenson, *Roman Provincial Administration* (2d ed.; Oxford: Blackwell, 1949).

J. Richardson, *Roman Provincial Administration: 227 B.C. to A.D. 117* (Inside the Ancient World; Basingstoke, UK: Macmillan Education, 1976).

H. T. F. Duckworth, "The Roman Provincial System," in: Foakes Jackson and Lake, *Beginnings,* 1. 171–217.

Graham Webster, *The Roman Imperial Army of the First and Second Centuries A.D.* (London: Black, 1969).

G. H. Stevenson, "The Imperial Administration," and "Army and Navy," in *CambAncHist* 10. 182–238.

portance to their office as having the mandate of the Roman people, and this had more than merely symbolic significance. The principate as an institution of peace and justice was upheld by a spirit that was different from the earlier oriental and Hellenistic monarchies.

An essential presupposition for the reorganization of the administration was the maintenance of the classes from which public servants were recruited. The censorship thus became a permanent office of the emperor, that is, the supervision of the class membership lists for the patricians and the equestrians. Through the right to admit suitable men to the Senate and through the marriage laws (senators had to marry, and those who had at least three children enjoyed a privileged status) the emperors sought to keep these classes viable. The appointment of patricians from the provinces, especially from the western provinces, though later also from Greece and elsewhere in the east, brought many Romans (and later also non-Romans) from other parts of the empire into the Senate.

The army was organized in such a way that its leadership was integrated into the civil service. This prevented the formation of a professional officer corps; the army instead became the training ground for future civil servants. It was also important that most of the legions were stationed in the border provinces: the administration of these provinces by the emperor was thus closely related to his military functions. At first the army had twenty-five legions, and later the number was raised to thirty. Each legion had six thousand soldiers, who were originally recruited from the Roman citizenry. In addition there were auxiliary troops recruited from the provinces, and a navy; soldiers who served in these branches of the army received Roman citizenship upon their honorable discharge. Each legion comprised ten cohorts, each cohort six centuries. A legion was commanded by a legate of the senatorial class. Under him served six military tribunes, of whom the first was a senatorial tribune, the other equestrians, as were also the commanders of the auxiliary troops. These officers served for only limited periods, although those of equestrian rank might serve longer, sometimes for life. The permanent officers of the army were the centurions who were always commoners for whom this was a lifetime profession. A special part of the army was the imperial guard, the praetorians, who had developed from an imperial bodyguard into an elite corps which also served as a kind of military academy; the senior centurions were often recruited from the praetorians.

In the public service career of the younger members of senatorial families, they first served in subordinate positions before entering the army as military tribunes for one or more years. After their return to civil service, they could advance through the offices of praetor and quaestor to the consulate. Since having the consulate was required to advance to the higher senatorial and imperial positions, there were each year not only the two regular consuls (*ordinarii*), but also additional appointments for consuls (*suffecti*) who served during the later months of that year. The most important offices for men from the equestrian class were those of the military tribune (who normally served longer than the senatorial tribunes) and of the prefect and procurator. These latter posts included a number of functions, from financial administration to the governance of a province. Unlike the senatorial public servants, those of equestrian rank normally served for many years in the same position and therefore formed the class of experienced, older officials who were well acquainted with their responsibilities.

Provincial administration was divided in such a way that the pacified provinces, which did not require a standing army, were administered by the Senate through a former consul, whose title was "proconsul" (ἀνθύ-πατος), and who stayed in office for only a year. These provinces included, among others, Africa, Greece, Asia, Bithynia, and Cyprus. The border provinces, however, which required the stationing of one or several legions, were under the direct authority of the emperor, who appointed a "legate" (ἡγεμών) as governor for each province. In addition, certain districts were administered by the emperor, through a "procurator" or "prefect" (in Greek also ἡγεμών or ἐπίτροπος); Judea was one of these districts. Egypt had a special status. Because of its significance, especially for Rome's grain supply, senators were not permitted to govern Egypt, which was instead directly governed by the emperor through a "prefect" of equestrian rank. In order to end the exploitation of the provinces once and for all, the imperial administrators received fixed salaries. The financial administration was reorganized accordingly. The finances of each province were supervised by a procurator who was directly responsible to the emperor. Estate and personal taxes were raised through his employees with the cooperation of the communities. All indirect taxes, however, were still farmed out to the highest-bidding applicant, a system which was not abolished until late II CE.

One important innovation in the legal system was the introduction of imperial jurisdiction. The administration of justice by the emperor and his appointed officials was added to the older courts of juries and replaced them to a large extent. Any lawsuit could be referred to the emperor, or the emperor could decide to transfer any legal proceeding to an imperial court before it was brought before another court. It was also possible to appeal a decision of a governor's court to the emperor. In cases of criminal law this was especialy important in the lawsuits *de repetundis* (charges against officials because of extortion and exploitation) and of lese majesty. The latter were suits for any violation of the interests of the Roman people and their authority (*crimen laesae maiestatis populi Romani*), which included the emperor and his family. Such lawsuits, therefore, concerned not only high treason, conspiracy, and instigation to war against the Roman people, but also libel against the emperor and refusal to sacrifice in the emperor cult. Only in rare cases during the time of the principate did this result in tyranny by the imperial administration of justice. It later provided, however, the juridical basis for the persecution of Christians. Only occasionally were Christians accused of crimes against religion because this category encompassed only the practice of magic and sacrilege (e.g., theft from a temple), but not the rejection of the emperor cult, or the refusal to participate in any other public cult. Proceedings against the Christians varied considerably with the attitude of each emperor, because in all areas of criminal justice (and often also in cases of civil law) the emperors directly influenced juridical administration through their edicts and legal advice.

(b) Commerce and Trade

The economic area of the Mediterranean Sea and the states surrounding it (§2.1–7) became a political unit through Roman rule, but the basic structures of economy and trade changed very little from the Hellenistic period (§2.2a–e; 2.7a–b). The economic centers, however, shifted to the west, and Rome became the new pivot of Mediterranean trade. This was due primarily to the enormous growth in the Roman demand for mass-

Bibliography to §6.3b

A. H. M. Jones, "Rome," in *The Ancient Empires and the Economy* (Troisième conférence internationale d'histoire économique, München, 1969; Paris, 1970) 81–104.

Tenney Frank (ed.), *An Economic Survey of Ancient Rome* (6 vols.; Baltimore: Johns Hopkins, 1933–40; reprint: Peterson, NJ: Pageant, 1959).

A. H. M. Jones, *The Roman Economy: Studies in Ancient Economic and Administrative History* (Essays ed. by P. A. Brunt; New York: Rowman and Littlefield, 1974).

F. Oertel, "The Economic Unification of the Mediterranean Region," in *CambAncHist* 10. 382–424.

Helen Jefferson Loane, *Industry and Commerce of the City of Rome (50 B.C.–200 A.D.)* (Baltimore: Johns Hopkins, 1938).

René Martin, *Recherches sur les agronomes latins; et leurs conceptions économiques et sociales* (Paris: Les Belles Lettres, 1971).

E. H. Warmington, *The Commerce between the Roman Empire and India* (Cambridge: Cambridge University, 1928; 2d ed. with new appendix: London: Curzon, and New York: Octagon Books, 1974).

J. Innes Miller, *The Spice Trade of the Roman Empire* (Oxford: Clarendon, 1969).

K. D. White, *Roman Farming* (London: Thames and Hudson, and Ithaca, NY: Cornell University, 1970).

M. P. Charlesworth, *Trade-Routes and Commerce of the Roman Empire* (2d ed.; Cambridge: Cambridge University, 1926; reprint: Chicago: Ares, 1974).

consumption goods and luxury articles. Roman agriculture had slowly shifted to the production of wine and oil, which were the primary crops of the huge landed estates with large armies of agricultural slaves. As a result, Italy, and especially the city of Rome, was permanently dependent upon grain imports from Sicily, North Africa, the countries around the Black Sea, and primarily from Egypt, the "granary" of Rome. Bad harvests in those countries led several times to crises in the grain supply (this happened, e.g., under both Claudius and Nero; see Acts 11:28) and to famines in other parts of the empire (like Greece) which relied upon imports from these main areas of grain production. The demand for luxury items greatly increased during the imperial period, with most of the imports going to Rome. As a consequence, trade with far-away areas, such as Scandinavia, Africa, and China, experienced considerable growth. Primary import items included perfumes, ointments, precious stones, incense, spices, and silk. Exotic animals were brought from central Africa and India, amber from the Baltic countries. Such trade, handled by independent merchants and middlemen, was very lucrative, while trade in mass-consumption goods became so unprofitable that the emperors had to provide subsidies and management.

Supplying Rome with the necessary foodstuffs was also a financial problem. Rome and Italy suffered from a chronic export deficit, which was made worse by Rome's great demand for luxury articles, and grew to astronomical figures under such emperors as Nero, who imported luxury items (perfumes, exotic animals) in large quantities for the imperial court and for public games. But the imperial purse also had to finance the supplies for the army in Rome and in the provinces. Another burden was the payment of salaries for the public service which had been instituted at the beginning of the imperial period. Exports from Italy were unable to bring enough money to Rome to balance the trade deficit. Though many industrial products had at first been exported to the provinces, such as pottery and glass, the rapid economic growth also meant that formerly underdeveloped provinces were able to meet their demand through their own production. The primary source of income for the imperial treasury, of course, was from taxes, which came primarily from the provinces. Roman citizens—the major portion of the Italian population—were exempt from direct taxation. In addition, the emperors could use the income from the imperial estates in Italy and in the provinces; with the end of the Julio-Claudian dynasty all its estates had become state property. But when all these resources still proved to be insufficient, the expedients of debasing the coinage and confiscating property were used in order to balance the imperial expenses (for the Roman monetary system, see §2.7c).

The shift in economic centers also implied changes in the trade centers and trade routes. Delos and Rhodes lost their significance as major eastern centers. But Ephesus, Antioch, and Alexandria, among others, maintained their importance as centers of reshipment because they were situated at the terminals of important trade routes from the inland areas. Corinth, refounded by Caesar and quickly rebuilt, soon assumed a leading role in the trade between the eastern and western Mediterranean because many merchants preferred to transfer their goods through Corinth rather than take the often dangerous sea route around the Peloponnesus. (The Corinthian canal through the Isthmus, began by Nero, was never completed in antiquity.) In the western Mediterranean, Carthage had lost much of its significance since the Punic Wars. The leading center of trade was Rome, which was directly connected with the sea through its port Ostia at the mouth of the Tiber; also competing was Naples and its port Puteoli. In addition to building up the major seaports, the emperors spent large amounts of money for the construction of roads. The Roman roads, which made even the most remote outpost accessible, belong to the most impressive accomplishments of antiquity. Most of them were paved and built in a straight line wherever possible. In difficult terrain, obstacles were surmounted by cutting away the rock face in the mountains, building daring viaducts across deep valleys, and firm dams through swamps. Postal stations, inns, and military posts were set up at regular intervals, though it was never completely possible to eliminate the menace of highway robbery. Itineraries and maps were available to indicate the distances, inns, and major points of interest along the way. A medieval copy of such a map from III (or IV) CE, known as the *Peutinger Table,* shows the entire inhabited world from Britain to India and China (the westernmost section is lost) with its network of roads, stations, and distances. Carriages, often quite comfortably equipped (some even had beds), were the primary means of conveyance, and could be rented in many places. Thus the roads served not only military purposes, but also the transportation of goods and tourism. The communications system was considerably improved through these roads. It has been estimated that the Roman government's mail service covered 75 km per day; messengers on horseback using the relay stations could cover as much as 100 km per day. Roman soldiers were expected to march 30 km daily. Even if a normal citizen could not use the government's mail service, travel and communication were made possible through these roads to a degree previously unparalleled in antiquity. This became a significant factor in the mission and expansion of Christianity.

(c) Social Problems

It has been said that the ultimate decline and fall of the Roman empire was caused by its inability to solve its social problems. These problems were, at least to some degree, an inheritance from the Hellenistic period (§2.3a–e), and were often a consequence of the unrestrained policies of exploitation during Rome's late republican period. It was now brought home that the newly conquered provinces had suffered immensely because of that exploitation, and also that only a small portion of the Roman population had benefited from it. Thus Rome was confronted with two tasks at the beginning of the imperial period: to provide an opportunity for recovery to the once wealthy provinces of the east, and to provide for the constantly growing masses of poor in Rome's population. The first task was solved rather quickly. The abolition of exploitation through a new system of imperial administration, remission of taxes, stimulation of building activity (temples, administrative buildings, roads, and ports), and the reestablishment of secure trade routes brought about a new economic upturn in many countries of the east, especially in the heavily populated and culturally developed western part of Asia Minor.

The second task was never fully mastered. The expansion of the large landed estates in Italy had dislodged large numbers of small farmers. Together with thousands of freedmen and countless poor immigrants from other provinces, they formed the plebs of the city of Rome. Caesar, Augustus, Claudius, and other emperors successfully settled many displaced farmers and veterans on state-owned properties in Italy and the western provinces, with the result that some areas experienced a gradual transition from the system of landed estates to a pattern of independent and tenant farmers who worked small parcels of land. But even energetic emperors did not dare to infringe on the large private estates in Italy. Social ills resulting from this situation have endured in southern Italy into modern times. The poor population of Rome constantly restored its numbers from uncontrollable sources despite all such settlement programs.

Bibliography to §6.3c

Ramsay MacMullen, *Roman Social Relations 50 B.C. to A.D. 284* (New Haven: Yale University, 1974).

Jean Gagé, *Les classes sociales dans l'empire romain* (Bibliothèque Historique; Paris: Payot, 1964).

J. P. V. D. Balsdon, *Romans and Aliens* (Chapel Hill, NC: University of North Carolina, 1979).

Idem, *Roman Women* (rev. ed.; London: Bodley Head, 1974).

B. Dobson, "The Centurionate and Social Mobility during the Principate," in: Claude Nicolet (ed.), *Recherches sur les structures sociales dans l'antiquité classique, Caen 25–26 avril 1969* (Paris: Centre National de la Recherche Scientifique, 1970) 99-116.

William L. Westermann, *The Slave Systems of Greek and Roman Antiquity* (MAPS 40; Philadelphia: American Philosophical Society, 1955; reprint, 1964).

W. W. Buckland, *The Roman Law of Slavery: The Condition of the Slave in Private Law from Augustus to Justinian* (Cambridge: Cambridge University, 1970).

Inscription of Slave Manumission from Lefkopetra

Clearly visible is one of three inscriptions cut into the face of the side support of a table, found near Lefkopetra on the road from Verria (ancient Beroea) to Kozens in Macedonia. The second inscription is visible below the first, the third (unrecognizable) is to the right. All three inscriptions record the manumission of a slave under the legal protection of the temple of the Mother of the Gods. The first inscription translates as follows:

For Good Fortune

To the Aboriginal Mother of the Gods: I, Marsidia Mamaris, according to a vow, have given a woman by the name of Tychike with any offspring which may be born to her to serve the goddess, and the goddess shall have power over her which is not to be violated. In the year 2ll of Augustus, which is also 327 (= 180 c.ᴇ.).

The free provision of grain for these impoverished masses remained a heavy burden for the treasury throughout the imperial period and caused social unrest on several occasions. Other big cities, to be sure, had similar problems, but they never reached the same proportions.

One of the greatest social ills which Rome inherited from the late republic was slavery (§2.3c). The many military conquests of II and I BCE brought hundreds of thousands of slaves to Italy. Whenever the wars did not supply sufficient quantities of slaves, pirates discovered that kidnapping and the slave trade were a lucrative source of income, and that Rome was unlikely to interfere. Thus slavery reached its peak in the last decades of the republic. Most of the slaves were employed in the landed estates, industry, and the mines, and the terrible lot of the agricultural slaves indeed caused revolts (§2.2c). Since the educational level of many slaves was comparatively high, slaves had little difficulty finding competent leaders for such uprisings. In any case, the transplantation of large parts of the populations of Greece, Asia Minor, and Syria to Italy and the western provinces because of the slave trade was an important factor in the spread of Greek culture in the western part of the empire. Educated slaves and those who were masters of some craft or business had a better chance than others to be freed, and slaves of Roman citizens received Roman citizenship upon their manumission. This contributed to the growth of a class of citizens in Rome and Italy who had a Greek education. Once the pirates had been suppressed and the military conquests had come to an end, the supply of new slaves dwindled. The increase in manumissions also contributed to the gradual decline of the number of slaves, until the institution of slavery lost its economic significance at the beginning of the Byzantine period. In fact, Augustus had already a severe problem in the rapid growth of the number of manumissions and enacted legislation designed to curb its practice. The emperors themselves indeed were the biggest slave-holders and continued to employ large numbers of slaves for the huge estates and industrial plants, even though the economic structures were otherwise changing in favor of small parcel farming and small workshop production. The emperors also used slaves in the various branches of the imperial administration, where they had good opportunities to advance and perhaps to occupy important official positions after their manumission.

Except for the provision of grain for Rome, there were few if any beginnings of a state welfare system. Trajan set up a fund from which orphans and children of poor citizens could receive stipends for their education. But on the whole, welfare was left to the communities and was therefore—often not to its own detriment—left to the private initiative of wealthy benefactors. Some cities employed physicians responsible for public health care, but only members of the wealthy upper class could afford regular medical attention. The emperor and the very rich had private physicians. The common people often had no other choice but to visit somewhat questionable wandering physicians, miracle workers, magicians, and astrologers, who were also often able to deceive members of the upper classes and even the emperor himself. Public hospitals did not exist. The numerous Asclepius sanctuaries which experienced a new flowering during the imperial period fulfilled an important function as private health spas and outpatient clinics, but they could not be compared to regular hospitals, which existed only for the army, and sometimes on estates employing a large number of slaves. Care for the aged was left to their families. The first beginnings of regular care for the aged can be found in the Christian institution of older widows, who could not remarry, and were thus cared for by the community. The establishment of almshouses, orphanages, and hospitals is owed to the Christian emperors and is due to the direct influence of the Christian churches.

(d) The Cities in the Roman Empire

The cities were the political and economic backbone of the Roman empire. Urbanization was the explicit policy of many emperors, especially Augustus and Vespasian, a policy that was carried out in many ways. Existing cities, especially in the east, were reconstituted, received special privileges, and were given financial support in emergency situations (e.g., after destruction from an earthquake). Some cities, such as Rhodes and Tarsus, were recognized as "free allied cities," meaning that they received the right to levy their own taxes, were immune from imperial taxation, and could govern themselves according to their own laws. Older cities, such as Damascus and Gerasa, were sometimes rebuilt according to the

Bibliography to §6.3d

Anthony D. Macro, "The Cities of Asia Minor under the Roman Imperium," *ANRW* II, 7, 2 (1980) 658–97.

A. H. M. Jones, "The Economic Life of the Towns of the Roman Empire," in idem, *The Roman Economy* (Oxford: Oxford University, 1974) 35–60.

Dieter Nörr, *Imperium und Polis in der hohen Principatszeit* (2d ed., München: Beck, 1969).

Ramsay MacMullen, *Enemies of the Roman Order* (Cambridge, MA: Harvard University, 1966).

A. H. M. Jones, *The Cities of the Eastern Roman Provinces* (2d ed.; Oxford: Clarendon, 1971).

P. A. Brunt, "The Roman Mob," in M. I. Finley (ed.), *Studies in Ancient Society* (London: Routledge and Kegan Paul, 1974) 74–102.

Clarence L. Lee, "Social Unrest and Primitive Christianity," in Stephen Benko and John J. O'Rourke, *The Catacombs and the Colosseum* (Valley Forge: Judson, 1971) 121–38.

Roman city plan or were completely reconstituted as Roman colonies: Caesar had already rebuilt Corinth as *Colonia Laus Julia Corinthus;* Philippi, through the settlement of veterans under Augustus, became *Colonia Augustia Julia Philippensium.* A *colonia* was privileged with the *ius Italicum,* which meant that its agricultural land was not subject to taxation, just as was the case wth the land of the Italian cities.

In addition to the older Greek colonies in the west, all situated on the coasts (§1.1a), the Romans founded a large number of cities, primarily in the inland areas of Gaul (Nîmes, Geneva, Lyon, Paris), Germany (Cologne, Mainz, Augsburg), and Britain (Colchester, Lincoln, London). Some of these cities were founded on the basis of military camps, while others developed out of trade centers. In Spain and Africa, Roman cities usually comprised new foundations of older Punic cities. The typical Roman city was laid out as a large square or rectangle, surrounded by walls. All the streets within this area followed a regular plan and met at right angles. One central road, usually running from east to west (the *decumanus*), was crossed by another main road running north-south (the *cardo*). This was the layout used to set up military camps and was thus adopted by the cities that often rose in their place in the subsequent period.

Corresponding to the Greek and Hellenistic city (§2.5a–b), the Roman city would also always include the area of its surrounding countryside. Its chief source of wealth lay in its agricultural lands, which were essential for the food supply of the city's population and provided most of the income for its aristocracy. Even more than in the Hellenistic period, the city government was considered the privilege of this landowning aristocracy, even if its members often lived on estates outside the city. The Roman imperial administration successfully discouraged the older Greek democratic city government in which administrative offices would ideally be open to all free citizens. Membership in the aristocracy was limited and strictly controlled (the class of the *decuriones,* normally a hundred citizens who formed the city council, was responsible for the election of the administrators, the confirmation of laws and regulations governing the city, and taxation). Such leadership insured greater stability within the Roman patronage system: the ruling aristocrats had their patrons in Rome to whom they could appeal; the patron was assured in turn of the support and loyalty of his clients. In the older Greek cities, the traditional names of the offices were preserved, while Roman titles were used in the "colonies," where the *duoviri* were the highest officials.

All other classes, whether they were citizens, freedmen, aliens, or slaves, were excluded from participation in the government and administration of their cities. Merchants, businessmen, and craftsmen might accumulate considerable wealth—though even the richest could not compare with the wealthier owners of agricultural estates—but they still would not be found among the aristocrats, the decurions. The only exceptions were in those few cities, such as Ostia, the port city of Rome, and Palmyra, the wealthy caravan city of Syria, that possessed very little land, but derived most of their livelihood from trade. On the other hand, decurions did not engage in trade and industry, and if they owned a manufacturing plant or shipping agency they would employ freedmen or slaves as their agents and managers. The actual heartbeat of the city was nonetheless its trade, business, and industry.

Beginning with Augustus, the Roman emperors made considerable efforts to revive the economic and industrial prosperity of the cities, especially in the Greek heartland. Augustus came to Samos several times, the third time for more than two years (21–19 BCE), in order to supervise the reorganization of Asia Minor. The newly proclaimed Pax Augusta came to be particularly effective in the highly developed manufacturing industries of this region—with Ephesus as the "first city of Asia." Donations of wealthy citizens played a significant role in the beautification of the city, such as those of T. Claudius Aristion in Ephesus (end of I CE), of Pantaenus in Athens (ca. 100 CE), and many others elsewhere, or of Romans who had become residents of Greek cities (e.g., the Vedii in Ephesus) and donated major buildings. Thefts of art objects—Nero stole hundreds from Greece and Pergamum—were no doubt resented but did not seriously endanger these cities' growing beauty and their increasing economic well-being. Urban populations became more numerous during I and II CE, and manufacturing and trade provided employment for large numbers of people.

It must be remembered that overland transportation of consumer goods was very expensive. Only special industrial products were not manufactured locally: textiles from Patrae and Tarsus, for example, or glass products from Egypt, which were exported even into distant areas. But, as a rule, each city had a large number of local factories. Some were small shops with only one or two employees, others large plants employing dozens of slaves or paid laborers. These workshops could produce all the goods necessary for local consumption, while at the same time they provided jobs and income for the majority of the city's population. Owners and workers, craftsmen and businessmen, merchants and even slaves constituted the large middle class of the cities. They were organized in associations (§2.3c), whose membership included wealthy owners of large stores and plants, as well as humble craftsmen; both free citizens as well as resident aliens, freedmen, and slaves could be found in their ranks.

During the first two centuries CE, this class was still willing to accept the Roman order. It also maintained considerable social mobility: even slaves could, in fact, be candidates for active participation in this class and might share in its opportunities once they became freedmen. There were, to be sure, various causes for social unrest that would repeatedly lead to tumultuous scenes, such as the revolt instigated by the Ephesian silversmiths described in Acts 19:23–41. Strikes by bakers and construction workers are reported from several cities. In the agricultural areas the hatred of the city, a feeling of exploitation, and the lack of patrons responsible for the welfare of rural clients contributed to unrest among the more impoverished farmers and farm workers. This led in the late II and III CE to violent protests against the Roman order. But in the cities, unrest had its source neither in the suppression of the impoverished proletariat nor among the salves. Rather, it arose in the middle class, sometimes fed by the disenchantment of impoverished members of the aristocracy. The local aristocracies (decurions), together with the Roman administrators (not to mention the legionnaires of the Roman army), were the only people who had control over the affairs of the city. For members of the middle class, there were little or no political opportunities, and their dependence upon the munificence of the aristocracy was almost complete, often even for their supply of bread. Unrest resulted from frustration and dissatisfaction. It could be triggered by incidents that seemed to threaten the economic well-being of any group within the middle class or any of their rights, but complaints about the quality of the games financed by members of the aristocracy could also lead to tumult. The Roman administration soon recognized that the associations in which most members of the middle class were organized could breed such unrest and often discouraged their formation; yet in most cases it had no choice but to acknowledge their existence, though withholding official recognition. In general, an uneasy equilibrium was maintained as long as economic prosperity prevailed. Once the political situation changed toward the end of II CE, and continuous wars both worsened the cities' economic opportunities and increased their financial burdens, unrest became more widespread.

From the beginning, Christianity found its converts neither among the rural population nor in the aristocracy, but in the middle class of the cities. Paul's description of the Corinthian church could be taken as an appropriate characterization of this class: "Not many wise, . . . not many powerful, not many of noble birth" (1 Cor 1:26). Like most of the associations, Christian churches clearly included a few wealthy people, along with larger numbers of craftsmen and working people (see 1 Thess 4:11–12) and some poor people and slaves. But these Christian "associations" in the cities of the Roman empire developed a system of mutual reliance and dependence that required greater sacrifices by the rich and thus created much more closely-knit communities (see 1 Tim 6:1719; *Hermas Sim.* 1). The further development of the structures of the churches clearly reflects the social situation of the middle class of the city and reveals various efforts to overcome its institutions and limitations.

4. ROMAN CULTURE AND HELLENISM

(a) The Hellenization of Roman Culture

The culture of the late Roman republic and imperial Rome was so deeply affected by the process of Hellenization that older Roman elements either disappeared or could be maintained only in modified forms, in constant tension with their Greek counterparts. Roman culture, especially during the time of its high flowering, cannot be understood without considering its Greek component. Greek influences reached Rome in various ways: first, from the Hellenized cities and Greek colonies in Sicily and southern Italy, which had already had numerous contacts with Rome in the early centuries of the Roman republic; second, through the influx of Greek education into the Roman upper classes during the time of the conquest of Greece, corresponding to a clearly visible enthusiasm of many Greeks for the constitution and organization of the Roman state; and third, through the mobility of the entire population of the Hellenized eastern provinces, as numerous immigrants came to the Roman Mediterranean as slaves, as soldiers in the army, or in the context of trade and commerce.

Most conspicuous was the spread of the Greek language. As early as the time of the later republic, all educated Romans were bilingual and could speak and read Greek as well as Latin. There seems to have been a renewed interest in Greek in II CE: the emperor Marcus Aurelius, scion of a Roman family from Spain, wrote his *Meditations* in Greek. During the

Bibliography to §6.4

Ludwig Bieler, *Geschichte der römischen Literatur* (3d ed.; 2 vols.; SG; Berlin: De Gruyter, 1972).

Manfred Fuhrmann (ed.), *Römische Literatur* (Neues Handbuch der Literaturwissenschaft 3; Frankfurt: Athenaion, 1974).

Eduard Norden, *Die römische Literatur* (6th ed.; Leipzig: Teubner, 1971).

Idem, *Die antike Kunstprosa* (5th ed.; Darmstadt: Wissenschaftliche Buchgesellschaft, 1958) 1. 156–343.

Chester G. Starr, *Civilization and the Caesars* (Ithaca: Cornell University, 1954).

Friedrich Klingner, *Römische Geisteswelt* (5th ed.; München: Ellermann, 1965).

M. L. Clarke, *The Roman Mind* (Cambridge, MA: Harvard University, 1956).

Ulrich Kahrstedt, *Kulturgeschichte der römischen Kaiserzeit* (2d ed.; Bern: Francke, 1958).

imperial period, merchants and soldiers from the western provinces could converse in Greek as well as those from the east. Since the Romans accepted Greek learning not only in the field of philosophy, but also in science and technology, the vocabulary of Latin was strongly influenced by Greek in most areas of specialized terminology. Tractates about the construction of war machines as well as philosophical literature were read in Greek. Roman poetry, historiography, philosophy, and rhetoric cannot be imagined without their Greek prototypes. Forms and methods were borrowed from the Greeks, and often topics and subject matter. Greek influences upon Roman culture were not limited to one particular period upon which an independent Roman development might have followed. Rather, Roman culture remained in constant juxtaposition to its Greek counterpart, which continued its own development and was repeatedly promoted by Roman officials, so that its influence was renewed time and again. Even later Roman writers and philosophers would often make recourse to older Greek models and prototypes, which they deemed more important than whatever had developed meanwhile in Latin tradition and language.

In the fine arts and in architecture, the Augustan renaissance was at the same time a renewal of Greek influence. Imitation of Greek architecture became the rule. The city of Rome as it presented itself in its public buildings became more and more a Hellenistic city. To be sure, in construction methods and in the practical utility of the buildings, typical Roman features are visible. Roman architects replaced the massive Greek constructions from hewn natural stones with walls made of rubble or bricks and mortar, covered with plaster or marble revetments. The most important Roman contribution to architecture was the introduction of the arch, which made it possible to construct roofs for large interior rooms without using an interior colonnade. Vaulted roofs are frequently found in the buildings which are most characteristically Roman, namely the Roman baths with their large vaulted halls, which became very popular in all parts of the Roman empire. The Roman amphitheaters could be built only by using large vaulted support structures for the upper rows of seats. The Christians later utilized arches and vaults in church architecture in order to construct the roofs and domes of their basilicas. Vaulted arches were also the basis for the viaducts and aqueducts which can still be found today in all areas to which Roman rule extended. But in numerous instances, the Roman materials and methods of construction directly copied earlier Greek buildings. Temples and sanctuaries built in the Roman period, often with financial support from the imperial treasury, followed the classic examples of hewn natural stones and flat roofs. An important change took place, however, in the design of the cities' central areas. In the

Greek period, the agora was open, with free access to the main streets of the city; now it became an enclosed square, the Roman forum, whose entrance was protected by special gates. Especially in the cities founded by the Romans, the main streets no longer connected the agora with other parts of the city, but were arranged according to a strict axial system coordinated to a central main street, which also determined the location of the most important buildings, thus imitating the pattern of the Roman military camp (*castrum*).

In painting and sculpture the Romans imitated the much-admired Greek prototypes. Famous classical works of sculpture were repeatedly copied. But a tendency toward realism, which can be observed as early as the Hellenistic period, intensified and often assumed almost grotesque features. Only rarely were subjects idealized as, for example, some Roman emperors as represented on coins. Roman paintings were dominated by themes from Greek mythology, which were also constantly used for the popular floor mosaics. As compared with their Greek prototypes, the mannerism in the ornamentation and decoration of Roman paintings is striking. Paintings of landscapes and architecture were very popular. The frequent appearance of the mock window is noteworthy, simulating an opening in the wall. The classicistic austerity of Augustus' time gave way to a playful dissolution of forms at the end of the Julio-Claudian period, but the following period saw a renewal in the return to classical ideals.

(b) Poetry

The beginnings of Latin literature are in each case related to the respective genre of Greek literature. The use of the Latin language for poetry began very early, but the forms and topics were largely borrowed from the Greek tradition. At first, Greek tragedies and comedies were presented in Latin translations (§3.4b). Their influence is visible in Ennius (239–169 BCE), who came from southern Italy and, after settling in Rome, belonged to the cultured circle of Scipio Aemilianus (§6.1c). Ennius wrote numerous tragedies and comedies; half of his tragedies are adaptations of Euripides (§3.4b). His epic poem on Roman history, written in hexameters, draws its prototypes from the epics of Homer. Somewhat earlier, Plautus (who died in 184 BCE) had written over a hundred comedies in Latin closely modelled on the works of the New Comedy of Greece, both in their form and in their themes, although they also contain some indigenous Roman elements. The comedies of the Libyan freedman Terence, written between 166 and 160 BCE, are all adaptations of the famous comedies of Menander (§3.4b). The situation just before the great flowering of Latin poetry in the time of Augustus is best illustrated by the didactic poem in six books *On nature* (almost completely preserved) of

Lucretius (97–55 BCE). This work demonstrates that the forms of Greek poetic art had become totally at home in the Latin language, and also how the ideas of Epicurean philosophy (§4.1c), which Lucretius shared, had made their inroads into Roman thought.

The discovery of a new horizon of experience which became characteristic of the Augustan era began with the "modern poets" (*Neoterici*) before the end of the republic. Most of the works from this circle are lost; but many poems of Catullus, who belonged to this circle, are preserved. Their form imitates the Alexandrian poetry of III BCE (§3.4b), but their themes go decidedly beyond these Greek prototypes. The goal is no longer the artistic reproduction in poetic form of any topic of human knowledge, but the expression of human desire and despair in the adverse experiences of the present. Friendship and hate, love and obscenity are felt so strongly

Bibliography to §6.4b: Texts

George E. Duckworth (ed.), *The Complete Roman Drama: All the Extant Comedies of Plautus and Terence . . . in a Variety of Translations* (New York: Random House, 1942).

Plautus: Latin text and English translation by Paul Nixon in LCL (5 vols.).

Terence: Latin text and English translation by John Sargeaunt in LCL (2 vols.).

Lucretius, *De rerum natura:* Latin text and English translation by W. H. D. Rouse in LCL.

Catullus and Tibullus: Latin text and English translation by F. W. Cornish in LCL.

Horace: Latin texts and English translation by H. Rushton Fairclough and C. E. Bennet in LCL (2 vols.).

Virgil, *Eclogues, Georgics,* and *Aeneid:* Latin text and English translation by H. Rushton Fairclough in LCL (2 vols.).

Propertius: Latin text and English translation by H. E. Butler in LCL.

Ovid: Latin texts and English translation by J. H. Mozley and others in LCL (6 vols.).

Lucan, *The Civil War:* Latin text and English translation by J. D. Duff in LCL.

Petronius, *Satiricum:* Latin text of fragments and English translation by Michael Heseltine in LCL.

Martial, *Epigrams:* Latin text and English translation by Walter C. A. Ker in LCL (2 vols.).

Juvenal and Persius: Latin text and English translation by George Gilbert Ramsay in LCL.

Bibliography to §6.4b: Studies

J. Wight Duff, "The Beginnings of Latin Literature," in *CambAncHist* 8. 388–422.

George E. Duckworth, *The Nature of Roman Comedy: A Study in Popular Entertainment* (Princeton: Princeton University, 1952).

Karl P. Harrington, *Catullus and His Influence* (New York: Longmans, Green, 1927).

J. K. Newman, *Augustus and the New Poetry* (Collection Latomus 88; Bruxelles: Berchem, 1967).

Z. F. D'Alton, *Horace and His Age* (New York, 1962)

A. G. Carrington, *Aspects of Martial's Epigrams* (Eton: Shakespeare Head, 1960).

Gilbert Highet, *Juvenal the Satirist* (Oxford: Clarendon, 1954).

that it is impossible not to hear the message: namely, the demand for a new world in which salvation and human fulfillment become a reality. Horace and Virgil endeavored in their poetry to understand the horizons of this new world and to describe its emergence, as they saw its signs appear in the events of the early years of Augustus. Horace (65–8 BCE) was the son of a freedman and first fought on the side of the assassins of Caesar. But after his reception into the circle of Augustus' friend Maecenas, he was converted from an indignant critic of the political situation into an enthusiastic messenger of the new age. In his satires, odes, lyric poetry, and letters he employed manifold theological, mythological, and cultural motifs, in order to assess the legitimacy of the new age and its ruler, as well as its possibilities for moral action and artistic production. Horace has been accused of having become a propagandist for Augustus, but he is more adequately understood if his work is seen as an attempt to explore the dimensions in which the present events can be seen as the beginnings of a time of justice and peace.

The eschatological character of these political events was expressed strongly by Virgil (70–19 BCE). He was the son of simple but well-to-do country people from the north of Italy, received a rhetorical and philosophical education, but never entered into the course of public offices. The favor of Maecenas and Augustus made it possible for him to devote himself to his poetical work fully and with the necessary leisure. In his *Bucolica* (*Eclogues*), Virgil used the genre of the Hellenistic pastoral poem (§3.4b) and connected it with mythical motifs in which the eschatological schema of primordial time versus endtime is especially evident. These poems, which were written by ca. 40 BCE, are filled with a prophetic view which surmounts the present and unequivocally expresses an expectation of the coming savior. The Christians afterwards understood the famous vision of the child's birth in the *Fourth Eclogue* as a prediction of Jesus' birth. Virgil's *Georgics* represent the genre of the Hellenistic didactic poem: the various branches of agriculture appear in a poetic description, and the material is taken from scholarly works about agriculture. But Virgil at the same time describes agricultural practice within the larger framework of a view of the whole world, of nature, and of its origin. This work, completed after many years of work in 29 BCE, and read in parts to Augustus during the same year, expresses the divine mission of the ruler more directly. The great work of Virgil's later life is the *Aeneid*, the masterwork of Latin epic. The destruction of Troy is related as a negative backdrop to the realized-eschatological time of salvation in the period of Augustus. In the *Aeneid*, Virgil took his starting point from the older Greek Homeric allegory, but did not simply develop it further, but recreated the epic material in such a way that the presentation of prehistoric events illumines the significance of Rome's history and of the salvific experience of the present. The epic repetition of the primordial time thus announces the presence of the eschatological time.

The generation of poets after Horace and Virgil belongs to a new period. The eschatological tension had been relaxed; the praise of the new order was a duty fulfilled more or less willingly. Propertius (50–15 BCE) and Tibullus (48–19 BCE) were elegaic poets who primarily dealt with the topic of love, though their personal experience was occasionally related to events of the present. Ovid (43 BCE–17 CE) discontinued his initial political career early on, and at the beginning of his poetic work he also wrote elegiac love poems. But in his later work, *Ars amatoria,* Ovid created a didactic poem which objectivizes love as a topic of elegy and thus makes love an art that can be taught. His *Metamorphoses* center on the question of the relationship of general human experience to a comprehensive view of past and present. The history of the world appears in successive pictures in chronological order, composed of a large variety of traditional Greek and Roman materials. To be sure, at the end of this picture, Ovid deals with the time of Augustus, but a heroic or mythological perspective is missing, and consequently the present is no longer seen under eschatological auspices. After Ovid was sentenced to exile in 8 CE (the reasons are not quite clear) he wrote poetry and letters from exile which express not only his grief due to his separation from Rome, but also contain references to the divine mission of the emperor, which sound like the repetition of a traditional court ceremonial. Hellenistic formulations of ruler worship thus enter into Latin literature for the first time, although Ovid still considered the emperor to be a human being, not a god.

Latin poetry experienced a second blossoming during the time of Nero, though it is evident that this poetry no longer had any intrinsic relationship to current political events. The most significant poet of this time was Lucan, a nephew of Seneca. He was only twenty-six years old when he was executed by Nero (§6.2a). Only an unfinished epic poem about the civil war between Caesar and Pompey, *Pharsalia,* is preserved of his work. Because of the poet's republican bias, the two main figures of his work become anti-heroes, so that one can speak of an anti-epic written in conscious contrast to Virgil's *Aeneid.* An analogous attitude is found in the work of Lucan's older contemporary Petronius, the esteemed advisor of Nero's amusements. Like Lucan, Petronius also belonged to the Roman nobility, and he shared his fate, being commanded by Nero to commit suicide in 66 CE. Petronius' *Satiricum,* preserved only in fragments, is a parody of an erotic romance (§3.4e). The prototypes of its heroes are taken from the Hellenistic romance, but they are changed into their opposite, that is, they are vulgar and perverse rather than noble and sublime.

Persius (34–62 CE) wrote satires which were published and revised after his early death by his teacher, the Stoic philosopher Cornutus. The satires treat moral and religious topics and soon made him a "classical" writer in this genre, whose work was commented on in late antiquity and still widely read in medieval times. The satirical orientation of poetry, moralizing and critical of its times, also appears among the later poets of the imperial period. Martial (ca. 40–103 CE) wrote only epigrams (his longest poem comprises fifty-one lines) in which he sends festive birthday greetings, grieves about the dead, attacks his contemporaries with spirited wit (using pseudonyms throughout), and lets other people of his time see themselves as they really are. Juvenal (ca. 70–150 CE) was the last great satirical poet of Rome. His satires are more biting than those of his predecessors, as he turns against hypocrisy and moral depravity, especially in the Roman upper classes. His power of keen observation is evident in the satires which are preserved; they are, therefore, important sources for the study of the society of his time.

(c) Cicero and Varro

The most influential men who determined the features of the amalgamation of Greek and Roman tradition and culture were Cicero and Varro. Both men played significant roles as politicians in the last period of the Roman republic, and their comprehensive literary works created the prototypes for many areas of cultural life in the imperial period and centuries to come.

1) *Cicero* (106–43 BCE), from the municipal aristocracy of Arpinum, studied Greek rhetoric and philosophy extensively, first in Rome, then in Athens (where his teacher was Antiochus of Ascalon), Smyrna, and Rhodes. After his return he entered on his political career. He began as quaestor in Sicily and reached the apex in his election as consul in the year 63 and in his exposure of Catiline's conspiracy. Though Cicero was still

Bibliography to §6.4c (1): Texts

Cicero: Latin texts and English translation by various authors in LCL (numerous volumes).

Bibliography to §6.4c (1): Studies

Thomas Alan Dorey (ed.), *Cicero* (New York: Basic Books, 1965).

Matthias Gelzer, *Cicero* (Wiesbaden: Steiner, 1969).

Karl Büchner, *Cicero* (Heidelberg: Winter, 1964).

R. E. Smith, *Cicero the Statesman* (London: Cambridge University, 1966).

F. R. Colwell, *Cicero and the Roman Republic* (4th ed.; Baltimore: Penguin, 1967).

Woldemar Görler, *Untersuchungen zu Ciceros Philosophie* (Heidelberg: Winter, 1974).

Alfons Weische, *Cicero und die Neue Akademie* (Münster/W.: Aschendorff, 1961).

politically active and not without influence during the later years of his life, most of his important literary works of that period were written with the clear knowledge that his own political ideal of a free republic, led by a responsible aristocracy, was at odds with the political realities.

Cicero's experience as an active politician gave him the opportunity to unite his thorough knowledge of the policies of the Roman Senate, administration, and law and to perfect his rhetorical and literary work in direct contact with all the developments of that critical period. For Cicero, public oratory was the most important instrument for exercising political influence, a privilege of the aristocracy, whose duty it was to direct the affairs of state, as indeed the republic had always been led by the persuasive words of their leaders. In Cicero's time, education in rhetoric was the most important preparation for public office. Greek teachers of rhetoric had offered instruction in Rome for many years; wealthy families sent their sons to Greece for further study. Although many Greek influences were already present in Roman rhetoric, Cicero clearly saw the deficiencies of this course of study: one borrowed from the Greek tradition whatever could be used successfully in legal and political oratory; the result was superficial education and men striving after effect. Cicero demanded that the orator should have a thorough general education, especially in Greek philosophy. He himself had intensively studied the classical philosophers and orators (Plato, Aristotle, Xenophon, Demosthenes). His extraordinary gift for language enabled him to render into Latin in a masterly manner whatever he learned from Greek literature. Thus he transformed Latin into a language of literature and philosophy. At the same time, his works reveal a new seriousness, which contrasts pleasantly with the artificiality of later Hellenistic rhetoric and is thoroughly Roman in character. Instead of boasting with the subtleties of specialized knowlege, Cicero demanded that orators display true knowledge of the subject matter, persuade through clarity of presentation, and reject rhetorical tricks. Even if considerations of political expediency sometimes caused Cicero to fall short of realizing this ideal in his speeches, his published works became the highest criterion and example for future generations.

As a philosopher Cicero depended upon developments in the philosophical schools of the late Hellenistic period, in which Skepticism had led to a levelling of the different school opinions. It had become more common to think that true happiness could be found only in removal from existing reality and from the attempt to derive knowledge from its interpretation (§4.1a–d). Scientific as well as dogmatic knowledge had become open to doubt, and it seemed that insights based upon probability were a satisfactory foundation for moral action. The result was eclecticism, that is, the admission that the individual was not obligated to think through an entire philosophical system and pledge allegiance to it. Rather, it was permissible to accept or reject any particular traditional opinion or insight of the philosophical schools, according to one's own judgment and experience of usefulness. On this basis Cicero not only created an authentically Latin philosophical language, he also legitimized the acceptance of Greek philosophy in the Roman world and paved its way. As a young man, Cicero had studied under the Academician Philo of Larissa, who had come to Rome after the disaster of the war with Mithridates (88 BCE). Throughout his life Cicero maintained a philosophical position of the modified Skepticism, which he had learned from Philo. For Cicero, the level of probability resulting from an evaluation of alternative courses was sufficient in choosing the right and moral actions. The criterion for this comparison and selection is ultimately one's own conscience, which by nature possesses ethical norms and knowledge of justice. In any case, action is superior to knowledge. Therefore, ethics is the primary subject of Cicero's philosophy. In this area, he clearly rejected only the opinions of the Epicureans, and was himself inclined toward Stoicism, though mostly to the more popular philosophical Stoicism which was distinguished by its practical applicability. A life lived according to nature is, therefore, based not on a strictly Stoic philosophical definition of the concept of nature, but on those things which in a more general understanding can be called "natural." The law of nature, for Cicero, is that which corresponds to the divine order of the world, to wise legislation, and to the healthy moral conscience. The final arbiter in decisions about a life led according to nature is thus, again, one's own ability of discernment, implanted in the human soul, whose divine origin Cicero never doubted. But equally important as a criterion is an action's political utility. Cicero had serious reservations regarding the whole system of Stoic ethics insofar as its consistent application would lead to an alienation from political responsibility. The eclecticism which characterizes all of Cicero's philosophical thinking demonstrates that he never intended to create a philosophical system. It is precisely for this reason that he was able, on the basis of his immense knowledge, his comprehensive studies, and his extensive literary activity, to present the study of Greek philosophy to the Roman world as useful and profitable, and thus to point a way to the *Interpretatio Romana* of the Greek tradition.

2) *Varro*. As Cicero had created a criterion for future generations in the Romanization of the Greek inheritance in rhetoric and philosophy, his somewhat older contemporary Varro (116–27 BCE) could boast of a similar accomplishment in the areas of cultural history and in the encyclopedic sciences. Varro's philosophical position was the same as Cicero's, an eclecticist who granted some possession of truth to all philosophical

schools and emphasized the superiority of virtue over all other goods. The primary accomplishment of Varro, however, was his brilliant mastery of several areas of scientific knowledge, which enabled him to recreate the entire scientific tradition of the Greek world in new Roman dress. Among his works, comprising more than fifty titles (only a small portion is preserved) are treatises on philology and grammar (twenty-five books on the Latin language), investigations in literature, the science of agriculture, number theory, systems of education, rhetoric, philosophy, civil law, history, and biography. His great encyclopedic work is a comprehensive presentation of the history of the culture, religion, and constitution of the Roman people, *Antiquitates rerum humanarum et divinarum,* in forty-one books, with an epitome of nine books. This became the basic encyclopedia of the history of culture and theology for the whole Roman world and was able to influence St. Augustine very deeply four centuries later. Varro's scientific universality compelled the Roman world to use the traditional Greek criteria of scientific and philosophical assessment for all areas of human experience.

(d) The Writing of History

1) *From Cato to Sallust.* Roman historiography began in III BCE with the works in the Greek language which sought to present a positive image of Rome to the Greek world (Greek works of that time also dealt with Roman history; see §3.4e). The first Roman history in Latin was written by the elder Cato (234–149 BCE), who was followed by the so-called "older annalists." The model for this type of historiography was the table erected annually by the pontifex maximus, listing all the unusual events of each year. Many of these Roman histories were written by leading politicians. They are characterized by an emphasis upon exemplary events and figures of the Roman past, but also treat contemporary events in the interests of political and moral education.

Bibliography to §6.4c (2): Texts

Varro, *De lingua latina:* Latin text and English translation by Roland G. Kent in LCL (2 vols.).

Varro, *Three Books on Agriculture* in: Cato and Varro, Latin texts and English translation by William Davis Hooper in LCL.

Burkhard Cordanus (ed.), *Varro Logistoricus über die Götterverehrung (Curio de cultu deorum)* (Würzburg: Triltsch, 1960). Edition and interpretation of fragments.

Bibliography to §6.4c (2): Studies

Jens Erik Skydsgaard, *Varro the Scholar* (Hafniae: Munksgaard, 1968).

Hallfried Dahlmann, *Varro und die hellenistische Sprachtheorie* (Problemata: Forschungen zur klassischen Philologie 5; Berlin: Weidmannsche Buchhandlung, 1932).

All these older works are lost, though much of their information has been absorbed by later Roman historians. Substantial portions of Roman histories are preserved from the period at the end of the republic and the time of Augustus. Caesar used as a model for his presentations of contemporary history the "commentary," i.e., the notebook of a magistrate about his official actions. In Caesar's employment of this genre the influence of the Hellenistic *hypomnēma* is visible as well as the typically Roman intention to advertise one's own political astuteness and mission. His commentaries on the Gallic War and the Civil War are historical works which renounce any unnecessary elaborations and were written with a masterly command of Latin prose. They reveal a rhetorical training for which utmost brevity and pregnancy are the most important instruments of persuasion—and to persuade others is exactly what Caesar sought to do with these works. Their strength derives from being not simply chronicles, but from using objective presentation as an instrument of political propaganda. Next to Caesar, the most influential historian was Sallust, Caesar's partisan and contemporary (86–34 BCE). In addition to historical monographs on the Jugurthan and Catilinarian wars, he wrote a history of the first half of his century, placing a single great personality in the center of each chapter. This type of presentation is an important stylistic instrument: Sallust not only described the sequence of events in the history of the state and its people, he also sought to communicate a judgment about the success and failure, justice and injustice, of the actions of leading

Bibliography to §6.4d

M. L. W. Laistner, *The Greater Roman Historians* (Berkeley, CA: University of California, 1947).

Thomas Alan Dorey (ed.), *Latin Historians* (London: Routledge and Kegan Paul, 1966).

A. D. Leeman, "Die römische Geschichtsschreibung," in: Manfred Fuhrmann (ed.), *Römische Literatur* (Neues Handbuch der Literaturwissenschaft 3; Frankfurt: Athenaion, 1974).

Erich Burck, "Grundzüge römischer Geschichtsauffassung und Geschichtsschreibung," *GWU* 25 (1974) 1–40.

Victor Pöschl (ed.), *Römische Geschichtsschreibung* (WdF 90; Darmstadt: Wissenschaftliche Buchgesellschaft, 1960).

Bibliography to §6.4d (1): Texts

Selected works of Sallustius: Latin text and English translation by J. C. Rolfe in LCL.
Caesar, *The Gallic War:* Latin text and English translation by H. J. Edwards in LCL.
Caesar, *The Civil Wars:* Latin text and English translation by A. G. Preskett in LCL.
Caesar, *The Alexandrian, African and Spanish Wars:* Latin text and English translation by A. G. Way in LCL.

Bibliography to §6.4d (1): Studies

Franz Bömer, "Der Commentarius," *Hermes* 81 (1953) 210–50.
Ronald Syme, *Sallust* (Berkeley, CA: University of California, 1964).

individuals. The works of Caesar and Sallust overcame the purely chronographic historiography and replaced it with a view of history which understood the past on the basis of the political commitment of the present, unafraid of making the contemporary historical experience its primary subject.

2) *Livy*. The only major work of Latin historiography from the time of the Augustan renaissance which is at least partially preserved is the Roman history *Ab urbe condita* of Livy (59 BCE–17 CE). Like many writers of his time (such as Virgil), he came from northern Italy. That Livy was not both a politician and historian at the same time was a new phenomenon in Latin historiography. Livy's work originally comprised 142 books, of which about one quarter is preserved; there are also some epitomes and tables of contents for the lost books. Only about half of the books were devoted to the time from the founding of Rome down to II BCE; the second half dealt with events from the time of the Gracchi to Augustus. In its external form, Livy's work renewed the tradition of the Roman annalists, but in language and style he was dependent upon Cicero, and thus achieved a high level in the art of historical narrative. It was Livy's intention to describe the ancient history of Rome as the model for the renewal under Augustus after the decline of the Civil War. In this respect Livy wrote in the interests of politics and was in complete agreement with Augustus, who was his patron. Apart from Livy nothing is preserved of the diversified historical literature from that time (about the non-Roman historians, see §3.4c). Even the universal history of Pompeius Trogus, a contemporary of Livy from Gaul, is lost. From the tables of contents which are preserved one can learn that he presented the history of other nations in such a way that all lines of development point to the realization of Roman rule over the whole world. The decades following after Augustus produced no significant historians. Possibly the history of Alexander of Curtius Rufus should be dated at the end of the Julio-Claudian period. This work reveals how strongly the invocation of Alexander the Great determined the spirit of that time.

3) *Josephus*. A renewal of historiography is visible at the end of I CE, but non-Roman authors have as much share in this renewal as Roman

Bibliography to §6.4d (2): Texts

Livy, *Ab urbe condita:* Latin text and English translation by B. O. Foster and others in LCL (14 vols.).

Bibliography to §6.4d (2): Studies

P. G. Walsh, *Livy: His Historical Aims and Methods* (Cambridge: Cambridge University, 1961).

Erich Burck, *Die Erzählungskunst des Titus Livius* (2d ed.; Berlin: Weidmann, 1964).

writers. Greek and Roman historians from now on belonged to the same general culture. This renewal was once more inspired by political engagements and political interests. Among the "barbarians" who published historical and ethnographic materials from their own cultures in Greek writings during the Hellenistic and Roman period (Berossus, Manetho, Fabius Pictor, and others), the Jewish historian Flavius Josephus occupies a special position. He was born in 37/38 CE and descended from the priestly nobility of Jerusalem. With respect to the political role which he played, he could not, to be sure, be compared with men like Polybius and Caesar, but in the political events of his time and people he played more than a minor role. In 64 Josephus went to Rome for negotiations with Roman authorities; after returning to his home country he became one of the commanders of the revolutionary Jewish army (66–67 CE), then a Roman prisoner. While in the Roman camp he prophesied that Vespasian would become emperor and was released when this prophecy became true. He remained in the camp as a friend and advisor of Titus until the end of the war. Later he lived in Rome, where he died shortly after 100 CE.

In his work about the *Jewish War,* Josephus tried to illuminate the background and causes of the war. Thus he began with the description of the conflict of the Jews with Antiochus IV Epiphanes and dealt in detail with the difficulties which the Roman procurators had created before the war began. The major part of the work is devoted to the events in which Josephus himself had participated and which his own lifetime encompassed. His second major work, *Jewish Antiquities,* was a kind of universal history of the Jewish people from the beginnings to his own time. This work exhibits the major shortcoming of Josephus' writing of history, something he shared, by the way, with other historians of his time: an

Bibliography to §6.4d (3): Texts

Josephus, *The Jewish War:* Greek text and English translation by H. St. J. Thackeray in LCL (3 vols.).

Josephus, *Antiquities:* Greek text and English translation by Ralph Marcus and others in LCL (9 vols.).

Josephus, *Life* and *Against Apion:* Greek text and English translation by H. St. J. Thackerary in LCL.

Nahum Glatzer (ed.), *Jerusalem and Rome: The Writings of Josephus* (New York: Meridian, 1960).

Bibliography to §6.4d (3): Studies

R. J. H. Shutt, *Studies in Josephus* (London: SPCK, 1961).

Harold W. Attridge, *The Interpretation of Biblical History in the Antiquitates Judaicae of Flavius Josephus* (HDR 7; Missoula: Scholars Press, 1976).

Otto Betz, Klaus Hacker, and Martin Hengel (eds.), *Josephus-Studien: Otto Michel zum 70. Geburtstag* (Göttingen: Vandenhoeck & Ruprecht, 1974).

Abraham Schalit (ed.), *Zur Josephus-Forschung* (WdF 84; Darmstadt: Wissenschaftliche Buchgesellschaft, 1973).

uncritical use of source materials (for the early times of Israel his only source is the Old Testament) which admits into his history not only valuable excerpts from reliable documents and sources, but also many miraculous and paradoxographical accounts. Political and cultural apologetic was the motive for Josephus' writing of history. This reflects the attitude of the time. The failure of the principate of I CE is compared to the greatness and dignity of more ancient times, and the attractiveness of the moral sense of a barbaric people is an important factor in such a comparison of past and present.

4) *Tacitus*. In this respect the closeness of Josephus to his younger contemporary Tacitus (born in 55 CE) is remarkable. Tacitus, the last of the great Latin historians of the imperial period, Roman senator, consul and proconsul, belonged to the elite of the politically experienced Roman nobility, against whose polished Latin prose the Greek style of Josephus would not survive a comparison. But Tacitus shares with Josephus an insight into the failures of the institutions of the imperial constitution of the Roman world rule, as well as an admission of its necessity. But while Josephus criticized the mistakes and mismanagement of the Roman administration of Palestine, Tacitus censures the entire imperial history of I CE, which comes to a head in the disaster of Domitian's tyrannical rule. Both major works of Tacitus (only partially preserved), the *Histories* and the *Annals*, deal with this period. Motivated by political engagement and moral protest, Tacitus devotes himself to recent history. But this writing of history no longer intervenes in the events of the present, as it is more apologetic than propagandistic. Accordingly, its moral criteria are drawn from the past, namely, from the ideals of the senatorial nobility of the Roman republic. The contradiction between these ideals from the past and the events and experiences from the time of the empire puts a characteristically pessimistic stamp on Tacitus' historical works. The purpose and objectives of another of his works, the *Germania,* are less clear. Probably this presentation of a barbaric people should be seen analo-

Bibliography to §6.4d (4): Texts

Tacitus, *Annals* and *Histories:* Latin text and English translation by Clifford H. Moore and John Jackson in LCL (4 vols.).

Tacitus, *Dialogus, Agricola,* and *Germania:* Latin texts and English translations by William Peterson in LCL.

Bibliography to §6.4d (4): Studies

Ronald Syme, *Tacitus* (2 vols.; Oxford: Clarendon, 1958).

Thomas Alan Dorey (ed.), *Tacitus* (London: Routledge, 1969).

Joseph Vogt, "Die Geschichtsschreibung des Tacitus: ihr Platz im römischen Geschichtsdenken und ihr Verständnis in der modernen Forschung," in: idem, *Orbis* (Freiburg: Herder, 1960). 128–48.

gously to his criticism of recent history in his two major works: there the criticism was based upon the ideals of the past; in the *Germania* these ideals are presented by way of describing a barbaric nation.

5) *Arrian and Dio Cassius.* Greek historiography experienced a late renaissance during II and III CE in the works of the two Bithynians Arrian and Dio Cassius. Arrian (ca. 90–170 CE), a student of the Stoic philosopher Epictetus, came from Nicomedia in Bithynia and was a politician and public servant of Rome under Hadrian (in 130 he was suffect consul). He published monographs and ethnographic works for which he used in part his own observations and experiences. But he became famous as a historian of Alexander. In contradistinction to the Alexander romance which was widespread at that time, Arrian restricted himself to using the works of Ptolemy and Aristobulus, the two oldest historians, both personal participants in Alexander's campaigns. To Arrian, who was himself a general and politician, these two works must have appeared as particularly trustworthy. His critical judgment as well as style of presentation, for which he had taken Xenophon as his model, have secured Arrian's reputation until today as the writer who has preserved the most reliable material about Alexander the Great. Dio Cassius (who died after 230 CE) from Nicaea in Bithynia occupied a number of high-ranking government positions and was full consul as the colleague of the emperor in 229 CE. His Roman history in eighty books (of which those about the imperial period are preserved) extended from the beginnings down to his own time and was written on the basis of many years of collecting materials and sources. It became the standard Roman history for the Greek-speaking world in subsequent centuries. The value and reliability of this work is debated. Dio Cassius was largely dependent upon Latin annalists, inserted numerous long speeches, and showed independent judgment only in the treatment of his own period. On the other hand, his work demonstrates that even in the later imperial period a politically engaged historian was capable of writing a large-scale historical work which overcame the pedestrian repetition of information and sources that characterized most of his predecessors.

Bibliography to §6.4d (5): Texts

Arrian, *Anabasis of Alexander* and *Indica:* Greek text and English translation by E. Iliff Robson in LCL (2 vols.).

Dio Cassius, *Roman History:* Greek text and English translation by Earnest Cary in LCL (9 vols.).

Bibliography to §6.4d (5): Studies

Fergus Millar, *A Study of Cassius Dio* (Oxford: Clarendon, 1964).

(e) Rhetoric and the Second Sophistic

1) *Quintilian.* In the realm of the Latin language, Cicero (§6.4c) continued to be the master and example of rhetoric. But Cicero's ideal that rhetoric was an art of the statesman lost its real meaning in the imperial period. After the end of the republic little room was left for this function of the rhetorical art. Instead, rhetoric became the primary subject of state-supported schooling and higher education. The greatest Roman master of rhetoric after Cicero was not a politician but a professor, Quintilian (35–100 CE). Patronized by Vespasian and Domitian, he became the first teacher of the Roman school of rhetoric who received a regular salary from the state. He was famous and widely recognized already during his lifetime (included among his students were such people as the younger Pliny). He wrote the last great textbook on rhetoric that antiquity produced and that is still completely preserved. In this *Institutio oratoria* Quintilian sought to reestablish the unity of the wise man and the statesman. With this renewal of the ancient Sophistic ideal, Quintilian was one of the pioneers of the Second Sophistic (see below). He emphasized that eloquence grants to everybody who seriously and intensively studies rhetoric the opportunity not only to serve the state in many ways, as politician, lawyer, and public servant, but also to be successful as a writer or historian, and to achieve fame and wealth in any case. This explains Quintilian's scornful rejection of the philosophers, for whom theoretical knowledge and moral education was an end in itself, and who had therefore withdrawn from the public into the gymnasia and schools.

Indeed, due to the impact of Nero's tyranny, whose victims had included Seneca, many young people from the Roman upper classes had withdrawn from the regular course of public service, and thus also from the appropriate rhetorical education; instead they attended the schools of the philosophers. Quintilian accused them of supposing that virtue could

Bibliography to §6.4e

George Kennedy, *The Art of Rhetoric in the Roman World 300 B.C.–300 A.D.* (Princeton: Princeton University, 1972).

Martin Lowther Clarke, *Rhetoric at Rome: A Historical Survey* (London: Cohen and West, 1966).

Jochen Bleiken, *Der Preis des Aelius Aristides auf das römische Weltreich* (NAWG.PH 1966,7; Göttingen: Vandenhoeck & Ruprecht, 1966).

Bibliography to §6.4e (1): Texts

Quintilian, *Institutio Oratoria:* Latin text and English translation by H. E. Butler in LCL (4 vols.).

Helmut Rahn (ed.), *Marcus Fabius Quintilianus: Ausbildung des Redners* (Texte zur Forschung 2; 2 vols.; Darmstadt: Wissenschaftliche Buchgesellschaft, 1972).

be learned through reflection about their own selves, and of fearing the demanding course of studies which a rhetorical education required. There could be a meaningful function for the philosophical tradition only as a part of a rhetorical education because education could be justified exclusively on the basis of its public utility. This motivation for taking over the Greek cultural inheritance reflects the general attitude of the Roman upper classes which prevailed until the time of Antoninus Pius. Marcus Aurelius was the first emperor who represented the turn away from rhetoric to philosophy. The Second Sophistic was largely based upon the attitudes of rhetoric as they appear in Quintilian. Quintilian himself, however, was then no longer influential, because the Second Sophistic drew its concepts not from Cicero but from older Greek ideals.

2) *Fronto.* In I CE the Numidian Fronto (ca. 100–175) was the most famous teacher of Latin rhetoric. Only some of his letters are preserved, while his speeches are lost. He became politically influential during the time of Hadrian; Antoninus Pius appointed him as the teacher of the future emperors Marcus Aurelius and Verus. But even though Fronto rejected philosophy, especially Stoicism, he was not spared the experience of having his student Marcus Aurelius, still a young man, pledge his allegiance to the Stoic philosophy of the former slave Epictetus.

3) *Second Sophistic.* During this time, Greek rhetoric experienced a renewal in what is known as the Second Sophistic. It originated in reflection upon the ideal of the politically active wise man, once taught by the old sophists of Athens, but it was also influenced by renewed interest in the Greek of classical Athens, interest which had grown during the two preceding centuries (§3.2b). The leading advocate of this style of Greek that follows the classical examples was Herodes Atticus (101–177 CE), from Marathon near Athens. He was immensely rich—a wealth which he used generously for various bequests, especially for building projects in Greece—and also politically active. His political influence was doubtlessly enhanced by the fact that his wife Regilla was related to Faustina, wife of the emperor Antoninus Pius. As the most brilliant orator of his time he became the teacher of Marcus Aurelius in Greek rhetoric. His rhetorical ideals were continued by his students, including Hadrian of Tyre (113–193 CE). A contemporary, Lollianus from Ephesus, also an orator and

Bibliography to §6.4e (2): Text

Fronto, *Letters:* Latin text and English translation by C. R. Haines in LCL (2 vols.).

Bibliography to §6.4e (3)

G. W. Bowersock, *Greek Sophists in the Roman Empire* (Oxford: Clarendon, 1969).

E. L. Bowie, "Greeks and Their Past in the Second Sophistic," in: M. I. Finley, *Studies in Ancient Society* (London: Routledge and Kegan Paul, 1974) 166–209.

politician, represented the same ideals of Atticism as the incumbent of the chair of rhetoric in Athens. But in the next generation, Hermogenes (160–225 CE) demonstrated that now also rhetoric was ready to abandon the ideal of political engagement and withdraw into self-reliant educational activity—without, however, making its peace with philosophy.

(f) The Stoics of the Imperial Period

1) *Seneca.* During II CE the emperors founded endowed chairs for all the old philosophical schools. But the Romans made substantial intellectual contributions only to Stoic philosophy. In its concentration upon ethical teaching, Stoicism became the typical Roman philosophy. This is visible already in Seneca (4 BCE–65 CE; see §6.2a), the first great Stoic philosopher of the imperial period. His concept of God was designed entirely in the interests of his moral doctrine. As providence, highest reason, and father of humankind, God made his will identical with the moral law. By fulfilling this law and purging oneself from all affections, one becomes identical with the deity. Seneca connects these thoughts with an anthropology that has Platonic features: only the soul is truly human and thus capable of equality with God; the body is the soul's prison, physical experiences nothing but agonies, and the duties of the political life unwelcome necessities. Philosophy can free the soul from this bondage because even relationships to one's fellow human beings are not established by means of the political structures, but only through the moral values which are the property of the soul. Friendship, loyalty, and general love of humanity also include the slave and therefore break all social conventions.

Bibliography to §6.4f

J. M. Rist, *Stoic Philosophy* (London: Cambridge University, 1969).

Max Pohlenz, *Die Stoa: Geschichte einer geistigen Bewegung* (2 vols.; 2d ed.; Göttingen: Vandenhoeck & Ruprecht, 1959).

Gregor Maurach (ed.), *Römische Philosophie* (WdF 193; Darmstadt Wissenschaftliche Buchgesellschaft, 1976).

Heinrich Greeven, *Das Hauptproblem der Sozialethik in der neueren Stoa und im Urchristentum* (Gütersloh: Bertelsmann, 1935).

Bibliography to §6.4f (1): Texts

Seneca, *Epistulae morales:* Latin text and English translation by Richard M. Gummore in LCL (3 vols.).

Seneca, *Moral Essays:* Latin text and English translation by John W. Basore in LCL (3 vols.).

Bibliography to §6.4f (1): Studies

Arnaldo Momigliano, "Seneca between Political and Contemplative Life," in: *Quarto contributo all storia degli studi classici e del mondo antico* (Rome: Edizioni di storie e letterature, 1969) 239–56.

2) *Musonius Rufus and Epictetus.* The standard form of Stoic philosophy of that time is represented by Musonius Rufus (ca. 30–100 CE), who was the teacher of Epictetus and of Dio of Prusa (§6.4h). He called for detachment from all political, social, and personal circumstances in order to center existence upon one's inner freedom. The ethical norms which are derived from this inner freedom regulate relations with all beings and things and thus replace the external political and social norms of behavior. Epictetus (ca. 55–135 CE), the only non-Roman among the leading Stoics of the imperial period, took his starting-point from these concepts of his teacher. Epictetus came from the Phrygian city of Hierapolis, had once been a slave, and dwelt in Rome at the time of the Flavian emperors. Expelled by Domitian, he founded a school in the large city of Nicopolis in western Greece. Epictetus' student Arrian (§6.4d) transcribed and published the lectures of his teacher (*Dissertations*), which exhibit the perfection of Stoic philosophy in its concentration upon ethical teaching. Logic and dialectics—not to mention rhetoric—are nothing but ancillary disciplines. The classical doctrines of older Stoic dogmatics are presupposed in their main outlines, but not further investigated. Epictetus strongly emphasized the universality of the deity, whose herald is the philosopher. The proclamation says: the human spirit is divine; whoever recognizes this will become a god. But this recognition can be realized only in the practical conduct of one's life. Such conduct requires the establishment of inner freedom as detachment from all external experiences and as the surrender of any and all attempts to change one's personal situation or the existing social conditions. Neither the most lowly work as a slave, nor the most honorable political office has any significance for the dignity and divinity of the human spirit. Epictetus knew only one single obligation: the general love of human beings. All human beings are brothers and sisters, which requires that they be treated with love and respect.

Bibliography to §6.4f (2): Texts

Cora E. Lutz (ed.), *Musonius Rufus "the Roman Socrates"* (New Haven: Yale University, 1947).

Epictetus, *Dissertations:* Greek text and English translation by W. A. Oldfather in LCL (2 vols.).

Bibliography to §6.4f (2): Studies

P. W. van der Horst, "Musonius Rufus and the New Testament," *NovT* 16 (1974) 306–15.

Rudolf Bultmann, "Das religiöse Moment in der ethischen Unterweisung des Epiktet und das Neue Testament," *ZNW* 13 (1912) 97–110; 177–91.

Herbert Braun, "Die Indifferenz gegenüber der Welt bei Paulus und bei Epiktet," in: idem, *Studien,* 159–67.

3) *Marcus Aurelius.* Born in 121 CE and emperor 161–180, Marcus Aurelius (§6.2c) received an excellent rhetorical education (§6.4e) designed to prepare him for the highest office in the empire. But when he was only twenty-five years old, he turned to philosophy. His philosophical *Meditations* were written during his later years which were marked by changing fortunes of war, constantly deteriorating political and economic conditions, and personal calamities in his family. Among all the Roman emperors there was none as highly educated and none as deeply committed to justice and veracity as Marcus Aurelius; his guiding-star was the former Phrygian slave Epictetus. Like Epictetus, Marcus Aurelius emphasized the rule of the whole world by divine providence, but had an even more radical conception of the mutability, inconstancy, and transitoriness of all things. Faced with the constantly changing course of all events, a human being has no choice but to submit to the divine will, even if this will brings forth what seems to be evil and ill-fated. But while reflecting upon their true selves, human beings can recognize that they are of God's family and therefore free to show love, clemency, and kindness to all other people. However, Marcus Aurelius saw this moral demand in a different perspective than Epictetus. For the emperor, it required actions which are directed to the world and which are not discouraged by ill fortune and failure. The *Meditations* of this emperor, written in Greek, pointing the way to the unity of faithfulness to oneself, fulfillment of duty, and submission to the divinely ordered fate, even came to favor among Christians (whom the emperor deeply despised) and gave consolation to many a troubled soul—not least in the military camp where Marcus Aurelius wrote many of his aphorisms.

(g) The Philosophical Marketplace

During the imperial period, expecially in II CE, the philosophical schools attempted to recover their classical ancestry. The Peripatetics wrote commentaries on Aristotle, the Stoics produced interpretations of

Bibliography to §6.4f (3): Text
Marcus Aurelius: Greek text and English translation by C. R. Haines in LCL.

Bibliography to §6.4g: Texts
Cartlidge and Dungan, *Documents,* 151–65.

Bibliography to §6.4g: Studies
Dieter Georgi, *Die Gegner des Paulus im 2. Korintherbrief: Studien zur religiösen Propaganda der Spätantike* (WMANT 11; Neukirchen-Vluyn: Neukirchener Verlag, 1964) 187–205; English translation forthcoming.
Otto Weinreich, *Antike Heilungswunder: Untersuchungen zum Wunderglauben der Griechen und Römer* (RVV 8,1; Berlin: De Gruyter, 1909; reprint, 1969).

Chrysippus, and the Platonist Albinus composed an epitome of Plato's philosophy. The real life of "philosophy," however, had left the schools and had gone into the marketplace and onto the streets of the big cities. Many people called themselves "philosophers": it was difficult to know whether a man offering his wisdom in the street was a god, a magician, the apostle of a new religion, or a true philosopher. In the imperial period the army of the wandering missionaries and philosophers had become legion. All of them competed with each other, advertised their art in order to attract disciples, outdid each other in demonstrations of their power, and were by no means disinclined to draw money out of peoples' pockets. Such missionaries competed even within the same religious or philosophical movement, as can be seen in the earliest Christian missionary efforts. Wherever Paul went, he was soon confronted with other Christian preachers who tried to outdo him with their performances. Much information about these marketplace philosophers comes to us only through their more educated literary opponents, because the philosophers who went out into the streets did not write; they relied on the spoken word, just as Christian missionaries and wandering preachers entrusted themselves not to the written word but to the effect of their oral message. It is not merely accidental that there is also direct written information preserved in letters, such as those of Paul. Paul's letters, to be sure, owe their existence to his special circumstances, which did not permit oral communication. But the very fact that Paul made use of the written medium of the letter in such circumstances reveals a new element which distinguishes his mission from the normal business of the philosophical market: Paul was concerned with the organization of communities and their enduring unity. Thus his letters were written for reasons which are very different from the motivations for writing in the established philosophical schools. Paul's letters are not didactic compositions but instruments of propaganda and community management.

Pagan, Christian, and Jewish philosophers of this sort did not address the educated establishment, but the common people, that is, anybody they could meet on the streets. The educated Platonist Celsus accused the Christian missionaries of squandering their message on the lowest classes of society. Origen was able to respond that the Cynic philosophers did exactly the same thing. Lucian, the fierce critic of all these propagandists and missionaries, described Peregrinus Proteus as a Cynic philosopher who became a Christian, but later defected in order to gather followers once more as a Cynic philosopher. Lucian's presentations, as well as those of Martial and Juvenal (§6.4b) and the Acts of the Apostles, also demonstrate that these missionaries were by no means prudish in the choice of their instruments of propaganda. This is true for Jews, Christians, and pagans alike. Foremost was the art and adroitness of public speech. Even if these preachers and philosophers adhered to quite different schools of thought, they agreed in their criticism of the existing conditions, in their attack upon the shallowness, vanity, and corruption of the bourgeois urban life, and in their moral summons. In addition to the public speech in which one pulled out all the stops, demonstration of one's possession of supernatural power was an important propaganda instrument. Miracles were performed not only by Christian missionaries, as described in the Acts of the Apostles and as Paul encounters them in the opponents of 2 Corinthians, but also by Jewish preachers, Neopythagorean philosophers, and by many other teachers, physicians, and magicians. The entire scale of miraculous deeds of power was commonly used, from magical tricks to predictions of the future, from horoscopes to the healing of diseases and maladies, even the raising of dead people. In those circles which were addressed by these philosophers of the marketplace, the power of speech and the greatness of miracle would have more profound effects than the depth and dignity of rational, moral, and religious insight.

The ancient and new insights of the philosophers and great thinkers were not in demand, but rather whatever could clarify the world and its powers as they affected peoples' everyday problems. Astral powers thus took the place of the old gods; new deities recommended themselves rather than critically tested philosophical doctrines; demonic forces were better explanations of the world than scientific knowledge. Simple moral rules for human behavior offered better advice than psychological insights into the motivations of human actions. The solution of the most pressing personal problems, even if by magical tricks, would be more readily accepted than demands for social reform. If Christianity wanted to keep its message competitive in this religious market, it had to enter into a critical debate with the laws of supply and demand of the marketplace. This is well attested in the Pauline correspondence which is preserved in 2 Corinthians (§9.3d).

It also became clear how difficult it was to draw the line between the imposter and the serious religious missionary. What was most in demand, and what would most easily attract people, were occultist phenomena, visions and ecstasies, exorcisms and conjurations, miracles and magic. The magical papyri (most of which come from Egypt) report the very diversified practices to control "power" or to receive predictions and revelations: manipulations of water or light, conjuration of dead people, spirits and gods, and the skillful handling of media. It could be dangerous to interfere with such operations: Acts 16:16ff reports that Paul and Silas were thrown into prison because they exorcised a spirit from a possessed slave girl, who had just proclaimed the apostles as "servants of the most high god." How grotesque such a situation could be is again well described by Luke in Act 14:8ff: it is by no means difficult for Barnabas and Paul to confirm the significance of the preaching by the performance of a miracle; but they have great difficulties in preventing the people from worshiping them as Zeus and Hermes. For a missionary to say "We are only human beings just like you" would certainly undermine his credibility. Paul's opponents in Corinth were much less scrupulous than Paul himself in using all available means of propaganda (miracles, visions, ecstases, rhetorical tricks, letters of recommendation). That such occultist and spiritualistic practices could even invade the philosophical schools is later evident in Neoplatonism. It is reported about Iamblichus that he levitated while praying, and of Proclus that he was surrounded by a halo when he was lecturing. A philosophy like Neoplatonism, which put great value upon asceticism, esteemed mystical power very highly, used magic wheels in order to speak with the gods, and knew magic rites in order to make rain, has close resemblances to a theosophy and to theurgy. The difference between philosophers and "philosophers" had become obliterated.

(h) Dio of Prusa, Plutarch, Lucian

Among the representatives of popular philosophy are several figures of the imperial period who did not belong to a particular philosophical school, but must be distinguished from the philosophers of the marketplace because of their comprehensive education and erudition, and their literary activity. It is characteristic that they were advocates of the Greek educational tradition, that they stood for propriety and morality in the name of philosophy, and that they primarily attempted to influence the comparatively broad middle class of the cities.

1) *Dio Cocceianus of Prusa.* Typical features of the popular philosophical wandering preacher are most clearly evident in Dio Cocceianus of Prusa, later known as Dio Chrysostom (ca. 40–120 CE). After his rhetorical education he was converted to philosophy, was exiled from Rome by Domitian, and for many years wandered from province to province as a Cynic preacher. Trajan called him back to Rome, where he came into

Bibliography to §6.4h (1): Texts

Dio Chrysostom: Greek text and English translation by J. W. Cohoon in LCL (5 vols.).
Grant, *Hellenistic Religions,* 162–66.

Bibliography to §6.4h (1): Studies

C. P. Jones, *The Roman World of Dio Chrysostom* (Cambridge, MA: Harvard University, 1978).
Hans von Arnim, *Leben und Werke des Dio von Prusa* (Berlin: Weidmann, 1898).

favor once more. Dio spent the last years of his life in his home city. Many of his speeches are preserved; they belong to the best and most instructive testimonies for the Cynic-Stoic ideal of the conduct of life. His description of the self-sufficiency (*autarkia*) of the philosopher is in harmony with the Pauline words: "I have learned to be content in whatever state I am. I know how to be abased, and I know how to abound. In any and all circumstances I have been initiated: plenty and hunger, abundance and want" (Phil 4:11–12). According to Dio, the passions, desires, and vices of humans are obstacles on the way to morality and self-sufficiency. But the philosopher's task is not only to preach moral improvement; as a pastor and counsellor he should also support people in their moral and practical problems. Dio connects a positive criticism of religion with his moral preaching. The philosopher must assist people in discovering the true meaning of the worship of the gods, which is not fully comprehended in the external adoration of divine images—although even this expresses a genuine desire of the human soul. Dio's Cynicism was not uncritical of the existing political situation. During the years of his exile in the east he actively agitated against the Flavian dynasty. But he was not a revolutionary; rather, his political propaganda sought to regain the classical ideals of morality and education, for which he frequently cites examples. Criticism of established social and religious conventions is at the same time a summons to obtain true humanity in moral freedom and in true piety.

2) *Plutarch*. The same basic moral and religious attitude can be found in Dio's contemporary, the much more learned Plutarch from Chaeronea in Boeotia (ca. 46/48–120/125 CE). Plutarch came from a noble family, studied philosophy in Athens (especially at the Academy), read voraciously and travelled extensively in Greece, Asia Minor, and Egypt.

Bibliography to §6.4h (2): Texts

Plutarch, *Moralia:* Greek text and English translation by Frank Cole Babbitt and others in LCL (15 vols.).

Plutarch, *The Lives:* Greek text and English translation by Bernadotte Perrin in LCL (11 vols.).

Bibliography to §6.4h (2): Studies

R. H. Barrow, *Plutarch and His Times* (Bloomington, IN: Indiana University, 1967).

Helge Almqvist, *Plutarch und das Neue Testament* (ASNU 15; Uppsala: Almqvist and Wiksell, 1946).

Hans Dieter Betz (ed.), *Plutarch's Theological Writings and Early Christian Literature* (SCHNT 3; Leiden: Brill, 1975).

Hans Dieter Betz (ed.), *Plutarch's Ethical Writings and Early Christian Literature* (SCHNT 4; Leiden: Brill, 1978).

Braun, "Plutarchs Kritik am Aberglauben im Lichte des Neuen Testaments," in: idem, *Studien*, 120–35.

Throughout his life he remained politically active in behalf of his home city. Such work as well as his rising fame as a writer resulted in several extended stays in Rome. When about fifty years old, he became a priest of Apollo in Delphi. In this context it is, of course, impossible to give anything like an adequate account of the work of this influential author. Only about half of his literary output is preserved, and even this still fills about six thousand pages in a modern edition. Many of his writings deal with scientific, philosophical, moral, educational, devotional, and religious subjects (collected today under the name *Moralia*). Another part of his literary work is made up of the famous parallel biographies; twenty-two are preserved, which begin with Theseus/Romulus and end with persons from I BCE. The purpose of Plutarch's literary work was moral education. He wanted to be understood not as an abstract scholar, but as friend, pastor, and physician. This is also true of his biographies, which are not written as examples of political activity, but as models of an attitude of life revealing true virtue and genuine piety; deterrent models are also presented.

In his philosophical positions, Plutarch was a Platonist, although he also assimilated many things from the Stoics and Aristotelians. But his plain admiration is given to Plato alone, because only with him does he find genuine religious attitudes and the true recognition of God. More than other writers of his time, Plutarch is a theologian, and he returns repeatedly to the question of the right interpretation of religion and religious traditions. He is in agreement with many of his contemporaries when he criticizes the view that the deity can be found in material images and in the myths of the poets. Rather, allegorical interpretation is required to comprehend the true, spiritual essence of the deity. Such insight is necessary if one seeks to evaluate the things of the world, to recognize moral forces which can assist human beings, and evil powers that threaten them. God has created the whole world and is its ordering and governing power. Nevertheless, the world is not of one piece: there are two world souls in the realm between God and matter, one higher soul which is good, and a lower soul which is evil. The latter determines the lower world beneath the moon, which is therefore subject to change and instability. The entire realm between God and humanity is occupied by demons, some of which possess divine power, while others share the vacillating world of sense-perception. The hierarchy of the demons' world is a kind of stepladder from the human world to God. Such views are not necessarily due to the influence of the older Academy, although the concepts of the dual world soul and demonology ultimately derive from Plato's student Xenocrates (§4.1a). Plutarch simply presents a Platonic world view which was widely accepted in his day. This includes a mitigated Platonism in anthropology and cosmology amplified by astrological concepts and the belief in demons that was widely shared by people of that age. But although Plutarch is convinced that evil rules in the sublunar world, he does not draw the same conclusions as the contemporary Christian Gnostics. He does not turn away from the world and its social and religious institutions; on the contrary, he commends a life which finds true, spiritual happiness in the mastery of the moral demands of marriage, family, the education of children, as well as in the faithful fulfillment of the duties of inherited religion. The Greek fathers of the ancient church, beginning with Clement of Alexandria, saw a kindred spirit in Plutarch and were fond of his writings.

3) *Lucian.* The third writer in this category is the Syrian Lucian from Samosata in Commagene (ca. 120–180 CE). Lucian represents both the general level of higher education, and also the increasing disenchantment with the once highly praised values of the classical Greek inheritance. In many respects he is the exact antithesis of Plutarch. Lucian exhibits biting irony where Plutarch is confident; he ridicules the old gods where the Delphic priest interprets them with profundity. Lucian was educated in rhetoric and began his career as a travelling orator, first in Ionia and Greece, then in Italy where he became famous, and in Gaul where he became rich. He did not understand his rhetorical performances as instruments of political or moral influence; rather, he merely intended to entertain his listeners with his criticism of the existing conditions, and his satirical speeches were designed to amuse the audience. But Lucian later revoked his commitment to rhetoric and was converted to philosophy and thus also to the dialogue as the genre of his literary work. Yet while the dialogue in its classical form had been the appropriate genre of philosophical reflection, with Lucian it became a tool for presenting the absurdities of philosophy and rhetoric, religion, and morality. Instead of philosophical considerations, Lucian's dialogues offer clever and witty comedy. In spite of his renunciation of rhetoric, Lucian never became a true disciple of philosophy. His nearest kin are the Cynics; Lucian is a master of the diatribe style and loves to quote Diogenes. He also shares with the Cynics the criticism of greed, luxury, debauchery, and intemperance, but he proclaims no moral ideal of his own. Lucian's assaults upon the charlatanism of religious propaganda are particularly sharp; especially well known are

Bibliography to §6.4h (3): Texts

Lucian: Greek text and English translation by A. M. Harmon and others in LCL (9 vols.).

Bibliography to §6.4h (3): Studies

Hans Dieter Betz, *Lukian von Samosata und das Neue Testament* (TU 76; Berlin: Akademie-Verlag, 1961).

his writings about the false prophet Alexander, who claimed to be a son of Asclepius and founded an oracle, and about the Cynic Peregrinus Proteus, a former Christian missionary who immolated himself publicly in Olympia. Lucian, an expert judge of his educated and uneducated contemporaries and a keen observer, has preserved a good deal of valuable information about the religions of his time: about the ancient cults; the Syrian Goddess; Hades and the judgment of the dead, the place of punishment of the evil-doers and the reward of good deeds; the conflict between fate and providence; astrology; migration of souls; and belief in miracles. Even though Lucian rarely says anything that is complimentary, whether about human beings, the gods, or religion in general, his writings (of which more than seventy are preserved), written in brilliant classical Greek— Lucian did not participate in the sophistry of the Atticists—are rarely boring, never edifying, always entertaining, and of incomparable value as a mirror of his time.

5. The Religions of the Roman Imperial Period

(a) Roman Religion and Foreign Cults

It is difficult to reconstruct ancient Roman religion and to grasp its essential features. Some information is preserved about rituals, festal calendars, and the worship of various gods and divine powers. Divinities were usually conceived of as abstract powers rather than as anthropo-

Bibliography to §6.5

Herbert Jennings Rose, *Ancient Roman Religion* (Hutchinson's University Library: World Religions 27; London and New York: Hutchinson's University Library, 1948).

Frederick C. Grant (ed.), *Ancient Roman Religion* (New York: Liberal Arts, 1957).

Kurt Latte, *Römische Religionsgeschichte* (HAW 5,4; München: Beck, 1960).

Nilsson, *Griechische Religion* 2.

John Ferguson, *The Religions of the Roman Empire* (London: Thames and Hudson, 1970).

Jean Beaujeau, *La religion romaine à l'apogée de l'Empire* (Paris: Les Belles Lettres, 1955).

W. Ward Fowler, *The Religious Experience of the Roman People* (London: Macmillan, 1933).

William Reginald Halliday, *Lectures on the History of Roman Religion* (Liverpool: University Press, 1922).

Carl Koch, *Religio: Studien zu Kult und Glauben der Römer* (ed. Otto Seel; Erlanger Beiträge zur Sprach- und Kunstwissenschaft 7; Nürnberg: Carl, 1960).

A. D. Nock, "Religious Developments from the Close of the Republic to the Death of Nero," in *CambAncHist* 10. 465–511.

Idem, "Studies in the Greco-Roman Beliefs of the Empire," in: idem, *Essays,* 1. 33–48.

Franz Cumont, *Oriental Religions in Roman Paganism* (New York: Dover, 1956).

morphic divine persons. However, under Etruscan and later under Greek influence, the Roman understanding of deities became somewhat more personalized and cult statues were introduced. Our oldest literary sources are already influenced by this Greek interpretation of the Roman deities. But *religio* was and remained for the Romans the exact observation of established rites on behalf of the whole political community. The fruitfulness of the fields, undisturbed peace and successful war, prosperity and health could be achieved in no other way, because everything was dependent upon the favor of those supernatural powers.

Piety (*pietas*)—and the Romans thought of themselves as the most pious people on earth—was not understood in terms of the religious experience of the individual, and mysticism was always viewed with great suspicion by the Romans. Rather, piety meant the faithful observation of ritual duties because the life of the individual, as well as of the community as a whole, was permeated by these divine powers, whether in birth, marriage, or death, the seasons of the year, popular assemblies, or warfare. In order to maintain the favor of the gods and to avert their curse, the most important instrument was prayer. Equally important was the observation of signs (*omina*) from which one could learn what the gods intended to do. The *augures,* a college of priests who were charged with the task of making these observations (from the motion of birds in flight, the appetite of the sacred chicken, and also lightning and thunder) and of giving advice accordingly, were held in high respect. On the other hand, magic and all those religious practices which the Romans called superstition (*superstitio*) were rejected. The latter term comprised everything that was alien to Roman religious practices, and it was therefore frequently used for foreign cults which had religious ceremonies that the Romans judged to be strange or undignified.

In general, however, Roman religion was quite open to other cults. Accepting new cults and previously unknown religious powers and including them in the official religion, or at least giving them space for an altar or a temple in the city, was felt to be very appropriate, in order to secure the favors of such new deities. Roman religion was syncretistic

Bibliography to §6.5a

Simeon L. Guterman, *Religious Toleration and Persecution in Ancient Rome* (London: Aiglon, 1951).

A. H. McDonald, "Rome and the Italian Confederation (200 to 186 B.C.)," *JRomS* 34 (1944) 11–33.

Martin P. Nilsson, *The Dionysiac Mysteries of the Hellenistic and Roman Age* (Lund: Gleerup, 1957; reprint: New York: Arno, 1975).

R. M. Ogilvie, *The Romans and Their Gods in the Age of Augustus* (London: Chatto and Windus, 1969).

already in its oldest known form. Etruscan elements had been accepted very early; in the triad of Jupiter, Juno, and Minerva, the last is probably of Etruscan origin (note also the Etruscan *haruspices,* priests who divined the future on the basis of inspecting the liver of sacrificed animals; they were officially recognized in the late republic). Among the Greek gods, Apollo was worshiped as early as v BCE. Asclepius (*Aesculapius*) was introduced to Rome in 293 BCE in order to fight a plague. The first oriental religion recognized in Rome was the cult of the Great Mother (Cybele), accepted in 204 BCE in a critical moment of the Second Punic War (but Romans were not permitted to participate in her orgiastic rites).

A grave and momentous turn in the Roman attitude towards foreign religions came with the Bacchanalian scandal of 186 BCE. Although both the *senatus consultum* about the Bacchanalia as well as the report of the historian Livy are preserved, it is still not quite clear what actually happened. Obviously the cult of Dionysus (§4.3f) had spread rapidly in Etruria and in the region of the city of Rome. Yet it did not come as a religion seeking official recognition, but as a mystery cult attracting proselytes without official sanction. Numerous new adherents had already been won, and "temples" (i.e., probably house sanctuaries) had already been founded in Rome and its environs. Initiation ceremonies were held at night, and men as well as women participated. Through some incident the whole affair received public attention. The Senate grew suspicious, fearing immorality and conspiracy, and intervened: all new "temples" were destroyed, the adherents were hunted down and many executed. The cult, however, was not completely outlawed, but only restricted and brought under the Senate's control. Henceforth the founding of a temple would require a permit, communal treasuries would not be allowed, and not more than five persons could participate in the ceremonies.

Rome would never lose its suspicion of any foreign cult which appeared to be a mystery religion. There was a deep-seated fear of magic and witchcraft and, in fact, anything which might appear to the Romans as superstition. Nevertheless, the mysteries of Dionysus/Bacchus remained popular in Italy and, after the end of the republic, gained new ground, especially in the upper classes of the population. In addition, other mystery religions were able to establish themselves in Rome, although often only with difficulty. The cult of Isis (§4.4a) had been brought to Rome by Egyptian immigrants in I BCE. The Senate intervened repeatedly: Isis temples or altars were destroyed by *senatus consultum* in 59, 58, 53, 50, and 48 BCE. In the year 28 BCE, Augustus outlawed private house sanctuaries of Isis, and in 19 CE, Tiberius had the Isis temple in Rome destroyed once more and the cult statue thrown into the Tiber. Finally, under Caligula, the Isis cult found permanent official recognition, and a double temple for Isis and Sarapis was built, though only on the Campus Martius outside of the *pomerium* (the old district of the city which was subject to special regulations and laws).

But even if imperial Rome was still opposed to the introduction of new cults into the city of Rome itself, there were no official restrictions pertaining to the expansion of these religions in the provinces of the Roman empire. To be sure, in order to establish a new temple, authorization from the government was required. That decision was usually left to the local authorities, however, which normally granted such privileges gladly, as the many Isis and Sarapis sanctuaries of the imperial period demonstrate. In many instances, it was only a question of the renewal of older privileges. The situation was quite different for religions which could not claim to possess ancient privileges and did not represent the national religious tradition of one of the many peoples of the Roman empire. Their propaganda and missionary activity would make such religions appear even more suspicious. Private meetings in secret which were not supervised by local authorities nor led by officially recognized priests were never welcome. The celebration of secret initiation rites, such as "mysteries" in the Isis temples or, which was increasingly the case, also in temples of other deities, would not be suspect because such temples were officially sanctioned, even if the mysteries were not accessible to everybody. But Christianity, which was spreading quickly in many areas, did not fit the Roman concept of a legitimate religion. One had learned to acquiesce in the existence of Jewish religious communities which were established in numerous cities, though ancient sources give no evidence for the modern hypothesis that the Jews enjoyed the status of a *religio licita,* a generally licensed religion. But the Jews had ancient privileges in most areas, even if these were not always uncontested, and they were a nation which could claim possession of a long tradition. Nonetheless, many gentiles liked to believe that the head of an ass was worshiped in the Jerusalem temple, and circumcision was considered a barbaric rite.

If Jews were suspect because they did not participate in the emperor cult, such refusal put the Christians into double jeopardy. To be sure, the Roman empire was not a police state and did not possess a worldwide organization of informers (such things existed only at certain times in Rome itself under emperors such as Nero). Christian itinerant missionaries were free to preach anywhere, just like other wandering preachers and philosophers of the streets and marketplace, and their followers would normally be left unmolested. Difficulties arose if local authorities had the impression that the Christians had caused unrest, or if competitors or malevolent outsiders denounced them to the magistrates. In such instances they would be brought to trial (often after long imprisonment), sentenced to corporal punishment, and expelled from the city. For this the Pauline letters give eloquent testimony; in the Acts of the Apostles such actions have been stylized to a fixed schematism of the missionary experience. Capital punishment was rarely used in such cases—otherwise Paul would probably never have made it much beyond Antioch. If Paul was indeed finally sentenced to death—and this must be assumed—that sentence was most likely based on the accusation that he had violated the sacred rights of the Jewish temple (§9.4c).

Scattered pieces of information about Christian missionaries from the first two generations of Christianity lead to the conclusion that many, for whatever reasons, suffered martyrdom; but not all of these death sentences can be attributed to Roman courts (cf., e.g., Acts 12:1–2; §8.3b). The Neronian persecution of the Christians in Rome (§6.2a) is an exception and must not be considered as typical for the attitude of the Roman authorities toward the Christians. The early Christian apologists tried to argue that the Christians were not a new religious sect but the legitimate heirs of the venerable ancient religion of Israel (§12.3a). But for a Roman official, this would not have been immediately evident. And besides, not all Christians would lay claim to the Old Testament in the same way. In any case, the emperor cult was to remain an unsolvable problem (see below on the further development of the relationship of Christianity to the Roman state, §12.1c, §12.3a, d–f).

(b) The Emperor Cult

The Roman emperor cult was not a homogeneous phenomenon, because it combined two different elements which remained in constant tension with each other: the fully developed Hellenistic royal cult (§1.5a–d) and native Roman concepts of the extraordinary personality. Whereas the

Bibliography to §6.5b

J. R. Fears, *Princeps a Diis Electus: The Divine Election of the Emperor as a Political Concept at Rome* (Papers and Monographs of the American Academy in Rome 26; Rome: American Academy, 1977).

Fritz Taeger, *CHARISMA: Studien zur Geschichte des antiken Herrscherkultes*, vol. 2: *Rom* (Stuttgart: Kohlhammer, 1960).

L. Ross Taylor, *The Divinity of the Roman Emperor* (Middletown, CT: American Philological Association, 1931; reprint: Philadelphia: Porcupine, 1975).

R. Mellor, *THEA RŌMĒ: The Worship of the Goddess Rome in the Greek World* (Hyp. 42; Göttingen: Vandenhoeck & Ruprecht, 1975).

Jürgen Deiniger, *Die Provinziallandtage der römischen Kaiserzeit von Augustus bis zum Ende des 3. Jahrhunderts n. Chr.* (München: Beck, 1965).

Antonie Wlosok (ed.), *Römischer Kaiserkult* (WdF 372; Darmstadt: Wissenschaftliche Buchgesellschaft, 1978).

Inez Scott Ryberg, *Rites of the State Religion in Roman Art* (Memoirs of the American Academy in Rome 2,2; Rome: American Academy, 1955).

Greek east saw the person of the ruler as the epiphany of a god, the Romans worshiped transcendent powers which, under special circumstances, might become active in exceptional human beings. Victorious Roman generals who took over the authority of government from the former Hellenistic rulers repeatedly received divine honors in the east (e.g., Sulla and Pompey); but in Rome itself great pains were taken not to treat these powerful leaders of the state as if they were gods. Therefore, the concept of the divinity of the living emperor gained ground in Rome only very slowly and under protest.

It is unclear what Caesar's position on the question of the emperor cult was. During the last years of his life the Senate voted several times special honors, some resulting from Caesar's own initiative, and these may have had some similarity to divine honors. In spite of the presence of Hellenistic features, there was a desire to establish a connection to more ancient Roman concepts. Caesar himself was deeply conscious of his mission, and his ideal of the ruler was Alexander the Great. On the other hand, he had little use for those mythical concepts of divinity upon which the worship of the ruler as a revealed god was founded. Rather, in typical Roman fashion he believed that his destiny belonged to his own *felicitas,* i.e., an impersonal power which showed itself in his deeds. Whatever the case may be, many people in Rome believed that Caesar was planning to be pronounced both king and god. The assassination of Caesar was intended to put an end to such developments. Instead it resulted in Caesar's divinization, spontaneously enacted by the people and later sanctioned by the Senate, which officially accepted Caesar among the gods of the state and erected an altar for him in the city (later a temple was built). The popular religious beliefs which soon grew around the person of Caesar included Hellenistic concepts of the divine ruler and his charisma.

Marc Antony did not share Caesar's caution and reticence: as soon as he reached the east, he demanded to be worshiped as a divine king and in typical Hellenistic fashion identified himself with a specific deity (Dionysus). His antagonist Octavian (Augustus) aptly took advantage of the negative Roman reaction to this move and from the beginning explored for himself a different option, seeking something which was more congenial to his own inclinations and which would correspond to traditional Roman concepts and customs. When he called himself "Son of the Divinized Caesar" (*divi filius*), he was not claiming divine sonship in the Greek sense, but, avoiding any mythological connotations, establishing his legitimate continuation of the inheritance, divine destiny, and mission of his adopted father Caesar. The title *Imperator Caesar,* which Augustus regularly used, also expressed the typical Roman concept that the office of the *imperator* possessed a numinous dignity; all that was new was the perma-

Inscription from the Roma-Augustus Temple in Athens

The temple whose fragments are now assembled behind the Parthenon on the Acropolis was built shortly after 27 B.C.E. The inscription on one of the epistyle blocks records the dedication by "the priest of the Goddess Rome and the Savior Augustus."

nent use of this title. The conferment of the name *Augustus* ("One who deserves reverence," an archaic Roman designation) by the Senate in 27 BCE clearly elevated its bearer to a position above the level of ordinary human beings; but it did not make him a god. Rather, it emphasized the superhuman dimensions of his *felicitas.*

Insofar as the official Roman emperor cult maintained the structures created by Augustus, it was not a cult of the divine person of the emperor. Its predominant features were rather the cult of Roma (the city of Rome as the symbol of the divinely sanctioned rule of Rome over the nations) and of the Divus Julius (Caesar). A relationship with the person of the living emperor was expressed in the cult of his *genius,* that is, his personal guardian deity, and of the *Lares Augusti,* the protecting deities of his house. Both practices are related to older Roman concepts. This is also the case in the worship of the powers acting through the person of the emperor as, for example, *pax* and *victoria,* which were not perceived as gods but as personalized powers. Augustus, instructed no doubt by political caution, but also by a genuine understanding of the Roman mind, thus distinguished the emperor cult of Rome from that of the Hellenistic idea of the worship of the god revealed in the person of the emperor; however, such distinctions were meaningless in the eastern provinces of the empire, and even in the west the Hellenistic concept would soon overshadow the official Roman version of the cult. Altars and temples consecrated to Augustus, as well as honorary inscriptions, differed in no way from those honoring the Olympian gods. After his death and the official divinization by the Senate, Augustus became the *Theos Sebastos,* the god Augustus. He was explicitly identified with other gods, especially with Zeus, and other members of the imperial family also received divine honors—a characteristic feature of the Hellenistic ruler cult. Asia Minor seems to have been the center for this Hellenistic interpretation of the emperor cult; in the western provinces, however, it is often unclear whether worship was accorded to the *genius* of Augustus or to himself as a god.

Under Augustus' successor, Tiberius, a conscious effort was made to discourage the cult of the living emperor. Tiberius made a point of not accepting divine honors offered to his own person, just as he also tried to restore the authority of the traditional institutions of the republic. Caligula, however, went to the opposite extreme. As soon as he became emperor, he demanded to be treated and worshiped as a god. As a consequence of this request, and despite the resistance of leading Roman circles, a new invasion of ideas from the Hellenistic ruler cult took place. At the same time, Caligula triggered the first serious conflicts between the emperor cult and other religions, because he went further than identifying himself with specific traditional deities and manipulating his own official acceptance among the gods of the Roman state; he also demanded that his cult statue be set up in the temples of other gods everywhere in the empire, even in the temple of Jerusalem and in Jewish synagogues (because of the prudent delaying tactics of the Syrian legate, this completely foolhardy demand was never carried out in Jerusalem).

After Caligula's assassination, Claudius returned to the policies of Augustus. Neither Claudius nor Nero was officially accepted among the gods of the Roman state during their lifetimes. But the forms of reverence for the living emperor which had been taken over from Hellenism had meanwhile become so widely accepted in the Roman upper classes that even the philosopher Seneca, in a petition written in exile, addressed the emperor Claudius in terms which left no doubt that he was indeed writing to a god. To be sure, many of the terms and phrases had already become worn-out formulas. They were also used in addresses to Nero, who flattered himself with the belief that such words were seriously meant. Vespasian, however, put a stop to all of this and unequivocally returned to the form of the emperor cult which had been created by Augustus: only an emperor who had been explicitly divinized after his death became one of the gods of the state. This form of the emperor cult became authoritative under later emperors until Marcus Aurelius, with the one exception of Domitian. When he demanded to be addressed as "Lord and God," he not only provoked the opposition of the Senate, but also appeared to the Christians as the dreaded beast from the abyss (Revelation of John 13). The persecution which the Roman church had to suffer (in 95 CE) is mentioned in *1 Clement*, written shortly after the events (it is doubtful, however, whether the consul of that year, T. Flavius Clemens, and his wife Domitilla were executed because of their Christian faith). But even if the emperors of II CE officially were not gods walking on earth, nobody was prevented from offering divine honors to an emperor, even in public. The proconsul Pliny placed the statue of the emperor next to those of the gods, so that renegade Christians could sacrifice to the emperor. And when Hadrian had finished building the temple of Zeus Olympius in Athens, delegations from many cities dedicated inscriptions which praised the "Olympian" Hadrian as a benefactor.

The emperor cult never became a new religion as such, or a substitute for religion during the first two centuries CE. This was well known to all, both the advocates of the emperor cult and its opponents. This cult was rather a supplementary glorification of the official religion which served the Roman state. No one was urged to accept the emperor cult as a replacement of his traditional religion. On the contrary, the Romans earnestly supported the veneration of all gods in their native cities and nations, and they expected those gods would in turn lend their support to the Roman state. When inscriptions speak about the emperor as "savior" and announce his "appearance" (*epiphania*) as a "gospel," praising him as the benefactor and bringer of peace to all humankind, the religious content of these terms is not directly comparable with the significance of the same terminology in Christian language. In official usage, such terminology soon became hackneyed language. Certainly, people were grateful for the establishment and preservation of peace by the emperor, and they by all means hoped that the gods or the powers of fate would continue to enable the emperor to secure peace and prosperity. But the idea that this Roman empire could be the fulfillment of humanity's religious longings was a thought which appeared like a brief flash at the beginning of the reign of Augustus, as, for instance, in the poems of Virgil. Afterwards everybody went back to his accustomed ways, sometimes still to the old gods, more often to one of the new religions, to the missionaries of the marketplace, to the philosophers, and not rarely to the magicians and astrologers.

The Christians nevertheless got into a serious conflict with the emperor cult, but this was neither designed nor understood by the Roman authorities. The Christian message from the beginning demanded exclusive loyalty. This loyalty did more than refer to the *one* God whose exclusive worship was an indisputable obligation, it was also irreconcilable with Rome's political world view. The Christian message sprang from the enthusiastic experience of faith in the coming of a new world. To be sure, the tension of this faith was soon relaxed, and the expectation of the coming of Christ in the near future might often disappear altogether. But the Christians remained citizens of a different world and had pledged allegiance to its ruler, Christ; this remained a constant part of the Christian conviction. Although Christianity was divided into bitterly feuding factions, nonetheless Gnostics, Montanists, Marcionites, and apologists were all united in that allegiance. Since the belief in other gods was already intolerable for the Christians, the admission of the emperor among the public gods of the state, designed to serve the preservation of the world and its institutions, was not only hubris and blasphemy, but a direct contradiction and challenge to Christ's sovereign authority. Of course, the Christians were quite prepared to compromise. They prayed on behalf of the emperor, and the apologists recommended the strict Christian morality as a virtue useful for the preservation of the state. But a true Christian would likely never sacrifice to the gods and to the emperor, as was explicitly stated already in Pliny's letter to Trajan (10.96; see §12.3d). Thus the emperor cult became the criterion by which the allegiance to Christ was tested.

(c) Mithras

Among the missionary religions which spread in the Mediterranean world during the imperial period, the cult of Mithras occupied a special place. Although Mithras was the most oriental god among the new deities, and although his cult was essentially celebrated in an exclusive mystery association—the Mithraic cult was a "mystery religion" in the strict sense of the word—Mithras was received by the Romans without resistance and, at the end of III CE, he even became the offical god of the Roman state. Originally Mithras was an Indo-Aryan god whose name meant "covenant." The spread of the Zoroastrian faith in Persia seems to have led to the suppression of Mithras. But the Achaemenid kings also worshiped Mithras, though they prohibited the characteristic bull sacrifices. In the Hellenistic period the names of members of the Parthian dynasties in Persia and of the rulers of Pontus, who were of Iranian origin, point to the continued veneration of Mithras (e.g., Mithridates). There were sanctuaries of Mithras during that period in many places of the east, including even Egypt. The magi, a priestly caste from Media, were this religion's cult officials. However, the Greeks also used this term for Babylonian priests and connected it with astral religion. Therefore, the occurrence of the term "magi" cannot always be taken as evidence for the Mithraic religion. Nothing indicates that the Mithraic cult of the Hellenistic period was a mystery religion, nor that its Iranian ingredients were instrumental in the development of the mysteries. It is quite possible that the Mithraic religion assumed the features of a mystery religion only during its migration to the west at the beginning of the Roman imperial period (§4.3e; 4.4d). How this happened and under what circumstances we do not know.

Bibliography to §6.5c

Grant, *Hellenistic Religions,* 147–49.

Franz Cumont, *The Mysteries of Mithra* (Chicago: Open Court, 1903).

M. J. Vermaseren, *Mithras: Geschichte eines Kultes* (UB 33; Stuttgart: Kohlhammer, 1965).

Esmé Wynne-Tyson, *Mithras: The Fellow in the Cap* (2d ed.; Fontwell, Sussex: Centaur, 1972).

Franz Cumont, "Mithra en Asie Mineure," in: Calder and Keil, *Anatolian Studies,* 67–76.

J. R. Hinnels (ed.), *Mithraic Studies* (2 vols.; Manchester: Manchester University, 1975).

Leroy A. Campbell, *Mithraic Iconography and Ideology* (EPRO 11; Leiden: Brill, 1968).

Alfred Schütze, *Mithras-Mysterien und Urchristentum* (Stuttgart: Urachhaus, 1972).

Robert Duthoy, *The Taurobolium* (EPRO 10; Leiden: Brill, 1969).

Gaston H. Halsberghe, *The Cult of Sol Invictus* (EPRO 23; Leiden: Brill, 1972).

Franz Altheim, *Der unbesiegte Gott: Heidentum und Christentum* (Hamburg: Rowohlt, 1957).

In any case, at the beginning of the Roman imperial period, Mithraic mysteries existed in many parts of the empire. According to Plutarch, Cilician pirates settled by Pompey in the west propagated the cult in the western provinces. Evidence for a widespread dissemination of Mithraism does not appear, however, until late in I CE. There can be no doubt that the worship of Mithras was the most important mystery religion of the pagan world during the whole imperial period and as late as IV CE. Sanctuaries of Mithras (*Mithrea*) have been discovered almost everywhere, especially in the border provinces, from the *Limes* in Germany to Mesopotamia (Dura Europus), but also less frequently in the interior provinces. There were probably as many as one hundred *Mithrea* in the city of Rome, and sixteen have been found in its port city of Ostia. Only men were initiated into the mysteries: thus this religion became the mystery cult of soldiers, sailors, and merchants. Membership was by no means limited to the lower classes, although regions in which the mobility of the population was not an important factor, and where the old family structures had survived, were less likely to open their doors to Mithras.

The cult legend of Mithras is only partially known, and then only insofar as it can be reconstructed from the numerous pictorial representations. Mithras is born from a rock on 25 December; shepherds bring gifts. While hunting Mithras meets the bull, overcomes it, and carries it into a cave, where he kills the bull with a short sword. From its blood and semen grows new life, but a snake tries to drink the blood and a scorpion poisons the semen. The sun, the moon, the planets, and the four winds witness the sacrifice; Mithras meets with the sun (= the god Helios/Sol), both eat the meat and drink the bull's blood and make a covenant; Sol kneels before Mithras, receives the accolade, and they shake hands. It is not known how this cult legend was related to the performances of the mystery celebration. The initiation into the mystery comprised seven steps, which probably corresponded to the seven planets. The initiate is called "reborn" and through an oath he becomes a soldier of Mithras. The highest step of the initiations was to be identified with the sun (Sol). Within the mystery association a strict order was maintained, wherein a hierarchical structure reflected the seven steps of initiation. Military discipline and subordination are mirrored in the mystery cult's organization. The order of initiation also demonstrates that elements of astral religion played a role. Finally, cosmic concepts appear in special initiations into the elements (fire, water, air), which existed in addition to the regular seven initiations.

The history of Mithraic religion reveals that Rome's official policies were quite able to accommodate a widely propagated eastern mystery cult. But it is not possible to define in legal terms why the cult of Mithras was accepted, and even increasingly promoted, whereas the Christians were persecuted. An important reason was probably the simple fact that major, influential parts of the population—which increasingly included the soldiers—were initiated into the mysteries of Mithras. During a period in which the army was constantly expanding its role in determining the fate of the empire, the ruling classes of Rome would find their social ideals in the Mithraic religion rather than in Christianity.

(d) Neopythagoreanism

The Pythagorean movement appeared once more in the late Hellenistic and Roman periods. These Pythagoreans based their teachings upon Pythagoras, philosopher, mathematician, and founder of a religious order, who was born in Samos ca. 570/560 BCE. After travels to Babylon and Egypt, Pythagoras was active in Croton in lower Italy from about 525/520 BCE. There he founded a philosophical order whose members had to live according to strict and partly ascetic rules. Pythagoras may have created this order not only for esoteric religious purposes, but also as an instrument of political power. This is reflected in the organization of the order, which was divided into "politicians" and "theoreticians"—this division is probably identical with the later distinction betwen "hearers" (akousmatikoi) and mathematicians. The first group was not obliged to observe all of the society's rules. After some initial success in several cities of southern Italy, where the Pythagoreans became the primary support for the ruling aristocracy, the group experienced catastrophic setbacks through the democratic revolutions of v BCE. It is not impossible that there was a short-lived recovery, though it did not have much effect. In any case, during the first two centuries of the Hellenistic period the Pythagoreans had ceased to exist. Thus it is highly unlikely that the later Neopythagoreans were the direct continuation of a still existent organization of the old Pythagoreans. There are, to be sure, pseudo-Pythagorean writings from the Hellenistic period; but these are pure fictions which belong to no

Bibliography to §6.5d: Texts

Holger Thesleff (ed.), *The Pythagorean Writings of the Hellenistic Period* (Åbo: Åbo Akademi, 1965).

Cartlidge and Dungan, *Documents,* 205–42.

Philostratus, *The Life of Apollonius of Tyana:* Greek text with English translation by F. C. Conybeare in LCL (2 vols.).

R. J. Penella (ed.), *The Letters of Apollonius of Tyana: A Critical Text with Prolegomena, Translation and Commentary* (Mn.Suppl. 56; Leiden: Brill, 1979).

Bibliography to §6.5d: Studies

G. Petzke, *Die Traditionen über Apollonius von Tyana und das Neue Testament* (SCHNT 1; Leiden: Brill, 1970).

particular school, and it is hardly possible to prove a relationship between the later Pythagoreans and these writings.

As a matter of fact, the Neopythagoreans had no strictly organized schools, and their doctrines were only partially Pythagorean. Orphic concepts (§4.2d) were frequently appropriated. Whatever one might point to as a specifically Pythagorean inheritance could have been learned without difficulty from Aristotle, because he (or one of his students) had collected the precepts of Pythagoras, the so-called *Akousmata* (the ancient Pythagoreans never fixed the teachings of their master in writing, but transmitted them only in oral form). According to this material, the Pythagorean tradition consisted of scientific definitions, wisdom sayings, and rules for conduct. The last group contained dietary laws which, due to the doctrine of the transmigration of souls, required a predominantly though not exclusively vegetarian diet; on the other hand, they also included rules for ritual purity (such as the need to wear white garments and no shoes when entering a temple, or the prohibition of the cremation of a corpse). Insofar as the Neopythagoreans resumed a life according to these rules, they would indeed have continued the ancient Pythagorean tradition. The symbolism of numbers developed by the Neopythagoreans, which was most characteristic of their interests, is also an inheritance of the mathematical endeavors of the old school. In the philosophical orientation, which was by no means uniform, the Neopythagoreans were eclectic, although primarily Platonists. They combined a Platonic dualism with the doctrine of the immortality of the soul and a very realistic belief in demons. To this point it would be difficult to distinguish them from other philosophers of their time. The Delphic priest Plutarch, the Jewish biblical scholar Philo, and the Christian apologist Justin shared all these views, and Philo and Plutarch moreover were as interested in number symbolism as the Pythagoreans. What distinguished the Neopythagoreans from other philosophers was their appropriation of certain religious undercurrents, especially concepts which derive from Orphism (§4.2d), such that Orphic and Neopythagorean concepts cannot always be differentiated (as, e.g., in views about the fate of the soul after death). All this the Neopythagoreans combined into a very peculiar ideal of the conduct of life, in which the power and superiority of the human self are visibly presented in the life of the philosopher. Since these philosophers often went from place to place as wandering preachers, they became a major factor in the propagation of a popularized Orphism and Platonism.

The best example for the ideal life of the Pythagorean is Philostratus' biography of the magician, ascetic, and philosopher *Apollonius of Tyana* (I CE). The picture which Philostratus draws is certainly idealized because he wanted to present the example of the perfect Pythagorean philosopher, although he certainy used earlier source materials. All the features of a life agreeing with the Pythagorean principles of conduct are mirrored in this biography of Apollonius. Indeed, the genre of the biography was far superior to that of a theoretical tractate about Pythagorean life: one should act charitably toward friends and toward the commonwealth, always knowing how to give others good advice; one should know how to worship the gods in the right way, not through sacrifices and festivals, but through turning away from the world of sense perception; one must recognize demons and drive them away; it is necessary to give account to oneself every day for all the deeds one has done, never to depart from righteousness, and always to trust the guidance of one's *daimonion*.

Apollonius appears as the incarnation of this ideal in Philostratus' biographical work. Dressed in a priestly garment of linen, he travels through many lands, always remaining faithful to his calling of serving the deity and doing good to human beings. He never eats meat, lest he should destroy some living thing; he never takes a bath, but frequently fasts. He drives out demons, heals the sick, predicts the future, and gives his advice where it is welcome, and also where it is not wanted (thus he does not always make friends). In many ways this ideal fulfills contemporary expectations very well. People were only too willing to believe in the presence of divine power and to be impressed by mysterious knowledge about the workings of supernatural powers. The ascetism and rigorous morality of the Pythagorean philosopher embodied a human greatness which transcended the limitations of everyday life, and opened a view into a possibility of existence which was more just and more consistent than most dealings in a world full of injustice. The biography of Apollonius (as also the many biographies of Pythagoras) could satisfy such expectations precisely because it was a religious legend of a saint. As distinct from Plutarch's parallel biographies, such legends do not intend to provide examples for moral decision-making, but reveal insights into the deeper connections of human existence with divine powers and invisible demonic energies. What the Neopythagoreans proclaimed was not philosophy, but rather religion.

(e) Astrology and Magic

After the discovery of Babylonian astrology in the Greek-speaking world at the beginnings of the Hellenistic period, astrology had strengthened the spreading beliefs in fate (§4.2c), but the new world view which is offered did not succeed in reaching broad circles of the population until the late Hellenistic and early imperial periods. In the beginning, astrology was a religion of the upper, educated classes. Horoscopes were expensive because they required comprehensive scientific investigations. But the introduction of the Julian calendar cleared the way for a more general dissemination of astrological concepts. Astrology was successful because it offered an opportunity to comprehend the laws and powers of the universe by means of a system that seemed scientifically valid. Since the political, social, and economic horizons of human experience had become so much wider, people understandably welcomed a revision of the traditional image of the cosmos, with the flat disc of the earth inhabited by human beings, the vaulted roof of the sky with the mansions of the gods above it, and the underworld below. Astronomy and astrology together made this revision possible: the earth became a sphere at the center of the constantly changing sublunar world; the place of the dead and of the souls, resuming older oriental concepts, was transferred to the upper regions of the air or the moon. The realm of the sun and the fixed stars, of light and the gods, of the fire and the spirit, was seen in immeasurable distances beyond the orbits of the planets. Even if human beings were exposed to the powers of the terrestrial world, they could be assured of their kinship with higher celestial powers. The human spirit belonged to the sun and the stars. Whoever learned to understand the laws of the universe could calculate the adverse powers of the lower regions and thus break the spells of the planets, which sought to block one's entrance to the august celestial realms above, the true home of the essential human self. And after all, such knowledge might even prove useful for the mastery of the various situations of human life.

Astrology did not enter the Hellenistic and Roman world as pseudo-religious quackery, but as scientifically approved insight into the true

Bibliography to §6.5e: Texts

Karl Preisendanz, *Papyri Graecae Magicae: Die griechischen Zauberpapyri* (2d ed. by Albert Henrichs; Stuttgart: Teubner, 1973-74).

Barrett, *Background*, 29-36.

Kee, *Origins*, 84-89.

Bibliography to §6.5e: Studies

Frederick H. Cramer, *Astrology in Roman Law and Politics* (MAPS 37; Philadelphia: American Philosophical Society, 1954).

Franz Cumont, *Astrology and Religion among the Greeks and Romans* (New York and London: Putnam's, 1912).

O. Neugebauer and H. B. van Hoesen, *Greek Horoscopes* (MAPS 48; Philadelphia: American Philosophical Society, 1959).

Hans Georg Gundel, *Weltbild und Astrologie in den griechischen Zauberpapyri* (München: Beck, 1968).

Eliane Massonneau, *La magie dans l'antiquité romain* (Paris: Sirey, 1934).

Albrecht Dieterich, *Abraxas: Studien zur Religionsgeschichte* (Leipzig: Teubner, 1891; reprint: Darmstadt: Wissenschaftliche Buchgesellschaft, 1973).

J. J. Hull, *Hellenistic Magic and the Synoptic Tradition* (SBT 2,28; London: SCM, 1974).

essence of the universe, an insight that was legitimized by the leading
scholars and systematized by the most learned philosophers. The reorganization of the Greek world of the eastern Mediterranean was another
important factor, and the establishment of peace after the long decades of
civil war by Augustus went hand in hand with the introduction of the
Julian calendar. This was a solar calendar designed by Julius Caesar on
the basis of scientific astronomy, and is essentially the calendar still in use
today. But the average citizen was probably not always conscious of the
fact that this calendar was the result of strictly astronomical computations.
Indeed, its introduction was as much expedited by religious beliefs about
the sun, as the naming of the days of the week according to the planets
ruling the first hour of each day was promoted by astrological supersti-
tions. The propagation of the festival of the New Year also rested on
astrological beliefs.

At the beginning of i CE everybody was acquainted with astrology, and
consciousness of the difference between astrology and scientific astronomy
was lost. Astrological symbols appeared widely in everyday life. Popularized astrological writings, easily accessible, made it possible to obtain
information about favorable and unfavorable days and hours without any
complicated calculations. Enough is preserved of these writings to obtain
an accurate image of their contents: prediction for each day according to
the times of the rising and setting of planets and stars, predictions based on
the position of the sun and the moon in the zodiac, lunar calendars with
information about each day of the lunar month, explanations for the
occurrence of earthquakes and thunderstorms, and, finally, character por-
traits and behavior patterns for individuals according to the planets which
determined the hour of their birth or conception. But even without reading such books it would have been difficult to avoid the influence of
astrological symbols. The orbits of planets, signs of the zodiac, and dis-
plays of the months and the seasons could be seen frequently on the walls
and doorposts of houses and in the mosaics decorating private and public
buildings. Augustus minted coins with the sign of the Capricorn, under
which he was born. The legions received ensigns with the zodiacal sign of
the month of the current emperor's birth.

Inevitably the image of the old and new gods would also be transformed
according to these quickly spreading astrological concepts. A copy of the
Artemis of the Ephesians from the Roman period (now in the museum in
Selcuk near Ephesus) shows the goddess with a necklace made of the
twelve signs of the zodiac. Gods were often presented with the radiate
crowns of the sun. But in addition to this new understanding of the gods
according to astrological concepts, cosmic powers were sometimes personified—clear evidence that the new world view did not conceive of the

universe as a mindless mechanism. The gods of the new religions represented astrological powers (for Isis and Sarapis, see §4.4a; for Mithras, §6.5c), and oriental prototypes seem to have given rise to the god Aion, a personification of eternity and infinity and the ruler of cosmic time. He stands next to the transcendent highest god as a second deity and embodies the continuous movement of the All, the revolution of the stars, of becoming and passing away, birth, death, and rebirth. Therefore his symbols are the snake that constantly rejuvenates itself and the phoenix that rises from the ashes for new life. Although there seem to have occasionally been specific cult sites for Aion, it is not possible to speak of an independent Aion religion. Rather, this god belongs to the general world view of that time: sometimes he was connected with other deities; in theogonies and cosmogonies he plays a role as the creator; in the Hermetic writings he is the first image and power of the highest god; in magical rites he is called upon as the origin of all energy. The widespread dissemination of astrological concepts is also demonstrated in Jewish and Christian writings of the period. The community of Qumran at the Dead Sea used a solar calendar. Apocalyptic writings are full of numbers, symbols, and cosmological images which are derived from astrology. When the Revelation of John (12:1ff) describes the vision of a woman who is dressed with the sun, stands on the moon, and is crowned with the twelve stars (the signs of the zodiac), it is evident that even Christianity could not escape the influence of astrological concepts of divine figures.

With astrology came its close relative, magic. To be sure, magic had always existed, submerged beneath the official cults and their rites, despised yet very much in demand. Magic characteristically remains in the shadow and does not have the same public standing as religion, even though magical and religious rites may be quite similar. The magician is not a priest or theologian who is publicly appointed or elected; he is a craftsman. His power does not rest upon a social institution and its sanctioned tradition, but upon the rules of his craft, which have been learned from a master technician through an apprenticeship and refined through practice. Religion is concerned with all those experiences of life which are significant for the political and social community, namely, for the polis or the state; thus religion deals with war and peace, guilt and expiation, seed and harvest, family and marriage. The magician, however, has learned to master the powers which lie outside this realm, powers of nature and energies of the cosmos, good and evil demons; he controls the delimitations of human existence: conception and birth, death and underworld, but also such "frontier" experiences as disease, personal calamities, illicit amorous adventures, and travel to foreign countries.

The developments of the late Hellenistic period created a situation in

which magic appeared to many people as more important and more en-
ticing than traditional religion. Two factors paved the way for magic. On
the one hand, philosophy had renounced its allegiance to the state and its
task of providing a political education; instead it had turned to nature, the
cosmos, the soul, and the afterlife. On the other hand, astrology had begun
its victorious advance, advertising its ability to disclose the relationship of
human fate to the powers of the stars. Thus astrology and magic became
allies, because magic had always understood its craft as an intervention
into the mysterious network of the powers of nature and cosmos. Things
celestial and terrestrial, stars and human beings, soul and body, spirit and
matter, word and sacrament, names and gods—all were seen as corresponding parts of the same "scientific" conformity to the principles of the
universe. If one knew the laws of the stars, their powers and names, and if
one knew their closely related counterparts in the terrestrial realm, one
could also influence the stars' powers by correctly manipulating the cosmic energies wherever they were accessible within things under human
control. In this way astrology made it possible for magic to come forward
with its new claim of being a craft which could influence the powers of the
universe. If the fate of human beings was determined by the stars, and if
good and evil demonic powers constantly interfered with human life,
magic offered to make the demons subservient to human interests and to
outwit the dictates of fate.

The magical papyri from the Roman period as well as scattered pieces
of information from other sources demonstrate that magical practice
would employ whatever was available. What was happening was an
unauthorized syncretism that knew no limits. Since any particular cosmic
power might have different names in the various religions, one was forced
to pronounce all of these names in order to adjure that power. Next to the
names of Greek gods one finds the names of Egyptian, Jewish (e.g., Iao =
Yahweh; Sabaoth) and other gods, as well as many mysterious, artificial
terms. The tried and trusty instruments of the craft, which are too numerous to recount here, were supplemented by new tools borrowed from any
and all religious traditions: transcriptions of Hebrew sentences into Greek
(which were then read from left to right, i.e., backwards), liturgical pieces
from the mystery religions of the east or Egypt, recitations of cosmogonies,
manipulations unhesitatingly borrowed from medical or scientific handbooks and combined with old magical practice or religious ritual. Because
this syncretistic process in magic was not restrained by the sanctions of
religious communities and institutions, oriental materials could infiltrate
without impediment. The proportion of Jewish materials in the magical
papyri is striking and is certainly related to the successful activities of

Jewish magicians and the wide distribution of Jewish magical books (often under the authority of Solomon).

It is difficult to overestimate the diffusion and success of magic during the Roman imperial period. Several attempts were made during I BCE to expel the "Chaldaeans" and sorcerers from Rome. But they returned and could be found everywhere, advertising their craft openly in the marketplace or covertly making known by word of mouth where they could be found. It apparently was not very difficult for anybody to seek out a wizard "philosopher," the priestess of a backstreet cult, or a useful magical book. How else could one manage to have an admired sweetheart yield to one's desires, get rid of a political opponent, be healed from a disease which no physician could cure, or make an important business trip despite ill omens! Magicians were badly needed, if people were unwilling to give up in the face of a menacing fate. Magic quickly conquered all classes of the society. Philosophy and religion were as powerless before magic as against the influence of astrology. When in the *Acts of John* the apostle drives out the bedbugs from the inn by his magic art, and when Peter and Simon Magus outdo each other in their conjuring tricks in the *Acts of Peter,* we might wonder whether the frequent accusations of magic in the religious competition in the marketplace do not have some justification. Astrology and magic together had certainly taught the missionary religions that they could be successful only if they could point a way to freedom from the fate of the stars, and to mastery over the demonic powers. Christian and Jewish missionary propaganda, as well as the Egyptian religion and the cult of Mithras, understood this very well. But only the Hermetic religion and Gnosticism incorporated the answer to this challenge into their religious program.

(f) Gnosticism and the Hermetic Religion

Magic could play tricks on the power of fate, but was unable to overcome it. It is true that beginning in the time of Augustus, the Roman empire offered a political program designed to guarantee the internal peace of the realm. This program was largely successful, and a long-lasting economic upturn was the consequence. The existing religions were promoted and strengthened. Political propaganda for the emperor cult was ubiquitous: emperor temples, statues, inscriptions, and coins were witnesses that nobody could miss. Nevertheless, conflicts with the older religions were rare. Few people would consider the propaganda for the emperor cult to be a message of religious salvation. This cult, though quite capable of elucidating the political mission of Rome, was in no position to make sense of the world for those inhabitants of the empire who were serious in their quest for meaning. Philosophy had already decided to bracket this question: metaphysics was not in demand in the schools. The Romans had long since focused their interests upon the political usefulness of philosophical ethics. One could certainly turn away from this world and its busy activities, reprimand its pompous pursuits and its craving for pleasure; one could withdraw into a skeptical distance from all things or become independent in the Cynic's contentedness. But alternately, one could join one of the new missionary movements which offered at least some answers to personal problems and questions.

1) *Gnosticism.* Only one religious movement, however, could claim the ability to answer every question with one single message: Gnosticism. The gnostic religion knew the answer to the central question: what is this world in which human beings live all about? The world was seen as the tragic product of a fateful movement or battle within the deity itself, and humanity, essentially a part of the transcendent deity, as caught in the middle of this tragic event, a foreigner in a world in which it has no business whatsoever. The problem of the world is that it exists at all.

Bibliography to §6.5f (1): Texts

James M. Robinson (ed.), *The Coptic Gnostic Library* (NHS; Leiden: Brill, in process of publication). Edition, translation, introduction, and notes of all writings from the Nag Hammadi Library.

Idem, *The Nag Hammadi Library in English* (Leiden: Brill, and New York: Harper, 1977). English translation with brief introductions of all writings from the Nag Hammadi Library.

Walther Völker (ed.), *Quellen zur Geschichte der christlichen Gnosis* (SQS 5; Tübingen: Mohr/Siebeck, 1932). Greek and Latin texts from the church fathers about the Gnostics.

Robert M. Grant (ed.), *Gnosticism: A Source Book of Heretical Writings from the Early Christian Period* (New York: Harper, 1961). English translations.

Foerster, *Gnosis,* vols. 1–2. English translations.

Bibliography to §6.5f (1): Introductions and Surveys

James M. Robinson, "The Coptic Gnostic Library Today," *NTS* 14 (1967/68) 356–401.

E. H. Pagels, "Gnosticism," *IDBSup* (1976) 364–68.

G. MacRae, "Nag Hammadi," *IDBSup* (1976) 613–19.

John Dart, *The Laughing Savior: The Discovery and Significance of the Nag Hammadi Gnostic Library* (New York: Harper, 1976).

Bibliography to §6.5f (1): Comprehensive treatments

Kurt Rudolf, *Die Gnosis: Wesen und Geschichte einer spätantiken Religion* (Göttingen: Vandenhoeck & Ruprecht, 1978). English translation forthcoming.

Hans Jonas, *The Gnostic Religion* (2d rev. ed.; Boston: Beacon, 1963).

Idem, *Gnosis und spätantiker Geist,* vol, 1: *Die mythologische Gnosis* (FRLANT 51; 1st ed.; 1934; 3d ed.; Göttingen: Vandenhoeck & Ruprecht, 1964), vol. 2: *Von der Mythologie zur mystischen Philosophie* (FRLANT 63; 1st ed.; 1954; 2d ed.; Göttingen: Vandenhoeck & Ruprecht, 1966).

Salvation would mean that the world would return to its nothingness, and that human beings would receive the freedom to return to their divine origin. But when human beings can recognize their true self, the world has already lost its power and its claim upon human existence. This is *gnosis,* knowledge, recognition of one's self and of God—which is one and the same thing. Since humans are caught in this world, imprisoned, ensnared, deluded, and blind, and since they are asleep or intoxicated by this world, a call from the outside is needed to awaken and make them conscious of their true identity. To issue this call in the world is the task of the revealer, the content of whose call is solely the message that human beings belong to God and are foreigners in this world. Those who bear this equality with God in themselves are able to hear this call and recognize themselves through it, with which recognition they are liberated. The remainder of the gnostic message serves to help one find one's way—not in this world, because that is nothing but a tragic abortion, an evil fiction. One must find answers to these questions: where did I come from? why am I here? how do I find my way back? Therefore the gnostic message speaks of the primordial divine beginning (theogony), the tragic and fateful ensnarement (cosmogony), and the "way" of return from the reality of the divine origin (eschatology).

For the historian of religion, however, this description of Gnosticism may not be satisfactory. The comparative history of religions seeks to describe developments, understand dependencies, and present new phen-

Bibliography to §6.5f (1): Studies

Barbara Aland (ed.), *Gnosis: Festschrift für Hans Jonas* (Göttingen: Vandenhoeck & Ruprecht, 1978).

Layton, *Rediscovery of Gnosticism,* vols. 1–2. Collection of conference papers.

Karl-Wolfgang Tröger (ed.), *Altes Testament—Frühjudentum—Gnosis: Neue Studien zu "Gnosis und Bibel"* (Berlin: Evangelische Verlagsanstalt, 1980).

Nock, "Gnosticism," in: idem, *Essays,* 2. 940–59.

Idem, "The Milieu of Gnosticism," in: idem, *Essays,* 1. 444–51.

George MacRae, "The Jewish Background of the Gnostic Sophia Myth," *NovT* 12 (1970) 86–101.

R. M. Grant, *Gnosticism and Early Christianity* (New York: Columbia University, 1959).

Haenchen, "Gab es eine vorchristliche Gnosis?" in: idem, *Gott und Mensch,* 265–98.

Kurt Rudolph (ed.), *Gnosis und Gnostizismus* (WdF 262; Darmstadt: Wissenschaftliche Buchgesellschaft, 1975).

Karlmann Beyschlag, *Simon Magus und die christliche Gnosis* (WUNT 16; Tübingen: Mohr, 1974).

Gershom Sholem, *Jewish Gnosticism, Merkabah Mysticism, and Talmudic Tradition* (2d ed.; New York: Jewish Theological Seminary of America, 1965).

David Scholer, *Nag Hammadi Bibliography, 1948–1969* (NHS 1; Leiden: Brill, 1971); continued as "Bibliographia Gnostica," *NovT* 1971ff.

omena in such a way that it is possible to recognize how they are related to or caused by older religious concepts. Yet the new religious insight of Gnosticism cannot clearly be derived from any one thing. In this respect, it is futile to ask whether Gnosticism derives from Judaism or from Christianity or from Platonism. Neither can the origin of Gnosticism be described in terms of specific historical dependencies and developments. The radical novelty of the gnostic insight makes this impossible. Nevertheless, the general question of its origin cannot be put aside. We do know that the gnostic religion came into existence at a period in history during which social and political identity had become problematic for many people. This became a particularly difficult problem because the previously existing social institutions, such as the polis or a nation state, had been religiously sanctioned and in this way drew their meaning. But now human beings were confronted with a world which was strange and unfamiliar, and which could no longer be meaningfully understood by means of the inherited religious beliefs. There was, to be sure, no lack of suggested solutions. The Stoics had said that people should learn to understand themselves as citizens of the world at large. New religions proclaimed deities which were said to be rulers of the whole universe. But the dominions and jurisdictions of these deities were not identical with the political powers to which the people of the Roman empire were subject. Moreover, if one directed one's gaze to the heavens and the celestial world, one learned that the air was populated by demons who were not necessarily well-disposed toward human beings, that the planets brought more evil days than good, and that the stars of the zodiac pronounced an ironclad law to which even the gods were subject. This experience of the world is the presupposition for the gnostic religion and its message. Gnosticism thus cannot be derived from anything but the experience of the world as a foreign place and of the liberating message of the divine call through which humans were able to recognize themselves and their true being.

But more precise statements can certainly be made about the language of the gnostic message. This is indeed the actual question in the debate about the origin of Gnosticism: in which language of the known religions of antiquity does the gnostic message appear for the first time? There is no question that gnostic writings were composed by authors who claimed to be Christian and who usually, though not always, believed that Jesus was the one who brought the gnostic message. That fact was known as early as II CE. In such writings gnostic faith is sometimes interwoven so closely with Christian traditions and language that it is difficult even today to remove the weeds without destroying the wheat. But many other things are also found in Christian gnostic writings which cannot be readily derived from Christian language and its concepts. Particularly striking are the theogonic and cosmogonic mythologies, the metaphysically based dualism, and the mythic description of the revealer figure.

The early Catholic father Hippolytus (III CE) accused the gnostic heretics of letting reprehensible doctrines from Greek philosophy mislead them into their heretical ideas. With respect to the dualism of the gnostics, Hippolytus was right, to the extent that later Christian gnostics did indeed present their teachings in the terms of Greek philosophy. But in a number of older gnostic writings mythological language and concepts predominate to such a degree that any attempt to show a philosophical derivation is doomed to fail. These mythological materials in the gnostic writings no doubt ultimately derive from the mythical traditions of the ancient Orient. We know very little, however, about the continuance and development of these traditions during the Hellenistic periods. Some features of gnostic dualism may be of Iranian origin, but our knowledge of the Persian religion during that period is so meager that the assumption of an Iranian salvation mystery as the predecessor of the gnostic religion is nothing but an unfounded guess. It is more probable that Canaanite creation myths were used in the formation of gnostic cosmogonies, but such a possible dependence is difficult to verify. However, as late as the Hellenistic and Roman imperial periods, Judaism gives testimony for the reception and critical elaboration of Canaanite and other oriental mythologies. Therefore, we might well ask whether the first testimonies for the development of early gnostic imagery do not in fact belong to the immediate neighborhood of the syncretistic Judaism of that period. It seems probable that this was indeed the case. Further clarification can be expected from the ongoing scholarly investigation of the newly discovered texts from Nag Hammadi (§10.1b; 10.5b; 11.2a).

At least the outlines of the development of gnostic concepts can be sketched with a considerable degree of certainty. If we stress the Jewish component, it should be remembered once again that this does not involve an attempt to "derive" Gnosticism from Judaism. Accepting the gnostic creed would always and at any time entail for a Jew a radical break with his God, the creator of heaven and earth and the lord of the history of Israel. "Deriving" Gnosticism from Judaism is just as improbable as deriving it from Christianity—although in the latter case, the Christian believer is in a much more difficult position because it was left to the fathers of the church to decide how the legitimate Christian beliefs should be defined. During the first and second Christian centuries it would have been much more difficult to find one's way through the labyrinth of various Christian beliefs. But one might still question whether a believing Jew of that time really was in any better position. One of the writings of the period, the Wisdom of Solomon, suggests not, because this book proclaims gnostic theology in a Jewish framework. To be sure, it did not take the step of rejecting the visible creation as a work of evil powers, but sees the wise man as a despised stranger in the world, to which he does not really belong, and where he abides until he recognizes the voice of wisdom in himself and thus his true divine origin (§5.3e). But others drew more radical conclusions. Whether or not they were Jews can be left undecided.

In any case, in the work of elaborating this declaration of the bankruptcy of the whole creation, and especially of the creation of the human race, the first book of the Bible acted as a midwife. Elements of Jewish biblical exegesis of the Hellenistic period are clearly involved. Philo of Alexandria demonstrates that one had learned to distinguish between the true and essential creation of humanity in the sphere of the divine (in the world of ideas in Platonic terms), and the creation of the earthly human beings, which are only secondary copies. Philo also testifies to efforts to understand the process of the unfolding of the divine world which preceded the formation of the visible world (§5.3f). If Philo did not allow the use of astrological and mythical speculations in his description of the creation, he imposed a restriction upon himself as a Jew and as a philosopher that would not necessarily obligate others, especially not in an age of the widespread recrudescence of myth. Philo is also very careful not to make any distinctions between the highest god and a creator god of lower rank, although he knows a figure who is the mediator of creation. But Plato's dialogue, *Timaeus,* in which the figure of a subordinate creator-god, the demiurge, plays a significant role, had long since become a philosophical textbook. Post-exilic Judaism, after all, had learned to understand the course of the world and the nature of humanity in dualistic terms. This dualism appeared in the form of popularized Platonic dualism which had become the decisive vernacular philosophical doctrine, and also in a mythological dualism which spoke about the battle between God and Belial, between an angel of light and an angel of darkness, between the power of evil in history and the transcendent power of God to be revealed in the future (§5.2b–c).

Mythical concepts of wisdom, cosmogony and astrology, dualism and Genesis interpretation, law and apocalypticism, God, demiurge, angels, demons, Satan—one could come to terms with any or all of these at random and eclectically and still remain a law-abiding Israelite, or become a Platonic philosopher, or a messianic fanatic. But to amalgamate all these elements into a new vision of the world and of salvation required a catalyst, which Gnosticism became. It seems that several of the books from the library at Nag Hammadi belong to the earliest period of mythological Gnosticism, in which Christian elements are either completely missing or were superficially introduced at a later date (§10.5b). In such works, such as the *Apocryphon of John,* one can still feel the ravenous appetite caused by this still new gnostic insight. The new formula made it possible to absorb just about everything and to stop short of nothing. Reading some selections of this writing causes something like giddiness. Words and terms which any rational theologian would presumably first weigh carefully are used in the predication of the father-god, recited at breathtaking speed: "For the perfect one is majestic, he is pure and immeasurable greatness. He is an aeon-giving Aeon, life-giving Life, blessedness-giving Blessed One, knowledge-giving Knowledge, goodness-giving Goodness, mercy and redemption-giving Mercy, grace-giving Grace. . . . His aeon is indestructible, at rest and in silence reposing and existing prior to everything," etc. (*Ap. John,* NHC II,1.4,1ff.). This is only a very small section.

What follows is a description of the incomprehensible movement into which god and the aeons fall; Greek terms (Ennoia, Pronoia, Autogenes) are connected with oriental names of gods and angels (Barbelo, Oriel, Daveithai, Pigeraadamas). Then comes the abortion of Sophia, and Yaltabaoth, the demiurge who creates the lower world according to the image of the divine aeons. At this point the author has reached the first verse of the Bible. What follows, however, is not a well-balanced exegesis, but once more the complicated activities of the demiurge and his aides in the creation of Adam. A very elaborate anatomical list is used here, and to each part of the human body an angel is assigned, all with names that are otherwise unknown in religious history. Sentences from Genesis 2–3 to which Philo would have devoted a whole series of commentaries are extemporaneously but pointedly interpreted in brief remarks, stating exactly those things which an upright Jewish exegete would never say under any circumstances, such as that the highest power of the abortive creation has intercourse with Eve and begets Elohim and Yahweh. This is either plain nonsense, or else an ingenious reevaluation of the tradition, unambiguously stating that this world of earthly existence is a monstrous and dangerous miscarriage. It is necessary to know this claim before one can hear the message which appears at the end of the book: "He who has ears, let him get up from deep sleep," and "guard yourself against the angels of poverty and the demons of chaos and all those who ensnare you."

This is, to be sure, only one of the many possible varieties of gnostic expression, yet is still a variant which is closely related to the language in which Gnosticism was first proclaimed. Mythological exegesis of the Book of Genesis is found repeatedly in numerous variations in gnostic writings. But there are other forms of gnostic ideas, including many which are not as offensive to traditional religion and philosophy to the same extent as is frequently the case in mythological Gnosticism. The gnostic message was amazingly well suited for "translation," but the offer of anarchy and the rejection of any meaning for this earthly life, however formulated, always lurks in the background. Gnosticism was particularly productive in the composition of songs and hymns (§10.5c). In such poetic works the description of the tragic event of creation is usually passed over. As an expression of piety, the hymn is best suited for describing the relationship of the human soul to the revealer in which it has found its true self. But the gnostic presuppositions also appear here: the revealer comes from a different world, which has nothing in common with the earthly realm, just as the redemption of the soul vanquishes all earthly powers. Sayings of Jesus were interpreted at a very early date as the call of the gnostic revealer. Traditional apocalyptic sayings were used to designate the transitoriness of the visible world. In the further development of the gnostic sayings tradition, statements about the creation and about the path to the heavenly home of the soul were added (see below on the *Gospel of Thomas* and the *Dialogue of the Savior*, §10.ab). In Jewish Christianity, Gnosticism seized upon the language and tradition of the interpretation of the law, thus dealing with the cosmological dimensions of the Jewish law and with the distinction between false and true pericopes since only the latter derive from the heavenly revealer who appeared in the figure of Moses (§10.4c). In the sources which are still preserved one also finds repeated attempts to reconcile gnostic concepts with analogous Christian traditions. This will be discussed later.

2) *Hermetic Writings*. Another collection of writings, the *Corpus Hermeticum*, mostly preserved in Greek, attempts a reconciliation of Gnos-

---

Bibliography to §6.5f (2): Texts

A. D. Nock and A.-J. Festugière, *Corpus Hermeticum* (4 vols.; Paris: Les Belles Lettres, 1945–54).

"Poimandres," in: Foerster, *Gnosis,* 1. 326–36.

Barrett, *Background,* 82–90.

Bibliography to §6.5f (2): Studies

A.-J. Festugière, *La révélation d'Hermès Trismégiste* (4 vols.; Paris: Gabalda, 1950–54).

G. van Moorsel, *The Mysteries of Hermes Trismegistus* (STRT 1; Domplein, Utrecht: Kemink en zoon, 1955).

Richard Reitzenstein, *Poimandres: Studien zur griechisch-ägyptischen und frühchristlichen Literatur* (Leipzig: Teubner, 1904; reprint: Darmstadt: Wissenschaftliche Buchgesellschaft, 1966).

Haenchen, "Aufbau und Theologie des 'Poimandres,'" in: idem, *Gott und Mensch,* 335–77.

Karl-Wolfgang Tröger, *Mysterienglaube und Gnosis in Corpus Hermeticum XIII* (TU 110; Berlin: Akademie-Verlag, 1971).

W. C. Grese, *Corpus Hermeticum XIII and Early Christian Literature* (SCHNT 5; Leiden: Brill, 1979).

ticism and philosophy. It contains more than two dozen books, in which the Greek god Hermes appears as the heavenly messenger, indeed more than just a messenger: he is revealer, father, personified reason (*nous*), and especially mystagogue, Hermes the Thrice-Greatest (Hermes Trismegistus). Most of the tractates were probably written in II CE by different authors, whose religious and philosophical position varies. But all the tractates have in common an offer of a syncretistic pagan philosophy of religion, which is presented as a revelation that can be taught. Some tractates promote philosophical gnostic teachings (especially I *Poimandres* and XXIII *Kore Kosmou;* there are also two Hermetic tractates among the writings of Nag Hammadi: NHC VI/6 and VI/8); others engage in a controversy with Gnosticism on behalf of an eclectic philosophical religion characterized by a moderated dualism and a pantheistic world view. Mythological statements about the generation of the world, whether as an act of creation, as a physical process, or as the product of emanations, are a major focus of these writings. Astrological speculations are used in almost every instance, sometimes with great elaboration. Religious concepts were drawn from the most diverse segments of Greek religion. But Jewish elements can also be recognized (e.g., in the creation story of *Poimandres*), and some Egyptian influences are present (e.g., Hermes is identified with the Egyptian god Tot).

It appears certain that the Hermetic writings presuppose a pagan Gnosticism which had developed not in the form of philosophical teachings, but as the message of salvation of religious groups which were organized as mystery associations. These writings do not argue in a philosophical manner, as would be expected in writings from a philosophical school, nor is the form of the dialogue used solely as an instrument of literary style. Rather, the dialogues mirror instructions in which the mystagogue introduces the secrets of the mystery initiation, and in which the one who is to be initiated learns the proper questions and answers. This original life situation also produced the many hymns, doxologies, prayers, and fixed proclamations of revelation which appear in these writings. What appears to be philosophical reflection is frequently the interpretation of religious traditions. In their present form, the Hermetic writings are probably no longer liturgical service books, but designed as "reading mysteries," which also are meant to contribute to the philosophical discussion. Was there, indeed, a pagan gnostic mystery religion, independent of Christianity? Traditional scholarship dealing with the *Corpus Hermeticum* often rejected such a conclusion. But in the context of the more recently discovered gnostic texts, it will be advisable once again to consider a positive answer to this question.

6. Palestine and Judaism in the Roman Imperial Period

(a) Herod the Great

In the year 63 BCE, on a Sabbath, Pompey entered the temple of Jerusalem after three months of siege (§5.1d). Hyrcanus was reinstated as high priest, but he was accountable to the Romans for his administration from now on. His brother Aristobulus, whose claim had not been recognized by Pompey, was led as a prisoner in Pompey's triumphal procession in Rome. Later he managed to escape to Judea, but was caught again and poisoned by the Pompeians because they considered him a partisan of Caesar. One of his sons, Alexander (the father of Mariamne, who later became Herod's wife), was decapitated; only his other son Antigonus was able to escape.

When Caesar followed Pompey to Egypt after the battle of Pharsalus, many cities and countries of the east which had previously supported Pompey defected to Caesar. Hyrcanus was among those who hastened to Egypt in order to support Caesar (who had run into difficulties after the murder of Pompey). Hyrcanus' adroit minister, the Idumean Antipater, sent troops to Egypt who rendered valuable service to Caesar. Hyrcanus

Bibliography to §6.6

E. Mary Smallwood, *The Jews under Roman Rule* (SJLA 20; Leiden: Brill, 1976).

Salo Wittmeyer Baron, *A Social and Religious History of the Jews* (vol. 2; 2d ed.; New York: Columbia University, 1966).

Félix Marie Abel, *Histoire de la Palestine depuis la conquête d'Alexandre jusqu'à l'invasion arabe* (vol. 1; Paris: Gabalda, 1952).

Samuel Sandmel, *The First Christian Century in Judaism and Christianity: Certainties and Uncertainties* (New York: Oxford University, 1969).

Joachim Jeremias, *Jerusalem in the Time of Jesus* (London: SCM; and Philadelphia: Fortress, 1969).

Michael Avi-Yonah and Z. Baras (eds.), *The Herodian Period* (The World History of the Jewish People 1,7; New Brunswick, NJ: Rutgers University, 1975).

Morton Smith, "Palestinian Judaism in the First Century," in: Moshe Davis (ed.), *Israel: Its Role in Civilization* (New York: Harper, 1955) 67–81.

David M. Rhoads, *Israel in Revolution: 6–74 C.E.: A Political History Based on the Writings of Josephus* (Philadelphia: Fortress, 1976).

See also the literature under §5, 5.1 and 2.

Bibliography to §6.6a

Stewart Perowne, *The Life and Times of Herod the Great* (London: Hodder and Stoughton, 1956).

Michael Grant, *Herod the Great* (New York: American Heritage, 1971).

Walter Otto, *Herodes* (Stuttgart: Metzler, 1913).

Abraham Shalit, *König Herodes: Der Mann und sein Werk* (Berlin: De Gruyter, 1969).

A. H. M. Jones, *The Herods of Judaea* (2d ed.; Oxford: Clarendon, 1967).

persuaded the powerful Jewish community of Alexandria to support the new ruler. In the following year Antigonus, the last surviving son of Aristobulus, also appeared before Caesar in Syria, in order to submit his claims to rule in Palestine and to the office of high priest in Jerusalem. But Caesar did not seem to trust him, preferring to rely upon Antipater, who had served him so well in Egypt. Thus he awarded Roman citizenship to Antipater and appointed him administrator of Judea, with the rank of Roman procurator. Hyrcanus was confirmed in the office of high priest and received the title of ethnarch. The area of Judea was enlarged and became an allied state, a status which included freedom from certain taxes. The walls of Jerusalem could be rebuilt. Antipater reorganized the administration of the country and appointed his son Phasael as governor (*strategos*) of Judea and Perea and his son Herod as governor of Galilee.

The year of Caesar's assassination (44 BCE) once more tested Antipater's political cleverness. The murderers of Caesar, Brutus and Cassius, attempting to gather an army in the eastern provinces, demanded his support, which they readily received. But the exploitation of the country for the support of Cassius' army increased the unrest in Palestine. Antipater was poisoned in a conspiracy. Later the Hasmonean Antigonus invaded Galilee, but was defeated by Antipater's son Herod. After the luck of Caesar's murderers ran out, Herod had to come to terms with Antony, the new master of the east, and he succeeded in spite of the resistance of Jerusalem. But as soon as Antony had gone to Egypt, the Parthians invaded Syria, and Antigonus was able to conquer Palestine with their help. Hyrcanus and Phasael fell into the hands of the Parthians through deceit. Phasael committed suicide when the Parthians wanted to hand him over to Antigonus. Hyrcanus had his ears cut off by his nephew Antigonus and was thus disqualified for his office as high priest. Herod had seen through the treachery of the Parthians and was able to flee after making his family secure in the fortress of Masada at the Dead Sea.

Antigonus now renewed the Hasmonean rule in Palestine and minted coins which proclaimed him as "High priest Mattathias" in Hebrew and as "King Antigonus" in Greek. But it was not long before the Romans began to take measures against the Parthian rule in Syria. Herod had travelled to Rome and had succeeded in obtaining the support of the triumvirs, whereupon the Senate appointed him king of Judea. As soon as the Romans had driven the Parthians out of Syria, Herod could assume his rule in Israel. Jerusalem was conquered and Antigonus killed; Herod was the master of the country. The conflict between Octavian and Antony, however, once more threatened Herod's position. Herod had been a favorite of Antony, who fled to Egypt after the battle of Actium and committed suicide. In a clever and impressive move Herod travelled to Rhodes, where

Octavian was staying, and laid his crown at the feet of the victor. Octavian accepted the gesture, reinstated Herod in his rights as king of Judea, and a year later added the Palestinian coast, Samaria, and Jericho to his realm (30 BCE). On a later occasion Herod also received the areas north and east of the Galilean Sea. This realm he ruled until his death in 4 BCE as an absolute despot and Augustus' faithful vassal.

HERODIANS AND PREFECTS

63 BCE	Pompey enters Jerusalem temple
63–40	Hyrcanus high priest, later ethnarch
40–38	Antigonus high priest and king
38–4	Herod the Great

Judea		*Galilee*	
4 BCE–6 CE	Archelaus	4 BCE–39 CE	Antipas tetrarch
6–41 CE	Prefects:		
6–9	Coponius		
9–12	Ambibulus		
12–15	Annius Rufus		
15–26	Valerius Gratus		
26–36	Pontius Pilatus		
36–37	Marcellus	39–41	Agrippa I

Palestine	
41–44	Agrippa I king
44–66	Procurators:
44–46	Fadus
46–48	Tiberius Alexander
48–52	Cumanus
53–58	Felix
58–62	Festus
62–64	Albinus
64–66	Gessius Florus
66–70(73)	Jewish War

Herod's loyalty to Augustus and to Rome was real. He did not, as did Antigonus shortly before, renew the old ideals of the Hasmonean rule. In his internal policies it soon became clear that he was emulating Augustus' policies of peace. Under Augustus Rome promoted the Greek cities, reconstituted them, and granted various privileges. Herod followed this example in his small kingdom. In the place of the ancient northern capital of Samaria, which had been refounded by Alexander but was destroyed by the Hasmoneans, Herod established a splendid city, calling it "Sebaste" in honor of Augustus; only now did Samaria experience its greatest flowering. On the Palestinian coast he built a completely new city, entirely in the Hellenistic style, which rose to become a significant port and later the seat of the Roman governor, and was called Caesarea in honor of Augustus Caesar. A number of other cities were reestablished or renewed. Herod's second concern was to strengthen the fortresses at the eastern border of his realm, including the fortress of Masada at the Dead Sea. Finally, Herod spent large sums of money for buildings in Jerusalem, most importantly for the erection of a new temple. Its foundations were enlarged (the famous Wailing Wall is part of these Herodian foundations), and the temple was completely rebuilt. Herod also attended to the other holy shrines of Israel, like the shrine of Abraham in Mamre, though he did not neglect the pagan cults in his country: a temple for the emperor cult was added to the shrine of Pan at the sources of the Jordan.

These extensive building projects demonstrate not only that Herod was capable of exacting large sums of money from his country, but also that there was an unusual prosperity and considerable economic growth in Palestine during his rule. After many years of war and unrest, peace had finally returned to the land of Israel, and all its inhabitants could profit from the blessings of the new age. Nevertheless, Herod never succeeded in his attempts to become reconciled with the Jewish people. The splendor and cruelty of his rule combined to establish his image as a tyrant. Although he eagerly supported the institutions of the Jewish religion, it was never forgotten that he was an Idumean (the Idumeans had been forcibly converted to Judaism by the Hasmoneans) and that his kingdom relied upon the favor of the Romans, whose rule remained a hated foreign dominion for the Jewish people. Neither the Pharisees nor the Sadducees seem to have supported Herod, although they had no choice but to acquiesce. The tragedies of Herod's family history apparently contributed to his bad reputation. He had his second wife, the Hasmonean Mariamne, put to death because he suspected that she had been involved in a conspiracy against him. Furthermore the former high priest Hyrcanus, the last Hasmonean, was murdered by Herod at the advanced age of eighty. At the end of his rule, Herod executed his two sons from his marriage with Mariamne (Alexander and Aristobulus; 7 BCE), and shortly before his death he eliminated his oldest son Antipater (4 BCE). Thus it is not surprising that Herod is remembered as the murderer of the children of Bethlehem (Matt 2:16–18). When he died unrest broke out in Palestine for the first time after several decades, while Rome discussed the question of his successor. Varus, who was legate of Syria at that time, had to move to Palestine with his army to suppress the insurrection. Several cities were destroyed and more than two thousand leaders of the uprising killed.

(b) Palestine under the Sons of Herod

In his testament Herod the Great had divided the land among his sons Archelaus, Antipas, and Philip. A delegation from Jerusalem tried to persuade Augustus not to continue this hated dynasty. But Augustus decided to recognize the testament of his long-standing friend and faithful vassal. Archelaus received Judea and Samaria, which amounted to about half of the territory that his father had ruled. He was awarded the title "ethnarch," with the promise that he would later become king, if his administration went well. This, however, was not the case; Archelaus was deposed in 6 CE and exiled to Vienne in Gaul. Archelaus is the "king" whom Joseph feared when he came back to Bethlehem from Egypt and instead moved to Nazareth in Galilee (Matt 2:22), where, however, another son of Herod ruled.

Antipas was appointed "tetrarch" of Galilee and Perea, which he ruled from 4 BCE to 39 CE. He was the true son of his father; cunning, cruel, but also fond of splendor, yet without true greatness. He continued his father's building program, first enlarged his capital, Sepphoris—only a few miles from Nazareth—then built a second on the shores of the Galilean Sea, which he called "Tiberias" in honor of the emperor (ca. 20 CE). This city had a predominantly pagan population, and it is interesting to note that Jesus apparently never went there. But in II CE, Tiberias became the metropolis of rabbinic Judaism. Antipas is the "Herod" mentioned in Luke 3:1 as tetrarch of Galilee; Jesus called him "this fox" (Luke 13:32). He also appears in Luke 23:6–16 as Jesus' sovereign, to whom Jesus is sent by Pilate for interrogation. Finally, Antipas is remembered by the New Testament gospels and by Josephus (*Ant.* 18.116–119) as the murderer of John the Baptist. Antipas was first married to a Nabatean princess; she left him, however, when she heard that Antipas intended to marry his niece Herodias (the sister of the later king Agrippa I, a granddaughter of Herod the Great and Mariamne), who was the wife of Antipas' brother Herod (Mark 6:14–19 erroneously calls her the wife of Philip, the tetrarch of Trachonitis; later copies of the gospel try to correct this mistake). John the Baptist had publicly attacked Antipas because of this scandal, an act which cost him his head. But according to the account of Josephus, it finally also cost Antipas his kingdom, because the separa-

Bibliography to §6.6b

Stewart Perowne, *The Later Herods* (London: Hodder and Stoughton, 1958; New York: Abingdon, 1959).

Harold W. Hoehner, *Herod Antipas* (Cambridge: Cambridge University, 1972).

tion from his former wife led to a further deterioration of relations with the neighboring kingdom of Nabatea. In repeated border wars, Antipas was finally beaten so badly by the Nabatean king Aretas (the same Aretas from whom Paul escaped at Damascus; 2 Cor 11:32) that the Syrian legate Vitellius had to come to his aid. This seems to have been the reason for his deposition and banishment to Lyon in Gaul by Caligula (39 CE), when Antipas applied to Rome to be awarded the title "king." It is not unlikely that Antipas' nephew Agrippa was involved in devising the accusations which were brought against him. In any case, Agrippa inherited his uncle's tetrachy (§6.6d).

The third of the successors of Herod the Great was his son Philip, who became tetrarch of the areas north and east of the Galilean Sea: Trachonitis, Gaulanitis, and Auranitis. He built his residence at the foot of Mt. Hermon and called it "Caesarea" in honor of Augustus; in order to distinguish this city from Caesarea Maritima on the Mediterranean Sea, it became known as Caesarea Philippi (see Mark 8:27f, the so-called confession of Peter at Caesarea Philippi). The large village of Bethsaida at the northern influx of the Jordan River into the Galilean Sea, mentioned several times in the gospels, was expanded into a city by Philip and called "Julia" in honor of Augustus' daughter. Not much is known about Philip's rule. He seems to have been a just and reasonable petty prince. His wife was his grand-niece Salome, the daughter of Herodias, who is said to have asked for the head of John the Baptist when she was at the court of Antipas. Philip died in 34 CE without leaving an heir.

(c) Judea under Roman Administration

After Archelaus had been deposed from office (6 CE), Augustus administered the districts of Judea, Samaria, and Idumea through a prefect (*praefectus cum iure gladii;* §6.3a) who was directly responsible to the emperor, but had to depend on the legate of Syria for military aid. The Syrian legate also remained the highest Roman administrator for the coastal area from Jamnia to Gaza and for the Decapolis. Quirinius (Luke 2:2) became the new legate of Syria, Coponius the first prefect of Judea. Because this was the first time that Judea had come under direct Roman administration, a "census" (ἀπογραφή) was made, that is, an establishment of tax records. Luke used the information about this census in order to provide a motive for the travel of Jesus' parents from Nazareth in Galilee to Bethlehem in Judea—a quite improbable assumption, because Nazareth did not belong to the area of direct Roman jurisdiction. The census in 6 CE caused rebellions, instigated by a radical Jewish group. The identity of this resistance movement is not clear. There is no evidence that it was made up of "Zealots," since Josephus uses this term exclusively for the terrorists under the leadership of John of Gishala at the beginning of the Jewish War. The seat of government for the new prefect became Caesarea (Maritima). Only during the high festival days did the prefect reside in Jerusalem; a strong permanent garrison was stationed in the fortress of Antonia, which was situated next to the temple. The other fortresses of the country were also garrisoned by Roman soldiers.

The country was divided into eleven toparchies, each headed by a Jewish sanhedrin (*synedrion*) with jurisdiction over all petty lawsuits. More important cases had to be referred to the sanhedrin in Jerusalem. The jurisdiction, however, of this central Jewish court was also limited. Accusations which involved the death penalty had to be brought before the prefect's court. The prefect was also responsible for the collection of direct taxes, which was accomplished through the salaried officials who were assisted by the local sanhedrins. Indirect taxes and customs duties were farmed out, as was customary then, to private tax collectors (publicans). This practice often gave rise to complaints and unrest. The tax farmers, who collaborated voluntarily with the Roman administration and frequently became quite wealthy, had a poor reputation, both in Judea and elsewhere (see the gospels' references to the despised publicans). The high priest was appointed by the prefect who otherwise did not interfere in the Jewish temple cult, public worship services, and the peculiarities of Jewish legal observance. The Roman soldiers were also advised not to take their ensigns with them into Jerusalem in order to avoid unnecessary offence to Jewish sensibilities.

The first two decades of the Roman administration of Judea seem to have been relatively free of friction; no major case of unrest is known before 26 CE. Pontius Pilate was sent to Judea in that year as the fifth prefect of the district. (The title *praefectus*, not *procurator*, is now attested for Pilate by an inscription found in Caesarea.) Difficulties mounted and incidents of unrest increased under his administration. He brought the Roman military ensigns into Jerusalem, but had to withdraw them because of widespread public protest. Tumults broke out when he began to build a major aqueduct meant to improve the water supply of Jerusalem, but Pilate quelled them ruthlessly. He did not hesitate to order on-the-spot executions by his soldiers, as is evident from the incident alluded to in Luke 13:1. Similarly, in the case of Jesus, Pilate was quick in sentencing and executing a potential agitator. When Pilate proceeded too recklessly and brutally against a movement of religious fanatics in Samaria, the Syrian legate Vitellius recommended that he be recalled. He had to appear in Rome to give account for his conduct of office. It seems that he was forced to commit suicide (36 CE).

(d) Agrippa I and Agrippa II

After Caligula had become emperor in 37 CE, one of his first official actions was to appoint his friend Agrippa, grandson of Herod the Great and Mariamne, to be tetrach of Abilene (a small district north of the sources of the Jordan) and of the country of Philip's tetrarchy, which had become vacant three years before. Two years later, Antipas was removed from his tetrarchy, and Agrippa, probably involved in his uncle's removal, became his successor. In the same year Caligula ordered that his statue should be placed in the temple of Jerusalem. In 40/41 CE the Syrian legate Petronius went to Palestine in order to lend force to the emperor's order, but he withdrew, realizing that to enforce the order would lead to revolution. But before Petronius and Agrippa could attempt to persuade the emperor to withdraw his mad order, Caligula was assassinated (§6.2a). Agrippa played a significant role in the choice of Claudius as Caligula's successor, who demonstrated his gratefulness by appointing the tetrarch of Galilee as king over all the former territories of his grandfather Herod the Great.

From 41 to 44 CE Agrippa I was king, by the grace of Rome, over the entire area of ancient Israel. In contrast to Herod the Great and his sons, Agrippa enjoyed the goodwill of the leading circles of the Jewish people, perhaps because he was a legitimate descendent of the old Hasmonean house through his grandmother Mariamne. In Jerusalem the king made great efforts to appear to be a pious and law-abiding Jew, promoting the Jewish religion forcefully, and taking measures against the enemies of Judaism according to the will of its Jerusalem leadership. For example, the apostle James, son of Zebedee, was executed by Agrippa, as is known from Acts 12:1ff. In his political capital Caesarea, on the other hand, Agrippa played the role of an oriental petty king. A conference with other Syrian petty kings was broken up by the Syrian legate because it looked like a conspiracy. The Syrian legate also prevented Agrippa from building a third city wall around Jerusalem. What kind of plans Agrippa would actually have finally pursued remains unknown, since he died unexpectedly from some disease in 44 CE.

Agrippa left a son of the same name who was still underage. Agrippa II did not become his father's successor even when he had reached his majority. Rather, in 50 CE he received Chalcis, a small principality in the northern part of the valley between the mountain ranges of Lebanon and Antilebanon. In 53 he was permitted to exchange Chalcis for the former tetrarchy of Philip. He also received Abilene, and later parts of Galilee along with Tiberias. In addition, he was given responsibility for the supervision of the temple in Jerusalem. Agrippa II kept his realm until his death in ca. 100 CE. He did not participate in the Jewish War, but remained loyal to the Romans. Agrippa II never played a significant political role. The author of the book of Acts remembers him as the king Agrippa who visited with the Roman procurator Festus during the trial of Paul, and who admits that Paul had almost persuaded him to become a Christian (Acts 25–26; esp. 26:28). At that time Agrippa was accompanied by his sister Berenice, formerly the wife of his uncle, who was said to have lived in incestuous relationship with her brother, and who later became the mistress of the Roman general Titus who afterwards became emperor.

(e) Palestine before the Fall of Jerusalem

After the death of Agrippa I, Rome organized the whole area of Palestine as a Roman province and made some attempts to gain firm control over this restless country. It is difficult to say whether these efforts had any success, because our primary sources for this period are the writings of the Jewish historian Josephus, who seeks to demonstrate that the blunders of an incompetent Roman administration were ultimately responsible for the destruction of his people. Therefore, we hear very little about those periods in the Roman administration in which peace prevailed. As far as the years immediately before the outbreak of the war are concerned, Josephus' contention seems to be justified.

The first procurator of this period was Fadus (44–46 CE). At the beginning of his administration he had to quell several minor rebellions with the help of the Syrian legate Cassius Longinus. He also forced the Jews to surrender the garments of the high priest, which had been in Jewish custody during the reign of Agrippa I (later they passed into the hands of Agrippa II). The insurrection of Theudas, incorrectly dated by the book of Acts in the time before the revolt of Judas the Galilean (6 CE; see Acts 5:36), seems to have occurred under Fadus' administration. Theudas, the leader of a messianic-prophetic movement, was executed. Fadus' successor was Tiberius Alexander (46–48 CE), scion of a rich Jewish family from Alexandria, and nephew of the philosopher Philo (he later became prefect of Egypt; see §5.3f). After him, Cumanus became procurator (48 CE).

In the year 51, a Jewish pilgrim to Jerusalem who dared to travel through Samaria was murdered by the Samaritans. The Jewish leaders in

Bibliography to §6.6e

David M. Rhoads, *Israel in Revolution: 6–74 C.E.* (Philadelphia: Fortress, 1976).

Martin Hengel, *Die Zeloten: Untersuchungen zur jüdischen Freiheitsbewegung in der Zeit von Herodes I. bis 70 n. Chr.* (AGSU 1; 2d ed.; Leiden: Brill, 1976).

Jerusalem demanded strict punishment of the guilty persons from Cumanus. When Cumanus did not comply, the Jews themselves undertook a
punitive expedition into Samaria, burned several villages, and massacred
the population. This time Cumanus became active, now taking measures
against the more recent troublemakers, namely, the Jews. This brought
the intervention of the Syrian legate Quadratus, who feared that the
conflict might become more widesprad. Quadratus made short work of the
whole affair and sent all parties involved to Rome to defend their cause
and to settle their quarrel: Cumanus, the leaders of the Jews, and the
leaders of the Samaritans. The negotiations apparently took place in
Rome during the summer and fall of the year 52. As a result, the high
priest Jonathan and the powerful imperial secretary Pallas agreed that
the Jews could return unpunished, if they petitioned the emperor to send
Pallas' brother Felix, a freedman, to Palestine as procurator. This turned
out to be a disastrous move. It was only through the favor of the powerful
Pallas that an incompetent former slave could be appointed to an office
which was traditionally reserved for a member of the equestrian class, and
only as long as Pallas' position in the imperial court was secure could
Felix hold on to his office as procurator.

Since Felix was probably appointed in the fall, he could scarcely have
assumed the duties of his office before the spring of 53 CE. It is at least in
part due to Felix's incompetence that the years of his administration were
filled with disturbances and tumults. During this period the Sicarii made
their first appearance, revolutionaries who carried daggers under their
clothing and used every possible opportunity to assassinate people suspected of collaboration with Rome. Felix cruelly suppressed a religious
uprising involving a huge crowd of people who went into the wilderness to
await the coming of the messiah, and an insurrection under the "Egyptian
prophet." Among the disturbances which were quelled by the Jewish
authorities in collaboration with the Roman administration was a tumult
in the temple caused by the Christian apostle Paul, who had been recognized there and was accused of having brought a gentile in with him. In
this case the procurator also intervened and Paul was arrested (§9.4b–c).

The dating of the end of Felix's term is problematic, which probably
means that an important date for Pauline chronology also remains uncertain. Acts 24:27 speaks of a period of two years after which Felix was
replaced by Festus, and by these "two years" it means the time of Paul's
imprisonment in Ceasarea. This would allow a dating of the imprisonment of Paul in the last years of the sixth decade, namely, 58–60. This
seems to be corroborated by Josephus, who has very little to tell about
Festus' administration, except that he died in office in 62; thus he apparently was procurator for only a very short period. Several scholars have

understood the "two years" of Acts 24:27 to refer to the time of Felix's procuratorship; in Luke's source this time period would not have been connected with Paul's imprisonment. In connection with this hypothesis, we could also mention Josephus' report that the Jewish authorities had accused Felix before Nero, but the intervention of his brother Pallas, at that time still in good standing with Nero, saved him from punishment (*Ant.* 29.182). Tacitus (*Ann.* 13.15) says that Pallas fell out of favor with Nero shortly before the murder of Britannicus in December of 55. Thus, this hypothesis concludes, Pallas' intervention on behalf of his brother and Felix's replacement as procurator must be dated no later than the fall of the year 53. Felix's administration would then be limited to the two years beginning in 53, and Paul would have been imprisoned in the summer of 55, brought to trial before Festus, and sent on to Rome shortly thereafter.

This combination of various data seems ingenious, but the difficulties which arise for Pauline chronology from it are considerable (§9.1c; 9.3b–c; 9.4b–c). The immensely rich Pallas probably did not lose all of his influence, even when he fell out of Nero's favor. Thus he might have intervened with the emperor on behalf of his brother at some later date. He was not put to death by Nero until 62. As will be argued below, the internal chronology of the Pauline mission suggests a somewhat later date for Paul's arrest in Jerusalem. On the other hand, the administration of Festus should not be calculated as too short a period. Probably it covered the years 58–62. The competent Burrus still held the reins of the Roman government at the end of the 50s, and the appointment of a competent procurator for the restless province of Palestine is therefore not unlikely during those years of Nero's rule. The fact that Festus was a qualified and prudent administrator may have been the reason for Josephus' silence about the years of his procuratorship.

Festus died in 62 while still in office, causing a vacancy which was used by the leaders of the Jewish community to do away with some unwelcome people. The Jewish sanhedrin did not have the authority to execute wrongdoers. As far as is known, such sentences were never passed by the sanhedrin, not even in the case of Jesus of Nazareth, who was sentenced by the Roman court of the procurator. The martyrdom of Stephen seems to be an exception (§8.3b); but Luke's sources apparently told of a case of lynching, not an orderly execution by the Jewish authorities. Another doubtful case is the execution of Jesus' brother James, which, however, took place during the vacancy after the death of the procurator Festus. Perhaps it was this event which prompted the Christian community of Jerusalem to emigrate to Pella; Pella was a city of the Decapolis which fell under the direct administration of the Syrian legate, while the rest of the country east of the Jordan was at that time subject to Agrippa II.

Albinus, sent from Rome as Festus' successor, was procurator from 62 to 64. According to the report of Josephus, he was incredibly corrupt, and his successor Gessius Florus (64–66) seems to have been even worse. His incompetence created a situation which provided every opportunity for the anti-Roman elements in the country to incite further unrest and consciously steer a course that would result in war with Rome. A feud between the Jewish and Greek parts of the population of Caesarea in 66 opened the hostilities of the Jewish War. Was the procurator hesitant to interfere? Did he simply not know what to do? It was the kind of conflict which could have been settled easily with a little good will on all sides. Construction work on a lot next to a synagogue had obstructed part of the synagogue's entrance. It remains inexplicable why Gessius Florus went to Jerusalem shortly afterwards and seized some of the temple's treasure—the situation was tense enough without such an outrageous action. When the population of Jerusalem protested, he permitted his soldiers to plunder the city. But Gessius Florus had to give way to the fury of the people and withdrew to Caesarea. Open rebellion was thus now a fact, and Josephus describes the events in such a way that the reader can have no doubt: the incredible stupidity and brutality of the Roman procurator was responsible for the actual outbreak of hostilities.

There can be little doubt that Josephus thereby had indeed pointed to one important factor which brought the beginning of the war. During the last years of Nero's rule the once well-functioning Roman administration had been severely impaired. Incompetent and disreputable lackeys had received responsible positions; supervision and control by the emperor and his closest associates had practically ceased to exist. The behavior of the procurator Gessius Florus is to that extent a typical product of the late-Neronian period. Nevertheless, it is necessary to reflect upon the reasons for the outbreak of the Jewish War from the Jewish side. The repeated messianic disturbances, including the activities of Jesus, prove that eschatological aspirations and hopes were by no means dead among the people, but exercised a considerable influence among wide circles of the population. In some instances the lower classes may have been those most prepared to follow the call of a messianic prophet. But at the beginning of the Jewish War, a radical political-eschatological spirit also took hold of the younger generation of the upper classes. The leader of the rebellion which threw Gessius Florus out of Jerusalem was the son of the high priest. Josephus, also a member of the upper class, tries of course in his presentation to emphasize his own wisdom and insight, but he cannot deny that he himself, just thirty years old, belonged to the aristocratic leaders of the rebellion: in the organization of the military resistance he became the commanding general of the Galilean army.

The whole summer of the year 66, while the Romans did nothing, was filled with negotiations in which the elders of the people, led by the high priest and supported by Agrippa II, tried to persuade the rebels to come around to a negotiated peace. But when the king's three thousand mounted soldiers, brought in to lend force to Agrippa's and the high priest's position, were driven out of Jerusalem, the Syrian legate Cestius Gallus decided to intervene (autumn of 66). He appeared before Jerusalem, but the rebels now held full power and control in the city. Cestius Gallus was not prepared for such strong resistance, and since he was unable to seize Jerusalem, he withdrew. His army was attacked by the rebels on its retreat and suffered heavy casualties. The legate himself could escape only with great difficulty. These events demonstrate that the Romans had to cope with more than the simple indignation of the people caused by the incompetence of a Roman procurator; rather, they were confronted with a movement that was inspired by revolutionary messianic ideas and that had the allegiance of large parts of the whole population.

Characteristic for the political messianism of the rebellion was the appearance of a group which Josephus calls the "Zealots." They cannot be related to any other messianic movement of an earlier period. Several of Josephus' remarks about the Zealots of the Jewish War reveal that they subscribed to a religious ideology which was more radical than the ideas of the young aristocratic leaders of the rebellion's first year. Josephus himself soon discovered that it was difficult to come to terms with one of the leaders of these Zealots, when he tried to build up the military organization of the Jewish resistance in Galilee: John of Gishala repeatedly frustrated his plans and also tried to persuade the leaders in Jerusalem to remove Josephus as commander-in-chief. Meanwhile, however, Nero had come to understand that something had to be done about the rebellion in Palestine. While he was spending his time in Greece "winning" one contest after the other in the various Greek games, Nero entrusted the suppression of the rebellion to the experienced general Vespasian. During the winter of 66/67 Vespasian gathered three legions and various auxiliary troops; he started the actual campaign in the spring of 67. Galilee was his first target. After a siege of several weeks, Josephus had to submit to the conquest of his main fortress at Jotapata. He surrendered himself to the Romans, and as a valuable prisoner and advisor he was kept in the camp of Vespasian, whom he prophesied would someday become emperor. John of Gishala, the leader of the Zealots, managed to escape to Jerusalem, where he succeeded in gaining the upper hand among the Jewish commanders.

While Jerusalem was dominated henceforth by often bloody feuds between the radical and moderate factions, Vespasian was able to conquer the major part of the country by the spring of 68—including Qumran, the seat of the Essenic community, which had joined the rebels. But the death of Nero in the summer of 68 and the struggle for his succession (§6.2a) delayed the further progress of the war. A radical group of Zealots led by Simon bar Giora managed to force their way into Jerusalem, and John of Gishala was compelled to share the command with this new leader. Vespasian began the siege of the capital in the spring of 69, though the continuing disturbance about Nero's succession brought a new interruption of the Roman war efforts. This gave a new respite to the revolutionaries which, however, was spent with internal quarrels. In the summer, Vespasian was proclaimed emperor and left the command of the operations in Judea to his son Titus. Since Titus now commanded four well-trained legions, the outcome could not be in doubt. The siege proper started in the spring of 70. By September, the several parts of Jerusalem had been conquered in succession. The temple went up in flames, though this was not intended by the conquerors. The temple's treasures, however, were saved and subsequently carried in the triumph of Titus as still depicted on the Arch of Titus in Rome. The last fortress, Masada, was not conquered until 73. When the defenders of Masada finally committed suicide in the face of their hopeless situation, the dream of political messianism was buried—at least for the time being. Jerusalem became the Roman city Aelia Capitolina, and no Jew was henceforth permitted to set foot within it. The Samaritan capital Shechem became Neapolis (Nablus). Those among the Pharisees who had not been compromised by the war gathered in the coastal city of Jamnia, attempting to build a new form of Judaism without the temple and its priests. As rabbinic Judaism it proved capable of outlasting the centuries.

(f) Judaism after the Destruction of Jerusalem

1) *Sources and Beginnings.* Almost no direct sources are preserved for the history of Judaism in the last part of I and throughout II CE. The oldest writings of rabbinic Judaism (the *Mishnah* and the older *Midrashim*; see below) were not put in written form until about 200 CE, with the traditions contained in these sources typically embedded in later school discussions and blended with legendary materials. Moreover, these writings show no interest in the historical situations of the traditions they preserve, but emphasize solely their legal value. As for the later Jewish apocalyptic writings (*4 Ezra* and *2 Baruch*, both from the end of I CE, and the *Apocalypse of Enoch,* preserved in Ethiopic, which was composed from older sources in II CE), it is quite uncertain how much and in what way they relate to rabbinic Judaism. The sparse information of the historians is anything but impartial; this is also true of Josephus' work on the *Jewish*

Antiquities, with its clearly pro-Pharisaic bent. We have gained interesting insights from the Jewish synagogues, of which many have been excavated quite recently, especially in Galilee, but also elsewhere. (Half a century ago, the synagogue of Dura Europus in Mesopotamia attracted much attention; the recent excavations of the synagogue in Sardis are also important.) But only rarely is it possible to date any of these synagogues as early as I CE; most were built between II and V CE.

Many problems also exist in determining the predecessors of the rabbinic Judaism which developed after the Jewish War. There is no doubt, to be sure, that rabbinic Judaism developed from the movement of the Pharisees (§5.2d). But this statement describes its predecessors both too narrowly and yet also too vaguely. The assumption of a succession of five pairs of rabbis extending from Simon the Just (who was high priest ca. 200 BCE; see §5.1b) to Hillel and Shammai explains very little—not to speak of the fiction of the "Great Synagogue" which is said to have been in existence since Ezra's time. It is necessary to recall two facts which gained great significance in Judaism during the Hellenistic period: the central position of the Bible (especially the five books of Moses) and the democratization of learning. In the ideal concept of the *synedrion* (Hebrew "sanhedrin"), projected into the time of Simon the Just, all classes of people are represented, which is an appropriate symbol for this movement in which many circles of Judaism participated, including the diaspora. Only the Sadducees stood aside from this process. With their literalistic

---

Bibliography to §6.6f

Michael Avi-Yonah, *Geschichte der Juden im Zeitalter des Talmuds* (Berlin: De Gruyter, 1962).

Johann Maier, *Geschichte der jüdischen Religion* (GLB; Berlin: De Gruyter, 1972) 92–211.

George Foot Moore, *Judaism in the First Centuries of the Christian Era: The Age of the Tannaim* (3 vols.; Cambridge, MA: Harvard University, 1927–30; reprint, 1966–67).

Jacob Neusner, *Early Rabbinic Judaism: Historical Studies in Religion, Literature and Art* (SJLA 13; Leiden: Brill, 1975).

Jean Juster, *Les Juifs dans l'empire romain* (2 vols.; Paris: Geuthner, 1914; reprint, 1965).

Wolfgang Harnisch, *Verhängnis und Verheissung der Geschichte: Untersuchungen zum Zeit- und Geschichtsverständnis im 4. Buch Esra und in der syrischen Baruchapokalypse* (FRLANT 97; Göttingen: Vandenhoeck & Ruprecht, 1969).

Hugo Mantel, *Studies in the History of the Sanhedrin* (HSS 17; Cambridge, MA: Harvard University, 1961).

Saul Lieberman, *Hellenism in Jewish Palestine: Studies in the Literary Transmission, Beliefs, and Manners of Palestine in the I Century B.C.E.–IV Century C.E.* (2d ed.; TSJTSA 18; New York: The Jewish Theological Seminary of America, 1962).

Gershom Sholem, *Gnosticism, Merkabah Mysticism, and Talmudic Tradition* (2d ed.; New York: Jewish Theological Seminary of America, 1965).

interpretation of the Bible, they were the guardians of the ancient religious institutions (temple, sacrifices; see §5.2a). During the Roman period, the Sadducees also bore the political responsibility, through their control over the Jerusalem sanhedrin, which was chaired by the high priest. But outside of Jerusalem, especially in the diaspora outside of Palestine, Jews had long since learned to adjust their religion to the new situation, and to solve moral, legal, and ritual questions on the basis of the ancient texts with the use of new methods of biblical exegesis. Thus a new tradition of interpretation was developed in the synagogues which was no longer controlled by the priests.

Certain traditions of interpretation were already fixed in I CE. But there was no uniformity, not even within the Pharisaic movement itself, to which Paul belonged as much as Hillel and Shammai. The sanhedrin in Jerusalem could not possibly have been interested as an institution in the creation of a unified tradition of interpretation. Its task, like that of the many local sanhedrins which were founded in the Roman districts of Palestine, was the immediate concern of fiscal and legal administration, for which it was accountable to the Roman authorities. Since the Sadducees also would have determined the ties to the temple ritual, there was little chance that the sanhedrin would concern itself with novel alternatives in biblical interpretation. The question has been much disputed whether there was also, in addition to the official Jerusalem sanhedrin, a private religious institution of a Pharisaic sanhedrin which was widely recognized among the Aramaic-speaking Jews. Such an organization might have proceeded from the Hasidim of the Maccabean period. In this case, the rabbinic sanhedrin of Jamnia could be seen as a continuation of this Pharisaic institution, not of the official sanhedrin of Jerusalem.

But the hypothesis of a special Pharisaic sanhedrin is burdened with too many difficulties. An obvious problem arises from the observation that the rabbis of Jamnia did not use the term "sanhedrin," but spoke of the "Law Court" (*Beth-Din*) headed by a president (*Nasi*) and a vice-president (*Ab Beth-Din*). Moreover, the leading Pharisees of Jerusalem would have been members of two sanhedrins, since they certainly belonged to the official sanhedrin. But, most of all, this hypothesis underestimates the creative power of the Jewish synagogue, which simultaneously was the center of a religious association and school house, the base of religious propaganda, and the house of worship (§5.1e). Of course, the synagogue was not capable of creating a worldwide unity in Judaism—it was a long road to that unity even after the founding of the *Beth-Din* in Jamnia. For the time being, the Alexandrian philosopher Philo had just as much place in the synagogue as Hillel from Babylon, or Jesus, Paul, and many Christians of the first generation. But there was unity in one respect: the question of the temple ritual was secondary to the interpretation of the Bible. The question of conduct, including problems of ritual purity, was the primary concern. The often complex legal discussions of questions of conduct (*halachah*), therefore, must have begun to be formed already before the destruction of the temple, not to mention the further development of proclamation (*haggadah*), mystical interpretation, and apocalyptic speculation.

2) *Hillel.* What would give to later rabbinic Judaism its characteristic mark was the practice of legal interpretation in the Babylonian synagogue. Hillel (who lived until about 20 CE) came from Babylon. He may have also studied in Jerusalem, but his exegetical principles, which together with his humaneness became determinative for rabbinic Judaism, reveal the diaspora situation, for which legislation related to the temple cult and to living conditions in an overwhelmingly Jewish country were of only academic interest. This perspective as well as his great gifts as a teacher made Hillel the father of rabbinic Judaism—much more so than his famous exegetical rules, like the conlusion *a minore ad maius* and the conclusion from analogy. In contrast, his often-quoted opponent Shammai represents a branch of Pharisaism which was closely related to the temple. Shammai is aristocratic, severe, and nationalistic. But Gamaliel I, Hillel's successor as the head of his school (probably a son of Hillel) had also become a member of the Jerusalem aristocracy. He was a member of the Jerusalem sanhedrin who became famous for his wisdom (and as such he appears in Acts 5:34–39), though he may have distanced himself sometimes from the prevailing opinion of that institution, as is indicated by the report of the Book of Acts. However, Gamaliel's son Simeon became the leader of the Pharisaic war party and was associated with the first government of the revolutionaries, although he later had to make room for a more radical leadership. This Pharisaic war party can be largely identified with the Shammaites with whom Simeon, grandson of Hillel, perished in the chaos of the Jewish war.

3) *From Yohanan ben Zakkai to Aqiba.* Judaism owes its new beginnings after the Jewish War to a man who, according to the tradition, was the colleague of Simeon ben Gamaliel in the leadership of the school in

Bibliography to §6.6f (3)

Jacob Neusner, *A Life of Rabban Yohanan ben Zakkai, ca. 1–80 C.E.* (SPB 6; 2d ed.; Leiden: Brill, 1970).

Idem, "In Quest of the Historical Rabban Yohanan ben Zakkai," *HTR* 59 (1966) 391–413.

Idem, "Studies in the Taqqanot of Yavneh," *HTR* 73 (1970) 183–98.

Louis Finkelstein, *Akiba: Scholar, Saint, and Martyr* (first published 1936; New York: Atheneum, 1970).

Jerusalem and himself a direct student of Hillel: Yohanan ben Zakkai. He disengaged himself from the war party at an early date. There are testimonies that he had protested against certain brutalities which were committed in the name of national liberation. Yohanan left Jerusalem in 68 CE, even before the end of the war, and risking his life went into the camp of Vespasian to request permission to settle in Jamnia (Yavneh, modern Yebna), on the coast of Palestine, in order to found a new school. It is quite credible that this happened with the explicit permission of the Romans. In view of the increasing gravity of the situation in Rome due to the disputed succession of Nero (§6.2a–b), Vespasian would certainly have been interested in encouraging a new, moderate Jewish leadership in Palestine. Other Jewish teachers who had not identified themselves with the national revolution, especially from the school of Hillel, joined Yohanan shortly before or after the end of the war. Other Jews were forcibly settled by the Romans in this area. This made it possible to reorganize Jewish religious life after the catastrophe of Jerusalem under Yohanan's leadership.

Everyone agreed at this moment in history that this catastrophe was a punishment for Israel's sins; this was the opinion not only of the Christians and the apocalyptic theologians (*4 Ezra* and *2 Baruch*), but also of Yohanan ben Zakkai and his colleagues. Yohanan also knew the answer: nothing but the strictest fulfillment of the law could bring recovery because it was disregard for the law that had brought unspeakable disaster. The problem was how the law could be fulfilled in this absence of an institution able to determine legal and cultic questions, since there was no longer a temple nor a sanhedrin. For the solution of this problem, Hillel's methods of interpretation and his principal rules of conduct (*halachah*), which came from the diaspora and had no necessary connection with the temple, became decisive. Yohanan ben Zakkai saw to it that they were accepted.

It can be assumed that the most important decisions of the reorganization were made already under Yohanan. These judgments concerned liturgical as well as legal questions. The new court, formed at Jamnia, thus claimed the authority to make decisions in areas which previously had been the domain of the priests. This involved especially the fixing of the Jewish calendar (the lunar calendar of Jerusalem was continued, requiring the intercalation of a thirteenth month every three years) and the determination of dates for the festivals. The important problem of "clean and unclean" was once and for all separated from the sacrificial cult of the temple—the sacrifices henceforth were of only academic interest— and thus removed from priestly jurisdiction. From now on only the word of the learned court of law was valid. The preservation of ritual purity was made an obligation for the conduct of all members of the Jewish community. The concept of the priesthood of all believers was just as strong here as in the New Testament (1 Pet 2:5). The Sadducees' interpretation of the law and their rejection of belief in the resurrection were repudiated.

So far the controversy between the two Pharisaic schools, the Hillelites and the Shammaites, had been solved in favor of the school of Hillel. But the battle with the Shammaites, who had earlier been more numerous than the Hillelites, had not come to an end, nor was the controversy with the Pharisaic war party a thing of the past. Gamaliel II, son of the former leader of the war party, Simeon ben Gamaliel (I), was one of the few former leaders of the war party who had escaped the Roman massacre after the destruction of Jerusalem. He came to Jamnia in about 80 and was elected *Nasi* of the *Beth-Din* before the death of the aged Yohanan ben Zakkai. The prestige of the family of Hillel, whose genealogy was soon traced back to David (cf. Matt 1:2–16), may have contributed to the fact that Gamaliel II received this position and was able to maintain it until 135, though not uncontested. The leadership of the *Beth-Din* in subsequent years also remained in the hands of the descendents of Hillel. Gamaliel's son Simeon was his successor (ca. 135–175), who was in turn succeeded by his son Judah, called "the Prince" (*HaNasi*; ca. 175–220). The period from the death of Hillel to the final redaction of the *Mishnah* by the patriarch Judah the Prince is called the time of the Tannaites, that is, of the "transmitters" or "teachers" (derived from the Aramaic term *tena* = "to repeat," "to transmit," which corresponds to the Hebrew *shanah*, from which the word "Mishnah" is derived). The two most important teachers of this time were R. Aqiba ben Joseph and R. Ishmael ben Elisha. Aqiba systematized the tradition of the *halachah* in six main sections, with numerous subdivisions which are still preserved in the later redaction of the *Mishnah*. The *halachah* became more strictly aligned with the Scripture, meaning that the traditional legal decisions had to be shown to agree with the Scripture. At the same time the principle of inspiration was intensified: all minutiae of Holy Scripture, to the very last letter, were deemed significant. In the development of the Greek Bible, the recension of Aquila corresponds most closely to this principle, because his translation follows the Hebrew text as closely as possible (§5.3b). Aquila was not only a contemporary of Aqiba, but perhaps also his student. Ishmael rejected Aqiba's literalism, recognizing the use of vernacular language in the Bible, and warning that details should not be emphasized too strongly in interpretation. Ishmael is credited with the expansion of Hillel's seven rules of interpretation. He modified Hillel's rules and divided them into the thirteen rules which were to become determinative for rabbinic Judaism.

After the year 70, the Roman administration did not interfere in the reorganization of Judaism, did not persecute the Jews, and did not disturb the activites of the *Beth-Din,* which sent messengers to other Jewish communities in an attempt to broaden its influence and thus gain more general recognition for its legal and liturgical decisions. It is an open question how quickly and to what extent this was achieved. Archeological finds and excavations seem to indicate that the influence of the rabbinic legal court was still limited during II through IV CE, especially in areas where Greek (and not Aramaic) was the spoken language, and where Hebrew was not in use even as the language of liturgy. To be sure, archeological evidence presents notorious difficulties for interpretation, but a few data are nonetheless clear. Jewish inscriptions from Asia Minor, for example, are written in Greek almost without exception until the early Byzantine period; there was no division for the seating of men and women in the Sardis synagogue, nor apparently in other synagogues; and the wall paintings from early III CE in the synagogue of Dura Europus violate the rabbinic prohibition of images as much as do the astrological symbols in the floor mosaics of Galilean synagogues. Nothing is known about the relationship of the court in Jamnia to those communities who kept the law and also confessed Christ (§10.4a–c), nor about its connection with Gnosticism, which certainly had its beginnings in the areas of Syria and Palestine. The formation of the gnostic interpretation of Genesis cannot be explained without the assumption of some contacts with the beginnings of rabbinic exegesis (§6.5f; 10.5b). Mystical, apocalyptic, and gnostic speculations were not unknown in Jamnia, as is evident from scattered information from later rabbinic sources (the studies of Gershom Sholem have brought new insights to the investigation of this problem). The image of a court which dealt exclusively with legal and halachic questions is certainly too narrow. The revision of the materials from the first period of the Tannaim that took place in the second half of II CE apparently purged many things which were no longer acceptable after the catastrophes of the Jewish insurrections of 116–117 and 132–135 CE.

4) *The Insurrections of the Second Century.* Despite the pacifist position of many of its leaders, and despite the principle that the study of

Bibliography to §6.6f (4)

Yigael Yadin, *Bar Kochba* (New York: Random House, 1971).

Judah Goldin, "The Period of the Talmud (135 B.C.E.–1035 C.E.)," in *The Jews: Their History, Culture, and Religion* (3d ed.; New York: Harper, 1960; 4th ed.; Schocken Books, 1970) 115–215.

Torah has a higher value than the national freedom of the Jewish people, the *Beth-Din* never renounced the expectation of a real, political fulfillment of messianic beliefs. The moderate leaders of the court in Jamnia were united with the nationalists in their desire to return to Jerusalem and rebuild the temple. In the second decade of II CE the Romans seemed willing to grant the fulfillment of this wish. But when Trajan in the end forbade the reconstruction of the temple after a long period of negotiation, militant nationalism prevailed over rational opinion. The insurrection began in the Cyrenaica and Egypt and also spread to Palestine. The bloody suppression of the insurrection also had consequences for the court in Jamnia. It was forced to move to Lod (Lydda, Ludd), and was deprived of important functions, such as the right to determine the calendar. In the years following this insurrection, the radical elements seem to have gained the upper hand, while the pacifist party led by Aqiba lost its influence. The last insurrection broke out when Hadrian made known his plans to build a temple for the Capitoline Jupiter on the site of the Jewish temple in the course of his reconstruction of Jerusalem. Within three years (132–135 CE), the Romans crushed the resistance of the messianic movement, whose leader had been called "Star of Jacob" at the beginning of the war and who is therefore remembered by the name of Bar Kochba.

The consequences were catastrophic. Hadrian well knew the religious motivations which had triggered the insurrection. In contrast to the aftermath of the Jewish War of 66-70, the Romans took measures which were directed against the very practice of the Jewish religion. Not only were the Jews forbidden to enter Jerusalem or even to approach it, but the prohibitions also included the practice of circumcision, the observance of the Sabbath and of the Jewish festivals, as well as instruction in Torah. The aged Aqiba, over ninety years old, suffered martyrdom when he refused to comply with the latter prohibition. The *Beth-Din* had ceased to exist. The Jewish population of Palestine had been massacred or expelled.

The legislation against the practice of the Jewish religion was somewhat mitigated under Antoninus Pius. As soon as it became possible to reconstitute the Jewish law court, the reorganization began in Galilee, where the *Beth-Din,* after several relocations, finally settled in Tiberias. Here the students of Aqiba continued and further elaborated the traditions from the first period of the Tannaim. Foremost among them was R. Meir, who had studied under both Ishmael and Aqiba, and who is primarily responsible for the form of the *Mishnah* as it was finally revised and fixed in written form by the patriarch Judah ca. 200 CE. This last period of the Tannaim made the decisions which would determine the course of rabbinic Judaism. This period also gave us the oldest rabbinic literature which is preserved, the *Mishnah,* the Tannaitic *midrashim,* and the *Tosephta.* These will be briefly described below.

5) *The Mishnah.* Interpretations of important laws were at first transmitted orally. Such traditions often begin with the opinions of Hillel (and Shammai) and add the opinions of later teachers. The fundamental elements of these discussions were essentially formed during the time of the reconstruction after 70 CE. During II CE it seems that written notes were also produced, that is, handbooks for private use and for the court's legal decisions. Aqiba created the division of the material into six main sections: *Zeraim* ("Seeds"—on agriculture and fruits of the field); *Moed* ("Festivals"); *Nashim* ("Women"—this section also contains the legislation on vows); *Nezikin* ("Damages"—civil and criminal law); *Kodashim* ("Hallowed Things"—sacrifice and ritual); *Tohoroth* ("Cleanness"—legislation about clean and unclean). This method of division is not purely systematic, but also reveals an interest in aids for memorization. Reshaped by R. Meir, the *Mishnah* was revised and edited in written form by the patriarch Judah. It became the standard collection of the legal discussions and decisions of the Tannaim, and was accepted not only in Palestine but also in Babylon, thus becoming the basis for both the Palestinian and for the Babylonian Talmuds.

6) *The Early Midrashim.* Alongside the legal decisions transmitted in a systematized fashion, no later than the early II CE legal commentaries on the individual books of the Bible began to be composed, beginning with

Bibliography to §6.6f (5–7): Texts

Herbert Danby, *The Mishna* (Oxford: Clarendon, 1933). Best available English translation.

Jacob Z. Lauterbach, *Mekilta de-Rabbi Ishmael* (3 vols.; The Schiff Library of Jewish Classics; Philadelphia: Jewish Publications Society, 1933–35). Hebrew text of Mekilta on Exodus with English translation.

Hermann Strack and Paul Billerbeck, *Kommentar zum Neuen Testament aus Talmud und Midrasch* (6 vols.; München: Beck, 1922–69).

Paul Levertoff, *Midrash Sifre on Numbers* (Translations of Early Documents 3: Rabbinic Texts; London: SPCK, 1926). Selections from Sifre on Numbers in English translation.

Kee, *Origins,* 136–44.

Bibliography to §6.6f (5): Introductions

Hermann L. Strack, *Introduction to the Talmud and Midrash* (Philadelphia: Jewish Publication Society, 1931; reprint: New York: Meridian, 1959).

Jacob Neusner, *Method and Meaning in Ancient Judaism* (Brown University: Brown Judaic Studies 10; Missoula: Scholars Press, 1979). A good introduction to the purpose and function of early Rabbinic literature.

Chanoch Albeck, *Einführung in die Mischna* (SJ 6; Berlin: De Gruyter, 1971).

H. A. Fischel, *Rabbinic Literature and Greco-Roman Philosophy: A Study of Epicurea and Rhetorica in Early Midrashic Writings* (SPB 21; Leiden: Brill, 1973).

the books of Exodus, Leviticus, Numbers, and Deuteronomy. The subjects and materials of these commentaries in the early period are predominantly halachic, that is, legal while preaching and narrative (*haggadah*) plays only a minor role in the early commentaries. The name for such a commentary is *midrash* (= "investigation"). The oldest commentaries which are preserved are known as *Mechilta, Sifra,* and *Sifre. Mechilta* is a commentary on Exodus, namely Exodus 12–23 and 31:12–17; 35:1–3. It has been assumed, therefore, that the commentary is not completely preserved. *Mechilta* quotes opinions of later rabbis, but its basis seems to be a commentary of R. Ishmael or of his school. *Sifra* (precisely *Sifra de-Be-Rab* = "Book of the School") is a running commentary on Leviticus, interpreting almost every sentence. It originated in the school of Aqiba, though its final redaction was made after the codification of the *Mishnah. Sifre* (*Sifre de-Be-Rab* = "Books of the School") designates two different works, namely a midrash on Numbers and a midrash on Deuteronomy. The former derives from the school of Ishmael; in *Sifre on Deuteronomy* the commentary on Deuteronomy 12–26 comes from the school of Aqiba. In both instances the parts which are preserved do not represent the full extent of the original commentaries.

7) *The Tosefta.* This is the name of a second collection of halachic materials from the Tannaitic period which was made at some time in addition to the *Mishnah.* The origin of this collection is debated. In the division of its materials the *Tosefta* follows the *Mishnah,* and the halachic rules are often the same as those in the *Mishnah.* In some sections the *Tosefta* is nothing but the presentation of additional materials (*Tosefta* = "Additions"), but it often preserves independent, parallel traditions which are particularly valuable, since the *Tosefta* did not have the same canonical status as the *Mishnah* and was therefore not subject to the same degree to the redaction of the later rabbinic editors.

Agora: The central square of the Greek city, surrounded by the public buildings, temples, and open halls with stores (stoas). People went here for business, leisure, and shopping. It also served for assemblies of the people and was considered a sacred place. See I 71.

Amanuensis: A secretary who would draft letters and take dictation. It is likely that the apostle Paul used an amanuensis for the composition of his correspondence.

Anacoluthon: Construction of sentences that are incomplete (e.g., without a predicate), either intentionally or accidentally.

Anthropos: The Greek word for "human being." It is often used to describe the celestial or spiritual and divine prototype for the creation of human beings. The *Anthropos* is thought of as bisexual or asexual and is sometimes considered as the redeemer, thus identified with the heavenly Christ.

Apocalypticism: Belief in the disclosure of the events of the future (restitution of Israel, cosmic catastrophe and creation of a new heaven and earth) through prophets who have received special revelations (visions). Such revelations are usually propagated through books, often considered mysterious and secret. Apocalypticism implies that the course of future events can be calculated. See I 230-34.

Apophthegma: A brief story, usually transmitted orally, in which a traditional saying of a famous person (Diogenes, Jesus, and others) forms the conclusion. In most cases, the saying is more original, while the narrative part of the apophthegma is subject to variation.

Aretalogy: The enumeration of the great deeds of a god or of a divinely inspired human being (a "divine man"). An aretalogy can appear in the form of a sequence of brief sentences, each describing a different *arete* ("powerful act" or "virtuous quality"), or in the form of a series of stories, such as miracle stories.

Colophon: A subscript to a work often found in ancient books; it gives the title of the work, sometimes also information about the author or the place of composition. Colophons are not original parts of such works but have been added by the scribe.

Cosmogony: Mythical descriptions of the birth or creation of the whole universe, either by a process of divine evolution or through interaction of various divine powers or substances, usually ending in the creation of heaven and earth.

Covenant formula: The genre visible in the presentations of the making of the covenant between God and Israel. It consists of a historical introduction (e.g., story of the Exodus), a basic command, individual stipulations (e.g., the decalogue), and curses and blessings. See I 256.

Diaspora: Part or all of a nation living away from its homeland in various other cities and countries. Especially used of Israelites living in the many cities of the Hellenistic world and the Roman Empire. See I 219-28.

Divine Man: Human beings endowed with special divine powers, thus transcending in their accomplishments the range of normal human abilities. Poets (e.g., Homer), philosophers, rulers, and miracle workers were considered divine men; sometimes also called "Son of God." See I 173.

Docetism: The belief that Christ could not really become human because of the insurmountable difference between the divine and the human world. It was therefore thought that Christ only "seemed" (Greek: *dokei*) to be human, but actually never gave up his divine nature and essence. See II 197.

Encratism: Abstention from sex, marriage, certain foods and drinks for religious reasons in order to avoid contamination from natural and earthly things. See II 122f. and the General Index under "Asceticism."

Eudaemonia: Usually translated "happiness." But the term expresses much more: the status of complete peace and imperturbability in this life. It is often commended as the ultimate goal of a philosophical and religious life.

Eschatology: The belief that there will be a divinely guided renewal of the world and society in the near future, often seen as beginning in the present time (realized eschatology). Eschatological beliefs may be connected with apocalyptic mythology, but can also be expressed in political terms or in terms of individualistic piety. See the General Index.

Etymology: The method used to explain the meaning of a term or word on the basis of its assumed original literal sense rather than on the basis of the context of its actual usage.

Form: The structure of units that are transmitted orally, such as sayings, miracle stories, and apophthegms.

Forum: The central square in a Roman city. Like the Greek agora, it is surrounded by administrative buildings and also serves as a market place. But it is usually built as an enclosed rectangular square with access gates allowing easy control of entry.

Genre: The structure of particular types of literature, such as letters, gospels, biographies.

Gymnasium: Special building units in Greek (and Roman) cities, normally large peristyle courts, surrounded by stoas, various rooms, small temples, and lecture halls. The gymnasia served as places of athletic training and competition as well as places of school and education.

Ithyphallic: "with raised phallus," i.e., with erect penis. Satyrs and donkeys in the company of the god Dionysus are usually presented in this way as well as some other gods like Priapus.

Kerygma: "Proclamation." Technical term for fixed formulations of the early Christian proclamation, such as the "kerygma of the death, resurrection, and exaltation of Jesus."

Leitourgia: The term for certain public offices in Greek cities, such as "president of the gymnasium." A *leitourgia* was considered a special honor, but also involved the expenditure of considerable amounts of money, e.g., endowing or paying for an athletic contest.

Manumission: The legal procedure for the freeing of a slave. It required the supervision of a public official or of a temple, the payment of certain sums of money, and the filing of the appropriate documents, which were sometimes published in the form of an inscription.

Modalism: A christological belief that fully identified God and Christ in their divine nature so that Christ became a certain "mode" of the being or presence of God himself. Later modalists were accused of saying that God the Father suffered on the cross.

Onomasticon: A method used in the composition of psalms, hymns, or wisdom lists: the first letter in each succeeding line or verse would be made to correspond to the order of the letters in the alphabet or in certain sacred names.

Parenesis: "Admonition." Used to designate certain traditional types of admonition and exhortation aimed at a proper religious and moral life. Most early Christian letters contain parenetical sections.

Parousia: Originally "coming" or "presence" of a divine being or of God. Later it was specifically used to designate the expected (second) coming of Jesus.

Pericope: Technical term for a segment of a biblical text, as it was "cut out" for liturgical reading in worship service. Pericopes are usually small, self-contained units, comprising not more than a part of the chapter of a biblical book.

Prescript: The opening of a letter, comprising the name of the sender and of the addressee as well as a greeting. See II 54-56.

Proem: The second section of a letter, following upon the prescript. It is formulated either as a thanksgiving prayer or as a doxology and may include more lengthy descriptions of the situation of the sender and of the status of the addressee. See II 54-56.

Protreptic: The invitation to enter upon a truly philosophical or religious life, to defend the qualities and virtues of such a life, and to describe the basic philosophical concepts by which it should be guided. See II 338-40.

Stichometry: A list in which the number of lines in each of the books in question is given. Ancient stichometries help us to estimate the length of writings that are lost or only preserved in fragments.

Stoa: Public buildings in ancient cities: a hall with a single or double colonnade, open on one side and often with a line of shops on the other side. But stoas did not only serve as shopping malls; they were also used as courthouses, picture galleries, lecture halls (like the Painted Stoa in Athens where Zeno, the founder of the "Stoic" philosophy, gave his lectures), and as places for general business and leisure. Often of large dimensions (several hundred feet long), they lined many squares, streets, and courts.

Syzygy: Mostly used with respect to mythical speculations in which the celestial, divine world is described as consisting of pairs, e.g., of a male and female in each cosmic aeon; it is also sometimes applied to the reconstruction of history. See II 207, 213.

Technitai: "Craftsmen." The term is used for the members of any profession that required a skill, be it bakers or actors or shipbuilders. They were usually organized in associations, such as the "Dionysiac Technitai" (the association of professional actors and dancers related to the theater under the protection of the god Dionysus).

Testament: A genre of literature. It is a modification of the covenant formula in which the historical introduction is replaced by the biographical description of an individual (patriarch or apostle). This individual, who may already be dead at the time of writing, then gives instructions and pronounces curses and blessings. See I 258.

Theogony: Mythical description of the evolution of the world of the gods in a primordial time, describing their origin, function, and power. Theogonies often recount dramatic celestial struggles, and they precede cosmogonies in many ancient myths.

Thiasos (pl. *thiasoi*): Term for an association with a particular religious commitment. The term is also used for secular associations organized under the protectorate of a deity.

Index

EARLY CHRISTIAN WRITINGS

This index lists only those page numbers where these writings are treated in detail. For other references, see the General Index. All page numbers refer to Volume II.

General Index

All writings are normally listed under the name of their assumed authors (except for the Pauline letters). Bold Roman numerals refer to volumes.

Authors Discussed in the Text

Bold Roman numerals indicate volume number.